WORLD POLITICS

WORLD POLITICS

POWER, INTERDEPENDENCE & DEPENDENCE

David G. Haglund

Director of the Centre for International Relations
Queen's University

Michael K. Hawes

Assistant Professor of Political Studies
Queen's University

HARCOURT BRACE JOVANOVICH, CANADA
TORONTO ORLANDO SAN DIEGO LONDON SYDNEY

Canadian Cataloguing in Publication Data

Main entry under title:
World politics : power, interdependence & dependence

Includes bibliographical references.
ISBN 0–7747–3127–3

1. World politics - 20th century. 2. International relations. I. Haglund, David G. II. Hawes, Michael K., 1954–

D443.W67 1990 327′.09′04 C89–094932–8

Publisher: David Dimmell
Acquisitions Editor: Heather McWhinney
Developmental Editor: Sandra Peltier
Publishing Services Manager: Karen Eakin
Managing Editor: Liz Radojkovic
Editorial Assistant: Robert Gordon
Copy Editor: Beverley Endersby
Cover and Interior Design: Angela Vaculik
Typesetting and Assembly: True to Type Inc.
Printing and Binding: John Deyell Company

Cover Art: Gerald Gladstone (1929–)
Untitled, 1963
oil on canvas
137.2 × 114.9 cm
Art Gallery of Ontario, Toronto

Printed in Canada
1 2 3 4 5 94 93 92 91 90

To our families

PREFACE

In the decades following World War II, a rough consensus emerged among those who followed international politics: the world divided into two ideological camps, security issues dominated the global policy agenda, Western economic priorities were established by the United States, and international organizations operated relatively successfully in a world of sovereign states. In the 1980s, however, the postwar political and economic consensus began to unravel. Over the course of 1989, the unravelling progressed at breakneck speed, with the dramatic developments in the Soviet Union and Eastern Europe putting an abrupt end to the bipolar, cold-war world. Economic pluralism and the relative economic decline of the United States have challenged the logic of a single global economy and the stability normally associated with strong leadership. The drive for democracy in much of the world, the emergence of a dynamic collection of successful industrial economies in Asia, the intractable poverty of Africa, and the prospect of environmental collapse are challenging the world we have come to know. The global policy agenda, once dominated by security issues, is now crowded and confused, with economic, environmental, and human-rights issues occupying a much more prominent place.

In many respects, despite the persistence of some important and enduring elements, change has become the single dominant feature of world politics. Consequently, it is increasingly important for us to comprehend both the new issues that have emerged and the various perspectives that have developed to provide us with analytical and conceptual tools for understanding the evolving international context.

Just as the world is changing, so too is our appreciation of it. It is a critical time for those of us who study world politics, a time to explore new perspectives and take stock of old ones, as well as to examine the state of the field and the extent of our knowledge. Our purpose in producing this book, which collects new material from a wide range of ideological and practical perspectives, is to provide students with an introduction to the key contemporary issues in world politics, the major analytical perspectives, and the main concepts and emerging issues in the increasingly complex world of international politics. Not surprisingly, textbooks tend to present the world from a particular perspective, and edited collections focus on issues. Our aim is to provide a book that reflects the current tension within the field of world politics — both between competing perspectives and between new and enduring themes.

World Politics: Power, Interdependence & Dependence is organized into four sections: The Politics of Power and Security, The Politics of Interdependence, The Politics of Dependence, and Perspectives on World Politics. No single book can fully capture the diversity of the field or include all the important issues. However, by organizing the material as we have and by working with new material, we have sought to include theoretical formulations ranging from classical theories of war to modern theories of co-operation, and to cover issues ranging from deterrence to economic integration, to technological dependence.

Throughout the process of planning the book, making decisions about organization and content, commissioning and editing the various chapters, and producing the final draft, we have proceeded from a single assumption: that there is a need for a balanced and comprehensive introductory textbook in international relations that recognizes the validity of competing perspectives and the importance and urgency of understanding change.

Many people have contributed to the development of this book. Working at Queen's University is both a productive and pleasant experience, not least because of the mix of bright, stimulating students and the institutional support provided by the university to its researchers. We should like to acknowledge especially Kay Ladouceur, who, along with Bernice Gallagher and Mary Kerr, patiently typed and retyped the manuscript. Marilyn Banting tirelessly supplied superb editorial assistance. We are particularly grateful to the Department of National Defence, which, through its Military and Strategic Studies Program, generously supports our Centre for International Relations. Our own work has also been supported by the Donner Canadian Foundation and the Canadian Institute for International Peace and Security. We are indebted to Heather McWhinney, Liz Radojkovic, Robert Gordon, and our project editor, Sandra Peltier, all of Harcourt Brace Jovanovich, Canada, for their professional and enthusiastic support. They were a pleasure to work with. Finally, we are grateful to our contributors, whose ideas we present to you in this volume.

David G. Haglund
Michael K. Hawes

CONTENTS

PREFACE vii

CONTRIBUTORS xi

LIST OF ABBREVIATIONS xii

INTRODUCTION: CONTEMPORARY ISSUES AND APPROACHES 1

PART I: THE POLITICS OF POWER AND SECURITY 15

The State and International Relations 16
Tom Keating

The Causes of War: How Does the Structure of the System Affect International Conflict? 38
Patrick James

Balances of Power: Analogy, Arguments, and Some Evidence 56
William B. Moul

The Theory and Practice of Deterrence 83
Paul Buteux

Arms Control 104
David Cox

Trading in Weapons: The Role of Arms Transfers in International Politics 129
Keith Krause

PART II: THE POLITICS OF INTERDEPENDENCE 153

Assessing the World Economy: The Rise and Fall of Bretton Woods 154
Michael K. Hawes

Integration, Interdependence, and Institutions: Approaches to International Order 173
Charles C. Pentland

Structural Change and Hegemonic Decline: Implications for National Governments 197
Michael K. Hawes

The Roles of the Multinational Enterprise in International Relations 224
David Leyton-Brown

International Sanctions 242
Margaret Doxey

State Capitalism 262
Maureen Appel Molot

Trade and Global Interdependence 283
Jock A. Finlayson

PART III: THE POLITICS OF DEPENDENCE 311

Economic Imperialism 312
Malcolm J. Grieve

Dependent Development in the New International Division of Labour: Prospects for Africa's Political Economy 333
Timothy M. Shaw

Technology and the New International Economic Order 361
Elizabeth Riddell-Dixon

The International Political Economy of Food and Agriculture 379
Andrew Fenton Cooper

The New Geopolitics of Minerals: The Changing Significance of Strategic Minerals 405
David G. Haglund

PART IV: PERSPECTIVES ON WORLD POLITICS 439

War and Empire: Thucydides and International Politics 440
Larry Pratt

Bridge Over Troubled Waters: Linking Strategic Studies and International Relations 456
Michel Fortmann and William L. George

History and Structure in the Theory of International Relations 482
R.B.J. Walker

Ethics and International Relations: A Critique of Cynical Realism 506
Constantine Melakopides

Opening Up the Black Box: The Decision-Making Approach to International Politics 531
Kim Richard Nossal

The Latest Wave: A Critical Review of Regime Literature 553
James F. Keeley

CONTRIBUTORS

Paul Buteux	*University of Manitoba*
Andrew Fenton Cooper	*University of Waterloo*
David Cox	*Queen's University*
Margaret Doxey	*Trent University*
Jock A. Finlayson	*Queen's University*
Michel Fortmann	*Université de Montréal*
William L. George	*Department of National Defence*
Malcolm J. Grieve	*Acadia University*
David G. Haglund	*Queen's University*
Michael K. Hawes	*Queen's University*
Patrick James	*McGill University*
Tom Keating	*University of Alberta*
James F. Keeley	*University of Calgary*
Keith Krause	*York University*
David Leyton-Brown	*York University*
Constantine Melakopides	*University of Manitoba*
Maureen Appel Molot	*Carleton University*
William B. Moul	*University of Waterloo*
Kim Richard Nossal	*McMaster University*
Charles C. Pentland	*Queen's University*
Larry Pratt	*University of Alberta*
Elizabeth Riddell-Dixon	*University of Western Ontario*
Timothy M. Shaw	*Dalhousie University*
R.B.J. Walker	*University of Victoria*

LIST OF ABBREVIATIONS

ABM	anti-ballistic missiles
ACP countries	African, Caribbean, and Pacific countries
ACDA	Arms Control and Disarmament Agency
ADB	African Development Bank
AIC	advanced industrial country
APPER	Africa's Priority Programme for Economic Recovery
ASEAN	Association of Southeast Asian Nations
BGS	British Geological Survey
BHN	Basic Human Needs
BNAC	British–North American Committee
CAP	Common Agricultural Policy
CAT Talks	Conventional Arms Transfer Talks
CCSBMDE	*See* CDE.
CD	Committee on Disarmament
CDE	Conference on Confidence- and Security-Building Measures and Disarmament in Europe
CGCT	Compagnie Générale de Construction Téléphonique
CIDA	Canadian International Development Agency
CIF	cost, insurance, and freight
CIIPS	Canadian Institute for International Peace and Security
CON index	concentration index
COW Project	Correlates of War Project
CREON	Comparative Research on the Events of Nations
CSBM	confidence- and security-building measure
CSCE	Conference on Security and Co-operation in Europe
CST	Conventional Stability Talks
CTB	comprehensive test ban
DISC	Domestic International Sales Corporation
DME	developed market economy
DND	Department of National Defence
EC	European Community
ECA	Economic Commission for Africa
EEC	European Economic Community
EEP	Export Enhancement Program
EFTA	European Free Trade Association
ENI	Ente Nazionale Idrocarburi
FAO	Food and Agricultural Organization
FOB	free on board

FTA	Canada–U.S. Free Trade Agreement
GATT	General Agreement on Tariffs and Trade
GDP	gross domestic product
GLCM	ground-launched cruise missile
GNP	gross national product
IAEA	International Atomic Energy Agency
IBRD	International Bank for Reconstruction and Development
ICBM	intercontinental ballistic missile
ICJ	International Court of Justice
IDS	Institute for Development Studies
IESI	International Economic Studies Institute
IDA	International Development Association
IMF	International Monetary Fund
INF	intermediate-range nuclear forces
INF Treaty	Intermediate Nuclear Forces Treaty
INI	Instituto Nacional de Industria
IPE	international political economy
IR	international relations
IRI	Instituto per la Riconstruzione Industriale
ITO	International Trade Organization
ITT	International Telephone and Telegraph
LDC	less-developed country
LPA	Lagos Plan of Action
MAD	mutual assured destruction
MBFR Talks	Mutual and Balanced Force Reduction Talks
MFA	Multi-Fibre Arrangement
MFN	most-favoured nation
MIRV	multiple independently targeted re-entry vehicle
MNC	multinational corporation
MNE	multinational enterprise
NAM	Non-Aligned Movement
NATO	North Atlantic Treaty Organization
NEB	National Enterprise Board
NDI	Network Density Index
NGO	nongovernmental organization
NICs	newly industrialized countries
NIEs	newly industrializing economies
NIEO	new international economic order
NPT	Non-Proliferation of Nuclear Weapons Treaty
NTB	nontariff trade barrier
NTM	national technical means

OAS	Organization of American States
OAU	Organization of African Unity
ODA	official development assistance
ODI	Overseas Development Institute
OECD	Organization for Economic Cooperation and Development
OEEC	Organization for European Economic Cooperation
OIAG	Österreichische Industrieverwaltungs AG
OMA	orderly market arrangements
OMV	Österreichische Mineraloelverwaltung AG
OPEC	Organization of the Petroleum Exporting Countries
OSI	on-site inspection
PDVSA	Petróleos de Venezuela
PQLI	Positive Quality of Work Life Index
PTBT	Partial Test Ban Treaty
QR	quantitative restriction
R&D	research and development
RIO	Reshaping the International Order
SAC	Strategic Air Command
SALT	Strategic Arms Limitation Talks
SDI	Strategic Defense Initiative
SEATO	Southeast Asia Treaty Organization
SGF	Société générale de financement
SIPRI	Stockholm International Peace Research Institute
SLBM	submarine-launched ballistic missile
SNECMA	Société nationale d'étude et de construction de moteurs d'avion
STABEX	Stabilization of Export Earnings
START	Strategic Arms Reduction Talks
TRIM	trade-related investment measure
TTBT	Threshold Test Ban Treaty
UDI	unilateral declaration of independence
UNCTAD	U.N. Conference on Trade and Development
UNESCO	U.N. Educational, Scientific, and Cultural Organization
UNIDO	U.N. Industrial Development Organization
UNITAR	U.N. Institute for Training and Research
UNRISD	U.N. Research Institute for Social Development
UNSSOD	U.N. Special Session on Disarmament
UNU	U.N. University
VEBA	Vereinigte Elektrizitaets und Bergwerks AB
VER	voluntary export restriction
VIAG	Vereinigte Industrie-Unternehmungen AG
VRA	voluntary restraint agreement

WHO	World Health Organization
WOMP	World Order Models Project
WTO	Warsaw Treaty Organization
ZANU	Zimbabwe African National Union
ZAPU	Zimbabwe African People's Union

INTRODUCTION: CONTEMPORARY ISSUES AND APPROACHES

By virtually all accounts, we are at a critical juncture in the history of the modern international system. The peace, prosperity, and stability that came to characterize the postwar international order — during the so-called long decade of the 1950s — has come under considerable pressure in recent decades. With respect to economic matters, we have witnessed the emergence of a different pattern of economic power, with new centres of production and finance and new forms of interdependence. The relative decline of American economic power and influence, the concomitant rise of Japan and the European Community (especially the Federal Republic of Germany), the powerful economic challenge posed by the newly industrializing economies (NIEs), and the seemingly insoluble problems of debt and development have rocked the postwar economic order to its very foundation. The Bretton Woods system, which was characterized by strong and stable leadership, a pattern of progressively more liberal trade and investment flows, and an established order for trade and payments, all but collapsed in the 1970s and early 1980s.

More recently, and perhaps more importantly, the political side of the postwar international order has undergone an equally dramatic and challenging transformation. At the centre of these changes lie the new realities in East-West relations. The ideological conflict between East and West, which was without question the most prominent and the most enduring feature of the postwar international order, has changed in profound and puzzling ways. First, during the 1970s, we went through a period of détente and convergence. Then, in the early 1980s, with the election of Ronald Reagan in the United States and the death of General Secretary Brezhnev in the Soviet Union, the cold war seemed to return with a vengeance. However, in more recent years, we have witnessed an even more dramatic reversal in the relationship between East and West and in the ideological differences that characterized the cold war. Driven largely by the efforts at political and economic reform in Mikhail Gorbachev's Soviet Union (not to mention recent advances toward democratization in Eastern and Central Europe and pressures in that direction in China), the international political order has found its way to a critical crossroads.

These profound changes in the international system, and among its constituent members, have generated equally profound challenges to both students and practitioners of world politics. The ever-widening interest in the field reflects both the enormity of the issues at hand (war and peace, stability and prosperity, and order and justice) and the increasingly complex and uncertain character of the international system.

As a field of study, international relations is less than a century old. However, its intrusion into virtually all levels of public and private life is one of the stark realities of the late 20th century. Efforts at securing peace, reducing conflict, guaranteeing economic well-being, encouraging equity, and maintaining order are no longer the exclusive prerogative of government leaders and senior civil servants, and they are no longer simply abstract concepts. They touch the lives and demand the attention of virtually all of the world's citizens. Not surprisingly, as a discipline, world politics is undergoing a boom of sorts. The tremendous popularity of recent books, such as Paul Kennedy's *The Rise and Fall of the Great Powers*,[1] supports the argument that study of world politics is eliciting a good deal of attention — at least in the industrialized countries of the West. These empirical works, especially those that are as substantial as Kennedy's, are extremely useful. However, we are also in need of scholarly work that systematically addresses both the conflicts and the continuities in the study of world politics and encourages informed publics to examine the international system in a sustained and critical fashion.

Competing Perspectives in the Study of World Politics

The primary aim of this book is to provide a unified and coherent approach to the study of world politics, an approach that accepts the logic of competing perspectives and the need to come to terms with a dynamic and complex collection of issues and actors. To this end, it is essential to have a clear and sustained understanding of how various ideological perspectives influence our thinking and direct the behaviour of political leaders and policy makers. While it is possible to locate many different analytic positions (and many variations on these positions), we have chosen to isolate the three main perspectives in the literature. For the sake of analytic convenience, we will refer to these three perspectives throughout this book as the power-politics or realist perspective, the interdependence perspective, and the dependence perspective. Other students of international relations have referred to these perspectives in slightly different terms, the most common distinction being between realist, liberal, and Marxist positions.[2]

There is basic agreement within the literature with respect to the main analytic distinctions between the three perspectives. The most important of these distinctions include the structure of the international system, the underlying logic or fundamental principles that characterize the system, and the distribution of power and influence (i.e., the relative status of the main actors). On the question of structure, the basic difference is quite clear: the realist-statist position posits a state-centric or interstate system, the interdependence perspective argues for a "transnational" or multicentric structure, and the dependence perspective suggests a systemic or global-centric structure. James Rosenau has captured this distinction quite clearly in his analysis of the three perspectives. He contends that

> the state-centric analysts presume a fragmented structure in which power is located in nation-states; those who adhere to a multi-centric approach picture an interdependent structure with power distributed among a variety of types of actors; and those who subscribe to a global-centric perspective view the system as having an integrated structure deriving from patterns of power distribution that have been in place for centuries.[3]

Similarly, each perspective is quite clear with respect to the underlying logic to which it adheres. The realist position maintains that the international system is characterized by anarchy and by the political competition for power and influence. The interdependence view holds that the system is characterized by the notion of complexity, although the system is basically orderly.[4] (It can also be distinguished by its pluralist or liberal character.) The dependence perspective, in contrast, is characterized by its reliance on the idea of historical patterns of trade and production and conflict. (This perspective is often associated with Marxist analysis, although such an association is not necessary.)

Finally, with respect to the composition of the international system and the distribution of power within it, the differences are equally clear cut. The realist perspective sees the system as being fragmented, with power distributed unequally among the actors (nation-states). The transnational-relations paradigm suggests that interdependence is the hallmark of the international system; power is distributed (somewhat more equally) among nation-states, multinational enterprises, international organizations, and other transnational coalitions. Lastly, according to the dependence perspective, the international system is highly integrated, with power distributed in terms of long historical patterns of global development.

While the most influential reviews in the field tend to support the basic idea that there are three main perspectives, they differ when it comes to the more subtle distinctions between the competing positions. For example, with respect to the transnational-relations perspective, Robert Cox focusses on the maintenance of the status quo and the "management of interdependence," rather than on the notions of multicentrism and pluralism. He prefers to call this the "establishment perspective,"[5] a term consistent with his overall view of what can, more generically, be called the "liberal perspective." In contrast, Robert Gilpin views this perspective in terms of the challenge posed to the nation-state by systemic pluralism and complexity. He sees this view as one best understood in terms of the "sovereignty at bay" thesis, where the principal conflict of our time is between the political forces of nationalism and the economic forces of internationalism.[6] Others, such as Stephen Krasner, stress the societal (domestic-interests) aspect of the liberal paradigm.[7] While each is, in essence, still looking at the same paradigm (and doubtless would agree to the basic distinctions outlined above), it is important to note that paradigmatic conflict is not characterized by simple ideological conflict. More often than not, the interpretation each analyst has of the three perspectives is coloured by his or her own preferred alternative and by a context-bound understanding of the debate.

What follows is a somewhat more detailed review of the competing perspectives in world politics. First, we review the basic premises of classic realism. Then, we proceed to an analysis of how the transnational-relations paradigm came to challenge the dominant realist view. This perspective, along with the interdependence bias that replaced the national-security focus of the realist perspective, was so pervasive in the 1970s that it succeeded in tipping the scales well over to the "liberal" side of the debate. Finally, we examine alternative perspectives, including the dependence perspective and the re-emergence of the realist position.

Political Realism: The Politics of Power and Security

Political realism, and the preoccupation with the politics of power and security, emerged in the pragmatic and nationalistic period that followed World War II. Its initial prominence in both the academic community and policy-making circles can be attributed to the decline of idealism and linked to the writings of Hans Morgenthau, George Kennann, E.H. Carr, and others.[8] This perspective understands the international system to be one in which independent sovereign states are in constant competition for power and influence. In this formulation, the central goal of every state is the pursuit of its national interest and the maximization of its power, relative to the other states in the system. The underlying premise here is that mankind is inherently evil and that man (and man-made institutions, such as the state) will attempt to enhance his position whenever the opportunity arises.

Realism portrays the international system as one composed of similar states, in which balancing the power or finding a systemic equilibrium is the main task of diplomatic activity. Balance-of-power theory, backed up empirically by the lessons of international relations in 19th-century Europe, goes hand in hand with the fundamental principles of realism. As Hedley Bull notes, "the very institutions of international society [are] the balance of power, international law, the diplomatic mechanism, the managerial system of great powers, and war."[9] Bull maintains that, of these institutions, the balance of power is the main support of international order. For realists, the international system has to be understood as a system of sovereign states that are in constant competition for scarce resources and political influence.

From this perspective, international politics must be perceived as anarchy or, at the very least, as organized violence. For realists, the conflict over the distribution of power within the system will inevitably lead to war, as war becomes the ultimate arbiter — the means by which the balance is restored. Nowhere is this point made more clearly than in Morgenthau's classic *Politics among Nations*, where he states that "all history shows that nations active in international politics are continuously preparing for, actively involved in, or recovering from organized violence in the form of war."[10] Similarly, Bull notes that "the chief function of the balance of power . . . is not to preserve peace, but to preserve the system of states itself. Preservation of the balance of power requires war."[11]

While this synopsis of the realist position is very brief, it is possible to summarize this perspective quite neatly by defining realism as an intellectual perspective that makes three interrelated assumptions. First, it assumes that states are the dominant, if not the exclusive, actors in international relations (the state-centric principle) and that states act as coherent units (the state-as-actor principle). Second, it assumes that force is a usable and effective instrument of foreign policy and that states will use force to enhance their relative position in the international system. And, finally, it assumes that there is a clear hierarchy of issues in world politics, headed by the military/security issue. In short, it asserts that "high politics" (military issues) dominate "low politics" (economic, social, and technical issues).

The classical-realist interpretation of world politics is quite straightforward. Political and diplomatic interactions between sovereign states constitute the core of international relations. The outcomes of these interactions, according to realist theory, are largely determined by the distribution of power in the system. The now-famous billiard-ball metaphor is a particularly apt representation of this view:

> The realist model of world politics was simple and elegant. An image of states as billiard balls, interacting within a specific arena and according to established rules, became increasingly prevalent. Once the implication of the metaphor was grasped, that there are only a few immutable patterns of behaviour in politics — billiard balls, after all, are not very complex phenomena — the principal preoccupation of statesmen became clear. They were to judge, by experience and intuition, the requisite amount of force to move one or another in a preferred direction.[12]

However, the most compelling feature of the realist perspective — its profoundly simple and parsimonious explanation of international political behaviour — proved, in time, to weaken its appeal. The realists' world of the 1950s and 1960s gave way to new realities in the early 1970s. The classical-realist view seemed far too limited in a world characterized by a general relaxation in East-West tensions, a dramatically expanded level of international economic activity, the prominence of nonstate actors, the increasing permeability of national boundaries, the breakdown of the Bretton Woods system, and the decline of U.S. hegemony.

Transnational Relations: The Politics of Interdependence

Around this time, and for many of these reasons, students and practitioners of international relations were actively looking for alternatives to the dominant realist view. The "world politics paradigm" of Robert O. Keohane and Joseph Nye, Jr., emerged as a direct paradigmatic challenge to the logic of realism.[13] It focussed on the importance of transnational society, rather than interstate relations. The world-politics paradigm was not designed to replace the realist perspective or to deny the relevance of interstate relations or the notions of power and national interest. Rather, this competing paradigm set out to extend the realists' understanding of contemporary international politics. It attempted to accomplish this task by introducing three specific amendments to realist theory. First, it maintained that states were not the only significant actors in world politics; that various transnational actors (i.e., nongovernmental actors that operate across national boundaries) are also important in world politics. Second, the world-politics paradigm added transgovernmental relations (i.e., direct interactions between agencies of different governments, where those agencies act relatively autonomously from central-government control) to state-to-state relations. Finally, this perspective suggested that there is a multiplicity of issues on the global policy agenda and that the military-security issue no longer dominates that agenda. And, even if the security issue was to dominate the agenda again, it would still be necessary to take into account other important issue areas.

By relaxing the state-centric assumption, the transnational-relations perspective was successful in directing our attention to one of the most important structural problems in world politics — the extreme asymmetry of global actors. Where realism assumes a system of relatively equal actors (all of which are states), the world-politics paradigm contends that the relations between the principal actors in world politics (both states and nonstate actors) are highly unequal. Transnational business activity, for example, has traditionally been distributed very unevenly, with virtually all important activity originating in (or providing disproportionate benefits to) the developed market economies. The myth of state sovereignty and the emphasis on security issues (which were perpetuated by the realists) make the world seem less imbalanced than it is.

In addition to the assertion that states are not the only important actors in world politics, the world-politics paradigm also relaxed the "state-as-actor" assumption, or the idea that national governments behave as single, unitary actors. The implication here is that international politics would include not only state-to-state relations and transnational relations but transgovernmental relations as well. Transgovernmental relations involve an increase in communications among governments. In particular, they draw attention to bureaucratic contacts taking place below the apex of power — pointing to the existence of a network of co-operative interactions among like-minded subunits of different governments. Moreover, transgovernmental relations involves considerably more than simple transgovernmental policy co-ordination. According to this argument, regularized policy co-ordination often leads to changes in attitudes, where governments cease to be seen as closed decision-making units, and to the creation of transgovernmental elite networks. The resulting networks or coalitions amount to an alliance of subunits of one government with like-minded agencies of other governments. International organizations, international regimes, economic summitry, and other forms of joint decision making have strengthened and legitimized this practice.

The transgovernmental dimension lends additional credibility to three important features of the transnational-relations perspective. First, the practical realization that conflict exists among various subunits of national governments in the foreign-policy decision-making process challenges the realists' claim that national governments make decisions unitarily and rationally. In fact, the world-politics paradigm is more in keeping with the bureaucratic-politics model of decision making, which suggests that national decisions are the result of a policy process characterized by conflict, compromise, and confusion among the constituent units of a national government. Some scholars see this connection as the crux of the transnational-relations perspective.

Finally, transgovernmental relations underscore the increasing permeability of the nation-state. While transnational activities make societies more sensitive to one another and to systemic factors, national governments are pressed to control this nongovernmental behaviour. Ironically, one possible result of these attempts to co-ordinate national policy is the further increase in direct bureaucratic contacts between subunits of different governments. These transgovernmental relations add to the external threat posed by transnational organizations by challenging the autonomy of the state from within.

In sum, the paradigmatic challenge posed by the world-politics paradigm introduced a number of important new factors to the study of world politics. These factors, which include the introduction of transnational and transgovernmental actors, the realization that bureaucratic politics applies in situations where interactions are transnational, and the notion of asymmetry, constitute an entirely new way of looking at world politics. The single largest point of departure between the two perspectives resides in the fact that the realist perspective focussed on the rhetoric of national security whereas the transnational-relations perspective is noted for its direct association with the notion of economic interdependence.

Globalism: The Politics of Dependence

Generally speaking, systemic theories of world politics are ones that share a global rather than a state-centric conceptualization of the field. The focal point of systems theory tends to be the structure of the system (rather than the political or economic processes that take place within it) — stressing the inequities in the relative distribution of power, influence, and economic well-being. This systems or structural perspective operates basically at two levels. The first level proceeds from what has come to be known as the "world systems" approach, stressing the broad historical development of the world economy, its resistance to change, and its continuing ability to determine the political and economic realities of individual members. The most notable theoretical construct to emerge from this particular school of thought is "world systems theory," which is most often associated with the work of Immanuel Wallerstein.[14] The second level, which also involves a systemic explanation, proceeds from the assumption that the system can largely be understood in terms of its leadership. It looks for sources of change in patterns of hegemonic ascendance and decline, long cycles, international regime change, and the dynamic interaction of the system and its constituent members.

World-systems theory poses a direct paradigmatic challenge to both the realist school of thought and the liberal perspective. The focus here is not on the state or some combination of national and transnational interactions, but on the system itself. More specifically, world-systems theory derives its theoretical legitimacy from an analysis of the historical development of the capitalist world economy. While there are realists who are committed to the use of the system as the principal focus for analysis, most "globalists" are more interested in the impact of change in the international system on the various social and economic formations than they are in the so-called state system. They base their analysis on the transhistoric economic and social context of global affairs. Explicit in this approach is the logic of historicism and a commitment to structuralism. Its attention to historicism (and the notion that system continuities give way slowly and erratically) further distinguishes this perspective from mainstream international political economy.

As we noted above, this approach can be traced largely to the work of Immanuel Wallerstein. For Wallerstein, the world economy can be understood primarily in terms of the historically conditioned, systemically promoted relationship between the core and the periphery (and the existence of a semiperiphery that operates as a buffer between exploiter and exploited). The system maintains political stability by virtue of the concentration of military power, the pervasiveness of the ideological commitment to the system, and the division of the system into the three tiers. From this perspective, the main thrust of scholarly activity centres on the historical evolution of the international system and on the continuing impact which the system has on individual members. While world-systems scholarship tends to focus on the former, there is a growing interest in understanding

> the functioning of a capitalist world economy [which] requires that groups pursue their economic interests within a single world market while seeking to distort this market for their benefit by organizing to exert influence on states, some of which are more powerful than others but none of which controls the world market in its entirety.[15]

The world-systems approach has, however, received a good deal of criticism in recent years. One of the most compelling of these criticisms is that Wallerstein's version of world-systems dynamics tends to be reductionist, undervaluing considerations of international politics such that the world system is seen in strictly economic terms. Wherever political phenomena occur, they tend to be "explained away" as a consequence of capitalist economic development. For the world-systems perspective, nation-states are instruments used by economically dominant groups. One alternative to this economic determinism is the "long cycle" explanation offered by George Modelski, William R. Thompson, and others.[16] The fundamental difference between the world-systems perspective and the long-cycle-of-world-leadership perspective is the reluctance of the latter to accept the logic that economic considerations are the prime source of structural change. The central assumption of the long-cycle theory is that the level of world order can more realistically be traced to the global political system's power structure.

More recently, a number of scholars have attempted to integrate or synthesize the logic of the two perspectives. In an insightful assessment of the fundamental differences between the state-power argument and the world-systems approach,

Christopher Chase-Dunn has argued that the systemic ordering of the international state system and the world economy are so intertwined as to constitute only one logic:

> Capitalism is best conceived as a peculiar combination of economic and political processes which operate at the level of the world economy as a whole. Thus the interstate system is the political side of capitalism, not an analytically autonomous system, and its survival is dependent upon the institutions which are associated with the capital-accumulation process.[17]

Change is still seen only in the long-term historical context, and world wars and the rise and fall of hegemonic powers as the violent reorganization of production relations on a world scale. If anything, Chase-Dunn tends to come down on the "material" side of the debate.

Chase-Dunn goes on to argue that the marriage of these two theoretical constructs produces what he calls the "modern world-systems" perspective. The main features of a modern world-systems perspective include an interstate system that is dependent on the institutions and opportunities presented by the world market for its survival; the division of sovereignty in the core (interimperial rivalry); the uneven nature of capitalist economic development; and the continuity of structural features of the system over long periods of time. Needless to say, this formulation has not been embraced by more traditional realists. Still, this synthesis has taken world-systems theory well beyond the much-criticized reductionism of Wallerstein. Moreover, the notion of integrating the broader logic of the world-systems or world-economy perspective with some elements of the interstate-system perspective has been extremely useful in coming to terms with an increasingly complex and uncertain international political system.

The Study of World Politics

The contrast between a realist image, an interdependence image, and, to a lesser extent, a dependence image has been a powerful theme in international relations scholarship in the late 1970s and throughout the 1980s. The emergence of the transnational-relations perspective and the rebirth of the historically conditioned dependence perspective have proved to be both workable alternatives to the logic of classical realism and important tools in understanding a world increasingly characterized by rapid change and by structural uncertainty. Interestingly, as the chapters in the final section of this book suggest, recent work in the field has led to the resurgence in realist thinking. An increasing number of students of world politics have come to believe that the preoccupation with transnational and global concerns may have obscured some of the more important and more enduring elements of the realist position. As Kal Holsti has noted,

> analysts have been so impressed by growing interdependence that they have ignored a simultaneous or parallel process that results in increased international fragmentation . . . while transactions between societies have indeed grown dramatically

> throughout this century, nationalism, separatism and international disintegration have also been prominent. . . . The two trends are taking place concurrently.[18]

The realist response to the transnational-relations challenge seems to have taken two specific forms. In the first place, there are those who are content to restate the classical-realist principles. Their argument rests on the assumption that the bulk of the literature employing the transnational-relations perspective has fundamentally misrepresented the realist position. The second type of response has employed the basic logic of realism (i.e., state-centrism, power politics, national interest) but focusses more on the role of the state and on economic factors. While the bulk of the recent literature emphasizes the second type of response, it would be useful to examine briefly the first, as it clearly spells out what we like to call "classical realism." In an intriguing essay on the connection between protectionism and the resistance to structural change in the world economy, Susan Strange has suggested that the realist school "from Hobbes to Kenneth Waltz and Hedley Bull is due for a revival."[19] And, indeed, a major restatement of the original realist position has occurred in the form of Hedley Bull's *The Anarchical Society* and Kenneth Waltz's *Theory of International Politics*.[20] Although Strange's prediction about the revival of realism seems quite accurate, her presumption that the conventional realists would pay greater attention to the economic issues that were of such great interest to the transnational-relations school seems somewhat less plausible. Both Waltz and Bull continue to explain international politics primarily in terms of strategic/military power and the number of units in the system, without reference to economics as an independent variable. Moreover, both understand security in very narrow terms.

To be sure, as we will see in this book, analyses of international relations that pay particular attention to the notions of power, national interest, and the structure of the system have come back into fashion. What we are witnessing, however, is not a return to the traditional balance-of-power realism (*à la* Morgenthau, Waltz, or Bull) but a swing back to structural explanations that deal, in many cases, specifically with the so-called new international politics of the 1970s and 1980s.

This second form of response to the transnational challenge can be found in recent writings that focus on the structure of the international system and its relationship to the state. This literature can be categorized generally as operating from a "modified realist," "neorealist," or "statist" position. The basic difference between this perspective and classical or traditional realism lies in the idea that "relative power capabilities are not the only state objective . . . economic wealth, for instance, could be an end in itself."[21] In addition, where classic realism all but denies the existence of economic interdependence, statism accepts the premise that increasing economic interdependence has exacerbated the need for the state to reassert its economic autonomy. In fact, the statist or modified-realist school has placed considerable emphasis on the role of the state in explaining change in the international political economy. Without doubt, the main proponents of this perspective are aware of their realist roots.

Despite the similarities with traditional realist thinking, the state-power argument and the realist position are not directly analogous. In fact, of the three central realist principles — that autonomous states dominate an interstate international system, that force is an effective and usable instrument of foreign policy, and that there is a clear hierarchy of issues on the global policy agenda headed up by the military/security issue — the statists really adhere only to the first. This point is worth pursuing as it is very important to our understanding of world politics not to confuse this statist position (which asserts quite clearly that there is a strong relationship between the world economy and national foreign economic policy) with the traditional or conventional realist perspective. However, as Robert Gilpin has so aptly argued, while a neorealist school of thought undoubtedly exists, there are important distinctions that must be made within this broad school of thought. These differences are elaborated throughout this book.

With respect to the first principle, where there is some agreement, the statists adopt what amounts to a much weaker position. As Krasner puts it, they are working from "an analytic perspective that treats the state as an autonomous actor, but one constrained by domestic as well as international structures."[22] Accepting these constraints allows for a more flexible commitment to both the state-as-actor and the state-centric assumptions (and, implicitly, recognizes the existence of transnational and transgovernmental relations). It would appear that neorealists and statists do not completely discount mass preferences, political parties, and elections, as some of their detractors suggest, although these are generally viewed as the result, and not as the cause, of government policy. On the second and third principles, there is much less agreement. While the statists would be likely to accept the maxim that military force is a usable and effective instrument of foreign policy, they would probably add that symbolic and economic power (both real and potential) are equally important (and, in recent years, more important) in pursuing the national interest. Moreover, as the chief proponents of the statist position have a demonstrated interest in economic issues, it goes without saying that the third principle of realism (a clearly organized hierarchy of issues, dominated by the military/security issue) is too restrictive for the state-power argument. Also, as many now subscribe to a comprehensive notion of security (which broadens the definition of security to include economic and environmental concerns), this distinction is simply less relevant than it was a decade or so ago.

If nothing else, this review of the competing paradigms in the study of world politics should serve to demonstrate the folly of rigidly adhering to any one of the three dominant perspectives. Clearly, as we will see throughout this volume, there is an ongoing debate among those who pursue a world-systems approach, those who adhere to a liberal position and attempt to find ways to manage interdependence, and those who view the international system in dynamic but statist terms. This volume explicitly addresses the conflicting ideological perspectives and competing approaches that characterize the study of world politics and attempts to put into some meaningful context the world in which we all must live.

NOTES

1. Paul Kennedy, *The Rise and Fall of the Great Powers: Economic Change and Military Conflict from 1500 to 2000* (London: Unwin Hyman, 1988).

2. Robert W. Cox, "Ideologies and the New International Economic Order: Reflections on Some Recent Literature," *International Organization* 33 (Spring 1979): 257–302; Robert Gilpin, "Three Models of the Future," *International Organization* 29 (Winter 1975): 37–60; Stephen Krasner, *Defending the National Interest* (Princeton: Princeton University Press, 1977); and, James Rosenau, "Order and Disorder in the Study of World Politics: Ten Essays in Search of Order," in *Globalism Versus Realism: International Relations' Third Debate*, ed. R. Maghroori and B. Ramberg (Boulder: Westview, 1982), 1–7.

3. Rosenau, "Order and Disorder in the Study of World Politics," 4.

4. On the notion of complexity in the international system, see the seminal article by Ernst Haas: "Turbulent Fields and the Theory of Regional Integration," *International Organization* 30 (Spring 1976): 173–212.

5. See Cox, "Ideologies and the NIEO."

6. See Gilpin, "Three Models of the Future." On the original formulation of the sovereignty-at-bay thesis, see Raymond Vernon, *Sovereignty at Bay* (New York: Basic, 1971).

7. See Krasner, *Defending the National Interest.*

8. See, especially, Hans Morgenthau, *Politics among Nations: The Struggle for Power and Peace* (New York: Knopf, 1948; 4th ed.: 1967); Kenneth Waltz, *Man, the State, and War* (New York: Columbia University Press, 1954); George F. Kennann, *Realities of American Foreign Policy* (Princeton: Princeton University Press, 1954); R. Niebuhr, *Moral Man and Immoral Society* (New York: Scribners, 1947); and, E.H. Carr, *The Twenty Years' Crisis: 1919–1939* (London: Macmillan, 1946).

9. See Hedley Bull, *The Anarchical Society: A Study of Order in World Politics* (New York: Columbia University Press, 1977), 74.

10. Morgenthau, *Politics among Nations*, 4th ed., 36.

11. Bull, *Anarchical Society*, 109.

12. Robert L. Rothstein, "On the Costs of Realism," in *Perspectives on World Politics*, ed. M. Smith, R. Little, and M. Shackleton (London: Croom-Helm, for the Open University, 1981), 389.

13. See Robert O. Keohane and Joseph Nye, Jr., *Transnational Relations and World Politics* (Cambridge: Harvard University Press, 1972).

14. See, in particular, Immanuel Wallerstein, "The Rise and Future Demise of the World Capitalist System: Concepts for Comparative Analysis," *Comparative Studies in Social History* 16, no. 4 (1974): 387–415; *The Modern World System* (New York: Academic, 1974); *The Capitalist World Economy* (Cambridge: Cambridge University Press, 1979); and *The Modern World System II: Mercantilism and the Consolidation of the European Economy* (New York: Academic, 1980).

15. Wallerstein, "The Rise and Future Demise," 401.

16. William R. Thompson, "Uneven Economic Growth, Systemic Challenges, and Global Wars," *International Studies Quarterly* 27 (September 1983): 341–55.

17. Christopher Chase-Dunn, "Interstate System and Capitalist World Economy: One Logic or Two?" *International Studies Quarterly* 25 (March 1981): 19–42.

18. Kal Holsti, "Change in the International System: Interdependence, Integration and Fragmentation," in *Change in the International System*, ed. O. Holsti, R. Siverson, and A. George (Boulder: Westview, 1980), 23.

19. Susan Strange, "The Management of Surplus Capacity: Or How Does Theory Stand Up to Protectionism 1970s Style?" *International Organization* 33 (Summer 1979): 309.

20. Bull, *Anarchical Society*, and Kenneth Waltz, *Theory of International Politics* (Reading, Mass.: Addison-Wesley, 1979).

21. Stephen Krasner, "Regimes and the Limits of Realism: Regimes as Autonomous Variables,"*International Organization* 36 (Spring 1982): 496.

22. Krasner, "Regimes and the Limits of Realism," 498.

PART I

THE POLITICS OF POWER AND SECURITY

In many respects the politics of power and security has been the mainstay of international relations scholarship. Not only have political leaders traditionally conceived of world politics in these terms, but war and peace are its most persistent themes, and the latter, that is, the avoidance of conflict (particularly armed conflict), is an abiding concern of all students of world politics. Insofar as scholars are concerned — from Machiavelli, through Hobbes, to those of the 20th century — power, security, and the national interest have been instrumental concepts in understanding the relations between and among states.

Given that conflict reflects the inability of sovereign states to resolve their competing interests, Part I begins with an examination of the state in international relations. Tom Keating argues that, while, in the late 20th century, the state is being challenged by new forms of political organization, there is a stubborn life and purpose in the nation-state, making it critical to understand why states go to war. Patrick James assesses the causes of war, paying particular attention to the role of the systemic power structure in the generation of conflict. Among the dimensions of that structure discussed are the concentration of capabilities among states and the configuration of alliances as political causes of war. The four following chapters attempt to come to terms with the various approaches to avoiding conflict. William Moul examines the classic balance-of-power argument, paying particular attention to historical evidence linking various balances of power to war, peace, and alliance-formation. Paul Buteux adopts a much more contemporary focus, assessing the role and importance of nuclear deterrence in world politics. David Cox addresses the utility of arms control, with particular reference to negotiations between the superpowers over nuclear weapons. Keith Krause examines one aspect of the proliferation of conventional weapons; namely, the arms trade.

While these writers generally concede that security remains the critical factor in any explanation of international (especially interstate) relations, and that realism remains the most compelling analytic tool, all posit the growing awareness that security must be conceived of in much broader terms.

THE STATE AND INTERNATIONAL RELATIONS

Tom Keating

International relations theory has been described as "a tradition of speculation about relations between states."[1] While this description may appear reasonable, there are many who would take exception to it. For them, international relations theory encompasses much more than simply interstate relations. Indeed, in the view of some, it is just a matter of time before we see the decline and eventual demise of the state. Recently, the discipline has been inundated with discussions about new actors and new agendas in international relations. The state is losing its attraction and its authority as new rivals appear. Transnational actors in the form of multinational business enterprises, religious and social movements, and supranational organizations such as the European Community are frequently cited as the rising stars on the world stage. Some writers even disavow the use of the term "international" on the grounds that it suggests a bias toward states and substitute in its place such words as "global," "world," and "transnational," each of which is intended to make clear that the subject of the discipline must not be limited to states but should also include nonstate actors.

In spite of these views, the state refuses to go away. Against claims to the contrary, the popularity of states and their seemingly insatiable appetite for intervention at home and activity abroad stand among the more pronounced trends of the 20th century. Indeed, it is somewhat surprising that arguments forecasting the demise of the state in international relations have received so much attention. Within the past 40 years the state system that emerged in Europe after the Middle Ages has expanded to encompass the entire planet. The wave of decolonization and independence movements in the postwar period has increased the number of states from about 50 to more than 160 in four decades. The majority of states that now exist achieved their political independence after 1945. In addition, there are many groups around the world — in Namibia, the Middle East, and Quebec, to cite a few examples — who, through violent or peaceful means, are aspiring to become states. Even the oceans have not been immune to state-building: states took advantage of the most recent round of negotiations on the law of the sea to expand their jurisdictional reach. In short, contrary to reports of its imminent demise, the state appears to be thriving.

This conclusion receives additional support from evidence of the expansion of the state's activities at home. In industrialized societies, the state has expanded dramatically over past centuries. Consider for a moment Mann's description of European states in their formative years and contrast it with the contemporary states of Europe:

> The states were the initially weak states of feudal Europe. In the twelfth century even the strongest of them absorbed less than two percent of GNP; they called out highly decentralized military levies of at most 10–20,000 men sometimes only for 30 days in the campaigning system; they could not tax in any regular way; they regulated only a small portion of total social disputes — they were, in fact, marginal to the social lives of most Europeans.[2]

The picture is quite different today. States are now able to maintain standing armies, some in the hundreds of thousands. They have extensive taxing powers and use these with impunity; more than one-third of the gross national products of industrialized societies pass through the state. In its relations with domestic society, the modern state has extended its grasp into many areas of social and economic activity. Most states now control a large portion of their educational systems. They also have programs governing the young, the aged, and the infirm. Few areas of life have been left unregulated, and the state has become the main source of sustenance and support for many, from cradle to grave. Wars and economic recessions, which have recurred in the 20th century, have further increased the scope and depth of the state's intervention in society. Even modern-day neoconservatives, such as the Reagan administration in the 1980s, who publicly decry big government, have been unable to resist the temptation to make use of the powers of the state.

> President Reagan when elected promised to reduce the power of the federal government and to turn the rising tide of state spending. Yet he has presided over fiscal deficits that broke all previous records, and over an increase in the powers of some key agencies like the Federal Reserve Board and the Comptroller of the Currency and over more protective intervention on behalf of uncompetitive American industries than had been seen for many years.[3]

Comparable patterns of state activity are apparent throughout the world.

The dramatic rise in state intervention in domestic society and the proliferation of states are facts that are difficult to reconcile with the claim that the state is in decline. Yet, this claim is not without some foundation. There is real evidence that there has been an expansion in the number and the competence of nonstate actors in the modern world. However, the presence of such actors is not a distinctly new phenomenon in international relations, and not all of these actors have great significance for the conduct of such relations. Yet, when the size and range of activities of multinational corporations exceed those of many states and when transnational groups are able to penetrate states and disrupt social, economic, and political life, it becomes difficult not to grant some importance to these nonstate actors and consider the challenges they do or could present to states. The contemporary international system thus contains an apparent paradox. States are very much alive and in many respects expanding their range of authority, and, at the same time, nonstate actors are proliferating and developing their competencies around the globe. If international relations theory remains "a tradition of speculation about relations between states" it must also be concerned with the alternatives to states and with those developments that may change interstate relations. Thus, before examining theories of the state and their relevance for international relations, we will assess the state in light of the challenges, academic and other, that have been made against it. All too frequently, discussions of the state and international relations have been conducted as if the state were unproblematic and required no further attention. There is, however, a good deal of evidence to suggest otherwise. More importantly, in examining theories of the state, it may be possible to account for the apparent paradox mentioned above.

Critical Assessments of the State

The proliferation of states in recent decades, the stubborn persistence of sovereignty in international relations, and the interventionist practices of states on the domestic front, all validate the view that the state has a central role in the world today. Yet, in spite of such evidence, one should not exaggerate the ability of states to control their own destiny. There are ever-increasing numbers of nonstate actors involved in international relations. Indeed, much attention has been devoted to the erosion of state sovereignty and the possibility that the authority of states is being usurped by these increasingly competent nonstate actors. Not all of these challenges to state sovereignty undermine the idea of states or the viability of a system of states. For example, many separatist or irredentist movements, such as those among Palestinians in the Middle East and Québécois within Canada, seek merely to replace a state that they consider unrepresentative with one that represents their unique cultural, religious, or political interests. Alternatively, a supranational organization, such as the European Community, aspiring to acquire sovereign authority over its member states, would, in effect, if it were to succeed (which is unlikely), create a single state to replace the existing member states. Indeed, the emerging European Community bureaucracy in Brussels is already in the process of replicating that which presently exists at the national level, including an agency to handle relations with other states. These examples suggest that some of the contemporary threats to the state are better viewed as challenges to particular states and not to the state system as such. In this respect they reaffirm the persistent attraction of the state as the basic unit of political organization in the contemporary world.

For some observers, these and other challenges to the state are indicators of the beginnings of a crisis in the state system. Critical commentary on the state and its utility as a concept for explaining international relations has reflected at least three different, but not necessarily distinct, types of considerations: empirical, normative, and analytical. The empirical concerns relate primarily to the developments in the contemporary international political economy that challenge the legitimacy and capacity of states to represent and to respond to societal demands. Many have questioned the legitimacy of the state because of its inability to respond to the needs and aspirations of various distinct cultural, linguistic, or ethnic communities that reside within a state's territorial boundaries. "The current demarcation of the globe into nation-states is in large measure the outcome of the last round of struggles between cultural groups that defined themselves as nations and insisted on their own states in which they could set the rules."[4] Obviously, "the current demarcation" has not met with universal acceptance. There are numerous examples of disaffected peoples around the globe who have sought, or are in the process of seeking, greater autonomy from existing states. As indicated above, these people usually seek to replace one state with another. The persistence of such demands, however, indicates to some the inability of states and the state system to respond to the level of cultural diversity that exists on this planet. Not only are attempts to reorganize the state system in a way that would respond to these demands likely to be unsuccessful, but the attempts themselves would be too threatening, given the likelihood of violence. Currently, there are at least 800 and as many as 7000 potential nationalist groups that have or might become political movements of consequence. This fact suggests to some a more permanent structural problem that cannot be accommodated within the existing state system.

A second set of criticisms is centred on the notion that many of the major problems threatening the stability of the international system require solutions that transcend the authority and capacity of sovereign states. The world faces a multitude of military, economic, social, and environmental problems that cannot be resolved unilaterally or at the local level. All such problems — from nuclear-weapons proliferation to exchange-rate stability to acid rain — resist resolution by unilateral action. In an age when the technology of modern weaponry facilitates the penetration of national boundaries, some have said that the state is incapable of guaranteeing security to its citizens. Confronted by increasing levels of interdependence (symmetrical or asymmetrical) many states lack the capacity to implement an effective national economic policy that addresses domestic demands. Instead, they are frequently forced to react and to adapt to events and policies that lie beyond the state's capacity to control. In addition, states must increasingly be prepared to face the prospects that their actions might be undermined by the practices of other states or multinational corporations. While state intervention has raised societal expectations in terms of welfare benefits, the state may be losing the capacity to provide such benefits. Many Western developed states are facing what some call a fiscal crisis. In simple terms, many states find that there is an increasingly large gap between their commitments and their capabilities. The principal effect of such crisis seems to be the further erosion of the legitimacy of the state, as individuals are forced to look for alternative sources of material as well as cultural benefits.

The potential for citizens to circumvent the state has expanded in direct proportion to technological developments in global transportation and communication. These developments enhance the ability of nonstate actors to link peoples in different parts of the world in ways that are beyond the influence of national governments. As a consequence, states encounter greater difficulty in sealing their borders against the incursion of these "foreign" ideas. The Canadian government, for example, has abandoned attempts to limit Canadians' access to U.S. television and radio since the technology that facilitates such access is beyond government control. As another illustration of this problem: much of the recent controversy within the U.N. Educational, Scientific, and Cultural Organization (UNESCO) has been centred on the New World Information Order, which seeks to legitimize state interference in various media to prevent the penetration of national societies by external actors. Many member-states are concerned that more powerful states or nonstate actors would employ these information technologies to subvert efforts to generate and maintain national loyalties. Modern technology has, of course, also been used by states to control their own citizens more effectively.

While many of these rivals to the state, such as religious movements, have always existed, their enhanced capacities for interference within the sphere of the state, especially given the nature of many contemporary problems that exist within that sphere, have provided such groups with both the incentive and the capability to mount a more sustained challenge to the state's ability to exercise effective authority than had been possible in the past. Based on these trends, it has been argued that there is an emerging crisis of authority in which the state is losing its ability to maintain the loyalty of its citizens and that these citizens, in turn, will be gently subverted by these transnational religious, economic, or social movements. In short, the state withers as transnationalism expands.

> Despite the revival of geopolitical imperatives and the renewed primacy of national security policy, it is clear that subnational and transnational entities simply will not go away. They have asserted themselves against the prerogatives of nation-states, compelled statesmen to respond to their concerns, and frequently bypassed the traditional state-to-state diplomatic arena, as they conduct their own transnational negotiations and confrontations. It is clear, in fact, that they will increasingly affect who gets what, when and how in the world system.[5]

A second, related consideration questions the value of states and the state system. This critical normative view holds the state responsible as the principal impediment to social progress. The state is seen as the primary perpetrator of violence and warfare in the world. States are also viewed as substantial barriers to justice, equality, cultural expression, and a stable and sustainable physical environment. These concerns have been expressed most consistently by such critics as Richard Falk, who is involved in the World Order Models Project: "The state and state system possess a declining functional capacity and legitimacy, while obscuring this decline behind an intensifying reliance on internal violence and international war-making."[6] The elimination of states and the nonviolent transformation of the state system through "gentle subversion" by more just, humane, and equitable social forces become matters of priority for these advocates. In short, states impede global co-operation and must be overcome. There is an implicit assumption here that the state system would be replaced by more "progressive" forms of social, economic, and political organization.

Drawing in part from the idealism that was prevalent in the interwar period, these writers look to a future without states in which individuals are guided by either some benevolent global despot or some universally shared ideal in which "reason" becomes sovereign, as espoused by Immanuel Kant. As interpreted by Walker this latter view would entail

> the growth of uniquely human capacities through reason allow[ing] for the gradual development of a universal kingdom of ends and the eventual replacement of legal constraints by freedom and morality alone. Thus just as individual men have a duty to move from a state of nature to civil society, so nations also have a duty to pass out of their state of nature into a relationship that is somehow analogous to that which joins individuals in civil society.[7]

Both the empirical and normative critiques caution against reliance on a state-centric approach for understanding international relations. A number of writers have advocated alternatives to this state-centric approach. They have expressed concerns that the state has become reified and that, in adopting a state-centric approach to analyzing international relations, students are confusing the façade of interstate relations with the real forces that are shaping world politics. Such views have been evident for some time and are prevalent in writings on integration, interdependence, transnationalism, world systems, and, most recently, international regimes. The principal target of these criticisms has been the work of realists who assert the pre-eminence of states and frequently do so with little concern for the nature of these states.

> The state is viewed as the "essential actor" whose interests, power, decisions, practices, and interactions with other states define and exhaust the scope and content of international politics as an autonomous sphere . . . there is no political life absent of states, prior to states, or independent of states. Political interests that are not reducible to state interests enter the international political realm only insofar as they are mediated by state interests.[8]

By focussing on the state, critics either undervalue or ignore completely the influence on activities of other social forces. Critics have also expressed concern that such terms as "the national interest" are used without qualification or even without consideration of the possibility that such interests might be unrepresentative of large segments of the population or even that they might represent political bargains worked out within a divided bureaucracy or between state elites and domestic groups. Instead, there is a tendency to consider the state as a unified rational actor that speaks with a single voice on behalf of society.

Working from an entirely different frame of reference, others have maintained that states are incidental in comparison to structural features of a "world capitalist system" and that a reliance on state-level explanations would be incomplete and misleading. From this perspective, "states appear as territorial subdivisions within gross economic sectors of the world economy, not as organizations able to mobilize forms of power other than economic interests."[9] The gist of all of these criticisms is that a more fruitful analysis of international relations would require that less attention be given to the state. The critics are, however, divided on what the alternative focus should be.

Resurrecting the State

Not surprisingly, many of these criticisms have been met with some skepticism. Among realists there is a widely held view that, despite all of the challenges to the state, little of substance has changed. Raymond Aron, for example, concluded that there was no reason to believe that "economic and technological interdependence among the various factions of humanity has definitely devalued the fact of . . . the existence of distinct states."[10] A more sustained response to these critics was made by Hedley Bull, who defended the state not only on empirical grounds but on moral ones as well.[11] As noted earlier there is much evidence to indicate that the state has successfully resisted these challenges, at least for the present, as it continues to expand spatially and administratively. This resistance might explain why, in recent years, there are signs of a resurgence of interest in the continuing importance of the state for understanding international relations. Fred Halliday is among those who have encouraged such a change, in part on the basis of research conducted in other disciplines such as sociology and history. "At the very time when the innovators and proponents of new paradigms within International Relations have been seeking to reject or reduce the salience of the state, the comparable trend within sociology has been to re-examine the state and to reassert its centrality in historical and contemporary contexts." Rather than dismissing the state or forecasting its eventual demise while attention is directed elsewhere, Halliday favours a more intensive examination of the nature of the state. "The argument is not about whether we are or are not state-centric but what we mean by the state."[12] The apparent paradox of persisting statism in the face of the pressing challenges referred to earlier supports such a position. Reconciling these alternative views of the state's role in international relations necessitates a closer examination of the role of the state — its origins and evolution, its position in the international system, its position in domestic society, and its sources of autonomy in the contemporary world.

The very idea that the state has been neglected in the study of international relations may strike some as odd. With the exception of the wave of critical works referred to earlier that questions the utility of a state-centric approach, most of the writing on international relations has focussed primarily, if not exclusively, on interstate relations. Prominent within these critical works are those of such realists as E.H. Carr, Hans Morgenthau, Hedley Bull, Martin Wight, Raymond Aron, Stanley Hoffmann, and J.D.B. Miller.[13] Many of their texts have been used in the classroom for decades and have influenced generations of students. Indeed, many believe that realism and its corresponding emphasis on the state are a dominant approach in the field.[14] Yet, despite the emphasis that these works have placed on the importance of the state, there is a tendency in at least some of these writings to treat it as ahistorical and unproblematic. Within this perspective the nature of the state is considered inconsequential in the study of international relations. This view is evident in the manner in which the state has been defined.

Most definitions identify people, territory, government, sovereignty, and international recognition as the constitutive elements of states. These characteristics are also emphasized in international law. The first article of the Montevideo Convention of 1933 stipulates: "the state as a person of international law should possess the following qualifications: (a) a permanent population; (b) a defined territory; (c) government; and, (d) the capacity to enter into relations with other states." Many who write from a realist perspective consider these qualifications to be all that is necessary to identify the state. As Northedge points out, "a state . . . is a territorial association of people recognized for purposes of law and diplomacy as a legally equal member of the system of states. It is in reality a means of organizing people for the purpose of their participation in the international system."[15] These definitions do not distinguish between different types of states, nor do they raise questions about the nature of the relationship between state and society. Instead, they view all states as sharing certain characteristics and imply that the state and society are coterminous. Yet, the state is not as simple and straightforward as these definitions suggest.

> The concept normally used in International Relations is not merely an analytical abstraction, but also one replete with legal and value assumptions (i.e., that states are equal, that they control their territory, that they represent their peoples). There could indeed be few concepts less "realistic" than that of the sovereign state in its conventional International Relations guise.[16]

Given the arguments raised against the state in the earlier section and these conceptual difficulties, there is good reason to look more closely at the state.

The Origins of States

States are the basic unit of political activity and organization in virtually all corners of the world. Boundary lines differentiate one territory from the next. Most people have little hesitation in identifying themselves as members of a particular state, as Canadians, Nigerians, Pakistanis, or Australians, for example. Indeed, Wight is probably correct when he asserts that "modern man in general has shown a stronger loyalty to the state than to church or class or any other international bond."[17] This has not always been the case. The state is a modern phenomenon. Its global reach has been completed only within the last few decades, the number of states having more than tripled since 1945.

The origins of the modern state system have been the subject of considerable discussion with respect to both chronology and substance. The chronology need not delay us here except to note that there is widespread agreement that the Peace of Westphalia (1648), which ended the bloody Thirty Years' War of religious conflict that had raged over Europe in the early 17th century, confirmed the mastery of sovereign states over the main rivals of church and empire.[18] Whether this situation was the beginning or the end of the establishment of a state system is not immediately relevant here. What is important to recognize is that the state, which is often considered to be a permanent fixture of international relations (i.e., it was, is, and always will be), is not only impermanent but has a relatively short history.

The emergence of the state and its subsequent evolution into a system of states that has since encompassed the globe have been conditioned by a mix of political, economic, and social circumstances. The state was in no sense preordained, and its future survival, while highly probable, is by no means a certainty. The state emerged as the pre-eminent player in international relations only after a lengthy and, at times, violent struggle with dynastic and other secular forces. The struggle, then as now, is one between unity and diversity. Since its emergence at the end of the Middle Ages, the European state system has been repeatedly challenged by contemporary aspirants to empire — Napoleon in the early 19th century and Hitler in our own, for example. There have always been those who would supplant the state and replace it with their own messianic vision, and there probably always will be. It is the more virulent and violent efforts to do so that have led realists such as Wight to look skeptically upon proposals to eliminate states and reform the international system. And, it is by no means certain that, having failed in the past, such attempts will fail in the future. Wight even expresses some uncertainty about whether interstate relations have been the norm in the history of international relations:

> It might well be asked why unrevolutionary international politics should be regarded as more normal than revolutionary, since the history of international society has been fairly equally divided between the two. . . . To describe either international revolution or power politics (unrevolutionary international politics) as "normal" is to make a statement of belief about the way international politics ought to go. Either the tendency towards establishing doctrinal and political unity is regarded as more important and fundamental, or the maintenance of national freedom and a balanced variety. But there are few greater errors in the study of international politics than to suppose that revolutionary doctrines have been discarded or are maintained only hypocritically for reasons of state.[19]

More important than the chronological limits to the modern state system are the substantive factors that led to its development and that have sustained it over time. Examining these factors not only sheds light on the current condition of states but it also identifies some persistent features of the interrelationship between state, society, and the international system. On the matter of origins, there are a number of disparate views. These differences cannot be resolved here, but it is helpful to identify some of the major issues in the various arguments because they reflect two competing views of the state and international relations.

Historians and sociologists point to the plurality of sources of power that began to emerge during the Middle Ages and cite the competition between these forces as the principal explanatory variable in the formation of states in Europe. Local political elites emerged in the contest between church and empire. In differentiating their activities and source of authority from those of the church and by expanding the administrative tasks they performed in local communities, these emerging political elites acquired the administrative control and the monetary and political support necessary to prevail over the previously dominant forces. Politics replaced social and economic forces in the early formation and subsequent development of European states. The emergence of states was not, according to their view, prior to the development of societies. Instead, as Hall argues, "the European state evolved slowly and doggedly in the midst of a pre-existent civil society. It is no capstone or predatory organization in large part because it was not a conquest state."[20] This is not to say that the state was unable to shape the society and the economy in which it evolved and operated. It does, however, consider the state in organic terms as growing out of society. It is the idea of an organic state that Hugo Grotius was defending when he developed his law of nations and wrote of the need to protect states. For Grotius, the state was "a complete association of free men, joined together for the enjoyment of rights and for their common interest" and in turn that these states existed in a wider community of shared values. Thus, his view holds that "the state system [is] a valid society of mutual rights and obligations."[21] Hall contrasts these European states, which were able to gain some power amid a plurality of competing interests, including the economy and the church, with alternative systems in China, India, and the Middle East. In these other systems there was no autonomous sphere of politics. To cite a contemporary example, in postrevolutionary Iran, the state has been wedded to the tenets of Islam. Politics is merged not only with theological principles and practices but with virtually all aspects of social and economic behaviour, given the inclusiveness of the Islamic religion.

An alternative to this view places a greater emphasis on the coercive powers of the state. "The story of the development of the European States–system in the seventeenth and eighteenth centuries is very largely a military one."[22] Michael Howard's history of European conflict emphasizes the role that conflict played in the development of the modern state. In order to acquire control over territory and to defend the territory once it had been acquired, local elites needed financial and other support to fill the ranks of the army and to supply the weapons. Arrangements with the local population became more regularized and complex as the demands of warfare increased. Mercenaries gave way to standing armies of nationals, who were considered more reliable. Patriotism was encouraged as a means of ensuring a cohesive and consistent body of support. The significance of war in state-formation has also been noted by others more critical than Howard. In Charles Tilly's view, war was a natural ally of the state in its attempts to secure compliance from local citizens. He likens state elites to contemporary protection rackets and maintains that "a portrait of war makers and state makers as coercive and self-seeking entrepreneurs bears a far greater resemblance to the facts (of state formation) than do its chief alternatives."[23] For Tilly, the state is best understood as a predator, taking control over a society rather than emerging from it. Importantly, the state's international activity in competition with other states, especially through warfare, aids the state in its efforts to secure this control and to maintain the compliance of its citizens. The state became the chief source of both physical and economic security for its citizens.

One of the most influential expressions of the role of force in the formation of the state came from Niccolò Machiavelli, the Florentine chancery official turned political philosopher, who became one of the main proponents of *raison d'état*. Having lived through the French invasion of 1494 and the Italian city-state's feeble response, which, in the view of one author, "had been an impressive demonstration of the decisive role of force in politics," it was not surprising that Machiavelli would emphasize the utility of force in establishing and protecting the state.[24] The idea of *raison d'état* justifies the use of force, and indeed any other tactic, against external and internal foes alike and excuses the state from any sort of ethical limits to its actions. *Raison d'état* holds that

> the well-being of the state and of its population is held to be the ultimate value and the goal; and power, maintenance of power, extension of power, is the indispensable means which must — without qualification — be procured. With qualification, in so far as it must even be procured if necessary at the expense of a complete disregard for moral and positive law.

Raison d'état was based on the assumption that the state was a necessary and desirable instrument and, further, that the state, in Meinecke's words "is bent upon power as men on nourishment."[25] Because all states shared these aspirations for power it became necessary for all states to possess the ability to use force to protect their independence. *Raison d'état* has been very influential, and aspects of the doctrine continue to appear in the works of contemporary realists. It was accorded considerable prominence in the writings of German statesmen and historians, who saw war as the ultimate expression of interstate politics. Bismarck is widely believed to have argued that "the great questions of our time will not be settled by resolutions and majority votes . . . but by blood and iron." In the 20th century, war and the state came to be linked, by some, with social Darwinism. A competitive state system meant that only the fittest would survive and that fitness was best determined on the field of battle. Needless to say, Hitler did much to discredit these ideas.

International Relations and the State

Most of those who have written on war and the state have emphasized the influence of international or external pressures on the formation and development of states. Historians such as Otto Hintze, Heinrich von Treitschke, and Leopold von Ranke have argued in support of the "primacy of foreign policy" in explaining how and why states formed as they did. As Mann suggests, these writers may have been ignored because some of them have been "associated with [the] rather unpleasant politics" mentioned above. They do, however, direct attention to one of the cornerstones of state power and autonomy. Moreover, in emphasizing the influence of external threats to the sovereignty of the state, these works are of particular relevance in considering the state and international relations. In a comment on the writings of Otto Hintze, Skocpol identifies the contribution of this tradition of scholarship:

> [It] leads us away from basic features common to all policies and toward consideration of the various ways in which state structures and actions are conditioned by historically changing transnational contexts. These contexts impinge on individual states through geopolitical relations of interstate domination and competition, through the international communication of ideals and models of public policy, through world economic patterns of trade, division of productive activities, investment flows, and international finance. States necessarily stand at the intersections between domestic sociopolitical orders and the transnational relations within which they must maneuver for survival and advantage in relation to other states.[26]

Viewed from this perspective, the state is conditioned by what Anthony Giddens has referred to as a "reflexively monitored set of relations between states." As a result, "'International relations' are not connections set up between pre-established states, which could maintain their sovereign power without them: they are the basis upon which nation-states exist at all."[27]

The "primacy of foreign policy" argument leads to a diminution of the influence that domestic social, political, or economic forces will have on the formation and subsequent development of the state. Hintze argues that the "form and spirit of the state's organization will not be determined solely by economic and social relations and clashes of interests, but primarily by the necessities of defense and offense, that is, by the organization of the army and of warfare."[28] Under this sort of arrangement, external pressures from the competing power balances force the domestic adjustments required to maintain the necessary capabilities to wage foreign wars. Internal adjustments are not merely incidental to external developments but are very directly conditioned by them. Hintze makes this point specifically when he writes that, compared to class conflict, "conflict between nations has been far more important; and throughout the ages pressure from without has been a determining influence on internal structure."[29] This argument could lead one to ignore completely the manner in which domestic politics have conditioned a particular state's response to these external pressures. It would also encourage an exaggerated view of the role of coercive force as a source of the state's authority. Mann, and others, caution against an overemphasis on the role of force in state-formation as it would be extremely reductionist. "The state is still nothing in itself: it is merely the embodiment of physical force in society . . . it is an arena in which military force is mobilized domestically and used domestically and, above all, internationally."[30] He argues that, while it is essential to take into account the important role that force has played, it is also necessary to look at other sources of state autonomy, such as ideology, administrative power, and politics. Rather than rely on a deterministic account of the connection between force and the formation of the state, force should be viewed as one among a set of factors.

In contrast to this "realist" portrayal of the state, with its emphasis on the competitive nature of the international system, and the importance of force in defining and sustaining states, is a view that stresses the more co-operative elements of interstate relations. Here, too, however, we find evidence that the international environment has had considerable influence on the formation of states. This more co-operative view of international relations finds its early articulation in the writings of Hugo Grotius, who emphasized the importance of international law in protecting the sovereignty of states. Sovereignty has been a central concept in the study of international relations. The concept received its first systematic treatment in the 16th and 17th centuries in the works of such scholars as Jean Bodin, Hugo Grotius, and Thomas Hobbes. Sovereignty is not, however, a physical condition that can be weighed and measured. It is a convention that was devised both to ratify and to justify the state's acquisition of power over its rivals. It is also subject to change. "Sovereignty, like any other human convention, is something that can be acquired and lost, claimed or denied, respected or violated, celebrated or condemned, changed or abandoned, and so forth. It is an historical phenomenon."[31] Today, sovereignty is considered by some to be a barrier to a sane global society; however, in this earlier period it was praised as a method of protecting states from the centralizing pressures of a unitary authority so that each could develop its own indigenous culture and values. The idea was that states reflected an empirical reality of pluralism within European society that needed to be protected and nurtured.

Sovereignty was not intended to define the nature of one's domestic politics but to ensure that these domestic politics were not interfered with by an external power. As Hintze described it, "the concept of sovereignty, as it emerged in France at the end of the sixteenth century, expresses not solely but primarily the notion of independence from both Emperor and Pope."[32] It is for this reason that sovereignty became linked to the principle of nonintervention, a principle that remains prominent to this day and has been enshrined in Article 2(7) of the Charter of the United Nations. The principle of nonintervention holds that the territory of each and every state should remain free from external interference. The fact that the principle has been breached at times in the practice of international relations should not lead to its summary dismissal. The retention of principles such as sovereignty and nonintervention are evidence of the manner in which states have sought to support and to reassert their own prominence and independence in the contemporary international system. While sovereignty can and does serve as an excuse for an internal abuse of power, it can also be a source of great strength for states. For example, Krasner has argued that "without sovereignty many poor and small areas would be placed in formally subservient, perhaps tributary, relationships with more powerful actors."[33] Sovereignty remains an important principle in international relations in part because states have by and large granted it importance and abided by it. Further evidence of this can be found in the latest expansion of the state system and the manner in which sovereignty has been extended to newly independent states.

As mentioned above, sovereignty was developed to protect states from external pressures that would leave them under the control of "foreign" powers. Its continued significance is reflected not only in the expansion and persistence of sovereign states in the international system but in the way the concept has been altered to adapt to changing circumstances. Indeed, it is the flexibility of the notion of sovereignty that has allowed the state system to prosper in spite of an increasing number of states with exceedingly limited capabilities. Although the state system has always had some weak members, the number of such states has increased dramatically and the gap between the weakest and the strongest as measured by various capabilities has grown considerably. Today, many states around the globe rest on very tenuous domestic foundations and would be unable to resist an invasion if threatened. This is not meant to imply that all new states are uniformly lacking in the capacity to exercise authority either domestically or in the face of external pressure. It is evident, however, that when states with populations and territories no bigger than large urban centres receive recognition as states they require more than their empirical capabilities to support their independence. What is required instead is the willingness of other members of the state system to accept as legitimate states that may lack the necessary capabilities to insure their own survival. For these states, sovereignty "is a right enjoyed to the extent that it is recognized to exist by other states."[34] As a consequence, sovereignty becomes a juridical as well as an empirical concept. The "legal fiction," as some might call it, has (as suggested by Krasner's comment above) been used by disadvantaged states to secure for themselves a presence in a world in which they would otherwise be shoved aside on the basis of their limited competence.

In examining the emergence of new states in the last few decades, Jackson has argued that, while many of these "quasi states" may lack the empirical basis of statehood (in the sense that they have limited capabilities for exercising control over their domestic populations and still less for being able to protect themselves if ever threatened by external force), they nevertheless have been able to acquire the legal basis of sovereignty. Jackson attributes this acquisition to the willingness on the part of existing states to extend sovereignty to these new states. He argues that this willingness reflects a commitment on the part of these established states to the idea of a state system based on widely shared procedural rules — an extension in effect, of Grotius's view of the European-states system of an earlier era. Unlike European states, which had some demonstrable characteristics of statehood, many of these new states have been protected in the hope that they will be able to develop such characteristics.[35] In the great wave of decolonization that swept the globe in the 1950s and 1960s the U.N. General Assembly unanimously adopted Resolution 1514, which (in addition to advocating self-determination and independence for all colonial peoples and territories) stated that the "inadequacy of political, economic, social or educational preparedness should never serve as a pretext for delaying independence." Because of the pervasiveness of states in the system, the viability of states in some Third World societies, the willingness of established states to admit these new states to the state system, and the lack of any acceptable alternative form of political organization, these newly independent territories became states. The universal acceptance of the sovereignty of many of these "quasi states" as evidenced by the respect for their territorial boundaries and their participation in organizations such as the United Nations stands as a persuasive statement on the commitment to sovereign statehood on the part of both old and new states. For these new states, and indeed for many established states as well, sovereignty has largely been conditioned by the state system. It results as much from the environment in which states operate as it does from the internal characteristics of any particular state, and therefore explains, at least in part, why the system can accept such tremendous diversity. It may also help to explain why states have persisted in the face of economic interdependence, transnationalism, the use of supranational organizations, and the changing technology of warfare.

Society and the State

The state is Janus-faced. It has an internally directed face in addition to the externally directed one that we have already discussed. It would, therefore, be misleading to consider simply the state's presence in the international system in accounting for its existence. As indicated earlier, much of the writing on international relations begins by conflating the state with society by assuming that, in matters of foreign policy, the two are coterminous. This realist view identifies states as the only major actors in international relations; it sees them as unitary actors, responding to the anarchic character of the international system and motivated principally by their own insecurity. Such a view ignores the state's relations with its domestic society, either concluding that it is irrelevant or assuming that the state is the embodiment of civil society and that, therefore, no further consideration is required. This approach has created the misleading impression that the national interest as defined by the state is unproblematic. To suggest that this view is misleading does not mean that the national interest is always unrepresentative of societal interests, merely that it is wrong to assume as much uncritically and to ignore the way in which in which these societal interests have been represented. Instead, it is important to recognize that, when making claims for autonomy in conducting international relations, the state may simply be seeking a rationale for ignoring the demands of societal interests. In Halliday's view such claims have meant "that states can be less responsive to, and representative of, their societies precisely because of their international role."[36] These concerns make it both necessary and useful to consider more closely the relationship between the state and civil society. While such considerations may appear to lie beyond the field of international relations, given the central place of states and the many arguments mentioned already, it should be evident that some consideration of the nature of states, and particularly their relations with domestic society, is vitally important for assessing the role of the state in international relations.

The issues that arise in discussing the nature of the state and its relations with domestic society are varied and complex but there is one point that is central to most of these commentaries: the autonomy of the state vis-à-vis societal interests. Is the state to be understood as having a lifeforce of its own, one rooted in international conflict and sustained by and very much a part of that ongoing conflict? Alternatively, is the state merely a passive agent of society, participating in international relations in response to the demands of various groups within society or of society as a whole? Or is the state, as Marxists would argue, merely acting at the behest of selected class interests to use the international system to reproduce the conditions at home that will protect those interests? Examining the links between state and society is necessary to assess these alternatives and to account for the foreign-policy activity of states.

It is both important and timely for students of international relations to acknowledge the influence that domestic politics have on interstate relations and, particularly, the effects of the state-societal relationship on the state's participation in international relations. Both liberals and Marxists have tended to discount the state in emphasizing the greater significance of societal groups or classes. These societally oriented accounts of state-societal relations are those most likely to forecast the eventual demise of the state. Liberals tend to suggest (and prescribe) a very limited role for the state. For liberals, progressive individualism will lead to the development of a social conscience and eventually allow for contracts to be secured without the mediation or formal sanction of the state. Foreign policy is seen to be constrained by domestic groups, and the state itself is frequently rendered incapable of rational action because of intrabureaucratic conflict over competing policy choices. In turn, contact between societies now residing in territorial states allowed to progress unfettered will emerge into a peaceful system based on a harmony of interests. This view was put forward by functionalists such as David Mitrany and has also been prominent in the more recent writings on transnationalism and interdependence.

For Marxists, the state will wither away once the class struggle has reached its ultimate conclusion. In the interim, the state is a mere reflection of the dominance of certain economic and social forces. Either these classes will rule on their own behalf, or political elites will operate the powers of the state in the interests of this dominant class. The net effect is that the state becomes the captured client of this class and has little room for independent action. The state is essentially apolitical and lacking in autonomy. Recent revisions to this view have accorded the state a limited realm of autonomy but the state is still seen as rooted firmly in society with no independent source of authority. At the international level, Marxists share the longer-term liberal idea that wars will disappear once their preferred economic forces gain power.

Both liberals and Marxists propose a passive state, one that responds to societal pressure and is incapable of controlling or shaping these pressures to meet its own independent objectives. Investigations into the origins of the state suggest a different view. "It is the necessity of managing state competition that has provided the opportunity for state elites to gain autonomous power free from the constraints often imposed upon them by civil society."[37] However, to argue that states can secure autonomy by turning to their international responsibilities is not to show how this is done. Conceived and nurtured through warfare, states require popular support, or at least acquiescence, to gather the implements of warfare. This requirement encouraged states to extend their presence in society through taxation and, later, conscription. In doing this the state was forced to make agreements with various domestic interests to insure their continuing support. Even those, like J.A. Hall, who consider the state to be organic, have noted the influence that international relations has had on state-societal relations. "Individual states did not exist in a vacuum. They were rather part of a competing state system, and it was that system, particularly the military organization it engendered, which played a considerable part in determining the character of individual states."[38] The working-out of these arrangements with domestic interests tended to vary from one state to the next, depending on local conditions.

Aristide Zolberg, for example, distinguishes between the process of state-formation in France and Britain. In addition to identifying the significant influence that external developments had in fostering the development and expansion of administrative structures in France and England, Zolberg has argued that the domestic context played a significant role in shaping the particular type of state structure that emerged. Thus, a consideration of these domestic conditions helps to account for the distinct constitutional and administrative paths that these two states have taken. In France, the necessity of conducting war to protect and expand territorial boundaries required not only a revenue base but also a sizeable army. Both encourage the emergence of a more centralized and authoritarian structure than developed in England, where the principal source of revenue was identified as the merchant class, who shared an interest with the state elites in advancing Britain's naval capacities. In turn, there was less need for a centralized administrative structure and more incentive and need to diffuse power to this merchant class. In both instances, the state elites were securing the capabilities for warfare in response to external pressures. The process differed, however, depending on domestic considerations. As Zolberg concludes, "even when the exigencies of a given strategic pattern led the central power to look within the country for a more efficient means of mobilizing the resources he needed the effects produced were by no means exclusively determined by the external stimulus."[39]

Tilly also has identified the importance of examining the manner in which states resolved conflicts with their respective domestic societies in order to maintain the necessary support to sustain their coercive capabilities. Such arrangements were not wholly dictated by state elites, but in some instances required compromises in the form of such things as representative institutions. The military organization, while remaining significant, was often forced to share influence with other, more domestically oriented institutions, and the state was at times required to share power with representative institutions that could in turn affect its future. Tilly goes on to argue that newer states have not been forced to make such elaborate arrangements with domestic interests because they have been granted coercive capabilities by external powers. The magnitude of weapons transfers that has taken place over the past few decades has, in Tilly's view, brought about a "great disproportion between military organization and all other forms of organization" in many of these new states. These states thus acquired military capabilities "without the same internal forging of mutual constraints between ruler and ruled."[40]

The need for states to secure domestic support to participate effectively in international relations takes on greater importance as societal interests become more susceptible to the influence of transnational forces. States have, however, shown an ability to respond to these changing conditions. Susan Strange has noted that the sources of state autonomy have changed over time. Initially, in her view, authority was derived from control over land and labour. State elites who were able to secure access to territory and to control this territory and utilize labour to generate revenue and armies were most likely to resist challenges to their authority.[41] More recently, land and labour have yielded to capital and knowledge. These developments are reflected in the change in the composition of the coercive force that the state uses to maintain its authority. Initially, states relied on mercenaries but, when these became too costly and unpredictable, the state turned to the mobilization of the masses through conscription. During the 20th century, conscripted armies have given way to technology as the state uses surveillance and sophisticated weaponry to maintain compliance at home and further its objectives abroad. This characterization suggests that the state has been successful in adapting to changing circumstances in maintaining its power.

In more specific terms, the ability of the particular states to acquire autonomy from societal interests on selected issues and the process by which this is done would seem to depend on the states, publics, and issues involved. Some have made a distinction between "weak" states and "strong" states on the basis of their ability to secure freedom of action from societal demands. Yet, as Putnam writes, "a more adequate account of the domestic determinants of foreign policy must stress politics: parties, social classes, interest groups (both economic and noneconomic), legislators, and even public opinion and elections, not simply executive officials and institutional arrangements."[42] Thus, it becomes important to distinguish not only between states and society but also between states and nations and governments. The process whereby states acquire the support or compliance of domestic groups will help to explain whether these groups are likely to go outside the state to challenge its authority. It will also determine the relative effectiveness of the state in pursuit of foreign-policy objectives. For these reasons it becomes an important subject matter for international politics.

The issue of state autonomy has consumed many pages in journals and academic textbooks in recent years but much of the discussion has been focussed on issues of domestic policy and considerably less on matters of foreign policy and international relations. There has been some recognition of the connections between the state's involvement in a competitive state system and its relations with domestic groups, factions, or classes. Skocpol considers the state's primacy in foreign policy as being of considerable importance in understanding how states gain and maintain autonomy from societal interests. Skocpol identifies three potential sources of state autonomy: the international orientation of states, their domestic function of keeping order, and the possibility that permanent organizations will have the capacity for and interest in devising and pursuing their own policies.[43] In considering Skocpol's sources of state autonomy, it is evident that the state's presence in the international system, its external face, is of considerable significance in enhancing state autonomy and, furthermore, that the state's activity in this international arena will have an effect on its relations with its own society. In short, the external face cannot be separated from the internal face of the state. Students of international politics have tended to neglect this very basic and significant fact. As a result there has been a tendency to separate international relations from domestic politics for purposes of analysis. Unfortunately, this tendency has encouraged only a false dichotomy between the two. Instead, as Skocpol and others have pointed out, there is a dynamic at work between the two sides of the state such that actions on one front have implications for those on the other. One has only to consider, for example, the extreme cases of revolution. Revolutions in such places as Russia in 1917 or Nicaragua in 1979 cannot be accounted for solely in terms of domestic issues and events; nor are their implications restricted to the domestic environment. Even policies designed primarily for the external environment are not without their impact on domestic concerns. The Concert of Europe was designed to establish international order, but this international order was also useful in supporting an internal order that had been threatened by the rise of republicanism in France. At present, the government of South Africa is engaged in a policy of destabilization of the front-line states of southern Africa in an effort to undermine the legitimacy of black-majority rule and to bolster the legitimacy of apartheid and their own white-minority government. "It is the preference for homogeneity in political arrangements for international legitimacy and stability that shows up both the crucial, if often understated, dependence of domestic power arrangements upon international factors, and the degree to which domestic factors, including the state–society relationship itself, influence the foreign policy of the states."[44] Given this, it is evident that the interactions between social forces and international relations are most often mediated by the state, and the degree of autonomy that the state can acquire to mediate these interactions in its own independent interests is dependent on both the domestic and the external context in which the state acts. Autonomy secured from one sector may impede autonomous action in the other sector. A state more constrained by the international environment will be less willing and able to respond to the demands of societal interests, and one controlled by domestic pressures will find little room for manoeuvring with other states. A theory of international relations must be attentive to such linkages.

Conclusion

Why is it useful for students of international relations to consider these theories of the state? First, international relations and the primacy of states therein have been discussed for too long without a theory of the state. It is important to remember, especially in this age where the withering power of the state is so frequently asserted, that the state emerged within an international as well as within a domestic framework. Its future is as much tied to that of its external environment as it is to that of the domestic society over which it governs. A more fruitful approach for considering the state's position in international politics is to recognize it as a distinct set of institutions that operates between domestic and external pressures. While states are not analytically prior to the international system, neither are they incidental to it. Instead, states, and the social forces amid which they have evolved, have developed in a dynamic historical and transnational process. The pattern of state–society–international system relations that has been worked out has both challenged the state and reinforced it, depending on the particular historical circumstances.

As this chapter suggests, the persistence of the state in international relations contradicts the growing presence and significance of challenges to the state system. By examining rather than making assumptions about the nature of the state and incorporating this examination into theories of international relations, it may be possible to understand if not reconcile this apparent paradox. It may also create an opportunity to move closer to Martin Wight's second objective of theory: "that theoretical inquiry into International Relations should [also] be focused upon the moral and normative presuppositions that underlie it."[45]

NOTES

1. Martin Wight, "Why Is There No International Theory?" in *Diplomatic Investigations*, ed. Martin Wight and Herbert Butterfield (Cambridge, Mass.: Harvard University Press, 1966), 17.

2. Michael Mann, "The Autonomous Power of the State," in *States in History*, ed. J.A. Hall (Oxford: Basil Blackwell, 1986), 133.

3. Susan Strange, "Supranationals and the State," in *States in History*, 291.

4. Seyom Brown, *New Forces, Old Forces, and the Future of World Politics* (Glenview, Ill.: Scott, Foresman, 1988), 12.

5. Seyom Brown, "New Forces Revisited: Lessons of a Turbulent Decade," *World Policy Journal* 1 (1984): 409.

6. Richard A. Falk, "Solving the Puzzles of Global Reform," *Alternatives* 11 (1986): 80.

7. R.B.J. Walker, "The Territorial State and the Theme of Gulliver," *International Journal* 39 (Summer 1984): 548.

8. Richard Ashley, "Three Modes of Economism," *International Studies Quarterly* 27 (December 1983): 470.

9. Anthony Giddens, *The Nation State and Violence* (Berkeley: University of California Press, 1985), 168. For an illustration of the "world system" argument, see I. Wallerstein, *The Modern World System* (New York: Academic Press, 1974).

10. Raymond Aron, *Peace and War* (New York: Praeger, 1968), 748.

11. Hedley Bull, *The Anarchical Society* (New York: Columbia University Press, 1977).

12. Fred Halliday, "State and Society in International Relations," *Millennium* 16 (1987): 217.

13. In addition to the works of Wight, Aron, and Bull cited above, see E.H. Carr, *The Twenty Years' Crisis, 1919–1939* (London: Macmillan, 1939); Hans Morgenthau, *Politics among Nations*, 6th ed. (New York: Knopf, 1985); Stanley Hoffmann, *Janus and Minerva* (Boulder, Colo.: Westview, 1987); J.D.B. Miller, *The World of States* (London: Croom Helm, 1981).

14. See K.J. Holsti, *The Dividing Discipline* (Boston: Allen and Unwin, 1985).

15. Northedge, cited in Halliday, "State and Society," 217.

16. Halliday, "State and Society," 219.

17. M. Wight, *Power Politics*, 2d ed. (Harmondsworth: Penguin, 1986), 25.

18. For some different views on this issue, see Joseph Strayer, *On the Medieval Origins of the Modern State* (Princeton: Princeton University Press, 1970), and Martin Wight, *Systems of States* (Leicester: Leicester University Press, 1977), especially chap. 5.

19. Wight, *Power Politics*, 92, 94.

20. J.A. Hall, *Powers and Liberties* (Harmondsworth: Penguin, 1986), 137.

21. Cited in Wight, *Systems of States*, 39.

22. Michael Howard, "War and the Nation-state," *Daedalus* 108 (1979): 101.

23. Charles Tilly, "War Making and State Making as Organized Crime," in *Bringing the State Back In*, ed. Peter B. Evans, Dietrich Rueschemeyer, and Theda Skocpol (Cambridge: Cambridge University Press, 1985), 169.

24. Felix Gilbert, *Machiavelli and Guicciardini* (Princeton: Princeton University Press, 1965), 129.

25. Friedrich Meinecke, *Machiavellism: The Doctrine of Raison d'État and Its Place in Modern History*, trans. Douglas Scott (London: Routledge and Kegan Paul, 1957), 2–3.

26. Theda Skocpol, "Bringing the State Back In: Current Research," in *Bringing the State Back In*, 8.

27. Giddens, *Nation State*, 263–64.

28. Otto Hintze, "Military Organization and State Organization," in *The Historical Essays of Otto Hintze*, ed. Felix Gilbert (New York: Oxford University Press, 1975), 215.

29. Hintze, "Military Organization," 183.

30. Michael Mann, "The Autonomous Power of the State," in *States in History*, 110–11.

31. Robert H. Jackson, "Quasi-states, Dual Regimes, and Neoclassical Theory," *International Organization* 41 (Autumn 1987): 522.

32. Hintze, "Formation of States and Constitutional Development," in *Historical Essays*, 167.

33. Stephen Krasner, "Regimes and the Limits of Realism," *International Organization* 36 (Spring 1982): 509.

34. Hedley Bull, "The State's Positive Role in World Affairs," *Daedalus* 108 (1979): 118.

35. This argument is a summary of Jackson's in "Quasi-states."

36. Halliday, "State and Society," 219.

37. J.A. Hall, "Introduction," in *States in History*, 8.

38. Hall, *Powers and Liberties*, 139.

39. Aristide Zolberg, "Strategic Interactions and the Formation of Modern States: France and England," *International Social Science Journal* 32, no. 4 (1980): 695.

40. Tilly, "War Making," 186.

41. Strange, "Supranationals."

42. Robert D. Putnam, "Diplomacy and Domestic Politics," *International Organization* 42 (1988): 432.

43. Skocpol, "Bringing the State Back In."

44. Halliday, "State and Society," 225.

45. Wight cited in Jackson, "Quasi-states," 549.

SELECT BIBLIOGRAPHY

Bull, H. *The Anarchical Society*. London: Macmillan, 1977.

Carnoy, Martin. *The State and Political Theory*. Princeton: Princeton University Press, 1984.

Cox, Robert. "Social Forces, States and World Orders: Beyond International Relations Theory." *Millennium* 10 (Summer 1981): 126–55.

Evans, Peter B., Dietrich Rueschemeyer, and Theda Skocpol, eds. *Bringing the State Back In*. Cambridge: Cambridge University Press, 1985.

Hall, J.A. *Powers and Liberties*. Harmondsworth: Penguin, 1986.

———, ed. *States in History*. Oxford: Basil Blackwell, 1986.

Hinsley, F.H. *Power and the Pursuit of Peace*. Cambridge: Cambridge University Press, 1963.

Howard, M. *War in European History*. Oxford: Oxford University Press, 1976.

Keohane, R., ed. *Neorealism and Its Critics*. New York: Columbia University Press, 1986.

Keohane, R., and J. Nye, eds. *Transnational Relations and World Politics*. Cambridge, Mass.: Harvard University Press, 1972.

Krasner, Stephen. *Defending the National Interest*. Princeton: Princeton University Press, 1978.

———. "Approaches to the State: Alternative Conceptions and Historical Dynamics." *Comparative Politics* 16 (January 1984): 223–46.

Mattingly, G. *Renaissance Diplomacy*. London: Jonathan Cape, 1955.

Meinecke, Friedrich. *Machiavellism: The Doctrine of Raison d'État and Its Place in Modern History*. Trans. D. Scott. London: Routledge and Kegan Paul, 1957.

Miller, J.D.B. *The World of States*. London: Croom Helm, 1981.

Strayer, J.R. *On the Medieval Origins of the Modern State*. Princeton: Princeton University Press, 1970.

Tilly, C. "Reflections on the History of European State-making." In *The Formation of National States in Europe*, ed. C. Tilly. Princeton: Princeton University Press, 1975.

Wight, M. *Systems of States*. Leicester: Leicester University Press, 1977.

THE CAUSES OF WAR: HOW DOES THE STRUCTURE OF THE SYSTEM AFFECT INTERNATIONAL CONFLICT?

Patrick James

Choosing a Level of Analysis

Within the politics of power and security, war represents the most intense form of competition. Although violent conflict has a long history, with the passage of time it becomes an ever-greater menace to survival. Nuclear weapons and other highly destructive inventions virtually guarantee that global war would result in unprecedented catastrophe. Presumably, lesser instances of strife, such as the protracted war in the Persian Gulf involving Iran and Iraq, can also produce extraordinary human and material losses. Furthermore, such conflicts have the potential to expand, possibly leading to superpower confrontation, as in the case of the Yom Kippur War of October 1973 in the Middle East. Thus, the practical relevance of studying the causes of war should require no further justification.

This chapter occupies a middle ground, constituting as it does a reassessment of some strands of research about war. Other strands — concerning, for example, diplomacy, arms trading, nationalism, and resource scarcity — deserving as they undoubtedly are of sustained attention, will not be treated here. Instead, this investigation will focus on one particular level of analysis. With regard to the meaning of "levels of analysis," scholars have tended to cluster their theorizing around the focal points articulated by Kenneth Waltz in his classic exposition on theories of war: the individual, the state, and the system. These options correspond, respectively, to (1) the role of the individual leader in the choice of peace or war; (2) internal characteristics of the state as an actor; and (3) the relationships among states in the international system.[1] The three points of interest have become known as levels of analysis because each represents a different degree of aggregation in identifying the determinants of international political behaviour.

To describe the influence of Waltz's taxonomy as paradigmatic would not be much of an exaggeration. This point becomes obvious from any type of survey of basic textbooks dealing with international relations. Even if Waltz's framework is viewed as a culmination of pre-existing tendencies in the literature on world politics, it can still serve as an invaluable system of categorization for theories of war. Of course, all purported explanations of war must somehow deal with individuals, states, and the international system. But, illustratively, Waltz's levels identify the most salient aspects of cause and effect within a given theory, and for that reason his framework remains useful.

In this chapter I choose to examine some of the numerous studies on war's origins undertaken at the *systemic* level. I do this for several reasons, both intellectual and practical. First, the systemic level is the natural point of departure from the standpoint of generality and economy of explanation. "Without prior systemic theory," as Keohane has observed, "unit-level analysis of world politics floats in an empirical and conceptual vacuum."[2] In developing theory, it is a basic principle that the simplest explanations should be considered first, and that building in complexity should be undertaken only as it becomes necessary. If enduring factors — most often found at the level of the international system — can at least partially explain the occurrence of war, then that would create a solid foundation for later, more complex theorizing.

Second, traditional realist or *realpolitik* theory and testing has tended to focus on the systemic level of aggregation. Distribution of power, interstate coalitions, and the like are most naturally discussed in a systemic context. National attributes and the traits of leaders (or small groups), by contrast, are less obviously related to power as a concept.

Third, and finally, there is a great need for clarification of the findings that currently exist at the systemic level. Sabrosky, to cite one of those who have identified that problem, has referred to the extent of literature on polarity and war as being matched "only by its indeterminacy."[3] Issues arising from concept-formation, contradictory hypotheses and evidence, and the relevance of findings, all require some reflection in order to enable us to move toward greater understanding.

Two further qualifications are in order here. One relates to the definition of war, the other to selection of a subset of systemic research for extended consideration. International war I identify by employing the Correlates of War (COW) Project definition. The project's defining conditions for international war, described by Small and Singer in a comprehensive data handbook, are elaborate. To present them in detail would be time-consuming and of little practical value, because they have been evaluated in a number of readily available sources. Only the two general criteria used by the COW Project to distinguish wars will be mentioned here: (1) the participants must be nation-states, and (2) the conflict must have led to 1,000 or more combat-related casualties.[4] Use of the Small and Singer conditions confers two advantages for analyses such as my own. First, the conditions are consistent with implicit (and explicit) definitions of war used in case studies and other literature. Second, much of the research that deals with more than one case of war is based upon COW data, now available for the period between 1816 and 1980. In that regard, the COW Project represents the most sustained research program in existence on the causes of war.

Among the many systemic studies that might be reviewed, a sizeable and interesting segment deals with the role of *structure* in the generation of conflict. Structure refers to the basic units of a system (meaning states, at the international level) and their arrangement within that system. It is possible to identify several strands of power-oriented research on structure and war, each focussing on the effects of a different set of variables: (1) the size of the system, often referring more specifically to the number of major powers; (2) the extent of alliance commitments; (3) the tightness and discreteness of those linkages; and (4) the concentration of power within the system.[5]

All of these aspects of structure will be considered in turn. A basic hypothesis will be identified in each instance, my overall objective being to determine the extent to which systemic structure can explain the occurrence of international war.

Poles and States

One of the principal aspects of structure is the number of poles in the international system. This concept has been the subject of some controversy; as Hart has observed, the debate over polarity and stability has "combined elements of what are called polarity and polarization." In more specific terms, Goldmann noted that "a clear distinction is not always made between the international power structure ('polarity') on the one hand and the structure of international interaction ('polarization') on the other."[6] Thus, within the realm of structure, there is a need for greater clarity among the frequently cited concepts of pole, polarity, and polarization.

With regard to the first of these designations, some degree of consensus seems to have emerged. Bueno de Mesquita identified the "number of poles, blocs, or clusters of nations in the system" as one of the two principal aspects of polarity to consider in the context of the causes of war.[7] Although that designation would appear to mix states and groups of states together, it represented an improvement over earlier treatments of polarity. Bueno de Mesquita separated the number of poles — or blocs of states — from the bonds linking states, most commonly assessed in terms of alliances. This distinction removes at least one source of confusion from the debate, since the nature of the alliance infrastructure then can be dealt with more effectively as a separate causal factor.

More precise designations are located in recent studies by Levy and Wayman. "Whereas size refers to the number of Great Powers," Levy has argued, "polarity is best defined in terms of the distribution of military capabilities among the Great Powers." In a like manner, Wayman identified two dimensions of polarity, describing power polarity in terms of the number of prominent power centres, and cluster polarity as referring essentially to the tightness and discreteness of coalitions.[8] Although the terminology is somewhat different — size versus power polarity — it is clear that, in each instance, the number of major powers is equated with the number of poles.

It is one thing to claim that the number of poles is a distinct structural factor, but what is the presumed linkage between poles and a systemic propensity toward war? The classic debate over that issue took shape 25 years ago, with bipolarity confronting multipolarity as a structural option.

Some have argued that bipolarity will promote stability and, more specifically, inhibit the outbreak of war. Waltz, the most persistent advocate of bipolarity, contends that a system with only two poles has several advantages.[9] First, with only two leading powers, there are no peripheries, and the system is simpler to manage. Second, all changes are deemed relevant by the two major actors as part of their competition, and thus developments are monitored rather closely. Third, recurrent crises are expected to provide a substitute for war, with disagreements being handled in an incremental fashion. Fourth, and finally, the preponderant power of the leading states should encourage them to act as system managers. Waltz argued that these features will inhibit the outbreak of highly destructive wars, although minor conflicts are expected almost as a matter of course.

Others have suggested that a system with more than two poles would be preferable. For example, Deutsch and Singer note that a larger set of vital actors would allow for a greater number of interaction opportunities. Such opportunities would make confrontation less likely, because each system member directs a smaller share of its attention to any particular other.[10] A further effect of the proliferation of central actors would be the "dampening" of arms races, given that there would be a lower level of dyadic confrontation in the system. By contrast, as Rosecrance has observed, in a world of two competing superpowers "each action by one will be viewed as a strategic gambit by the other." The resulting danger of misperception thus would be very high, along with the likelihood of an arms race. Cooper summarized the presumed advantages of multipolarity, observing that it "lessens the total nature of war, reduces arms spending, facilitates increased contacts between nations, and plays down ideology."[11]

Several studies have used aggregate data on international war to assess the relative merits of various numbers of poles in a system. Haas studied stability and polarity in a regional context, identified 21 geographic subsystems, and examined their patterns of stratification and instability from the 18th century onward. He defined stratification as the degree of concentration of capabilities within a subsystem, effectively identifying a set of major powers, and conceived of instability in terms of "rates of incidence of warfare." His results were not directly comparable to those of the other studies reviewed here — for example, the data transcend the compilation from COW — but they do possess a certain degree of similarity. Haas summarized his discoveries in the following manner:

> The choice between bipolar versus multipolar arrangements now seems clear. If a state or group of states is willing to accept long wars that are won by aggressor states, bipolarity provides an escape from the more war-prone character of historical multipolar subsystems. Multipolarity entails more violence, more countries at war and more casualties; bipolarity brings fewer but longer wars.[12]

Such mixed results, as will become apparent, are by no means anomalous within this program of testing.

Singer, Bremer, and Stuckey conducted bivariate testing that linked the number of poles to the pervasiveness of war. They used COW Project data for the period from 1820 to 1965 and probed for intercentury differences. Singer and his associates measured the concentration of capabilities among the major powers, with a lower level corresponding to a greater degree of multipolarity. With regard to the dependent variable, warlikeness, they measured the average annual amount of war underway in the system at half-decade intervals. In the 19th century, bipolarity showed a positive linkage to the pervasiveness of war, the reverse being true in the current century.[13]

Cannizzo replicated the study by Singer's team, offering a different treatment of the dependent variable. Within a state-centred perspective, she measured the "average annual nation-months of interstate war in which a given major power was involved." Like others, Cannizzo found an intercentury breakpoint within the period from 1816 to 1965. In the 19th century, the concentration of power in the system — a measurement of its extent of bipolarity — predicted toward war involvement for the individual state much less accurately than it had for the collectivity of major powers. In the 20th century, a major power's involvement in war tended to follow "periods of parity and rapid change toward parity," although the model could explain 50 percent of the variance in warlikeness for only one state, China.[14]

Using data on war from the COW Project for the period from 1824 to 1938, Ostrom and Aldrich found the probability of war to be "moderately large" in a bipolar system; minimal with three poles; greater with four and five actors; and drastically lower with six powers. A more sophisticated, regression-type analysis of the same data (known as "probit" analysis) supported a combination of the "Balancer [i.e., N = 3] and Deutsch–Singer hypotheses." This pattern, with the probability of war being lower with either three or more than five great powers, is consistent with the initial set of results obtained by Ostrom and Aldrich.[15] Levy investigated the impact of the number of poles on several indicators of war over a very long time span. Using several sources, including data from the COW Project and Sorokin's impressive compilation, he assembled a list of wars from 1495 to 1975 involving the great powers. Striving for a comprehensive measurement of systemic war-proneness, Levy relied on three indicators: "the *frequency* of war is the number of wars in a given period. *Magnitude* refers to the total nation-years of war among participating Powers and reflects its spatial-temporal scope. The *severity* of war reflects its human destructiveness and is measured by the number of battle fatalities." Using several statistical measures, Levy found no connection involving war and the number of poles in a system, ranging from four to eight. "It is precisely *because* the size of the Great Power system has varied so little," he concluded, "that it cannot account for significant variations in stability."[16]

Using COW Project data through 1965, Wayman also examined the impact of the number of poles on the magnitude (i.e., nation-years or -months) and frequency of interstate wars fought by major powers. He used a measure of power concentration based on the share of major-power capabilities held by the two greatest powers, considering a system to be "power bipolar" when that share exceeded 50 percent of the total. Although Wayman found the multipolar years to be "slightly less war prone," 75 percent of the wars within those years were of high magnitude, with the percentage being reversed for the bipolar wars.[17]

Although it has received less attention than did the number of major powers, the sheer number of actors in the system is a complementary aspect of structure. Deutsch and Singer argued that a greater number of states in the system would lead to more interaction opportunities. This property, in turn, would tend to lower the amount of confrontation. Similarly, Thompson, Rasler, and Li identified the stabilizing role of "multiple actors and issue areas" as a basic component of the "pluralistic process" in world politics.[18] These studies suggest, in theoretical terms, that a larger international system would tend to experience less war.

However, Most and Starr have demonstrated that expansion of the system's size may have a different impact than expected. Consider a system with a specific number of major powers. A dyad in this system, using the terminology of Most and Starr, is balanced if it consists of two approximately equal states, and is unbalanced otherwise. The number of unbalanced dyads in the system, then, is regarded as an indicator of potential for war. Of course, that is a problematic assumption, but it ultimately does not affect the line of argument. Most and Starr use a system with three major powers to illustrate some unexpected effects: "simple expansion of system size — in addition to changes in the number of major powers — has a dramatic effect on the numbers of imbalanced and balanced dyads. *Tripolar* systems with 3, 5, 10 and 15 nations would have 0, 6, 21 and 36 imbalanced dyads respectively."[19] Thus, viewed in terms of dyadic interactions, it is not obvious that a larger system should be less war-prone. Opportunities for aggression may even increase with a greater number of states, depending on the distribution of capabilities. For example, a further proliferation of weak states in Africa might simply create new and inviting targets for more-established powers on the continent. If, by contrast, *parity* is inherently more dangerous, then an increasing number of balanced dyads, within a larger system, would be the source of worry.

Taken together, the evidence about the number of poles and states in the system is complex and should be interpreted with caution. The results appear to be quite sensitive to the specific approach adopted toward measurement. With respect to the number of poles, the most visible pattern is that which favours bipolarity, specifically in the 20th century. Several studies produced evidence that a system with two central powers would be less prone to damage from warfare (especially in the current century), while no study resulted in uniform support for multipolarity. It, therefore, is not clear that movement away from bipolarity would be a welcome development.

Perhaps the best prospects for stabilizing the contemporary international system rest in conflict management and negotiations conducted by the superpowers. The recent Intermediate Nuclear Forces (INF) Treaty could be cited as one promising development, perhaps setting the stage for other superpower arrangements. Along a similar line of reasoning, it is difficult to imagine the superpowers' task of stabilization becoming easier with new states joining the system.

What, then, can we conclude from an assessment of the evidence pertaining to the number of poles and states in the system? The data seem to suggest one important lesson: hypotheses that link individual structural variables to the occurrence of war are likely to provide only a partial explanation at best. Such factors as the number of states and poles within the system eventually must be brought together in a more comprehensive approach toward structure and war.

Alliance Pervasiveness

When we turn to alliances, or the arrangement of units in the system, we confront the most important issue in considering how the magnitude or extent of commitments might be linked to the occurrence of war. In a highly influential study, Singer and Small hypothesized that a greater number of alliance commitments in the international system would result in more experience of warfare. Pursuing a line of argument that parallelled Adam Smith's "invisible hand" within a market, they asserted that "anything which restrains or inhibits free or vigorous pursuit of the separate national interests will limit the efficacy of the stabilizing mechanism. And among those arrangements seen as most likely to so inhibit that pursuit are formal alliances." To test that proposition, Singer and Small used six measurements of the pervasiveness of alliances, including the percentage of overall dyads exhausted by alliance commitments, to represent the independent variable. Using COW data through 1945, they charted the magnitude and severity (nation-months and battle deaths, respectively) of war that began within three different periods following measurement of the alliance configuration. These time lags — one, three, and five years — showed recognition of how little was known about the impact of alliance aggregation on dependent variables such as the outbreak and intensity of war.

Singer and Small produced a wide range of correlations, with results for all independent states (subject to constraints on data) and separately for those involved in the central European subsystem. They also subdivided the data by century, with findings for the periods 1815–99 and 1900–1945, respectively. From the complex tables of statistics, Singer and Small produced the following summary:

> Regardless of the war-onset measure we use, the pattern is similar. Whether it is nation-months of war or battle-connected deaths, whether the data are for the total system or the central one only, and whether they reflect all members of the system or major powers only, when alliance aggregation or bipolarity [i.e., pervasiveness of major-power defensive pacts] in the nineteenth century increases, the amount of war experienced by the system goes down, and vice versa. And in the twentieth century, the greater the alliance aggregation or bipolarity in the system, the more war it experiences.[20]

Thus, another intercentury difference is revealed: the 20th century is consistent with the conventional wisdom about the pervasiveness of alliances, while the 19th century is not.

Ostrom and Hoole conducted a similar, COW-based investigation of alliance aggregation and war. For each year from 1816 to 1965, they calculated the ratio of defence dyads and dyads of interstate war, respectively, to the size of the system. Using statistical procedures that differed from those of Singer and Small, they found no connection between the two ratios. However, Ostrom and Hoole also compared the percentage of states in the system involved in alliances with five measurements of war magnitude. The results from this phase of testing parallelled those of Singer and Small.[21]

Thompson, Rasler, and Li investigated the linkage between interaction opportunities and war from 1816 to 1965, using COW data. They measured the independent variable with a Network Density Index (NDI), which "involves computing the actual number of internodal connections (alliance commitments) as a proportion of all possible internodal connections." Thompson and associates assessed the amount of war in the system in two ways: (1) the number of wars ongoing; and (2) nation-months of wars ongoing. A statistical analysis of the data, with a three-year time lag, partially confirmed the results from Singer and Small. Reducing interaction opportunities predicted toward war for 1919–39 and the reverse (albeit weakly) for 1816–1914. However, for 1946–65 the expected linkage did not hold.[22] Collectively, these results pointed to the need for further testing, in order to produce more coherent findings.

Focussing on the great powers from 1495 to 1975, Levy probed the connection between war and international military alliances. He used a wide range of measurements for the former, among them, frequency, duration, and number of great powers involved. For the last named, Levy focussed on the number of alliances and the number of powers forming alliances. From rank-order correlations he found that alliance-formation is associated with relatively low levels of war, measured in various ways. However, he also computed "the proportion of alliances followed by war within five years and the proportion of wars preceded by alliances within five years," as more specific tests of the general hypothesis. "With the exception of the nineteenth century," Levy found that "defensive and neutrality alliances when they have occurred, have been excellent predictors of wars involving (or between) the Great Powers, appearing thus to have nearly constituted sufficient conditions for war in some periods." Attempting to synthesize the results, Levy suggested that alliances should occupy the role of an intervening variable in a more comprehensive model of international conflict.[23] In other words, intercentury and other differences and patterns probably reflect underlying environmental factors, as opposed to the direct impact of alliances.

Siverson and Sullivan examined alliances and war in a different context. They focussed on the initial dyad in each war, in order to more directly observe the onset of the latter, and also developed a "baseline population" to permit more meaningful comparison. Among the 50 wars from 1815 to 1965 identified by the COW Project, 59 of the 100 initial participants did not have an alliance.

This result is inconsistent with the usual logic regarding interaction opportunities and war. However, Siverson and Sullivan also discovered an interaction effect involving alliances and power status: "major powers with alliances are more likely to be an initial war participant than major powers without allies" and "minor powers with an alliance were less likely to be an initial war participant than minor powers without an alliance."[24] This difference suggests that the argument about the pervasiveness of coalitions formulated by Deutsch and Singer may be more relevant to major powers, because alliances reduce flexibility for such actors. By contrast, alliances provide security for minor powers, which tend to be less autonomous in the first place.

Schroeder's historical analysis of European diplomacy also is relevant to the question of alliances and war. Concerned with the 19th century, he argued that the treaty system of 1815 and the network of small powers on the Continent combined to make the area relatively stable.[25] The Concert of Europe operated flexibly and its members shared an interest in preserving the autonomy of small states. Rather than removing interaction opportunities, the Concert nurtured cooperative linkages among the powers. Schroeder's evidence is consistent with the conclusion reached by Levy; alliances will manifest underlying intentions and are less likely to have independent effects on the outbreak of war.

Several points emerge from the review of research on the extent of alliance commitments and the occurrence of war. There is a relatively consistent difference between the 19th and 20th centuries. Alliances appear to correlate with stability in the previous century; in the present one, the reverse seems to be true. Once again, the need for a more comprehensive model of structure and conflict — to account for such differences — becomes apparent.

Within such a framework, the pervasiveness of alliance commitments logically would occupy the role of an intervening variable. Coalitions, after all, tend to reflect the prior objectives of participating states, especially the major powers. Perhaps in the current century, alliances are more likely to represent explicit commitments toward the defence of endangered client states, while in the previous century, alliance-formation reflected the stereotypical game of "musical chairs" associated with a highly flexible system. Some of the especially unsuccessful alliances of the 20th century — such as those involving France and small powers in Eastern Europe during the 1930s — tend to confirm that hypothesized difference. In short, the sources of alliance-formation should receive more attention in a renewed attempt to link more comprehensively systemic structure to international conflict.

Tightness and Discreteness of Alliance Commitments

With regard to the specific properties of alliance configurations, there is a consensus on the two factors to consider and their likely effects. "Polarization," according to Goldmann, "is a process characterized by an increase in positive interaction between certain members of the system and a decrease in positive interaction between them and other members of the system." On an equally general note, Jackson urged scholars to "reverse the concept polarization for description of patterns of interaction, i.e., the structure(s) of conflict in the system." This formulation became more explicit with Bueno de Mesquita's dimensions of discreteness and tightness, referring to the distance separating clusters of states and their degree of cohesion around the respective poles in the system. Similarly, Rapkin and Thompson referred to the "extent to which a system's actors form two separate subsystems or blocs with inter-bloc and intra-bloc interaction being characterized, predominately and respectively, by conflict and cooperation."[26] Efforts toward testing the effects of polarization on the outbreak of war have focussed primarily on discreteness and tightness, as just described.

There also is agreement with regard to the presumed impact of each of these structural attributes. Greater tightness and discreteness are uniformly expected to result in a higher amount of war in the system. In that regard, the standard historical reference is August 1914. As the two camps within Europe drew farther away from each other, while simultaneously showing greater internal cohesiveness, the opportunity to prevent disaster slipped away. World War I ensued.

Wallace used COW Project data to assess the impact of polarization on the magnitude (nation-months) and severity (battle deaths) of war within a given time frame. His polarization index encompassed tightness and discreteness:

> where the system is highly polarized, the great majority of nations will be clustered in as few as two tightly knit groups at a considerable distance from one another. On the other hand, where polarization is low, the nations will form many loose clusters distributed in random fashion throughout the [geographical] space.

Wallace correlated the index with the indicators of war over the usual 150-year period — and segments of it — but found only negligible connections. He then tested a more complex model and found support for a curvilinear linkage. Very low and high levels of polarization predicted toward war, with the best system being one that is moderately polarized.[27]

Investigating the impact of polarization on violent conflict, Bueno de Mesquita used two measurements of the occurrence of war from the COW data set "1816–1965: interstate and major power wars." Using statistical procedures, he measured tightness and discreteness (along with the change in each) on the basis of alliance commitments. Highly similar states ended up in the same cluster, at various distances from those in other clusters. Closer proximity among the states in a cluster represents tightness, while discreteness corresponds to the relative distance from other groupings.

A variation on one of the above-noted structural factors had by far the most significant connection to the occurrence of war in the 20th century. Increasing systemic tightness correlated positively with war: "Eighty-nine percent of the twentieth-century periods of declining tightness preceded years in which no war began, while 84 percent of the wars in the twentieth century began in years following a five-year rise in systemic tightness." Bueno de Mesquita also found that the duration of war in the current century could be predicted best by the change in tightness.[28]

Wayman hypothesized that "cluster bipolarity" — analogous to high levels of tightness and discreteness in the system — would be associated with subsequent warfare. This proposition followed from the fact that "two important conflict-reducing agents — namely, intermediary relationships and cross-cutting cleavages — exist in a cluster multipolar setting but are eliminated in a cluster bipolar one." Using the magnitude and frequency of war as dependent variables, he found support for the hypothesis in the 20th century, but the reverse obtained for the 19th century.[29]

There is some degree of consistency among the preceding studies. Wayman found an intercentury difference, with the linkage of cluster bipolarity to war in the 20th century running parallel to the discoveries by Bueno de Mesquita about increasing systemic tightness, and by Wallace regarding very high levels of polarization. When polarization becomes more precise — meaning that the configuration of alliances tightens or already is highly visible — the danger of war is greater. Concerning Wallace's finding that very low polarization also increases the risk of war, and the similar linkage uncovered by Wayman for the previous century, these patterns may be related to the earlier discoveries about the effects of alliance pervasiveness. Given the flexible system of bargaining within 19th-century Europe, more alliances may have meant more stabilizing factors in operation, with extremely "loose" alliances being less helpful than more obvious connections.

Concentration of Power

With regard to the concentration of power, the question ultimately becomes a philosophical one. On the one hand, consider Lord Acton's dictum: "Power tends to corrupt and absolute power corrupts absolutely." On the other, recall Hardin's equally discomforting analysis of the Tragedy of the Commons.[30] With power widely distributed, the public good — in the classic example of the Tragedy, land under collective administration — suffers because of the uniform pursuit of individual interests. The spectre of hegemonic war argues against concentration of power, while danger of collective irresponsibility would suggest its value.

Within the study referred to earlier, Singer, Bremer, and Stuckey assessed the impact of *changes* in power concentration on major-power war. In the 19th century, greater concentration of capabilities is associated with the amount of war in progress, while the reverse is true for the 20th century. Cannizzo's state-level replication exhibited the same pattern, although with much stronger results for the present than for the previous century.[31]

Siverson and Sullivan produced a comprehensive summary of research on power concentration and war. Whether state-level, dyadic, or systemic in nature, the studies in their review (with one exception) supported the notion that "power parity produces war." However, Siverson and Sullivan urged caution in interpreting that result, because the studies concerned have "drawn their data from extremely restricted samples" or "transformed the data in a way that restricts variance in the indicators of power."[32]

Stoll and Champion suggested a more complex linkage involving power concentration and war. They hypothesized that "the 'coefficient' governing the relationship between capability concentration and international conflict is not constant, but is itself determined by the proportion of the capability in the system held by satisfied powers." With a low proportion of the capabilities held by satisfied powers, war becomes more likely when the concentration factor is high, because a disparity would tend to favour revisionist states. When a moderate percentage of power is held by satisfied states, less war is expected; of course, a high proportion of capabilities among satisfied states would be more stable if power also was concentrated. Stoll and Champion used expert-generated data to measure the respective satisfaction levels among states and relied on the COW Project for data on the amount of war from 1820 to 1965. Their model is supported by the data, without the usual intercentury difference, although it underestimated the magnitude of World War I significantly.[33]

Considered collectively, research on the concentration of power tends to link a diffuse distribution to the occurrence of war, most notably in the current century. This result is consistent with the earlier conclusions reached about multipolarity. Perhaps the most interesting aspect to consider is the insight from Stoll and Champion that the *intentions* of those holding power are likely to intervene and complicate any mechanical connection that is identified with regard to concentration and war. Once again, the potential utility of a more comprehensive outlook on structural factors is suggested by closer examination of a presumably bivariate linkage.

A Summary of Findings and Directions for Further Research

Some of the more salient patterns from the four areas of inquiry may now be identified. In the current century, multipolarity and a less-concentrated distribution of power are linked to the occurrence of war. Alliance-formation and tightening of existing commitments also are associated with systemic war-proneness. On the basis of these results, a bipolar system with a concentrated distribution of power and a few loose alliances may be described as the preferred structure.

However, there are at least three reasons why the preceding generalization about structure and war should be regarded with caution. The role of necessary versus sufficient conditions, unknown multivariate effects, and causal factors from other levels of analysis suggest that, at best, only a partial answer has been obtained.

First, the results from the four areas of testing collectively say more about the necessary — as opposed to sufficient — conditions for war.[34] Changes toward tightness in alliance configurations and more diffuse distribution of power do not, to be more precise, guarantee interstate warfare. Rather, it is appropriate to view these developments as reducing environmental constraints on the decision by the leadership of a given state to choose war over peace. For example, suppose that more clearly defined coalitions and greater uncertainty about relative power (in the latter sense, a trend toward parity) had emerged in an international system. A higher *probability* of both confrontation and misjudgement about the likely outcome of war might be the result, tending to encourage the outbreak of violent conflict.

There is a second reason to be wary of reading too much into the patterns that have emerged from the record of primarily aggregate testing. Intervening variables may have a profound effect on presumably straightforward linkages involving war and individual aspects of structure. The role played by the pervasiveness of alliances in the system, to cite an example already noted, is likely to depend on the intentions behind their formation. Similarly, whether or not those with capabilities are satisfied with the system should have a mediating effect on the linkage of power concentration to war. In sum, multivariate effects are as yet poorly understood because a comprehensive model of structure and conflict — incorporating a full range of independent, intervening, and dependent variables — has yet to be specified and tested.

Related to the preceding point is a third, more general, concern about developing a thorough explanation of the causes of war. Factors from other levels of analysis — the individual and state — must be incorporated, especially when the investigation turns to specific cases. While Singer has argued that models focussing on national attributes "do little in accounting for the distribution of war across cases, regions, and time," Siverson and Sullivan respond by observing that "power distribution by itself" is unlikely to be a "sufficient variable in accounting for war."[35] These two points of view do not necessarily pose a contradiction. For a specific instance of war, the system may have presented the opportunity to act, given the statics and dynamics of power endowments and coalitions. Within the state, other factors may help to explain the exact timing and scale of a war. The greatest value of systemic theory, to return to the point made by Keohane, is to reveal general patterns that may exist and thereby counteract the tendency to see every case as uniquely determined by the traits of individual leaders or national character.

Having argued that a more comprehensive model of structure and war should be developed, it is appropriate to conclude with some preliminary suggestions for its composition and testing. It would be interesting to construct a dynamic model, perhaps beginning with two independent variables: change in (1) the concentration of power, and (2) the number of poles. (The latter might be assessed along a continuum, ranging from extreme bipolarity through greater degrees of multipolarity.) As an intervening variable, movement in the tightness of alliances is a natural choice, based on previous findings. Dependent variables could include several indicators of war, such as frequency, duration, and magnitude. This approach would take into account the previously exhibited sensitivity of findings to measurement of the occurrence of war. It also might be interesting to see whether the combination of structural variables would predict other forms of conflict, such as international crisis.[36]

It is beyond the scope of this review to be more precise about a comprehensive model of structure and conflict. Measurement, selection of data, and testing procedures would all require more detailed treatment. However, it is interesting to speculate on the war propensity of the international system in the near future, guided by the independent and intervening variables.

With regard to the independent variables, the impressionistic evidence is somewhat discouraging. The number of power centres appears to be moving away from the long-established level of two. Each of the commonly identified contenders for polar status, however, still seems to be missing at least one ingredient. China's overall military effectiveness remains problematic, at least relative to the superpowers, as a result of a lag in technology. For Japan, potential military capacity is impressive, but the proportion of revenue devoted to that sector remains small. Finally, the states of Western Europe lack political integration and do not appear to be moving toward it with any great speed. In sum, the potentially dangerous effects associated with multipolarity in the current century do not appear to be on the immediate horizon, despite a relative decline in stature for the two leading powers.

More straightforward is the pattern of change in the concentration of power. Middle powers have been gaining, at least in relative terms, on those closer to the apex of the pyramid. Unfortunately, that trend does not reflect disarmament among the elite. Instead, many Third World states have increased military capabilities over the last two decades, especially in the already volatile subsystem of the Middle East. It is likely that the diffusion of capabilities, as would be suggested by the aggregate studies, is not a welcome development at this stage in history.

For the intervening variable, tightness in alliance commitments, the outlook is more promising. The tight structure of the post–World War II era has not entirely unravelled, but East-West confrontation is certainly at a lower level than in the past. The superpower-centred alliances, for example, SEATO, NATO, and WTO, either have disbanded or have become less hierarchical in nature. Some prominent states, such as China, are no longer overwhelmingly associated with one of the blocs, although sympathies in one direction or the other may still exist. Overall, the pattern of change in alliances would not appear to be threatening at this time, based on the linkages revealed in aggregate testing. Of course, it always is possible that unanticipated mediating effects could be dangerous, but that question cannot be answered on the basis of existing research.

To conclude, systemic factors do seem to have implications for the occurrence of war. In the late 20th century, the pattern of power endowments and coalitions does not look especially threatening. Although such environmental factors do not entirely determine what will happen next, there is some reassurance in the fact that properties of the system may constrain the resort to arms. At the very least, greater understanding of the impact of the system on world politics may help to anticipate and even deal with conflicts in the future.

NOTES

1. Kenneth N. Waltz, *Man, the State, and War* (New York: Columbia University Press, 1959).

2. Robert O. Keohane, *After Hegemony: Cooperation and Discord in the World Political Economy* (Princeton: Princeton University Press, 1984), 25–26.

3. Alan Ned Sabrosky, "Introduction: Polarity and War," in *Polarity and War: The Changing Structure of International Conflict*, ed. Alan Ned Sabrosky (Boulder, Colo., and London: Westview, 1985), 3.

4. The specific rules of categorization derived from the two general criteria are discussed at length in Melvin Small and J. David Singer, *Resort to Arms: International and Civil Wars, 1816–1980* (Beverly Hills: Sage Publications, 1982), 31–61.

5. David Garnham, "The Causes of War: Systemic Findings," in *Polarity and War*, 7.

6. Jeffrey A. Hart, "Power and Polarity in the International System," in *Polarity and War*, 33; Kjell Goldmann, *Tension and Détente in Bipolar Europe* (Stockholm: Scandinavian University Books, 1974), 103.

7. Bruce Bueno de Mesquita, "Systemic Polarization and the Occurrence and Duration of War," in *Explaining War: Selected Papers from the Correlates of War Project*, ed. J. David Singer et al. (Beverly Hills and London: Sage, 1979), 114; see also "Theories of International Conflict: An Analysis and an Appraisal," in *Handbook of Political Conflict: Theory and Research*, ed. Ted Robert Gurr (New York: The Free Press, 1980), 381. Østergaard, describing the world of the 1980s as one of "multipolarity," reveals a similar perspective: "The key states are the USA, the Soviet Union, Japan and two groups of states, the EEC and the Third World." See Clemens Østergaard, "Multipolarity and Modernization: Sources of China's Foreign Policy in the 1980s," *Cooperation and Conflict* 18, no. 4 (1983): 249.

8. Jack S. Levy, "Size and Stability in the Modern Great Power System," *International Interactions* 10 (1984): 345; Frank Wayman, "Bipolarity, Multipolarity, and the Threat of War," in *Polarity and War*, 118–19.

9. Kenneth N. Waltz, "The Stability of a Bipolar World," *Daedalus* 93 (Summer 1964): 882–87. Other advocates of bipolarity have included William H. Riker, *The Theory of Political Coalitions* (New Haven: Yale University Press, 1962); Steven L. Spiegel, "Bimodality and the International Order: Paradox of Parity," *Public Policy* 18 (1970): 383–412; and Ciro E. Zoppo, "Nuclear Technology, Multipolarity and International Stability," *World Politics* 18 (July 1966): 579–606.

10. Karl W. Deutsch and J. David Singer, "Multipolar Power Systems and International Stability," *World Politics* 16 (April 1964): 390–406. Among the others who have advocated multipolarity are Raymond Aron, *Peace and War* (Garden City, N.Y.: Doubleday, 1966), and Stanley Hoffmann, *Gulliver's Troubles, or the Setting of American Foreign Policy* (New York: McGraw-Hill, 1968).

11. Richard N. Rosecrance, "Bipolarity, Multipolarity, and the Future," *Journal of Conflict Resolution* 10, no. 3 (1966): 314–27; John F. Cooper, "The Advantages of a Multipolar

International System: An Analysis of Theory and Practice," *International Studies* 14, no. 3 (1975): 415.

12. Michael Haas, "International Subsystems: Stability and Polarity," *American Political Science Review* 64 (March 1970): 99–100, 121.

13. J. David Singer, Stuart Bremer, and John Stuckey, "Capability Distribution, Uncertainty, and Major Power War, 1820–1965," in *Explaining War*, 165–69, 173.

14. Cynthia Cannizzo, "Capability Distribution and Major-Power War Experience, 1816–1965," *Orbis* 21 (Winter 1978): 951–53, 957.

15. Charles W. Ostrom, Jr., and John H. Aldrich, "The Relationship Between Size and Stability in the Major Power International System," *American Journal of Political Science* 22 (1978): 762–63.

16. Levy, "Size and Stability," 349, 350–52.

17. Wayman, "Bipolarity, Multipolarity, and the Threat of War," 126, 131.

18. Deutsch and Singer, "Multipolar Power Systems and International Stability"; William R. Thompson, Karen A. Rasler, and Richard P. Y. Li, "Systemic Interaction Opportunities and War Behavior," *International Interactions* 7 (1980): 59.

19. Benjamin A. Most and Harvey Starr, "Polarity, Preponderance and Power Parity in the Generation of International Conflict," *International Interactions* 13 (1987): 235. Emphasis added.

20. J. David Singer and Melvin Small, "Alliance Aggregation and the Onset of War, 1815–1945," in *Quantitative International Politics*, ed. J. David Singer (New York: The Free Press, 1966), 249, 283.

21. Charles W. Ostrom, Jr., and Francis W. Hoole, "Alliances and War Revisited: A Research Note," *International Studies Quarterly* 22 (June 1978): 215–35.

22. Thompson, Rasler, and Li, "Systemic Interaction Opportunities," 63, 77.

23. Jack S. Levy, "Alliance Formation and War Behavior: An Analysis of the Great Powers, 1495–1975," *Journal of Conflict Resolution* 25, no. 4 (1981): 596–97, 612.

24. Randolph M. Siverson and Michael Sullivan, "Alliances and War: A New Examination of an Old Problem," *Conflict Management and Peace Science* 8 (1984): 5–6, 10–12.

25. Less relevant to the current issue of alliances is the third factor identified by Schroeder: the relatively insular nature of European politics in that era. See Paul W. Schroeder, "The 19th-Century International System: Changes in the Structure," *World Politics* 39 (October 1986): 1–26.

26. Goldmann, *Tension and Détente*, 107; William D. Jackson, "Polarity in International Systems: A Conceptual Note," *International Interactions* 4 (1977): 92; Bueno de Mesquita, "Systemic Polarization," 126; David P. Rapkin and William R. Thompson, "A Comparative Note on Two Alternative Indexes of Bipolarization," *International Interactions* 6 (1980): 378.

27. Michael D. Wallace, "Alliance Polarization, Cross-Cutting, and International War, 1815–1964: A Measurement Procedure and Some Preliminary Evidence," in *Explaining War*, 97, 105.

28. Bueno de Mesquita, "Systemic Polarization," 126, 131, 136.

29. Wayman, "Bipolarity, Multipolarity, and the Threat of War," 122, 133.

30. John Bartlett, ed., *Familiar Quotations*, 15th ed. (Boston and Toronto: Little, Brown, 1980), 615; Garrett Hardin, "The Tragedy of the Commons," in *Managing the Commons*, ed. Garrett Hardin and John Baden (San Francisco: W.H. Freeman, 1977).

31. Singer et al., "Capability Distribution," 173; Cannizzo, "Capability Distribution," 954.

32. Randolph M. Siverson and Michael P. Sullivan, "The Distribution of Power and the Onset of War," *Journal of Conflict Resolution* 27 (September 1983): 491.

33. Richard J. Stoll and Michael Champion, "Capability Concentration, Alliance Bonding, and Conflict Among the Major Powers," in *Polarity and War*, 77–87.

34. For a discussion of power attributes as necessary conditions for war see Wolf-Dieter Eberwein, "The Quantitative Study of International Conflict: Quantity and Quality? — An Assessment of Empirical Research," *Journal of Peace Research* 18, no. 1 (1981): 19–38.

35. J. David Singer, "Confrontational Behavior and Escalation to War 1816–1980: A Research Plan," *Journal of Peace Research* 19, no. 1 (1982): 37; Siverson and Sullivan, "The Distribution of Power," 475.

36. For initial efforts to assess the impact of structure on crisis-generated instability, see Michael Brecher and Patrick James, "Polarity, Stability and Crisis: State of the Art and New Directions," and Michael Brecher, Jonathan Wilkenfeld, and Patrick James, "Polarity, Stability and Crisis: Weighing the Evidence," in *The Analysis of Crises in the Twentieth Century*, ed. Michael Brecher and Jonathan Wilkenfeld (Oxford and New York: Pergamon, 1989).

SELECT BIBLIOGRAPHY

Albertini, Luigi. *The Origins of the War of 1914*. 3 vols. Trans. and ed. Isabella M. Massey. London: Oxford University Press, 1952–57.

Bueno de Mesquita, Bruce. *The War Trap*. New Haven: Yale University Press, 1981.

Choucri, Nazli, and Robert C. North. *Nations in Conflict*. San Francisco: W.H. Freeman, 1975.

Deutsch, Karl W., and J. David Singer. "Multipolar Power Systems and International Stability." *World Politics* 16 (April 1964): 390–406.

Holsti, Ole R. *Crisis Escalation War*. Montreal: McGill-Queen's University Press, 1972.

Organski, A.F.K., and Jacek Kugler. *The War Ledger*. Chicago and London: University of Chicago Press, 1980.

Richardson, Lewis F. *Arms and Insecurity*. Pittsburgh: Boxwood, 1960.

Rosecrance, Richard N. "Bipolarity, Multipolarity, and the Future." *Journal of Conflict Resolution* 10, no. 3 (1966): 314–27.

Russett, Bruce M., ed. *Peace, War, and Numbers*. Beverly Hills: Sage, 1972.

Small, Melvin, and J. David Singer. *Resort to Arms: International and Civil Wars, 1816–1980*. Beverly Hills: Sage, 1982.

Smoke, Richard. *War: Controlling Escalation.* Cambridge, Mass., and London: Harvard University Press, 1977.

Stoessinger, John G. *Why Nations Go to War.* 4th ed. New York: St. Martin's Press, 1985.

Waltz, Kenneth N. *Man, the State, and War.* New York: Columbia University Press, 1959.

———. "The Stability of a Bipolar World." *Daedalus* 93 (Summer 1964): 881–909.

Wright, Quincy. *A Study of War.* 2d ed. Chicago: University of Chicago Press, 1965.

BALANCES OF POWER: ANALOGY, ARGUMENTS, AND SOME EVIDENCE

William B. Moul

The "balance of power" is a hardy notion, basic to many understandings of politics among states. That much is not in dispute. Most other things concerning this expression, however — What is the balance of power? What is it supposed to do? Has it or has it not done what it is supposed to do? — remain contentious. The words themselves inhabit a confusing middle ground between being an evocative metaphor that fixes thoughts time after time and being so well worn of connotation that they can no longer be considered metaphorical at all. Perhaps for a time in Europe, during the 17th century, when the modern state system was being established, the phrase "balance of power" did possess the mark of a good metaphor, in the same way that Adam Smith's "invisible hand" leading self-interested individuals to promote the public interest would a century later. Soon after, however, the phrase became hackneyed, and Richard Cobden's harangue on balance-of-power thinking was as well deserved in 1836 as it was overdue:

> [The concept is] not a fallacy, a mistake, an imposture, it is an undescribed, indescribable, incomprehensible nothing; mere words, conveying to the mind not ideas, but sounds like those equally barren syllables which our ancestors put together for the purpose of puzzling themselves about words in the shape of *Prester John* or the *philosopher's stone*!
>
> [The theory is] mere chimera — a creation of the politician's brain — a phantasm, without definite form or tangible existence — a mere conjunction of syllables, forming words which convey sound without meaning.[1]

This mere chimera remained Cobden's favourite target during his 30 years of public life, and like-minded persons found good reason to repeat his words during the century and a half since they first were published. However, as metaphor, the "balance of power," a tough old phrase, is not dead.

Although much shorter than that of theoretical literature, the trail of empirical literature regarding the balance of power is likewise confused and inconsistent. Different notions of what it is have led to different evidence, and hence to different findings. Such a result could be expected. What could not be expected is that agreements on what the balance of power is would lead to different findings drawn from the same sorts of evidence. For example, some quantitative studies have found that an equal balance of power maintains interstate peace; others, that a decided imbalance preserves peace. Some find one way at one time and another way at a different time; some, that a balance of power kept the peace for one type of state and not for a different type. Finally, some find nothing much at all.

As the mix of the findings suggests, replacing anecdotes from diplomatic history with quantitative data has not replaced confusion with cumulative knowledge. Furthermore, the self-consciously scientific approach of the quantitative work has added controversies over proper method to controversies over the substance of "the balance of power." As we will see, there is irony in the fact that, currently, the most prominent balance-of-power theorists pay little attention to statistical studies such as those to which I have alluded, while those who do quantitative research pay little attention to the "state arithmetic" practised by early statisticians.

The purpose of this chapter is to evaluate arguments and evidence connecting various balances of power to war, peace, and alliance formations. Some of the confusion about what, if anything, "the balance of power" is and what any balance of power is supposed to do can be reduced by keeping close to the physical analogies. The discussion is in three parts: first, an account of various descriptive usages of the term bound to the physical analogy; second, prominent and cogently contrary arguments connecting those "balance of power" descriptions to war, peace, and alliances; and third, evidence from some systematic studies of the great powers. Although Martin Wight denotes seven distinct uses of the phrase in one of his classic essays on the balance of power (and nine in a later essay), and A.F. Pollard suggests that there are thousands of others, the focus here is on two themes: the measurement of power of states among states and the role of balancers, or third parties, in a division of power.[2] The central balance-of-power arguments hinge on the uncertainty inherent in the measurement of power so that methodological and measurement matters raised in the first part prepare the way for the substance of the second part. Some data are better than others, and discussion of method and measurement provides criteria for selecting the evidence considered in the third part.

Like the many balance-of-power theorists, I concentrate on the great powers during the 1815–1939 period. The ending of World War II forced a distinction between great powers and superpowers and, parallel to it, a distinction between a balance of power and a balance of terror. Some argue that the latter distinction is a matter of words, involving nothing new or fundamental. To quote from Geoffrey Blainey's otherwise excellent analysis of interstate war: "the idea of a balance of terror is highly appropriate today, but it was appropriate a century ago."[3] This is wrong. One reason why the contention is wrong can be appreciated if we keep to the balance analogy.

Balances and the Problem of Measurement in Politics

A simple balance is a lever consisting of a uniform beam suspended at its centre upon an edge, with two pans of equal weight suspended in identical positions from opposite ends of the beam. The midpoint of the beam, where it pivots on the edge, is the centre of gravity and is called the "fulcrum." The balance is said to be in equilibrium when the beam is parallel to a level surface. Put more formally, equilibrium occurs when the force in one direction is equal to the force in the opposite direction. The word *equilibrium* derives from "equi" (equal) and "libra" (balance, as in the zodiacal constellation named "the Scales"). The abbreviations for pound sterling and pound weight are also etymological remnants of this derivation. The weight of a body is the force of gravity operating on that body and can be determined when the object to be weighed is placed in one pan and weights of known magnitude are added to the second pan until the balance is in equilibrium. The weight of the object is then equal to the magnitude of the weights added. If there are no standard weights, the relative weights of objects can be assessed.

The balance device was already ancient in the 17th century, and its figurative usages in politics and law were as old then as they were commonplace. At that time the use of the word *balance* extended to include measuring devices based on different physical principles, and from this usage *balance of power* secured a place in the vocabulary of diplomacy and international law. The implication that the magnitude of political power of a state among states could be assessed as if it were the weight of an object suited a time of profound advances in mechanics and mathematics as well as of the invention of state arithmetic or statistics. This was the age of Newton and of those who stood on his shoulders. The "balance of power" suggested possibilities for a political arithmetic where political principles could be expressed in the manner of physical laws, "in Terms of *Number*, *Weight*, or *Measure*" instead of in "comparative and superlative words." Such were the sentiments of Sir William Petty, student and disciple of Thomas Hobbes, a founder of the Royal Society, and collaborator of John Graunt. It is from the latter's analyses of London's Bills of Mortality that we trace the modern science of statistics. Unlike those of his collaborator, Petty's analyses mixed politics and numbers freely in many essays on the methods he called *Political Arithmetick*. For example, in a pamphlet of that name, Petty sought to convince his king that subsidies from France were unnecessary by demonstrating that the "People and Territories of the King of England . . . a small Country, and few People, may . . . be equivalent in Wealth and Strength, to a far greater People, and Territory," namely France.[4]

War tied wealth and strength closely in new ways during the 17th century in Europe. There were few years without war, and the scale of organized violence made for increases in the size and centralization of state power. In turn, the financial reorganization of the state made possible the employment of novel, sophisticated military techniques. As a result, warfare and the threat of war demanded further financial and administrative change in order to pull more resources from the country to sustain military scale. "War lays a burden on the reeling state, / And peace does nothing to relieve the weight."[5] The burden provided practical employment for statistics and the statisticians who wielded them.

The word *statistik* itself was coined by Gottfried Achenwall, a Göttingen professor of politics and public administration whom we would put on the "qualitative" rather than the "quantitative" side of the debates over proper method in the study of politics. In Germany, state arithmetic was less numerical than was its equivalent in Britain, and Achenwall and those who followed him did not "devote themselves so much to enumeration and computation as to verbal descriptions of the political situation and all facts of [political] interest." They "looked with considerable unfriendliness and displeasure upon the 'Table-statistician'," those whom today we would call statisticians.[6] The quantitative/qualitative controversies over the proper method for studying interstate politics are almost as old as modern interstate politics.

In elementary usage, "the balance of power" assesses, quantitatively or not, the ability of state A to do something that state B would prefer that it not do. In an anarchical world of armed and insecure states, where war is the ultimate power relationship, assessing fighting strength is an essential task. Estimates of fighting power are estimates of the course of a war, if such a war were to occur. In large part, they are made by combining and weighing the capabilities or wherewithal of opposing sides. Such judgements are inherently uncertain. As Hans J. Morgenthau writes, "to chart the course of the stream [of power] and of the different currents that compose it, and to anticipate the changes in their direction and speed, is the ideal task of the observer."[7] This ideal cannot be achieved because there is no standard unit of power comparable to pounds weight or pounds sterling. Power among states is always relative, never absolute.

Balancing books involves different sorts of assessments from those used in balancing power. Morgenthau, as did some other balance-of-power thinkers before him, raised this difference to a matter of high principle: quantitative and qualitative are deemed to be "irreconcilable approaches to the study of international politics."[8] Why this might be so is not put clearly. Morgenthau declares that power itself, as defined above, "can be experienced, evaluated, guessed at, but that [it] is not susceptible to quantification." To assess or to balance power is to make an "historical and necessarily qualitative judgement." One can agree while finding no irreconcilable differences in method. Judgements of fighting power must be historical, if for no other reason than the fact that past performance is our purchase on estimates of future conditional outcomes. We can agree also that such judgements are necessarily qualitative once we recognize how restrictively Morgenthau confines quantitative measurement.

Measurement is the assigning of numbers to a property of an object, an event, or a person according to rules. These rules tell the properties of the number system (such as name, order, distance) we use and, thereby, what information our measures can carry. If we use numbers to name categories, any number will do, since any number would carry no additional information. Arithmetic with such numbers would be foolish. If the numbers are assigned to distances between standard units, such as dollars, beginning with zero where there are none, the numbers would not be arbitrary. The resulting system of measurement could carry all the information of the number system and allow any arithmetical operation. Morgenthau compares power and wealth in order to illustrate that there is no such system of measurement for power while there is one for wealth. Therefore, political arithmetic is very different from ordinary arithmetic. However, to restrict quantitative analysis in this way is to overlook the use of numbers for ordering states in a balance of power and for recording the orders so that a range of very useful logical techniques can be made available. Indeed, inherently qualitative judgements should be recorded so that the judgements can be counted, weighed, and compared or correlated with the observations of whatever balance-of-power theories purport to explain. "Always, we might as well face it, the shadow of the statistician hovers in the background; *always* the actuary will have the final word" balancing the books on balances of power.[9]

Lack of a precise system of measurement does not mean lack of measurement; rough measurement is still measurement. Judges of the relative power of opposing sides always have at the least two choices: first, one side is stronger than the other; second, one is not stronger than the other. The scale of a balance of power is something more than "comparative and superlative words," but it is less than the "*Number*, *Weight*, or *Measure*" Petty had hoped to build. Furthermore, balances of power fall outside the common classification of scales of measurement to which statistical techniques are geared: nominal (e.g., Asian/non-Asian state), ordinal (e.g., a pecking order), interval (e.g., Celsius temperature), or ratio (e.g., income in dollars). It lies between ordinal and interval and has a natural zero point as does the ratio scale (at the equilibrium of no difference in forces). Unlike, however, the ratio or interval or ordinal scales, balances need not be transitive. A transitive relationship is one in which, for instance, A is greater than B, B is greater than C, and, therefore, A is greater than C. Balances of power among three states, A, B, and C, on the other hand, could find that A is greater than B and B is greater than C, but A is less than C. The unwary use of quantitative techniques that presume a specific transitive scale leads to mistakes of political arithmetic.

Placing them in their proper perspective requires that these arguments about balances of power and measurement be put more generally. Power is relative not only from one state to another but from one circumstance to another. Political power is always bound by context. Resources potent in one situation need not be as potent in another. For example, the number of nuclear-tipped ICBMS is not relevant if the prospect is a distant land war against a state without ICBMS; a pack of nuclear-powered submarines might cost as much as an army but the one could not be substituted for the other in the same way that the money used to purchase either could. To measure power capabilities with little regard to specifics of what can be used against whom is to grab at a frail notion of power.

To switch metaphors, money is liquid; power capabilities are shaped by circumstances. This is very clear when a state has an ally, and the ally's ability to fight has to be considered in the balance. Whatever the "balance of power" is thought to be, it involves alliances, and alliances complicate political arithmetic. Consider a pair of articles of the 1902 alliance between two important island empires off the Eurasian land-mass, which prepared the ground for a Russo-Japanese war within two years. The *casus foederis* of this Anglo-Japanese alliance was defined more clearly than in many other alliance treaties; and as in many other treaties, the participants anticipated more than one future situation. One article stated that should one party "become involved in war with another Power, the other High Contracting party will maintain a strict neutrality, and use its efforts to prevent other Powers from joining in hostilities." The next provided for a coalition in the event of a war between Japan and two other states.[10] These articles did not and do not lend themselves to arithmetic abstracted from context. What David Baldwin cogently argues with respect to resources of individual states applies with greater force to combinations in alliances: "*No political power resource begins to approach the degree of fungibility of money.* Political power resources are relatively low in fungibility; that is precisely why specification of scope and domain is so essential."[11]

Baldwin appropriated the word *fungible* from Scottish law, where it is associated with the image of a judge holding a balance in hand. Some commodity is fungible insofar as it can function in place of another; to quote a dictionary definition that reminds us of Petty's political arithmetic, fungibles are equivalent in "number, weight and measure." When assessing power capabilities, equivalence is to be investigated, not presumed, because identical items (such as gross national products, sizes of armed forces, or amounts of military expenditures) are to be compared. To presume identical items to be equivalent is to forget that the analogy is about a comparison of weights of diverse items. To be equivalent is to have the same result; identical power capabilities might well have different results in different contexts. Such is usually the case in the social sciences. To argue, as do some students of the balance of power, that to include such contextual information is to abandon "attempts to judge the adequacy of theories across historical and temporal contexts" begs the question of the adequacy of any test in any particular circumstances.[12] The basic methodological distinction between internal and external validity must not be overlooked. Without attention to context when assessing the balance of power, internal validity is undermined, and internal validity is the sine qua non of external validity or generalization. To test a theory requires equivalent, not identical measures. Unfortunately, much quantitative work disregards these distinctions, making measurement more a matter of definition than of inference. Such poor definitions excite the ire of those who insist on irreconcilable qualitative and quantitative approaches to balances of power, rather than on better measurement in the place of poorer measurement.

The outcome of war provides the direct measure of fighting power. Except when measured so directly, the measurement of fighting power is inferred or indirect, and the validity of context-dependent inferences must be tested. Consider the use of gross-national-product statistics as the measure of power capabilities. One reason why this practice is common is that such data are readily available for large numbers of states. To include more cases is to be more general, but what is suited to so many circumstances might be ill-suited to any particular ones so that the generality of the index undercuts specific uses. Generality is a theoretical virtue, but not always a measurement virtue. A.F.K. Organski and Jacek Kugler illustrate this point when comparing the ratios of GNP values of the victors and losers in hard-fought wars during recent times: GNP Davids often defeated GNP Goliaths because Davids were more able to tax the resources that GNP statistics assess in the marketplace. GNP provides a poor measure when the political and organizational capacities of opposing states differ. With other states in other circumstances, Organski and Kugler champion the use of GNP statistics to weigh power capabilities.[13]

Geography and Other Qualifications

Although the image of the simple balance suggests a form of political arithmetic, the more general mechanism, the lever, suggests forms of political geometry to complicate any political arithmetic. Canakya Kautilya formalized the geometry of power politics in the third century B.C., when he described circles, rings, or *mandalas* of neighbours in his *Arthashastra*. The basic principle, a widely recognized one embedded in the folk wisdom of many peoples, is that neighbours are enemies, and enemies of enemies are natural allies. Borders are fighting places, and the system of weights and counterweights known to some as the odd/even number principle — odd and even being enemies, like numbers being allies — and to others as the sandwich system or the "double policy," is fundamental to understanding the outlines of interstate conflict and co-operation.[14]

The mandalas and the number line of odd and even digits presume the weights of states to be identical in order to focus on variations in position. In contrast, the equal-arm balance "controls" for position in order to focus on weight. Other levers vary locations and weights because the force applied depends upon distance and weight. The force is governed by the law of the lever, and there is a political principle analogous to the mechanical one. The mechanical law is that the force equals weight times the length of the effort arm (the distance between the fulcrum to where the weight rests): the farther from the fulcrum, the stronger the force to be applied to the other end. The political principle is the converse because, unlike a lever that allows one to act at a distance, states must overcome distance in order to act. Kenneth Boulding calls this "the great principle of *the further the weaker*. The amount by which the competitive power of a party diminishes per mile movement away from home is the loss-of-power gradient."[15] The loss-of-power gradient is exceedingly steep where there are geopolitical barriers and buffers such as other states, mountains, or seas separating states. For this reason, we could find that the weight of power capabilities of A is greater than that of its neighbour B, and the power capabilities of B greater than those of its neighbour C, but that A is not stronger than C because B separates them.

Separation and distance vary with geography, politics, and technology. Given A, B, and C, all in a row, if A and B or B and C were to ally, the barrier between A and C could become a conduit. Consider the alliance between France and

Sardinia-Piedmont, which, as it were, put France alongside Austria on the Italian peninsula in 1859. Think of the Russo-Japanese war example mentioned above. The loss-of-power gradient across the many thousands of kilometres of the Russian Empire varied with the construction, completion, and quality of railways through Siberia; the availability of rail lines in China; and the conclusion of the alliance with the United Kingdom, which served to keep the Russian fleet on the longest route possible from Europe around Africa to northeast Africa.

In general, barriers and distance favour the defence; technology to overcome barriers and to enhance firepower favours the offence, with modern military technology, especially, enhancing the latter.[16] Near the beginnings of the modern European-state system, the amphibious Netherlands republic, far smaller than either imperial Spain, from which it had revolted, or the aggressive France of Louis XIV, could breach the dikes and turn the country into an island, a marshland into a quagmire. In 1940, at the eclipse of the European-dominated state system, the "great bog of Europe" provided no safety for those in Rotterdam. As Bertold Brecht wrote at the time,

> Out of the libraries
> Emerge the butchers.
> Pressing their children closer
> Mothers stand and humbly search
> The skies for the inventions of learned men.
> The designers sit
> Hunched in the drawing offices:
> One wrong figure, and the enemy's cities
> Will remain undestroyed.[17]

The distinction between defensive and offensive capabilities is not always as clear-cut as that between barriers of mud or water and heavy bomber aircraft. This does not mean that the distinction is of no use. The clarity of the distinction and, concomitantly, the extent of a security dilemma — that what one does to defend oneself thereby threatens another — is a variable of obvious importance in balance-of-power arguments.[18] War was first industrialized during the 19th century, and with the technological impetus to offence and the murkiness of the offence/defence distinction, we would expect security dilemmas to be ever-present dangers, and interstate wars to be frequent. This has not happened. When compared to the century before, war was rare in 19th-century Europe. Many credit the long peace to the "balance of power." There is a similar argument to account for the post-1945 period of great-power peace, the longest such period. We will examine peace by balance of power or by balance of terror below.

There are many more qualifications to balance-of-power capabilities than those mentioned here, which make the political arithmetic appear more difficult than it often is. Oftentimes, whatever the qualifications, disparities in power are plain for all to see. When they are not plain, when reasonable well-qualified judgements of observers on each side differ, the fair (dare I say "balanced"?) assessment would be rough equality. As it happens, one use of the word *balance* refers to the taking into account of all that should be considered, while another refers to a situation in which matters are wavering, with their outcome in doubt or suspenseful. The ability or inability to decide which of two sides would fare better in war is the information that we require to test our balance-of-power arguments. Those who must decide a state's fate if war were to occur demand more than that, of course, but to repeat Morgenthau's caution, such demands are "ideal." In the present, "rational calculation of the relative strength of several nations, which is the very lifeblood of the balance of power, becomes a series of guesses the correctness of which can be ascertained only in retrospect."[19] Morgenthau extracts one basic balance-of-power argument about peace and war from the uncertainty inherent in any measurement of power. There is another argument to be found there. To appreciate each of these arguments, let us consider more descriptions of "the balance of power."

Balance as Equality of Sides

In some arguments the "balance of power" refers to any distribution of power among states, sometimes a synonym for the status quo, if not for the state system itself. More often still, the reference is to particular types of distribution of states or positions in such distributions. The most general of those descriptions is that a balance of power is "a state of affairs such that no one power is in a position where it is preponderant and can lay down the law to others."[20] The more narrow, and thereby more informative, description is an equality or equilibrium of power. The latter usage is straightforward, provided that an eye is kept on the state among states, not some other unit of analysis. Pulled by statistical technique, eyes do stray from the analogy and the proper unit of analysis — the state among states — to the pair of states or to the group of states.

One function of statistical methods is to summarize observations on large numbers of cases, and some judge the number of states to be insufficient for statistical analysis. The solution is to generate large numbers of cases from much smaller numbers of states by describing all possible pairs of states: i.e., 50 states can be made to yield more than 1200 pairs — $(N[N-1])/2$. This solution, indeed the "problem" itself, bears the mark of a table statistician rather than the good sense of a political arithmetician. A sound political arithmetician would point out that there are three parties to any political conflict: those engaged on one side; those engaged on the other side; and the bystanders attracted by the commotion. Conflict is contagious, and because the extent of bystander involvement determines the outcome of conflict, bystanders are a part of the calculus of all conflicts.[21] But, there is no room for bystanders in the dyad.

Balance-of-power arguments concern states, not pairs of states in a fanciful netherworld where each party to a pair is tied exclusively to the other, disconnected from all others including itself on the $N-1$ occasions when it is paired with another. These strange worlds of dyads often hide well in tables of statistics meant to test balance-of-power arguments. In one version developed recently to test a balance-of-power theory of war and peace rooted in alliances and counter-alliances, the 1914 France/Germany dyad is taken to be unrelated to the 1914 Russia/Germany dyad and the 1914 United Kingdom/Germany dyad, and so on, save for any Austro-Hungarian dyads excluded because there are no GNP statistics. We should expect such a chaotic world to yield inconclusive evidence. So it has. Organski and Kugler report that "the major powers seem to fight, whether they are weaker, as strong as, or stronger than their opponents."[22] Whether or not there is any pattern in the less chaotic world of states among states remains to be seen.

TABLE 1 Distributions of Percent Shares of Power Capabilities

State	Shares T	Shares T+1	Shares T+2	Shares T+3
A	0.200	0.500	0.500	0.600
B	0.200	0.200	0.250	0.100
C	0.200	0.200	0.150	0.100
D	0.200	0.050	0.065	0.100
E	0.200	0.050	0.035	0.100
Total	1.000	1.000	1.000	1.000
CON	0.000	0.411	0.419	0.500

Where analyses of dyads chop interstate relations into too many pieces, analyses of groups or systems of states run the risk of papering over interstate relations. For example, an approximately equal distribution of power among states may hide very unequal arrangements between some states. Consider the following illustrations using the CON index devised by James L. Ray and J. David Singer to test the same balance-of-power arguments that Organski and Kugler had set out to test. There are four decimal percentage distributions of power capabilities involving five states. CON, shortened from "concentration," ranges from 0.000, where all are equal, to 1.000, where one has all. Therefore, CON is 0.000 at T, where the shares are identical, and increases as the difference between the largest and the smallest increases. According to the argument to be tested, equality of capabilities leads to decisional uncertainty concerning the victor if war were to occur. Whether or not the wavering "balance" of uncertainty made by the "balance" or equality in the balance of power deters war is the question Singer and his colleagues seek to answer. The difficulty with the procedure is that CON bears no relationship to uncertainty induced by equalities or balances among states except when the values are very close to the extremes of 1.000 and 0.000. CON at T+2 is much the same as CON at T+1, but the balances between states differ: two pairs of equal states at T+1 (B and C; D and E) and no equal pairs at T+2. At T+3 where there is a four-way equality, CON is 0.500, suggesting less equality than at T+1 and T+2.

In their often-cited study, Singer, Stuart Bremer, and John Stuckey report such small values of CON to be correlated with small amounts of warfare for the 19th-century great powers and with large amounts of warfare during the

20th century. They speculate, and lead others to speculate, upon why states were able to keep to the balance-of-power norms in one century but not in the other.[23] The speculation is bound to be fruitless because they provide no good evidence that what is to be explained did happen. To speak of the balance-of-power "system" without ambiguity is to speak of actions or positions of states among states, not of a state aggregate.

Balances and Balancers

One of the oldest uses of the word *balance* is to refer to the authority to decide. Within states, those in authority hold the balance because they determine the measures. Among states those who hold the balance can command by countering one side, not the other. So declares Geffray Fenton in the dedication to Queen Elizabeth of his translation of Francesco Guicciardini's history of war among Italian states: "And lastly [God] hath erected your seate upon a high hill or sanctuarie, and put into your hands the ballance of power and justice, to peaze and counterpeaze [appease and counterpoise] at your will the actions and counsels of all the Christian Kingdomes of your time."[24] The power of the balancer depends upon the effect of the weight it could add to each side once the others have divided. The balancer, the ultimate bystander to any conflict, is the key to much balance-of-power thinking and to much balance-of-power confusion.

Watch what happens when describing three simple arrangements of three states — A, B, and C. The distribution of A = B = C would be balanced, not only because the three states are equal, and no one is preponderant, but because there is the *prospect* that A, B, or C could alter any balance between the other two. If two were to join against one, the distribution of power would not be equal or in equilibrium: any AB or BC or AC coalition would be preponderant. In other words, a balanced distribution is one in which there is the threat that the state holding the balance could make a decidedly unequal distribution. The assessment of fighting power is an assessment of prospects. Thus, the decidedly unequal distribution of A greater than B greater than C, but A less than (B + C) is balanced because B or C could hold the balance in a conflict with A and any two would be superior to the one without an ally. No matter what is the arrangement of states in the present, a balance of power exists if the prospect includes the possibility of the weaker being made stronger than, or equal to, a potential opponent by a coalition with the third party. If A is greater than B and greater than C, but A = (B + C), there is a balance of power because BC is equal to A, and any other coalition would be stronger than one alone. Now, look back over these uses of the phrase "balance of power." They lie as if on a Möbius strip: starting with any distribution of power, to equality, through the half-twist at equilibrium, to inequality, and arriving back where we started at almost any arrangement of states and coalitions of states. The task at hand is to make some theoretical sense of such a pliable notion.

Theoretical Presumptions

Although the balance image is a very general one, some keep it to particular times, depending on the character of states or the intentions of statesmen. There is said to be little balancing of power if there is no one attentive to the collective interest rather than to self-interest. Consider the balance-of-power thinking in two standard studies, one of 16th-century Italy and the other of European states during the Napoleonic Wars two centuries later.

Those who credit the translation of Guicciardini's history with the importation of balance-of-power thinking to Elizabethan England must contend with Garrett Mattingly's magnificent history of Renaissance diplomacy. He found little balance-of-power thinking to be exported from 16th-century Italy. Mattingly portrayed the dynastic competition of princes among whom state interest was personal. Princes did not seek equilibrium; allies were sought "not just to balance the strongest power, but to outweigh it." Rather than equilibrium, the common principle was "little more than that the biggest dog gets the meatiest bone, and others help themselves in the order of size." "It is hard to be sure," Mattingly understated, "that the sixteenth century appreciated the full beauty of a balanced system." The implication was that this full beauty depended upon less-selfish, less-brazen ambitions and interests to be found later. Why they should be found later is hard to understand because, as Mattingly concludes, the personal power of princes gave way to the "voracious, amoral, man-made monsters, the Leviathans."[25] Why should such monsters intend or be able to act for the collective good in a Hobbesian world where war made states, and states made war?

The "bigger dog/bigger bone" rule is never far from the surface in Gullick's masterful account, in *Europe's Classical Balance of Power*, of the arrangement of states raised in coalitions to defeat Napoleonic France and in congress at Vienna to draw a new political map of Europe. However, to conclude, as Gullick does, that "the history of the congress must be written largely in terms of state interest *vs.* equilibrium, but with the greater emphasis on equilibrium" is to complicate matters that Occam's razor would keep simple. In Gullick's words, "while state interest repeatedly diverted individual statesmen from equilibrist policies, there were always other statesmen present to check these excursions and redirect them along balance lines."[26] In other words, the interests of competing great powers conflicted, and the pattern of the settlement was the result of opposing forces. There is no need to invoke the opposition between state interests and collective interests.

A balance of power, however defined, is a consequence of relations among independent states, some of which are more powerful than others. The assumption that calculations of security and of interest are much the same, no matter the time or place or character of the states, is reasonable and simple. Simplicity is a cardinal theoretical virtue. There is no need to posit states of good character or of poor character or to root the actions of states in flaws of human nature (as do many balance-of-power theorists), or in anything other than the anarchy of armed independent organizations. We can now examine balance-of-power theories proper.

Whatever the balance of power is, within it are alliances and the possibilities of alliance. Whatever the balance of power is to do — keep states independent, maintain stability or peace — the central proposition is that the weak mobilize in coalition when threatened by a would-be-preponderant state. "Otherwise," as *Europe's Catechism* instructed, "there is but one Potentate, and the others are only a kind of Vassals to him."[27] As obvious as the logic might appear to some, there is a contrary reasoning that is as obvious to others. According to some cold warriors of one insecure superpower, power attracts rather than repels. Rather than seek to balance, weak states tend to "bandwagon," to use the term taken from U.S. domestic politics. To "bandwagon" is to jump on board in order to join an apparent success, and states are thought to tilt toward those that are up and coming. States bandwagon in order to share in the spoils of the successful or to appease the more powerful. Stephen Walt, who examines the question of balancing or bandwagoning in the post-1945 Middle East, offers the alliance between Germany and the USSR in August 1939 as the best historical illustration of bandwagoning logic. The example suggests another, more cogent line of argument.

There is a mobilization of bias with an alliance to form a coalition, but the alliance between Germany and the USSR in 1939 did not provide for a coalition. Each party intended to immobilize the other, not to mobilize together. The agreement committed each party to benevolent neutrality in the event that "one should become the object of belligerent action" but *not* to a coalition.[28] Germany then attacked Poland, and Poland and its great-power allies declared war on Germany, not the USSR. Shortly thereafter, the USSR, as set out in the alliance, took a part of Poland, and demanded suzerainty from the Baltic republics once within the Czar's domain. When Finland resisted, the USSR found itself in difficulty during the Winter War. Let us examine the strategies of great-power rivals such as the USSR and Germany in conflict with states such as Finland, Latvia, and Poland. Later we can expand the argument to explain why some conflicts between strong and weak states expanded to great power–versus–great power wars while most did not.

Estimates of how others would act if war were to occur between the strong and weak are fundamental to a decision to wage war, and alliance commitments are a means of reducing decisional uncertainty concerning the scope of conflict, and "every change in scope has a bias."[29] The strong would hesitate when pressing the weak because of the prospect of a third party's intervening on the weaker side. To keep the balance tilted in its favour, any prudent would-be predator must seek to limit the scope of conflict by restraining third parties, particularly stronger rivals. An alliance agreement with the stronger third party could function as a restraint on that party. It would enable a predator to manage a conflict of interest with that great-power rival in order to pursue a conflict with a non–great power opponent. Machiavelli advised that a prince "ought never to make common cause with one more powerful than himself to injure another, unless necessity forces him to it."[30] While an alliance is often necessary, there is no need to make common cause, as is true in a coalition. The predator requires the tolerance, not the capabilities, of a rival.

For its part, the rival of a would-be predator allies with that state to restrain it in order to limit unfavourable changes in the distribution of power. In practice this might mean that a rival allies to prevent escalation to war, to restrict gains from war, or to share in those gains. The rival's toleration of change and, thereby, the firmness of the alliance restraints a would-be predator need apply depend upon the existing structure of great-power conflict (polarized or not), and the location of the conflict (centre or periphery). Together the two axes define the importance of the weaker to alterations in the distribution of power. The fate of the weak on the periphery is less likely to concern other great powers than if the weak were at the centre. At the centre, the weak increase in importance to the strong, relative to the polarization of conflict. Moreover, with polarization in the centre, disputes at the periphery are brought thereto. These crude power-politics calculations suggest the possibility of three geopolitical circumstances as well as corresponding alliance formations, if a great power were to make war on a much weaker state.

Situation 1 Weak state in periphery and no polarization of great-power conflict: no alliance required by would-be predator, few are expected, and those few are expected to be ententes or understandings, not neutrality pacts.

Situation 2 Weak state in periphery and great-power conflict polarized, or weak state in centre and great-power conflict not polarized: alliance of restraint, such as an entente, is necessary.

Situation 3 Weak state in centre and great-power conflict polarized: a prudent predator requires a very firm commitment not to intervene — provision for neutrality — but such a commitment from a rival would be very exceptional.

As in the Germany–USSR case, one example of an exceptional circumstance is when other roughly equal and hostile third parties exist. Just as threats and side payments can bind coalition partners, they can also bind rivals to an agreement not to form a coalition, as they did in August 1939.

Balances and Peace

When explaining war and peace, balance-of-power theorists often appear to resist putting the "balance of power" in jeopardy. For example, it is common to claim that the relatively peaceful time in Europe, from the defeat of Napoleon to 1914, was the result of a balance of power. After 100 years this balance eroded. According to David Fromkin, "it was not the balance of power, but the erosion of the balance, that led to the outbreak of the 1914 war." Why, you might ask, did it break down? Fromkin replies: "One answer is that [the balance of power] dictates no longer were followed by the leaders of the principal European states." Why not? Bismarck's departure and the relative decline of the United Kingdom are mentioned. Still, the question "Why peace for so long?" remains. And, why war in 1914? Again, because the balance broke down. "Perhaps the more important answer," writes Fromkin, "is that in the end, whenever that might be, the balance of power always breaks down."[31] How do you know that it broke down? War.

Such circularity appears difficult to avoid in the argument of Hans Morgenthau, the most prominent of balance-of-power theorists. Morgenthau declares the balance of power to be "inevitable" and "essential." A "state of affairs in which power is distributed among several nations with approximate equality" keeps peace, but also encourages war. It is, he points out, "not hard to see that most of the wars that have been fought since the beginning of the modern state system have their origin in the balance of power." In contrast, however, it "will forever be impossible to prove or disprove" that the balance kept the peace "because one cannot retrace the course of history, taking a hypothetical situation [no balance of power] as one's point of departure." The presumption is that a balance of power is ever present, keeping such peace, and that "the instability of the international balance of power is due not to the faultiness of the principle but to the particular conditions under which the principle must operate in a society of sovereign nations."[32] The tendency toward circular reasoning can be arrested if we consider two particular conditions, the independence of states and the absence of a system of measurement of fighting power, because they permit a cogent alternative argument. In turn, competing arguments allow room for empirical tests.

The first argument — made by Morgenthau, Quincy Wright, Martin Wight, and a host of other balance-of-power theorists — is that the uncertainty inherent in the assessment of power discourages escalation of conflict to war far more often than not. However, given the lack of precision in assessing one's fate if war were to occur, the stability of any balance of power becomes precarious. Morgenthau put this part of the argument clearly:

> Since no nation can be sure that its calculation of the distribution of power at any particular moment in history is correct, it must at least make sure that, whatever errors it may commit, they will not put the nation at a disadvantage in the contest for power. . . . since in a balance-of-power system all nations live in constant fear lest their rivals deprive them, at the first opportune moment, of their power position, all nations have a vital interest in anticipating such a development and doing unto others what they do not want others to do unto them.[33]

The logic loosely fits the conflict spiral between opposing alliances in August 1914 and the choosing of allies in August 1939. In 1914 the rough equality that had kept peace for so long ended in war. In 1939, to follow Martin Wight's account, European great-power

> relationships fell into an equilateral triangle; and it was possible for different observers to convince themselves that destiny would be fulfilled by the alliance of the Western Powers with Russia to encircle Germany, or of Russia with Germany to overbalance

the Western Powers, or of the Western Powers with the Fascist Powers against the interests of Russia.[34]

With the alliance between the USSR and Germany, what was balanced became unbalanced and war resulted.

TABLE 2 War and Peace in Eight Types of Triad: Balance of Power 1

Type	Power Distribution	Expected Coalition	Balanced?	Expectations
1	A = B = C	None	Yes	PEACE; if coalition any pair, then war
2	A > B B = C A < (B + C)	None	Yes	PEACE; if coalition B–C, then war
3	A < B B = C	None	Yes	PEACE; if coalition A–C or A–B, then war
4	A > (B + C) B = C	B–C	No	WAR; A versus B or C or B–C
5	A > B > C A < (B + C)	None	Yes	PEACE; if coalition the minimal B–C, then war
6	A > B > C A > (B + C)	B–C	No	WAR; A versus B or C or B–C
7	A > B > C A = (B + C)	B–C	Yes	PEACE
8	A = (B + C) B = C	B–C	Yes	PEACE

SOURCE: Adapted from Theodore Caplow, *Two Against One: Coalitions in Triads* (Englewood Cliffs: Prentice-Hall, 1968), figs. 1:4 and 3:1; Moul, "Balances of Power and European Great Power War, 1815–1939: A Suggestion and Some Evidence," *Canadian Journal of Political Science* 18 (September 1985): table 1.

Table 2 describes what would be expected in an equilateral triangle and in various other triads of states. Threats are expected from a stronger side, and alliances are formed to aggregate capabilities of the weaker against the stronger in minimal winning coalitions. The uncertainty of victory or defeat in balanced distributions encourages peace, whereas the certainty of victory in an unbalanced distribution is the prelude to war. A distribution of power is balanced insofar as: (1) the sides are equal (Type 1 triad); or (2) any future coalition would be a winning coalition (types 1, 2, 3, and 5); or (3) any future coalition would divide power equally (types 7 and 8).

These common criteria of "balance" admit a number of unwelcome inconsistencies into the argument. Consider the power distribution in Type 7, where A is greater than B, which is greater than C, and A = (B + C). We could say, as above, that the uncertainty of victory would deter A from war on B or C because A = (B + C). However, B would be deterred from attacking C because of the strong possibility of encountering an overwhelming A–C coalition. "Certainty" of defeat, rather than "uncertainty" of victory or defeat is the apt characterization of the situation. Similarly, in the Type 2 triad, we would be inclined to say that the prospect of meeting a much stronger B–C coalition would inhibit A. Of course, if such a B–C coalition were to form, war would be expected to follow. In the final analysis, however, these inconsistencies concerning the place of the variable "decisional uncertainty" in the argument are a sign of theoretical weakness. One advantage of the following balance-of-power argument is that it is consistent.

Balances and War

The second argument is that the certainty of the outcome should war occur keeps the peace, while uncertainty of defeat or victory on each side encourages escalation to war. Rough equality creates uncertainty, and, with reason, each side can judge itself able to fare better than the other. When material capabilities are roughly equal, the judgements are likely to fall upon more subjective qualities. This is where the so-called crucial intangibles supposedly resistant to measurement count. As Morgenthau points out, the political arithmetic of power is always certain "in retrospect," that is, after the fighting. War is the measure of fighting power, and the political arithmetic of the breakout of peace is as straightforward: war orders the combatants into categories of "victorious" and "defeated," and as long as there is little uncertainty of the outcome should war recur, peace is kept. The plainly stronger have no need to fight to get their way, and are able to tolerate concessions to the weak while the weak would be foolish to fight the obviously much stronger opponent. Georg Simmel put the relationship between measurement of fighting power and actual fighting succinctly: "The most effective prerequisite for preventing struggle, the exact knowledge of the comparative strength of the two parties, is very often attainable only by the actual fighting out of the conflict."[35]

The expectations of war or peace as well as alliance formations in various types of triads drawn from Simmel's paradox are described in the last column of Table 3. In the third column are the expectations from the first balance-of-power argument. The expectations are contrary in most cases, and where they are not, as they appear to be in Type 7, different reasoning leads to similar conclusions. According to the first argument, the equality between A and a B–C coalition in Type 7 maintains peace. According to the second argument, the clarity of the hierarchy A greater than B, which is greater than C (in types 6 and 7) maintains peace, just as possible ambiguities in the hierarchy in Type 5 encourage warfare. Rough equality between states produces decisional uncertainty, uncertainty of defeat or victory makes war likely, and alliances are used to spread or to contain the conflict. The general rule in alliance-formation is to form alliances of restraint with those stronger states capable of tipping the balance to the other side, and alliances to aggregate power capabilities with those weaker states in minimally winning coalitions. Thus, in Type 3, advantage would be

TABLE 3 [illegible], Peace, and Alliance-Formation

[illegible]	[illegible]	**Expectations Argument 1**	**Expectations Argument 2**
[illegible]	[illegible]	PEACE; if coalition any pair, then war	WAR between any pair and alliance of restraint with other
[illegible]	[illegible]	PEACE; if coalition B–C, then war	WAR; B versus C and alliance of restraint (B–A or C–A)
[illegible]	[illegible]	PEACE; if coalition A–C or A–B, then war	WAR; B versus C and A–C or A–B coalition
[illegible]	[illegible]	WAR; A versus B or C or B–C	WAR; B versus C, alliance of restraint "up" to A
[illegible]	[illegible]	PEACE; if coalition the minimal B–C, then war	WAR; too close to call. A versus B in alliance with C; or B versus C and alliance of restraint with A
6	[illegible]	[illegible]R; A versus B or [illegible]r B–C	PEACE; no alliance
7	[illegible]	[illegible]CE	PEACE
8	[illegible]	[illegible]	WAR; B versus C and A–B or A–C alliance of restraint

with the state able to form a coalition with the much weaker state A, and, in Type 1, there would be an advantage to the one of the three rough equals able to make an agreement of benevolent neutrality with another.

The second balance-of-power argument is consistent regarding the role of decisional uncertainty and peace or war, and is also more informative than the first argument. Consider the predictions in the Type 4 triad. According to the common balance-of-power argument there will be war — perhaps A against B, from which A against C would follow in due course (perhaps the other way around), perhaps A versus the B–C coalition. The more possibilities, the less informative the argument. According to the more informative argument, war is likely between B and C, and much more likely if one or the other were to arrange an alliance of restraint with the much stronger A. As you can see, this is in keeping with the argument concerning alliance-formation in the three geopolitical circumstances made above. Together they suggest why some wars are duels and others involve many states. To predict who would fight whom, who would ally in what type of alliance with whom, and which wars are likely to expand to include others is to provide much room for many empirical errors. In principle, the more room for errors, the more informative the theory. In practice, the more informative theory is the one that better stands up to tests presented by the sound evidence.

Arguments and Evidence

The evidence considered here consists of findings from a small number of systematic empirical analyses of balances of power, alliance-formation, and war or peace. Many other empirical studies are excluded because of the ways in which balances of power are measured. The inconsistent findings noted earlier are the products of measurements of the balance of power in terms of power capabilities without reference to geopolitical context, including alliance formations. When the measurement is made sound by comparing various power capabilities in the proper context, the evidence points in one direction. Also excluded here are studies of alliance formations that count the number of alliances or of allies without reference to who allied with whom or to what allies agreed to do. Unless the scope and domain of an alliance agreement are considered, it is impossible to assess the impact of the alliance on a balance of power or the impact of the balance of power on the kind of alliance formed.

Although there are many historical studies of individual alliances and a smaller number of systematic studies of the consequences of alliances, there are few systematic studies of the politics of alliance-formation. Stephen Walt's recent work on the origins of alliances in the Middle East from 1955 to 1979 is the only sustained analysis of the merits of balance versus bandwagon logics of alliance-formation. From the evidence he assembles on the 36 alliances formed among Middle Eastern states and between those regional states and great powers active in the region, Walt concludes that states ally to balance against the most serious threat rather than to bandwagon with the strong and successful. Each superpower, as expected, allied to balance the power of the other superpower, but Walt found that the regional states themselves were preoccupied with threats from nearby states and "relatively unconcerned about the global balance of power."[36] This difference in attention is the empirical basis for Walt's theoretical distinction between a balance of threat and a balance of power.

According to Walt, if the balance-of-power theory had merit, one would expect states to react to the balance-of-power capabilities between the superpowers. Since they did not do so, he prefers to credit his evidence to his "balance of threat theory." However, a distinction between his balance-of-threat argument and balance-of-power thinking discussed in this chapter appears to be a forced one. Given the arguments described here, we would expect regional states to be more concerned with those threats from the powerful states nearby than with those that are far away, behind geopolitical barriers. Thought of in this way, the distinction Walt makes appears to be less a theoretical one than a matter of proper measurement of various balances of power. Context is crucial to measurement, and the weight of power varies with context.

Paul Schroeder is also critical of balance-of-power thinking in his survey of great-power alliances during the 1815–1939 period. Arguing that balance-of-power thinking supposes alliances to be only a means to aggregate power, he finds that "the desire for capability aggregation against an outside threat has not always played a vital role in the formation of alliances." States do use alliances to mobilize power, and they use them to immobilize power. All great-power alliances since the Congress of Vienna "in some measure" functioned to restrain or to control the actions of the alliance participants themselves. While the "perception of a threat from another power might lead a state to try either to form an alliance *against* that power, in order to meet the threat by capability-aggregation," it might also, says Schroeder, cause it "to ally *with* that power, in order to manage the threat."[37] He finds that the use of alliances as restraints has encouraged peace. Like many other reasonable generalizations about peace and war, this one invites specification.

Many of the alliances Schroeder surveys could be used to restrain the participants, not to aggregate capabilities, because they did not provide for a coalition. These alliances were ententes, neutrality pacts, and nonaggression agreements. When we examine conflicts between a predatory great power and a much weaker state, we find that a conflict was more likely to escalate to war if the predatory state had such an alliance of restraint with a stronger great-power rival. The two cross-tabulations in Table 4 summarize some of the evidence. The one to the left-hand side describes the relationship between the presence of an alliance of restraint and the escalation to war of 66 unequal conflicts between a predatory great power and a lesser power during the 1815–1939 period. Each of the conflicts involved the use of force or the explicit threat of violence by the great power in order to alter the political status quo. Fifteen conflicts escalated to war. In two-thirds of those conflicts, the great power had prepared the way with an alliance of restraint with a stronger great-power rival.

TABLE 4 Alliances of Restraint and Escalation to War: Great Powers versus Non-Great Powers, 1815–1939

	All Conflicts (N = 66)		**"Central" Conflicts (N = 41)**	
	Alliance of Restraint	**No Alliance of Restraint**	**Alliance of Restraint**	**No Alliance of Restraint**
Escalated to War	10	5	8	2
Did Not Escalate to War	13	38	10	21
	Yule's Q = 0.71 Phi = 0.36 Phi square = 0.13		Yule's Q = 0.79 Phi = 0.41 Phi square = 0.17	

SOURCE: William B. Moul, "Great Power Nondefense Alliances and the Escalation to War of Conflicts Between Unequals, 1815–1939," *International Interactions* 15 (1988): tables 4 and 6.

The strength of any restraint varied with the three geopolitical circumstances outlined earlier. When the weaker state was at the European centre and the great powers were polarized (Situation 1), the few alliances that formed tended to provide for benevolent neutrality if war should occur. When the weaker state was in the periphery while great powers were polarized or when the weak target was at the centre while there was no great-power polarization (Situation 2), alliances tended to be more vague ententes. When the weaker state was at the periphery and there was no great-power polarization (Situation 3), alliances were more likely to be formed than not, and those formed were vague understandings. The proportion of conflicts that escalated to war increases from 66 to 80 percent when the conflicts in Situation 3 are excluded from the cross-tabulation at the right-hand side of Table 4. They are excluded because the formation of an alliance of restraint is not expected in all cases when the weak state is at the periphery and there is no great-power polarization.

As both cross-tabulations indicate, not all alliances of restraint led to escalation to war. Alliances of restraint appear to be more a necessary than a sufficient condition of warfare. The size of the Yule's Q values (indicating strong relationships from war to the presence of an alliance) and the differences between them and the values of the phi co-efficients (indicating mutual association) state this conclusion more succinctly. Isolation of the weak by collaboration of the strong is a partial theory of interstate relations because it provides no good explanation of why some great powers were predatory at some, but not other, times.[38]

According to the common balance-of-power argument, imbalances in power encourage the preponderant state to be predatory and make warfare most likely while equality of power makes it less likely. Good evidence provides no support for this equibalance-to-peace argument. Clear imbalances between European great powers between 1815 and 1939 were times of peace between them, while equibalances often ended in war.[39] Table 5 describes some of this evidence. There were 58 cases of conflict during the 1815–1939 period in which one great power

TABLE 5 Balances of Power and the Escalation of Serious Conflicts Among Nonseparated European Great Powers, 1815–1939

	Great Power–versus–Great Power War	No Great Power–versus–Great Power War	Total
Power Capabilities Ratio "Equal"	5	1865 PRU/AUS 1911 FR,UK/GER 1912 RUS/AUS 1938 FR,UK/GER	9
Power Capabilities Ratio "Unequal"	1859 FR/AUS	26	27
Total number of conflicts	6	30	36

Yule's Q = 0.94
Phi = 0.60
Phi square = 0.36

SOURCE: William B. Moul, "Balances of Power and the Escalation to War of Serious Disputes among the European Great Powers," *American Journal of Political Science* 32 (May 1988): table 5.

used force against another great power or made the threat of violence plain. "Equal" or "unequal" assessments of the balance are determined by a weighing of military and economic capabilities of opposing sides, qualified by indicators of the political capacity to use the capabilities tallied, by various alliance formations, and by geopolitical circumstances. One feature of political geography proves to be fundamental: not one of the 22 disputes in which there were geopolitical barriers escalated to war. In the 36 instances where geopolitical barriers could not help to keep the peace, inequalities in power capabilities inhibited war. Of the 6 disputes that escalated to war, 5 were disputes in which the opposing sides were roughly equal. Simmel's insight on the paradoxical relationship between the imprecision inherent in the measurement of fighting power and the occurrence of a fight is historically well grounded.

The four instances of rough equality in fighting power and the keeping of peace demonstrate that the presence of a balance of power is not sufficient to predict escalation to war. Notice, however, the pattern of the contrary instances identified in the upper right-hand cell of the table. The rough equals that did not fight in 1865, 1911, 1912, and 1938 did fight within three years of the dispute that had not escalated to war. The subsequent changes in alliance formations appear to have been crucial to the occurrence of war in 1866, 1914, and 1939. When rough equals were at the top of the great-power hierarchy, as was the case in the 20th-century disputes listed in Table 5, coalitions were formed or made stronger with states lower down in the rank order. When the rough equals were low in the ranks, the conflict escalated after the formation of an alliance of restraint with a stronger state. Such was the case after the 1865 dispute between Austria and Prussia.

This pattern of types of alliance formations — coalitions to mobilize and other agreements to immobilize power, varying with positions in the great-power ranks — provides a ready explanation of why some wars were widely participated in, and some were duels.[40] In turn, the number of states fighting influenced the duration of the fighting, and duration is related to severity. Longer wars were more bloody than shorter wars — how much more bloody depended upon when the states fought. The history of modern warfare is the history of organizational and technological innovations to make killing people easy and to administer pain and destruction speedily on an ever-larger scale.

Balances of Power and Terror

When the scale of possible destruction makes plain the threat of mutually assured destruction, the phrase "balance of terror" is more apt than "balance of power." Some strategists and scholars, including historian Geoffrey Blainey, who provides much evidence and insight on the incidence and duration of interstate war, disagree. Accordingly, to substitute "balance of terror" for "balance of power" is, at best, to add to the confusion dogging the older phrase. At worst, it is to encourage an extremely dangerous historical ignorance. As Blainey declares, "In each generation during the last two and one-half centuries many men thought their own era was unique and therefore could learn little from the past; but their belief was disproved."[41] Although there is no doubt that future generations will see our time as not having been unique, they should be able to recognize the profound differences nuclear weapons did make. The balance analogy itself indicates what makes our time unlike any earlier time.

The period since the establishment of superpowers among great powers is the longest period of peace among great powers since great-power status itself was entrenched in 1815. The prospects should conflict escalate to war made plain by preponderant power encouraged peace between great powers during the 1815–1939 period and peace between great powers polarized by two superpowers during the 15 or so years after the deployment of the "absolute weapon."[42] Until the 1960s, the United States maintained a substantial military and industrial advantage over the USSR, including the capabilities to leave much of populated Eurasia a "smoking, radiating ruin at the end of two hours."[43] When each side possessed a secure second-strike capability, the consequences, if superpower war were to occur, were only too obvious. Thus, marked inequality in fighting power, assured destruction of one side, and mutually assured destruction *all* encourage peace. Rough balances of power make war more likely; rough balances of terror do not.

If we wish to speak of "the balance of terror" before the 1960s, we should recognize that it was always unequal, tied tightly to an inequality in power. Victims of terror are just that — victims — helpless, powerless people, vulnerable because the state is without defences. In 1940, German bombers attacked Rotterdam after the government had capitulated; in 1943, the Royal Air Force made the firestorm of Hamburg after Operation Window Pane rendered German radar defences ineffective; in 1945, a single bomber aircraft met no resistance when dropping Fat Man and Little Boy on Japanese cities. No balance of terror was ever equal until each superpower, regardless of military victory or defeat, had the ability to administer unprecedented pain and destruction on the other. However, with that ability, the balance analogy fails: "X, regardless of how much more superior it is to Y, here equals Y."[44] The nuclear weapon is the "absolute weapon" because the damage that could be done is unconditional or independent of the damage done by the weapons of the opposing side. Power is always relative; terror is far less so.

Conclusion

Those who take "the balance of power" to be a fundamental principle and those who find it dangerous nonsense all agree that the phrase is politically potent. Morgenthau and Cobden, among many others, describe how the words enhance justifications and rationalizations for all sorts of state actions. Those who seek to explain those actions find the "balance" much easier to evoke than to put to theoretical service. Many balance-of-power theories do not work at all. Absorbing contrary empirical evidence, they avoid the risk of error, and succumb to truism. Such are the muddled generalities Cobden attacked. Some of them remain popular. If they were all that could be drawn from the metaphor, we, like Cobden, should avoid the words *balance of power.* There is more. The metaphor does inform good explanations of peace, war, and alliance formations. The trouble is that there are many cogent competing balance-of-power theories. However, the proper measurements with which to assess competing explanations are the measures that attend to the connotations of "balance." The analogy is very useful when separating poorly made data from well-constructed evidence. The "balance of power" proves to be a tough old phrase with theoretical and methodological bite.

NOTES

1. *Russia, 1836*, reprinted in *The Political Writings of Richard Cobden* (London: T. Fisher Unwin, 1903), 1:197–98, 202.

2. Martin Wight, "The Balance of Power," in his *Power Politics* (London: Royal Institute of International Affairs, 1946); rev. ed., ed. Hedley Bull and Carsten Holbraad (Harmondsworth: Pelican Books, 1979); "The Balance of Power," in *Diplomatic Investigations*, ed. Herbert Butterfield and Martin Wight (London: Allen and Unwin, 1966). See also A.F. Pollard, "The Balance of Power," *Journal of the British Institute of International Affairs* 2 (March 1923): 51–64.

3. Geoffrey Blainey, *The Causes of War* (New York: Free Press, 1974), 121.

4. "Political Arithmetic," printed in 1690, reprinted in Charles Henry Hull, ed., *Political and Economic Writings of Sir William Petty* (New York: Augustus M. Kelly, 1963), vol. 1.

5. William Cowper, "Expostulation," in *Cowper: Verse and Letters*, ed. Brian Spiller (Cambridge, Mass.: Harvard University Press, 1986), 247. The couplet was noticed first in Michael Mann, *The Sources of Social Power*, vol. 1: *A History of Power from the Beginning to A.D. 1760* (Cambridge, Mass.: Cambridge University Press, 1986), 486.

6. Helen M. Walker, *Studies in the History of Statistical Method* (Baltimore: Williams and Wilkins, 1931), 32.

7. Hans J. Morgenthau, *Politics among Nations*, 4th rev. ed. (New York: Knopf, 1967), 147.

8. Hans J. Morgenthau, "International Relations: Quantitative and Qualitative Approaches," in *A Design for International Relations Research: Scope, Theory, Methods, and Relevance*, ed. Norman D. Palmer (Philadelphia: The American Academy of Political and Social Science, October 1970), 67.

9. Paul E. Meehl, *Clinical versus Statistical Prediction: A Theoretical Analysis and a Review of the Evidence* (Minneapolis: University of Minnesota Press, 1954), 138. See also Donald N. McCloskey, *The Rhetoric of Economics* (London: Wheatsheaf Books, 1986).

10. Treaty text in Michael Hurst, ed., *Key Treaties for the Great Powers, 1814–1914* (New York: St. Martin's, 1972), 726–27.

11. David A. Baldwin, "Power Analysis and World Politics," *World Politics* 31 (January 1979): 166.

12. As do Alan Alexandroff, Richard Rosecrance, and Arthur Stein, "History, Quantitative Analysis, and the Balance of Power," *Journal of Conflict Resolution* 31 (March 1977): 52.

13. A.F.K. Organski and Jacek Kugler, *The War Ledger* (Chicago: University of Chicago Press, 1980), cf. 30–38 and 64–102. Take care to notice that varying the measures of power capabilities to fit the circumstances does not reduce the number of cases for analysis. A balance-of-power judgement is a rough ratio of the capabilities of opposing sides, and a ratio is a "pure" number, independent of units compared. No matter of what materials balances of power are made, they can be tallied together. See my "Measuring the 'Balances of Power': A Look at Some Numbers," *Review of International Studies* (in press), for a comparison of various quantitative assessments.

14. See Heinrich Zimmer, *Philosophies of India* (New York: Meridian, 1956), for an account of Kautilya's philosophy of success. Zimmer wrote in 1942, and demonstrated the relevance of Kautilya's words to modern European interstate politics.

15. Kenneth Boulding, *Conflict and Defense: A General Theory* (New York: Harper and Brothers, 1962), 78–79.

16. George Quester, *Offense and Defense in the International System* (New York: John Wiley, 1977).

17. Bertold Brecht, "1940," in *Bertold Brecht Poems* (London: Eyre Methuen, 1976), 347.

18. Robert Jervis, "Cooperation under the Security Dilemma," *World Politics* 30 (January 1978):167–214.

19. Morgenthau, *Politics among Nations*, 198.

20. Emerich de Vattel, as quoted in Hedley Bull, *The Anarchical Society* (New York: Columbia University Press, 1977), 101.

21. The political arithmeticians I have in mind are E.E. Schattschneider and Georg Simmel. See Schattschneider, *The Semisovereign People* (Hinsdale, Ill.: Dryden, 1975); and Lewis Coser's exposition and elaboration of Simmel's ideas in *Functions of Social Conflict* (New York: Free Press, 1956).

22. Organski and Kugler, *The War Ledger*, 51. That alliances and the role of balancer are thought to be crucial to any balance-of-power theory is stated clearly by Organski in the "Balance of Power" chapter of his *World Politics* (New York: Knopf, 1968).

23. Singer, Bremer, and Stuckey, "Capability Distribution, Uncertainty, and Major Power War, 1820–1965," in *Peace, War, and Numbers*, ed. Bruce M. Russett (Beverly Hills: Sage, 1972). The merits of the CON index are described in James Lee Ray and J. David Singer, "Measuring the Concentration of Power in the International System," *Sociological Methods and Research* 1 (1973): 403–36.

24. See Martin Wight, "Balance of Power," in *Diplomatic Investigations*, 164.

25. Garrett Mattingly, *Renaissance Diplomacy* (Boston: Houghton Mifflin, 1954), 163, 293.

26. Edward Vose Gullick, *Europe's Classical Balance of Power* (New York: W.W. Norton, 1955), 304.

27. *Europe's Catechism* (London: 1741), as found in Gullick, *Europe's Classical Balance of Power*, 2.

28. Texts found in Arnold J. Toynbee, ed., *Documents on International Affairs, 1939–1946*, vol. 1: *March–September 1939* (London: Oxford University Press, 1951), 408.

29. Schnattschneider, *Semisovereign People*, 4.

30. Niccolò Machiavelli, *The Prince and The Discourses*, ed. Luigi Ricci (New York: Modern Library, 1950), 84.

31. David Fromkin, *The Independence of Nations* (New York: Praeger, 1981), 145.

32. Morgenthau, *Politics among Nations*, 161.

33. Morgenthau, *Politics among Nations*, 202.

34. Martin Wight, "The Balance of Power," in *The World in March 1939, Survey 1939–1946*, ed. Arnold Toynbee and Frank T. Ashton-Gwatkin (Oxford: Oxford University Press, 1952), 530.

35. Cited in Coser, *Functions of Social Conflict*, 133.

36. Stephen M. Walt, *The Origins of Alliances* (Ithaca, N.Y.: Cornell University Press, 1987), 158.

37. Paul Schroeder, "Alliances 1815–1945: Weapons of Power and Tools of Management," in *Historical Dimensions of National Security Problems*, ed. Klaus Knorr (Lawrence, Kansas: University of Kansas, 1976), 230.

38. William B. Moul, "European Great Power *Pacta de Contrahendo* and Interstate Imperial War, 1815–1939: Suggestions of Pattern," *Canadian Journal of Political Science* 16 (March 1983): 81–102.

39. William B. Moul, "Balances of Power and European Great Power War, 1815–1939: A Suggestion and Some Evidence," *Canadian Journal of Political Science* 18 (September 1985): 481–527.

40. Blainey, *Causes of War.*

41. Blainey, *Causes of War*, ix.

42. Bernard Brodie, ed., *The Absolute Weapon: Atomic Power and World Order* (New York: Harcourt Brace, 1946).

43. David Alan Rosenburg, "'A Smoking Radiating Ruin at the End of Two Hours': Documents on American Plans for Nuclear War with the Soviet Union, 1954–1955," *International Security* 6 (Winter 1981–82): 3–38.

44. Hans J. Morgenthau, "Four Paradoxes of Nuclear Strategy," *American Political Science Review* 58 (March 1964): 23–35.

SELECT BIBLIOGRAPHY

Baldwin, David A. "Power Analysis and World Politics." *World Politics* 31 (January 1979):161–94.

Bull, Hedley. *The Anarchical Society: A Study of Order in World Politics*. New York: Columbia University Press, 1977.

Claude, Jr., Inis L. *Power and International Relations*. New York: Random House, 1962.

Dehlio, Ludwig. *The Precarious Balance: Four Centuries of the European Power Struggle*. (1948). New York: Knopf, 1962.

Gulick, Edward Vose. *Europe's Classical Balance of Power: A Case History of the Theory and Practice of One of the Great Concepts of European Statecraft*. New York: W.W. Norton, 1967.

Haas, Ernst B. "The Balance of Power: Prescription, Concept, or Propaganda." *World Politics* 5 (July 1953): 442–71.

Morgenthau, Hans J. *Politics among Nations*. New York: Knopf, 1967.

Moul, William B. "Balances of Power and the Escalation to War of Serious Disputes among the European Great Powers, 1815–1939: Some Evidence." *American Journal of Political Science* 32 (May 1988): 241–75.

Vincent, R.J., and Moorhead Wright, eds. "The Balance of Power." Special Issue of *Review of International Studies* (March 1989).

Waltz, Kenneth N. *Theory of International Politics*. Reading, Mass.: Addison-Wesley, 1979.

Wight, Martin. "The Balance of Power." Chapter 7 in *Diplomatic Investigations: Essays in the Theory of International Politics*, ed. Herbert Butterfield and Martin Wight. London: Allen and Unwin, 1966.

THE THEORY AND PRACTICE OF DETERRENCE

Paul Buteux

Deterrence is essentially a very simple concept. It refers to the adoption by states of policies and strategies that seek, through the manipulation of threats, to stop an adversary or putative enemy from doing what he might otherwise do. Broadly, there are two ways in which this might be done: first, by denying the adversary the prospect of ever achieving his objective; second, by threatening retaliatory punishment on a scale that is grossly disproportionate to the objectives sought. For our purposes, both methods are about the threat to use force in order to counter the possible threat or use of force by others.

The first method is known sometimes as "deterrence by denial," and the second one, as "deterrence by threat of punishment."[1] Deterrence by denial is frequently equated with the concept of defence, but in doing so in fact a crucial difference is ignored, one between defending against an actual resort to force on the part of an adversary and dissuading an adversary from launching a military challenge. In the latter case, deterrence is achieved by a perceived ability to defeat the challenge or, alternatively, by an ability to raise the costs of a victorious challenge to a level incommensurate with the purpose of resorting to military force in the first place. It is the element of *dissuasion* that distinguishes deterrence by denial from the concept of defence. It is the attempt to affect the calculations of those contemplating the use of force that is essential to deterrence, not the successful exercise of force on the battlefield in defence of values under attack. In contrast, although it, too, seeks to dissuade an adversary from challenging, by threat or use of force, values that the deterrer wishes to protect, deterrence by threat of punishment does so not by a manifest capacity to deny, but by a manifest capacity to hurt the adversary by retaliation. Thomas Schelling has termed this "the threat of punitive violence," the capacity to inflict pain and suffering on an adversary in order to persuade him that the use of force is simply not worthwhile.[2]

"Deterrence by denial" is inherent in any capacity for self-defence, and except for the self-conscious recognition that a capacity to defend may dissuade an enemy from resorting to force, there is nothing particularly new or distinctive about the concept. In fact, in classical strategy it was taken for granted. Classical strategists were interested in the coercive possibilities of the punitive use of force, but they were not interested, by and large, in the punitive threat of force as a means of dissuasion. Insofar as classical strategy was concerned with the deterrent possibilities of force, these were implied in the basic right of any state *to threaten war.* Hence, only since the end of World War II has deterrence become a central concern of strategic studies, and for one fundamental reason: with the advent of nuclear weapons, it became possible to threaten an adversary with appalling levels of destruction without first having to achieve victory on the battlefield. Thus, for the first time in history, it became possible to conceive of deterrence without reference to defence. *Deterrence* in its contemporary usage is a product of the nuclear age.

In principle, it is possible to apply the notion of deterrence to any situation in which threats are used to dissuade others from the exploitation of force. Indeed, there is a group of scholars, mainly American, who have done this with reference to U.S. foreign policy.[3] But only in the field of nuclear strategy has deterrence become the central focus of study. Nuclear weapons have created contemporary strategy, nuclear weapons provide the moral and political dilemmas to which deterrence has been one policy response, and nuclear weapons make the contemporary concept of deterrence possible. Thus, the analysis of deterrence undertaken in this chapter, unless otherwise stated, is that of *nuclear* deterrence.

The term "deterrence" is used in a variety of ways: it is used in connection with theories of rational decision making; it is used to describe a state of affairs; and, finally, it is used to describe particular kinds of policies and strategies of national security. Within this last context, policies and doctrines have evolved over time, and so it is also possible to speak of the "history" of deterrence. A later section of this chapter will outline this historical evolution.

The Theory of Deterrence

With respect to its theoretical status, deterrence is understood best not as a theory of causal explanation, but rather as a theory of rational decision. What it purports to do is explain the *logic* of strategic decision.[4] This distinction is important to bear in mind since many critics of deterrence have questioned the validity of the concept on empirical grounds; that is, they have made the claim that decision makers do not, in fact, behave in the rational way that deterrence theory assumes. In doing so, many such critics commit a "category mistake," since deterrence theory is primarily about the construction of strategic models and is not a theory about actual behaviour. Such critics confuse the theory of deterrence with actual policies and strategies of deterrence, and with why deterrence works (or does not work) in particular situations. The practice of deterrence should be distinguished from the logical elaboration of the concept.

As a theory of rational decision, deterrence has been much influenced by "formalistic" approaches. Two of the most important of those whom Lawrence Freedman has termed the "formal strategists" were Thomas Schelling and Herman Kahn.[5] The methods and insights, derived directly or indirectly from game theory, that Schelling applied to the problem of deterrence are now pervasive in the literature.[6] In contrast, Kahn, through his exhaustive analysis of various "scenarios," elaboration of various "types" of deterrence, and development of "escalation ladders," provided many of the metaphors and terms that colour the language of deterrence. In addition, his pretensions to a dispassionate, "scientific" approach to the problems of nuclear deterrence and the consequences of nuclear war made him the model for "Dr. Strangelove" and his work, a convenient, albeit highly misleading, basis for the caricature of nuclear strategy.[7]

The paradigm case for the formal strategist is that of deterrence by threat of punishment, and the key concern, that of determining what kind of threats are likely to be effective in persuading an adversary not to resort to force. This concern, which has obvious policy implications, becomes even more salient in situations where each adversary is vulnerable to devastation by the other. The requirements of deterrence may be said to involve the following elements: capability, intention and will, communicability, cost-effectiveness, and credibility.

Of these requirements, capability is seemingly the most straightforward. Quite simply, in order to deter, it is necessary to have the means of implementing a threat. Of course, it is always possible to bluff, as Khrushchev did at the time of the Cuban missile crisis when he greatly exaggerated Soviet strategic capabilities, but this tack is not a sound basis for statesmanship and may lead to political defeat or even military catastrophe if the bluff is called. In the 1960s, the United States approached the issue of capability by asking the question "How much is enough?" The answer was a capacity for the "assured destruction" of the enemy even after being subject to a first strike directed against one's own nuclear forces (a "counterforce" strike). What constituted assured destruction against the Soviet Union was determined, somewhat arbitrarily, by the then secretary of defense, Robert McNamara, as a capacity to destroy about 33 percent of the Soviet population and at least 50 percent of Soviet industry. This capacity, in turn, was thought to require the United States to have the means of delivering a nuclear strike against an appropriate array of targets equivalent to 400 megatons in yield even after suffering a Soviet counterforce first strike. Such means was deemed to meet the requirements of an "assured-destruction, second-strike capability."

As a measure of capability, the notion of "assured destruction" is not without its problems. First, there is the question of what size and character of nuclear forces are required in order to have confidence that one possesses a capacity for assured destruction. Such factors, as the evolution of the U.S. nuclear-force structure after the early 1960s shows, are not necessarily easy to determine. With emphasis being placed on second-strike capability, the vulnerability of one's nuclear forces to a first strike becomes a crucial concern. Nuclear forces have to be designed and deployed in such a way that they are sufficiently invulnerable to pre-emption so as to be able to retaliate on a scale sufficient to threaten the enemy with unacceptable destruction. Thus, the United States justifies the mix of bombers, submarines, and land-based missiles in hardened silos that make up its strategic deterrent force (the so-called strategic triad) on the grounds that such a mix makes the prospect of strategic pre-emption impossible. The result has been a strategic force much larger than that required to deliver an equivalent 400-megaton strike against the Soviet Union.

Second, there is the problem of deciding what it is that any given force structure is supposed to deter. In the case of the assured-destruction criterion, the specific object was to deter a Soviet first strike against the strategic nuclear-force structure of the United States. But such a military threat was the least likely one that the United States faced, and it is not clear that a country's capacity to eliminate an enemy as a functioning political society, even after that country itself has been eliminated, constitutes an effective deterrent to other kinds of military challenge. More fundamentally, questions arise as to whether nuclear forces are designed simply to deter direct aggression, or, more generally, to deter military threats to values and interests that lie outside the physical security of the national territory itself. Above all, in terms of its political salience, the United States was faced with the problem of deterring threats to its European allies in NATO while itself being vulnerable to nuclear reprisal (the problem of "extended deterrence"). More generally still, the object of deterrence may be to maintain a given international system, that is, to ensure somehow the maintenance of the status quo. Finally, it is possible to ask whether a policy of deterrence is about war avoidance, or whether it is about the threat to punish specific transgressions against one's interests.

Thus, questions concerning intention and will arise. What actions are intended to be deterred and does the will to implement the threat exist? The capacity to implement a threat may be useless if there is no will or intention to do so when circumstances require. Of course, the putative enemy may not know that intention and will are lacking, and the very physical impressiveness of the forces deployed against him may be sufficient to deter, but the theory of deterrence suggests that it is advisable to convince an enemy that in fact the will to implement the threat exists. It is easier to convince the enemy of such will if the interests at stake are clearly seen to be vital ones. In addition, a reputation for resolve may assist in convincing others that the necessary intention and will exist. In this respect, it is possible to suggest that much of U.S. foreign policy since the end of World War II has been influenced by the belief that it is necessary to convince others, allies and adversaries alike, that the United States will stand by its commitments and, if necessary, follow through on its threats. Thus, one sees the emphasis on demonstrating resolve, and the willingness to employ military force over issues that might otherwise seem to be of little intrinsic importance.

Consequently, it is necessary to communicate to an adversary that there exist the capability, will, and intention of carrying out a threat. That this is not always easy to do is demonstrated in the voluminous literature on international crises. In the real world, there exist enormous opportunities for misperception, misunderstanding, irrationality, and sheer desperation that can lead to a threat's being ignored or misinterpreted, or simply not being perceived at all.[8] Empirical and historical studies of this problem have been devoted mostly to the question of conventional deterrence, where it has been shown that communication failure is not uncommon during international crises, but the problem is clearly of great relevance to nuclear deterrence as well.

In the case of nuclear deterrence, the problem of communication failure is probably less acute than in the conventional case, for the discounting of a threat has to be measured against the consequences of miscalculation. Within the context of a confrontation between nuclear-armed adversaries, awareness of the likely consequences of nuclear war is high. The risk of a threat's being carried out may be perceived as low, but must be balanced against the consequences of the threat's actually being implemented. Expected gains from an action must be balanced against the costs of an opponent's actually carrying out a threatened response. Such balancing may be termed the "cost-effectiveness" consideration. In other words, deterrence theory postulates that statesmen enter into some form of cost-benefit analysis in which the expected benefits of an action are discounted against the possible costs of carrying it out. If the benefits are thought to be less than the costs incurred if the adversary implements a deterrent threat, then deterrence holds. But, there is one further consideration that operates: that the estimate of costs will be weighted against the likelihood that the adversary will actually carry out the threatened response.

Deterrence theory argues that, against a nuclear-armed adversary, caution is enjoined, since, regardless of the degree of specificity of a threat, or the clarity or otherwise with which it might be communicated, statesmen cannot but be aware of the unacceptable costs of being wrong. This consideration has led many observers to suggest that among nuclear-armed adversaries, a form of "nuclear learning" has taken place in which the awareness of the consequences of nuclear war has led them to place the avoidance of nuclear confrontation at the centre of their relations.[9] Thus, following the summit meeting between Mikhail Gorbachev and Ronald Reagan in Geneva in 1985, both leaders could sign a communiqué in which they recognized that "nuclear war cannot be won and must never be fought." Of course, if this is truly the case then the question arises as to whether a policy of deterrence is necessary at all. This issue will be addressed later.

All of the above considerations — capability, will and intention, communicability, and cost-effectiveness — may be said to determine the *credibility* of a deterrent threat. At first glance, it appears that credibility ultimately depends on convincing an opponent that there is a good chance that the threat will actually be carried out. How good this chance must be is a matter of considerable controversy, and the position adopted on this issue has important policy implications. But, from the perspective of deterrence theory, if all of the factors entering into credibility are positive, then effective deterrence is deemed to operate.

However, credibility must be perceived not only by the opponent but also by the deterrer. The deterrer must decide whether, in fact, to carry out a threat in the light of the consequences for him of doing so. Those responsible for making the deterrent threat are subject to a cost-benefit calculus as well. If the likely consequence is his own destruction, then the deterrer may be inhibited in following through, and the phenomenon of "self-deterrence" may operate. Obviously, this consideration is important in situations where adversaries are mutually vulnerable, and where a nuclear power, as is the case with the United States, is seeking to "extend" deterrence to its allies. Here, so it is argued, the factor of "uncertainty" comes into play. Deterrence is sustained in these circumstances because, although it may be irrational for a deterrer to carry out his threat, the opponent can never know that, in fact, the deterrer will not act irrationally. The consequences of being wrong are so great that the uncertainty generated is sufficient to sustain deterrence. Schelling placed considerable emphasis on the role of uncertainty in his analysis of conflict, and he summarized the idea in his aphorism "the threat that leaves something to chance." The deterrer, in effect, makes a threat in circumstances in which a decision on whether to implement it is not entirely under the threatener's control. There is the risk that, if the deterrer is challenged, things may simply get out of hand.[10] Once, however, the factor of uncertainty is brought into deterrence, its status as a theory of rational decision is compromised.

Deterrence as a State of Affairs

Although the assumptions of rationality that underlie much of the formal theory of deterrence have been widely challenged, few would assert that policies of nuclear deterrence are thereby necessarily ineffective. All the nuclear powers practise policies of deterrence, and all who face the possibility of being involved in a nuclear confrontation are conscious of the risks involved.

Patrick Morgan draws a distinction between "immediate" and "general" deterrence, which is helpful in sorting out the role of deterrence in international relations. "Immediate deterrence" refers to situations in which at least one of the parties to a confrontation is considering the use of force while another is making a threat of retaliation in order to prevent it. In short, at least one side of the confrontation perceives that war threatens. "General deterrence," however, refers to a situation in which opponents maintain forces as an insurance against each other and to regulate their relationship, but in which none is actually contemplating the immediate threat or actual use of force. The latter state of affairs clearly characterizes the normal circumstances of the nuclear powers in general, and the superpowers in particular. The actual use of threats of nuclear retaliation in specific confrontations has been very limited in the nuclear age, but, as Morgan points out, deterrence theory has been developed almost exclusively "by hypothesizing an abstract world of immediate deterrence."[11]

This hypothetical basis of deterrence in itself is not surprising. There are specific interests and values that are impossible to defend against nuclear attack, but the threat to these may, nevertheless, be deterred. The fact that these interests may not be threatened at any particular time does not mean that, in an uncertain world, the capacity to deter if necessary is not required. And it is the crisis that might lead to nuclear war that constitutes the greatest threat to national survival and the greatest test of deterrence. In this case, it is natural that attention has been directed primarily to the analysis of immediate deterrence. Nonetheless, the more general problem of challenge and confrontation in a nuclear environment has not been ignored by deterrence theory. Two concepts have loomed large in this respect: first, the idea of bargaining in a nuclear context, and, second, the idea of stability.

Numerous commentators have observed that, even when nuclear threats have not been made, since 1945 all competition and confrontations between major powers have taken place in the shadow of nuclear weapons. Political objectives, diplomatic gestures, and military deployments have been affected by their existence. At the same time, although statesmen have sought to avoid nuclear war, they have sought also to promote their political interests at the expense of others or in competition with them. In these circumstances, nuclear threats have not been absent; sometimes they have been made explicitly, but more frequently in great-power confrontations the very presence of nuclear weapons and the rhetoric employed in conjunction with them has been sufficient to generate the ambivalent threat that the opponent risks nuclear war. The role played by such threats in actual crises and confrontations is not always clear, and, as the historical record opens up, it appears that what once were thought to be occasions where clear-cut nuclear deterrent threats worked were, in fact, not so.[12]

In the real world of deterrence, another problem that arises is that from one perspective what one side considers to be a deterrent threat against unwarranted action on the part of another, may, from the other's perspective, appear as an attempt to *compel* him to adopt forms of behaviour that he would prefer not to adopt.[13] The obverse side of deterrence is what Schelling has termed "compellence": not stopping an opponent from doing something you do not want him to do, but forcing him to do something he does not want to do.[14] Although deterrence and compellence may be conceptually distinct, in practice the distinction may be not at all clear to the participants. There are normative components at work here: deterrence is "good" and compellence is "bad."

Part of the problem is that it is difficult to know whether deterrence has worked or not. If an opponent does not actually mount a military challenge and appears to back down from a confrontation, it is not necessarily the case that this demonstrates the effectiveness of deterrence — or of compellence, for that matter. It may be that the opponent did not intend a military challenge in the first place. There are logical problems in explaining events that did not happen. However, and mindful of Sherlock Holmes's observation to Watson that the significant thing about the dog was that it did not bark, may we not infer that nuclear weapons might have had something to do with the fact that, in the postwar confrontation between East and West, direct armed conflict between the superpowers has been avoided?

But, for all the incentive that the nuclear powers have had to avoid nuclear war, all at various times have sought strategic and foreign-policy advantage from the possession of nuclear weapons. All, in one way or another, have stressed that their purpose was to deter; all have sought to avoid being subject to "nuclear blackmail"; but all, in so doing, have attempted to alter the international environment in ways favourable to their interests by exploiting the generalized threat posed by nuclear weapons. Despite the claims by some critics of nuclear strategy that the utility of nuclear weapons is limited to the deterrence of their use by others, statesmen have persistently sought to reap political advantage from them. They have done this, not so much by the making of direct threats, as through the formulation of declaratory policy and nuclear doctrine, and through choices about nuclear posture, with the object of affecting the choices and options of others. General, rather than immediate, deterrence has provided the context of nuclear bargaining.

In the contemporary international system, nuclear weapons seem to have operated as a factor preventing war between the major powers rather than as one preventing particular cases of "aggression." To the extent that nuclear weapons deter what might be termed "central" or "systemic" war between the great powers, then, of course, it is logically entailed that aggression is deterred as well. But, one further criticism that can be made of the formal theory of deterrence is that it has little or nothing to say about how wars start. In the West, at least, the theory of deterrence has been presented almost exclusively in terms of preventing premeditated aggression, regardless of the fact that, in modern times, few wars can be said to have started in such an unequivocal way. The model of World War II, beginning, as it did, with Hitler's assault on Poland, and its extension with Japan's attack on Pearl Harbor, has had a significant effect on thinking about what it is that nuclear weapons are supposed to deter and how they are supposed to do it.

In the United States, for the purposes of formal strategy, aggression has tended to be defined in terms of challenges to the status quo. Given the persistence in U.S. foreign policy of the strategic objective of "containing" the power and expansion of the Soviet Union, this view of aggression is understandable. In a situation of mutual vulnerability between the superpowers, it is understandable also that the formal strategists have given attention to the notion of stability, understood as a state of affairs in which premeditated aggression, nuclear first use, or changes in the strategic balance are minimized. Three related conceptions of nuclear stability have been developed: *strategic stability*, *crisis stability*, and *arms-race stability*.

Strategic stability is said to exist when both sides are secure in their possession of a second-strike capability; in other words, both sides are mutually vulnerable and mutual deterrence is deemed to operate. Crisis stability is held to exist when it is unlikely that a situation can arise in which one (if not both) of the parties to a confrontation in which war appears to be a distinct possibility fears that it may be subject to a pre-emptive counterforce attack. That is, although both sides may possess reserve forces that could survive such an attack, nonetheless to act pre-emptively may seem preferable to receiving the full power of the opponent's nuclear arsenal. Although the results may still be catastrophic, the act of pre-emption may appear to be less catastrophic than not invoking it. Where both sides are tempted to act pre-emptively, even though they might prefer not to go to war at all, a situation would arise akin to Schelling's "reciprocal fear of surprise attack";[15] such a situation is regarded as highly unstable for mutual deterrence. Finally, arms-race stability concerns a situation in which both strategic and crisis stability exist, but in which one side (or both sides) begins to acquire and deploy weapons that potentially may threaten strategic or crisis stability. Such perceptions are likely to encourage an arms race and guide it in particular directions.[16]

With respect to both strategic and crisis stability, the key to a stable situation is the possession of secure second-strike forces. Thus, it can be argued that, although the Soviet Union developed operational forces of intercontinental range in the late 1950s, it was not until a decade later that Soviet strategic forces were of a size and character to provide a secure second-strike, assured-destruction capability. Thus, at the time, the Soviet Union's declaratory strategy placed considerable emphasis on surprise and pre-emption in the event that war appeared imminent. The Soviet Union sought to deter by threatening to initiate a central strategic exchange. From the U.S. point of view, this could only appear to be destabilizing. As the size and accuracy of Soviet strategic forces increased during the 1970s, a number of American critics of U.S. strategic policy became concerned at the counterforce threat that Soviet forces posed to the land-based intercontinental-missile component of the U.S. strategic triad. They asserted that a "window of vulnerability" was emerging that would enable the Soviet Union to eliminate U.S. ICBMs in a surprise attack and then hold U.S. cities hostage to a U.S. reprisal. This, it was believed, would give the Soviet Union considerable bargaining leverage in the event of a crisis. In turn, the United States might be forced to adopt policies, such as "launch on warning," that themselves would be destabilizing in a crisis. It is a concern with stability that has been the basis of many criticisms of the Strategic Defense Initiative; the deployment by the United States of strategic defences could be interpreted by the Soviet Union as a challenge to its assured-destruction capability and thus would force the Soviet Union to adopt countermeasures to it that would "fuel the arms race."

Two points are worth noting about these notions of stability. First, they assume that deterrence is a bilateral affair, and, second, their approach to stability is mechanistic rather than political. Since the dominant nuclear relationship in the international system is that between the United States and Soviet Union, and the balance between them is a major structural component in the system, emphasis on their mutual-deterrence relationship is to be expected. However, it should not be forgotten that there are five declared nuclear powers, and, even in the case of France and Britain, which are allied with the United States, deterrent policies of varying degrees of independence are pursued. In the case of China, allied to neither of the superpowers, a completely autonomous nuclear policy has been developed. If we take note also of such ambiguously nuclear powers as Israel and India, then the possibility of the emergence of a multipolar international deterrent system cannot be discounted. As yet, however, multipolar deterrence does not operate internationally, and currently, the deterrent relationships of the existing nuclear powers are all dyadic ones. Still, conceptions of stability based upon bilateral relationships are already highly abstracted from the complexities of the real world.

The second point is that these definitions of stability are based on the technological characteristics of nuclear forces and do not take into account political relations. Again, this is a common criticism of deterrence theory — that it is technical and static, rather than dynamic and political in character. This criticism frequently misses the mark since, as has been pointed out, formal deterrence theory is about the logic of nuclear strategy and is not a theory of international politics; nonetheless, it may be pertinent to deterrence as a state of affairs in the international system. In the case of nuclear stability, it is worth pointing out that policy prescriptions based upon these notions may not reflect very well the actual dynamics of conflict in international politics. It is also worth pointing out that they tend to ignore the operational dimensions of strategy. The formal notion of strategic stability, like the formal notion of nuclear deterrence, has little to say about how crises develop and about how they may lead to war. Moreover, the technical characteristics of nuclear forces that are supposed to determine whether stability exists or not are usually unrelated to how they might actually be used in war. The discussion frequently does not get beyond whether counterforce or countervalue targeting (the targeting of industry and population centres) is stabilizing or destabilizing. Quite frequently, the elaboration of these questions takes nuclear strategy far away from the world of international politics and into the realm of "nuclear theology."

The Evolution of Nuclear Deterrence

Deterrence operates in the international system, not only as a state of affairs in the sense of "general deterrence," and perhaps occasionally in the sense of "immediate deterrence," but it is also a policy practised by all the nuclear powers. The fact that states have adopted such policies does not mean necessarily that they subscribe to the formal theory of deterrence adumbrated in this chapter. This theory has been developed primarily by Americans (with the considerable assistance in the early years of the British) largely in response to U.S. preoccupations and policy concerns.[17] Other nuclear powers have developed their own theories of deterrence, which depart in greater or lesser ways from the primarily U.S. model. There is, in any theory of deterrence, an underlying normative and political agenda, and this, together with their different economic and geostrategic situations, accounts for the different strategic doctrines that underlie the deterrent postures adopted by the nuclear powers.

In examining the evolution of policies of nuclear deterrence, it is as well necessary to make a distinction between those of the superpowers and those of the lesser nuclear powers. The superpowers have sought much more ambitious objectives from their nuclear forces than have France, Britain, and, as far as can be determined, China. The strategic doctrine that has been applied to the nuclear forces of the lesser nuclear powers is that of "minimum deterrence," the requirements of which are defined in terms of the possession of second-strike forces sufficient to deter a nuclear attack, even by a superpower. For minimum deterrence, an assured-destruction capability on the scale possessed by the superpowers is not required (though all the lesser nuclear powers have notions of sufficiency that have tended to become greater as their nuclear arsenals have improved in size and performance). Rather, the ability is sought to threaten a degree of punitive harm that is disproportionate to any political or material gains that the adversary might achieve by a resort to nuclear threats. Thus arises the idea, much favoured by the French, of "proportional deterrence." It is not necessary to destroy an adversary, such as the Soviet Union, as a functioning society in order to deter; instead, it is sufficient to be able to inflict considerable and painful damage that would seriously weaken the adversary in relation to other nuclear powers, and to demonstrate the will to do so. Such demonstration of will is achieved by restricting deterrent threats only to situations in which national survival is at risk. The French describe this as "la dissuasion du faible au fort" (the deterrence by the weak of the strong).

This form of deterrence places emphasis on countervalue rather than counterforce targeting. The British, for example, in their fledgling nuclear program of the 1950s, defined their minimum deterrent requirements in terms of an ability to attack successfully such targets as would rapidly and decisively affect the Soviet Union's ability to wage war. Settling such requirements has meant an ability to attack key elements in Soviet state power, such as the central agencies of political order in the Soviet Union and key military-industrial complexes. In practice, this attack capability extends to perhaps 20 major military-industrial targets in the Soviet Union. Above all, the British have deployed and designed their forces in such a way as to be confident at the very least of being able to attack Moscow. Similarly, the French have stressed the countervalue threat posed by their strategic nuclear forces, and as their strategic forces have grown they have adopted similar targeting criteria.[18] Though very little is known of China's targeting doctrine, the current size and capabilities of Chinese strategic nuclear forces leads to the suspicion that they, too, have little option but to adopt countervalue targeting.

At this stage, the role of shorter-range, so-called tactical, nuclear forces has not been addressed. All the operational nuclear powers possess them, but, for the lesser powers, their contribution to minimum deterrence is not always clear. These are forces that could not be used against the adversary's strategic targets, but would be directed against forces in the field and their means of communication (interdiction targeting). The Chinese have been silent on their use; the French term them "prestrategic" weapons and have rationalized their possession as providing for a final demonstration of resolve before resort to the strategic deterrent, while the British fit them into NATO targeting arrangements as part of the alliance's strategic concept of flexible response.

For all of the intricacies and problems associated with the lesser nuclear powers, for obvious reasons it is the arsenals and doctrines of the two superpowers that dominate the literature on deterrence. The evolution of their nuclear strategies has passed through a number of phases since the first atomic bombs were dropped on Hiroshima and Nagasaki in August 1945, and these phases can be related to changes in such variables as the state of the strategic balance, technology, foreign-policy objectives, and perceptions of the overall balance of power (what the Soviet Union terms the "correlation of forces").

For the United States, a number of commentators have identified three "waves" or phases in the evolution of strategic doctrine.[19] The first wave corresponded to the advent of nuclear weapons and the possession by the Americans of a fleeting nuclear monopoly. Theorizing, in contrast to operational doctrine, was concerned with the implications of nuclear weapons for war and for international relations generally. The second wave was a response to the Soviet Union's becoming a nuclear power. This wave was marked by the Soviet Union's successful nuclear test in 1949, followed by the build-up of an arsenal of atomic and hydrogen weapons during the 1950s. The emergence of the Soviet Union as a nuclear power highlighted for the United States the problem of "extended deterrence." The third wave corresponds to the emergence of strategic "parity" between the United States and the Soviet Union, which may be said to have been formally recognized with the signature of the first strategic arms-limitation agreements (SALT I) in 1972. This wave has been marked by a continuing search for nuclear arms-control agreements between the superpowers, by a vigorous debate over nuclear war-fighting strategies, and by a revival of interest in strategic-missile defence. Finally, I would argue that the U.S. doctrine is now entering a fourth phase in which the legitimacy of deterrence is increasingly being questioned on ethical, political, and strategic grounds, and in which elements of nuclear disarmament are becoming politically relevant for the first time (as opposed to the empty rhetoric that has characterized disarmament, for example, in debate in the U.N. since its founding conference in 1945). Although this can be speculation only, it may well be that the United States will move in the direction of "finite deterrence."

During the period of U.S. nuclear monopoly, that country's strategic doctrine drew little distinction between deterrence and defence. With the emergence of the cold war, the major military threat confronting U.S. interests was perceived to be that posed by the Soviet Union to its allies, and in particular to Western Europe. In the event of war, nuclear weapons would be used to weaken the enemy by strategic bombing, while conventional forces would attempt to defend against attack until strategic bombing had taken effect, and the enemy would then be defeated. This strategy was classic deterrence by denial; the enemy is deterred by the threat of ultimate defeat. However, critics pointed out that nuclear weapons were not simply more effective conventional weapons, but represented a revolutionary development in the technology of warfare. If two adversaries possessed nuclear weapons, then each risked a level of destruction incompatible with any political objectives war might serve. As early as 1946, the American naval historian and strategist Bernard Brodie made his famous statement: "Thus far the purpose of our military establishment has been to win wars. From now on its chief purpose must be to avert them. It can have almost no other useful purpose."[20]

The doctrine of deterrence by denial did not long survive the advent of the Soviet Union as a nuclear power. During the Eisenhower administration, the United States attempted to exploit its clear nuclear superiority by adopting in

1952–53 the policy of "massive retaliation."[21] In effect, the United States sought to deter threats to its allies and interests, not by fighting a limited conventional war, as in Korea, or engaging in a more destructive replay of World War II in Europe, but by threatening to retaliate "massively" and by "means of our choosing." Here, for the first time, was a clear expression of a doctrine of deterrence by threat of punishment. However, almost immediately, the new doctrine was criticized on the grounds that, as a deterrent to lesser aggressions, and to ambiguous and limited probes, the threat to retaliate massively was simply not credible, and, as the United States itself became vulnerable to Soviet retaliation, its implementation could be disastrous.

The problem of U.S. vulnerability to retaliation became acute with the development by both sides of the intercontinental-range nuclear missile coupled with warheads of enormous destructive power. Under the Kennedy administration, and under the influence of Robert McNamara as secretary of defense, massive retaliation was abandoned and two ultimately contradictory lines of policy developed. After a brief false start in which the United States tried to impose a "city avoidance" targeting doctrine on the Soviet Union, two linked, but nonetheless distinctive, strategies emerged. In Europe, in order to maintain the credibility of extended deterrence under conditions of mutual vulnerability, the NATO allies were persuaded to accept a deterrence posture based upon a combination of deterrence by denial and deterrence by threat of punishment, which came to be known as the strategic concept of "flexible response." With respect to the balance of strategic forces between the United States and the Soviet Union, the doctrine of mutual assured destruction (MAD) evolved.

The actual implementation of flexible response had undergone many metamorphoses since its formal adoption by NATO in 1967, but its essential components as a deterrent strategy remain unchanged. These consist of a commitment to a robust "forward defence" by conventional means, backed up by thc threat to use nuclear weapons first in the event that conventional defence fails. The second component of flexible response is an ability to respond militarily in an appropriate manner to any level of violence initiated by the enemy and, if necessary, to escalate the level of violence in order to dissuade the attacker from continuing with his assault. Here, the notions of "escalation" and "intrawar deterrence" enter into the equation. The politics of flexible response have focussed on persistent attempts by the Americans to persuade reluctant European allies to make greater efforts at conventional defence in order to raise the "threshold" at which the use of nuclear weapons might be contemplated, and on the degree of allied consultation and control that would be involved in any decision on nuclear use.[22] Flexible response has also provided the framework within which a role has been found for the thousands of "tactical" nuclear weapons deployed in Europe since the 1950s. These not only provide in theory a nuclear option short of the use of strategic weapons, but also provide the means of "coupling" defence and deterrence in Europe with American strategic forces. Hence, the NATO "triad" of conventional, theatre nuclear, and strategic nuclear forces that are said to provide a seamless web of deterrence from conventional defence to strategic retaliation.

With its emphasis on conventional defence, the first use of nuclear weapons as a demonstration of resolve, and the prospect of escalation, NATO has adopted a doctrine of deterrence that is a hybrid between denial and punishment.

By way of contrast, during the second phase, the United States moved toward an outright-punishment strategy as far as its strategic forces were concerned. As the technology of long-range missiles and their warheads improved, leading to improvements in response times and accuracy of several orders of magnitude, the United States was confronted with the reality that there was no escape from the vulnerability of American society to devastation. Neither suggestions for massive programs of civil defence nor those for anti-ballistic missile (ABM) systems offered an escape. Thus, the key to the U.S. posture was confidence in its second-strike assured-destruction capability.

Since it was clear that the Soviet Union also possessed similar capabilities, U.S. thinking focussed on maintaining the stability of MAD. Two key political and strategic implications flowed from this: first, that under MAD it made absolutely no sense to threaten the first use of strategic nuclear weapons; hence the emphasis on the possession of flexible options in Europe that provided the U.S. president with at least the possibility of a wider range of choice than suicide or surrender in the event that NATO faced conventional defeat; second, arms control was seen as a means of maintaining the stability of the mutual-deterrent relationship. Thus, in this period, arms control not only became central to the strategic relationship between the Soviet Union and the United States, but was central to the political relationship as well. It is for this reason that in Soviet-American relations détente and progress on arms control have gone together. As arms control became an important independent factor in the interaction of the strategic forces of the two superpowers, tensions and contradictions between the U.S. strategic posture and extended deterrence were underlined.

During the first two phases in the evolution of American strategic doctrine, the Soviet Union adopted a very different approach to the problem of security in the nuclear age. Essentially, the Soviet Union adopted a declaratory doctrine that corresponded to deterrence by denial, though, in noting this, it is important to bear in mind that at no time has the Soviet Union accepted Western theories of deterrence.[23] Rather, in Soviet writings on the subject, the political meaning of war is always stressed. Thus, U.S. notions of stability based upon the technical characteristics of weapons have been rejected, as have American attempts to determine the "rules of nuclear engagement" through such means as limited counterforce targeting and controlled escalation.

Soviet security policy vis-à-vis the United States has been based quite explicitly upon a war-avoidance strategy involving a combination of political and military measures. Since war between the superpowers, by definition, can arise only from the actions of the imperialist powers, they can be deterred from starting it only by the establishment of an overall correlation of forces that would deny them victory. Clearly, the military balance is an important determinant of this correlation of forces. Thus, the Soviet Union's declaratory strategy has stressed the ability of the Soviet Union to deny an enemy victory (*sderzhivanie*) and to respond with punishing retaliation (*ustrashenie*).

Until the late 1960s, the period corresponding to the first two phases of American strategic doctrine, and the period in which the USSR could be said to be strategically inferior to the United States, military writers in the Soviet Union tended to place greater emphasis on *ustrashenie* than they did subsequently, but the emphasis on war avoidance was explicit from the 1956 Twentieth Party Congress onwards, when Khrushchev revived the Leninist notion of "peaceful coexistence." But though the Soviet Union in its military doctrine (which has a particular meaning in Soviet military thought) stressed war avoidance, the Soviet military insisted that, should war occur, then the progressive forces of socialism ultimately would emerge victorious. For most of this period, such views probably represented the triumph of hope over reality, but the Soviet Union, through its ability to hold Western Europe hostage to its conventional strength, and its efforts to build strategic forces that were comparable in size and quality to those of the United States, sought successfully to create a strategic posture that conformed to its definition of the requirements of security. The Soviet Union was determined to undermine U.S. strategic superiority.

It was the Soviet Union's march to strategic parity that led to the SALT I agreements in 1972. From the Soviet point of view, SALT I represented the acceptance by the United States of strategic equality, while, from the American perspective, the agreements confirmed the strategic doctrine of mutual assured destruction. Unfortunately for the United States, neither SALT I nor the follow-on SALT II negotiations led to a stable balance at lower levels of strategic nuclear weapons. Instead, the 1970s saw the introduction of new technologies by both sides that increased the capabilities of their strategic nuclear forces, but did nothing to diminish their mutual vulnerability. In addition, parity simply underlined the problems of extended deterrence for the United States and its allies. Thus, increasingly during the 1970s, the United States moved into the third phase of the evolution of its strategic doctrine.

This phase was marked initially by a search for ways in which the United States could posture its nuclear forces so as to make extended deterrence credible under conditions of parity. This search led to an emphasis on the possession of nuclear options short of an all-out nuclear exchange. This doctrine of "limited nuclear options," which emerged in 1974, led, in turn, to revisions in targeting doctrine and to the exploitation of increasing warhead accuracies for counterforce targeting. In effect, if extended deterrence was to remain credible, the United States should possess the ability to fight a limited and, if necessary, protracted nuclear war. There were three major difficulties with this approach, however. First, the key to a strategy of limited nuclear options was an ability to attack Soviet strategic missiles in their hardened silos; but, despite improvements in American strategic forces, the United States, in fact, possessed only a limited ability to do so. Second, the idea of fighting a limited nuclear war was repugnant to all except those steeped in the arcana of contemporary strategic doctrine; the idea was thus politically unpopular in the United States and a political liability for relations with America's allies in Europe. Third, the Soviet Union, by means of its own strategic build-up and by its declaratory strategy, undermined the credibility of the new doctrine.[24] It was not until the advent of the Reagan administration in 1981 that the United States made a whole-hearted attempt to provide the means to implement what had become known as the "countervailing strategy." The ultimate failure of this attempt provides the basis for suggesting that the United States is now entering a fourth phase in the evolution of its strategic doctrine.

Also in response to parity, important changes were occurring in Soviet strategic doctrine at this time. The Soviet Union began to signal that it had eschewed the notion of victory in nuclear war. Brezhnev's speech at Tula in 1977 may be taken as a watershed in this respect, for, in it, the Soviet leader stated that his country was not seeking strategic superiority, as many American commentators were claiming, but simply parity. On the same occasion, Brezhnev also disclaimed any intention on the part of the Soviet Union ever to launch a first strike. Subsequent developments of this theme by Soviet military commentators, with their emphasis on the existence of parity and the need to maintain it through arms control, were clear indicators that the Soviet Union had built the reality, if not the conception, of mutual assured destruction into its military thinking.[25]

The new Soviet line reflected a specific political agenda related to ongoing strategic arms-control negotiations and the new Carter administration, but it also reflected growing concerns about the direction being taken by U.S. strategic doctrine. For, at this time, somewhat ironically, American critics of contemporary U.S. doctrine and arms-control policy were arguing that Soviet doctrine held that victory in nuclear war was possible, envisaged the possibility of nuclear warfighting, and recognized the possibility of exploiting the vulnerability of the U.S. land-based ICBMs to a pre-emptive strike. With the adoption, in 1980, of the "countervailing strategy" in the light of this interpretation, the U.S. administration defined the requirements of its deterrence policy as being able to convince the Soviet Union that, at a variety of levels of exchange, the United States possessed "countervailing" strategic options that would either defeat aggression or result in costs to the aggressor that would far exceed any political gains.[26] In effect, the United States attempted to maintain a credible link, under conditions of parity, between its strategic forces and extended deterrence by stressing a targeting doctrine that allowed for a flexible response, even at the strategic level. The announcement of the countervailing strategy followed closely the NATO "two-track" decision of December 1979 to deploy modern intermediate-range nuclear forces (INF) in Europe if an arms-control agreement covering weapons of this range could not be negotiated with the Soviet Union.

The Reagan administration's military build-up of the early 1980s was entirely compatible with the strategic policies of its predecessor and, at the same time, incompatible with arms control. The result was a major deterioration in Soviet-American relations, and concern on the part of the Soviet Union that the new U.S. policies would undermine the strategic gains that it had made over the previous decade. Moreover, the announcement of the American Strategic Defense Initiative (SDI), in March 1983, raised genuine and additional fears that the United States was seeking to gain a first-strike advantage and restoration of strategic superiority. The SDI challenged two long-standing Soviet objectives: first, that if war were to occur in Europe, nuclear strikes involving the territory of the Soviet Union must be avoided; and, second, to obtain U.S. acceptance of the Soviet interpretation of the political and strategic implications of parity.[27]

The Soviet response was to launch a major "peace offensive" in Europe, and to spell out even more clearly than in the past its rejection of the notion that nuclear war could be fought and won. The change of leadership in Moscow and the advent of Gorbachev to power, when coupled with new directions in U.S. policy after the re-election of Ronald Reagan in November 1984, provided the political conditions for the signature, in December 1987, of the treaty eliminating worldwide their longer- and shorter-range intermediate missiles (those with ranges of between 500 and 5500 kilometres). The treaty was significant in a number of ways, not least because it was the first agreement between the superpowers to incorporate a substantial measure of nuclear disarmament, but also because it represented a major retreat from the objective of strengthening the link between U.S. strategic forces and extended deterrence. Indeed, a number of developments have called into question the whole basis of Western deterrence policy in Europe. Among these may be cited the acceptance of the Soviet position on nuclear war at the 1985 Geneva summit; the agreement in principle that the next strategic arms-control agreement should aim for a 50 percent reduction in the size of the superpowers' current nuclear arsenals, and the inability of the United States to solve the problem of the vulnerability of its land-based strategic forces in a manner compatible with the countervailing strategy.

The weakened link between U.S. strategic forces and the security commitment to Europe, and the commitment to further measures of nuclear disarmament, provides evidence that the United States may be entering a fourth phase in the development of its strategic doctrine. The continued interest in ballistic missile defences is compatible with this trend, though the ambitions of then-president Ronald Reagan to make nuclear weapons obsolete when he launched his "Star Wars" initiative have long been abandoned. Certain forms of ballistic-missile defence are compatible with mutual deterrence premised on an assured-destruction, second-strike capability, and they would not necessarily threaten any of the forms of strategic stability. However, as the Soviet reaction demonstrated, ballistic-missile defences coupled to war-fighting strategies would not be compatible with MAD. If the Soviet-American strategic relationship does become based on the acceptance by both sides that neither can unilaterally upset the fact of their mutual vulnerability, then the way is open for the United States, and for the Soviet Union, to adopt a posture that approximates one of "finite deterrence."

Finite deterrence provides one answer to the question "How much is enough?" Such a policy accepts that the only function of nuclear weapons is to deter their use by others. Threats of first use and the attempt to extend deterrence by the threat of controlled and limited strategic reprisal are simply too dangerous to be credible. Beyond the point of confidence in the possession of an assured-destruction capability, numbers of weapons do not matter, and concern with the numerical strategic balance becomes irrelevant. According to the argument, extended deterrence may nonetheless operate in circumstances where the interests at stake are great and where there is a clear conventional military commitment to defend them. This is so because any conflict between nuclear-armed adversaries involves the possibility of something going wrong and the nuclear threshold being crossed despite the intentions of those involved (the "uncertainty" principle). In the context of NATO, as long as the United States indicates its commitment to European security by maintaining substantial conventional forces in Europe, and if the European allies provide forces capable of conducting a strong conventional defence, then European security is assured.[28]

Given the contemporary strategic situation in Europe, it is possible to argue that, de facto, this is a close approximation of the present basis of allied security.[29] Nonetheless, it is unlikely that the United States will, or could, adopt a full-fledged posture of finite deterrence. Above all, such a strategy would be incompatible with NATO's strategic concept of flexible response. For all its current lack of credibility, the political costs to the alliance of abandoning or developing an alternative to flexible response would be too great. Any formal revision of flexible response probably would occur only as a result of major agreements on arms control in Europe. Second, it is very unlikely that any U.S. president would abandon the search for further choice between "suicide or surrender." Some form of flexible targeting always will be built into the U.S. strategic arsenal.

Nonetheless, the United States does seem to be abandoning some of the more demanding roles it has traditionally applied to nuclear deterrence, and the likely signature of a strategic arms-control agreement that requires a substantial measure of disarmament will reinforce this trend. As well, the legitimacy of deterrence as a policy for all but direct threats to territorial integrity is increasingly being questioned in all Western countries. This, again, limits the ability of governments to exploit deterrence for wider political purposes. Perhaps, then, a more restricted role for nuclear threats in support of foreign policy is emerging.

Nevertheless, the genie cannot be put back into the bottle; nuclear weapons have become part of the fabric of the international system. Even though the theory of deterrence, and the ethical basis for it, have been subject to telling criticism, those states that possess nuclear weapons, by necessity, will continue to base their security policies on nuclear deterrence. What has become increasingly questionable is whether it is possible or wise to attempt to exploit them for purposes of *compellence*. In a world of nuclear weapons, the avoidance of nuclear war has become a political and moral imperative. The destructiveness of nuclear weapons, and the emerging consensus that their use could not serve any political purpose, that they are incompatible with the Clausewitzian notion of war as the servant of politics, have resulted in a situation in which those states that operate in a nuclear environment have little choice but to act prudently and avoid nuclear confrontation. One of the major paradoxes of the nuclear age is that, through unprecedented threats of mutual destruction, policies of deterrence have provided the means of enforcing the political virtues of restraint and prudence in international politics.

NOTES

1. The distinction between "deterrence by denial" and "deterrence by threat of punishment" is credited usually to Glenn H. Snyder, *Deterrence and Defence: Toward a Theory of National Security* (Princeton: Princeton University Press, 1961), 3–15.

2. Thomas C. Schelling, *Arms and Influence* (New Haven and London: Yale University Press, 1966), 17–19.

3. For example, Alexander L. George and Richard Smoke, *Deterrence in American Foreign Policy* (New York: Columbia University Press, 1974).

4. Stephen Maxwell, "Rationality in Deterrence," *Adelphi Papers* 50 (London: International Institute for Strategic Studies, August 1968): 3–4.

5. Lawrence Freedman, *The Evolution of Nuclear Strategy* (New York: St. Martin's, 1981), 175–89.

6. In addition to *Arms and Influence*, see Thomas C. Schelling, *Strategy of Conflict* (New York: Oxford University Press, 1960).

7. Herman Kahn, *On Thermonuclear War*, 2d ed. (New York: Free Press, 1969; originally published by Princeton University Press, 1960); *Thinking about the Unthinkable* (New York: Horizon, 1962); *On Escalation: Metaphors and Scenarios* (New York: Praeger, 1965).

8. This issue is thoroughly explored in Robert Jervis, Richard Ned Lebow, and Janice Gross Stein, *Psychology and Deterrence* (Baltimore: Johns Hopkins University Press, 1985).

9. See, for example, Joseph S. Nye, Jr., "Nuclear Learning," *International Organization* 41 (Summer 1987): 371–402; and Michael Mandelbaum, *The Nuclear Revolution* (Cambridge: Cambridge University Press, 1981), especially chaps. 5 and 8.

10. Schelling, *Strategy of Conflict*, 187–90.

11. Patrick M. Morgan, *Deterrence: A Conceptual Analysis* (Beverly Hills: Sage, 1977), 28–29.

12. Richard K. Betts, *Nuclear Blackmail and Nuclear Balance* (Washington, D.C.: The Brookings Institution, 1987). See also the article by Marc Trachtenberg, Roger Dingman, and Rosemary J. Foot, "Truman, Eisenhower and the Uses of Atomic Superiority," *International Security* 13 (Winter 1988–89): 5–112.

13. Betts, *Nuclear Blackmail and Nuclear Balance*, 6.

14. Schelling, *Arms and Influence*, 69–74.

15. Schelling, *Strategy of Conflict*, 207–8.

16. Leon V. Sigal, *Nuclear Forces in Europe* (Washington, D.C.: The Brookings Institution, 1984), 9–10.

17. Barry Buzan has suggested that the formulation of retaliatory-deterrence theory has been primarily a Western and, more specifically, an Anglo-Saxon phenomenon because

of the particular historical and strategic circumstances that the United States and Britain faced at the end of World War II. They were status-quo powers faced with the problem of managing international security in a nuclear environment. *An Introduction to Strategic Studies* (New York: St. Martin's, 1987), 138–42.

18. An analysis of British and French strategic forces in order to determine whether they are capable of meeting such targeting requirements is beyond the scope of this chapter. Suffice it to say that, at the end of the 1960s, the British possessed such a capability and the French did not. Since then French forces have grown while those of Britiain have declined. The modernization of their strategic forces planned by the French and British will almost certainly restore this capability for the British and confirm it for the French.

19. Buzan, *An Introduction to Strategic Studies*, 143–60. Robert Jervis has suggested that similarly there have been three waves in deterrence theory: "Deterrence Theory Revisited," *World Politics* 31 (January 1979): 289–324.

20. Bernard Brodie, *The Absolute Weapon: Atomic Power and World Order* (New York: Harcourt Brace, 1946), 76.

21. Massive retaliation has been much misunderstood. The doctrine was not as simple as frequently portrayed, and as a strategy involved more than simply threatening to deal with Soviet "aggression" anywhere with a massive attack on the Soviet homeland. A succinct discussion can be found in Freedman, *The Evolution of Nuclear Strategy*, 76–88.

22. For the genesis of flexible response, see Jane E. Stromseth, *The Origins of Flexible Response: NATO's Debate Over Strategy in the 1960s* (New York: St. Martin's, 1988). For the issue of allied consultation and control of nuclear weapons, see Paul Buteux, *The Politics of Nuclear Consultation in NATO 1965–80* (Cambridge: Cambridge University Press, 1983).

23. Indeed, there is no word in Russian that corresponds unequivocally to the English word "deterrence." It should be noted that there does not appear to be an exact equivalent in Chinese either; also, the French word "dissuasion" takes on different nuances from "deterrence" in French theories of deterrence.

24. An excellent account of the labyrinthine contortions of U.S. strategic doctrine in this period is provided by Warner Schilling, "U.S. Strategic Nuclear Concepts in the 1970s: The Search for Sufficiently Equivalent Countervailing Parity," *International Security* 6 (Fall 1981): 49–79.

25. Raymond L. Garthoff, "Mutual Deterrence, Parity and Strategic Arms Limitation in Soviet Policy," in *Soviet Military Thinking*, ed. Derek Leebaert (London: Allen and Unwin, 1981), 104–10.

26. Walter Slocombe, "The Countervailing Strategy," *International Security* 5 (Spring 1981): 21. (Slocombe was one of those responsible for drafting the countervailing strategy.)

27. The thesis that these were key Soviet objectives is argued exhaustively in Michael MccGwire, *Military Objectives in Soviet Foreign Policy* (Washington, D.C.: The Brookings Institution, 1987).

28. The arguments for finite deterrence have been restated in Robert Jervis, *The Illogic of American Nuclear Strategy* (Ithaca, N.Y., and London: Cornell University Press, 1984);

and Morton Halperin, *Nuclear Fallacy: Dispelling the Myth of Nuclear Strategy* (Cambridge, Mass.: Ballinger, 1987).

29. Paul Buteux, "NATO, No First Use and Conventional Deterrence," in *Deterrence in the 1980s: Crisis and Dilemma*, ed. R.B. Byers (London: Croom Helm, 1985), 166–82.

SELECT BIBLIOGRAPHY

Betts, Richard K. *Nuclear Blackmail and Nuclear Balance*. Washington, D.C.: The Brookings Institution, 1987.

Brodie, Bernard. "The Anatomy of Deterrence." *World Politics* 11 (January 1959): 173–91.

Byers, Rod, ed. *Deterrence in the 1980s: Crisis and Dilemma*. London: Croom Helm, 1985.

Craig, Gordon, and Alexander L. George. *Force and Statecraft: Diplomatic Problems of Our Time*. London: Oxford University Press, 1983.

Freedman, Lawrence. *The Evolution of Nuclear Strategy*. New York: St. Martin's, 1981.

Holloway, David. *The Soviet Union and the Arms Race*. New Haven, Conn.: Yale University Press, 1983.

Jervis, Robert. "Deterrence Theory Revisited." *World Politics* 31 (January 1979): 289–324.

Malone, Peter. *The British Nuclear Deterrent*. London: Croom Helm, 1984.

Mandelbaum, Michael. *The Nuclear Revolution*. Cambridge: Cambridge University Press, 1981.

Morgan, Patrick. *Deterrence: A Conceptual Analysis*. Beverly Hills: Sage, 1971.

Yost, David S. "France's Deterrent Posture and Security in Europe." *Adelphi Papers* 194–95. London: International Institute for Strategic Studies, 1984–85.

ARMS CONTROL

David Cox

A newcomer to the study of arms control might be forgiven for assuming that the activity is entirely contemporary. Since the early 1970s, arms-control negotiations have centred on the superpower negotiations on nuclear weapons. In the 1980s the debate has been dominated by "Star Wars": the pros and cons of space-based laser stations with fighting mirrors, battle stations the size of an executive desk and capable of shooting down the entire Soviet land-based strategic-missile force, and other exotica have provided a futuristic quality to the debate about arms control that has captured the imagination of the public, as, indeed, it did that of former president Ronald Reagan. It must first be noted, therefore, that arms control has a long if somewhat mixed pedigree.

Ironically, Canada has a modest claim to have been present at the creation of the process. Most accounts of the contemporary history of arms control begin with the Rush–Bagot Treaty of 1817, in which the British Empire and the United States agreed to reduce and limit their naval forces on the Great Lakes. As the heir to that treaty, in 1940, at a time when the United States was still a neutral, Canada requested permission from Washington to sail newly constructed naval vessels from the Great Lakes shipyards through the St. Lawrence River and into the battle of the Atlantic, thereby paying its respects to the legal axiom on which, ultimately, the strength of all arms-control agreements must rest: *pacta sunt servanda.*

Not all subsequent naval arms-control agreements were as long-lived or as scrupulously observed. The Washington Naval Treaty of 1922, for example, was considered to be one of the great hopes for arms control in the interwar period, limiting the shipbuilding programs and capital ships of the great naval powers. It was peremptorily abrogated by Japan in 1934, when national policy objectives overrode international commitments. Juxtaposed, these two examples immediately raise some of the central problems posed in the quest to limit national military establishments by international agreement. Under what circumstances, and with what motivations, do states find it in their interest to negotiate mutual limits on armaments? How can they be sure that the other parties will comply with such agreements? And what protection is there against the possibility that the agreement will be suddenly abrogated?

The prenuclear, pre-1945 attempts at arms control by the great powers offer an impressive storehouse of experience with the political circumstances conducive to success and failure in arms control. To begin, it reminds us of the slow rate of progress. The 20th century in arms control was introduced with the two international peace conferences held at The Hague in 1899 and 1907. These conferences made significant progress in codifying the humanitarian rules of warfare, but had little impact on the slaughter during World War I, including that resulting from the use of chemical weapons. After World War I, convinced that the war had been precipitated by the arms race between the European great powers, the League of Nations turned to arms control and disarmament as a solution to the destructive competition that had beset Europe before 1914. Proposals were made to control arms transfers (some 70 years later the issue is still on the agenda of the United Nations), to reach agreement on limits to national-defence expenditures, to expand the naval limits first agreed to in the Washington Treaty of 1922, and (in another thoroughly contemporary issue) to ban the first use of chemical weapons.

In the late 1920s, faced with the disintegration of the European system created by the Treaty of Versailles, arms-control proposals, paradoxically, became ever more ambitious. The 1928 Pact of Paris (more commonly known as the Kellogg–Briand Pact) called for the renunciation of war, and its signatories pledged to settle all disputes through peaceful means. The first World Disarmament Conference, convened in Paris in 1932 under the auspices of the League of Nations, and attended by the largest number of states ever gathered in a single conference, had as its objective a universal reduction and limitation on all types of armaments. The disarmament conference continued for four years until, faced in 1936 with German rearmament and withdrawal from the League, it was suspended and soon forgotten. The lesson seemed clear: arms control was not a cure for irreconcilable political differences, and the solution for widening political disputes could not be found in ever-more-grandiose plans for arms control and disarmament.[1]

Nevertheless, immediately after World War II, at a time of growing division between the United States and the Soviet Union, and in the aftermath of the use of the atomic bomb against Japan, one more grand scheme was offered to the newly created United Nations. The Baruch Plan proposed the creation of an international atomic-energy authority that would control, with enforcement powers, the production and management of fissionable materials. Once such a system was in place, the United States argued, it would be possible to dismantle existing stocks of atomic weapons. Prior to the Baruch Plan, even-more-ambitious proposals had been made by atomic scientists deeply concerned about the spread of atomic-weapons technology. James Conant, the science administrator for the Manhattan Project, echoed the thoughts of many of his colleagues in proposing an international atomic-energy agency to strictly control access to atomic materials and technology. Conant went farther than any other proponent of international control: the international authority, he argued, should enjoy unconditional right of entry into any country, with its own army to enforce its authority.

In the last resort, it should use atomic weapons to enforce its rules and, if countries such as the United States or Britain tried to seize the commission's arsenal of atomic weapons, the arsenal guards would repel them, if necessary, by using atomic weapons. The arsenal was to be stored in Canada, and the atomic guards would be empowered to use the weapons against the host country if it sought to interfere.[2]

As with the prewar schemes, the Baruch Plan foundered on the growing antipathy and distrust of the United States and the Soviet Union. In retrospect, it is tempting to see this and the ambitious proposals of the interwar period as the work of unrelenting idealists incapable of coming to terms with political realities. In fact, the pre–World War II experiences revealed most of the arguments still made by proponents of arms control, exposed the practical difficulties involved in implementing complex proposals, and, above all, raised the fundamental political problems concerning the feasibility of arms-control restraints. In what circumstances is it likely that states will enter into, and abide by, agreements that impose restraints on their development of military forces? "Realists" accuse the designers of grand blueprints for disarmament of entirely ignoring political considerations. In turn, however, these critics tend to argue that arms-control measures can be successful only after political conflicts have been resolved. Sophisticated proponents of arms control have attempted to reject both of these positions. Writing in 1962, Hedley Bull argued the point in the following terms:

> Arms control is significant only among states that are politically opposed and divided, and the existence of political division and tension need not be an obstacle to it. On the other hand, the political conditions may allow a system of arms control, or they may not. Unless the powers concerned want a system of arms control; unless there is a measure of détente among them sufficient to allow such a system; unless they are prepared to accept the military situation among them which the arms control system legitimises and preserves, and can agree and remain agreed about what this situation will be, there can be little place for arms control.[3]

It is clear that Bull's political conditions were not present in the interwar years, despite the enormous efforts of arms-control advocates to present rational solutions to political decision makers. It is also apparent that the early years of the atomic era were equally inhospitable to the delicate balance of mutual interest and antipathy that, Bull seems to suggest, is the meagre soil in which arms-control processes may take hold. It remains to be seen whether the current period of arms control, which may be dated from about 1957 to the present, provides a more enduring and evolutionary base for arms-control regimes.

Superpower Arms-Control Negotiations

The United States and the Soviet Union have been negotiating strategic nuclear arms-control agreements more or less continuously for the past 30 years. As John Newhouse, one of the early chroniclers of the Strategic Arms Limitation Talks (SALT) has argued, the process has become akin to the Congress of Vienna, a continuing forum for the negotiation if not resolution of great-power differences.[4]

If this was true by the end of the period, however, it was not so at the beginning. U.S. interest in bilateral strategic arms negotiations developed out of the mounting concern (some would say obsession) of a small number of U.S. defence intellectuals in the mid-1950s with the vulnerability of U.S. strategic nuclear forces to surprise attack. Working primarily at the Rand Corporation, they argued that U.S. retaliatory forces, then consisting primarily of heavy bombers, were vulnerable to a surprise attack on their bases, and that, as a consequence, in a time of acute crisis, an opponent would have a strong incentive to launch such a surprise attack. The situation would become even more serious, they argued, with the deployment of ICBMs.[5]

Despite some skepticism, including especially that of General Curtis LeMay, then chief of the Strategic Air Command (SAC), this line of reasoning found official support in the Gaither Committee report of 1957. Created under the authority of the National Security Council, the Gaither Committee reflected the concern that SAC was vulnerable to a surprise attack in a noncrisis situation, and that vulnerable nuclear forces gave strong incentives to strike first. While the Gaither Committee anticipated with foreboding a period at the beginning of the 1960s when, it was believed, the Soviets would enjoy ICBM superiority, the immediate requirement was to take steps to reduce bomber vulnerability. In a broader context, however, the superiority of the United States in 1957 (soon to be lost, the Gaither Committee wrongly believed) might provide the best opportunity to initiate serious discussions with the Soviets.[6]

From such concerns came the impetus for the Surprise Attack Conference of 1958, convened by President Eisenhower and General Secretary Khrushchev to consider "measures to safeguard against surprise attack." Curiously, the conference was organized on East-West rather than bilateral-superpower lines. Canada, as the geographic ally now key to U.S. efforts to ensure early warning of Soviet bomber attack, joined Great Britain, France, and West Germany on the West's negotiating team. (It was the last occasion on which such issues of direct concern to the superpowers' strategic arsenals were negotiated in a multilateral forum.) There was no specific outcome to the negotiations held in Geneva, but the exchange of views influenced both the development of strategic nuclear arsenals and the definition of critical issues for arms control in the decade ahead.[7]

In regard to nuclear forces, the vulnerability issue could be solved largely by national decision making. The United States, for example, had in hand the navy's development of the Polaris submarine, which, able to fire ballistic missiles while submerged, was essentially untargetable. On land, it cancelled the slow-to-fuel Atlas intercontinental ballistic missile (ICBM), and replaced it with the solid-fuelled Minuteman, so named for its rapid reaction time. Subsequently, the Minuteman was placed in hardened silos designed to withstand a Soviet first strike. Somewhat more laboriously, the Soviets followed in U.S. footsteps, building a less efficient but probably adequate first generation of ballistic missile–carrying submarines, and progressively deploying a large ICBM force in hardened silos. From an arms-control viewpoint, these force developments were stabilizing, since they reinforced the idea that each side might support the strategic-force security of the other by building forces that did not themselves increase the incentive to pre-empt. Doctrinally, secretary of defense Robert McNamara gave explicit formulation to the process in the concept of mutual assured destruction (MAD), a calculation of guaranteed survivable forces that would be able to inflict unacceptable damage on the opponent no matter how catastrophic the blow initially absorbed.[8]

In terms of arms-control negotiations, two tangible results followed from this line of reasoning. The first was a confidence-building measure. Stimulated by the unwelcome experience of the Cuban missile crisis, President Kennedy and General Secretary Khrushchev agreed in 1963 to establish the Direct Communications Link (the hot line) between Moscow and Washington for use in times of emergency. The arrangement has flourished. In 1971 a further agreement was concluded, providing for improvements in the efficiency and reliability of the hot line. In 1988 the Moscow summit resulted in an agreement to establish mutually manned risk-reduction centres in the two capitals as a logical extension of the concept.[9]

More importantly, the view that each side should support the other's development of secure, offensive forces led to the 1972 Anti-Ballistic Missile Treaty. If the greatest threat to crisis stability, as McNamara and others believed, was the vulnerability of strategic retaliatory forces, then it also followed that a partial defence against those retaliatory forces increased their vulnerability. In the late 1950s the United States gave high priority to the search for an active defence against ballistic missiles, focussing on the development of the family of Nike anti-ballistic missiles (ABMs). By 1966 proponents of the system, spurred on by the public display of a large interceptor missile in Moscow, were ready to claim success, and the Joint Chiefs of Staff sought appropriations authority for the deployment of the Nike-X system. The first great ABM debate in the United States ensued.

At the heart of the U.S. debate between 1966 and the signing of the ABM Treaty in 1972 were two basic questions. First, from a technical point of view, how effective was the system? Second, would an ABM system lead to an upward spiral in the arms race and increase the danger of pre-emption in crisis situations? During the Johnson and Nixon administrations a clear consensus emerged on the first question. The Nike-X (afterwards, the Sprint-Spartan) system was fragile, and could not be expected to ward off a determined attack. It followed, therefore, that it would be most effective against a retaliatory attack that had already been severely degraded by a U.S. strike against Soviet strategic forces.

The proponents of the McNamara doctrine now had their answer to the second question. A partially effective ABM defence would make offensive forces more vulnerable, thus encouraging a proliferation of offensive forces and increasing the incentive to use those forces in a first strike, or even, in the worst of scenarios, in a bolt-from-the-blue attack that would deny strategic warning to the ABM defence. If each side was indeed to support the security of the other's strategic forces, as McNamara had argued, ballistic-missile defences should be banned or limited.

In 1967, apparently persuaded of this reasoning but under severe pressure from Congress to begin deployment of an ABM defence, President Johnson invited the Soviets to discuss mutual limitations on ABM defences. The Soviets agreed, with the proviso that the discussions cover both offensive and defensive weapons, making clear their view that the principal threat lay in the burgeoning of offensive forces rather than, as the Soviets then perceived the strategic confrontation, the essentially defensive character of ABM systems. President Johnson was unable to shake the Soviets from their insistence on the prior importance of offensive strategic forces and, while still seeking to open negotiations, in September 1967 he authorized the deployment of a "thin" ABM system (called Sentinel) to provide a limited population defence against accidental launch or a third-party (Chinese) attack.

Richard Nixon modified the Johnson policy in 1969 only by renaming the ABM deployment (now to be called Safeguard rather than Sentinel), and declaring it to be for the point defence of U.S. military assets, including both missile silos and the National Command Authority, rather than a regional defence against a Chinese attack. At the same time, Nixon pursued the Johnson initiative with the Soviets. Four years later, in September 1972, President Nixon and General Secretary Brezhnev signed the ABM Treaty, which was to be of unlimited duration, and the five-year Interim Agreement on Strategic Offensive Forces. Collectively, the treaty and the agreement are referred to as SALT I.[10]

The ABM Treaty effectively crowned the efforts of the 1960s to safeguard the strategic offensive forces of both sides. Until the reinterpretation debate initiated by the Reagan administration in 1985, the negotiators of the ABM Treaty believed that they had placed strict limits not only on the deployment of ABM defences, but also on the development and testing of ABM technologies. Article I of the treaty pledged the parties "not to deploy ABM systems for a defense of the territory of the country and not to provide a base for such a defense." Article III permitted two ABM sites, one to be in and around the national-capital region, but severely limited the radars and interceptors that could be deployed at these sites (subsequently, in 1974, the parties agreed to reduce the number to one permitted site). Finally, Article V appeared to arrest ABM development by requiring the parties "not to develop, test or deploy ABM systems or components which are sea-based, air-based, space-based, or mobile land-based." The treaty specifically permitted the modernization of the ABM systems deployed under the terms of the treaty, but prevented qualitative changes such as multiple-launch or -reload capabilities, which might transform the permitted site from a point defence to an area of regional defence.

In sum, the ABM Treaty appeared to entrench the arms-control concept that had evolved from the Surprise Attack Conference of 1958. Its central approach was to promote crisis stability by encouraging the development of secure second-strike forces, which in turn was premised on the judgement that effective defences against a determined strategic nuclear attack could not be achieved. The first ABM debate challenged that judgement, but, in the outcome, reaffirmed it in the form of the ABM Treaty. The other side of the coin, however, was the approach to offensive strategic forces. After the Interim Agreement, which was signed at the same time as the ABM Treaty, bilateral-superpower negotiations focussed on this question until, on March 23, 1983, President Reagan declared his vision of a world made safe from nuclear war by the advanced technologies of ballistic-missile defence.

SALT I

In 1963, at the time when Robert McNamara was effectively lecturing the Washington community on the grim virtues of mutual assured destruction, the Soviets had reason for grave misgivings. The Cuban missile crisis began with the Soviets' attempt to circumvent their strategic inferiority by placing missiles in Cuba, and ended with the recognition on both sides that strategic-offensive superiority rested with the United States. Thereafter, the Soviets embarked on a massive building program that continued through the 1960s, and left them, at the end of the decade, with a larger ICBM force than that of the United States, which nevertheless retained its superiority in the two other legs of the strategic triad, ballistic-missile submarines and heavy bombers.

Along the way a consensus emerged in Washington that strategic nuclear superiority was no longer feasible, and that some form of superpower parity was an acceptable, or in any case inevitable, outcome of the strategic-arms competition. With the linkage between offensive and defensive weapons clearly established in the preliminary negotiating skirmishes of the Johnson administration, the SALT I negotiations between 1969 and 1972 focussed not so much on the principle of offensive-force constraints, but on the trade-offs that were necessary to balance two significantly different force structures. Lagging behind the United States in ballistic-missile submarine technology, the Soviet Union opted to develop and deploy very large ICBMs for which the United States had no equivalent. Even though the state-of-the-art "heavy" Soviet ICBM — originally the SS-9 but later the first version of the SS-18 — lacked the accuracy to destroy U.S. missile silos, by 1970 voices in Congress were expressing the concern with such missiles that afterwards came to dominate the U.S. domestic debate. Conversely, the Soviets began with their own definition of a strategic weapon, which they abandoned only after hard negotiation: they argued that a strategic weapon was one that could hit the territory of the Soviet Union, and therefore included in the count all such NATO and U.S. forward-based systems in Europe.

Shadowing the SALT I negotiations, moreover, was a technological development that was closely linked to the search for effective ABM defences. The United States was well advanced in the development of multiple, independently targetable re-entry vehicles (MIRVs), which meant that a freeze on the number of ballistic-missile launchers might nevertheless permit a dramatic expansion in the number of deployed, deliverable nuclear warheads. In Washington, some of the keenest exponents of MAD and its attendant focus on secure retaliatory forces were also strong supporters of MIRV technological development. For them, MIRV was the hedge against a Soviet ABM system, and possibly the stick that would bring the

Soviets to the ABM Treaty. Convinced that the Soviets lagged in the development of MIRV technology, U.S. negotiators failed to see the potential for the MIRVing of the Soviet heavy ICBMs until it was too late to prevent their deployment.[11]

Having failed to reach agreement on the long-term control of strategic offensive forces as the twin of the ABM Treaty, the two sides compromised on the Interim Agreement. This agreement was to last for five years, at which point it would be replaced by a treaty limiting offensive weapons. The agreement essentially froze ballistic-missile forces, permitting those in existence and under construction. It permitted the introduction of new SLBMs ("stable" missiles because they increased the security of offensive forces), but only in exchange for the dismantlement of an existing ICBM or SLBM. Under the terms of the agreement, the United States was permitted 710 SLBM launchers on 44 submarines and 1054 ICBMs; the Soviet Union was initially permitted 740 SLBMs, and 1618 ICBMs deployed and under construction.

The Interim Agreement did not apply to heavy bombers (the United States had about 600, and the Soviet Union, 150 less-capable bombers). It permitted modernization, did not address the question of intermediate-range delivery systems once the Soviets withdrew their demand that forward-based systems be included, and, perhaps most importantly, failed to deal with MIRVs. At the time, the negotiators could accept these shortcomings because the Interim Agreement was a stop-gap. Article XI of the ABM Treaty obliged the parties "to continue active negotiations for limitations on strategic offensive arms." SALT II was intended to be the treaty that would fulfil that obligation, and set in place the companion to the ABM Treaty.

SALT II and START

The SALT II negotiations began promptly in November 1972, and although the problems already foreshadowed in the Interim Agreement complicated the negotiations, progress the first two years was encouraging. At Vladivostok, in November 1974, General Secretary Brezhnev and President Ford recorded their agreement on the principles of a SALT II agreement. It was agreed that the treaty would be of ten years' duration, and would be based on certain key provisions, of which the most important were as follows:

- a ceiling of 2400 on strategic nuclear-delivery vehicles, including heavy bombers;
- an aggregate limit of 1320 on MIRVed systems;
- a continuation of the ban on new land-based ICBMs (thereby implying a ban on additional Soviet "heavy" ICBMs);
- limits on the deployment of new types of strategic offensive arms; and
- the incorporation of previously agreed principles of verification.

In the Vladivostok accord, therefore, the Soviets finally abandoned their preferred definition of "strategic," and therewith the proposal to count forward-based systems, while the United States abandoned its demand that the Soviets reduce the number of deployed heavy missiles. Thereafter, progress in SALT II was tortuous, with major disagreements persisting on the question of how to count the new Soviet Backfire bomber and the air-launched cruise missiles scheduled to be deployed on B-52s. However, President Carter was strongly committed to the SALT process, and, under the aggressive direction of Paul Warnke, the director of the U.S. Arms Control and Disarmament Agency (ACDA), the negotiations were pursued with renewed vigour from 1977 to 1979. Carter and Brezhnev finally signed the SALT II Treaty in Vienna, in June 1979, only to find that, in the United States, domestic support for the process had eroded to the point where it was no longer possible to achieve Senate consent to the ratification of the treaty.[12]

Although a number of factors influenced the Senate ratification debate in the fall of 1979 — regional conflicts and the personal popularity of President Carter after the debacle in Iran being high on the list — from an arms-control point of view it was apparent that the broad consensus achieved in the mid-1960s had broken down. On the one hand, SALT II supporters stuck to the view that the treaty provided "essential equivalence" in strategic nuclear arms. They argued that the agreement would prevent an open-ended arms race where no victory was in sight, while at the same time permitting the maintenance of a balanced and secure nuclear capability. The opponents, now rallying to the Republican cause in the 1980 election, took a more dismal view of Soviet intentions, and claimed that the treaty would permit the Soviets to pursue strategic superiority. In particular, they fastened on the failure to reduce the 308 SS-18s that formed the core of the Soviet ICBM arsenal. Now MIRVed with ten warheads, and qualitatively more accurate than the earlier SS-9, the SS-18s were seen by the SALT critics, the most influential of whom came to dominate the Reagan administration's approach to arms control, as a force designed and deployed to destroy the U.S. land-based ICBMs. As the Republican presidential candidate, Reagan declared the SALT II Treaty to be "fatally flawed," and pledged not to return it to the Senate should he become president.

In fact, in office President Reagan continued the Carter policy of abiding by the terms of the SALT II Treaty, which was to be in force to the end of 1985. The Reagan administration combined de facto acceptance of SALT II with a continuing attack on the merits of the SALT approach to arms control, and the untrustworthiness of the Soviets.[13] Despite the refusal of the United States to reintroduce the treaty for ratification by the Senate, the Soviets declared themselves to be in compliance with the treaty, and intent on maintaining the prescribed limits after the treaty's expiration. In this context, balanced precariously between the constraints of an unratified treaty and the prospect of constrained force modernization, the tense early years of Reagan's confrontation with the Soviet Union gave way to the arms-control agreements of the Reagan–Gorbachev summits.

After the SALT II debacle and the election of President Reagan, bilateral nuclear-arms negotiations resumed in November 1982. While the major achievement of the negotiations in the Reagan presidency was the INF Treaty, which eliminated from the superpower arsenals intermediate-range (between 500 and 5500 kilometres) missiles, the ongoing search for strategic stability centred on the Strategic Arms Reduction Talks (START). As its title implied, the Reagan approach focussed, not on aggregate limits, as pursued by the SALT negotiators, but on deep reductions in strategic forces. In particular, U.S. negotiators insisted that there should be deep reductions in the number of Soviet SS-18s, which, it was argued, held at risk the entire force of U.S. ICBMS.

After several years of fruitless negotiations, and a dramatic lurch at the Reykjavik summit toward the total elimination of ballistic missiles, in 1987 the negotiators in Geneva came very close to an agreement heralded as a 50 percent reduction in strategic weapons. As described in the December 1987 Washington summit communiqué, the principles of the agreement included the following:

- ceilings of no more than 1600 strategic offensive delivery systems;
- no more than 6000 warheads on these 1600 delivery systems;
- a sublimit of 4900 on the aggregate number of ICBM and SLBM warheads within the 6000 total;
- a sublimit of 154 "heavy" missiles to carry not more than 1540 warheads; and
- a limit on the total throw-weight of these delivery vehicles such that, after the prescribed reductions, the aggregate throw-weight of Soviet ICBMS and SLBMS will be approximately 50 percent less than current Soviet levels, with the new limit not to be exceeded by either side thereafter.[14]

Despite considerable negotiating efforts between the Washington summit of December 1987 and the Moscow summit of June 1988, it proved impossible to reach agreement on a draft treaty before President Reagan left office. In addition to the intricate details that the negotiation required — a START agreement will be significantly more complicated than SALT II because of the need to agree on verification procedures for the dismantlement of missiles — several major disagreements barred the way to agreement. Of these, familiar debates about the cruise missiles were prominent. But from a doctrinal point of view, the stumbling block was the U.S. insistence on continuing with the search for ballistic-missile defence. From the Soviet point of view, this was inconsistent with the attempt to reduce offensive forces. In the new U.S. position, a stable nuclear future would combine ballistic-missile defence with reduced offensive forces.

Despite this fundamental disagreement, there appeared to be continuing negotiating opportunities. The U.S. position was mitigated by continuing debate about the feasibility of ABM defences, and the reality of tightening defence budgets. The Soviets gave clear indications that compromises were possible that would protect the ABM Treaty while permitting greater flexibility in SDI research. It was not clear, therefore, that the START formula would unravel because of the disagreement on strategic defences, while, in the light of the START principles, the Reagan administration's attack on the ABM Treaty appeared to lose ground in the domestic debate within the United States.[15]

Looking back over the period from the 1958 Surprise Attack Conference to the beginning of the Reagan administration in 1981, therefore, the structure of superpower bilateral arms-control measures is clear. Through a process of almost continuous negotiation, both formal and informal, the two sides took measures to ensure that they developed mutually recognizable force structures that, as a minimum, would reduce the incentive to pre-empt in times of crisis. Beyond that basic objective, the two sides struggled to accept and give substance to the judgement that nuclear superiority for purposes of total victory over the opponent could not be achieved. In these circumstances an unrestricted quantitative arms race seemed both profligate and pointless, and likely, in any event, to undermine the principle of secure offensive forces. The setpiece in this structure was the ABM Treaty, which appeared to entrench the acceptance of vulnerability as the basis for stability. Like the SALT process in general, the ABM Treaty was rudely shaken by the Reagan administration. It remained to be seen, however, whether the Reagan upheaval had reversed the previous 20 years of arms-control logic, or merely tested its resilience in the light of political and technological challenges.

Alliance Approaches to Arms Control

It was suggested earlier that, since the Kennedy–Khrushchev period, nuclear-arms control has been almost entirely dealt with in the bilateral-superpower context. As recent dramatic evidence of this, one need only point to the Intermediate Nuclear Forces (INF) Treaty, in which, negotiating alone, the United States reached agreement with the Soviet Union on a range of issues vital to the European allies. These included, for example, arrangements to permit Soviet inspectors on the territories of those European allies (Britain, Holland, Belgium, West Germany, and Italy) that were hosts to the ground-launched cruise missiles (GLCMs) and Pershing IIs.[16]

The logic of this situation was inadvertently argued by the Soviets themselves in their early and intermittently repeated claim that INF and forward-based nuclear systems were "strategic" because they could reach the territory of the Soviet Union. Whatever its merits from a Soviet point of view, this definition of "strategic" appeared intended to divide NATO, since it threw into the SALT negotiation nuclear forces that were designed to underline the nuclear linkage between the United States and European NATO. Having resisted this decoupling, the United States took the view in SALT that it could not negotiate on behalf of the British and French, who were responsible for the disposal of their own nuclear forces. Britain and France, however, have resolutely refused to discuss their nuclear forces with the Soviet Union on the grounds that only when the superpower arsenals are reduced to a fraction of their present size will they be comparable with the much smaller French and British forces.[17]

Consequently, the range of nuclear issues negotiated by the United States in bilateral discussions means that, in effect, it negotiates on behalf of the alliance. In turn, procedures for consultation within the alliance are at a premium. Meetings of the NATO Council and foreign ministers, therefore, have become an important forum for registering the internal consensus reached by NATO on arms-control issues.[18] For the most powerful members of NATO, their input into collective decisions is such that their influence and ability to assert national viewpoints is beyond doubt. For the smaller states in the alliance, such as Canada, however, the effects are twofold. First, influencing U.S. policy is most likely to be effective when there is a concerted view advanced by the allies. For example, the Canadian concern in 1985 not to see the United States break out of the SALT II limits was undoubtedly more effective because it was part of a broader allied concern. However, the obligation to pursue and abide by allied consensus leaves little room for national positions on nuclear-arms control, and little incentive to take on the United States when opinions differ.

In the Canadian case, for example, possible strategic nuclear-force structures raise important issues for Canadian defence and arms-control policy. The encouragement of "slow-flying" bombers and cruise missiles as an element in the nuclear triad raises issues about the strategic significance of the air and sea approaches to Canada, which may have a crucial effect on future Canadian defence policy. From a Canadian point of view, strict limits on both air-launched and sea-launched cruise missiles would reduce these problems and make less critical the search for advanced surveillance systems capable of identifying and tracking the small, radar-eluding cruise missiles. Similar considerations apply to the U.S. quest for ballistic-missile defences: there is a strong prospect that many of the surveillance and attack systems under study would require or benefit from Canadian participation or co-operation, but this in turn has not resulted in a vigorous Canadian view on the merits of the program or the requirements of strategic stability.[19] In short, within the logic of the alliance an independent voice on such issues is difficult to assert. Faced with the prospect of a bleak reception in Washington, and the charge that such unilateral interventions constitute impediments to the broader task of forging an alliance consensus, only a determined government can find the will to assert a national viewpoint.

If it is the case that, in nuclear matters, NATO is a forum for the generation of internal consensus rather than direct negotiation with the Soviet Union, in conventional arms control in Europe the alliances have served as the principal structures for arms-control negotiations. In regard to Europe, two negotiations have dominated the arms-control agenda since the early 1970s: the Mutual and Balanced Force Reduction (MBFR) Talks, and the Conference on Confidence and Security Building Measures and Disarmament in Europe (CCSBMDE, or, in its shorter but less accurate version, the CDE).

The MBFR Talks began in Vienna in 1973, and dragged on for 13 years with little or no progress, until they were mercifully put to rest in 1986. The talks involved 19 nations drawn entirely from NATO and the Warsaw Treaty Organization (WTO), and concentrated on discussions of military manpower and arms-control reductions in a defined geographic area of central Europe that included the Benelux countries, West Germany, East Germany, Poland, and Czechoslovakia. Bogged down, for the most part, in arid debates about the numbers of military personnel to be counted (Is a cook a soldier if in uniform, but not if the army hires civilians?), the MBFR talks nevertheless illustrated the extreme complexity of negotiations for conventional-force reductions in Europe, beginning with the complexities of establishing a database, continuing with the geographic asymmetries that give the Soviet Union a clear advantage in introducing new forces into the area, and ending with the stringent requirements for effective verification.[20]

By comparison, the CDE has proved to be a remarkable success story. Like the SALT process, moreover, it illustrates the extent to which arms control has become an established structure in East-West diplomatic relations. The CDE was established by the European nations, together with the United States and Canada, which comprise the Conference on Security and Co-operation in Europe (CSCE). It will be noted, therefore, that unlike MBFR, which is set up bloc to bloc, the CDE comprises the nations of Europe. While the alliances have played a dominant role in the CDE negotiations, the presence of the European neutrals and the larger geographic area encompassed by the negotiations provided a flexibility, and, in the case of the neutrals, a leavening not present in the MBFR talks.

The CDE began discussions in Stockholm in January 1984. Its mandate was not to negotiate troop reductions in Europe, but to discuss confidence- and security-building measures (CSBMs) that would reduce the threat of attack and minimize the possibility of hostilities initiated through misunderstanding of the other side's military preparations. On September 22, 1986, after three years of arduous and frequently unproductive negotiations, a landmark agreement was reached at the 178th Plenary Session of the CDE. The terms required the signatories to give notice of large-scale troop manoeuvres, to permit foreign inspection of troop manoeuvres, to provide an annual calendar of military exercise in Europe, and to provide up to two years' advance notice of very-large-scale troop manoeuvres involving up to 70 000 men.[21]

In the light of the stagnation of the MBFR talks, in 1987 there was much debate about the prospect of turning the CDE into a forum that would also address troop reductions.[22] The issue was complicated, however, by the inclusion of the European neutrals and nonaligned in the Stockholm talks. During 1987, therefore, negotiations focussed on the appropriate forum for the continuation of the negotiations in conventional-force reductions. In 1988, agreement was reached that both negotiations should continue, but this time with both located in Vienna. Moreover, the Conventional Stability Talks (CST), as the successor to the MBFR Talks was now called, were to address troop reductions from the Atlantic to the Urals, thus providing a larger geographic context for the negotiations, and, in principle, greater flexibility. As the skirmishes over the still-elusive database demonstrated, however, there was little prospect of early success.

Multilateral Arms Control

The structure of bilateral and alliance arms-control negotiations reveals an elaborate and well-established approach to the management, however imperfect, of the East-West military confrontation. By comparison, although it is possible to list a number of significant non-European regional arms-control agreements — the Antarctic Treaty, the Treaty of Tlateloco, and the Treaty of Raratonga are immediate examples — it is clear that the arms-control experience of the post-1945 world has focussed primarily on the issues arising from the superpower military confrontation.

Multilateral approaches to arms-control, mainly but not exclusively sponsored by the United Nations, in part reflect that primary focus. Where an agreement sought by the superpowers requires the support of the larger international community, they have been able to co-operate in mobilizing multilateral commitment to the agreement. The Partial Test Ban Treaty (PTBT), the Non-Proliferation of Nuclear Weapons Treaty (NPT), and, currently under negotiation, a chemical-weapons treaty may be understood in this light. Conversely, both on nuclear issues and on broader issues of the international control of armaments, a large group of states have sought to use multilateral negotiations to influence the arms-control agenda and to persuade the superpowers and their allies to address issues of concern to the larger community of states. These approaches have centred predominantly on the variety of U.N. bodies mandated to deal with arms control and disarmament. As the Partial Test Ban Treaty and the Non-Proliferation of Nuclear Weapons Treaty illustrate, however, treaties deposited at the United Nations and opened to signature also provide leverage to the larger community of states.

In 1954 growing public concern about the fall-out resulting from Soviet and U.S. atmospheric testing peaked in the reaction to the U.S. Bravo test in the South Pacific. Bravo produced twice the anticipated yield, and showered radioactive fall-out over a wide area of the Pacific, including Japan. The incident served to focus international public opposition to atmospheric testing, and to stimulate the anti-nuclear movement among scientists and the general public. At the same time, influential individuals in government began to see a nuclear test ban as the first and logical step toward a comprehensive East-West discussion of arms-control issues. Additionally, U.S. defence analysts may have come to believe that the U.S. lead in testing and sophistication of nuclear weapon-design would diminish thereafter, as the Soviet testing program accelerated with the increasing availability of nuclear fuels.[23]

In addition to these domestic and national-security considerations, however, both superpowers could see a larger advantage in a test ban. A comprehensive test ban might prevent or at least inhibit the spread of nuclear-weapon technology to third parties: in the mid-1950s, the first targets of this nonproliferation strategy were France and China, but in the long term it was evident that nuclear weapons would gradually spread to other countries unless steps were taken to restrain this process. Negotiations on a comprehensive test ban began in 1958, and continued for three years. At times apparently very close to a draft treaty, the negotiations foundered, ostensibly on the inability to agree on an issue that afterwards came to be a sticking point in many superpower negotiations: the verification measures necessary for the implementation of the treaty, and, in particular, the U.S. insistence that on-site inspections were necessary to ensure adequate monitoring of compliance with the treaty provisions.

In the light of the subsequent 25-year effort to negotiate a comprehensive test ban (CTB), it is reasonable to argue that throughout the period there have been powerful interests in the United States that, as the Reagan administration explicitly accepted in 1982, oppose a CTB on national-security grounds. In the late 1950s, however, the negotiators came very close to an agreement despite these constraints. The negotiators were unable to resolve the inspection issues, and the Soviets' decision to abandon their test moratorium in 1961 brought the negotiations to a halt; they were resumed again after the Cuban missile crisis, when Kennedy and Khrushchev turned to arms-control agreements as a means of improving superpower relations after the missile confrontation. Still unable to agree on a CTB, in a three-week period the negotiators drafted the Partial Test Ban Treaty, which was signed in Moscow in August 1963.

The PTBT solved the health hazard produced by atmospheric testing by banning nuclear tests in the atmosphere, in outer space, and underwater. It permitted testing underground, as long as radioactivity did not vent from the tests across international boundaries. Because the parties were confident that tests in the banned environments were detectable by national means, no further verification measures were stipulated as necessary in the treaty. And finally, although the original parties to the treaty asserted their right to a veto on amendments, the treaty was open to signature. By January 1987, 116 states had signed the PTBT, though not, perhaps predictably, the two states at whom it was initially aimed: France and China.

As the technology and design refinement of nuclear weapons has spread, the 1958–61 negotiations have taken on the appearance of a crucial missed opportunity. Underground testing brought with it inconveniences, but it has not prevented the superpowers from carrying out more than 900 nuclear tests since signing the PTBT. Moreover, the continued testing programs have done little to create a political environment in which potential possessing states might be constrained from crossing the nuclear threshold. In the preamble to the PTBT, the original parties declared their commitment to continue negotiations leading to the "permanent banning of all nuclear test explosions." Although progress in this regard was desultory after 1963, in 1974, again seeking an arms-control agreement that would symbolize the superpower search for improved relations, President Ford and General Secretary Brezhnev signed the Threshold Test Ban Treaty, which limited the yields of underground explosions to 150 kilotons. While it is doubtful that the limit imposed any significant military constraint on weapon development, the TTBT could be pointed to as a further step in the progress toward a comprehensive ban, an objective reiterated in the preamble to the TTBT. The TTBT continued to be a source of controversy; Reagan administration spokesmen repeatedly accused the Soviets of violating the 150-kiloton threshold, an accusation that has been consistently refuted in independent scientific testimony to congressional committees.[24]

The NPT

As a measure designed to constrain nuclear proliferation, the PTBT was a missed opportunity, but it did not end the superpower search to enlist the support of the international community to control the spread of nuclear weapons. After the signing of the PTBT in 1963, the United States and the Soviet Union led a four-year multilateral negotiation that, in July 1968, led to the signing of the Non-Proliferation of Nuclear Weapons Treaty (NPT). Despite fears that the NPT would receive little support from the non-nuclear states, by 1985 the treaty had 124 signatories, including all the NATO members except France, and all members of the WTO. While the support for the NPT is impressive, particularly in the light of the controversial distinction between nuclear and non-nuclear states, the list of nonsignatories is ominous, since it is effectively a list of states with nuclear aspirations and capabilities, including, in addition to France and China, Israel, India, Pakistan, South Africa, Argentina, and Brazil.[25]

The NPT created two classes of signatories: nuclear-possessing states and non-possessing states. The treaty builds on this distinction by requiring nuclear-weapon states "not to transfer to any recipient whatsoever nuclear weapons or other nuclear explosive devices . . . and not in any way to assist, encourage, or induce any non–nuclear-weapon State to manufacture or otherwise acquire nuclear weapons" (Article I). Similarly, the nonpossessing states undertake reciprocal obligations in Article II not to receive, manufacture, or otherwise acquire nuclear weapons. At the same time, the treaty recognizes the right of all states to participate in the benefits derived from the peaceful uses of nuclear energy, and initiates a complex regime, under the management of the International Atomic Energy Agency (IAEA), to safeguard the transfer of nuclear technology and materials for peaceful purposes.

The creation of the classes of states in the NPT was accepted by the non-possessors, as the list of signatories demonstrates, but it has produced strains in the 20 years since the treaty was opened to signature. The preamble to the NPT recalled the determination of the PTBT signatories to ban all nuclear tests, and registered the intention of the signatories "to achieve at the earliest possible date the cessation of the nuclear arms race." Moreover, Article VI of the treaty required the parties to negotiate "effective measures" for nuclear and general disarmament. In the five-year review conferences required by the treaty, charges that the nuclear-possessing states have failed to comply with both the preamble and Article VI have dominated the discussions, with the prospect of an increasing rift between the Western nuclear states (the United States and Britain), and the large number of neutral and nonaligned signatories. While the NPT regime is threatened more directly by the nuclear-threshold states that have not signed the treaty, as the end of the 25-year term of the treaty approaches (it must be renewed or lapse in 1995), increasing recriminations between the two classes of signatories may well undermine the fragile political consensus that underlay the treaty in 1968.[26]

The Machinery of the United Nations

Every year the First (Political) Committee of the General Assembly considers an array of resolutions relating to arms control and disarmament, and reports to the General Assembly. Debate in the First Committee is often helpful in revealing the arms-control policies of U.N. members where, otherwise, the governments in question might not formulate a position or even address such questions as a comprehensive nuclear freeze, radiological weapons, and other persistent issues on the international arms-control agenda. Neither the General Assembly nor the First Committee, however, has been able to set the arms-control agenda of the international community, a role, whether in bilateral or multilateral negotiations, that has been jealously guarded by the leading military powers.

In contrast, the annual debates of the United Nations have served to broaden the knowledge and experience of the smaller U.N. members, and to provide a forum for the states affected directly or indirectly by the military, and particularly nuclear, policies of the great powers. For the large group of neutral and nonaligned states, therefore, the General Assembly and its various committees have become the principal vehicle for asserting their position on arms-control issues, and, indeed, for broadening the arms-control agenda beyond that which the superpowers and their allies find convenient to address. Issues such as the relationship between disarmament and development, proposals for reducing world military expenditures, nuclear weapon–free zones, an arms-trade register, and an international satellite-monitoring agency may not be received with favour by the states whose support is essential for their promotion, but without the U.N. forum there would be little opportunity for the nonaligned to raise this broader agenda or to assert their presence in arms-control issues.

It would be misleading, however, to suggest that multilateral activities are mainly declaratory. Since the 1950s a sequence of disarmament committees, not all U.N.-mandated, has engaged in working negotiations on arms-control agreements that require multilateral co-operation if they are to be implemented successfully. The current group is the Geneva-based Committee on Disarmament (CD), which was established after the first Special Session on Disarmament in 1978 (UNSSOD I). The CD comprises 40 states, including all five nuclear-weapon states, other militarily significant states, and a balance of regional and geographic groupings. It was not set up as a U.N. body, but works closely with the General Assembly and the secretary general.

Amongst the ad-hoc working groups of the CD, the one on chemical weapons is perhaps the most important. In 1984, then vice-president George Bush tabled a U.S. draft treaty in the CD, calling for exceptionally stringent ("anytime, anywhere") on-site inspection provisions, considered for some time to be quite unacceptable to the Soviets. However, in 1987, General Secretary Gorbachev signalled Soviet willingness to accept intrusive on-site inspection measures in a variety of arms-control negotiations, including chemical weapons. Although the provisions of the U.S. draft treaty are unlikely to be the final consensus (the United States is itself uncomfortable with the "anytime, anywhere" formula), the

CD has within its reach a draft treaty on chemical weapons, which, if finally agreed upon and opened to signature, would be a dramatic achievement for multilateral diplomacy.[27]

A less prominent but valuable activity in the CD relates to the verification of a comprehensive or very-low–yield nuclear-weapon test ban. Although the CD has not been mandated to produce a draft CTB, it has created a group of scientific experts to consider the monitoring requirements of a CTB. In addition to the bilateral-monitoring provisions that would need to be agreed upon by the superpowers, it is generally accepted that a ban on underground testing would require a global seismic and data-transmission system. To be effective, the global system would require careful choice of sites for seismic stations, the standardization of instruments, and a complex set of international facilities for near real-time data-transmission and -interpretation. Such a system would be impossible without close co-operation among the participating states. The CD is well-suited both to generate the technical requirements for the system and to explore the prospects for political co-operation.

In such activities it is clear that, while the multilateral agenda cannot move forward without the approval of the superpowers, there is considerable scope for technical and diplomatic initiatives by the smaller powers. In the group of scientific experts, for example, Canadian and Swedish scientists have taken the initiative in developing an international seismological-verification system.[28] In chemical weapons, the smaller industrialized states are themselves important actors since they have chemical facilities with a weapons potential. The exploration of the requirements of a draft treaty, and the acceptability of the intrusive verification measures required, have given the smaller states a key role in the negotiations. In part because of these experiences, Canada and other countries have sought to facilitate the arms-control process in general by establishing programs to resolve or clarify the verification requirements of different arms-control treaty regimes, including possible future treaties as well as those currently under negotiation.

Verification and Compliance

In the 1958–61 period, negotiations for a comprehensive test ban foundered on U.S. insistence that the treaty provide for mandatory on-site inspections. As indicated above, the Partial Test Ban Treaty of 1963, the first faltering step in a series of superpower arms-control agreements, contained no verification provisions because the banned environments could be effectively monitored by national technical means (NTM). With the increasing sophistication of satellite monitoring, the ABM Treaty, the interim agreement, and SALT II were all negotiated on the basis that NTM provided sufficient means of verification. Article XV of the SALT II Treaty, for example, explicitly identifies national technical means as the method for assuring compliance with the treaty, and obliges the parties not to interfere with NTM necessary to ensure verification of the agreement.

In other negotiating areas, however, measures other than NTM are necessary. These areas include a comprehensive or very-low–yield test ban, conventional-force reductions, confidence building measures of the kind agreed to in the Stockholm Conference, chemical-weapon and nuclear-weapon treaties (such as the INF Treaty and the START proposals) that involve the destruction of missiles and, even more particularly, of warheads. All of these areas require verification measures beyond NTM. The first step beyond NTM is to establish co-operative measures to facilitate verification. Article XII of the INF Treaty, for example, requires the parties to open road-mobile missile shelters for satellite inspection. In addition, since the beginning of the test-ban negotiations, the United States and its allies have traditionally insisted on the necessity of mandatory on-site inspections (OSIs). Although the Soviet Union did not reject out of hand the principle of mandatory OSIs, the traditional Soviet position has been that U.S. insistence on mandatory OSIs had more to do with intelligence gathering than verification, and the Soviets have either rejected such provisions completely, or sought to keep them to a minimum.

These ongoing issues concerning verification have become considerably more important since 1983, when the U.S. Senate required an Executive Branch report on Soviet compliance with existing treaties. In response, the Reagan administration issued the first of several statements identifying a long list of alleged Soviet acts of noncompliance with existing treaties.[29] The most important of these concerned the phased-array radar at Krasnoyarsk, which is alleged to be a violation of the ABM Treaty insofar as the treaty does not permit the construction of such radars except at the periphery of the country. Whatever the purposes of the Krasnoyarsk radar — the Soviet motives in building it remain obscure — it has clearly embarrassed the Soviets, who have belatedly admitted that it is a violation of the ABM Treaty. Almost all other charges of noncompliance, however, have proved to be either contentious (in the sense of relating to "grey areas" of treaty interpretation), unproven (as in the allegations that the Soviets were developing biological weapons at facilities in Sverdlovsk),[30] or trivial (as, for example, in the reciprocal charges that the parties have permitted the venting of underground nuclear explosions across national boundaries). Nevertheless, the continuing debate, particularly in the U.S. Senate, about Soviet noncompliance has sharpened the requirement for future verification procedures that will give high-confidence assurance that the signatories are in compliance with arms-control treaty obligations.

Verifying the INF Treaty

The INF Treaty concluded in December 1987 requires the two sides to eliminate all intermediate and shorter-range nuclear missiles with ranges from 500 to 5500 kilometres. In order to do this, the parties have committed themselves to a detailed process of step-by-step verification extending over a period of 13 years. It should be emphasized that, despite the significant breakthrough in reaching agreement on OSIs, the principal means of verifying the INF Treaty, as with the previous SALT agreements, will be through national technical means (NTM). Article XII of the treaty, for example, echoing the SALT agreements, requires that the parties not interfere with legitimate NTM. However, attention has inevitably centred on the innovating provisions of the treaty that provide for on-site inspection in order to ensure that the destruction of INF missiles is carried out in accordance with the detailed provisions of the treaty. These inspections give both sides the right to visit operating locations to confirm the data provided in the Memorandum of Understanding, to confirm the elimination of missiles and launchers in accordance with the agreed-upon schedule, and to initiate a number of short-notice challenge inspections of operating locations for a period of 13 years to confirm that INF missiles have not been reintroduced.[31]

Further, the treaty also provides for a limited form of perimeter-factory monitoring. The United States is entitled to monitor the Votkinsk factory that produces stages for both the SS-20 and the SS-25 (a mobile ICBM not covered by the treaty). The Soviet Union is entitled to monitor the Magna, Utah, plant that once made boosters for the Pershing II, and more recently produces components for the MX and Trident missiles. This arrangement falls far short of the initial demands by U.S. secretary of defense Caspar Weinberger that factories would need to be open to inspection as if by bank inspectors, implying an unlimited right to inspect. It reflects, however, the sober second thoughts of the Reagan administration in 1987 as they contemplated all the implications of Soviet inspectors roaming freely across the NATO European countries, the United States, and even Canada. The factory-monitoring provisions, therefore, are modest but they open the possibility that future agreements, particularly in chemical weapons, where factory monitoring will be essential, may be able to exploit the opening created by the INF Treaty.

In the December 1987 Washington communiqué issued after the signing of the INF Treaty, extensive reference was also made to the verification requirements of a future START treaty. The general principles agreed in the communiqué drew heavily on the verification provisions of the INF Treaty. As with INF, the parties agreed to a data exchange identifying the numbers, location, and support facilities of the weapons to be limited by the proposed START treaty. The parties agreed in principle to on-site inspections to include a one-time inspection of the bases identified in the data exchange, on-site observation of the elimination of weapons, and short-notice challenge inspections of remaining missile sites permitted by the treaty, and of missile sites previously dismantled in accordance with the treaty. The communiqué also called for co-operative measures more far-reaching than the INF Treaty to facilitate surveillance by national technical means. Finally, and remembering that, unlike the case under the INF Treaty, production facilities for missiles covered by START would remain after the agreement, the parties agreed to continuous monitoring of critical production facilities, suggesting factory monitoring considerably more intrusive than that called for in the INF Treaty.[32]

Issues of verification and compliance, therefore, have provided both the low and the high points of Soviet-American arms-control negotiations in the Reagan era. In 1985 the entire structure of SALT and the ABM Treaty was at issue as a consequence of the policies of the Reagan administration. By 1988 the INF Treaty and the START principles promised not only significant arms reductions, but breakthroughs in accepted approaches to verification that held promise of verification regimes for other spheres, in particular chemical-weapons and conventional-force reductions.

Conclusion

This survey suggests that a layered structure of arms-control negotiations has developed in the contemporary international system. At the centre is the bilateral negotiation between the superpowers that, whatever its substantive success, has become a bellwether of détente. The Reagan attacks on the SALT process, in particular the threat to the ABM Treaty and the decision not to abide by the SALT II limits after the expiration of the agreement in 1985, marked the low point of Soviet-American relations in the 1980s. They were followed, however, by the INF Treaty, an agreement to establish a jointly managed risk-reduction centre, and marked progress toward a START agreement. Each side evidently needed these agreements for both domestic- and foreign-policy reasons. It appears, therefore, that there is a robustness to the bilateral arms-control process that is likely to ensure its continuation, whatever the vagaries of the superpower relationship.

Much the same might be said of the second tier of negotiations, which are focussed on conventional arms control in Europe. Thirteen years of drearily unproductive negotiations in the MBFR Talks did not lessen the European interest in alliance negotiations. The success of the 35-nation CDE, moreover, holds out the prospect that more far-reaching arms-control measures are also possible in Europe. However slow the pace, therefore, the new round of Conventional Stability Talks has emerged as another distinctive feature of the arms-control landscape, even if the political need to avoid the appearance of failure is as great as the will to achieve early progress. Such talks place a premium on the prior negotiation of alliance consensus. If not managed carefully by the alliance leader, they reveal fundamental divergences of view among the leading NATO members that further slow the prospect of meaningful negotiation with the WTO. For small powers such as Canada, therefore, these talks within the talks offer a seat at the NATO table, but little room to present independent views for fear of retarding the complex process of negotiating alliance bargaining positions.

The third layer of arms-control negotiations is the multilateral one, centred on the United Nations and associated bodies such as the CD. Although these negotiations may be more easily dismissed as a forum in which a large number of states without military power espouse high-minded principles that cannot possibly be implemented, closer examination suggests that the multilateral forum is a vital part of the structure. To begin, certain central arms-control measures, in particular the NPT, a chemical-weapons convention, and a comprehensive test ban, cannot be implemented without multilateral agreement. A wide range of other issues, such as efforts to control the spread of ballistic-missile technology, also need multilateral support if they are to be successful. Leadership in the multilateral forum, therefore, is essential. It is here that the smaller industrialized Western powers have a more distinctive opportunity to influence events. Diplomatically, they may be able to moderate the more extreme positions of Third World countries and to shade the more unyielding responses of the major Western countries. Scientifically, they are in a position, as at the CD, to provide leadership in determining the feasibility of arms-control and verification proposals, and staff work in preparing the way for future agreements.

NOTES

1. A valuable short summary of pre-1945 efforts toward multilateral arms control may be found in Jozef Goldblat, *Arms Control Agreements: A Handbook* (New York: Praeger, 1983), chap. 1.

2. The story is told in Martin Sherwin, "How Well They Meant," *Bulletin of the Atomic Scientists* (August 1985): 9–15. A fuller account of the political debate among the Manhattan Project scientists may be found in Richard Rhodes, *The Making of the Atomic Bomb* (New York: Simon and Schuster, 1986), especially 749–89.

3. Hedley Bull, *The Control of the Arms Race* (London: Institute for Strategic Studies, 1961), 10.

4. John Newhouse, *Cold Dawn: The Story of SALT* (New York: Holt Rinehart, 1973). Newhouse suggests (p. 2) that "SALT could develop a cumulative impact on the world system comparable to the Congress of Vienna, whose achievement was to spare Europe any major bloodletting for 100 years. Such is the hope."

5. The Rand Study was an internal document, R-290, *Protecting US Power to Strike Back in the 1950s and 1960s*, dated September 1, 1956. The study was the basis for the widely cited article by Albert Wohlstetter, "The Delicate Balance of Terror," *Foreign Affairs* 38 (January 1959): 211–34.

6. A brief account of the Gaither Committee report may be found in Lawrence Freedman, *The Evolution of Nuclear Strategy* (New York: St. Martin's, 1983), 160–63.

7. The significance of the Surprise Attack Conference is discussed in Thomas Schelling, "What Went Wrong with Arms Control?," in *Essays in Arms Control and National Security*, ed. B.F. Halloran (Washington: U.S. Arms Control and Disarmament Agency, 1986), 335–51.

8. An informed and sympathetic description of the development of MAD can be found in W.W. Kaufman, *The McNamara Strategy* (New York: Harper and Row, 1974).

9. The broader issue of measures against accidents was also dealt with in SALT I. For a brief summary of this set of measures, see Andrew Bennett, "The Accidents Measures Agreement," in *Superpower Arms Control: Setting the Record Straight*, ed. Albert Carnesale and Richard N. Haass (Cambridge, Mass.: Ballinger, 1987), 41–65.

10. A contemporary assessment of the first ABM debate, largely critical, can be found in *ABM: An Evaluation of the Decision to Deploy an Anti-Ballistic Missile System*, ed.

Abram Chayes and Jerome B. Wiesner (New York: Signet Books, 1969). Gerard Smith, *Doubletalk: The Story of SALT I* (Garden City, N.Y.: Doubleday, 1980), is a first-hand account by the U.S. chief negotiator. In addition to Newhouse, *Cold Dawn: The Story of SALT*, an excellent summary of the SALT I negotiation may be found in National Academy of Sciences, *Nuclear Arms Control: Background and Issues* (Washington, D.C.: National Academy Press, 1985), chaps. 2 and 5.

11. An excellent summary account of the development of the U.S. MIRV program can be found in Herbert York, "Multiple Warhead Missiles," in *Progress in Arms Control?* ed. Bruce Russett and Bruce Blair (San Francisco: W.H. Freeman, 1979), 122–32. York's first sentences graphically state the problem: "From 1945 to 1970 the number of nuclear warheads in the U.S. strategic arsenal went from zero to about 4000. From 1970 to mid-1975 the number will increase to almost 10,000."

12. As the title suggests, a blow-by-blow account of the SALT II negotiations can be found in Strobe Talbott, *Endgame: The Inside Story of SALT II* (New York: Harper and Row, 1980). For a useful short summary, see Stephen J. Flanagan, "SALT II," in *Superpower Arms Control*, chap. 5.

13. The United States formally exceeded the SALT II limits on November 28, 1986, when it rolled out the 131st B-52 converted to a cruise-missile carrier. The deployment exceeded the SALT II limit of 1320 MIRVed delivery vehicles.

14. For a summary of the START negotiations and related issues, see David Cox, *A Review of the Geneva Negotiations 1987–88* (Ottawa: Background Paper, Canadian Institute for International Peace and Security [CIIPS], 1989). The official U.S. view of the negotiations is described in Caspar Weinberger, "Arms Reductions and Deterrence," *Foreign Affairs* 66 (Spring 1988): 700–719.

15. The fundamental issues in the ABM Treaty debate are reviewed in T. Longstreth, J. Pike, and J. Rhinelander, *The Impact of US and Soviet Ballistic Missiles Defense Programs on the ABM Treaty* (Washington, D.C.: National Campaign to Save the ABM Treaty, 1985). For opposing views on the treaty interpretation, see S. Nunn, "The ABM Reinterpretation Issue," and A.D. Sofaer, "The ABM Treaty: Legal Analysis in the Political Cauldron," *Washington Quarterly* (Autumn 1987): 45–78.

16. For details on the INF Treaty, see "Summary and Text of the INF Treaty and Protocols," *Arms Control Today* (January/February 1988): 1–16. Leon V. Sigal, "The Long and the Short of It: Allied Ambivalence About a Zero INF Deal," *Arms Control Today* (May 1987): 10–13, offers a brief assessment of the alliance differences on the INF Treaty.

17. For an overview of the British and French nuclear forces, see Lawrence Freedman, "The Small Nuclear Powers," in *Ballistic Missiles Defense*, ed. A.B. Carter and D.N. Schwartz (Washington, D.C.: The Brookings Institution, 1984). For a discussion of the arms-control implications, see Jonathan Alford, "The Place of British and French Nuclear Weapons in Arms Control," *International Affairs* 59 (Autumn 1983): 569–74.

18. A comprehensive survey of NATO consultation processes may be found in Paul Buteux, *The Politics of Nuclear Consultation in NATO 1965–80* (New York: Cambridge University Press, 1983). For a more recent assessment, see Daniel Charles, *Nuclear Planning in NATO* (Cambridge, Mass.: Ballinger, 1987).

19. Canadian policies in this regard are discussed in John Barrett, "Arms Control and Canada's Security Policy," *International Journal* 42 (Autumn 1987): 731–68.

20. The fundamental questions are discussed in R.D. Blackwill, "Conceptual Problems of Conventional Arms Control," and J. Snyder, "Limiting Offensive Conventional Forces: Soviet Proposals and Western Options," in *International Security* 12 (Spring 1988): 28–77.

21. For an account of the Stockholm Agreement, see James Goodby, "To Reduce the Risk of War — The Stockholm Negotiation," in *Confidence-Building Measures and International Security*, ed. R.B. Byers et al. (New York: Institute for East-West Security Studies, 1987), 39–54. An account of one of the first inspections under the agreement is given in Department of State Bulletin, November 1987: "US Inspects Soviet Military Exercise."

22. These issues are chronicled in the yearbooks of the Stockholm International Peace Research Institute (SIPRI). A briefer comment may be found in J. Borawski, "Farewell to MBFR," *Arms Control Today* (May 1987): 17–19.

23. An authoritative account of these issues can be found in Glenn T. Seaborg, *Kennedy, Khrushchev, and the Test Ban* (Berkeley: University of California Press, 1981).

24. An overview of the issues arising in the efforts to secure a comprehensive test ban may be found in Jozef Goldblat and David Cox, *The Debate About Nuclear Weapon Tests* (Ottawa: Canadian Institute for International Peace and Security, 1988). For a critique of the administration's position on Soviet testing, see L.R. Sykes and D.M. Davis, "The Yields of Soviet Strategic Weapons," *Scientific American* (January 1987): 29–37.

25. An overview of the issues involved in the spread of nuclear weapons may be found in Leonard Spector, *The New Nuclear Nations* (New York: Vintage Books, 1985).

26. For an assessment of the 1985 Review Conference, see *World Armaments and Disarmament: SIPRI Yearbook 1986* (New York: Oxford University Press, 1986).

27. For background on multilateral approaches to a chemical-weapons ban, see N. Sims, *International Organisation for Chemical Disarmament* (New York: SIPRI, Oxford University Press, 1987).

28. The proposal is discussed in Peter W. Basham and Ola Dahlman, "International Seismological Verification," in *Nuclear Weapon Tests: Prohibition or Limitation?* ed. Jozef Goldblat and David Cox (New York: Oxford University Press, 1988).

29. For a comprehensive assessment of the compliance issues, see Gloria Duffy, ed., *Compliance and the Future of Arms Control* (Cambridge, Mass.: Ballinger, 1988).

30. A painstaking account of the Sverdlovsk case is contained in Elisa D. Harris, "Sverdlovsk and Yellow Rain: Two Cases of Soviet Non-Compliance?" *International Security* 11 (Spring 1987): 41–95. Harris concludes that "neither the yellow rain charges against the Soviet Union nor the US explanation for the anthrax outbreak at Sverdlovsk is supported by the evidence available in the public domain."

31. The INF Treaty and its implications are discussed in a series of articles by the chief negotiators, Maynard Glitman and Alexei Obukhov, and others, in *The United Nations Review Disarmament* (Winter 1987–88): 1–61.

32. An overview of the Soviet approach to verification in START is contained in *Verifying Arms Control Agreements: The Soviet View*, prepared by the Congressional Research Service for the Committee on Foreign Affairs, U.S. House of Representatives (Washington, D.C.: May 1987).

SELECT BIBLIOGRAPHY

Bull, Hedley. *The Control of the Arms Race*. London: Institute for Strategic Studies, 1961.

Barrett, John. "Arms Control and Canada's Security Policy." *International Journal* 42 (Autumn 1987): 731–68.

Carnesale, Albert, and Richard N. Haass, eds. *Superpower Arms Control: Setting the Record Straight*. Cambridge, Mass.: Ballinger, 1987.

Goldblat, Jozef. *Arms Control Agreements: A Handbook*. New York: Praeger, 1983.

Goldblat, Jozef, and David Cox. *The Debate About Nuclear Weapon Tests*. Ottawa: Canadian Institute for International Peace and Security, 1988.

Halloran, B.F., ed. *Essays in Arms Control and National Security*. Washington: U.S. Arms Control and Disarmament Agency, 1986.

Newhouse, John. *Cold Dawn: The Story of SALT*. New York: Holt Rinehart, 1973.

Russett, Bruce, and Bruce Blair, eds. *Progress in Arms Control?* San Francisco: W.H. Freeman, 1979.

Seaborg, Glenn T. *Kennedy, Khrushchev, and the Test Ban*. Berkeley: University of California Press, 1981.

Talbott, Strobe. *Endgame: The Inside Story of SALT II*. New York: Harper and Row, 1980.

TRADING IN WEAPONS: THE ROLE OF ARMS TRANSFERS IN INTERNATIONAL POLITICS

Keith Krause

Arms sales are foreign policy writ large.

Our foreign policy is in large part arms sales; that's true. Every other week we are selling something to someone.[1]

Arms transfers are a crucial aspect of the warp and woof of international politics.[2] In 1986, about $37 billion worth of arms were bought and sold, and the vast majority of these weapons went to Third World states.[3] This traffic in arms has more than *quadrupled* in real terms since 1963. These transfers are conducted for many reasons, and analysts only poorly understand what motivations drive the international arms-transfer system. For the recipients, arms purchases are a crucial aspect of defence and security policy, as only the advanced industrial states have the know-how and resources to produce all the weapons they need for their armed forces. What other states cannot produce, they are forced to buy on the market.

This fact gives the suppliers of arms an opportunity to exercise influence over their clients, but it also makes the arms trade intensely political. As former president of Tanzania Julius Nyerere put it,

> the selling of arms is something which a country does only when it wants to support and strengthen the regime or group to whom the sale is made . . . the sale of any arms is a declaration of support — an implied alliance of a kind. You can trade with people you dislike; you can have diplomatic relations with governments you disapprove of; you can sit in conference with those nations whose policies you abhor. But you do not sell arms without saying . . . "we will be on their side in the case of any conflict."[4]

It is this use of arms transfers as a tool of foreign policy that makes them interesting to international relations scholars. When one moves away from the abstract models of power and influence presented in introductory texts, it is quickly apparent that arms sales are one of the few tools decision makers in the United

States or Soviet Union possess to influence the foreign-policy behaviour or overall political orientation of client states. The existence of an arms-transfer relationship is often taken as sufficient evidence to describe a state as a "client" of either superpower. How this influence might be exercised, and indeed whether or not it actually exists, is another murky area.

Of course, the story is even more complex than this suggests. For some suppliers, political influence is less important than the economic or military gains to be had from selling arms. For some recipients, the weapons purchased have little to do with possible external threats faced by the state, and much more to do with maintaining an autocratic regime or leader in power against the wishes of the people. Massive purchases of advanced weapons and high levels of defence spending can also distort government priorities, drawing on resources that could possibly be used for other development goals, such as village electrification or the construction of schools. All of these possibilities raise ethical concerns that must be dealt with: weapons that kill are not purely economic goods to be bought and sold, as are copper, computers, or coffee.

This chapter will explore these various aspects of arms-transfer relationships. It will also use the focus on arms transfers (ignoring economic relations, foreign aid, diplomatic relations, and so forth) as a sort of microcosm to untangle and illuminate some more general and thorny issues in international relations. But to begin, one needs a clear picture of the current scope of the international arms trade.

The Scope of the Arms Trade

In 1986, there were 40 sellers and 107 buyers in the international arms market. Most of these participants were minor players, and the top few buyers and sellers accounted for the majority of weapons bought and sold. Tables 1 and 2 outline the distribution of suppliers' shares and the top-ten recipients for the most recent period.

TABLE 1 Arms Suppliers, 1982–86

Suppliers	**Market Share** *(percent)*
Soviet Union	38
United States	23
France	9
Britain	3
West Germany	3
Italy	2
China	3
Other Developed	5
Other Warsaw Pact	3
Developing	11

SOURCE: U.S. Arms Control and Disarmament Agency, *World Military Expenditures and Arms Transfers* (Washington, D.C.: U.S. Arms Control and Disarmament Agency, 1987).

TABLE 2 Top-Ten Arms Recipients, 1982–86

Recipient	Dollar Value *(in millions of dollars)*	Percentage
Iraq	31 740	14
Saudi Arabia	16 715	7
Syria	10 830	5
Libya	10 160	5
India	9 275	4
Iran	8 405	4
Cuba	7 830	3
Egypt	7 640	3
Vietnam	6 935	3
Soviet Union	5 550	2

SOURCE: U.S. Arms Control and Disarmament Agency, *World Military Expenditures and Arms Transfers* (Washington, D.C.: U.S. Arms Control and Disarmament Agency, 1987).

Together, the top-five recipients accounted for 35 percent and the top-ten recipients, 51 percent, of total global arms transfers. This makes clear that the "global" increase in arms sales of the past two decades is really a much more localized phenomenon, as many parts of the world have not dramatically increased their arms purchases. A glance at the top-ten recipients shows that six of them

TABLE 3 Distribution of Global Arms Deliveries to Regions, 1963–67 and 1982–86

Region	1963–67	1982–86	(% World Population)	(% World GNP)
Africa	4.2	13.9	10.6	2.5
E. Asia	28.7	10.6	34.1	14.8
S. Asia	6.8	6.4	20.8	1.8
L. America	3.1	7.6	8.3	4.9
N. America	3.0	1.6	5.4	30.0
M. East	9.2	40.0	3.3	3.2
Oceania	2.0	1.4	0.5	1.4
NATO Europe	20.3	8.3	6.9	16.7
Warsaw Pact	19.1	8.1	8.0	20.8
Other Europe	3.6	1.8	2.0	3.8
Developed	41.7	19.5	23.1	80.1
Developing	58.3	80.5	76.9	19.9

Regions are classified as follows:

Africa: does not include Egypt.
East Asia: Mongolia, both Koreas, China, Taiwan, Japan, and from Burma to Indonesia.
South Asia: Afghanistan, India, Pakistan, Nepal, Bangladesh, Sri Lanka.
Latin America: Mexico south, all Caribbean states.
North America: Canada and the United States.
Middle East: Egypt to the Persian Gulf, Iran, and Cyprus.
Oceania: Australia, New Zealand, Fiji, Papua-New Guinea.
Other Europe: Albania, Austria, Finland, Ireland, Malta, Spain, Sweden, Switzerland, and Yugoslavia.
Developed: all of NATO, except Greece and Turkey; all of the Warsaw Pact except Bulgaria; Japan, Australia, New Zealand, Finland, Austria, Ireland, Sweden, and Switzerland.
Developing: all others.

SOURCE: U.S. Arms Control and Disarmament Agency, *World Military Expenditures and Arms Transfers* (Washington, D.C.: U.S. Arms Control and Disarmament Agency, 1987).

are located in the Middle East (broadly defined); this suggests that the increase in arms purchases can be largely accounted for by sales to that strife-torn region.

Table 3, which presents a breakdown of global transfers by region at two different times, confirms this suspicion.

In the 1960s, the main arms purchasers were concentrated in Eastern and Western Europe, and in East Asia (as a result of the Indochina–Vietnam war). In the late 1960s and 1970s the focus shifted away from Europe, and an increasing proportion of sales went to the newly independent states in the Third World. Thus, East Asia and Europe saw their share of arms purchases decline between 1963 and 1986, while the Middle East and Africa shot to the top of the list. This shift is all the more striking, given that Africa and the Middle East account for less than 15 percent of the total world's population and less than 6 percent of its economic wealth, yet they purchase more than half of the arms sold.

The most rapid period of increased sales to the Middle East occurred just before and after the oil-price increases of 1973 and 1978. Not surprisingly in a region rife with conflicts, some of the petrodollars were used to purchase top-of-the-line arsenals. The most extreme example of this was the Shah's Iran, which between 1973 and 1979 purchased more than $11 billion in arms. By the time of the Shah's downfall, Iran possessed 445 combat planes, 1975 tanks, and 27 large naval vessels. For comparison, the French military had 460 combat planes, 2270 tanks, and 68 major surface ships (and a population of 53 million, compared with 40 million in Iran)! The Shah intended to build Iran into a regional power that could exercise dominant influence in the Persian Gulf. As he told British journalist Anthony Sampson in 1975, "I hope my good friends in Europe and the United States and elsewhere will finally understand that there is absolutely no difference between Iran and France, Britain and Germany."[5] The Shah's stated intention coincided perfectly with American desires for a regional "policeman" to look after its interests.

Saudi Arabia, Iraq, and the smaller Persian Gulf states all responded to this massive arms build-up and embarked on large arms-purchasing programs. In the core Middle East (Egypt, Israel, Jordan, and Syria), huge demands for arms resulted from the 1967, 1970, 1973, and 1982 Arab-Israeli wars. In North Africa, both oil-rich Algeria and Libya purchased large amounts of weapons. In southern Africa, the main customers were Angola and Mozambique, which, after winning their independence in 1975 and becoming clients of the Soviet Union, found themselves embroiled in continuing civil wars against American- or South African–supported rebels.

But noting that the arms trade is concentrated between a few major buyers and sellers should not lead us to neglect the general increase in spending on weapons and the military throughout the underdeveloped world. About 87 states spent more in constant-dollar terms on their military establishments in 1986 than in 1977. Roughly 44 increased their real spending on arms imports in that decade.[6] Although the absolute levels of arms sales to a state such as Bangladesh or North Yemen may be small in a global context, it is perhaps large enough to distort significantly development priorities in those countries.

With this thumbnail sketch of the global arms market, we can now turn to examine in more detail the motives driving both suppliers and recipients in the international arms market.

The Suppliers' Motives

Arms exports can bring a wide range of political, military, and economic benefits to supplier states. A "rough" checklist of the possible benefits would look like this:

Political Benefits

- provide influence over key leaders and elites in recipient countries
- symbolize a commitment to a client's security and stability
- exclude the influence of other states
- assist a regime in protecting itself against internal threats
- provide leverage to pursue diplomatic objectives
- create or maintain a regional balance of power
- create or maintain a regional presence

Economic Benefits

- provide foreign exchange and positively affect the balance of payments
- reduce the cost of weapons for one's own forces through economies of scale
- maintain employment in defence-related industries
- recover research and development costs

Military Benefits

- act as a quid pro quo for military bases or special privileges
- assist friends and allies to maintain defences against a common threat
- substitute for direct military involvement
- provide testing for new weapons systems

Naturally, not all suppliers seek the same benefits, and the same mix does not apply to every arms-transfer relationship. But there are some patterns, and one way of breaking down the different types of suppliers is to examine the different benefits they seek, as well as the different arms-industry structure they possess. When one does this, one discovers that there are actually three different "tiers" of suppliers in the arms market that can be distinguished by the size of their market shares and their motives for selling arms. The differences between the tiers has the unfortunate side-effect of sharply limiting the possibilities for international restraint on arms transfers for reasons that will become evident below.

First-Tier Suppliers

The first tier includes only the United States and Soviet Union. The two superpowers together account for 61 percent of global transfers in the most recent period, although this share has been slowly declining since the 1960s. Other than their huge market share, there are four other characteristics that distinguish the first-tier suppliers.

First, they are capable of mass-producing the entire range of modern, sophisticated weapons, including a large variety of jet aircraft (fighters, bombers, tankers, transports, trainers, and various combinations of these), a range of missiles (air-to-air, surface-to-air, surface-to-surface missiles), main battle tanks, anti-tank weapons, and air-defence systems. Many of these systems are designed to work together as a package (such as jet fighters and air-defence systems), which increases the attractiveness of the United States or Soviet Union as a supplier. If a stable supply relationship is already in existence, this huge "warehouse" of arms can save clients the trouble of "shopping around" for items that match their arsenal.

Second, the domestic military demand in the United States and Soviet Union is so high that exports are only a small percentage of total production, although this varies from item to item and from year to year. Very few individual American firms depend on exports for their well-being: between 1982 and 1985, only 6 percent of the total sales of the top-ten defence contractors was exported.[7] The Soviet Union exports a higher proportion of its total production, but, in its command economy, military production and arms export decisions are not taken with economic benefits foremost in mind. The result is that neither first-tier supplier is economically dependent on either the jobs or the export revenue generated by arms sales. For the United States, a complete ban on foreign military sales would cause a drop in GNP of less than 1 percent, and an increase in unemployment of less than 0.5 percent.

The third distinct feature of first-tier suppliers is that they are the only ones prepared to supply large quantities of weapons "free" as grants, or on subsidized financial terms. For example, the Soviets recently signed with India a $1.7-billion arms package with a 17-year loan at 2.5 percent interest rate — a heavy subsidy indeed! The United States in 1985 provided guaranteed loans or grants for more than $5 billion of its arms sales. Fourth, as a corollary to this, the United States and Soviet Union are the only suppliers who attempt to use their arms-transfer relationships as a means of political leverage or influence over their clients. I will return to this point below.

Who are the main clients of the United States and Soviet Union? Not surprisingly, the Soviets sell weapons to fewer states than does the United States (46 in the 1982–86 period), preferring to concentrate their efforts on close allies and states with which they have signed "friendship and co-operation" treaties. Their main customers are Vietnam, Iraq, Syria, India, and Cuba. But not all Soviet customers are "satellite states": although Cuba, Mongolia, and Vietnam fit into this category, many recent buyers of Soviet weapons, such as India, Iraq,

Jordan, and Peru, have varying degrees of attachment to the "international socialist commonwealth" (or no attachment at all). In contrast, the United States sells weapons to more states: 76 in 1982–86. Again, its most prominent clients (Israel, Egypt, Saudi Arabia, Japan) are political or military allies, and some other clients are cultivated for the military benefits they will provide (Somalia, Oman, Morocco, the Philippines). But, as with the Soviet Union, many other customers of American arms (such as Indonesia, Kuwait, and Pakistan) cannot be called shining members of the "free world" in any meaningful sense.

Second-Tier Suppliers

The second-tier suppliers are the industrial states of Western and Eastern Europe (West Germany, Britain, France, Italy, Spain, Czechoslovakia, and Poland), as well as other industrialized states such as Canada, Japan, and Sweden. Together, these states hold about 24 percent of the arms market. The three most prominent members are France, Britain, and West Germany, and their experience with arms-transfer policy is typical enough to describe all suppliers in this category, with two exceptions mentioned below.

The post-1945 history of French and British foreign policy is a difficult tale of attempts to meet a wide range of goals with an ever-shrinking amount of resources. Today, with their empires gone and their global economic status eclipsed by West Germany and Japan, it is difficult to remember that, after World War II, Britain and France viewed themselves as charter members of the "great power" club, able to wield influence around the world. This status was enshrined by permanent membership (and a veto) on the U.N. Security Council.

The shrinking of resources affected defence industries as much as other sectors. With little co-operation between Western European states on defence production in the 1950s and 1960s, each country (Britain, France, and West Germany at first, joined later by Italy and Spain) attempted to produce the entire range of military equipment and stay at the forefront of innovations in military technology. It was felt that a country that could not produce the weapons needed to defend itself was severely compromising its national sovereignty. Defending national sovereignty in a changing world required large investments in military research and development (R&D) and close co-operation between the defence industry, the government, and the military establishment.

The difficulties this investment commitment created became most apparent in France, which shifted to a position of foreign-policy independence under President de Gaulle in the 1960s (coincident with its withdrawal from the unified military command of NATO). As a consequence, national defence industries had to be maintained to protect national autonomy and supply the French military. But, two factors made this commitment increasingly difficult and costly to maintain. First, the small size of the military in France (relative to that of the superpowers) meant that the unit-cost of individual weapons systems would be higher. The cost per plane of an advanced jet fighter is simply much lower if one can build 1000 rather than 100. So, France, like all other European states, started at a relative disadvantage. Second, increasing financial pressures in the late 1960s and 1970s reduced the amount of money available to the military to purchase new weapons systems, putting further pressure on the arms industries.

The outcome was predictable. To reduce the costs of the *political* commitment to an autonomous national defence industry, European arms producers had to pursue aggressively arms exports, especially of their most sophisticated weapons. In practice, this meant increased sales to Third World states. One of the first examples of this occurred in 1967, when the French broke an earlier American embargo on introducing supersonic jet fighters to South America. The Americans had refused to sell the F-5 to any state in the region and requested co-operation from NATO partners. Both the British and the French, however, broke the embargo, with the French selling the Peruvians the Mirage V.[8] After 1973, this second-tier penetration of the Third World market was widespread, and by the 1980s, 83 percent of Germany's, 82 percent of Britain's, and 85 percent of France's arms exports went to the Third World.

One result is that arms manufacturers in second-tier suppliers are much more dependent on exports for their survival. In France, the Dassault company, which produces the Mirage fighter planes, regularly exports more than 60 percent of its production. In 1977, 70 percent of British Aerospace's orders were for export. Dependence on successful export sales is so great that the French defence minister even instructed the military to "take export potential into account when choosing military equipment": a classic case of the tail wagging the dog![9]

Many critics crudely claim that second-tier suppliers are driven by purely economic motivations, and that this makes their arms-transfer policies somehow "immoral." It is true that second-tier suppliers are concerned more with the "economic" than with the "political" benefits of arms transfers (in fact, there is almost never a political quid pro quo attached to their sales), but behind this economic motivation lies a domestic political consideration: the maintenance of national-defence industries as a means to establish sovereign independence. For a country such as France or Britain to forswear arms exports would put drastic pressure on its defence establishment, and consequently on its foreign policy. At a time when the American commitment to Western Europe is less certain than ever, such a renunciation would force the European NATO states to become more dependent on American resources. As French president François Mitterrand put it (after reversing his position against French sales of "offensive" weapons to the Third World), "Since 1981, I have become aware of the reality of the French nation. We support our effort of national independence with a . . . defence establishment which must have the means [to carry out its missions]. . . . to have these means, we must have access to foreign markets."[10] Perhaps the only way to overcome this obstacle is through greater European political co-operation on defence matters, which could lead to production sharing among West European states. Already such a situation has occurred to some extent: Britain, Italy, and Germany jointly produce a fighter plane; Germany and France make surface-to-air missiles; Germany and Spain make helicopters. But any expansion of this co-operation does not come easily to states with a long history of mutual suspicion and traditions of jealously guarded national autonomy.

Second-tier suppliers tend to have a broader range of clients than do first-tier suppliers (although not necessarily more of them). States such as Saudi Arabia or Kuwait, which can afford to pay for their weapons, turn to the Europeans to avoid the political entanglements and pressures that come with a relationship with a first-tier supplier. Other states, such as Iraq or India, purchase weapons from both first- and second-tier suppliers (the Soviet Union and France) to demonstrate partial independence from political pressures. Clients that have been politically pressured through embargoes or other threats also tend to turn to second-tier suppliers to diversify their sources of arms. Finally, international "pariahs" or outcasts, such as Chile, Burma, and Zaire, buy mainly from second-tier suppliers.

There are two subclasses of second-tier states that should be mentioned here: the East European suppliers and the restrictive Western suppliers. The first category includes Poland, Czechoslovakia, and (to a lesser extent) Rumania. These states each have a history of arms production that predates their membership in the Soviet bloc after World War II. Since then, their arms production has been integrated into the larger needs of the Warsaw Pact, and they do not generally make arms sales without Soviet permission.[11] But the pressure to make sales often comes from the Poles or Czechs themselves who do not wish to let their factories lie idle if customers willing to pay hard currency are available. As well, the Soviets have found it useful to "cover their tracks" on occasion, supplying arms through their East European clients rather than directly. The most famous example was the 1955 arms-for-cotton deal between Egypt and Czechoslovakia, which marked the entry of the Soviet Union into Middle East politics.

The second subcategory, the restrictive suppliers, includes Canada, West Germany, Japan, Switzerland, and Sweden. Each of these suppliers, for various historical and political reasons (the World War II experience of Germany and Japan; the neutrality of Sweden and Switzerland; the general foreign-policy thrust of Canada), sells arms only under certain controlled conditions. West Germany, for example, refused until 1982 to sell weapons to "areas of tension"; Canada refuses to supply weapons to countries engaged in hostilities or with persistent human-rights violations.

But these restrictive suppliers are not immune from the pressure to export either. In each case, one can find dramatic, often illegal, violations of the restraint policy. Swedish and Swiss firms have been implicated in arms deals to Iran or Iraq during the recent war. West Germany has circumvented its own policy through its coproduction deals: a multibillion-dollar deal signed between Britain and Saudi Arabia for the jointly produced Tornado fighter-bomber would *not* have passed through Germany's export policy. And Canada supplies large amounts of weapons components to American firms; the final product often ends up in Third World conflicts. The restrictive suppliers, with the exception of Germany, have relatively small market shares. If they abandoned their restraint policies they could expand their arms exports, but this would most likely merely redistribute the shares within the second tier rather than result in any radical restructuring of the international arms market.

Third-Tier Suppliers

The most rapidly expanding suppliers have been those of the third tier: their share of the market has grown from 4 percent in 1963–66 to 11 percent in 1982–86. Such unlikely states as Singapore, Chile, South Korea, and Israel have joined newly industrializing states such as Brazil, Yugoslavia, Turkey, and China as significant, if small, arms suppliers. The main importance of third-tier suppliers lies not in the size of their arms exports, but in their potential to disrupt and complicate any attempts to restrict the arms trade.

The diverse third-tier states have different motives for exporting arms. Some third-tier suppliers deliberately pursue arms exports as part of an overall development strategy. Large developing states, such as Brazil, Turkey, and Yugoslavia, look at the 19th-century experience of Prussia, Russia, or Italy and deduce that a "modern" export-based arms industry can help to catalyze industrial development (as well as being a source of scarce hard currency). Government support for one significant industry (for example, armoured vehicles) produces demand for advanced metallurgy, sophisticated engineering, explosives development, motor vehicles, and so forth. All of these sectors of the economy produce valuable civilian goods (trucks, cars, mining technology, bridge-building expertise), and if an arms industry can stimulate these sectors to greater production and prevent a "brain drain" of skilled personnel, it would be a valuable economic asset indeed! This logic appears to be the driving force behind the rapid expansion of Brazil's arms industry, and it also spurred efforts in Egypt in the 1970s (in co-operation with the wealthy oil-producing states) to establish a large arms industry for the Arab states of the region.

In the case of international "pariah" states (Israel, Taiwan, South Africa), arms exports help offset the cost of the independent national arms industries that they have been forced to develop to cope with international embargoes or other supply restrictions. Finally, there are third-tier states who merely have small industrial enclaves producing one or two easily exportable items. Pakistan, Chile, and Argentina fit into this category. Here, the arms industry is supported for the limited political and economic benefits it brings, but it has no broader role to play.

None of the third-tier suppliers can produce top-of-the-line weapons systems in all major categories of weapons, but some of them come close in one or two areas. Israel, for example, spent several billion dollars (much of it in grants from the United States) to develop the Lavi, an indigenously designed and built fighter plane that would rival the best offered by Britain, France, or the United States. A prototype was built, but the cost per plane was so high that the project was finally cancelled in 1987, amid much controversy. This plane would almost certainly have had to be exported to bring its cost down to manageable levels, and even then it was not affordable. But that Israel, a state with only four million people and a relatively small high-tech industrial base, could even embark on such a venture illustrates the seriousness with which many states take such matters.[12]

For the most part, however, the weapons produced by third-tier suppliers are inexpensive, rugged, and unsophisticated. These are precisely the kinds of weapons needed by ill-trained armies operating under difficult conditions. This makes the weapons of third-tier suppliers increasingly attractive to Third World clients, and as many of these states start making more "appropriate" military purchases (avoiding sophisticated but useless "prestige" weapons) these suppliers will find a continued high demand for their wares.

The Recipients' Motives

It is less difficult to analyze the motives of the states that receive weapons. Although there are roughly five main motives that may predominate in any specific case, there is no real geographic or political pattern to the examples one finds.

The first and most "genuine" motive is the need for security and defence. States purchase arms to protect their citizens and way of life from possible aggression by other states. This is the public justification given for most arms purchases, and one cannot deny that it is valid in many cases. One of the sources of increased arms transfers since 1960 has been decolonization: newly independent states in Africa and Asia have had to assume responsibility for their own defence for the first time in more than a century. Although the ideal of no military forces is attractive to some states, most have found that a certain amount of money must be spent on national defence. The result has been a transformation of former small colonial "constabularies" or national police forces in states such as Kenya, Burma, or Togo into national armies, navies, and air forces.

This process had the inadvertent result of triggering many small arms races. Preparations that are intended to be defensive often appear to neighbours to have offensive purposes, and thus an action-reaction cycle of arms purchases can be triggered in the absence of any intention on either side to start a war. This inability to distinguish between offensive and defensive military preparation is called by analysts the "security dilemma": responsible leaders must assume the worst about possible opponents, but assuming the worst can create an arms race that leaves all parties poorer, and no more secure. An example of such a case was the Latin American race to acquire supersonic jet fighters in the 1960s mentioned above. Peru was the first state to acquire such planes; by 1975, Argentina, Brazil, Chile, and Venezuela had followed suit. No war broke out, none was intended, and all states were forced to spend more than they would have wanted on national defence.

The second motive for acquiring arms is to fight a war. Most acquisitions of arms in the Arab-Israeli conflict since 1955 have been governed by this motive. Egypt turned to the Soviet Union for arms in 1955 because the weapons (and the quantities) it wanted were being refused by the United States. Israel became almost totally dependent upon American weapons after the 1967 war. Later, when Egypt discovered that the Soviets were not willing to supply arms of the quantities or types needed to defeat Israel on the battlefield, it turned back to the United

States to achieve a diplomatic solution to its problems. More recently, Syria's massive stockpile of Soviet weapons was used in its confrontations with Israel in the 1982 Lebanon war.

The arms races triggered by this motive are the most costly and most dramatic. When a conflict can be anticipated, small differences in the quality and quantity of weapons on hand at the outset can make a great deal of difference in the outcome. Major Third World conflicts, at least until the Iran–Iraq war, did not tend to be long and drawn out: the 1967 Arab-Israeli war lasted six days; the 1973 war, less than three weeks. Because most of these states have no domestic arms industries to fall back on, and because suppliers can be reluctant to make massive deliveries during a war, most recipients anticipating a conflict attempt to build their weapons stockpiles as large as possible to avoid this crippling dependence.

The third motive for acquiring arms is to use them to maintain one's position of power against *internal* threats. These threats can come in the form of an ethnic or religious minority agitating for independence, political insurgents of the right or left, or simply political discontent with authoritarian and repressive rulers. Each of these internal threats can develop into civil war. The Sikhs in India, the Karens in Burma, and the Tamils in Sri Lanka are examples of the first threat. The contras in Nicaragua, the UNITA movement in Angola, and the "Sendero Luminoso" (Shining Path) in Peru are examples of the second. Uganda under Idi Amin, Chile under Pinochet, and Iran under the Shah are examples of the last type of internal threat. Supplying arms to states in this category is a tricky business, for seldom does a supplier want to be associated with television images of a government suppressing and killing its citizens. To support the central government, if it happens to be a close or reliable ally, requires that the reality of complex internal conflicts be simplified into a left-right battle against the forces of either "international communist expansionism" or "international imperialism."

The fourth motive for the acquisition of modern weapons is to use the military as a tool to "modernize" society. In many countries in Africa and Asia, the military is considered the only "modern" social and political institution that can provide a focus for the growth of national identity against a historical backdrop of interethnic, interreligious, or intertribal rivalry. In addition, it is an important vehicle for educating and training individuals in technical skills that can be used outside the military. Finally, it socializes its members to a "modern" worldview with hierarchical, ordered, and punctual relationships that are based on efficiency and merit, not background and family ties.

This, at least, is the theory.[13] In practice, such arguments were (and are) used to justify military rule in Third World states on the grounds that civilian politicians and bureaucrats do not have the power to transcend their tribal, ethnic, or religious loyalties. Nigeria is the best example of military rule under such conditions. Naturally, if the military is to govern a country on the road to modernization, it must itself possess "modern" weapons and training. Large purchases of advanced weapons can follow from this logic.

The final general category of motives is simply "prestige." States that wish to assume a higher profile on the world stage often assume that military prowess is the ticket to a better role. If one can fly a squadron of advanced fighter planes over the capital on independence day, this is, much like a national airline and national palace, a sign of power. Thus, states such as Libya, Saudi Arabia, and Venezuela find themselves with sophisticated arsenals that either cannot be maintained or operated (because of a lack of trained pilots and maintenance people) or are more sophisticated than can be justified by any obvious military threats. Civilian politicians who govern under the shadow of the military are also often forced to "buy" the loyalty of the military with modern weapons.

One can guess what happens when these motives are mingled. One state may purchase weapons for reasons of prestige or to suppress internal dissent, yet its neighbours inevitably interpret this act, because of the security dilemma, as a possible threat. An expensive and unnecessary arms race may be triggered, and the result might even be an armed conflict. It is difficult to see how this downward action-reaction spiral can be stopped.

The Evolution of the International Arms-Transfer System

The picture painted above gives a static "snapshot" of the international arms market. Unfortunately, it might leave one with a misleading image of a declining role for first-tier suppliers at the expense of second-tier and third-tier suppliers. It might also leave the impression that arms transfers are a purely modern phenomenon, the result of forces at work in the post-1945 world. These misperceptions need to be corrected with a better historical perspective.

The first recorded arms transfers go back to the early modern period, in the 14th and 15th centuries. Before that, individual soldiers were responsible for supplying their own weapons, and the production of swords and armour varied little across the known world. But with the invention of cannon and gunpowder, technological "gaps" appeared, and states that had mastered new technologies (and the political and social organization that went with them) were able to gain ascendancy over their rivals. They also possessed a scarce "good" (technological know-how) that created an international market, in much the same way as other markets for scarce goods were established. In Europe, the Italian city-states were eclipsed: they did not have the money, the human resources, or the territorial base needed to mount a strong defence (or offence). The initiative shifted to England, the Low Countries (the Netherlands and Belgium), and the Germanic states. Weapons were traded between these states and other lesser powers, often to seal treaties or military alliances. Other states, such as France, Sweden, and Spain, tried to create a large-scale arms industry by importing skilled craftsmen. Even farther out, on the fringes, the Ottoman Empire struggled to copy European technology. Thus, one already finds our three tiers of arms production.

The same pattern manifested itself in the Industrial Revolution, when the "three-tiered" structure of the arms market made itself clearer. Britain, France, and Germany were the three industrial giants of the 19th century, the largest arms exporters, and the main players in European politics. Russia and Japan were in the second tier, struggling to build an advanced military and industrial base and participating in the imperial battles. States such as Italy, Spain, and Austria-Hungary made up the third tier. They were lesser players in both the arms market and the international politics of the day, and they tended to see an arms industry as a catalyst for industrial development.[14]

One interesting development during the Industrial Revolution was the concentration of arms production in the hands of "private" firms that sold to all customers with little regard for their political complexion. This "free market" was a departure from previous practice in which governments closely supervised all aspects of arms production, exports, and imports. But the free market did not long survive the intensification of political rivalries in the last half of the 1900s. The giant German firm Krupp was forced to choose between good relations with its government (and many contracts) and its main customer, Russia. British firms were forced to cancel some sales of their most advanced products. And French arms sales to allies in central Europe were backed by loans raised on the Paris stock exchange with the support of the government.

Thus, arms sales became again a reflection of prevailing patterns of international politics and an index of great-power status. World War I, which marked the culmination of the great-power rivalry in so many spheres, was to speed up this reversion. After the war, the shocked and battered publics sought some understanding of the "causes" of the seemingly senseless carnage, and their attention focussed quickly on the role of the private international arms dealers: the "merchants of death." This search for scapegoats turned into a witch hunt, with a Senate investigation in the United States and a royal commission in Britain. This excerpt from a popular magazine gives a flavour of public sentiment of the time:

> In 1899 British soldiers were shot down by British guns that British armaments firms had sold to the Boers . . . in 1914 . . . German soldiers were killed by German guns manned by the armies of King Albert and Czar Nicholas II . . . Bulgarian troops turned French 75s on French *poilus* [and] . . . China has been pleased to use excellent Japanese guns for the purpose of killing excellent Japanese soldiers . . . detail upon detail, incident upon incident, illustrate how well the armament makers apply the two axioms of their business: when there are wars, prolong them; when there is peace, disturb it.[15]

As with all conspiracy theories, this one confused cause with effect and concealed more than it revealed. The arms trade was indeed prominent in the international politics leading up to the war, but it merely *reflected* the power of states and their pattern of alliances; it did not create these realities.

When one looks at current developments in the arms market, it is tempting to speculate that the United States and Soviet Union will continue to lose their share of the market to second- and third-tier states. But the history of the last century tells us this is unlikely. The absence of a clear second and third tier in the first few decades after 1945 was an aberration, a product of the wartime collapse of the traditional second tier, the rapid American and Soviet rise to superpower status, and the underdeveloped (and colonized) state of much of the rest of the globe. The evolution of the last three decades reflects the re-establishment of a "normal" pattern, rather than a dramatic change in the nature of the arms market.

Underlying the three tiers is the persistent reality of "technological power" that causes the arms market to have its particular structure and plays a major subterranean role in long-term change in international politics. Looking at who sells what to whom in the arms business is a good way to gain a glimpse of this "technological power," as military innovation is a surface manifestation of it. First-tier states, today the United States and Soviet Union, are the locus of military technological innovation, whether it be nuclear weapons, Stealth bombers, cruise missiles, or computer guidance systems. Second-tier states have much of the same innovative ability, but neither the money nor the human resources to stay at the forefront in all sectors. Third-tier states struggle merely to keep up with older developments and are never innovators by themselves.

But the pace of technological innovation is not constant throughout history. When it slows, lesser states have an opportunity to "catch up": they can reap the benefits of the leaders' mistakes and new technologies tend to become cheaper with time (the development of the personal computer being an excellent example). During this period, technology is "diffused" from advanced to lesser states. If technological change were to stop altogether, then over time all that would be important to determine the relative power of states would be their population and resource base.

In the arms industry, the mechanism for diffusion is the coproduction or licensed production contract. Instead of delivering finished weapons, a supplier agrees to build certain components in the buyer's country, or even to sell simply the weapon blueprints and the help of a few technicians. In this way, a client can move up the various stages of the "ladder of production," which occur roughly as follows:

1. assembly of arms;
2. licensed production of components;
3. production of complete systems under licence;
4. reverse engineering or indigenous modification of foreign designs;
5. indigenous design and production.[16]

This was certainly the pattern of the 19th and early 20th centuries, and in today's arms trade one sees a similar development. The number of licensed production and coproduction deals between advanced and developing states has increased steadily, from 18 in the 1959–67 period to 52 in the 1977–84 period.[17] But even with this help the client never catches up completely, for the frontier of advanced technology moves ever away. Whether or not the pace of technological change will continue to be rapid is, however, impossible to predict.

Arms Transfers and Influence

The important role played by arms transfers as a tool of influence for first-tier suppliers has already been mentioned. In addition to economic and military benefits, arms transfers have been justified as providing suppliers with a wide range of political influence over clients' foreign-policy behaviour. But one must ask precisely what kind of influence can be "purchased" with arms-transfer relationships and how useful they are as a foreign-policy tool. A simplified list of the possible benefits that have been claimed by decision makers is as follows:

1. to support diplomatic efforts to resolve regional conflicts by maintaining local balances and enhancing access and influence vis-à-vis the parties;
2. to influence the political orientation of nations that control strategic resources;
3. to help maintain regional balances to avert war or political shifts;
4. to enhance the quality and interoperability of the defence capabilities of major allies;
5. to promote self-sufficiency in deterrence and defence;
6. to strengthen the internal security and stability of recipients;
7. to limit the influence of the other superpower and maintain the balance of conventional arms;
8. to enhance access to and influence over government and military elites;
9. to provide leverage and influence over individual governments on specific issues of immediate concern.[18]

From this tangle of justifications, one can unravel three different kinds of influence that suppliers exercise. The first can be called "bargaining power": gaining direct leverage, through the use of threats of punishment and/or promises of rewards, on specific foreign-policy issues of importance to the patron. These threats and promises can include: approval for a specific badly needed item, a reduction of the amount of arms given as "grant aid" or on concessionary terms, a slowing down of the approval process, a cutting off of supplies of spare parts, or an increased overall flow of arms. In each case, the change in the arms-transfer "pipeline" would be tied to a specific policy goal sought by the arms supplier. Bargaining power corresponds to item 9 on the list of influence benefits.

Examples of attempted exercises of bargaining power are numerous. The most prominent ones are associated with the Arab-Israeli conflict, where both superpowers have attempted at various times to force their clients to take specific steps to end the conflict. During the 1973 war, when Israel was in dire need of an arms airlift, Henry Kissinger (the American secretary of state) used this dependency to win eventual Israeli agreement to a ceasefire. The Soviet Union employed the same arm-twisting tactics with its clients Syria and Egypt.[19] After the war, Kissinger used a complex combination of threats and promises to bring Israel to sign limited agreements (the Sinai I, Golan Heights, and Sinai II agreements) that brought the conflict to a close.[20] In each case, movement can be connected, at least loosely, to American manipulation of the arms-transfer relationship.

The second type of influence can be called "structural power," and it encompasses items 1, 3, and 4 on the list. It is more subtle and difficult to find, as it does not manifest itself in direct threats and promises. Rather, a patron exercising structural power changes the range of policy options facing the client to make certain ones more or less attractive (or even out of the question), without any direct confrontation with the client. The best example of this was the behaviour of the Soviet Union toward Egypt between 1955 and 1970. Arms shipments were carefully calibrated to avoid giving Egypt the ability to defeat Israel militarily. Repeated Egyptian requests (especially after the 1967 defeat) for certain types of weapons, such as long-range bombers or surface-to-surface missiles that could strike Israeli cities, were always refused. There were, of course, other reasons why Egypt and the other Arab states failed to defeat Israel, but if one imagines what might have happened had the Arab states been able to obtain the quantity and types of arms they desired, Soviet restraint becomes clear.

The United States has similar (but declining) influence over certain of its clients. In the case of Saudi Arabia, until recent massive Saudi purchases of British fighter planes, the Saudi air force was completely dependent upon American technicians and parts to keep its sophisticated planes flying. The bulk of the Saudi air force could operate for only a few days without American help, thus severely limiting the use to which the Saudis could put it (especially in offensive strikes against Israel). Even so, the pro-Israel lobby in the United States opposed further American sales to Saudi Arabia to the point that the Saudis turned elsewhere for arms.

The third kind of influence can be called "penetrative power," and it describes a supplier's attempts to alter the client's definition of its military or political interests by affecting its internal political process: items 2, 6, and 8 on the list. In other words, the supplier attempts to make the client's "worldview" conform to its own. Examples of this would be American attempts in the 1980s to unite its Middle Eastern clients (Israel, Saudi Arabia, Jordan, Egypt) in a "strategic consensus" against "international communism," or Soviet attempts to radicalize the leadership of African states such as Somalia, Ethiopia, Angola, and Mozambique. In neither case did the attempt wholly succeed in suppressing regional or internal conflicts: Israel and Saudi Arabia do not perceive international communism as the main threat; Somalia and Ethiopia were more interested in fighting each other than in joining as fraternal socialist partners.

The most obvious way to exercise penetrative power is to support a rebel movement that overthrows an established government and changes the state's foreign-policy orientation. This is more or less what happened in Ethiopia and Angola. Alternatively, one can supply arms (and other support) to a friendly government to keep it from losing power. The best recent examples of this are Soviet support for the communist government in Afghanistan (which went far beyond arms transfers) and, perhaps, American aid to the government in El Salvador. A more subtle means of exercising penetrative power is to "socialize" the views of the leadership elite (often the military) through military training programs in which foreign officers are trained in the United States or Soviet Union. In all cases, the exercise of power is not directed toward specific goals, but is intended to "point" the client in the correct direction, in the hope that specific outcomes follow.

The three types of influence can be summarized this way: bargaining power tries to persuade a "rational" client to select a specific policy option through threats or promises; structural power attempts to affect the options themselves, removing or adding to the list; and penetrative power operates "inside" the client, by altering the client's perception of its interests with no reference to specific policy choices. Unfortunately, most descriptions of how power is exercised between states ignore both structural and penetrative power and treat both the overall "structure" of the situation and the client's definition of its interests as something *outside* the exercise of power. But both are possible influence targets for an arms supplier as the list of benefits given above demonstrates.

The United States and Soviet Union have at different times pursued all three types of influence. Of course, arms transfers are not the only influence tool used by the superpowers: foreign aid, economic tools, diplomacy, and traditional military instruments are all available. But, in the modern world, where the direct use of force is usually condemned and where economic tools are costly and difficult to manipulate, arms transfers stand out as a means of influence often used by the superpowers.

The effectiveness of a particular exercise of one of the three types of power outlined depends on a range of factors too broad to be easily analyzed. But many of them come to mind immediately:

- a rich client can easily turn to other suppliers;
- an industrialized client can build a domestic arms industry;
- a resourceful client can scrounge in the world markets for spare parts and weapons;
- a politically stable client can resist attempts to affect its policy-making process;
- a politically sophisticated client can detect in what ways its military options are being limited and take steps to surmount these limits.

It is obvious that evaluating what kind of influence has been exercised, and how effective it has been, is a difficult task for analysts that requires far more than the simple collection of data on weapons flows.

The Control of Arms Transfers

Against this backdrop, it is not surprising that efforts to control the international arms trade have had limited success, whether they have been unilateral, limited multilateral, or international. The first real international efforts (other than arrangements between one or two states to restrict the flow of arms to a third) took place after World War I and were a direct result of the search for a cause to that war. The Covenant of the League of Nations, which emerged from the Versailles Peace Conference, began the process by stating that "the manufacture by private enterprise of munitions and implements of war is open to grave objections."[21] Further negotiations toward prohibiting arms exports, save in exceptional cases (and with public licences), continued throughout the early 1920s. All that emerged from these efforts, however, was a League of Nations voluntary register of arms exports and a series of disarmament conferences that had no impact on the slide into World War II.

The reasons for this failure strike a chord today: those states that could not produce their own weapons saw restrictions on the arms trade as an unfair means of intervention, and they argued that publishing statistics on the arms trade *without* publishing details of individual national defence efforts was discriminatory. In addition, many suppliers saw political advantage to supplying arms to friends and allies. Finally, in the absence of absolute unanimity on restricting arms exports, suppliers resorted to the argument that if they did not sell the arms, someone else would.

Post-1945 efforts at controlling the arms trade have been much less ambitious. Various proposals have been made in the United Nations for a comprehensive register of international arms transactions. This would be a means to bring the spotlight to bear on the activities of free-spending governments and, through the pressure of domestic and international public opinion, would perhaps put a brake on spending. Proponents of a register see it operating much as Amnesty International does in the human-rights sphere. But the most serious obstacle to such a register is that disclosure would have to be voluntary, unless the United Nations set up a special information-gathering unit. The record of voluntary disclosure on military matters is dismal: only 20 states now comply with a voluntary U.N. register of military expenditures (Canada being one of them). Furthermore, an information-gathering unit would be politically too sensitive for the United Nations and would duplicate the efforts of the International Institute for Strategic Studies, the Stockholm International Peace Research Institute, and other such nonpartisan bodies.

In the limited multilateral arena, the most important effort has been the Conventional Arms Transfer (CAT) Talks between the Soviet Union and the United States that were started by President Carter. The initial impetus for talks was the sense in the United States that its own arms sales had gone out of control in the last years of the Nixon–Ford presidency. As one official put it, "Henry [Kissinger] used to hand out weapons like hostess gifts. We would think we had sales to Country X sealed off and then Henry would come back from some trip and tell us he had just agreed to supply another billion or so in arms to them."[22] The Shah of Iran, for example, was given a blank cheque to purchase *any* non-nuclear weapons in the American arsenal. Uncontrolled sales meant that even American political interests were being compromised, so unilateral reductions in transfers were part of the Carter plan.

But even with this self-interested motivation, the CAT Talks quickly stalled. The Soviets were willing to talk, but it is not clear they would have agreed to any major restraints. The British and French refused to participate in the talks until after an American-Soviet deal had been worked out, and it is doubtful that they would have agreed to any deal that required them to reduce their arms exports (although both the French Socialist and the British Labour parties have voiced opposition to their countries' participation in the arms trade). The real stumbling block, however, was the American internal political process. As long as only general global reductions were being discussed, special interests were not hurt; as soon as specific regional restrictions (such as in Latin America or the Middle East) came on the agenda, the American consensus collapsed.

Over the long term, one need not be as pessimistic as history would suggest. All arms-control efforts are part of a complex process that requires much "learning" by all participants before they can be successful, and previous failures have taught some important lessons. The main focus of attention in the future will not be on large-scale reductions of transfers, but on such limited issues as restrictions on the export of technology that can be used for nuclear weapons (such as advanced surface-to-surface missiles) or arrangements covering specific geographic areas that are agreed to by both suppliers and recipients (such as an informal deal in the Middle East or the Persian Gulf).

Conclusion

Predicting the future pattern of the international arms trade is an impossible business, but history and recent experience give us some guidance. The massive expansion in arms transfers that occurred between 1960 and 1980 has already slowed significantly, and one should not expect much of an increase in the near future. Major protracted wars (such as the Iran–Iraq war) do boost significantly the demand for arms (Iran and Iraq alone accounted for *18 percent* of overall arms sales at the height of the conflict), but the main reasons for the growth in worldwide arsenals, the new independence of states in Africa and Asia and the sudden wealth accruing to oil-rich states, no longer play a role in driving demand. In addition, the crushing debt burden of many Third World states makes huge purchases on easy credit less likely.

For the suppliers, this slower growth means increasingly cutthroat competition for business. The competition between the first and second tiers, and between the second and third tiers, will inevitably push some states out of the business. It will be especially hard on second-tier suppliers, such as France or Britain, that are trying to preserve an independent high-technology domestic defence industry in all sectors. Third-tier states will continue to nibble away at the fringes of the market, and their presence makes it increasingly difficult to implement any comprehensive embargoes. During the recent Iran–Iraq war, for example, Iran was able to remain well supplied with arms, despite a near-total embargo by major Eastern and Western arms suppliers.

The United States and Soviet Union are somewhat immune from this pressure, but they will suffer in other ways. Their ability to use the promise of weapons (or threats of embargoes) as a tool of influence works best in an "oligopolistic" market with few competing suppliers. As the technology of weapons manufacture continues to spread, more and more states are able to nullify the political advantage either superpower can seek from its arms-transfer relationships. This must be seen as part and parcel of the overall diffusion of power in the modern international system.

Whatever the specifics of the market, one can be certain that arms will continue to be controversial items of trade, totally unlike copper and bananas. In an international "self-help" system, where each state must fend for itself and where conflicts appear inevitable, weapons are an essential ingredient in any state's policy for survival. Those states that cannot produce their own weapons must purchase them, becoming, in the process, entangled in a web of dependence and interdependence that has enormous implications for foreign policy and international diplomacy.

NOTES

1. First statement: Andrew Pierre, "Arms Sales: The New Diplomacy," *Foreign Affairs* 60 (Winter 1981–82): 267; second statement: unidentified White House official quoted in "Divisions in Diplomacy," *Time*, March 1, 1982.

2. I use the more general term "arms transfers" because it includes not only weapons that are sold, but those that are given as gifts or grants.

3. All statistics, unless otherwise noted, are derived from various issues of the U.S. Arms Control and Disarmament Agency, *World Military Expenditures and Arms Transfers*, published annually since the late 1960s.

4. Quoted in Bruce Arlinghaus, *Arms for Africa* (Toronto: Lexington Books, 1983), 6.

5. Quoted in Anthony Sampson, *The Arms Bazaar* (London: Hodder and Stoughton, 1977), 253.

6. *Constant* or *real* dollars subtract the effect of inflation; *current* dollars are the actual dollars spent in a given year before eliminating the effects of inflation. Only an increase in constant or real spending is significant.

7. *Aviation Week and Space Technology*, February 9, 1987.

8. For the full story on the Latin American embargo, see John Stanley and Maurice Pearton, *The International Trade in Arms* (London: Chatto and Windus, 1972), chap. 11.

9. This was contained in a 1969 directive from France's defence minister Michel Debré to the military. Stockholm International Peace Research Institute, *The Arms Trade with the Third World* (Stockholm: Almqvist and Wiksell, 1971), 257.

10. Mark Rubin, "French Arms and the Third World," in *East-West Rivalry in the Third World*, ed. Robert Clawsen (Wilmington: Scholarly Resources Inc., 1986), 176, quoting President Mitterrand from *Le Monde*, October 2–3, 1983.

11. There are some interesting exceptions to this. During the Iran–Iraq war, the Rumanians supplied Egypt with T-55 tanks, which found their way to Iraq at a time when Iraq was being embargoed by the Soviets. The Soviets managed to stop this after roughly 50 out of 200 tanks had made their way to Egypt. Stockholm International Peace Research Institute, *World Armaments and Disarmament Yearbook,· 1985* (London: Oxford University Press, 1986), 400.

12. For the controversial Lavi procurement, see Galen Perras, "Israel and the Lavi Fighter-Aircraft: The Lion Falls to Earth," in *The Defence Industrial Base and the West*, ed. David G. Haglund (London: Routledge, 1989), 170–209.

13. For a discussion of the "military as modernizer" theory, see Samuel Huntington, *Political Order in Changing Societies* (New Haven: Yale University Press, 1968).

14. The odd state out is Austria-Hungary, which was a major political player but nevertheless in the throes of a long decline.

15. "Arms and Men," *Fortune* 9 (March 1934): 52, 120.

16. Andrew Ross, *Arms Production in Developing Countries: The Continuing Proliferation of Conventional Weapons* (Santa Monica: Rand Corporation, 1981), N-1615-AF: 4–5.

17. From Michael Brzoska and Thomas Ohlson, *Arms Production in the Third World* (London: Taylor and Francis, 1986), 306–49.

18. This is a paraphrase of the list presented by secretary of state Cyrus Vance in his "Report to Congress on Arms Transfer Policy," June 30, 1977, summarized in Paul Hammond et al., *The Reluctant Supplier: U.S. Decision Making for Arms Sales* (Cambridge, Mass.: Oelgeschlager, Gunn and Hain, 1983), 32–33.

19. To win Syria's acceptance the Soviet ambassador even turned around ships sailing toward Syria and threatened to send Soviet technicians home.

20. Among the many sources of information on this war the most accessible is William Quandt, *Decade of Decisions* (Los Angeles: University of California Press, 1977).

21. Article 8, paragraph 5, of the League of Nations Covenant.

22. Jo Husbands, "How the United States Makes Foreign Military Sales," in *Arms Transfers in the Modern World*, ed. Stephanie Neuman and Robert Harkavy (New York: Praeger, 1980), 171.

SELECT BIBLIOGRAPHY

Brzoska, Michael, and Thomas Ohlson. *Arms Transfers to the Third World, 1971–1985*. Oxford: Oxford University Press, 1987.

Hammond, Paul; David Luscher; Michael Salomone; and Norman Graham, eds. *The Reluctant Supplier*. Cambridge, Mass.: Oelgeschlager, Gunn and Hain, 1983.

Katz, James, ed. *Arms Production in Developing Countries*. Lexington: D.C. Heath, 1984.
Klare, Michael. *The American Arms Supermarket*. Austin: University of Texas Press, 1984.
Kolodziej, Edward. "France and the Arms Trade." *International Affairs* (London) 56 (January 1980): 54–72.
———. *The Making and Marketing of Arms: The French Experience*. Princeton: Princeton University Press, 1987.
Kramer, Mark. "Soviet Arms Transfers to the Third World." *Problems of Communism* 36 (September–October 1987): 52–68.
Menon, Rajan. "The Soviet Union, the Arms Trade, and the Third World." *Soviet Studies* 24 (July 1982): 377–96.
Neuman, Stephanie. "Arms, Aid and the Superpowers." *Foreign Affairs* 66 (Summer 1988): 1044–66.
———. "International Stratification and Third World Military Industries." *International Organization* 38 (Winter 1984): 167–97.
Neuman, Stephanie, and Robert Harkavy, eds. *Arms Transfers in the Modern World*. New York: Praeger, 1980.
Pierre, Andrew. "Arms Sales: The New Diplomacy." *Foreign Affairs* 60 (Winter 1981–82): 266–304.
———. *Arms Transfers and American Foreign Policy*. New York: New York University Press, 1979.
———. *The Global Politics of Arms Sales*. Princeton: Princeton University Press, 1981.
Stanley, John, and Maurice Pearton. *The International Trade in Arms*. London: Chatto and Windus, 1972.
Stockholm International Peace Research Institute. *The Arms Trade with the Third World*. Stockholm: Almqvist and Wiksell, 1971.
———. *World Armaments and Disarmament Yearbook*. London: Oxford University Press, annual.

PART II

THE POLITICS OF INTERDEPENDENCE

Following from the pioneering work of Robert Keohane and Joseph Nye, Jr., in the early 1970s, there has been a great deal of concern among both students and practitioners of world politics over the vagaries of economic interdependence. The interdependence theme challenges the three key realist assumptions: that states are unitary actors; that force is always a usable and effective instrument of foreign policy; and that the global policy agenda is dominated by security concerns. Students of interdependence tend to focus on international economic relations and regularized patterns of co-operative behaviour. The advent of détente in the late 1960s and the more recent relaxation of East-West tensions, largely as a result of Gorbachev's glasnost initiative, have lent a great deal of credibility to the interdependence argument and, consequently, economic, cultural, and environmental security have become much more pressing concerns.

While all of the chapters in Part II are concerned with both the foreign economic activity of individual states and the changes in the structure of the international political economy, each approaches the problem from a slightly different perspective. Michael Hawes systematically examines the nature and structure of the postwar world economy, arguing that the main challenge to the Bretton Woods system has to do with declining American influence and with fundamental structural uncertainty. Charles Pentland offers an intellectual history of interdependence, tracing international relations scholarship from the concern over integration to more recent work on international organizations and international regimes. Hawes's second chapter offers a framework for systematically addressing the impact of structural change at the level of the international system on the direction and content of national foreign economic policy. David Leyton Brown examines the various approaches used to understand the multinational enterprise. Margaret Doxey takes the behaviour of individual states one step farther in her assessment of the prominence and utility of international sanctions. Maureen Molot examines the debate over how best to enhance national welfare in the context of increasingly internationalized capital and production. Jock Finlayson notes that trade is an increasingly important issue for political scientists as it provides much insight into the nature and the extent of the trend toward global interdependence.

ASSESSING THE WORLD ECONOMY: THE RISE AND FALL OF BRETTON WOODS

Michael K. Hawes

This chapter sets out to review the nature of the Bretton Woods system and to examine recent structural changes in the world economy. The extent and character of these changes, which, we will argue, have resulted in the collapse of the particular system of trade and payments that emerged in the immediate postwar period (commonly known as the Bretton Woods system), are central to our understanding of contemporary international relations. In particular, two assumptions are critical to the thesis of this chapter. First, the fundamental structural changes that took place in the world economy during the 1970s have intensified in the 1980s to the point where (while institutional arrangements remain broadly intact) order is increasingly threatened by structural uncertainty. Moreover, it is quite clear now that these changes cannot be explained in strictly cyclical terms.[1] Second, any explanation of national trade policy has to be understood within the context of a significant global struggle for productive advantage, markets, and employment.[2]

The specific structural changes that we will discuss in this chapter must also be understood in terms of the broader social, economic, and political forces that have emerged during the past two decades. These forces include not only the practical changes that result from modernization (i.e., the technological and economic changes) but the social and ideological responses to these changes. They include, *inter alia*: the diminution of economic growth in the developed market economies (DMEs); the increasing economic conflict among and between those economies; the absolute growth in the number of sovereign states in the system; shifts in competitive forces, including the levelling out of economic advantage in the West and the emergence of the so-called newly industrializing economies (NIEs); the introduction and proliferation of new technologies; the mounting antipathy toward and distrust of "big government"; the unravelling of the postwar consensus on the validity and utility of international organizations; and the fiscal crisis of the modern welfare state.[3]

This chapter is divided into five sections. It begins by examining the Bretton Woods system itself, focussing on the structural realities of the world economy in its halcyon days between 1945 and 1968. It proceeds then to a discussion of the collapse of the Bretton Woods system, declining U.S. hegemony, and the fragmentation and disorder that characterized the 1970s. In the subsequent sections it addresses two of the most critical structural changes — the changing international division of labour and the growth of protectionism. In particular, it focusses on the resistance to structural change in the developed market economies (DMEs). It then moves on to an analysis of the world economy in the 1980s and to a discussion of the pervasive structural uncertainty that has come to characterize the 1980s.

The Bretton Woods System, 1945–1968

In the two decades following World War II, the world economy was both prosperous and stable. Western governments arranged a set of rules and institutions at Bretton Woods, New Hampshire, in July 1944 that effectively regulated the global economy, controlled conflict, and encouraged growth. It was a period characterized by stable exchange rates, under the auspices of the International Monetary Fund (IMF), increasing trade liberalization through the General Agreement on Tariffs and Trade (GATT), and political stability courtesy of American leadership and the United Nations system. Overall, growth in the world economy averaged a healthy 5 percent per annum, while world trade grew at roughly 7 percent per year. The system functioned quite well so long as economic power remained concentrated in a small number of states and the United States remained willing and able to maintain its leadership role.

The logic of the Bretton Woods system was simple and elegant. International organizations would harmonize trade and monetary relations — thereby avoiding the economic autarchy that was blamed for the great depression in the 1930s. These same organizations would be in a position to avoid the problems arising out of reparations payments. And, finally, the agreement allowed the United States the upper hand in these organizations in exchange for reconstruction funding, technological development, and military support. The articles of agreement at Bretton Woods set out a system of fixed exchange rates, where the IMF would act as a central banker (i.e., maintaining fixed rates and controlling liquidity). The International Bank for Reconstruction and Development (IBRD) was to provide a systemic source of equilibrium through aid and development funding. The United Nations was established one year later in San Francisco, and the General Agreement on Tariffs and Trade, which replaced the ill-fated International Trade Organization, came into being in 1947.

According to Michael Hudson, the Bretton Woods system was a compromise that met almost everyone's needs — at least everyone in the developed market economies.

> Both Europe and America looked forward to a cosmopolitan One Worldism that seemed to dovetail neatly into U.S. economic objectives while providing substantial inducements to Europe in the form of foreign aid, U.S. military support, and a reciprocal demand for exports. However, the textbook principles underlying the postwar

> economic order rested on the simplistic hope that the economic and political self-interests of nations might easily complement each other without much sacrifice of any single nation's economic potential or established interests. Prosperity for all would be promoted through a harmonious specialization of world labour and production, with the gains shared equitably among nations.[4]

Indeed, not only did the Bretton Woods system presume that economic conflict could be avoided, it assumed that the major actors and their goals would remain the same. Moreover, it assumed that the United States would always be willing and able to provide leadership.

There were three essential features of the Bretton Woods system: the monetary regime, the trade regime, and U.S. leadership. And, while trade and the character of the system are the main focus of this chapter, it is important to remember that the Bretton Woods system was essentially a framework for monetary order.[5] In simple terms, it involved an institutional interconnection between the IMF and the IBRD to guarantee international liquidity (financing) and adjustment (loans) in a regime or system, characterized by easy convertibility and stable exchange rates. It presumed that global monetary solutions should be dealt with at the systemic level. At the time, the war-torn European economies were in no position to pursue either national or market solutions.

Until 1960, the United States was able to maintain full control over the international monetary system. International liquidity was maintained by a constant infusion of U.S. dollars, while adjustment was achieved through the Marshall Plan. However, by 1960, the United States found itself with a serious balance-of-payments deficit, a shortage of reserve currency, and dwindling gold reserves. As a consequence, the period between 1960 and 1968 witnessed the beginnings of group management. The IMF, the Organization for Economic Cooperation and Development (OECD), and the "group of 10" (finance ministers from the 10 key DMEs) played a much larger role in the late 1960s and the 1970s. By the end of the decade, as the following analysis suggests, the global monetary regime had unravelled completely.

The trade side of the postwar economic order was largely designed to avoid the protectionism and beggar-thy-neighbour policies of the 1930s. There was, however, much less agreement on the question of an appropriate institutional framework when it came to trade. The United States was strongly in favour of a direct trade equivalent to the IMF. In 1945 the U.S. secretary of state introduced a set of rules for tariffs, preferences, quantitative restrictions, and subsidies, and provided for the establishment of the International Trade Organization (ITO). The Truman administration was not able to sell the idea either at home or abroad. After complex negotiations with the Europeans (especially the British), the Havana Charter was drafted in 1947. However, the U.S. Congress was so viscerally opposed to the charter that the Truman administration never introduced it.

The Havana Charter was effectively replaced by a "temporary" treaty that was set up to expedite tariff reductions while the Havana Charter was being ratified. This treaty, known as the General Agreement on Tariffs and Trade, became the statement of international consensus on trade by default. The United States had significant surplus capacity and was anxious to underwrite domestic employment and economic growth through an open international trade regime. This regime was easily accomplished with Europe through the European recovery program. The arrangement with Japan was somewhat more complex. The United States went to great lengths to assure most-favoured-nation status for Japan, eventually succeeding in convincing its European allies that Japan should become a contracting party to the GATT. However, even after Japan formally entered the GATT in 1955, many of the contracting parties invoked Article 35, thereby denying Japan nondiscriminatory status. In response, the U.S. market simply absorbed a larger share of Japanese exports, leading, in this instance, by example. The United States was determined to keep Japan in the American-led global capitalist system (and was ultimately successful in doing so). Ironically, it was Japan that would come to pose the greatest challenge to U.S. economic pre-eminence.

The trade regime, characterized by successive rounds of the GATT and tariff liberalization, worked relatively well until the late 1960s. Unlike that of the monetary regime, the overall framework governing trade relations has not altered substantially. However, the GATT has been relatively ineffective in the 1970s and 1980s, the main successes occurring on tariffs while the main impediments are increasingly associated with nontariff issues and trade in services

The final dominant feature of the Bretton Woods system has to do with leadership. More specifically it has to do with U.S. hegemony during the period in question. In the postwar period, the United States was the most powerful country on the face of the globe, both militarily and economically. The height of this hegemonic leadership was realized during what Robert O. Keohane has called the "long decade of the 1950s" — beginning with the Truman Doctrine and the Marshall Plan in 1947 and concluding with the Interest Equalization Tax, the test ban treaty, and the assassination of President Kennedy in 1963.[6] During this period, the United States orchestrated the reconstruction and growth of an open capitalist world economy around the Bretton Woods agreement and in the context of the cold war. In Keohane's words,

> it is hardly any wonder that American students of international political economy often seem to view the 1950s with nostalgia. In those years, it is argued, foreign economic policy was harnessed to responsible leadership rather than to the search for petty and often ephemeral gains at the expense of one's allies and trading partners. During the "long decade" the United States used its own vast political and economic resources to construct the basis for a strategy of "hegemonic leadership" — in which the United States provided benefits for its allies but also imposed constraints upon them.[7]

Hegemony can be defined in both economic and political terms. "An economically hegemonic power can better be defined as one with a comparative advantage in goods with high value added, yielding relatively high wages and profits," whereas a politically hegemonic power can be defined as "one that is powerful enough to maintain the essential rules governing interstate relations, and [is] willing to do so."[8] However, as suggested elsewhere in this volume, these are necessary but not sufficient conditions for hegemonic stability. A truly hegemonic system must include some notion of ideological consensus.[9] In short, the United States pursued a hegemonic leadership strategy between 1945 and 1968 that created and sustained a stable, prosperous, and open world economy.[10] During this period, the United States had both the authority and the desire to control the international economic regimes that were established at Bretton Woods, while their Western partners saw no reason to challenge such a system.

For our purposes, one of the most important features of the Bretton Woods system was the dramatic growth in world trade. Through the GATT process, the advanced industrial countries managed to systematically reduce the tariffs and quotas that impeded trade between them. In contrast to the 1913–48 period, in which trade grew at an average of less than 0.5 percent per year, world trade jumped to an average 7 percent per year in the 1948–73 period. In the two successive periods, world trade declined once again — dropping to 3.5 percent in the 1973–81 period and 3.5 percent in the 1982–88 period. The global recession of 1981–82 tends to distort the most recent figures. World trade actually contracted by 2.3 percent in 1982, followed by a healthy 8.8 percent increase in 1983, and levelled out at around 5 percent in the late 1980s. It is instructive to note that even during the post-recession boom in the mid-1980s, growth in world trade did not consistently reach the levels achieved during the heyday of the Bretton Woods system.

Hegemonic Decline and Systemic Fragmentation, 1968–1980

By the mid-1960s it was clear that the Bretton Woods system was on the verge of collapse. Many factors have been advanced to explain its demise, including the failure of the United States to maintain its leadership role; growing monetary interdependence, which exaggerated each state's vulnerability to systemic shocks; the increasing internationalization of production; and the changing realities of the postwar political system. Between 1968 and 1971, the system went through a period of crisis. The United States abandoned its commitment to monetary and trade order, co-operation between the group of 10 deteriorated, and confidence in the international system reached an all-time low.

The collapse of the Bretton Woods system of trade and payments is normally traced to the August 15, 1971, announcement of Richard Nixon's so-called New Economic Policy. Faced with depleted gold stocks, massive outstanding foreign-dollar holdings, the reality of a mounting trade deficit, and increasing unemployment and inflation, Nixon chose to (unilaterally) bring the Bretton Woods system to an end.

> By late summer 1971 benign neglect was no longer a sustainable policy. There was a decline in the American gold stock to $10 billion versus outstanding foreign dollar holdings estimated at about $80 billion, a worsening in the balance of trade, rampant

> inflation, and widespread unemployment. There were also political problems due to the economic situation and pressure to do something not only from the Democrats but also from the Republicans, who had an eye to the 1972 elections.
>
> On August 15, 1971, President Nixon — without consulting the other members of the international monetary system and, indeed, without consulting his own State Department — announced his New Economic Policy: henceforth, the dollar would no longer be convertible into gold, and the United States would impose a 10 per cent surcharge on dutiable imports. August 15, 1971, marked the end of the Bretton Woods period.[11]

The collapse of the monetary system, the deterioration of U.S. power and influence, the onset of détente, and the increasingly competitive position of Europe and Japan have had a dramatic impact on the global trade regime. Domestic economic pressures in the United States also had a significant effect on global trade. The combination of inward-looking macroeconomic policies, the 10 percent import surcharge, the creation of the Domestic International Sales Corporation (DISC), and the shifting balance of American domestic politics in favour of an openly protectionist Congress had the (unintended) effect of undermining confidence in the trade regime. As we will discuss later in this chapter, neomercantilist or protectionist trade policies increased in frequency and popularity throughout the system — particularly in the DMEs and most particularly in the United States. Moreover, the pursuit of these policies by the major trading states created a self-perpetuating phenomenon, exacerbating both economic *and* political conflict.

While the specific economic (and ideological) conditions that led to the collapse of the Bretton Woods system are relatively easy to enumerate, the extent of their impact is less obvious. Moreover, the forces that carried structural change in the 1970s are quite a bit more complex. Broadly speaking, these forces of change have to do with the growth of interdependence, the spread of pluralism, and the reality of inflation.[12]

On the surface, economic interdependence is a strikingly simple concept. According to Robert Keohane and Joseph Nye, "interdependence, most simply defined, means mutual dependence (and dependence, simply defined, means external reliance). . . . Where there are reciprocal (although not necessarily symmetrical) costly effects of transactions, there is interdependence. Where interactions do not have significant costly effects, there is simply interconnectedness."[13] Vulnerability to external phenomena (even after domestic measures had been taken to offset the negative consequences) effectively meant that economic policies in the DMEs were increasingly influenced by events over which the national government had little control. The result was that as national economies became more sensitive (and vulnerable) to external phenomena, domestic opposition to an open world economy rose. Interdependence has had an especially severe impact on employment-intensive sunset-industry sectors such as steel and textiles, encouraging them to pressure their governments into pursuing more protectionist trade and monetary policies. In short, interdependence was one of the dominant forces of change in the 1970s, and managing interdependence was at once the main problem and the most likely solution for the foreign economic problems of DMEs in the 1970s. As Tim Shaw notes,

> interdependence as doctrine and ideology has been the major response of the North to significant changes in the world political economy, particularly the ending of the postwar period of growth, the high price of oil, the impact of transnationalism and the communications revolution, and the new awareness of ecological constraints.[14]

The second broad force, which will be treated in detail below, is pluralism. Pluralism resulted primarily from the breakdown in U.S. hegemony. Shifting power and influence at the political level manifest themselves at the economic level through the levelling out of competitive advantage in the West and the relative success of the newly industrializing economies.[15] With respect to the world economy, multilateral management became the order of the day. A system of multiple supportership — formalized by the introduction of the annual Western economic summit at Rambouillet, France, in November 1975[16] — emerged during the 1970s. And, while the United States remained the most powerful state in the system, it lacked both the authority and the influence to make systemic decisions unilaterally.

The third broad force operating in the aftermath of the Bretton Woods collapse has to do with the twin themes of inflation and recession. For a number of reasons, undoubtedly including systemic disorder, the 1970s was a period of significant inflation and subsequent recession.[17] In a stable and expanding world economy, the benefits of trade liberalization were self-evident. However, under conditions of economic decline and disorder, exactly the opposite logic obtained. During economic crisis and uncertainty, states tend to fall back on protection and other forms of narrow self-interest. With respect to trade, inflation posed a collection of problems. In addition to the traditional beggar-thy-neighbour problem, some states also restricted exports in an attempt to export inflation.

While it is exceedingly difficult to determine at what point the system actually "fractured" (i.e., when the ideological consensus that characterized Bretton Woods broke down),[18] or exactly what the forces that propelled change in the 1970s were, what is important here is the idea that the end of Bretton Woods translated into significant structural change in the world economy. The world economy in the 1970s was characterized by a general economic malaise that could be traced to the lack of confidence in the system and the absence of stable international monetary, trade, and energy regimes. In addition, energy-price increases fostered stagnation and inflation (especially in the DMEs), which led to increasing levels of protectionism, to excess liquidity, to decreasing competitiveness and productivity, and to increasing economic uncertainty and instability.

The New International Division of Labour

Susan Strange has argued that the most fundamental change of all has occurred in the production structure.[19] The world economy is no longer simply a collection of economically autonomous national producers who engage in mutually beneficial trade. Rather, the concentration of large sums of capital in the hands of multinational business enterprises, their increasing ability to transfer that money from market to market, dramatic improvements in technology and communications, the increasing use of synthetics and substitutes for various resources, and gains in the technology of production have led to the genuine "internationalization of production." When Judd Polk coined the term in 1968, he estimated that roughly 30 percent of the world's industrial output could be understood in terms of international production. Strange suggests that, by 1985, this figure had reached 50 percent.[20] Moreover, as production has become increasingly international, there has been an important shift in the source of foreign direct investment and in the nationality of multinational enterprises (MNEs). Before 1970 more than two-thirds of all foreign direct investment originated in the United States. By the end of the decade, that figure had dropped below 50 percent.[21] And, as the 1980s unfolded, a larger and larger amount of investment capital came from Japan. At the same time, a surprisingly large number of Japanese, German, and South Korean MNEs entered the scene. Moreover, as most MNEs source at least some of their capital locally, it is reasonable to believe that this phenomenon is more widespread than these figures indicate.

Among other things, this increasing internationalization of production was seen to exacerbate the conflict between national capital and international capital. Many students of world politics have argued that this phenomenon has significantly reduced the ability of national governments to respond to the reality of mounting economic interdependence and has left them vulnerable to forces beyond their control.[22] By contrast, more recent neomercantilist analysis has argued that the state has reasserted itself in the face of these transnational challenges.[23] Perhaps the most significant implication of the internationalization of production is that it has provided the context for changes in the international division of labour. Over the past 15 years or so, there have been fundamental shifts in the international competitive positions of both the developed countries and the less-developed countries. In the first place, the virtual monopoly that the United States once had on technology-intensive industrial production is no longer a reality. In fact, owing largely to the maturing of the Japanese and West German economies, competitiveness among the most advanced industrial countries has effectively evened out. In fact, in some sectors, depending on the measures employed, it is reasonable to argue that Japanese industry is more competitive than its American counterpart. Second, there has been a dramatic growth in the competitive position of the Asian NIEs (particularly South Korea, Taiwan, Singapore, and Hong Kong) in the areas of standard technology, labour-intensive manufactured goods, such as clothing, and in industrial materials, such as steel and copper. Finally, another group of NIEs has emerged to pursue standard-technology industrial production while the original, more advanced NIEs follow Japan into more capital-intensive industries. As Michael Webb and Mark Zacher note,

> many commentators have remarked on the loss by the United States of its status as the undisputed world leader in industrial technology and innovation. Western Eu-

> rope and Japan reduced this gap during the 1960s with the help of foreign direct investment from U.S. transnational corporations (TNCs), imported and licensed U.S. technology and, especially in the case of Japan, supportive government policies. Since the 1970s, Japan has increasingly become the world's industrial pacesetter as a result of government industrial strategies aimed at developing international pre-eminence in selected advanced manufacturing sectors. . . . The second major change in competitive advantage has been the emergence of the newly industrializing countries (NICs) as producers and exporters of certain high volume, standard technology, manufactured goods that require relatively large imputs of low skilled labour relative to capital and natural resources. Textile, clothing and footwear were among the first sectors affected by competition from these new producers. To these the NICs have since added competitive advantages in steel, shipbuilding, automobile parts, consumer electronics, and other relatively simple consumer goods. The range of goods that can be competitively produced in the NICs is expected to broaden further during the 1980s as their technology becomes more widely diffused, capital more abundant, and labour more highly skilled. [24]

An examination of the relative factor endowments of the advanced industrial countries (AICs; DMEs) and some of the NIEs demonstrates these claims quite dramatically (see Table 1). For example, given the nature of capital-intensive high-technology production in the United States, it is not surprising that, in 1980, the United States had 33.6 percent of the world's capital and some 50.7 percent of the world's research-and-development scientists. These are impressive figures. However, when compared with the 1963 figures of 41.9 percent and 62.5 percent, respectively, it is clear that the United States is losing its pre-eminence in this area. Japan has been the obvious beneficiary of much of this shift. Japan's share of total world capital rose from 7.1 percent in 1963 to 15.5 percent in 1980, while its share of R&D scientists rose from 16.2 percent to 23.0 percent over the same period. The figures for Argentina, Brazil, Mexico, India, Hong Kong, and Korea are also very interesting. This group of NIEs experienced significant shifts in their share of the world's capital (from 6.2 percent in 1963 to 10.1 percent in 1980) and in their share of skilled workers. With respect to labour, they experienced significant increases in their share of the world's semi-skilled labour (from 24.8 percent to 30.5 percent during the period in question) and a more modest but equally significant increase in their share of skilled labour (from 19.3 percent to 22.0 percent).[25]

The growth of capital in the NIEs has slowed down considerably since the debt crisis and global recession of the early 1980s. However, while the drop in the price of oil has exacerbated the debt position of many of these NIEs, the growth of capital has continued in the Southeast Asian group and will undoubtedly strengthen and expand the steel and automobile industries there. The significant growth of semi-skilled labour is also important as it contributes to the comparative advantage of labour-intensive industrial production, which continues to overshadow the outdated, high-wage industries in the AICs. To quote Susan Strange, "the new international division of labour appears to be unstoppable. The movement of manufacturing industry to the Third World is structural not cyclical."[26]

TABLE 1 Relative Factor Endowments of Major AICS, 1963 and 1980 (Each Country's Endowment as a Percentage of World Total)[1]

	Year	Capital[2]	Skilled Labour[3]	Semi-skilled Labour[4]	Unskilled Labour[5]	Arable Land[6]	R&D Scientists[7]
UNITED STATES	1963	41.9%	29.4%	18.3%	0.60%	27.4%	62.5%
	1980	33.6	27.7	19.1	0.19	29.3	50.7
CANADA	1963	3.8	2.5	1.7	0.06	6.5	1.6
	1980	3.9	2.9	2.1	0.03	6.1	1.8
Japan	1963	7.1	7.8	12.6	0.30	0.9	6.2
	1980	15.5	8.7	11.5	0.25	0.8	23.0
France	1963	7.1	6.6	5.3	0.11	3.2	6.1
	1980	7.5	6.0	3.9	0.06	2.6	6.0
Germany	1963	9.1	7.1	6.8	0.14	1.3	7.5
	1980	7.7	6.9	5.5	0.08	1.1	10.0
United Kingdom	1963	5.6	7.0	6.5	0.14	1.1	6.1
	1980	4.5	5.1	4.9	0.07	1.0	8.5
Total of six major AICS	1963	74.6	60.4	51.2	1.35	40.4	100.0
	1980	72.7	57.3	47.0	0.68	40.9	100.0
Six NICS[8]	1963	6.2	19.3	24.8	86.7	37.2	n.a.
	1980	10.1	22.0	30.5	87.9	36.7	n.a.

1 Computed from a set of 34 countries, which, in 1980, accounted for over 85 percent of the GDP in noncentrally planned economies.
2 Based on real gross domestic investment.
3 Based on the number of workers in professional and technical categories.
4 Based on the number of literate workers not categorized as professional or technical.
5 Based on the number of illiterate workers.
6 Based on measurement of long acres in different climatic zones.
7 Initial year is 1967 and final year is 1979. Percentages are based on total R&D personnel from the six countries shown as provided by the National Science Foundation.
8 NICS represented in the 34 country sample were Argentina, Brazil, Mexico, India, Hong Kong, and Korea.

SOURCE: John Mutti and Peter Morici, *Changing Patterns of U.S. Industrial Activity and Comparative Advantage* (Washington: National Planning Association, Committee on Changing International Realities, 1983), 8.

The political, economic, and social consequences of this shift in the international division of labour have been extremely far-reaching in the AICs. The employment implications alone have served to heighten the economic crisis in the modern welfare state. In short, this shift in comparative advantage toward the NIEs poses a serious challenge to all of the DMEs.

Protectionism and the Avoidance of Structural Change

These changes in the production structure and the international division of labour have prompted the DMEs — especially the United States — to take steps to soften the domestic consequences of these changes. Quite simply, this phenomenon has translated into a significant increase in the use and promotion of protectionist policies. In particular, the DMEs have increasingly turned to the use of nontariff barriers (NTBS) such as antidumping action, countervailing duties, and voluntary export restrictions (VERS) or voluntary restraint agreements (VRAS). Fuelled by the recession of the early 1980s, the reality of rising structural unemployment in the DMES, the staggering trade deficit of the United States (which exceeded $200 billion in 1988), and mounting global surplus capacity in most of the standard-technology industries, protectionism increased quite dramatically in the 1970s and 1980s. In the Western world, unemployment has been at the heart of rising demands for protection. By 1983 unemployment had reached staggering proportions. The unemployment rate was 9.6 percent in the United States, 11.5 percent in the United Kingdom, and 11.9 percent in Canada.[27] Not surprisingly, unemployment was highest in those industries that were most susceptible to foreign competition. For instance, at the height of the recession, when total U.S. unemployment had reached some 10.6 percent, unemployment in the steel and auto industries stood at 29.2 and 23.2 percent, respectively.[28] While unemployment is down somewhat in the DMES, employment replaced inflation as the key political issue of the decade. And, as Joan Spero points out, "a growing public awareness of the impact of foreign competition on import competing industries [has]increased the pressure for protectionist solutions."[29]

Global surplus capacity, combined with the increasingly competitive position of offshore producers and the reality of rising interdependence, encouraged powerful unions, such as the AFL-CIO and the United Autoworkers of America, to join forces with domestic producers in their drive for protection. This protection is especially evident in certain key labour-intensive industrial sectors, particularly the automobile, steel, footwear, and consumer electronic industries.

In footwear, for example, the United States negotiated orderly market arrangements (OMAS) with Taiwan and South Korea in 1977. Beginning in 1978, Canada imposed footwear quotas on imports from all Third World nations. In 1979, the United Kingdom followed suit, imposing a blanket quota on all non-rubber footwear. Italy and France also negotiated various OMAS and voluntary export restrictions (VERS) with the principal Third World footwear producers. The story in the automobile industry was very similar. Led by the United Kingdom, who began monitoring Japanese imports in 1975, and followed by France's VER agreement with Japan in 1977, virtually all the key industrial countries instituted some form of quota system on incoming Japanese automobiles. In 1981, the United States, Canada, and West Germany all negotiated VERS with Japan.

To a large extent the recent rise in protectionism can be traced to the United States. Once the main proponent of a liberal and open international-trading order, U.S. policy systematically changed in the direction of closure during the 1970s. Beginning with Nixon's 1971 New Economic Policy, which included a 10 percent across-the-board import surcharge, the forces of protectionism moved steadily forward. Support for the *proposed* Trade Act of 1970 (the Mills bill) and the *proposed* Foreign Trade and Investment Act of 1972 (the Burke–Hartke bill) demonstrated quite clearly that certain elements in the Congress were prepared to forsake the postwar liberal trade arrangement in exchange for solutions to domestic problems. And, while the trade legislation that was eventually adopted (the Trade Act of 1974 and 1979) was somewhat tamer, it did provide specific remedies with respect to unfairly traded imports.[30] In addition to provisions for antidumping and countervailing duties, which can be imposed in the case of injury from unfairly traded imports under section 301, the Trade Act of 1974 also introduced an "escape clause" (section 201) that provides for action against imports even when they have not been deemed to have been traded unfairly. While the "test" of injury is generally more stringent in section 301 cases than in 201 cases, section 201 has effectively broadened the ability of Congress to provide protection for their import-competing constituents. And, while the most vociferous forces of protectionism have been kept at bay, the U.S. Trade Act of 1988 introduced a "super 301" clause targeted mainly at Japan and the Asian NIEs.

Broadly speaking, the recent rise in protectionism in the United States can be linked to four specific phenomena. First, it has to do with the overvalued U.S. dollar, which, combined with high wages and poorer productivity, has made American goods and services increasingly less competitive. Second, the United States has (perhaps justifiably) reacted strongly to trade restrictions imposed by their developed-country trading partners. This perception is heightened by the realization that, while the United States was running $150 billion-plus trade deficits in the mid and late 1980s, Japan had a growing trade surplus — reaching more than $80 billion by 1986. Third, there is a growing feeling in the United States that a great many low-cost imports from the NIEs are being subsidized by their national governments and therefore being traded "unfairly" into the United States. Finally, there is a fundamental underlying division within the United States between the administration and international capital, on the one hand, and some parts of Congress and domestic capital (nationally organized industry), on the other. Charles Maier has argued that the resolution of this internal conflict, in favour of the international interests, was the foundation for the Bretton Woods system.[31] This being the case, it is hardly surprising that as productivity and economic growth has declined, the conflict over the appropriate direction of foreign economic policy has resurfaced.

Protectionist pressures in the United States have led to friction between it and its major trade partners — particularly Japan and the European Community — which has, in turn, promoted the spiral of protectionism. The continuing reliance on nontariff barriers negotiated outside of the framework of the GATT has contributed to a global trading system that is determined less and less by market forces. The bottom line is that there has been a drift toward "managed trade." In manufactures, which account for roughly 40 percent of total world trade, the ratio of managed trade to total trade has risen from 13 percent in 1974 to 30 percent in 1982. Moreover, this movement toward managed trade does not appear to be abating in any way as larger political considerations continue to play a significant role in the trading policies of both developed and developing countries.[32]

Finally, the resistance to structural change in the DMEs has been exaggerated by the reality of a world in which postindustrial production is inconsistent with an economy and a polity geared toward full employment. Moreover, the rapid rise in technology and communications has increased the capital input required for each unit of output, thereby providing the producer with a greater incentive for protection.

The World Economy in the 1980s

By the end of the decade, it was clear that the Bretton Woods system, as it was constituted in the long decade of the 1950s, was not to be resurrected and that the economic changes and challenges of the 1970s were anything but transitory, especially during the "great recession" of 1981–82, and that a new international economic order was taking shape. The central features of the world economy in the 1980s derive from the changes that took shape in the 1970s. As Gilbert Winham and Denis Stairs note, "irreversible forces of technological, economic, and social change are sweeping through the world. They are transforming economic relationships, altering long-held expectations for national economic prospects, and putting a great deal of pressure on established economic institutions and existing international organizations."[33] In short, the world economy in the 1980s can best be understood within the context of turbulence and uncertainty. This complexity and uncertainty is demonstrated by the extensive "catalogue" of crises that make up the economic history of the first half of the 1980s. These crises include, among others, the global debt crisis; the global recession of 1981–82; the persistence of protectionism; the continual evolution of a new international division of labour; fundamental changes in the energy structure; and the re-emergence of the United States and its renewed desire to take the lead in the global economy. A brief review of these crises should prove useful in demonstrating both the direction and the importance of structural change at the level of the world economy.

In many ways the debt crisis was to the 1980s what the energy crisis was to the 1970s. The main focus of the debt crisis has been the middle-income developing countries in Latin America. The combined debt of Mexico, Brazil, Argentina, and Venezuela constitutes more than 80 percent of the region's debt and a little more than 40 percent of total Third World debt. These four countries, along with South Korea and the Philippines, are the world's largest debtors.

The onset of this crisis, which can be traced to the collapse of the Mexican peso in 1982, has been both the major source of economic disruption and dislocation in the Third World and the source of pervasive instability in the international financial structure. The debt crisis emerged from the complex collection of forces that were operating in the 1970s. Among other things, excess liquidity in the world banking system (owing largely to the decline of business activity in the OECD region) along with strong growth prospects for most of the NIEs led to excessive borrowing in many of these countries. Unfortunately, coincident with this heavy short-term borrowing, the NIEs were faced with a severe global recession, a significant decline in oil revenues, and persistently high real interest rates in the developed (creditor) countries.[34] Many of the Latin America debtors, who were on the verge of default in 1983 and 1984, have managed to ride out their predicament. Collective support, bridge financing, IMF-sponsored rescheduling, and strictly enforced domestic austerity measures have managed to stave off collapse. However, the domestic consequences of these measures threaten to produce an even more serious crisis. In the spring of 1984, the *New York Times* suggested that "a new Latin American debt crisis is brewing, probably more perilous and certainly more political than in the recent past [and] this time the issue is whether Latin America's four biggest debtor nations can achieve economic recovery and political stability while continuing to make huge interest payments on their foreign debts."[35]

Debt has played a crucial role in recent economic summits. At the Toronto summit in 1988, the crowning achievement was a package that would write off much of the debt for sub-Saharan African countries. The real challenge, however, has been to address the middle-income developing-country debt, which threatens the stability of the international financial system.

At roughly the same time, the DMEs were facing a more direct and perhaps more fundamental challenge to their economic well-being. From the second quarter of 1981 through to the fourth quarter of 1982, the world entered its most severe economic downturn since the great depression of the 1930s. Real growth in GNP in the OECD area, which had averaged 5.4 percent per annum between 1966 and 1973, dropped to less than 2 percent in 1981 and actually contracted by 0.3 percent in 1984. Unemployment climbed steadily, reaching highs of 11.5 and 11.9 percent in the United Kingdom and Canada, respectively, in 1983. Interest rates rose dramatically as well, rising from an average of 7.4 percent in the seven major DMEs in 1978 to more than 14 percent in 1981.[36] Moreover, even after the nominal rates dropped, real interest rates remained at historically unprecedented highs. Real interest rates in the seven principal DMEs averaged 6.0 percent between 1982 and 1985, as compared with figures well below 2.0 percent in the preceding decade.

Many factors can be brought to bear in explaining the recession of 1981–82. The main reasons seem to focus on the costs of battling the energy-price–induced inflation of the 1970s, the loss of confidence in the system in the 1970s, the decline in U.S. leadership, and the dramatic increase in protection. A more direct cause, to be sure, was U.S. macroeconomic policy. The American "supply-side" response to mounting trade and budgetary deficits led directly to a restriction of domestic (and international) money and the correspondingly high interest rates. In short, the United States was pursuing an expansionary fiscal policy along with a contractionary monetary policy. What this meant for other DMEs was that international liquidity was seriously reduced, domestic interest rates went through the roof, and investment dollars flooded into the United States.

While 1983–86 was a period of dramatic growth and recovery in the world economy, though not evenly spread out, the real problems associated with the recession have not been resolved. Despite steady GNP growth and good progress on the price-inflation front, the main economic problems that existed in 1982 and 1983 continued to trouble the world economy at the end of the decade. Unemployment remained high in virtually all countries and continued to rise in some. Budget deficits continued to plague most OECD countries — especially the United States, Canada, and Italy. The value of the U.S. dollar remained disturbingly high, leading to overvalued U.S. exports, undervalued imports, and ultimately, to significant current-account imbalances.

Tensions on the international-trade scene continued to mount, with protectionist interventions becoming increasingly common. The forces of protectionism were especially strong in the United States. At the same time, along with the fiscal and monetary crises, the global trading environment in the 1980s continued to be reshaped by a number of critical forces. The internationalization of production and changes in the new international division of labour continued to represent strong forces of change. In addition, until the opening of the Uruguay Round in 1986, trade liberalization under the GATT had ground to a complete standstill.[37]

In short, the reality of the world economy in the 1980s suggests that the forces of change that emerged in the 1970s have translated into long-term pervasive change in the structure of the world economy. The reality is structural uncertainty and a fundamentally flawed and unstable global economy. The debt crisis remains a serious problem, real interest rates remain disturbingly high, the unemployment problem in most of the OECD countries has not been resolved, the fiscal crisis of the state stands as a dangerous threat to the economic union and the development prospects of key industrial states, protection continues without much resistance, and inflation threatens to re-emerge.

Conclusion: The Pattern of Structural Change

In sum, the breakdown of the Bretton Woods system precipitated a series of significant changes in the global economy. Attempts at rebuilding the system or "adjusting" to new realities in the 1970s have given way to the realization, in the 1980s, that a new order is emerging. It is, however, an order characterized by uncertainty and instability. It is a system in which economic management is lacking, and unresolved economic crises are commonplace. This uncertainty is pervasive. It exists in all the primary structures (the security, production, monetary, and knowledge structures) and in the secondary structures, such as trade, as well. To quote Stairs and Winham, "the general sense of uncertainty and loss of control is a worldwide problem."[38]

The events of the 1970s and 1980s not only changed the structure of the world economy, but undermined the principal assumptions that characterized the postwar economic order. It was no longer apparent that an international economic system that gives power to the market is compatible with an international political system that gives power to states, or even that the two are separable. States tend to find themselves in conflict with an open trade environment when governments see national goals as inconsistent with systemic goals, and when a hegemonic structure is no longer in place. It is also no longer apparent that open and co-operative international trade and monetary structures offer all the participants in the system the best opportunity for progress and development. Finally, the logic that international organizations will necessarily improve the international political economy is no longer conceded.

NOTES

1. The underlying argument here is that the Bretton Woods system characterized a specific historical period that has come to a close. The main debate now centres on the extent of the decline of U.S. hegemony and on the composition, character, and stability of a nonhegemonic world economy. The literature on structural change in the world economy and hegemonic decline is enormous. For a thoughtful introduction, see David P. Calleo, *The Imperious Economy* (Princeton: Princeton University Press, 1982); Susan Strange, "Still an Extraordinary Power: America's Role in a Global Monetary System," in *Political Economy of International and Domestic Monetary Relations*, ed. R. Lombra and W. Witte (Ames: Iowa State University Press, 1982), 73–93; and R.O. Keohane, *After Hegemony: Cooperation and Discord in the World Political Economy* (Princeton: Princeton University Press, 1984).

2. Peter Morici, *The Global Competitive Struggle: Challenges to the United States and Canada* (Washington and Toronto: Canadian-American Committee, 1984).

3. The classic statement on the fiscal crisis in the modern welfare state is J. O'Connor, *The Fiscal Crisis of the State* (New York: St. Martin's, 1973). See also Mary Kaldor, *The Disintegrating West* (Harmondsworth: Penguin, 1979); Fred Block, *The Origins of International Economic Disorder* (Berkeley: University of California Press, 1977); and R.C.O. Mathews, *Slower Economic Growth in the Western World* (Stanford: Stanford University Press, 1982).

4. Michael Hudson, *Global Fracture: The New International Economic Order* (New York: Harper and Row, 1977), 9.

5. On international monetary order, see D.P. Calleo, ed., *Money and the Coming World Order* (New York: New York University Press, 1976); Charles P. Kindleberger, *The World in Depression, 1929–39* (Berkeley: University of California Press, 1973); and David Calleo and Susan Strange, "Money and World Politics," in *Paths to International Political Economy*, ed. S. Strange (London: Allen and Unwin, 1984), 91–125.

6. Robert O. Keohane, "Hegemonic Leadership and U.S. Foreign Policy in the Long Decade of the 1950s," in *America in a Changing World Political Economy*, ed. William P. Avery and David R. Rapkin (New York: Longman, 1982), 49–76.

7. Keohane, "Hegemonic Leadership," 49.

8. Keohane, "Hegemonic Leadership," 50.

9. While it is unnecessary to repeat the discussion offered in other chapters, it is critical to remember that a hegemonic power leads most effectively by consensus as opposed to coercion. See Michael K. Hawes, "Structural Change and Hegemonic Decline: Implications for National Governments," in this volume.

10. One of the best examinations of the U.S. strategy can be found in Fred Hirsch and Michael Doyle, "Politicization in the World Economy: Necessary Conditions for an International Economic Order," in *Alternatives to Monetary Disorder*, ed. F. Hirsch, M. Doyle, and E. Morse (New York: McGraw-Hill, for the Council on Foreign Relations, 1977).

11. Joan E. Spero, *The Politics of International Economic Relations*, 3d ed. (New York: St. Martin's, 1985), 54–55.

12. See R.J. Gordon and J. Pelkmans, *Challenges to Interdependent Economies: The Industrial West in the Coming Decade* (New York: McGraw-Hill, for the Council on Foreign Relations, 1979); and Harold K. Jacobson, *Networks of Interdependence*, 2d ed. (New York: Random House, 1984).

13. Robert O. Keohane and Joseph Nye, Jr., *Power and Interdependence* (Boston: Little, Brown, 1977), 8–9.

14. Tim Shaw, *Toward an International Political Economy for the 1980s: From Dependence to Interdependence* (Halifax: Centre for Foreign Policy Studies, Dalhousie University, 1980), 7.

15. It is extremely difficult to determine which was cause and which was effect in this instance — whether the breakdown of U.S. hegemony aided the economic rise of Japan and the Federal Republic of Germany or whether their rise contributed to the breakdown of the Bretton Woods sytem.

16. See G. DeMenil and A.M. Solomon, *Economic Summitry* (New York: Council on Foreign Relations, 1983), and R. Putnam and Nicholas Bayne, *Hanging Together: The Seven Power Summits* (Cambridge, Mass.: Harvard University Press, 1984).

17. See Robert O. Keohane, "Economics, Inflation, and the Role of the State: Political Implications of the McCracken Report," *World Politics* 31 (October 1978): 108–28.

18. Some students of international political economy argue that the Bretton Woods system depended very heavily on the notion of consensus (or ideological hegemony). See, in particular, Robert W. Cox, "Gramsci, Hegemony and International Relations: An Essay in Method," *Millennium* 12, no. 2 (1983): 162–75; and Arthur Stein, "The Hegemon's Dilemma: Great Britain, the United States, and the International Economic Order," *International Organization* 38 (Spring 1984): 335–86.

19. Susan Strange, "The Global Political Economy," *International Journal* 39 (Spring 1984): 273.

20. Strange, "Global Political Economy," 273.

21. Strange, "Global Political Economy," 274.

22. The classic statement on the "sovereignty at bay" thesis is Raymond Vernon, *Sovereignty at Bay* (New York: Basic, 1971).

23. On the current state of the debate, see David Leyton-Brown, "The Nation-State and Multinational Enterprise: Erosion or Assertion?" *Behind the Headlines* 60 (September

1982): 1–16. For a summary of implications of internationalized production and capital dependence in the Canadian context, see Michael K. Hawes, *Principal Power, Middle Power, or Satellite: Competing Perspectives in the Study of Canadian Foreign Policy* (Toronto: University of Toronto Press, 1984), 22–23.

24. M. Webb and M. Zacher, "Canada's Export Trade in a Changing International Environment," in *Canada and the International Political/Economic Environment*, ed. D. Stairs and G. Winham (Toronto: University of Toronto Press, 1985), 94–95.

25. See Morici, *Global Competitive Struggle*, 13.

26. Susan Strange, "Protectionism and World Politics," *International Organization* 39 (Spring 1985): 248.

27. Michael Hawes, "The National Economy," *Canadian Annual Review of Politics and Public Affairs, 1983*, ed. R.B. Byers (Toronto: University of Toronto Press, 1985), 135.

28. Spero, *Politics of International Economic Relations*, 118.

29. Spero, *Politics of International Economic Relations*, 118.

30. See, among others, Rodney de C. Grey, *United States Trade Policy Legislation: A Canadian View* (Montreal: The Institute for Research on Public Policy, 1985).

31. Charles S. Maier, "The Politics of Productivity: Foundations of American International Economic Policy after World War II," in *Between Power and Plenty: Foreign Economic Policies of Advanced Industrial Countries*, ed. Peter J. Katzenstein (Madison: University of Wisconsin Press, 1978), 23–50.

32. On protection and the drift toward managed trade, see R. Blackhurst, M. Nicolas, and J. Tumlir, *Trade Liberalization, Protectionism, and Interdependence*, GATT Studies in Inter-Trade (Geneva: 1977); Melvyn B. Krauss, *The New Protectionism: The Welfare State and International Trade* (New York: New York University Press, 1978); G. Helleiner, G. Franko, and H.B. Junz, eds., *Protectionism and Industrial Adjustment* (Paris: Atlantic Institute, 1980); and Robert Axelrod, *The Evolution of Cooperation* (New York: Basic Books, 1984).

33. Denis Stairs and Gilbert R. Winham, "Canada and the International Political/Economic Environment: An Introduction," in *Canada and the International Political/Economic Environment*.

34. See Jonathan D. Aronson, "Muddling Through the Debt Decade," in *An International Political Economy*, International Political Economy Yearbook, vol. 1, ed. W. Ladd Hollist and F. LaMond Tullis (Boulder, Colo.: Westview, 1985), 127–52.

35. *New York Times*, March 11, 1984: F1.

36. International Monetary Fund, *World Economic Outlook, 1985* (Washington: April 1985), 120.

37. On the U.S. response to the multilateral trade agenda, see C. Michael Aho and Jonathan D. Aronson, *Trade Talks: America Better Listen* (New York: Council on Foreign Relations, 1985).

38. Stairs and Winham, "Canada and the International Political/Economic Environment," 2.

SELECT BIBLIOGRAPHY

Block, Fred. *The Origins of International Economic Disorder.* Berkeley: University of California Press, 1977.

Calleo, David P. *The Imperious Economy.* Princeton: Princeton University Press, 1982.

———, ed. *Money and the Coming World Order.* New York: New York University Press, 1976.

Calleo, David, and Susan Strange. "Money and World Politics." In *Paths to International Political Economy,* ed. S. Strange. London: Allen and Unwin, 1984.

Gilpin, R. *The Political Economy of International Relations.* Princeton: Princeton University Press, 1987.

———. *War and Change in World Politics.* Cambridge: Cambridge University Press, 1981.

Goldthorpe, J.H., ed. *Order and Conflict in Contemporary Capitalism.* Oxford: Oxford University Press, 1984.

Hudson, Michael. *Global Fracture: The New International Economic Order.* New York: Harper and Row, 1977.

Kaldor, Mary. *The Disintegrating West.* Harmondsworth: Penguin, 1979.

Keohane, R.O. *After Hegemony: Cooperation and Discord in the World Political Economy.* Princeton: Princeton University Press, 1984.

———. "Hegemonic Leadership and U.S. Foreign Policy in the Long Decade of the 1950s." In *America in a Changing World Political Economy,* ed. William P. Avery and David R. Rapkin. New York: Longman, 1982.

Kindleberger, Charles P. *The World in Depression, 1929–39.* Berkeley: University of California Press, 1973.

Mathews, R.C.O. *Slower Economic Growth in the Western World.* Stanford: Stanford University Press, 1982.

Morici, Peter. *The Global Competitive Struggle: Challenges to the United States and Canada.* Washington and Toronto: Canadian-American Committee, 1984.

O'Connor, J. *The Fiscal Crisis of the State.* New York: St. Martin's, 1973.

Spero, Joan E. *The Politics of International Economic Relations.* 3d ed. New York: St. Martin's, 1985.

Strange, Susan. "The Global Political Economy," *International Journal* 39 (Spring 1984): 273.

———. "Protectionism and World Politics," *International Organization* 39 (Spring 1985): 248.

———. "Still an Extraordinary Power: America's Role in a Global Monetary System." In *Political Economy of International and Domestic Monetary Relations,* ed. R. Lombra and W. Witte. Ames: Iowa State University Press, 1982.

INTEGRATION, INTERDEPENDENCE, AND INSTITUTIONS: APPROACHES TO INTERNATIONAL ORDER

Charles C. Pentland

At the very heart of modern international relations lies a paradox — the existence of order in a setting of anarchy. Although such order is evident in many international systems throughout history, even prevailing in some for long periods of time, it has never been assured. The paradox, therefore, is not just an intellectual curiosity but a moral and political problem at once timeless and urgent. This chapter will explore some responses to the paradox of order in anarchy in the theory and practice of international relations since World War II. It will suggest that, in the remarkably innovative work on integration theory and interdependence that led up to the current preoccupation with regime analysis, there are some fundamental theoretical debates that go back to the very origins of today's international system.

As understood here, international order is not simply any persistent pattern or structure, as it is sometimes held to be by realists.[1] Here the reference is to purposive organization or institutionalized co-operation among states. The central question, then, is not why there may be a discernible structure or pattern in the superficially chaotic rivalry among sovereign states — as interesting as that question is. Rather, the issue is how, and why, in the absence of overarching authority and in the presence of a powerful tradition of egoism and self-help, states pursue and achieve institutionalized co-operation. The two questions are both important, and they are related. It is the latter that will be the main concern in what follows.

From the very origins of modern international relations onward, attempts to account for the incidence of co-operation in the "anarchical society" of world politics fall into three broad theoretical traditions, among which there has at times been vigorous debate. The first of these traditions, arguably the most ancient and the most familiar, is *political realism*.[2] Its proponents hold that, like almost everything else, international organizations and co-operation are a reflection of the patterns of power in the international system and of competing or converging national interests. Since these patterns and interests are in constant flux, co-operation is usually contingent and fragile; the only firm base for international institutions is a long-term coincidence of fundamental national interests, something all too rare in international history. The diagnosis is sombre, and the prognosis for long-term international co-operation, given the unchanging nature of man, the state, and the state system, is pessimistic.

The second theoretical tradition is, to use Joseph Grieco's label, *liberal institutionalism.*[3] In its most recent forms, as he notes, this school of thought accepts the basic realist premises that states are the major actors in world politics and that they act as rational, unitary agents. While even explicitly denying that states can sometimes be so construed, earlier versions of liberal institutionalism did claim that observers and practitioners of international politics now had to take account of the new realities of "complex interdependence" to which traditional realism was insensitive. These "new realities" included transnational and transgovernmental relations, the fragmentation of the modern state into various subnational interests, and the rise of welfare issues relative to military-security issues on national agendas. Liberal institutionalism has a long pedigree, going back at least to utilitarianism, the technocratic politics of Saint-Simon, the 19th-century Manchester School, and Fabian socialism. Its most recent manifestations, as we shall see, are functionalism, neofunctionalism, and theories of interdependence. Its hallmark is cautious, pragmatic optimism about the prospects for institutionalized co-operation among states.

The third tradition is *cosmopolitanism*, or, more familiarly, *idealism.*[4] It can be traced back to the writings of reactionary observers who, from the late Middle Ages to the 17th century, deplored the fragmentation of empire and Christendom into a system of sovereign states. From the 18th century onward, its proponents have cast their eyes forward to a time when, in the name of humanity, nation-states and national interests would be transformed, or even transcended. This tradition includes most schemes for world peace, world government, and the international rule of law. Their common theme is that the threat of war, the prevalence of distributive injustice on a global scale, and, most recently, environmental decay signal the bankruptcy of the nation-state system.[5] Institutionalized co-operation among states is but the start of a process that, driven by the imperative of human survival and sustained by increasing evidence of our shared conditions, must culminate in the complete transformation of world politics.

The paradox of international co-operation to which these three theoretical traditions respond in their very different ways would perhaps seem less worthy of extensive analysis were it not clear to most observers that the incidence of institutionalized collaboration and co-operation among states has been on the rise since the middle of the 19th century and has been especially striking since World War II. Heightening the paradox of the anarchic society is the fact that this surge in international co-operation, as measured by such indices as the rate of creation of intergovernmental and nongovernmental international organizations, has coincided with the proliferation of nation-states (the United Nations began with 50 members; it now has 159).[6] Moreover, national governments have at their disposal unprecedented capabilities, and the techniques and technology of national protection (whether economic or military) have achieved new heights of sophistication. These developments can only add to the significance of the ongoing three-way debate among realists, liberal institutionalists, and idealists about the causes, effects, and prospects of international co-operation.

It would be misleading to suggest that international co-operation was unknown in international relations in the early modern period, from the 17th to the 19th century. Nations collaborated readily in the alliances characteristic of the multipolar balance of power, although with little sense of permanent commitment (indeed, quite the reverse was the norm) and with nothing in the way of international institutions. To the strategic considerations that normally underlay the formation of these alliances were added a range of commercial, dynastic, and religious links among states that somewhat blurred the brutal clarity of the state system. But such interdependence was minimal and far from complex. On the whole, the realist language of power politics and national interest seemed sufficient to account for whatever co-operation occurred.

In the 19th century, however, after the settlement of the Napoleonic Wars, the realist tradition began to be challenged as new, institutionalized forms of international collaboration emerged. It is true that, in matters of military security, alliances continued to be the dominant form of co-operation, explicable in realist terms. But the Concert of Europe, created after the settlement of 1815, represented a new form of institutionalized response by the great powers to what they defined, at least initially, as a common security problem. It was possible, in exaggerating the urgency and the commonality of that problem, to put an idealist gloss on the Concert and interpret it as the beginning of a new age, as some of its contemporaries did. From the more distant vantage point of the late 20th century, liberal internationalists, too, have attempted to appropriate the Concert as an early example of a security regime. Still, realism has probably prevailed in this skirmish: minimally institutionalized, the Concert represented the relatively short-lived convergence of great-power interests in a stable postwar order. It co-existed with, indeed was animated by, balance-of-power politics. In short, it was nothing realism could not handle.[7]

A more significant long-term challenge to realism emerged later in the 19th century in the debate led by the Manchester School over the expansion of international commerce. In the writings of Cobden, Bright, and others, the argument that unfettered exchange among the world's nations is a prerequisite of peace raised the profile of liberal institutionalism.[8] Along with trade, the rise, later in the century, of public international unions, such as the International Telegraphic Union and the Universal Postal Union, to facilitate international co-operation in technical matters of communication, seemed to be concrete evidence that interdependence among nations was on the rise and that a correspondingly higher level of institutionalized co-operation was both necessary and desirable. Liberal institutionalism now seemed to be gaining a firmer empirical basis for its claims.

Some of the same trends also served to fuel a surge in international idealism. More important to this movement, however, was the increased brutality and destructiveness of war in the latter part of the 19th century. Mass mobilization and sophisticated military technology seemed to be transforming war definitively from a legitimate instrument of balance-of-power diplomacy to an uncontrollable scourge of humanity. Peace groups — religious or secular, scientific or mystical — produced innumerable publications advocating, at the least, legal and institutional controls on warfare, but more frequently arguing that the real danger was the state system itself, and the absence of some form of world government.

The effect of World War I was to focus attention and expectations concerning international organizations on the League of Nations.[9] Not surprisingly, the League became the object of close scrutiny from the three theoretical perspectives, each reading it differently. Idealists saw in it the beginnings of world government. At the very least they expected the judicial system of The Hague, backed by League sanctions, to usher in the international rule of law. Liberal institutionalists celebrated the construction of collective security as a workable security regime. The creation of the International Labour Office (later the International Labour Organization), along with the public international unions, seemed as well to herald a new era of functional co-operation. Realists, finally, were free to interpret collective security and sanctions as a concentration of power to deter and, if necessary, defeat challenges to the new international order. The unanimity principle governing the League was to them a sound recognition of sovereignty and an assurance that the League's purpose was to preserve, not transcend, the state system.

The 1920s were arguably the high-water mark of idealism. The League had its minor successes in conflict management, and it seemed possible to hope for progress in the area of disarmament and in the development of international law. For believers in the progress of international institutions, disappointed as they had been in the failure to negotiate improvements in the League Covenant's provisions for collective security, the Kellogg–Briand pact of 1928, in definitively outlawing recourse to war for the first time, represented the triumph of modern reason over old-fashioned power politics.

Realism, eclipsed by idealism in the 1920s, reappeared in full light in the "low, dishonest decade" of the 1930s; the critique of the Versailles arrangements and the analysis of interwar power politics by E.H. Carr, Martin Wight, and others had a powerful impact on contemporary views of international order.[10] The League did, from the vantage point of the late 1930s, look like an insufficient coalition of status-quo powers. Was it surprising that, for varying reasons, Germany, Japan, Italy, and the Soviet Union showed it little respect? Indeed, much realist commentary went beyond criticizing the League and its supporters as beset by the beguiling illusion that they had advanced beyond power politics, and argued more controversially that an international order that was both unjust and fragile deserved the challenge it faced. The former version counselled rearmament; the latter, appeasement.

While realists and idealists debated these issues, liberal institutionalism was putting down roots in both theory and practice. Drawing on the experience of the public international unions and of wartime allied co-operation, David Mitrany and others began to formulate a view of "international government" based on the new imperatives of social and economic co-operation.[11] The League itself recognized these imperatives, and its own delinquency, in the Bruce Report commissioned in the late 1930s.[12] But functionalism had to await the next war to gain the ear of governments.

After World War II the three-way debate resumed, in much the same terms as it had in the interwar period. If the voice of idealism was somewhat muted, the explanation perhaps lay in the lessons drawn from the League's fate and in the care taken to prune illusions about the demise of power politics from the design of the United Nations — an exercise aided by the wartime experience of negotiating the postwar order and, for the Western powers at least, by Soviet behaviour during and immediately after the war. Nevertheless, the idealist impulse to negotiate general and complete disarmament, to refine and develop international law into an effective instrument, and to propose some form of international authority to regulate nuclear and environmental threats, remained in the wings, occasionally venturing onstage in times of acute crisis.

As a doctrine of international order, however, realism dominated the field in the early postwar years, and through several mutations its influence has persisted, albeit somewhat diminished, into the 1980s. American realists' respect for the United Nations and for regional security arrangements varied with their perceived effectiveness as a form of supplementary countervailing power in the service of containment. In rhetoric, the North Atlantic Treaty Organization and other alliances could supplement the U.N. system of collective security; in reality the U.N. was no substitute for alliances, for deterrence, or, if necessary, for the unilateral exercise of power.[13]

Liberal institutionalism, particularly in the form of functionalism, came into the postwar era with a new authority and legitimacy. Functionalism became the orthodoxy of the U.N.'s new array of specialized agencies and played, as we shall see, a formative role in the process of European integration. As international institutions — mainly concerned with economic, social, and technical tasks — proliferated, and international interdependence became more intense, particularly among the Western nations, liberal institutionalism evolved from functionalism into integration theory and on into theories of interdependence, from which position it then re-engaged a debate with new strains of realism. (This story will be developed later in the chapter.)

If the postwar debate over international order is broadly reminiscent of the interwar debate, it nevertheless took some interesting turns in the context of two developments unique to the post-1945 period. The first of these is the rise of Western European integration in the 1950s and 1960s. The second is the continued growth of economic interdependence among Western nations to an unprecedented complexity and intensity, which began to elicit much analysis in the 1970s and gave rise, in turn, to a more broadly focussed concern with international regimes. It is to these two especially fruitful developments in the theory and practice of international organization that the rest of this chapter is devoted.

Integration

Reduced to its fundamentals, international integration is the process whereby two or more sovereign states undertake to transform their relationship into an enduring form of economic and political community.[14] There has always been controversy as to the precise nature of that community, that is, the extent to which it should approximate a new supranational entity with powers transferred to it from the constituent states. To this classic federalist vision, the alternatives usually advanced are either a loose network of functional collaboration that often evades precise institutional definition but that explicitly rejects the state-building model or a "security community" in which participant states retain their formal sovereignty, although interdependence is high and the expectation of war, low.

There is, in the literature on integration, a second debate, cutting across the lines of the first, over how states are to move from the condition of international anarchy to whatever form of integrated community is envisaged. The broad distinction here is between those stressing the primacy of politics, with all the implications of high-level decision, drama, and indeterminacy, and those stressing the motive force of economic, social, and technological change, who tend to see the integration process as piecemeal, incremental, and inevitable.

In these various distinctions and the debates surrounding them it is not hard to hear echoes of realism, liberal institutionalism, and idealism. Indeed the story of Western European integration since World War II resonates with some classic themes, although the variations played on them by European policy makers and their academic observers sometimes make them hard to recognize at first.

In the early postwar years the dominant approach to European integration was *federalism*. One expression of the broad rejection of nationalism and the trappings of international war and diplomacy that, as noted earlier, is characteristic of the immediate aftermath of a cataclysmic conflict, European federalism, like world federalism, was a direct descendant of the idealist tradition. Less a systematic political theory of integration than a program for action and a political movement, European federalism provided, in those early years, a clear vision of the goal of integration, a method derived from a reading of the history of federations, and a strong dose of ideological commitment to a "new Europe."[15] In the classic formulation, integration entailed the creation of a supranational government, a United States of Europe (how that Europe was to be defined geographically was another matter) with sufficient constitutional authority, material power, and popular legitimacy to meet its constituents' shared needs for both security and welfare. The member-states would retain jurisdiction in those fields that they did not consider, in their collective judgement, appropriate or necessary to consign to the new central authority. Unitary supranational government was seen as neither possible nor desirable. On the contrary, European federalists placed great importance on the traditional virtues of unity in diversity.

Impressed by the depth of their economic and military vulnerability, European federalists took to heart the dictum that "the most dangerous way to cross a chasm is one step at a time."[16] Integration, in their view, should be a virtual constitutional revolution, a collective political act in which governments, under extreme pressure, negotiate a treaty to become the constitutional foundation of the new European state. The imagery is, ironically, straight from Hobbes: anarchic Western Europe, threatened with attack from without, exhausted by its cycle of internal wars of "all against all" (or France against Germany), its economy in ruins, must submit itself to a higher power that embodies its own collective will to survive.[17] It must, argued the federalists, and history suggests it can. Whether by intergovernmental negotiation or by a popularly based constituent assembly, or some combination of these, Europe will cross the threshold between international anarchy and federal government.

The early postwar years lent some plausibility to this strikingly idealist view of European integration. As a political movement, federalism cut across national boundaries and across the political spectrum and built up considerable momentum between 1945 and 1948. In the latter year, an impressive congress was held in The Hague, attracting political leaders from across the continent. Among its achievements was the design for a Council of Europe with many supranational features, seen as the framework in which the institutions of federal Europe were to take shape. Within a year, however, federalist hopes had begun to fade, undermined by Britain's resistance to supranationalism, and by the beginning of economic recovery and the formation of NATO, both of which lessened Europeans' sense of emergency and hence the lure of radical federal solutions.[18]

Like the broader idealist traditions of which it is part, European federalism exercised little direct influence once the immediate postwar crisis was past. Federalists could take some satisfaction that their vision of a supranational European state as the goal of integration was appropriated by Jean Monnet and the neofunctionalists, whose approach dominated the field through the 1960s. But their methods were, by and large, dismissed as unrealistic and they found themselves relegated to the role of commentator and conscience, occasionally coming out of obscurity to propose federalist solutions to problems the European Community encountered. For example, in the early 1970s, when the Community was experiencing difficulty moving beyond the customs union toward the full common market and economic union envisaged in the Treaty of Rome, federalists argued that this showed the limitations of gradualism: what was needed was a new act of political will, expressed in the form of a new or revised treaty and some far-reaching reforms to the Community.[19] A decade or so later, federalist initiatives along these lines, mainly through the European Parliament, did play some part in the negotiations leading to the Single European Act of 1986. But the institutional reforms and the increase in the Community's supranational powers embodied in the act fall well short of federalist aspirations.[20]

The chief rival of federalism as an approach to European integration in the early postwar years was *functionalism*. Rooted not in idealism but in the liberal-institutionalist tradition, functionalism embodies a very different view of the ends and the means of integration. Functionalists see integration as the slow accumulation, through co-operative international efforts at problem solving in specific economic, social, and technical sectors, of international agencies to which governments transfer real, although circumscribed, powers. David Mitrany, the central theorist and promoter of functionalism, refers to "technical self-determination," whereby the nature of the shared functional need dictates the type of international institution appropriate to meet it.[21] As the network of functional institutions develops, it is argued, the material and psychological bases of international conflict are gradually eroded and a practical, interest-based form of international governance, a "working peace system," emerges almost by stealth.

Like federalism, functionalism starts from the premise that the nation-state and the state system are inadequate instruments for human welfare and that they are dangerous for human security. Unlike federalism, however, functionalism embodies a deep suspicion of political or constitutional solutions, and a predisposition to technocracy and economic determinism. Functionalists expect no miraculous overnight political conversions on the part of governments, even in Hobbesian conditions of extremity. Rather, they rely on national self-interest to lure states into an array of enduring co-operative institutions. Functionalists tend to argue that a secular increase in global rationalization and interdependence is at work, visible in economics, science, communications, and ecology, and that growing tension between these forces, on the one hand, and national parochialism and protectionism, on the other, can only ultimately be resolved in favour of the former.[22] The key to the process is the enlightened self-interest of governments and their ability to transfer the lessons of co-operation from one sector to another ("spillover"). The process of integration, viewed this way, is cumulative and self-reinforcing.[23]

Since institutional form is determined by functional need, it is clear that functionalists will reject federalist notions of a constitutional design for integration set out in advance. Consistent with their suspicion of politics, functionalists are also troubled by the territorial, state-building element in classic European federalism. A United States of Europe, they argue, with its rigid constitution, its armed forces, its state apparatus, and its demarcated territory, might pose a greater security threat than present arrangements while at the same time discouraging functional solutions to a number of problems that go beyond Europe's capacity. Nothing could be more opposed to functionalism's organic, open, and evolutionary approach to international integration.

Like federalism, functionalism had some limited but real successes in early postwar Europe. Its theoretical language aside, functionalism was, after all, a doctrine held by eminently practical men, many of them steeped in the experience of international economic and social agencies, interallied co-operation, and national planning. It seemed a short step, then, to adapt these ideas to the Western European setting.

In most cases, nevertheless, functionalism took hold only after more ambitious schemes had failed. The U.N.'s Economic Commission for Europe, soon precluded by the cold war from promoting East-West economic integration, settled into making a modest but useful contribution through a variety of committees for economic and technical co-operation. The OEEC, once the French gave up trying to vest it with supranational authority, developed an effective functionalist-style system of "horizontal" and "vertical" committees for the collective administration of Western European recovery. The Council of Europe, its federalist dreams over, evolved quietly into a functionalist workshop preoccupied with such issues as the environment, transportation, and human rights.[24]

Less directly, functionalist theory forms a critical link in the intellectual history of the liberal-institutional tradition. Through the scholarly writings of David Mitrany and Ernst Haas,[25] in particular, and through the political work of Jean Monnet, functionalism drew together a set of scattered and preliminary ideas based on the experience of international interdependence and co-operation in the late 19th and early 20th centuries, gave them a certain clarity and cohesion, and so laid the foundations of some important theoretical developments in the 1950s and 1960s. One of these, as we shall see later, was the concept of transnational politics, out of which developed ideas of complex interdependence. Its more immediate impact was felt, however, in integration theory, with the rise of neofunctionalism to pre-eminence in the field.

Neofunctionalism is a view of integration that combines federalist purposes with a functionalist strategy. Originating in the mid-1950s, in Haas's work on the European Coal and Steel Community,[26] it provided an original and compelling explanation of the dynamics of economic and political integration. As an academic theory it was primarily an American construct, drawing on then-prevailing notions about decision making, bargaining, interest-group pluralism, and political development. In the mind of Monnet and his colleagues, however, neofunctionalism (although he did not use the term) originated as a set of precepts for political action, a pragmatic doctrine for the achievement of a federal Europe by incremental, functional means. In European policy circles practice took precedence over the clear articulation of the ideas behind it. This remained so, at least, until the academic theories circulated back to Community officials, who then eagerly embraced neofunctionalism as a kind of unofficial ideology, an elegant rationalization of the messy technical and political processes through which they sought to advance integration.[27]

For neofunctionalists the objective of the integration process was, at least until the late 1960s, a federal or supranational state. In his memoirs, Monnet is clear on this point: a strong federal authority was needed to attack shared economic problems, to offset Soviet power, to work with the United States in an Atlantic community, and to restore Europe's international status.[28] Haas, in his early work, described the aim as "a new political community, superimposed over the pre-existing ones."[29] In their later work, however, Haas and other scholars became less forthright on this issue. They began to define integration more broadly and implicitly less demandingly, as the creation of collective decision-making processes or of "institutions to which governments delegate decision-making authority and/or through which they decide jointly via more familiar intergovernmental negotiation."[30] In the face of mounting evidence that a strong supranational order was far from inevitable, neofunctionalists began to concede other possibilities, although references to "authority-legitimacy transfer" and "organizational development" made it clear where their preferences lay.[31]

To this federalist image of the objective, neofunctionalists grafted a version of the functionalist strategy of integration that, in their eyes at least, was more politically sophisticated than the original. In this synthesis lie both the explanatory power and the political attraction of the theory. The influence of functionalism, with its liberal-institutionalist baggage, is evident in (1) the emphasis on the compelling integrative force of rising economic and technological interdependence among states; (2) the choice of a gradualist, piecemeal strategy of integration through collaboration on specific functional tasks; (3) the notion of an indirect, long-term attack on national sovereignty through appeals to the enlightened self-interest of governments, interest groups, and the public; (4) the concept of spill-over, in which lessons, attitudes, and practices of integration spread from sector to sector; and (5) the focus on institutional development as the central measure of the progress of integration.

Where the old and the new functionalism differ over strategy is primarily in the latter's embrace of the political, which is dictated partly by its acceptance of federalist objectives and makes neofunctionalism essentially a theory of supranational state-building and not just an approach to the management of international interdependence through a "working peace system." More importantly, while technical, material, and administrative factors are held to play a background role in integration, politics is clearly at centre stage. The key players are politicians, international (European) officials, national bureaucrats, and interest groups coalescing and bargaining in complex international, transnational, transgovernmental, and national patterns. These political processes occur in the context of broad intergovernmental agreement about the need to integrate, and of a "permissive consensus" in public opinion.[32] "Spillover," moreover, is not taken to be automatic and technically driven, but is contrived and negotiated by political actors seeking to maximize advantage. As it impinges more and more on sectors at the core of national sovereignty, integration is expected to become more and more politicized, its process marked by periodic crises. Neofunctionalists do concede, however, that the political and institutional context loads the dice in favour of positive integrative outcomes.

The experience of European integration from the mid-1950s to the late 1960s seemed to show that this liberal-institutional approach was on to something. The European Community (resulting from a merger negotiated in 1965 among the Coal and Steel Community, the Atomic Energy Community, and the Economic Community) seemed to have devised an innovative political method, and of the sort just described, in implementing the customs union 18 months ahead of schedule, constructing the complex and delicate Common Agricultural Policy (CAP), and establishing the free movement of labour by the end of the 1960s.[33] Despite some worrisome crises over British entry and over the powers of the Commission and the European Parliament, the 1960s saw a steady expansion of the Community's scope of activity and of the powers of its central institutions.

As the Community entered the 1970s, however, it became increasingly evident that neofunctionalism had some serious limitations as an explanation of European integration and a handbook for those pursuing it. The debate over the first enlargement (the entry of the United Kingdom, Denmark, and Ireland, finally achieved in 1973) as well as the effort (begun in 1969) to move toward economic and monetary union raised political issues that seemed qualitatively different from those relating to the customs union in the earlier "transitional period" (1958–69). The neofunctionalist approach seemed unable to account for, or cope with, this high-stakes version of politics. It also became clear that neofunctionalism had paid insufficient attention to the broader international setting in which the Europeans were attempting integration.[34] The 1970s saw the end of over a decade of global economic expansion (fuelled by cheap energy), low inflation, and unemployment. That difficult decade also indicated that uncritical American support for European integration could no longer be assumed (nor, for that matter, could Soviet hostility, which had long been the other major external motive force). As a result — and viewed from today's vantage the point seems even stronger — the 1960s looked like an especially benign environment for European integration, an exceptional period on which it was probably unwise to base a general theory. This new sense of the limits of neofunctionalism was confirmed by the numerous failures of attempts to transplant its methods and explanations to regional integration in the Third World.[35]

If neofunctionalism lay firmly in the tradition of liberal institutionalism, its main challenger during its period of pre-eminence (roughly 1958–70) drew at least some inspiration from realism. The *confederal* (or *pluralist*) approach began from the premise that international integration and national consolidation were complementary, not antagonistic, processes. Whereas the other three approaches all assumed that integration was a zero-sum game in which the new central institutions could gain power and authority only at the expense of the constituent governments, confederalism envisaged an increase in governing capacities at both levels, accompanied by increases in communication and exchange among the states. A united Europe could, in this view, be expected to consist of intensely interdependent states that, while retaining their sovereignty, had designed intergovernmental institutions and procedures for making joint decisions and had ruled out the use of force in resolving their differences.[36] Supranational institutions were simply unnecessary, and predictions about the demise of the nation-state ran counter to the evidence of recent history.

The link with realism is, in fact, this respect for the intractable character of national interests and power. But liberal institutionalism finds an echo as well. There is something of 19th-century liberalism in the notion that international order is best served by the full realization of national self-determination and development, and by the encouragement of international commerce and communication. In the work of Karl Deutsch, which provides the empirical basis and the theoretical rationale for the confederal model (which he calls the "pluralistic security community"), such notions are deeply embedded. In his historical and comparative study of integration, Deutsch concludes that pluralistic (i.e., confederal) communities require fewer resources to establish, may be more durable, and, if the purpose of integration is to establish peace, sufficient to the task. Amalgamation into a new federal or unitary state may prove not only difficult but unnecessary.[37]

How is this version of international community to be achieved? Like federalists, confederalists place much emphasis on the interplay of political elites in a context of rising and mutually rewarding transactions and communications among states. In contrast, however, they avoid federalist-style "leaps of faith"; rather, the progress and prospects for integration at any time can be read in the empirical data that measure interdependence and the pattern of political attitudes.[38] In principle, such indices could predict the emergence of a supranational state. In practice, they show a parallel rise of national and international institutional capacities.

This sort of analysis has always found happy resonance in a number of European capitals where supranational visions of integration have been viewed with suspicion. The British and Scandinavian preference for simple intergovernmental co-operation was the rock on which early postwar federalist schemes foundered. Throughout the 1950s and beyond, the United Kingdom, resisting all efforts to be drawn into the European Community, proposed a series of intergovernmental alternatives to it — notably in the abortive free-trade–area proposals of the late 1950s and subsequently in the creation of the European Free Trade Association (EFTA).[39] Within the Community itself, de Gaulle's France waged war on what it saw as the excessively supranational pretensions of the U.N. Economic Commission. The French government provoked crises and promoted schemes to move the Community in a confederal direction, by curbing or vetoing the application of provisions for supranationality (such as majority voting in the Council of Ministers) or by proposing new intergovernmental organizations into which the Community might be folded. Some of these stratagems succeeded, such as the Luxembourg compromise of 1966, which deferred majority voting until the mid-1980s. Others did not, but their long-term effects were felt.[40]

In the 1970s, in fact, the confederal view of European integration began to gain more of a hearing. It became accepted as a form of pragmatic realism appropriate to integration in a difficult decade. In 1970, a rigorously intergovernmental arrangement for foreign-policy co-operation was set up parallel to Community institutions. In 1973, the British gained entry, reinforcing the partisans of pragmatic confederalism. Most importantly, in 1975, much of the real power of policy initiative shifted from the weakened U.N. Economic Commission to the newly minted European Council, an institutionalized thrice-yearly summit meeting of the Community's leaders. European integration, it was then argued, had now entered a "confederal phase."[41]

It may in fact be more accurate to say that from the mid-1970s until the mid-1980s it made little sense to use the language of integration at all in order to interpret what was happening in Western Europe. In retrospect, confederal Europe is perhaps better seen as a brief transition to a phase in which the Community, like the rest of the Western world, came to be reinterpreted from the perspective of interdependence theory. It is to that theme that we now turn.

The concept of interdependence as mutual sensitivity and vulnerability among nations has a long pedigree in international relations. As mentioned earlier, the idea that linkages among states are on the increase and that they are to some degree altering the character of international relations has always been fundamental to the liberal-institutional perspective in international order. The term appeared here and there in literature of both liberal-institutional and idealist inspiration prior to World War II and by the 1960s had become a staple of Western political rhetoric.[42] Not until the 1970s, however, did the concept come under the close scrutiny of international relations scholars.

The American economist Richard Cooper is generally credited with beginning the transformation of interdependence into the central focus of liberal-international political economy. His book *The Economics of Interdependence*, published in 1968,[43] highlighted the problems created for Western industrialized nations by the size and rate of growth since World War II of trade, investment, and other economic exchanges among them. In the early 1970s, political scientists began trying to define interdependence more precisely and to develop in more testable form the propositions being put forward about its trends and political effects. By the end of the decade, critical argument and empirical analysis related to interdependence had become a major occupation of international relations theorists. Although most of this work was based in the liberal-institutional tradition, realists and idealists were obliged, in their very different ways, to come to terms with interdependence as well.

What accounts for the enthusiasm with which international relations scholars picked up the idea of interdependence at that time? In the first place, policy makers and academics, especially in the United States, were rapidly becoming aware of international trade, monetary investment, and energy relationships as closely linked to, rather than distinct from, foreign policy, and causing increasing political problems both at home and abroad. Economic interdependence of this sort was hardly news in most other countries, especially ones, like Canada, with relatively small, open economies in which trade and foreign investment were large relative to GDP. But, by the late 1960s, the trade and balance-of-payments deficits and the problems of the dollar had sensitized Americans to an unprecedented extent to their economic vulnerability. As in other matters before and since, Canadians and others then witnessed the always-impressive spectacle of American scholars excitedly discovering something the rest of the world had long taken for granted, and transforming it into a productive and innovative academic industry.

A second reason for the emergence of the interdependence theme in the 1970s lay in the growing influence of Marxist and Latin American dependency perspectives in the emerging field of international political economy and the search for a liberal alternative with a sound conceptual and empirical base. Analysis of bargaining relationships and of the institutionalized management of interdependence seemed to provide an appropriate research agenda for this purpose.

A third reason was the perceived intellectual bankruptcy of the liberal-institutional approaches to international organization that had prevailed in the

1950s and 1960s. As we have seen, integration theory had begun to run out of steam (and credibility) by the early 1970s. The European Community seemed to be an example, not of regional integration on the march but rather of a complex interdependence among industrialized nations. The analysis of interdependence — its dimensions, its effects, its management — devoid of the teleological baggage of neofunctionalist integration theory, seemed an attractive way out of the theoretical impasse in which liberal institutionalism found itself. Scholars such as Ernst Haas and Joseph Nye, who had begun their careers studying integration, led the way in attempting to take the political science of interdependence in more systematic theoretical directions.[44]

For all intents and purposes, the empirical focus of this emergent field of interdependence studies was the postwar Western industrialized world. In principle, the approach could also be applied to international relationships, where the general levels of economic development and exchange seemed lower than in the West, and some attempts were made to examine East-West relations, North-South relations, or even relations among less-developed countries, through these lenses. On the whole, however, scholarly attention centred on Western Europe, Canadian-American relations, and various other groupings of the Western industrialized nations, such as the OECD or the Atlantic Community.

With respect to Western Europe, the dominant view from the mid-1970s on took the Community to be, first and foremost, a system of collective policy making for a group of unusually interdependent states.[45] Unlike almost all previous analytical approaches to the Community, this one showed little interest in the ultimate political form to which it might evolve, or in how it was moving along that path. Integration, as purpose or as process, was scarcely mentioned. Instead, the Community was accepted as an untidy, flawed, but relatively stable political system, a unique blend of supranational, transnational, intergovernmental, and domestic political processes. What mattered was not what it might become but what it was, and did, here and now.

This literature, policy-oriented and theoretically unpretentious, consists largely of close empirical studies of European Community policy in sectors such as agriculture, competition and industrial policy, monetary policy, trade, and aid, drawing cautious generalizations as to how the Community works. The aim is to account for its capacity to arrive at acceptable collective decisions in some cases and not in others, to explain why specific policies such as the CAP have taken the form they have and why the Community has proved more effective in implementing policy in some sectors than in others.

Among the general conclusions that arise from these analyses are the following, which paint a portrait of complex interdependence:

1. National governments remain major players, however constrained they are by Community institutions and processes. They have adapted and expanded their capacities in order to function more effectively in the Community context. There is a symbiotic, not a zero-sum relationship between Community and national policy making.

2. There is no uniform Community policy process but rather a whole range of distinct sectors or "tracks" — a pattern reinforced by bureaucratic structures and the technical character of policy. Issue linkage is rare. Moreover, the predominant mode of collective decision varies from sector to sector — intergovernmental in one, supranational in another, transnational or based on patron-client relationships in another.
3. The formal institutions and processes often explain less about Community decisions and policies than do the informal relationships and "back-channel" networks of national and Community-level officials.
4. In many respects, Community policy making resembles national politics, considering the importance in each of interest groups, public opinion, bureaucratic politics, and patron-client relationships between regulatory bodies and those they regulate.

This portrait of the Community in the 1970s and early 1980s, while perhaps not pleasing to committed integrationists, does at least show an established, working system of collective policy making among highly interdependent states. Neo-functionalists taking heart from the recent energetic campaign to achieve a fully liberalized "internal market" in the Community by 1992 may mount a challenge to this "interdependence" perspective, but the burden of proof would seem now to be on them.

Canadian-American relations have provided a second fertile field for the empirical analysis of interdependence. As far back as the 19th century, studies of these relations have made much of the close interconnection of the two societies, although use of the term "interdependence" was rare and more often than not the conclusions drawn were more in conformity with theories of dependency or integration.[46] Indeed, the interdependence perspective on Canadian-American relations has been engaged, tacitly or openly, in debate with both of those schools of thought almost from the outset. Some of the first empirical analyses of interdependence carried out in the late 1960s and early 1970s concerned Canadian-American relations, notably the volume edited by Fox, Hero, and Nye, *Canada and the United States: Transnational and Transgovernmental Relations.*[47] A few years later Keohane and Nye noted that, while Canadian-American relations were hardly a typical case from which to generalize about world politics, they were arguably the most likely to conform to the "ideal type" of complex interdependence. Examination of the relationship, they claimed, would allow them to analyze the "political processes of complex interdependence in practice: to see how they have changed over time, and how they affect the outcomes of high-level political conflicts in which military force plays no role."[48]

According to Keohane and Nye, complex interdependence has three principal characteristics. First, societies are connected by multiple channels — interstate, transgovernmental, and transnational. Second, the agenda of interstate relations consists of multiple issues not arranged in a clear or consistent hierarchy. Military security does not always have priority, and the distinction between domestic and foreign policy is blurred. Third, the threat or deployment of military force is not an important factor in the relationship.[49] Given this definition, it is not surprising that Canadian-American relations should be seen as a prime testing ground, particularly for propositions relating complex interdependence to negotiating behaviour and outcomes, and to institutional development and integration.

Regional and bilateral studies have dominated the empirical analysis of interdependence. Given Richard Cooper's concern with the economic relationships of the Western industrialized nations, it is a little surprising that more work has not been done on the politics of broader multilateral interdependence in the Atlantic community or the OECD. Part of the reason may lie in the methodological difficulties of measuring and testing interdependence among more than two nations.[50] It may also be that until the establishment of the Western "summits" in 1975 and the general intensification of bilateral and multilateral negotiations and consultations that the Western world experienced from the mid-1970s on, the institutions and processes of collective decisions that might have provided a benchmark for measuring the impact of interdependence upon international behaviour were lacking.

Whenever a term such as "power" or "interdependence" moves from popular, general usage to narrower, scholarly applications, it raises difficult problems of definition. It would clearly be insufficient for theoretical purposes to work with a definition of interdependence that simply indicated that the actions of each state affected the others in some measure. The point is to distinguish interdependence from "normal" international relations, if possible by some sort of qualitative threshold.

Early approaches to definitions were not entirely successful in this respect. Oran Young defined interdependence as "the extent to which events occurring in any one part or within any given component unit of a world system affect (either physically or perceptually) events taking place in each of the other parts or component units of the system." Its opposite was therefore autonomy or isolation.[51] A few years later, a leading theorist of interdependence defined it in terms of "the outcome of specified actions of two or more parties . . . when such actions are mutually contingent."[52] Each of these formulations is broad enough to embrace a number of subcategories, for example, physical and perceptual (or felt) interdependence for Young, and strategic, systemic, and collective-goods interdependence for Morse. But they also pass over the distinction between mutual dependence, on the one hand, and mutual sensitivity, on the other, which later writings showed to be of some significance. Keohane and Nye defined "sensitivity interdependence" as degrees of mutual responsiveness within a given policy framework — "how quickly do changes in one country bring costly change in another country, and how great are the costly effects?" "Vulnerability" interdependence, in contrast, rests on the relative availability and costliness of alternatives; in other words, it refers to a state's liability to suffer costs imposed by external events even after policies have been altered.[53] While Keohane and Nye pay some attention to sensitivity, it is clear that vulnerability, more closely related to considerations of power and strategic choice, is really at the heart of their approach.

In an important article published in 1980, Baldwin acknowledged the existence of these same two themes running through general and scholarly usage. The central idea, he argues, has always been that of mutual dependence, or "relations that would be mutually costly to forego."[54] Complicating matters, however, is a second notion in general usage and insisted upon rather unhelpfully by economists such as Cooper, of dependence or interdependence as a situation where "an effect is contingent on or conditioned by something else."[55] Despite claims about the long pedigree and theoretical significance of this "sensitivity" definition, Baldwin argues persuasively that interdependence seen as mutual vulnerability, or referring to mutual relationships that would be costly to break, is the more usual, and useful, concept, especially for international relations. Such terms as mutual "influence," "responsiveness," and "sensitivity" are sufficient for the other kinds of relationships.

Proponents of both the broader and the narrower definitions of interdependence agree on the importance of being able to measure it, so as to test statements about its growth and significance. Most frequently used are economic indices such as the size of the "foreign sector" (e.g., trade, investment) relative to the economy as a whole. For Cooper, economic interdependence is "the dollar value of economic transactions among regions or countries, either in absolute terms, or relative to their total transactions."[56] Others have sought more refined indicators of the covariance of events in one society with those elsewhere. Rosecrance and his colleagues, for example, measured "horizontal interdependence" as transactions in money, people, and goods among nations, and "vertical interdependence" as the responses of one nation to another in terms of factor prices. Only the second, it seems, really comes close to an index of interdependence (as distinct from what *produces* that interdependence), and even here it is sensitivity more than vulnerability that is being measured.[57] Indeed, the more one's concerns move to the latter, and to its more directly political and strategic aspects, the more difficult the precise measurement of interdependence becomes.

Questions of measurement are important in relation to claims that international interdependence is low or high, rising or falling, and has certain consequences for foreign policy and for the future of the international system. Without doing too much violence to the nuances of various views, we can divide most scholars into two groups on these issues — one that sees interdependence as high, rising, and revolutionary in importance, and another that sees it as declining or fluctuating, and overrated as a force in international relations. Not surprisingly, idealists and liberal institutionalists tend to be found in the first group, realists in the second.

For most of the first group, the steady rise in interdependence over the last century or so among the industrialized nations has to do with the process of economic modernization with its syndrome of industrialization, international division of labour, and domestic pluralism. It may well be that interdependence has reached, or soon will reach, the limits of its growth. In any case, decline is unlikely, and even if it achieves a plateau, the political consequences may continue to unfold for some time yet. Idealists of the "global village" stripe clearly have the most far-reaching and optimistic sense of the likely effects. Among liberal institutionalists, there is a "modernist" wing, identified with Morse and Young, that accepts some idealist or globalist notions about the continuing development and the long-term transformational impact of interdependence, and a more cautious, mainstream view, associated with Keohane and Nye, that looks toward realism and emphasizes the role of power and national interest.[58]

Some scholars in the second group claim that by conventional measures of the size of the foreign sector, interdependence among industrialized nations has fallen through most of the 20th century. The argument is not necessarily that it has become insignificant, but that it is markedly lower today than in the late 19th century, and that there is no theoretical basis for expecting an upturn.[59] A more nuanced view, associated with Rosecrance, Katzenstein, and others, denies both secular rise and secular decline over the century. Katzenstein observes, from the 1950s onward, a dramatic reversal of the decline in international transactions, while Rosecrance sees a series of shorter-phase cycles over the century.[60] These data may give some comfort to realists, but they are certainly not incompatible with a liberal-institutionalist perspective.

Kenneth Waltz, however, has argued that the theoretical logic and the empirical evidence backing claims that interdependence is high, rising, and acts as a pacifying, constraining force on nations, are not persuasive.[61] He is particularly critical of related claims that the United States is more vulnerable, sensitive, and constrained than hitherto, and hence is less of a superpower than it once was. Another realist, Robert Gilpin, argues in a similar vein that there is no historical evidence that trade and economic interdependence "create bonds of mutual interest and a vested interest in international pace and thus have a moderating influence on international relations."[62]

Such arguments notwithstanding, liberal institutionalists have continued to explore the relationships between interdependence, foreign policy, and change in the international system. With respect to the making of foreign policy, interdependence does seem to change the cost calculations governments make in considering options, while the interdependence syndrome of domestic fragmentation and transnational linkage politics threatens loss of control and blurs the line between the domestic and the external.

In contrast to realists, who assert that relative overall power is the best predictor of bargaining outcomes, liberal institutionalists claim to show that interdependence can alter significantly the context and structure of negotiations. In Canadian-American relations, they argue, Canada has got its way in bilateral disputes more frequently than the straight calculus of power would predict. The same can be said of the smaller members of the European Community in dealing with France, Britain, and West Germany. Complex interdependence, it seems, provides opportunities for adept and single-minded smaller powers to "win" in specific issue areas that may matter enormously to them but occupy less of the greater power's attention and resources.

As to the effects of interdependence on the nation-states and the prospects for the transformation of international relations into a truly "global politics," realists are predictably skeptical of idealist claims. Whether trade "aggravates or moderates conflicts," writes Gilpin, "is dependent on the political circumstances. . . . No generalizations on the relationship of economic interdependence and political behaviour appear possible."[63] This view is consistent with realist assumptions about the primacy of politics and the immutable pattern of interstate relations. Part of the difference between realists and idealists on this issue is also related to how each views the empirical evidence of interdependence. The former tend to insist that nations' behaviour demonstrates mutual vulnerability — a characteristic both difficult to measure and likely to fluctuate over time — while the latter are content to infer interdependence and the growth of community from the quantitative increase in international linkages.

Liberal institutionalists sidestep this inconclusive debate by focussing on the undeniable pressures for collective international management that flow from perceptions of increased interdependence. Most would accept that interdependence, both physical and "felt," has been on the rise since World War II at least. If it does not pose a threat to the continuation of the nation-state or the state system, it does provide new constraints and opportunities for governments seeking to maximize their interests in the international political economy. For the last decade or more, liberal institutionalists have turned their attention to international regimes as a response to the need to manage interdependence collectively. Something of a consensus definition has been established, which holds that regimes are "sets of implicit or explicit principles, norms, rules, and decision-making procedures around which actors' expectations converge in a given area of international relations."[64] The chapter in this volume by James Keeley examines the regime approach in detail. It is, however, worth noting here by way of conclusion that the concept of regime has brought liberal institutionalists squarely back to themes of international governance from which they had tended to wander after the decline of integration theory. Some realists or structuralists question the introduction of regimes as an intervening explanatory variable lying between the power structure and international behaviour; others doubt some regime analysts' claim to have incorporated realist notions of egoistic self-interest into their approach.[65] Whatever the merits of these arguments, the evolution from integration to interdependence to regime analysis has undeniably transformed the classic debate about international order into more productive terms for both theory and policy.

NOTES

1. For a modern realist notion of structure, see K.N. Waltz, *Theory of International Politics* (Don Mills, Ont.: Addison-Wesley, 1979), chap. 5.

2. The classic realist text remains H.J. Morgenthau, *Politics among Nations*, 5th ed., rev. (New York: Knopf, 1978). On international institutions see chaps. 27 and 28.

3. J.M. Grieco, "Anarchy and the Limits of Cooperation: A Realist Critique of the Newest Liberal Institutionalism," *International Organization* 42 (Summer 1988): 485–507.

4. "Idealism" or utopianism are the traditional terms, sometimes used pejoratively in realist writings, e.g., E.H. Carr, *The Twenty Years' Crisis 1919–1939*, (London: Macmillan 1939), and R.E. Osgood, *Ideals and Self-Interest in America's Foreign Relations* (Chicago: University of Chicago Press, 1953). "Cosmopolitanism" has been given new currency by Charles Beitz. See his *Political Theory and International Relations* (Princeton: Princeton University Press, 1979).

5. An excellent historical review of this tradition is in F.H. Hinsley, *Power and the Pursuit of Peace* (Cambridge: Cambridge University Press, 1963), part I.

6. For data on the rise of international intergovernmental and nongovernmental organizations, see J.D. Singer and M. Wallace, "Intergovernmental Organization in the Global System 1815–1964: A Quantitative Description," *International Organization* 24 (Spring 1970): 239–87, and K. Skjelsbaek, "The Growth of International Nongovernmental Organization in the Twentieth Century," *International Organization* 25 (Summer 1971): 420–42. For an update to the late 1970s, see C.C. Pentland, "Building Global Institutions," in *Issues in Global Politics*, ed. R.G. Boyd and C.C. Pentland (New York: Free Press, 1981), 331–36.

7. For a range of views on the Concert, see E.V. Gulick, *Europe's Classical Balance of Power* (New York: Norton, 1955); C. Holbraad, *The Concert of Europe* (London: Longman, 1970); and R.B. Elrod, "The Concert of Europe: A Fresh Look at an International System," *World Politics* 28 (January 1976):159–74.

8. See Hinsley, *Power and the Pursuit of Peace*, chap. 6, and F.M. Russell, *Theories of International Relations* (New York: D. Appleton-Century, 1936), chap. 14.

9. The best account of the League remains F.P. Walters, *A History of the League of Nations* (London: Oxford University Press, 1952). See also A. Zimmern, *The League of Nations and the Rule of Law 1918–1935* (London: Macmillan, 1936).

10. Carr, *Twenty Years' Crisis*; M. Wight, *Power Politics* (London: Royal Institute of International Affairs, 1946).

11. D. Mitrany, *The Progress of International Government* (London: Allen and Unwin, 1933).

12. "The Development of International Cooperation in Economic and Social Affairs," *Special Supplement to the Monthly Summary of the League of Nations* (Geneva: League of Nations, 1939).

13. On shifting American attitudes to the U.N., in particular, see T.M. Franck, *Nation Against Nation* (New York: Oxford University Press, 1985).

14. For an earlier formulation along the same lines, see C.C. Pentland, *International Theory and European Integration* (New York: Free Press, 1973).

15. See A. Zurcher, *The Struggle to Unite Europe 1940–1958* (New York: New York University Press, 1958); and H. Brugmans, *L'Idée Européenne 1920–1970* (Bruges: de Tempel, 1970).

16. Quoted in J.P. Sewell, *Functionalism and World Politics* (Princeton: Princeton University Press, 1966), 315.

17. For a classic critique of federalist proposals for world order, see I.L. Claude, Jr., *Swords into Plowshares*, 4th ed. (New York: Random House, 1971), chap. 18.

18. For a history of early postwar developments, see R. Mayne, *The Recovery of Europe* (London: Weidenfeld and Nicolson, 1970), and Zurcher, *Struggle to Unite Europe.*

19. See, for example, J. Pinder and R. Pryce, *Europe After de Gaulle* (Harmondsworth: Penguin, 1969); and A. Spinelli, *The European Adventure* (London: Knight, 1972).

20. On the Single European Act, see *Bulletin of the European Communities Supplement 1/87* (Luxembourg: 1987), s-23; and J. de Ruyt, *L'Acte Unique Européenne* (Brussels: Eds. de l'Université de Bruxelles, 1987).

21. D. Mitrany, *A Working Peace System* (Chicago: Quadrangle, 1966), 72–73.

22. For an exposition and critique of this position, see Sewell, *Functionalism*, chap. 2.

23. D. Mitrany, "The Prospect of European Integration: Federal or Functional?" *Journal of Common Market Studies* 4 (December 1965): 119–49.

24. For a survey of these organizations, see M. Palmer et al., eds., *European Unity: A Survey of the European Organizations* (London: Allen and Unwin, 1968), chaps. 2, 3, and 4.

25. E.B. Haas, *The Uniting of Europe* (Stanford: Stanford University Press, 1958), and *Beyond the Nation-State* (Stanford: Stanford University Press, 1964).

26. Haas, *Uniting of Europe.*

27. On the interplay between neofunctionalist theory and the self-perception of Community officials, see P.C. Schmitter, "A Revised Theory of Regional Integration," *International Organization* 24 (Autumn 1970): 838.

28. J. Monnet, *Mémoires* (Paris: Fayard, 1976), 393–95.

29. Haas, *Uniting of Europe*, 16.

30. L.N. Lindberg, "Political Integration as a Multidimensional Phenomenon Requiring Multivariate Measurement," *International Organization* 24 (Autumn 1970): 652.

31. E.B. Haas, "The Study of Regional Integration: Reflections on the Joy and Anguish of Pre-Theorizing," *International Organization* 24 (Autumn 1970): 631–66; and P.C. Schmitter, "The 'Organizational Development' of International Organization," *International Organization* 25 (Autumn 1971): 917–37.

32. L.N. Lindberg and S.A. Scheingold, *Europe's Would-Be Polity* (Englewood Cliffs, N.J.: Prentice-Hall, 1970), chap. 2.

33. For a contemporary neofunctionalist analysis of this progress, see L.N. Lindberg, *The Political Dynamics of European Economic Integration* (Stanford: Stanford University Press, 1963).

34. E.B. Haas, *The Obsolescence of Regional Integration Theory* (Berkeley: Institute of International Studies, 1975).

35. For a critical commentary on these attempts, see W.A. Axline, "Underdevelopment, Dependence and Integration: The Politics of Regionalism in the Third World," *International Organization* 31 (Winter 1977): 83–105.

36. Pentland, *International Theory and European Integration*, chap. 2, develops and criticizes this model, there labelled "pluralism" after Deutsch's concept of the "pluralistic security Community."

37. K.W. Deutsch et al., *Political Community and the North Atlantic Area* (Princeton: Princeton University Press, 1957).

38. See, for example, the empirical assessment of the state of integration in K.W. Deutsch et al., *France, Germany and the Western Alliance* (New York: Charles Scribner's Sons, 1967).

39. M. Camps, *Britain and the European Community 1955–1963* (Oxford: Oxford University Press, 1964).

40. On French policy toward supranationalism, see N. Heathcote, "The Crisis of European Supranationality," *Journal of Common Market Studies* 5 (December 1986): 140–71; and S.J. Bodenheimer, *Political Union: A Microcosm of European Politics 1960–1966* (Leyden: Sijthoff, 1967).

41. P.G. Taylor, "The Politics of the European Communities: The Confederal Phase," *World Politics* 27 (April 1975): 336–60.

42. For a pre–World War II work, see R. Muir, *The Interdependent World and Its Problems* (London: Constable, 1932).

43. R.N. Cooper, *The Economics of Interdependence* (New York: McGraw-Hill, 1968).

44. R.O. Keohane and J.S. Nye, Jr., "International Interdependence and Integration," in *Handbook of Political Science*, vol. 8, ed. F.I. Greenstein and N.W. Polsby (Reading, Mass.: Addison-Wesley, 1975), 363–414; E.B. Haas, "Turbulent Fields and the Theory of Regional Integration," *International Organization* 30 (Spring 1976): esp. 208–12.

45. H. Wallace, W. Wallace, and C. Webb, eds., *Policy-Making in the European Community*, 2d ed. (New York: John Wiley and Sons, 1983), is representative of this approach.

46. See, for example, G. Smith, *Canada and the Canadian Question* (Toronto: Hunter and Rose, 1891).

47. A.B. Fox, A.O. Hero, Jr., and J.S. Nye, eds., "Canada and the United States: Transnational and Transgovernmental Relations," special issue of *International Organization* 28 (Autumn 1974): 595–1033.

48. R.O. Keohane and J.S. Nye, Jr., *Power and Interdependence* (Boston: Little, Brown, 1977), 165–66.

49. Keohane and Nye, *Power and Interdependence*, 24–29.

50. See M.A. Tetrault, "Measuring Interdependence," *International Organization* 34 (Summer 1980): 429–43.

51. O.R. Young, "Interdependencies in World Politics," *International Journal* 24 (Autumn 1969): 726.

52. E.L. Morse, *Foreign Policy and Interdependence in Gaullist France* (Princeton: Princeton University Press, 1973), 56.

53. Keohane and Nye, *Power and Interdependence*, 12–13.

54. D.A. Baldwin, "Interdependence and Power: A Conceptual Analysis," *International Organization* 34 (Autumn 1980): 487.

55. Baldwin, "Interdependence and Power," 475.

56. R.N. Cooper, "Economic Interdependence and Foreign Policy in the Seventies," *World Politics* 24 (January 1972): 159.

57. R. Rosecrance et al., "Whither Interdependence?" *International Organization* 31 (Summer 1977): 425–71. For a critique, see Tetrault, "Measuring Interdependence."

58. R.O. Keohane and J.S. Nye, Jr., "Power and Interdependence Revisited," *International Organization* 41 (Autumn 1987): 725–53.

59. K.W. Deutsch and A. Eckstein, "National Industrialization and the Declining Share of the International Economic Sector 1890–1959," *World Politics* 13 (January 1961): 267–99.

60. P.J. Katzenstein, "International Interdependence: Some Long-Term Trends and Recent Changes," *International Organization* 29 (Autumn 1975): 1021–1034.

61. K.N. Waltz, "The Myth of National Interdependence," in *The International Corporation*, ed. C.P. Kindleberger (Cambridge, Mass.: MIT Press, 1970), 205–23; and Waltz, *Theory of International Politics*, chap. 7.

62. R. Gilpin, *The Political Economy of International Relations* (Princeton: Princeton University Press, 1987), 56–57.

63. Gilpin, *Political Economy of International Relations*, 57–58.

64. S.D. Krasner, "Structural Causes and Regime Consequences: Regimes as Intervening Variables," *International Organization* 36 (Spring 1982): 186.

65. Grieco, "Anarchy and the Limits of Cooperation," 495–503.

SELECT BIBLIOGRAPHY

Archer, C. *International Organization*. London: Allen and Unwin, 1983.

Baldwin, D.A. "Interdependence and Power: A Conceptual Analysis." *International Organization* 34 (Autumn 1980): 471–506.

Bennett, A.L. *International Organization*. 3d ed. Englewood Cliffs, N.J.: Prentice-Hall, 1984.

Bull, H. *The Anarchical Society*. London: Macmillan, 1977.

Carr, E.H. *The Twenty Years' Crisis 1919–1939*. London: Macmillan, 1939.

Claude, Jr., I.L. *Swords into Plowshares*. New York: Random House, 1971.

Cooper, R.N. *The Economics of Interdependence*. New York: McGraw-Hill, 1968.

Deutsch, K.W.; Sidney A. Burrell; Robert A. Kann; Maurice Lee, Jr.; Martin Lichtermann; Raymond E. Lindgren; Francis L. Loewenhein; and Richard W. Van Wagenen. *Political Community and the North Atlantic Area*. Princeton: Princeton University Press, 1957.

Diehl, P., ed. *The Politics of International Organizations: Patterns and Insights*. Chicago: Irwin-Dorsay, 1989.

Grieco, J.M. "Anarchy and the Limits of Cooperation: A Realist Critique of the Newest Liberal Institutionalism." *International Organization* 42 (Summer 1988): 485–508.

Haas, E.B. *The Obsolescence of Regional Integration Theory.* Berkeley: Institute of International Studies, 1975.
———. *The Uniting of Europe.* Stanford: Stanford University Press, 1958.
Hinsley, F.H. *Power and the Pursuit of Peace.* Cambridge: Cambridge University Press, 1963.
Keohane, R.O., and J.S. Nye, Jr. *Power and Interdependence.* Boston: Little, Brown, 1977.
———. "Power and Interdependence Revisited." *International Organization* 41 (Autumn 1987): 725–53.
Mitrany, D. *A Working Peace System.* Chicago: Quadrangle, 1966.
Pentland, C.C. *International Theory and European Integration.* New York: Free Press, 1973.
Wallace, H.; W. Wallace; and C. Webb, eds. *Policy-Making in the European Community.* 2d ed. New York: John Wiley and Sons, 1983.
Waltz, K.N. *Theory of International Politics.* Don Mills, Ont.: Addison-Wesley, 1979.

STRUCTURAL CHANGE AND HEGEMONIC DECLINE: IMPLICATIONS FOR NATIONAL GOVERNMENTS

Michael K. Hawes

The purpose of this chapter is to provide a foundation for systematically assessing the impact of structural change at the level of the international economy on the direction and content of national foreign economic policy. More specifically, it attempts to elaborate an analytic framework that is aimed at exploring the relationship between structural change in the postwar world economy (understood as exogenous incentives and constraints) and trade policy in advanced developed market economies (DMEs). The focus is on how global structural change has affected the individual members of the system[1] and how they have responded to these changes. It is important to note that this "analytic framework" or model does not pretend to be a comprehensive or parsimonious theory. Our aim here is not to pursue a deductive theory of international relations[2] — through positivist methods or otherwise. Nor, although the model is more consistent with "historically sensitive" explanations of foreign policy and world politics, does it conform to the limitations of broad cyclical theory. Rather, as a particular theoretical framework, it represents the beginnings of a systemic model that attempts to bring together the unique insights of a structuralist position with the breadth and historicism of an international political-economy approach.

In a seminal and frequently cited article entitled "Pre-theories and Theories of Foreign Policy,"[3] James Rosenau introduced the notion that, in order to understand the external behaviour of states, one had to understand the sources of foreign policy. These "imputs" (to use Rosenau's language), which gave shape and direction to the foreign-policy behaviour of individual states, included external influences, societal pressures, role expectations, individual or personal factors, and governmental realities. Following Rosenau's invitation to address the various sources of foreign policy, students of world politics began to shift away from the traditional systemic (external) and role-determined explanations[4] and concentrated on societal and governmental sources of foreign policy. Following the pioneering work of Graham Allison and other proponents of the bureaucratic-politics paradigm,[5] domestic considerations became paramount in the study of foreign policy. In fact, the enthusiasm that the North American political-science community demonstrated for these societally generated, process-oriented explanations of foreign policy in the 1970s was really quite dramatic.

Interestingly, despite the influence of Robert Keohane and Joseph Nye's work, and their insistence that strategies of foreign economic policy depended on the interplay of domestic and international forces,[6] the preoccupation with domestic sources has been particularly pronounced. Liberals and realists alike continued to adhere to the view that states can be differentiated fundamentally in terms of their domestic structures and that these differences account for unique national responses to similar international phenomena.[7] While this is an eminently sensible position, and one generally consistent with the theoretical position that will be outlined below, the problem is that an uncritical commitment to this notion tends to "trivialize" the importance of external sources.

More recently, scholarly treatments of foreign policy in general and trade policy in particular (especially that of non-hegemonic Western states) have continued to emphasize the impact of domestic sources. Whether from a public-choice or pluralist perspective that focusses on the role of competition among domestic interests and sees governments rationally responding to competing interests within society, or from a more subtle view that sees foreign economic policy as the result of complex economic and political inequalities within society, the tendency has been to focus on the internal dynamics of foreign economic policy — largely from a process orientation. While there are many examples of this position, an interesting example from the Canadian case is Kim Richard Nossal's treatment of bureaucratic politics in the Canadian context and his examination, with Michael Atkinson, of the Canadian fighter-aircraft decision.[8] This argument attaches a great deal of importance to internal considerations and precious little to external, systemically determined sources of foreign policy.

Others have been less willing to pursue arguments that rely too heavily on either the systemic level of analysis or the state level. In an introduction to a recent collection of essays, William Avery and David Rapkin have argued that "the two levels of analysis must be employed in a complementary fashion."[9] However, as David Lake has perceptively noted, "comparatively little attention has been devoted to the international [or systemic] sources of foreign economic policy in individual countries."[10] Much needs to be done, Lake argues, to understand the important ways in which international economic structures shape individual foreign policies. In his study of the United States between 1887 and 1934, for example, Lake argues that "the [principal] source of American foreign policy . . . was to be found within the international political economy."[11]

To see foreign economic policy strictly in domestic terms (focussing on the domestic demand for protection, economic security, and the machinations of the domestic-policy process) seems to be far too limiting. The position advanced here is that the impact of external forces on advanced DMEs is considerable (and not just on the weaker states) and that this influence has been mounting as the world economy has become more diffused and fragmented. From this perspective, any discussion of national foreign economic policy must take place within the context of a significant global struggle for productive advantage, markets, and employment.

In the broadest sense, this model argues that an increasingly unstable world economy populated with or characterized by increasingly weak and ineffective international economic institutions (international organizations) and a fragile international economic structure has translated into greater *constraints* on the direction and content of foreign economic policy in advanced DMEs. In other words, within the context of a stable, highly structured world economy — such as existed prior to 1968 — DMEs tended to have a great deal of freedom in terms of their responses to external pressures *and*, beginning in the early 1970s, the governments of DMEs have been increasingly constrained by structural rigidities and by instability in the world economy. In simple terms, in an increasingly fragmented and interdependent world, the foreign economic policies of advanced DMEs are becoming more vulnerable to external influences.

Interestingly, this perspective appears to be in direct contrast to the thesis of an earlier attempt to understand the relationship between international and domestic sources of foreign economic policy. According to this view,

> international and domestic factors have been closely intertwined in the historical evolution of the international political economy since the middle of the nineteenth century. . . . But the relative weight of domestic structures in the shaping of foreign economic policy increased in periods of hegemonic decline. As long as the distribution of power in the international political economy was not in question, strategies of foreign economic policy were conditioned primarily by the structure of the international political economy. But when the structure could no longer be taken for granted, as is true today, the relative importance of domestic forces in shaping foreign economic policy increased.[12]

It is important to note, however, that the position taken by Peter Katzenstein (and by the contributors to his book) does not differ that radically from the one offered here. Although he clearly saw domestic structures as more directly relevant during periods of systemic instability (and this chapter suggests the opposite), he did recognize the fact that "the international context in which these countries found themselves in turn influenced their domestic structures."[13] In short, as does Katzenstein, this chapter argues that the dynamic relationship between domestic and external sources of foreign economic policy has not been captured in the literature. Katzenstein's position is that "the literature on foreign economic policy [has], in recent years, unduly discounted the influence of domestic forces."[14] This analysis, partly because of the influence of Katzenstein's *Between Power and Plenty*, suggests that it is external forces that are now being undervalued.

The argument that domestic and international sources are inextricably linked, and that they *both* influence foreign economic policy, cannot be overstated. The model outlined in this chapter does not in any way intend to propose an exclusively "systemic" understanding of national foreign economic policy. However, it is essential to remember that domestic politics and governmental-process explanations must operate within the framework and limitations provided by external systemic influences. In other words, the framework we are proposing is fundamental to an understanding of foreign economic policy in DMEs because it contextualizes the formulation of this policy by addressing the impact of external influences — and that it is a natural and necessary complement to analysis carried out at the level of the state.

This chapter sets out to provide a theoretical framework that focusses on the importance of external phenomena while retaining a commitment to the notion that different domestic structures and different historical realities are also critical explanatory factors in the articulation of a state's foreign economic policy. Specifically, it begins by examining the "roots" of the modified structural perspective through a detailed analysis of the hegemonic-stability theory. After exploring this model, which tends to focus on the origins of structural change in the world economy, it proceeds to an assessment of the modified structural model and to a discussion of the importance of examining the effects or implications of systemic change. Finally, the chapter concludes by examining the importance of systemic explanations and the need to understand structural change.

The Theory of Hegemonic Stability

The modified structural model presented in this chapter derives from systemic models of world politics, which are leadership-based. In particular, the theoretical argument can be traced to an acceptance of the fundamental premise behind the hegemonic-stability thesis. This model, championed by Charles Kindleberger, Robert Keohane, Robert Gilpin, and others,[15] basically argues that "variations in global order and stability [can be] attributed to variations in the systemic distribution of power resources and capabilities, with a unipolar/hegemonic distribution associated with higher levels of order and stability."[16] More specifically, our argument conforms to the second part of the main premise — that hegemonic systems tend to be more stable. In addition, there is a general commitment to the two main assumptions that follow from that premise. First, that during periods of hegemonic ascendance, open international trade and investment regimes (which provide a disproportionate share of benefits to the hegemon) will flourish. And, second, that during periods of hegemonic decline and instability, closure or protectionism will tend to prevail.

The hegemonic-stability thesis is a structural model of systemic change that focusses on the role of leadership and on the structure of the international economic system. This model rests on three premises. The first, as outlined above, suggests that order in world politics is typically created and sustained by the existence of a single dominant power (which is at once a world power and a lead economy). The second premise contends that the maintenance of order requires continuing hegemony. As Charles Kindleberger has noted, "for the world economy to be stabilized, there has to be a stabilizer, one stabilizer."[17] The third premise asserts that change in the international system reflects changes in the capabilities and resources of the various actors — in particular, the hegemon. In sum, according to this theory, a concentration of power would tend to lead to systemic stability (especially in collective-goods cases such as money, where the hegemon would clearly bear the burden of provision in exchange for the lion's share of the benefits), whereas a fragmentation of power and influence would lead to systemic instability.[18] The hegemonic-stability thesis would tell us, therefore, to look for sources of systemic erosion or decline in changes in the relative capabilities of the individual members of the system. In short, this is a "basic force" model in which outcomes largely reflect the capabilities of the various actors.[19]

The main proponents of the theory have been somewhat vague about what constitutes a hegemon. In fact, the tendency has been to define hegemony by historical example (i.e., the United States after World War II or Great Britain in the latter part of the 19th century) as opposed to a discussion of what features a state must possess to be considered hegemonic. In *After Hegemony*, Keohane is much clearer about what constitutes a hegemon. He suggests that,

> to be considered hegemonic in the world political economy, . . . a country must have access to crucial raw materials, control major sources of capital, maintain a large market for imports, and hold comparative advantages in goods with high value added, yielding relatively high wages and profits. It must be stronger, on these dimensions taken as a whole, than any other country.[20]

From a practical point of view, the hegemonic-stability theory has two critical implications — the first relating to international economic co-operation and the second to the international division of labour.

With respect to co-operation, this chapter suggests that hegemonic powers have the capacity to maintain effective international economic regimes. In other words, "strong international economic regimes depend on hegemonic power."[21] "International regimes are defined as principles, norms, rules, and decision-making procedures around which actor expectations converge in a given issue-area."[22] The logic of the hegemonic-stability theory suggests that the more hegemonic the system, the more precise and well-obeyed these principles, rules, norms, and procedures will be. More specifically, it suggests that recent historical experience (in particular, the declining economic influence of the United States and the apparent decline in patterns of regularized co-operative behaviour in the international political economy) offers at least prima facie support for the theory of hegemonic stability.

Despite the attention of many contemporary international relations theorists, regime analysis has come under substantial criticism. Proponents of the conventional structural position, in particular, view "regime" as a completely pernicious concept. Susan Strange's critique of regime analysis, for example, asks "whether the concept of regime is really useful to students of international political economy or world politics; and whether it may even be negative in its influence."[23] She challenges the validity of the regime concept on five separate counts. These challenges or "dragons," as she calls them, are: (1) that the study of regimes is a fad, with little if any long-term heuristic value; (2) that the concept is imprecise and woolly; (3) that it is value-biased, implying certain things that should not be assumed; (4) that it misrepresents the fundamental character of the international system, emphasizing the static at the expense of the dynamic; and (5) that it suffers from tunnel-vision, remaining committed to a limited, state-centric view of the world.[24] Moreover, Strange contends that the concept is yet another attempt by mainstream North American political science to formulate a tidy general theory of world politics.

While many of these criticisms can be levelled against the hegemonic-stability theory itself (and not just the related notion of international economic regimes), our concern here is less with international co-operation than it is with the implications that the theory of hegemonic stability has for the international division of labour. In other words, our primary concern is with how the erosion of a hegemonic system might affect economic and political relations between the individual members of that system.

On this score the model is quite clear. Eventually the productive superiority of the hegemon will be eroded and productive capabilities will tend to "even out." Primarily through trade, foreign investment, and product imitation, the productive advantages (technology, management skills, marketing skills, innovation, etc.) of the hegemon become dissipated. Ironically, the rate of change in the international division of labour in hegemonic systems is actually accelerated by the character of the system. The implications of this acceleration are critical to the predictions of the model and to our commitment to its broader principles. First, as the hegemon's capabilities decline so, too, do its abilities to exercise leadership and its desire to underwrite the costs of that leadership. Second, the diffusion of core production tends to facilitate global surplus capacity in key consumer-goods industries such as steel and automobiles. In turn, states are encouraged to take unilateral action, which leads to greater protectionism and to closure. Finally, both the institutional and the ideological foundations of the hegemonic order are called into question.[25]

There are, however, a number of problems with this characterization. In a perceptive assessment of the utility of the hegemonic-stability thesis, Timothy McKeown has pointed the way to a number of serious conceptual difficulties.[26] Among other things, these problems include imprecise terminology, the inability of the model to account for other actors, the failure to clearly explain the role of power, and the inability to make anything but the most general predictions.

To begin with, there is clearly a problem with respect to the precision of terminology — in particular, the key concept. One is never quite clear at what point a state becomes hegemonic or ceases to be hegemonic. Keohane, Gilpin, Avery and Rapkin, Kindleberger, and others we have discussed are clear in their commitment to the idea that the United States is a hegemonic power in decline. None, however, is very clear with respect to when, and under what circumstances, the hegemonic order will no longer be hegemonic. Moreover, while few would disagree that the decline of American economic power is relative, the question of what one measures this decline against is carefully avoided. Is it relative to an earlier period in history or to some as-yet-unspecified criterion for how much power a hegemon requires to maintain order? Not surprisingly, there are those, such as Susan Strange and Bruce Russett, who are not convinced that there has been a significant attenuation in the relative power of the United States.[27] As Russett points out in a recent article in *International Organization*,

> the standards against which to measure the American decline are seldom made clear. Part of the difficulty stems from a lack of agreement about how much power is necessary to produce "hegemony". Unless there is some rather sharp step-level jump at which hegemony comes into existence or is lost (a level that has never been specified), relative power is necessarily distributed continuously. The theoretical problem is basic: there is always room for argument about whether a given degree of superiority is enough to produce particular (and also rarely well specified) results.[28]

Another problem has to do with the role of power in the model. There is no question that the hegemonic-stability theory is a "power as resources" or basic-force theory that attempts to link specific state capabilities with behaviour.[29] Surprisingly, there has been little agreement on what the relevant dimensions of power are. And, even if there is general agreement that the key capabilities are access to crucial raw materials, control over major sources of capital, a large market for imports, and comparative advantage in important goods with high value added,[30] we are still faced with some very tricky problems. First, with respect to American power, how do we measure the decline? Which "instruments" do we use to determine how fast and how far the United States has fallen? Are all these instruments consistent? What time frame do we use to get a proper comparative perspective? The problem is obvious. There is no clear way to "quantify" the decline of American power. The second, and more important, problem relates back to the matter of imprecise terminology. Even if we could measure the decline of American power, at what point does that decline become *significant*?[31] Finally, and perhaps most importantly, how does the "power" of the hegemon translate into systemic "influence"? As McKeown correctly notes, "the critical challenge to the hegemonic state is to win the adherence of its important rivals to the open system; the challenge to hegemonic stability theory is to explain how the hegemonic state manages this victory."[32] To put it in stark terms, the question is, how does the hegemon use its preponderant capabilities to influence the other members of the system?

Here, at least from our point of view, a critical distinction must be made. We must differentiate between a "pure power" or coercive version of hegemony and a Gramscian or ideological version of hegemony. The former suggests that a hegemon can, for all intents and purposes, "coerce" other members of the system into accepting a certain order. This version of hegemonic stability suggests that

> in the early years, at least, the United States was such a powerful hegemon that it could skew the division of private goods in its favour and *enforce* "adequate" burden sharing for collective goods by other noncommunist states. The United States, according to this interpretation, in effect provided something functionally equivalent to the coercive mechanism of central government that insures the provision of collective goods within nation-states. In this sense American hegemony was essentially imposed

> and maintained by political-economic coercion, though not largely by the threat or fact of physical violence.[33]

This idea of "coercive hegemony" is most clearly represented in the work of Kindleberger, Krasner, and Gilpin, and in earlier versions of Keohane's argument.[34] In essence, they all argue that a hegemon provides the collective good of international economic stability through the establishment and maintenance of a liberal trade and monetary order and that it does so primarily by forcing or inducing others to adhere to liberal trade, exchange, and investment practices in their own foreign economic policies. Thus, for them, hegemony is necessary for the emergence of a liberal trade order, and coercion (of some nature) is necessary for its survival.

Concern over the hegemon's ability to actually *enforce* or coerce openness has led a good many analysts to suggest the need for a wider definition of hegemony.[35] As Fred Lawson suggests, "it seems unlikely that the possession of substantial capabilities is by itself sufficient to define international hegemony. A truly hegemonic power is one that is able to manipulate both the structure and the agenda of international relations in such a way that serious challenges to its predominance do not arise."[36] According to this logic, it is essential that we expand our understanding of what constitutes hegemony, provide an alternative explanation, or do both. One important alternative utilizes Gramscian notions of influence to provide an understanding of hegemony that focusses on the cultural and ideological dimensions of power and leadership. For Robert W. Cox, an important proponent of this view, hegemony can be understood as "the temporary universalization in thought of a particular power structure, thought not as domination but as the necessary order of things."[37] In other words, "a hegemonial structure of world order is one in which power takes a primarily consensual form, as distinguished from a non-hegemonic order in which there are manifestly rival powers and no power has been able to establish the legitimacy of its dominance."[38] According to this formulation, the hegemon need not coerce its principal rivals. Their adherence is given freely because they believe that the order is legitimate and that participation is beneficial.

In the context of the global political economy in the post–World War II period this understanding of hegemony seems to be particularly powerful. The resolution of the war effectively put an end to the dominant political cultures of Europe and Japan. Given this vacuum, American culture and ideology virtually took the world by storm. As the world became more "Americanized," a definite convergence took place — desires, ideals, and preferences that were once uniquely American gained wider acceptance. As Russett points out,

> pervasive American cultural influence was part of a structural transformation of the international system. It meant that in many cases Americans would be able to retain substantial control over essential outcomes without having to exert power over others overtly. Rather, others' values were already conditioned to be compatible with American wishes in ways that would benefit Americans as well as themselves.[39]

While it is extremely difficult to document, the erosion of this kind of consensus is particularly important since it offers an explanation of global structural change, which gives us some clues as to why the system is characterized by increasing instability even though its principal regimes are formally intact, and the United States remains the most powerful state (in terms of economic, political, and military capabilities). This point is especially important for our discussion of the implications of declining hegemony on individual states. In very general terms, if the coercive version of hegemony were comprehensive, hegemonic decline would suggest two types of action to both rivals and supporters — seek out alternative leadership or attempt to reaffirm the existing leadership. There would be little reason to pursue alternative structures. However, if the Gramscian version of hegemony is more compelling, the loss of consensus would have very serious implications for the individual members of the system. The most likely course would be to seek alternatives to the liberal, multilateral order — alternatives that were far more consistent with national priorities. In short, autarchic and protectionist trade policies would be more likely responses to a situation where the ideological basis of the liberal, multilateral system was undermined than they would be to crises in leadership. Alternatively, consensus could be generated for a collection of principles without the need to resort to a single coercive hegemon.

Another important difficulty with the hegemonic-stability model has to do with the way in which it conceptualizes growth and change. Although some proponents of the model suggest that hegemonic order is itself the principal source of expansion, the model tends to promote a broad cyclical view of history in which "the conclusion of one hegemonic war is the beginning of growth, expansion, and eventual decline."[40] These "long cycles" or "long waves" can be traced to the writings of Nikoli Kondratieff, Joseph Schumpeter, Walt Rostow, and, more recently, George Modelski.[41] Modelski suggests that long-wave theory tells us that growth occurs through "alternating periods of expansion in the polity with periods of growth in the economy."[42] There are, however, two serious theoretical difficulties here. First, the nature of technological innovation (which promotes growth in the economy) is not well understood by any of the long-cycle theorists. Second, and more directly relevant to our purposes, this cyclical view of history is extremely deterministic. Even though the politico-economic model of long cycles suggests the necessity of placing strategic emphasis on political innovation at this time, it also suggests that virtually nothing can halt the cycle's natural progression. Moreover, as some of the Marxist interpretations suggest, these long waves may in fact be determined by forces intrinsic to global capitalism.[43] If this were the case, the outcome of hegemonic systems would actually be determined exogenously.

However, despite the theoretical ambiguity associated with long-cycle theory, there are two very important implications that this has for our understanding of contemporary international relations. First, it emphasizes the importance of a historical perspective (even though we will be examining "within-cycle change" and its impact on individual states). And, second, it directs our attention to national political responses to hegemonic decline. Both are crucial to our analysis of the effects of global structural change.

Finally, the hegemonic-stability theory does not deal in any systematic fashion with the motivations and capabilities of non-hegemonic rivals. Nor does it account for the impact that declining hegemony has had on the other members of the system. In short, the literature deals exclusively with the relationship between the hegemon and the system. This problem is, however, one that need not persist. Taking the first steps toward resolving the problem requires broadening the research agenda to include the implications of hegemonic decline (i.e., to examine effects as well as causes). Moreover, it requires a good deal of theoretical innovation. The advantage of the hegemonic-stability thesis (even with its many conceptual difficulties) rests with the claim that to understand the impact of global structural change on advanced DMEs we must view them "within the context of an international system in which a hegemonic power is in decline."[44] Moreover, when we add cultural and ideological dimensions to the notion of hegemony, it becomes a far more intriguing and potentially useful theoretical concept. In short, the hegemonic-stability thesis provides the context of global structural change. We intend to extend the analytic enterprise by examining the *impact* of that change.

The Modified Structural Model: Global Structural Change and the Implications for National Governments

By reversing the logic of the hegemonic-stability model and examining the *effects* of structural change in the world economy on national foreign economic policy, the modified structural model pursues an alternative path for research — one that has received little attention in the scholarly literature. In the language of positive social science, this alternative would make structural change in the world economy the independent variable and examine its impact on the content and direction of national action (the dependent variable), which, in this case, would be foreign economic policy. Put more simply, the modified structural model attempts to locate the primary *sources* of foreign economic policy by examining the relationship between change in the international political economy and changes in national foreign economic policy.

There has been surprisingly little research done examining the impact of hegemonic decline (or ascendance, for that matter) on the other members of the international system. There has been a good deal of interesting work on the relationship between structural change in the capitalist world economy and the plight of the less-developed countries (LDCs).[45] And, more recently, through the development of the theory of associated dependent development, there has been research that explores the relationship between the capitalist world economy and the newly industrializing economies (NIEs).[46] There has *not*, however, been much attention paid to the relationship between changes in the international political economy and the foreign economic policies of advanced DMEs.

David Lake has done some interesting pioneering work in this area. In his 1983 *World Politics* article,[47] Lake examines systemic influences on U.S. foreign economic policy in the 1887–1934 period. Lake's central thesis is that, while the system did conform to the broad predictions of the hegemonic-stability theory, the tendency has been to overlook both the interesting and the important role played by "system supporters" and the impact that the redistribution of power and influence has had for these states. More specifically, he argues that "American foreign economic policy, and policy change during the period 1887–1934, was shaped in important ways by the international economic structure."[48]

Lake contends that much of the literature on hegemonic stability follows from the collective-goods or public-goods argument,[49] which distinguishes between three types of states — "hegemonic leaders," "spoilers," and "free riders." The first category requires no further explanation. Spoilers (or rivals) tend to be large states that may, at some point, see some advantage in challenging the hegemon. At present, the most obvious example of a potential spoiler is Japan. Finally, free riders are smaller states that take advantage of the benefits of collective goods (systemic stability) but do not contribute to its provision. Lake contends that this characterization ignores an important type of systemic actor. What is needed is a fourth category — one that he calls "system supporters."

> Supporters are middle sized countries of high relative productivity. . . . Supporters cannot unilaterally lead the international economy, nor — unlike the hegemonic leader — are they willing to accept high short-term costs for long-term gains. Rather, supporters seek to balance their short-term costs and benefits, and prefer to bargain for collective movement toward specified goals. Supporters . . . are not subject to the same constraints of leadership; they will protect their least competitive industries whenever possible.[50]

The notion of "supportership" is an important one for two reasons. First, it aids in defining and understanding a certain type of state — one that is neither a direct rival to the hegemon (either real or potential) nor completely impotent when it comes to the management of the international system. Hegemons and supporters have a symbiotic relationship. Hegemons require the firm backing of these states to legitimize the existing order, while the supporters gain a great deal from systemic stability without expending many resources. In short, by recognizing the supportership role we are much farther ahead in understanding how certain middle-range advanced DMEs deal with systemic incentives and constraints and suggest when and why these influences might be most critical. Second, the notion is important as it suggests the possibility that some form of collective leadership (i.e., multiple supportership) can act as a bridge from one particular order to another. Alternatively, it can provide a means by which the hegemon can attempt to restore consensus and re-establish its hegemonic leadership. In practical terms, this may account for the modest successes experienced by the economic-summit process.

There are, of course, different levels of supportership. For instance, in the context of "Pax Americana" and the Bretton Woods system, Canada has been an important supporter (especially in ideological/cultural terms) while Austria, Australia, Sweden, and others have been less influential. Not surprisingly, we could also expect that Canada's pre-eminence as a supporter (at least in symbolic terms) would make it more vulnerable to systemic influences.

Lake goes on to argue that, during periods of systemic stability, we could expect a certain amount of "free riding" from these supporters. Conversely, during periods of hegemonic decline, we could expect them to be more constrained by the need to collectively maintain order (or, at the very least, to provide moral support to the hegemon).

This position forms the basis of our model. However, Lake does not go nearly far enough in his examination of systemic influences and external sources of foreign economic policy. The modified structural model of systemic influence that is presented here attempts to *extend* the theoretical insights gleaned from the hegemonic-stability thesis and the related notion of supportership. In order to facilitate such extension, we will present four general propositions that focus on the relationship between global structural change and national foreign economic policy. Beyond these propositions are a number of specific incentives and constraints that structural change in the global economy has suggested.

The general propositions are as follows:

1. During periods of hegemonic ascendance, we should expect a relatively stable international economic order to prevail, accompanied by an open multilateral trade regime. However, during periods of hegemonic decline, the tendency would be toward closure and protectionism.
2. During periods of hegemonic ascendance/systemic stability we can expect systemic supporters to capitalize on their freedom from systemic constraints. In particular, we could expect that these states would maintain relatively high levels of protection while aggressively taking advantage of the open international trade regime.
3. The modified structural model would expect that, during the initial phase of hegemonic decline (delegitimation),[51] widespread protectionism would be accompanied by frantic and often contradictory attempts at the national level to avoid the additional constraints that instability in the world economy brings. However, it would also suggest that these new constraints would themselves severely limit the effectiveness of many policy options designed to escape them. Attempts at putting the world economy "back together" would likely be made without much attention to whether it would be possible or even desirable to do so.
4. We could also expect that middle-sized DMEs (especially declared system supporters) would openly commit themselves to more liberal trade policies while, at the same time, pursuing more protectionist measures. Specifically, we could expect such states to make strong formal commitments to multilateral trade negotiations and the process of tariff liberalization, while aggressively pursuing such policies as export subsidization, import substitution, the negotiation of bilateral voluntary export restraints (VERs), institutional change, the pursuit of specific institutional alternatives such as bilateral free-trade agreements and/or other elements of a national industrial strategy.

For all of these propositions, the question of timing is crucial. It is clear that there is a significant "gap" between the actual decline of a hegemonic power and systemic change. Specifying the extent and duration of this gap is immensely difficult since it depends on the notion of consensus (which is very difficult to operationalize). Delegitimation begins when members of the existing order no longer accept the hegemon's leadership and the prevailing regimes without question. The tendency, however, is to remain publicly committed to the existing order for some (indeterminate) period of time. Moreover, the "down side" of the hegemonic cycle may proceed for decades before a hegemon is no longer relatively more powerful than its rivals. Nonetheless, for our purposes, it is the *breakdown* of consensus that indicates the beginning of hegemonic decline. It is also possible, as suggested earlier, that the principles underlying the current liberal order are now firmly embedded in the consciousness of virtually all constituent members of the international system.

By modifying and extending the basic assumptions of the hegemonic-stability theory in this way we have arrived at a qualitatively new theoretical formulation. The four propositions presented above constitute the core of this model. However, for the model to have any practical explanatory value we must be more specific about the incentives and constraints that change in the international political economy suggests for national foreign economic policy.

These constraints and incentives will allow us to examine directly the main challenge of this model: that is, how global structural change (i.e., the onset of a more diffuse, multicentric system) has affected trade policy in advanced DMEs. Before discussing each of them separately, it is useful to enumerate the main constraints and incentives. The constraints include increasing economic interdependence, the internationalization of production (and capital), changes in the international division of labour, and increasing economic uncertainty. In terms of incentives, there are at least two important opportunities coincident with the breakdown of hegemony. The first is the possibility for various states to overcome existing "dependence" relationships. The second involves the possibility of moving beyond existing expectations of role.

Constraints

A stable, hegemonic (liberal) international order is advantageous for advanced DMEs in the sense that it provides a buffer against external shocks. In a stable international order with strong and effective international economic regimes (such as existed between 1945 and 1968), these regimes tended to "contain" or absorb disruptions. Periods of hegemonic decline and systemic instability, however, leave national economies vulnerable and increasingly less insulated from shocks that occur elsewhere in the system (such as energy-price increases, inflation, unemployment, and recession). In short, managing economic interdependence has become an intractable problem for advanced DMEs.[52]

In general terms this problem represents the most critical (although least specific) constraint facing national governments in DMEs. Unlike periods of systemic stability, those of hegemonic decline and systemic instability force national governments to intervene more often and more directly in their national economies simply to maintain an "even keel." This is especially true for DMEs with smaller, export-led economies, when the tendency is to run head-long into a lingering commitment to multilateralism. The catch-22 is that state intervention is increasingly futile when intervention and protectionism are the order of the day.

On a related note, the increasing *internationalization of production*[53] (manifest through the exponential rise in foreign direct investment) tends to reduce the ability of national governments to respond to this increasing vulnerability. The sovereignty-at-bay argument, first articulated by Raymond Vernon, is the clearest and simplest statement of this problem.[54] In short, when a national economy is inundated by foreign direct investment, it becomes dependent on decisions taken abroad for its economic success. The following are the central characteristics of this capital dependence.

1. Significant amounts of foreign direct investment often lead to a parent-subsidiary or branch-plant setting. Normally this involves a decline in local decision-making authority and a corresponding increase in that of the foreign multinational enterprises.
2. If the parent company is operating in other markets, subsidiaries often become merely one component in a larger whole. This leads to overspecialization and often involves problems with transfer pricing and the distribution of profits. Re-exporting also tends to decrease the amount of domestic value added.
3. Growth of indigenous research and development (R&D) is often stifled, since large multinationals tend to concentrate R&D in their home market. This means that technological competence, product innovation, and management skills in the branch-plant economy fail to keep pace with the marketplace.
4. Monetary policies are increasingly tied to access to foreign capital markets. For example, interest rates will have an exaggerated sensitivity to those in the parent companies' country.
5. Excessive foreign direct investment usually leads to balance-of-payments problems. Heavy investment inevitably leads to substantial dividend outflows to the country where the capital originated.[55]

The net effect is a national economy that is increasingly dependent on external forces and a national government that is increasingly unable to respond against those forces.

Additional constraints arise from structural changes in the *international division of labour.* Coincident with the breakdown of the Bretton Woods system there have been dramatic changes in the international division of labour. Three phenomena are particularly noteworthy: the advent of the communications and technology revolution (which some argue is analogous to the industrial revolution), the maturing of the Japanese and West German economies, and the emergence of the newly industrializing economies (NIEs) as effective and competitive producers of consumer durables. These three factors have put enormous pressures on the established DMEs in terms of their ability to maintain an internationally competitive position. One consequence of these phenomena is that national capital (i.e., domestic producers) in these countries has acquired more leverage in its demands for additional protection. Structural changes of this sort in the international division of labour have translated directly into greater protectionism. Moreover, as a defence mechanism, we have a real movement in the direction of bilateralism.

Finally, the *economic uncertainty* associated with systemic instability in the international political economy tends to provide further constraints for national governments. In particular, a heightened level of uncertainty may encourage export-led economies to pursue broader markets and diversify their export trade. In many ways, however, the implications of increased economic instability are contradictory to the implications of structural change in the international division of labour. Competing pressures have arisen from this tension. On the one hand, the new international division of labour has encouraged the advanced DMEs to unite, to form integrated regional markets designed to meet competition from the NIEs. Recent examples of this movement toward bilateralism and regional integration include the Canada-U.S. Free Trade Agreement (FTA) of 1989 and the attempt to "complete" the common market through "Europe 1992." On the other hand, instability in the global economy has encouraged many DMEs to broaden their economic activity, reducing their dependence on traditional markets and sources of capital, thereby improving their chances for future economic success. The difference, as our general propositions suggest, is that the latter tends to be a short-term situation (an initial reaction to systemic instability), whereas the idea that structural change would promote "pairing up" among DMEs is a more likely long-term response.

Incentives

The analysis presented here also allows that hegemonic decline and systemic change could provide opportunities for some states. Changing global production and trading patterns may allow some advanced DMEs to break out of existing relationships that, in some cases, are nothing less than institutionalized dependence. The opportunity for these states lies in the evolution of an international economic order where they would have a good deal more flexibility and autonomy. The risk to these states is that, while they may be dependent on the hegemon under the existing order, they may be even less independent under a new order. In essence, although the incentives exist for greater long-term autonomy and independent economic growth, it would seem that the immediate constraints (associated with uncertainty and the lack of competitiveness) would provide a strong deterrent to withdrawing one's support from the existing institutional arrangements.

On a related point, there would seem to be a strong incentive for most governments in advanced DMEs to encourage the process of "privatization" and deregulation so as to capitalize more fully on their comparative advantages and enhance their competitive position. The argument, especially in the United States and Great Britain, is that innovation and productive advantage have suffered under the weight of the welfare state and that private-sector economic growth is where Western comparative advantage still resides. Western governments in the 1980s have increasingly moved to a position where they are playing a smaller role in actual economic production and exchange and a larger role in establishing an appropriate framework for interstate commerce. Arrangements such as the FTA and the consolidation of regional markets seem to be the most attractive options.

Statism, Historicism, and the Modified Structural Model of Systemic Influence

Having discussed the origins of the model, the general propositions, and the specific incentives and constraints, it remains to differentiate (on theoretical grounds) this model from its intellectual predecessors. Four critical differences exist between this model and the theory of hegemonic stability. They can be summarized as follows. First, our model does not share the statist bias of the hegemonic stability thesis. Second, it is more broadly and more genuinely historical. Third, it perceives structural changes in terms of primary and secondary structures as opposed simply to regime change. And, finally, it is not committed to positivism as a methodology for understanding the implications of hegemonic decline. Rather, it sets out in an interactive way to comprehend how the breakdown of the Bretton Woods system and the decline of American hegemony affected specific advanced industrial economies.

Statism

To begin with, although it is clearly structural, this formulation has moved beyond the "statist" bias of the hegemonic-stability thesis to an unequivocally systemic orientation. It still retains a commitment to the importance of the state — accepting the recent argument that "the state will once again become a major area of scholarly discourse."[56] However, it stresses the way in which the system influences the state, rather than the reverse.

Unlike the hegemonic-stability thesis and the statist perspective, our model does not conceive of the state as completely autonomous. According to Krasner, "the statist paradigm views the state as an autonomous actor [whose] objectives cannot be reduced to some summation of private desires."[57] Eric Nordlinger takes this position even farther when he argues that "the democratic state is frequently autonomous in translating its own preferences into authoritative actions, and markedly autonomous in doing so even when they diverge from those held by the politically weightiest groups in civil society."[58] Two fundamental assertions are inherent in this interpretation of the statist position — that the state is autonomous from civil society and that the state is largely autonomous from external forces. Implicitly, the statist model assumes that the state behaves as a unified or rational actor.

With respect to the first assertion, the distinction between our position and the statist position hangs primarily on the *extent* of state autonomy. We would accept the general notion that the state is autonomous from civil society on foreign-policy issues, with the caveat that certain issues would allow the state *less* autonomy. For instance, the state would be more autonomous on foreign-policy matters than it would be on social-welfare issues.[59] In addition, it would seem that the "type" of state is critical when it comes to autonomy from societal forces — even for foreign-policy matters.[60] We would argue that the middle-range, advanced DMEs (system supporters) are clearly more autonomous from societal forces, if only because they are too vulnerable to external forces to allow domestic forces to play an important role. The historical development of the state in question would also play an important role in determining its autonomy from civil society.[61] For example, in contrast to Western European states, the United States and Canada clearly have a historically conditioned commitment to pluralism. We also need to draw a distinction here between the impetus for foreign-policy behaviour and policy formulation (with the latter being the more receptive to domestic influences) and between relatively independent domestic structures and externally conditioned domestic structures.

With respect to the question of state autonomy from external forces, our principal thesis is that the "context" of foreign economic policy in advanced DMEs is shaped in important ways by external forces and that the *fundamental* sources of foreign economic policy can be found in the international political economy. Close examination of modern states reveals that truly independent (i.e., isolationist) states are very rare. Interdependence (both economic and strategic) is a reality in the contemporary international system. Moreover, the extent to which external forces affect an individual state's foreign economic policy will depend on the level of stability in the world economy at that particular time, on the historical direction of systemic forces, and on patterns of state behaviour.

The notion that the state is autonomous from both civil society and the international system is, at best, a dubious one. It certainly leaves some doubt as to where national preferences originate. It is instructive to note that the lengthy debate between structural and instrumental Marxists on the relative autonomy of the state ultimately arrived at the realization that "beyond the differences that were expressed in these discussions [the Miliband–Poulantzas debates], there was also a fundamental measure of agreement that the state was decisively constrained by forces external to it, and that these constraints originated in the national and international capitalist context in which it operated."[62]

We would also distinguish our model from the pure statist perspective with respect to the third assertion — that the state is a unified, rational actor. There are two fundamental distinctions that we would make. The first is that the state will *not* always act in a rational and unified fashion — although under some circumstances it has the capacity to do so. It is worth repeating that there are critical distinctions that need to be made between different types of states, different issue areas, and different historical "moments." The second distinction is that the state will tend to view or interpret external *sources* of foreign policy as a unified actor, whereas the manner in which it responds to these influences will likely involve a less coherent position. Finally, it is important to note that many proponents of the hegemonic-stability thesis — for example, Keohane — proceed from a rational-choice position and simply accept the fact that systemic theory requires acceptance of "a purely hypothetical notion of rationality that does not accurately model actual processes of human choice."[63] Our model, however, proceeds from a subjective bias. States are composed of collections of individuals and organizations that (under particular circumstances) take on a collective (and independent) existence and behave as a monolithic whole.

Another important theoretical difference that requires clarification is the way in which we conceive of the international system. Unlike the traditional realists, who adhere to the fundamental logic of an interstate system (albeit a more sophisticated "layered" or "tectonic plate" image as opposed to the classic "billiard ball" version),[64] our formulation views the international system as more than the sum of its parts. In other words, the international system has an independent existence — both politically and materially — and it has an historical reality. In this context one needs to understand change in the world economy in a larger historical context. It is not simply changes in the existing distribution of power and influence that lead to structural change in the world economy. In other words, this model follows a Gramscian/ideological view of hegemony (where various forces can undermine the existing order) as opposed to a strictly realist interpretation, which sees structural change exclusively as the result of changes in the relative capabilities of the major states.

Structural Change

This brings us to the matter of how we conceive of international structures and structural change. The hegemonic-stability theory understands global structures largely in terms of international regimes. Regimes can be defined as "principles, norms, rules and decision-making procedures around which actor expectations converge in a given issue area."[65] These issue areas have been defined very broadly, including, among others, a monetary regime, a trade regime, a security regime, an oil regime, and a nonproliferation regime. Statists see the concept as advancing our understanding of the impact of the distribution of state power on some external environment. In other words, the impact of the state on the international system can be measured through the creation and maintenance of stable international regimes. They would suggest that the implications and limitations of hegemonic power could be tested through an examination of the effectiveness and durability of particular regimes. According to this thesis, regime creation usually takes place at times of fundamental discontinuity in the system (such as immediately following global war or global depression). The logic is that powerful states will create regimes in an attempt to enhance their own interests.

The theory of hegemonic stability suggests that, as a hegemon loses influence and as the order it created fragments, the international economic regimes associated with that order will break down. The fundamental flaw with this line of reasoning lies in the fact that this assumption does not square with the empirical reality of the 1970s — especially with respect to the so-called trade regime.[66] The hegemonic-stability thesis simply cannot come to terms with why international economic disorder and regime decay in the 1970s have not been as extensive as the theory would suggest.[67]

Before we proceed to our alternative conception of structures and structural change, it is important to take note of some shared ground. First, we would accept the argument that significant structural change in the international system tends to occur during periods of fundamental disequilibrium in the system. Second, we accept the logic that powerful states will pursue international economic structures that provide the most benefit for themselves. However, we find that the concept is much too broadly conceived. It simply does not adequately differentiate between the various international economic structures. Moreover, it tells us very little about how the international system (once constituted) affects other states.

An alternative method of understanding structural change has been formulated by Susan Strange.[68] She argues that the global political economy must be understood in terms of four primary structures (the security structure, the production structure, the information structure, and the monetary structure) and a number of secondary structures. Her thesis rests on the premise that trade in the international system has to be seen as a secondary structure and, as such, as extremely vulnerable to changes in the primary structures. The "tremendous changes which have taken place in financial markets" along with "the major structural changes in the international division of labour" will, *in time*, have a profound effect on the global trading environment.[69] It is not unreasonable, then, to see a continuing commitment to the liberal trade order in the short term (at least until the impact of changes in primary structures filters down to the secondary structures).

Our model begins with the idea that structural change occurs during periods of fundamental systemic disequilibrium and the belief that powerful states will use that opportunity to create international structures that are conducive to their own interests and *extends* those ideas through the notion of primary and secondary structures. This combination seems especially useful in accounting for "lags" between general systemic disorder (i.e., the beginnings of hegemonic decline) and the decay of specific structures, and is much more consistent with the reality of the 1970s. In particular, it is helpful in comprehending how and why the disintegration of the international monetary structure was much more extensive than the decline of the trade structure. Also, it points to changes in the production structure as the principal source of change in the international political economy in the 1970s and 1980s and suggests how these changes might affect individual states. Specifically, it tells us to look to the new international division of labour and to the internationalization of production to understand the impact of structural changes on advanced DMEs. Another critical feature of this formulation is that it differentiates between exclusively multilateral structures (such as the GATT and the IMF) and structures such as the FTA that have an important bilateral dimension. Finally, it suggests that these changes in the primary structures are structural and not cyclical.

Conclusion

In short, this is a structural model that abstracts from the hegemonic-stability thesis primarily in terms of reversing the logic of state influence on the international system and examining systemic influence on state behaviour. It does not focus on the *origins* of structural change in the world economy. What it does do is try to understand how these changes affect individual states. In other words, this type of analysis goes beyond the intra- and subnational "sources of state behaviour and emphasizes the constraints and incentives that the international system poses for its constituent national units."[70]

The modified structural perspective is founded on four general propositions. First, that during periods of hegemonic ascendance a stable international economic order and open multilateral trade regime will prevail. Conversely, during periods of hegemonic decline the tendency will be toward closure and protectionism. Second, during periods of hegemonic ascendance we could expect system supporters to capitalize on their freedom from systemic constraints. Third, the modified structural model would suggest that, during periods of delegitimation, DMEs would avoid attempts to escape the additional constraints imposed by systemic instability. And, fourth, we can expect some contradiction in policies (responses) from advanced DMEs. There is likely to be a great deal of tension between "national" pressures to protect and the broader ideological commitment to the liberal international order.

Furthermore, the modified structural model suggests a number of specific incentives and constraints. These include increasing economic interdependence, the internationalization of production (and capital), changes in the international division of labour, economic uncertainty, the opportunity to press beyond existing structural and institutional boundaries, the incentives for governments to pursue more flexible economic policies with respect to business-government relations, and the mounting tensions in advanced DMEs between supporting a declining order and taking a gamble on new structures and practices.

This chapter has also attempted to clarify a number of important theoretical considerations. First, while it accepts the importance of the state in scholarly discourse, the model goes beyond the state-centric and state-as-actor principles and adopts a genuinely systemic orientation. In doing so, it reaffirms our commitment to subjectivity, to the importance of historical analysis, and to an international political economy composed of many competing forces. In addition, the foregoing discussion has served to clarify our position on the autonomy of the capitalist state. Specifically, it maintains that the state is relatively autonomous from civil society — albeit less so for some issues — and that it is anything but autonomous with respect to systemic influences. This logic also requires differentiation between various types of states — with middle-range, advanced DMEs being more autonomous from civil society on foreign-policy matters and somewhat less autonomous from external constraints. We have also distinguished between different states on the grounds of historical experience. Second, we discussed how this model conceives of the international system as one with an independent, historically conditioned existence. This distinction reaffirms our understanding of a Gramscian or consensual interpretation of hegemony. Finally, this chapter has explored the way in which the notion of primary structures and secondary structures extends the basic premises of the regime concept. In particular, the model adheres to the argument that trade is a secondary or second-order structure that undergoes transformation primarily as a response to change in the primary structures. Specifically, this transformation is linked to changes in the international division of labour, the internationalization of production, and changes in the knowledge/information structure, which lead to more general change.

NOTES

1. For our purposes, at least insofar as this chapter is concerned, these members are nation-states. It is important, however, to remember that other (mostly transnational) actors exist and that this perspective should prove useful in understanding the impact of external, systemic phenomena on their behaviour.

2. Formal deductive theory attempts to organize hypotheses that have been deduced from general principles into a grand explanation that would support empirical generalizations.

3. J.N. Rosenau, "Pre-theories and Theories of Foreign Policy," in *Approaches to Comparative and International Politics*, ed. R. Barry Farrell (Evanston, Ill.: Northwestern University Press, 1966), 27–92.

4. Realist analysis treated the foreign-policy behaviour of monolithic states largely in terms of systemic (i.e., balance-of-power) and role (i.e., national-interest) explanations.

5. See, in particular, Graham Allison's *Essence of Decision: Explaining the Cuban Missile Crisis* (Boston: Little, Brown, 1971).

6. See Robert O. Keohane and Joseph S. Nye, Jr., *Power and Interdependence* (Boston: Little, Brown, 1977), 6–7.

7. See Peter J. Katzenstein, "Introduction: Domestic and International Forces and Strategies of Foreign Economic Policy," in *Between Power and Plenty: Foreign Economic Policies of Advanced Industrial States*, ed. Peter J. Katzenstein (Madison: University of Wisconsin Press, 1978), 4.

8. K.R. Nossal, "Allison Through the (Ottawa) Looking Glass," *Canadian Public Administration* 22 (Winter 1979): 610–26; and M. Atkinson and K.R. Nossal, "Bureaucratic Politics and the New Fighter Aircraft Decision," *Canadian Public Administration* 24 (Winter 1981): 531–62.

9. David P. Rapkin and William P. Avery, "U.S. International Economic Policy in a Period of Hegemonic Decline," in *America in a Changing World Political Economy*, ed. William P. Avery and David P. Rapkin (New York: Longman, 1982), 7.

10. David A. Lake, "International Economic Structures and American Foreign Policy, 1887–1934," *World Politics* 35 (July 1983): 517–18.

11. Lake, "International Economic Structures," 518.

12. Katzenstein, "Introduction: Domestic and International Forces," 11.

13. Katzenstein, "Introduction: Domestic and International Forces," 11.

14. Katzenstein, "Introduction: Domestic and International Forces," 4.

15. In particular, see Charles P. Kindleberger, *The World in Depression, 1929–1939* (Berkeley: University of California Press, 1973); Charles P. Kindleberger, "Dominance and Leadership in the International Economy," *International Studies Quarterly* 25 (June 1981): 242–54; Charles P. Kindleberger, "On the Rise and Decline of Nations," *International Studies Quarterly* 27 (March 1983): 5–10; Stephen Krasner, "American Policy and Global Economic Stability," in *America in a Changing World Political Economy*, 29–48; Robert Gilpin, *War and Change in World Politics* (Cambridge: Cambridge University Press, 1981); Robert O. Keohane, "The Theory of Hegemonic Stability and Changes in International Economic Regimes, 1967–1977," in *Change in the International System*, ed. O. Holsti, R. Siverson, and A. George (Boulder, Colo.: Westview, 1980), 131–62; Robert O. Keohane, "Hegemonic Leadership and U.S. Foreign Policy in the Long Decade of the 1950s," in *America in a Changing World Political Economy*, 49–76; Robert O. Keohane, "Theory of World Politics: Structural Realism and Beyond," in *Political Science: The State of the Discipline*, ed. A. Finifter (Washington, D.C.: American Political Science Association, 1983), 503–40; Robert O. Keohane, *After Hegemony: Cooperation and Discord in the World Political Economy* (Princeton: Princeton University Press, 1984); and David P. Calleo, *The Imperious Economy* (Cambridge, Mass.: Harvard University Press, 1982).

It is worth noting that there are various interpretations of the hegemonic-stability thesis. However, it is generally conceded that Kindleberger's *World in Depression* epitomizes the original collective-goods argument, that Keohane's article in *Change in the International System* is the most fundamental statement, and that Keohane's *After Hegemony* is the most sophisticated and coherent response to the challenges of a post-hegemonic world. See also Paul Kennedy, *The Rise and Fall of the Great Powers: Economic Change and Military Conflict from 1500–2000* (London: Unwin Hyman, 1988).

16. Rapkin and Avery, "U.S. International Economic Policy in a Period of Hegemonic Decline," 16.

17. Kindleberger, *World in Depression*, 305.

18. Keohane, "Theory of Hegemonic Stability," 136.

19. Keohane, "Theory of Hegemonic Stability," 136.

20. Keohane, *After Hegemony*, 33–34.

21. Keohane, "Theory of Hegemonic Stability," 136.

22. Stephen Krasner, "Structural Causes and Regime Consequences: Regimes as Intervening Variables," *International Organization* 36 (Spring 1982): 185. There has been a great deal of debate in the literature over the usefulness of the notion of international economic regimes. For our purposes, however, it is a secondary matter. We are concerned primarily with the impact of the system on individual states here and not on the viability of international economic co-operation in a non-hegemonic world. See, especially, Stephen D. Krasner, ed., *International Regimes* (Ithaca: Cornell University Press, 1983; originally published as a special issue of *International Organization*, Spring 1982); Keohane's *After Hegemony*, and James Keeley, "The Latest Wave: A Critical Review of Regime Literature," in this volume.

23. Susan Strange, "*Cave! Hic Dragones*: A Critique of Regime Analysis," *International Organization* 36 (Spring 1982): 479.

24. Strange, "*Cave!*" 479.

25. David Rapkin and William Avery, "America in the World Political Economy: Prognosis, Prescriptions, and Questions for Future Research," in *America in a Changing World Political Economy*, 237. There is, understandably, some disagreement among students of the hegemonic-stability thesis on this last point. The critical question raised by regime analysis is whether the decline of hegemonic power necessarily precipitates the decline of international economic institutions or regimes. Robert Keohane, for example, obviously has a strong commitment to the notion that international economic co-operation can take place "after hegemony." Others, such as John Ruggie, have argued that the underlying logic of international regimes (i.e., liberalism) is embedded in the international order. See John Ruggie, "International Regimes, Transactions and Change: Embedded Liberalism in the Postwar Economic Order," *International Organization* 36 (Spring 1982): 379–416.

26. Timothy J. McKeown, "Hegemonic Stability Theory and 19th Century Tariff Levels in Europe," *International Organization* 37 (Winter 1983): 73–91.

27. See Susan Strange, "Still an Extraordinary Power: America's Role in the Global Monetary System," in *Political Economy of International and Domestic Monetary Relations*, ed. R. Lombra and W. Witte (Ames: Iowa University Press, 1982), 73–93; and Bruce Russett, "The Mysterious Case of Vanishing Hegemony: Or, Is Mark Twain Really Dead?" *International Organization* 39 (Spring 1985): 207–231.

28. Russett, "Mysterious Case of Vanishing Hegemony," 209.

29. See Keohane, "Theory of Hegemonic Stability."

30. Keohane, *After Hegemony*, 33–34. Implicit in Keohane's assessment, one would assume, are military capabilities and technological capabilities. An earlier, but far more thorough, discussion of the relevant dimensions of state power can be found in Stephen D. Krasner, *Defending the National Interest: Raw Material Investment and U.S. Foreign Policy* (Princeton: Princeton University Press, 1978).

31. For a fascinating review of declining American capabilities, see Mark E. Rupert and David P. Rapkin, "The Erosion of U.S. Leadership Capabilities," in *Rhythms in International Politics and Economics*, ed. Paul Johnson and W.R. Thompson (New York: Praeger, 1985).

32. McKeown, "Hegemonic Stability Theory," 77.

33. Russett, "Mysterious Case of Vanishing Hegemony," 228.

34. See, for example, Krasner, "State Power and the Structure of International Trade"; Gilpin, *War and Change in World Politics*; and Keohane, "Theory of Hegemonic Stability."

35. See, among others, Arthur Stein, "The Hegemon's Dilemma: Great Britain, the United States, and the International Economic Order," *International Organization* 38 (Spring 1984): 335–86.

36. Fred H. Lawson, "Hegemony and the Structure of International Trade Reassessed: A View from Arabia," *International Organization* 37 (Spring 1983): 335.

37. Robert W. Cox, "Production and Hegemony: An Approach Toward a Problematic," paper presented at the International Political Science Association's annual meeting, Moscow 1979, 1.

38. Robert W. Cox, "Social Forces, States, and World Order: Beyond International Relations Theory," *Millennium* 10, no. 2 (1981): 153, note 27. See, also, Robert W. Cox, "Gramsci, Hegemony and International Relations: An Essay in Method," *Millennium* 12, no. 2 (1983): 162–75.

39. Russett, "Mysterious Case of Vanishing Hegemony," 229.

40. Gilpin, *War and Change in World Politics*, 210.

41. See, among others, N.D. Kondratieff, "The Long Waves in Economic Life," *Review of Economic Statistics* 17, no. 6 (1935): 105–115; Joseph Schumpeter, *The Theory of Economic Development: An Inquiry into Profits, Capital, Credit, Interest and the Business Cycle*, trans. R. Opie (Cambridge, Mass.: Harvard University Press, 1951; originally published in 1934); Walt W. Rostow, *The World Economy: History and Prospect* (Austin: University of Texas Press, 1978); George Modelski, "Long Cycles and the Strategy of U.S. International Economic Policy," in *America in a Changing World Political Economy*, 97–116; George Modelski, "The Long Cycle of Global Politics and the Nation-State," *Comparative Studies in Society and History* 20 (April 1978): 214–35.

42. Modelski, "Long Cycles and the Strategy of U.S. International Economic Policy," 108.

43. See Ernst Mandel, *Late Capital* (London: New Left Books, 1975), especially chaps. 4 and 6.

44. Avery and Rapkin, "U.S. International Economic Policy in a Period of Hegemonic Decline," 6.

45. In particular, I am thinking of the dependency literature. Dependency is a structural model that attempts to explain the historical process that has integrated the periphery (or hinterland) into the global capitalist economy. The theory is holistic and structural — beginning with the core/periphery framework and proceeding to an attempt to explain the historical interaction between the core and the periphery. According to the model, underdevelopment is generated by the same historical processes that generate development, namely the development of capitalism itself. The classic (if simplistic) statement of this theory can be found in André Gunder Frank, "The Development of Underdevelopment," *Monthly Review* (September 1966): 17–30. For a more thorough discussion, see James Caporaso, "Dependence, Dependency, and Power in the Global System," *International Organization* 32 (Winter 1978): 13–43.

46. To date, this argument has largely been confined to the Latin American NIEs (especially Brazil). It is entirely plausible, however, that it can be applied to other NIEs and to some middle-range, advanced DMEs with interesting results. See F.H. Cardoso, "Associated Dependent Development: Theoretical and Practical Implications," in *Authoritarian Brazil: Origins, Policy and Future*, ed. A. Stepan (New Haven: Yale University Press, 1973); F.H. Cardoso and E. Faletto, *Dependency and Development in Latin America* (Berkeley: University of California Press, 1979); and Peter Evans, *Dependent Development: The Alliance of Multinational, State, and Local Capital in Brazil* (Princeton: Princeton University Press, 1979).

47. See David Lake, "International Economic Structures and American Foreign Economic Policy, 1887–1934," *World Politics* 35 (July 1983): 517–43.

48. Lake, "International Economic Structures," 518.

49. Kindleberger adheres most closely to the collective-goods approach. More recent treatments of the hegemonic-stability theory (especially Gilpin's 1981 book *War and Change in World Politics*) focus more directly on the interests of the leader.

50. Lake, "International Economic Structures," 521–22.

51. "Delegitimation" here refers to the breakdown of consensus. In other words, the system ceases to be genuinely hegemonic when the potential rivals and the supporters no longer accept the existing order without question. The dominant power/lead economy may still possess a disproportionately large amount of power and influence (measured by actual capabilities) for a long time. We must remember, however, that one possible resolution to the crisis of delegitimation is the reinstatement of hegemonic order. Another, as we have discussed, is some form of group leadership. Still another would be the ascent of a rival.

52. There is a voluminous and fascinating literature on international economic interdependence. Among others, see Richard Cooper, *The Economics of Interdependence: Economic Policy in the Atlantic Community* (New York: McGraw-Hill, 1968); Oran Young, "Interdependencies in World Politics," *International Journal* 24 (Autumn 1969): 726–50; Edward Morse, "Interdependence and World Affairs," in *World Politics: An Introduction*, ed. J. Rosenau, Kenneth Thompson, and Gavin Boyd (New York: Free Press, 1976); Keohane and Nye, Jr., *Power and Interdependence*; and Harold K. Jacobson, *Networks of Interdependence* (New York: Knopf, 1979).

53. On the internationalization of production, see S. Hymer, "The Multinational Corporation and the Law of Uneven Development," in *Economics and World Order*, ed. J. Bhagwati (London: Macmillan, 1972), 113–40.

54. On the sovereignty-at-bay thesis, see Raymond Vernon, *Sovereignty at Bay* (New York: Basic Books, 1971); Raymond Vernon, *Storm Over the Multinationals* (Cambridge, Mass.: Harvard University Press, 1977); and Raymond Vernon, "Sovereignty at Bay Ten Years After," *International Organization* 35 (Summer 1981): 517–29.

55. Michael Hawes, *Principal Power, Middle Power, or Satellite? Competing Perspectives in the Study of Canadian Foreign Policy* (Toronto: University of Toronto Press, for York University, 1984 and 1987), 22–23.

56. Stephen Krasner, "Approaches to the State: Alternative Conceptions and Historical Dynamic," *Comparative Politics* 16 (1984): 243–44.

57. Krasner, *Defending the National Interest*, 5–6.

58. Eric Nordlinger, *The Autonomy of the Democratic State* (Cambridge, Mass.: Harvard University Press, 1981), 203.

59. Nordlinger retains his commitment to the autonomy of the state even in instances where the state's preferences are divergent from influential societal preferences.

60. For a fascinating account of the autonomy of the state that differentiates between capitalist states (primarily in terms of their historical development), see Robert Solo, "The Formation and Transformation of States," in *An International Political Economy*, ed. W. Ladd Hollist and F. LaMond Tullis (Boulder, Colo.: Westview, 1985), 69–86.

61. See Stuart Hall, "The State in Question," in *The Idea of the Modern State*, ed. G. McLennan, D. Held, and S. Hall (Milton Keynes: Open University Press, 1984), 1–28.

62. Ralph Miliband, "State Power and Class Interests," in *Class Power and State Power* (London: New Left, 1983), 64.

63. Keohane, *After Hegemony*, 29.

64. On the image of tectonic plates, see Stephen Krasner, "Regimes and the Limits of Realism: Regimes as Autonomous Variables," *International Organization* 36 (Spring 1982): 497–510.

65. Stephen Krasner, "Structural Causes and Regime Consequences," *International Organization* 36 (Spring 1982): 185.

66. See, in particular, Krasner, "State Power and the Structure of International Trade"; and Keohane, "Theory of Hegemonic Stability."

67. Specific conceptual difficulties associated with the notion of international regimes have been dealt with in detail earlier in this chapter. Our purpose here is to distinguish this explanation of structural change from our own.

68. Susan Strange, "The Global Political Economy," *International Journal* 39 (Spring 1984): 267–83; and Susan Strange, "Protectionism and World Politics," *International Organization* 39 (Spring 1985): 233–59.

69. Strange, "Protectionism and World Politics," 243.

70. Rapkin and Avery, "U.S. Economic Policy in a Period of Hegemonic Decline," 7.

SELECT BIBLIOGRAPHY

Avery, William P., and David P. Rapkin, eds. *America in a Changing World Political Economy*. New York: Longman, 1982.

Bhagwati J., ed. *Economics and World Order*. London: Macmillan, 1972.

Calleo, David P. *The Imperious Economy*. Cambridge, Mass.: Harvard University Press, 1982.

Cooper, Richard. *The Economics of Interdependence: Economic Policy in the Atlantic Community*. New York: McGraw-Hill, 1968.

Cox, Robert W. "Social Forces, States, and World Order: Beyond International Relations Theory." *Millennium* 10, no. 2 (1981): 126–55.

Gilpin, Robert. *War and Change in World Politics*. Cambridge: Cambridge University Press, 1981.

Goldthorpe, J.H., ed. *Order and Conflict in Contemporary Capitalism*. Oxford: Oxford University Press, 1984.

Katzenstein, Peter J., ed. *Between Power and Plenty: Foreign Economic Policies of Advanced Industrial States*. Madison: University of Wisconsin Press, 1978.

Keohane, Robert O. *After Hegemony: Cooperation and Discord in the World Political Economy*. Princeton: Princeton University Press, 1984.

———. "Hegemonic Leadership and U.S. Foreign Policy in the 'Long Decade' of the 1950s." In *America in a Changing World Political Economy*.

———. "The Theory of Hegemonic Stability and Changes in International Economic Regimes, 1967–1977." In *Change in the International System*, ed. O. Holsti, R. Siverson, and A. George. Boulder, Colo.: Westview, 1980.

Keohane, Robert O., and Joseph S. Nye, Jr. *Power and Interdependence*. Boston: Little, Brown, 1977.

Kindleberger, Charles P. *The World in Depression, 1929–1939*. Berkeley: University of California Press, 1973.

———. "Dominance and Leadership in the International Economy." *International Studies Quarterly* 25 (June 1981): 242–54.

Kennedy, Paul. *The Rise and Fall of the Great Powers: Economic Change and Military Conflict from 1500 to 2000*. London: Unwin Hyman, 1988.

Krasner, Stephen D., ed. *International Regimes*. Ithaca: Cornell University Press, 1983.

Lake, David A. "International Economic Structures and American Foreign Policy, 1887–1934." *World Politics* 35 (July 1983): 517–18.

Lombra, R., and W. Witte, eds. *Political Economy of International and Domestic Monetary Relations*. Ames: Iowa University Press, 1982.

Modelski, George. "The Long Cycle of Global Politics and the Nation-State." *Comparative Studies in Society and History* 20 (April 1978): 214–35.

Ruggie, John. "International Regimes, Transactions and Change: Embedded Liberalism in the Postwar Economic Order." *International Organization* 36 (Spring 1982): 379–416.

Rupert, Mark E., and David P. Rapkin. "The Erosion of U.S. Leadership Capabilities." In *Rhythms in International Politics and Economics*, ed. Paul Johnson and W.R. Thompson. New York: Praeger, 1985.

Russett, Bruce. "The Mysterious Case of Vanishing Hegemony: Or, Is Mark Twain Really Dead?" *International Organization* 39 (Spring 1985): 207–31.

Stein, Arthur. "The Hegemon's Dilemma: Great Britain, the United States, and the International Economic Order." *International Organization* 38 (Spring 1984): 335–86.

THE ROLES OF THE MULTINATIONAL ENTERPRISE IN INTERNATIONAL RELATIONS

David Leyton-Brown

The multinational enterprise (MNE) is one of the most interesting political phenomena of the postwar world. The spread of foreign direct investment and the internationalization of production have transformed the nature of the international economy, and have also complicated, if not transformed, international politics. The MNE is not a consequence of this transformation and complication, but a contributing cause of it. This chapter will examine the role(s) played by the MNE in international relations, in an attempt to shed some light on the ensuing changes in the global economy.

One can study the MNE from several different theoretical perspectives. The dominant perspectives informing the study of international relations — realism and neo-realism — would be attentive to the opportunities and constraints for the only actors considered to matter — states. Marxist political economy would address the internationalization of capital and the classes and social forces related to it. Dependency theory would concern itself with the internal underdevelopment and the external dependency of the Third World for which the MNE is the cause, or at least the carrier. Here, we will adopt the transnational-relations perspective, because of the analytic utility of the hypotheses generated by that approach.

In the early 1970s, Joseph Nye and Robert Keohane produced a pathbreaking work that recognized the inadequacy of the state-centric view that had characterized the realist approach to international relations.[1] Their contribution was not to deny the importance of interstate relations, but to assert the additional importance of a previously underemphasized residual category. They argued that "transnational relations should be included in any complete analysis of world politics." Transnational relations can be defined as "contacts, coalitions and interactions across state boundaries that are not controlled by the central foreign policy organs of governments."[2] At about the same time, Samuel Huntington defined transnational organizations as having three characteristics — a hierarchically organized, centrally directed bureaucracy; a set of specialized and technical functions; and the performance of those functions across one or more international boundaries.[3]

The identification of transnational relations alone would hardly have warranted the impact that Nye and Keohane had on the scholarly community. Rather, that impact resulted from the agenda of new questions opened up by the attention focussed on transnational relations and transnational organizations. In particular, Nye and Keohane hypothesized five effects that could be expected to follow from the existence of and increase in transnational relations.[4] Two of these are of particular relevance to the study of the multinational enterprise: transnational relations may create new instruments for influence for use by some governments over others; and, transnational organizations may emerge as autonomous actors in world politics with private foreign policies. These two hypothesized effects serve as the organizing principles for this chapter. They serve to focus attention on how the MNE can be used as an instrument of government policy, and how it can be understood as an autonomous actor, operating in pursuit of its own corporate interests and objectives, which may be indifferent to or in conflict with the official policies of governments.

MNE: Nature and Origins

Before proceeding to an examination of the roles played by the MNE in international relations, it is necessary first to establish just what an MNE is, and how and why it came to be. The reader will have noticed that the term used here is "the multinational enterprise" rather than the possibly more familiar one, "the multinational corporation." The reason is not some idiosyncratic preference, but a recognition that a corporation has a precise legal identity, and some multinationals are not, strictly speaking, corporations. All, however, are business enterprises. Of more importance is the question of which business enterprises should be labelled as multinational. A review of the literature reveals considerable confusion, as various authors focus upon different characteristics to distinguish the MNE from its domestic counterparts. These differences often result from the different analytic objectives of the authors involved, or from the concerns of the different academic disciplines they represent.

The most common criterion used to identify the MNE is *structure*, and the most common structural variable is the conduct of business operations in more than one country. The group of eminent persons convened by the Secretary-General of the United Nations offered such a structural definition, which encompasses all enterprises operating in more than one country. According to the group's report: "Multinational corporations are enterprises which own or control production or service facilities outside the country in which they are based. Such enterprises are not always incorporated or private; they can also be co-operatives or state-owned enterprises."[5]

A more restrictive structural criterion was adopted by the Multinational Enterprise Project of the Harvard Business School, directed for many years by Raymond Vernon.[6] This project established the twin criteria of large size (because of the conviction that small firms have small impact and warrant only limited attention) and geographical spread of foreign operations. These criteria were operationalized for United States–based manufacturing and extractive enterprises as membership on the *Fortune* magazine list of the 500 largest industrial firms, and ownership or control of manufacturing or extractive subsidiaries in six or more foreign countries. Accordingly, some enterprises covered by the U.N. definition were excluded here, because their foreign operations were confined to only one or two other countries, or because their foreign operations were only in the areas of sales or of technology licensing. By these criteria, the Multinational Enterprise Project identified some 187 U.S. MNEs in the mid-1960s.

Still other authors have offered additional structural criteria.[7] Some argued that it is the structure of ownership rather than the structure of operations that matters, and considered an enterprise to be multinational only if its ownership was dispersed among persons from many nations. By that criterion, Exxon or General Motors are U.S. enterprises rather than multinational enterprises, regardless of how many foreign subsidiaries they may have. By similar logic, other authors have termed an enterprise multinational only if its top management is drawn from many countries, rather than only, or even primarily, from the parent country.

A second definitional criterion is that of *performance*. By this criterion, an enterprise is multinational if some absolute amount or relative proportion of the firm's resources or overall business is devoted to its foreign operations, indicating that its foreign operations matter significantly to it. The firm's multinational performance could be measured by assets, earnings, sales, or number of employees abroad. The greatest difficulty with this approach is that the identification of relevant items is imprecise, as is the threshold between a national enterprise with some overseas operations and an MNE.

Finally, some authors use the criterion of *behaviour*, by which an enterprise is considered multinational if it thinks and behaves internationally, emphasizing global rather than national profit. This definitional criterion is hard to apply in practice, and runs the risk of tautology. It could fall into the circular reasoning that an enterprise is multinational if it behaves like a multinational enterprise. However, there are some objective behavioural indicators to which an analyst can turn. Clear evidence of multinational identity is provided by the presence of a vertically integrated production-and-distribution chain, in which the same MNE owns or controls subsidiaries involved in the different stages of the production process, from mining and refining of ore through manufacturing and assembly of components, to sale of the finished product. Other behavioural evidence is provided by the central control and integration of affiliate operations.

These considerations lead into the kind of definition that is of most interest and use to political scientists. An MNE can perhaps best be understood as a large business enterprise that directly owns or controls foreign subsidiaries responsive to, if not totally controlled by, decisions of the parent firm, and whose decision domain does not necessarily coincide with state boundaries.

Even if it is clear whether or not an enterprise is multinational, it still remains to be established why it has become so. Not surprisingly, the answer to that question is also complex. Leaving aside the qualitatively different explanations for the phenomenon of foreign direct investment and the internationalization of capital, which would be offered by proponents of Marxist political economy, different types of MNEs invest abroad for different reasons.

MNEs involved in the business of resource extraction seem primarily defensive in their investment behaviour. The structure of the various resource-extraction industries is oligopolistic, characterized by a small number of large firms. These firms tend to travel the world like a flock of sheep, all investing wherever one invests, in order to defend against any of their number's monopolizing a new source of supply. As the successive moves of the international oil MNEs into Indonesia or the North Sea have demonstrated, all MNEs in a given extractive industry are likely to emulate the others' actions, in order that the oligopolistic balance may be maintained.

Investments in manufacturing MNEs have taken place for both defensive and aggressive reasons. Defensive manufacturing investments typically follow a pattern of risk avoidance. An MNE might invest to acquire or establish a foreign subsidiary if it is imitating its competitor's behaviour so as not to lose market share (similar to the defensive investment strategy in resource-extraction industries), or if it is seeking to secure the vertical integration of production, by eliminating its vulnerability to disruption of supplies from an outside source.

Aggressive investment strategies have in the past followed the pattern of the product life-cycle, or have involved the exploitation of some temporary advantage. The product-cycle model developed by Raymond Vernon[8] presumed an initial innovation that allowed a parent (normally U.S.) firm to produce for its domestic market. As production expanded, the firm began to export some of that production to markets abroad. Over time, these foreign markets came to matter more and more to the profitability of the firm. The export penetration of the foreign markets stimulated local business to develop competitive substitutes for that local market. Eventually, the advantages of local production (i.e., low transportation costs) and, perhaps, tariff protection came to outweigh the advantages for the initial producer in volume of production and brand-name identification, and the increasingly important foreign market was in jeopardy. Following the traditional wisdom that investment is a substitute for trade, the U.S. firm was impelled to establish a subsidiary in (or near) the foreign market, so as to locate behind the tariff wall, and to reduce transportation costs to the market. Eventually, local producers improved their production processes to the extent that they could be entirely cost competitive with the production of the U.S. subsidiary; however, by that time the U.S. firm had developed a new product (having devoted its research-and-development efforts to new-product innovation while its foreign competitors were trying to replicate existing products). Thus, the entire cycle began again, except that this time the U.S. firm already had its foreign subsidiary in place, so the shift from export to local production could come sooner.

This product-cycle model provides a satisfactory explanation for the spread of U.S. investment in the 20 years following World War II, but its relevance ended as the United States ceased to be the unquestioned technological leader. Now innovations occur in many countries, and the cycles go in all directions. Innovation tends to be company-specific rather than country-based, and the pace of technological change as well as diffusion of new products to markets is much faster. Nonetheless, firms still aggressively seek to exploit temporary advantages, and invest abroad to do so.

The phenomenon of the internationalization of production is a related explanation for foreign investment. Where once MNEs invested to position themselves behind tariff walls, today they are more likely to invest to locate their facilities where the cost of factors of production such as raw materials or labour can be minimized. Vertically integrated production is one manifestation of this thinking. A logical consequence is the recent establishment of "export platforms" in certain developing countries, in which low-wage production occurs entirely for the MNE's home market, rather than for local consumption.

MNEs as an Instrument of Government Policy

An MNE can be used as an instrument of government policy in a variety of ways. Host governments can seek to realize some of their economic-policy objectives through the presence and operation in their territory of foreign-owned MNEs. Similarly, parent governments have demonstrated an ability to achieve some of their economic-policy objectives through control over or influence on the foreign operations of MNEs based in their countries. Politically more interesting are situations where parent governments, or in some cases even host governments, are able to use MNEs to exert influence over other governments.

The MNE represents a cluster of capital, technology, management, marketing, and revenue that can offer many benefits sought by governments. Government-policy objectives concerning economic growth and development can be furthered by the activities of MNEs within a country.

The capital inflow offered by MNEs can be an important part of the efforts by some governments to alleviate balance-of-payments difficulties. However, the initial investment may or may not involve substantial capital inflow, as the capital in question is frequently raised from local sources. Nevertheless, some governments have required that investment capital be imported, and, in some other cases, MNEs have offered to import capital in return for concessions of some other kind from the host government. Regardless of the initial capital inflow, however, the future activities of the MNE can have positive balance-of-payments effects. In the long term, imports of technology or management services may be effectively subsidized, and imports of components of final products may be reduced or even eliminated (to be replaced by local production by the subsidiary). Any expansion of exports, whether to regional or distant markets, will further benefit the balance of trade and, hence, the balance of payments. Of course, repatriation of profits or unfairly priced interaffiliate transfers pose a threat to the balance of payments, but it is commonly in the long-term interest of both the MNE and the host government for profitable economic activity to continue and expand.

Economic growth and development can also be advanced by some intangibles brought into the country by the MNE. Frequently, there is access to technology that is more modern, and available on more favourable terms, than that available under licence. The research and development possible for an MNE with a large resource base often exceeds that which governments themselves are able to undertake.

General economic growth and development is frequently expected to result from the infusion of management skills and by the stimulus to competition and efficiency that the MNE represents. MNEs are often marked by management techniques more aggressive and efficient than those prevailing in the domestic industry. The presence of a foreign-owned MNE can spread such skills, not only to its own employees, but to suppliers and competitors, and through personnel mobility, throughout the entire economy. So long as the MNE itself does not monopolize the local industry in which it operates, it can serve as a competitive spur to its domestic counterparts, breaking up traditional monopolies, pressing down prices, and boosting efficiency to the benefit of the economy as a whole.

There can also be benefits to economic growth and development resulting from increased employment and from location in underdeveloped regions. So long as the investment does not simply result in a change of ownership of an existing domestic enterprise, the entry and expansion of an MNE offers increased employment opportunities to the host country. The presumed greater mobility of the MNE as compared to its smaller domestic competitors attracts governments to encourage its location in peripheral regions, to support regional-development policies. Finally, the taxes and royalties paid by the MNE represent a source of revenue that might be significant for some governments. If the MNE, as promised, increases the level and volume of economic activity in the country, it will likely generate greater tax and royalty revenues.

The benefits discussed thus far are desirable for governments of most states, whether developed or developing. Nearly all governments seek capital inflow, economic growth and development, increased technological and managerial competence in its workforce, more jobs, and regional development. However, a particular subset of these goals is most relevant for governments of developing countries. Capital for rudimentary industrialization is often locally available, and mature technologies are often available under licence. Developing governments particularly desire the market access, government revenue, and foreign exchange that are promised by the MNE. These may simply not be available from domestic sources.

Of course, this discussion has only presented the positive side of the picture. These have been the benefits that governments seek to maximize, in accordance with their policy objectives. Most governments in the world, even of most communist countries, have demonstrably looked to MNEs to provide such benefits. Nevertheless, governments simultaneously will try to minimize disadvantages and costs resulting from the presence of foreign-owned MNEs, some of which will be discussed below. It would be easy enough to avoid the costs, if one were willing at the same time to forgo the presumed or desired benefits. Only a handful of autarchic or self-reliant countries, such as Albania and Burma, have shown themselves willing to do so. The competitive bidding of incentives by governments to attract investment attests to the enthusiasm most governments feel for the presence and activity of foreign-owned MNEs on their territory.

Parent governments can also seek to achieve economic-policy objectives through MNEs. The government that has done this most explicitly has been that of the United States, but in different ways other parent states, such as Japan, France, and even Canada, have done the same.

The U.S. government has resorted to extraterritorial application of some of its domestic laws to require compliance by foreign subsidiaries of U.S. MNEs.[9] A principal example is U.S. antitrust law, intended to prevent restraint upon U.S. business, whether that restraint occurs domestically or in a foreign country. U.S. companies have been required by U.S. courts to divest themselves of certain foreign subsidiaries, or to refrain from planned foreign mergers or acquisitions, in order to prevent restriction of competition in the United States, but without regard to the impact on the foreign economy concerned or the wishes of its government. Restraint upon U.S. trade has been interpreted by U.S. courts to include both restriction on the ability of U.S. companies to export from the United States and uncompetitive treatment of U.S. consumers by enterprises exporting to the United States from foreign locations. The presence within U.S. jurisdiction of the parent enterprise gives the U.S. government leverage to impose its antitrust policy on the operations of subsidiaries in foreign countries.

The U.S. government has also used the overseas operations of U.S.-owned MNEs to effect its balance-of-payments policies. In 1965, faced with a mounting balance-of-payments deficit, the U.S. government issued voluntary guidelines to 600 (later 900) corporations to decrease net capital outflow from the United States by expanding exports, limiting direct investment in developed countries, increasing the proportion of foreign investment financed through borrowing abroad, and increasing the return capital flow to the United States of foreign earnings and short-term assets. Thus, the U.S. government was seeking to dictate, or at least influence, the investment, procurement, and profit-repatriation policies of subsidiaries of U.S. MNEs in order to improve its own balance-of-payments situation. In 1968, the guidelines were made mandatory. Subsequent policy measures to affect the foreign activities of U.S. MNEs for balance-of-payments purposes included the 10 percent tariff surcharge announced by President Nixon on August 15, 1971, to reduce imports and encourage production in the United States, and the Domestic International Sales Corporation (DISC) legislation, intended to encourage U.S. companies to produce in the United States for export rather than produce abroad in foreign subsidiaries.

All that has been discussed thus far has involved a government using MNEs as a policy instrument to pursue policy objectives that ultimately are internal in character. It is also possible, as Nye and Keohane hypothesized, for a government to use MNEs as a lever of influence over other governments.

The most visible effort by the United States as parent government to the majority of the world's MNEs has been the extraterritorial application of export controls to constrain the behaviour of foreign subsidiaries. Through the Trading with the Enemy Act and the Export Administration Act, the U.S. government has sought to prohibit certain dealings by foreign subsidiaries of U.S. MNEs with proscribed foreign countries, whether or not those dealings would have been legal or even encouraged under host-government policy.

On the surface, such export controls would appear to be a classic illustration of Nye and Keohane's hypothesis. The U.S. government has used the policy instruments at its disposal to inflict economic harm on its adversaries, and has denied them access to financial and commercial interactions in which U.S. MNEs play so large a part. Nonetheless, the amount of harm actually visited upon the target countries, whether they be large (i.e., the Soviet Union or China) or small (i.e., Cuba or Vietnam) has been limited, and certainly smaller than the occasional political harm to the relationship between the United States and its allies whose companies were prevented by U.S. law from acting as they would have otherwise.[10] It does appear that the principal motivation of the U.S. government in the extraterritorial application of its export-controls policy has been to ensure nondiscriminatory treatment of U.S. enterprises that do and do not have foreign subsidiaries, rather than to inflict maximum economic damage on the target country.

While examples are rare, it is also possible for the parent government to seek to affect the behaviour of a subsidiary so as to pursue goals in the relationship with the government in which the subsidiary is located. Such a situation occurred in the 1960s, when the U.S. government ordered IBM to forbid its French subsidiary to sell to the French government for use in the French nuclear-weapons development program a computer manufactured in France but including some U.S.-made components. The sale was prevented, and the development of French nuclear weapons was delayed, though not halted. The U.S. government did something similar in its attempts to destabilize the governments of Chile under Allende and of Iran under the Ayatollah Khomeini.

It is also possible for the government of the host country to use the presence on its territory of foreign-owned MNEs as a lever of influence vis-à-vis the parent government. A foreign-owned subsidiary is simultaneously an outpost and a hostage, and economic interdependence can sometimes be made to work to the advantage of the smaller party. An example occurred in the early 1970s, when the Canadian government created a useful precedent that strengthened its claim to jurisdiction over the Northwest Passage by persuading a U.S. multinational to accept the authority of the Arctic Waters Pollution Prevention Act, against the express wishes of the U.S. State Department.[11]

As these examples demonstrate, while the results may be modest or mixed, both host and parent governments do seek to use MNEs as instruments of their policies. That, however, is not the only role played by the MNE in international relations. It is now appropriate to turn to an examination of the challenges posed for governments and societies arising from the autonomous behaviour of the MNE in pursuit of its corporate interests.

The MNE as an Autonomous Actor

Governments have concerns about their interactions with MNEs not only because those enterprises may be used as levers of policy influence by other governments, or because of incompatibility or conflict between the policy objectives of that government and other governments, but also because of the characteristics and behaviour of the MNE itself. Many of these concerns are common to all host governments, but governments of developing countries have some particular concerns. Even parent governments must sometimes confront the challenges and problems posed by MNEs that act, at least in part, autonomously in pursuit of their corporate interests and objectives.

The positive economic effects governments hope that MNEs will produce in their countries have already been discussed. There are also negative economic, political, and social effects that governments hope to avoid, or at least minimize. These cluster in four areas — industrial dominance, technological dependence, disruption to government economic policy and planning, and disturbing of local culture and lifestyle.

Fears that MNEs will dominate the local economy derive from the economic size of the MNE, and the presumed advantages that size brings. Foreign-owned subsidiaries, through their own profitability, and backed by the financial resources of their parents, are thought to be able to devote greater resources to research and development and to reinvestment for expansion, allowing them to innovate more rapidly and thus increase their dominant position in the economy. They tend to be situated in the most profitable, growing, and technologically innovative sectors of the economy, assuring to themselves the spinoff benefits of new discoveries, and ensuring that their economic domination would become even more pronounced in future. There is a tendency to re-create in the host country a miniature replica of the oligopolistic structure of the parent industry, with all leading MNEs in the sector having subsidiaries in the local economy and, thus, freezing out local competition. This combination of size and sectoral location can lead to disruptive rather than constructive effects on the pattern of competition in the local economy. They can import and impose industrial and management techniques that disturb local standards and practices, simply because they are familiar to the foreign management of the MNE. Rather than stimulating improved competitive practices among their domestic counterparts, they might swamp their competitors because of their size. They might enjoy "unfair" competitive advantages over local firms in the same industry, because of access to the financial resources of the parent enterprise with its global profit cushion, and because, as a subsidiary of a recognized and respected MNE, they may gain preferred access to local capital from lenders and investors. Because of its ability to overwhelm competition, the MNE may then be able to engage in uncompetitive behaviour and hinder rather than aid national economic growth and development, through raising prices to garner monopoly profits, absorbing local capital, developing or importing inappropriate technology, and employing foreign rather than local management.

Of course, size is not entirely equivalent to power. The power of governments rests on other than economic capabilities, and, even in the economic realm, size carries with it certain diseconomies as well as economies of scale. Nevertheless, the size of the MNE presence in a host economy may give it advantages over its competitors that could perpetuate its dominance over the economic sector, and its potential to challenge or disregard the government.

The fears concerning technological dependence are related to the issue of size, but are in some ways distinct. All governments are actively concerned to increase the amount of research and development (R&D) conducted by firms within their countries, because of the conviction that the prospects for increased international competitiveness and economic growth in future rest upon process and product innovation in the present. However, as the product-cycle model described earlier implicitly showed, there was a widespread assumption that technological dependence, once achieved, would be self-perpetuating. Governments were concerned that R&D would be conducted primarily abroad, in the laboratories of the parent enterprise, to the initial and primary benefit of the parent economy. The technology imported or applied by an MNE might well be inappropriate to the resource endowment of the local country or to its level of workforce training or consumer tastes, but might be nonetheless preferred by the MNE because of its compatibility with products or production processes elsewhere, or simply because it is what the MNE is used to. Because of its ability to devote greater resources to R&D or, through a brain-drain phenomenon, divert scientific efforts onto its own agenda, the MNE was feared to have the capacity to determine the products to be produced and the techniques to be used in the local economy. The concern was that the benefits of innovation would be enjoyed first in the parent country of the MNE, and only later be spread to host countries, thus consigning them to a perpetual second place in the technological sweepstakes.

This concern has not been entirely laid to rest, but it has undergone some modification in two areas. In the first place, governments, especially those in developed countries, have put considerable emphasis on the enhancement of their national R&D capabilities. MNEs have frequently been asked for, or have offered, increased local R&D as a condition for investment approval. The growing practice of granting world product mandates to subsidiaries, covering everything from R&D through production to marketing, is consistent with this trend. In the second place, as the declining usefulness of the product-cycle model shows, innovative capability has ceased to be identifiable exclusively at the national level, and is increasingly becoming company-specific. Some of the most economically significant innovations in recent years (i.e., in the computer field) have been made by relatively small firms, which became large as a result of their discoveries. The technological sweepstakes seem to be a series of hundred-metre dashes rather than a single marathon.

The ability of the MNE to disregard or disturb government policy and planning is ultimately the greatest source of concern for governments. National control of the economy may be imperilled by the ability of the MNE to make decisions affecting the welfare, efficiency, and growth of that economy for reasons of its own, and to circumvent the constraints and incentives of government policy. This loss of control by governments over the realization of their economic objectives is in part a consequence of the interdependence of the modern international economy; it is also in part a reflection of the uncertainty surrounding the autonomous role of the MNE.

Foreign-owned MNEs may be unresponsive to government policy and planning because they are accustomed to a different pattern of government-business relations in their country of origin, or because they may measure government incentives and constraints against their corporate global interests rather than against national goals. The literature on the MNE is replete with cases of MNE behaviour that ran counter to government policy goals, because the goals pursued by the MNE were different.

A classic example occurred in 1967 when the Chrysler-owned Rootes Motor Company of the United Kingdom concluded a rapid wage settlement with striking workers in excess of the British government's wage-restraint program of the time, thereby dooming that program to failure, because of the importance of its British plants to the continentally integrated production and marketing system. The wage-pause program made perfectly good sense to the British government in the context of the attempt to combat inflation in the United Kingdom. The need to halt the strike made perfectly good sense to Chrysler in a context where the strike closed not only the British plants but also those throughout Europe, which were dependent upon the continued supply of parts and components from British affiliates. Chrysler/Rootes must be seen not as deliberately contravening government policy, but simply as having been less concerned with it than with its own corporate interests.

Similar examples can be cited from countries around the world, where an MNE decided to close a plant that the government wished to have kept operating, to make new investments in locations or sectors where the government would have preferred it not to occur, to draw on its foreign financial resources to invest in industrial expansion when the government's fiscal and monetary policy was designed to cool down the economy, to increase imports from affiliates after a government's exchange-rate devaluation had endeavoured to increase exports and reduce imports, to allocate export markets to its subsidiaries regardless of government policy to increase trade with particular prospective trading partners, to adjust transfer prices for interaffiliate trade so as to minimize the tax paid in a high-tax jurisdiction when the government concerned was seeking to increase its tax revenue, or to accelerate or delay interaffiliate payments or even shift vast amounts of liquid assets in order to profit from anticipated exchange-rate fluctuations when the government was seeking to dampen capital movements and restore exchange-rate stability. In all of these cases, the goal of the MNE was not to defeat the government but to protect and advance its own interests, which lie in a different decision domain than that of the government of a nation-state.

There have been occasions when an MNE has pitted itself directly against a government. The United Fruit Company in Guatemala, International Telephone and Telegraph (ITT) in Chile, and Union Minière in Katanga are rare but instructive examples of direct political challenge from the MNE to a government. These cases are exceptions to the rule. Normally, the problems encountered by host governments lie in the areas of incompatible goals and practices.

Certain issue areas are common to the experience of many host governments with the MNE as autonomous actor.[12] Many governments encounter problems with subsidiaries importing labour-relations practices familiar and comfortable to the parent company, but foreign and disruptive to the experience of the host economy. Differences over the extent to which labour contracts are considered legally binding, over the notice and assistance to be provided to workers in the case of layoffs, over the receptivity to collective-bargaining and strike action, or over social expectations and conventions regarding hours of work and the like have arisen in country after country. Also, regardless of the degree of openness to foreign investment or the sophistication of a screening mechanism for investment approval, there are widespread examples in almost every jurisdiction of proposed takeovers or new investments that have become the subject of intense public negotiation and political pressure between MNE and government. The initial entry of an MNE into a country can be the occasion for some political difficulty.

The prospect that the MNE might alter the culture and lifestyle of the host country is an alarming one for governments of both developed and developing countries. The spectre of cultural homogenization, or "coca-colonization," looms over all citizens and governments concerned to preserve their distinctive and traditional way of life in the face of pressures to adopt values, tastes, and practices compatible with the production and marketing activities of MNEs. Many of these social and cultural effects result from underlying factors such as modernization and the imperatives of an industrial or postindustrial society. Nevertheless, in many eyes the MNE is seen as the channel through which cultural and social effects are transmitted.

The concerns about social and cultural effects are often vague and undefined, but some themes can be identified. They tend to be most pronounced in developing countries, where the contrast between traditional cultural patterns and modern industrial values and lifestyle is greatest, and where the presence of the MNE is proportionately larger. Nevertheless, the difference is only one of degree rather than kind. In either case, it is important to recognize that traditional culture is not necessarily "better" in some intrinsic case, but different. Arguments can be conducted about whether citizens will be better or worse off changing traditional values and behaviour, but the change will be imposed rather than self-selected.

One of the changes resulting from the presences and activity of the MNE in a local society can be an alteration in the existing social-class structure. By stimulating the movement of the peasantry from subsistence agriculture into wage-earning employment, and by advantaging a new managerial/entrepreneurial class that may not be drawn from the ranks of traditional political leaders or small merchants, the MNE can be responsible for setting in motion a new pattern of class relations in traditional societies. In a related manner, the MNE can have an impact on economic inequalities and social or ethnic stratification. Social cleavages between rich and poor, between regions of the country, or between the city and the countryside can be aggravated.

The socioeconomic system can be altered by the presence and activity of the MNE. This situation is perhaps most evident when a previously self-sufficient society is led to replace its subsistence agricultural sector with one geared to the production of cash crops for export. The result can be the monetarization of the entire economy, as it becomes increasingly impossible to function or survive without a money-earning occupation, and the replacement of cheaper, locally produced food with more expensive imported food, on which the country becomes dependent.

A related result is the impact on knowledge and skills of the citizens of the developing country. The training of a relatively unskilled labour force can disseminate that knowledge and those skills more widely through the entire population, creating a new favoured social class, and imbuing employees with the MNE's rules and norms, which are implicitly (if not explicitly) seen to be associated with progress and prosperity. An associated phenomenon is the increasing dependence of many countries on information provided by and through the MNE. The large presence of MNEs in the communications media (news organizations; publishers; radio, television, and film producers) and the overwhelmingly Western bias and content in the news, entertainment, and advertising they convey make their impact inescapable.

Perhaps the most striking cultural impact of all is the structuring of consumption patterns in the host society.[13] The MNE has a direct interest in implanting consumption-oriented values, and creating a consumer demand for certain goods and services (which they provide) for which there was none before. Through advertising and marketing, as well as more subtle social symbolism, societies are led to value manufactured products over cheaper and more traditional items. Through a process sometimes labelled "taste transfer,"[14] brand-name products come to be intrinsically desirable. The commercial interests of the MNE require that the consumption patterns of its host societies conform to its production capabilities.

These concerns about industrial dominance, technological dependence, disruption of government policy and planning, and cultural effects are present to a greater or lesser extent in all host countries. Developed countries have a more diversified economy in which the presence of any single MNE is unlikely to dominate, and generally find themselves in the position of being simultaneously host and parents to MNEs. Their governments are driven to find a balance between the benefits and costs of MNE activity that does not set a precedent for action injurious to the interests of their own MNEs abroad. Developing countries, by contrast, can experience far more disruption and dependence as a result of MNE activity, and their concerns, and responses, can be more sharply focussed.

With regard to industrial dominance, developing countries are particularly concerned about the challenge posed by the reproduction in their economies of the oligopolistic structure of the parent industry (the so-called miniature-replica effect), and about the possible decline in local entrepreneurship. The presence of 13 automobile companies producing in Argentina, when the size of the local market would justify one, or at most two, large-scale automobile assembly plants, suggests an inefficient economy. High tariffs and other measures to encourage import substitution and local production by subsidiaries can foster inefficiency, increase dependence on costly imported components, and perpetuate industrial dominance. Whether local entrepreneurship is inhibited or assisted will depend largely on what former owners do after their local companies are taken over by MNEs — if they use the proceeds to start new enterprises, the economy and society will benefit; if they retire on the proceeds, or become employees in the subsidiary, entrepreneurship will decline.

The concerns of developing countries regarding technological dependence focus particularly on the possible inappropriateness of the technology used by the MNE. Even when the developing economy is characterized by abundant and inexpensive labour, the MNE typically will prefer capital-intensive technology, because that is what its production processes are designed for.

Developing-country concerns about disruption of national economic policies and planning typically revolve around efforts by the MNE to avoid revenue payments to the government (through tax evasion, artificial transfer prices, etc.), and the ability of the MNE to insulate itself from the effect of local policy instruments because of its access to foreign resources. Because of the economic and political influence an MNE is more likely to generate in a developing country, its ability to bring direct pressure on the government to make or change policies can often be great.

Concerns about social and cultural effects are particularly pronounced in developing countries, probably because those effects are bound up in the whole unstable transition of modernization and industrialization. Developing countries are particularly vulnerable to the creation of geographical and sociological enclaves, to the exacerbation of social cleavages, and to the emphasis on private production and consumption that can drive out traditional socioeconomic patterns and public alternatives.

The prominence of these concerns has made developing-country governments more likely than those of developed ones to threaten or resort to nationalization and expropriation.[15] Even so, expropriation was widespread only in the relatively brief historical period from 1968 to 1975.[16] Since then it has declined as developing-country governments have become more sophisticated in their understanding of the benefits and costs of MNE operations, and more capable in the design and implementation of regulatory controls when ownership itself is not the issue. The obsolescing bargain has become more prevalent than outright expropriation, as governments have learned the wisdom of squeezing the golden goose to make it lay more golden eggs, rather than killing it. Permissive policies with high incentives to attract investment give way to round after round of new requirements to extract more benefits at lower cost once the investment has proved profitable, and the MNE is likely to comply rather than forgo the profit. Progressive rounds of renegotiation typically involve, first, laws of general application, such as tax, land-use, and labour practices; second, improved linkages between the foreign investor and the local economy, such as increased purchasing from local suppliers; and third, participation of the government in ownership and management decisions.[17]

Even if expropriation has become less common than before, it still occurs. What is more, local instability or policy changes (along the lines of the obsolescing bargain) can have major implications for the profitability of the MNE. In response,

MNEs have created an entire industry of political-risk analysts, forecasting the location of possible threats to their interests and counselling appropriate defensive and deterrent responses.

Host governments can respond to these challenges posed by the autonomous MNE either at the moment of entry of the investment or with respect to continuing operations. Developing-country governments with relatively little bargaining leverage at the moment of entry have, for the most part, tended to follow the strategy of the obsolescing bargain. Governments of developed countries have made efforts to monitor or regulate ongoing MNE operations, but in general have tended to use their control over access to exact favourable commitments from foreign MNEs through a screening process of some kind.[18]

While the parent government can more readily use the MNE as an instrument of policy, it is not immune to the challenges of negative effects on its society, economy, and policy from the autonomous action of the MNE. Some concerns, especially regarding disruption to government policies and planning, are qualitatively similar to those of host governments. Other concerns are specific to the situation of a parent country.

The U.S. labour movement has complained that the tendency of American MNEs to locate production in lower-wage countries is costing the United States jobs. This has led to political pressure to restrict foreign investment abroad, increase production at home, and prevent the "deindustrialization" of the United States. Investment may be a substitute for trade, but critics charge that it involves an export of jobs.

Similar concerns are voiced about technology transfer. At the same time that host countries want to increase their technological capabilities, parent countries (especially the United States) are becoming concerned that technology is being made available to other countries too rapidly through subsidiaries or licensing arrangements, thus denying the innovator the traditional opportunity to benefit commercially from the innovation. Export markets are lost, competitive advantages are lost, and again jobs in the parent country are jeopardized.

While host governments have concerns about the capital drain of profits and dividends remitted to the parent, parent governments have concerns that not enough capital is repatriated. The outflow of investment capital can pose a strain for the balance of payments, and so long as profits earned abroad are reinvested rather than repatriated, there is no benefit to the parent country's balance of payments, or tax revenue to its government.

Finally, there are questions about the impact of the MNE on the foreign policy of the parent government. There is an extensive literature on U.S. economic imperialism that charges that U.S. foreign policy is designed and implemented so as to advance the interests of capital, represented in MNEs. Some radical critics argue that U.S. foreign policy is instrumentally determined by members of the capitalist elite occupying positions of power or influencing those that do so. Others contend that the relationship is structural, with the state acting through its policies to reinforce the predominance of the capitalist system. Still others identify economic interests (typically investments, markets, and sources of supply), which foreign policy will be designed to protect.

Conclusion

The changes wrought by the MNE are many and varied. There is no single description that captures the role of the MNE in international relations. If asked whether the MNE is an instrument of government policy or an autonomous actor capable of challenging government policy, one must answer, both. But this answer is far from unsatisfying. It speaks to the richness and complexity of the modern world, and the analytic delight involved in tracing the roles and interactions of actors in individual situations and relationships.

Clearly, the MNE matters. What is more, it matters in different ways, depending on the time, and on the circumstances. Our knowledge of this subject has progressed beyond the point where the case must be made that the MNE is important enough to study. The task at hand is to refine our understanding, and to shed more light on what the MNE does, how it interacts with governments of different kinds, and what the consequences are. In short, the task is to engage in analytic study that will advance knowledge.

In the modern world, knowledge is power. The power of the MNE derives from its combination of capital, technology, management, and marketing. At least three of the four are knowledge-based. The ability of governments, international organizations, and nongovernmental actors to control or countervail the power of the MNE must also rest upon knowledge of the nature and implications of the MNE.

The world, as complex as it is, will not remain static. The MNE will change, in structure and in strategy. So, too, will the relationships between the MNE and other actors (principally states). How favourable will be the outcomes of those changes will depend in no small part on the adequacy of knowledge about the MNE and its present and possible roles.

NOTES

1. Robert O. Keohane and Joseph S. Nye, Jr., eds., *Transnational Relations and World Politics* (Cambridge, Mass.: Harvard University Press, 1972).

2. Joseph S. Nye, Jr., and Robert O. Keohane, "Transnational Relations and World Politics: An Introduction," in *Transnational Relations and World Politics*, xi.

3. Samuel P. Huntington, "Transnational Organizations in World Politics," *World Politics* 25 (April 1973): 333–68.

4. Nye and Keohane, "Transnational Relations," xvii-xxii.

5. United Nations Department of Economic and Social Affairs, *Multinational Corporations in World Development* (New York: United Nations, 1973), Annex II:4–6.

6. Raymond Vernon, *Sovereignty at Bay: The Multinational Spread of U.S. Enterprises* (New York: Basic Books, 1971), chap. 1.

7. Yair Aharoni, "On the Definition of a Multinational Corporation," in *The Multinational Enterprise in Transition*, ed. A. Kapoor and Phillip D. Grub (Princeton: Darwin, 1972), 3–20.

8. Vernon, *Sovereignty at Bay*, 65–77.

9. David Leyton-Brown, "Extraterritoriality in Canadian-American Relations," *International Journal* 36 (Winter 1980–81): 185–207.

10. David Leyton-Brown, "Extraterritoriality in Trade Sanctions," in *The Utility of International Economic Sanctions*, ed. David Leyton-Brown (London: Croom Helm, 1987), 261–62.

11. David Leyton-Brown, "Canada and Multinational Enterprise," in *Foremost Nation: Canadian Foreign Policy in a Changing World*, ed. Norman Hillmer and Garth Stevenson (Toronto: McClelland and Stewart, 1977), 78.

12. David Leyton-Brown, "Canada, France and Britain as Hosts to Multinationals," *International Perspectives* (September/October 1975): 39–43.

13. Jean-Louis Reiffers et al., *Transnational Corporations and Endogenous Development* (Paris: UNESCO, 1982), esp. chap. 4.

14. Steven Langdon, "Multinational Corporations, Taste Transfer and Underdevelopment: A Case Study from Kenya," *Review of African Political Economy* 2 (1975): 12–35.

15. This comparison is not absolute, as governments in developed countries have been known on occasion to do the same. For example, the provincial governments of Saskatchewan and Quebec nationalized the foreign-owned potash and asbestos industries, respectively.

16. Stephen J. Kobrin, "Expropriation as an Attempt to Control Foreign Firms in LDCs: Trends from 1960 to 1979," *International Studies Quarterly* 28 (1984): 344–45.

17. Joan Edelman Spero, *The Politics of International Economic Relations*, 2d ed. (New York: St. Martin's, 1981), 239.

18. A. E. Safarian, *Governments and Multinationals: Policies in the Developed Countries* (Washington, D.C.: British–North American Committee, 1983).

SELECT BIBLIOGRAPHY

Ball, George W., ed. *Global Companies: The Political Economy of World Business*. Englewood Cliffs, N.J.: Prentice-Hall, 1975.

Barnet, Richard J., and Ronald E. Muller. *Global Reach: The Power of the Multinational Corporations*. New York: Simon and Schuster, 1974.

Behrman, Jack N. *National Interests and the Multinational Enterprise: Tensions Among the North Atlantic Countries*. Englewood Cliffs, N.J.: Prentice-Hall, 1970.

Bergsten, C.F.; T. Horst; and T. Moran. *American Multinationals and American Interests*. Washington, D.C.: The Brookings Institution, 1978.

Blake, David H., and Robert S. Walters. *The Politics of Global Economic Relations*. 3d ed. Englewood Cliffs, N.J.: Prentice-Hall, 1987.

Fry, Earl H. *The Politics of International Investment*. New York: McGraw-Hill, 1983.

Gilpin, Robert. *U.S. Power and the Multinational Corporation: The Political Economy of Foreign Direct Investment*. New York: Basic, 1975.

Gladwin, Thomas N., and Ingo Walter. *Multinationals Under Fire: Lessons in the Management of Conflict*. New York: John Wiley and Sons, 1980.

Modelski, George, ed. *Transnational Corporations and World Order*. San Francisco: W.H. Freeman, 1979.

Safarian, A.E. *Governments and Multinationals: Policies in the Developed Countries*. Washington, D.C.: British–North American Committee, 1983.

Said, Abdul A., and Luiz R. Simmons, eds. *The New Sovereigns: Multinational Corporations as World Powers*. Englewood Cliffs, N.J.: Prentice-Hall, 1975.

Spero, Joan Edelman. *The Politics of International Economic Relations*. 3d ed. New York: St. Martin's, 1985.

Vernon, Raymond. *Sovereignty at Bay: The Multinational Spread of U.S. Enterprises*. New York: Basic Books, 1971.

———. *Storm Over the Multinationals: The Real Issues*. Cambridge Mass.: Harvard University Press, 1977.

INTERNATIONAL SANCTIONS

Margaret Doxey

Sanctions in Theory and Practice

International sanctions, and particularly international economic sanctions, have become a prominent feature of statecraft in recent years. They have been adopted within the framework of international organizations such as the United Nations, the Organization of American States (OAS), and the Arab League, and also by individual states and groups of states outside of these frameworks. Whether sanctions should be imposed, and, if they are, whether they will be effective, are often matters of heated debate in governmental and nongovernmental circles; arguments about the pros and cons of sanctions against South Africa have been particularly intense. For students of international politics, it is important that the complexities of the subject be carefully explored, both through analysis of ideas about sanctioning and through examination of cases where sanctions have actually been employed.

The first tasks in studying international sanctions are to clarify the meaning of the term, to draw up a typology of possible measures, and to review the question of sponsorship. Next, it is useful to outline some important cases where sanctions have been employed. Such an outline will provide a basis for discussion of such crucial factors as the intentions of governments in sponsoring sanctions, their choice of measures, and the extent of participation in application. Case studies also permit some retrospective assessment, both of target vulnerability and the effects of sanctions in a wider context, and provide lessons of experience that can be helpful to policy makers.

Definitional Problems

One of the difficulties encountered in studying international sanctions derives from the wide range of meanings that are attributed to the term. It is too restrictive to limit use of the word *sanction* to penalties imposed for violations of international law, but it is both confusing and incorrect to equate "sanctions" with all acts of foreign policy that have a negative intent. Self-serving policies pursued with the object of gaining advantages over other states should not be given a sanctions "label"; this label should be reserved for penalties imposed in response to government action that ignores international standards of behaviour or breaks international obligations that have been accepted on a bilateral or multilateral basis. International law may, indeed, have been violated, as was the case in 1979–80 when the Iranian government failed to protect personnel and property at the U.S. embassy in Tehran. Alternatively, or additionally, the behaviour of the target may be censured on other grounds: for instance, apartheid in South Africa clearly violates standards of international morality.

Problems of "labelling" do not arise in cases of multilateral sanctions sponsored by such bodies as the United Nations, the Commonwealth, or the OAS, but where measures are taken unilaterally, as is frequently the case, matters are often less clear-cut, and it is sometimes difficult to draw a sharp line between a penalty for "wrongdoing," which is correctly termed a "sanction," and other negative measures. Governments that impose such measures on other states like to call them "sanctions" in order to invest them with an aura of righteousness, highlighting misconduct on the part of the target, but perceptions of misconduct may be subjective and the justification for a punitive response, either to support community values or as self-help, may be controversial. There are undoubtedly grey areas in sanctioning, as some of the cases discussed later in this chapter will show, but commercial and financial measures deliberately designed to advance the economic interests of one state at the expense of others should not be called sanctions; nor should economic warfare (whether "hot" or "cold") that seeks to limit or destroy the enemy's military capability. It is interesting to note that neither the strategic embargoes imposed on the Soviet Union and other communist countries by members of the Western alliance since 1947 nor the Arab oil embargoes initiated after the 1973 Middle East war were labelled sanctions.

A Typology of Sanctions

Although economic sanctions are those most frequently used and discussed, it is important to note that a very wide range of measures can serve as sanctions in particular cases. They can be imposed singly or in a package and can be progressively intensified or scaled down as circumstances require. At the mild end of the spectrum are verbal protests and diplomatic and cultural measures; in the middle, restrictions on communication, transportation, and travel, and the familiar battery of commercial and financial measures; and, at the severe end of the scale, blockades and other measures involving the use of force.

A detailed list of nonviolent measures is given in Table 1 (page 244). It includes organizational penalties that are self-enforcing; all other measures require action by individual governments to bring them into effect.

Sponsorship of Sanctions

As already noted, international sanctions can be sponsored by international organizations against members and sometimes against nonmembers. They can also be adopted on a unilateral basis by one government, or by a number of

TABLE 1 Typology of Negative Nonviolent Sanctions

1. Diplomatic and Political Measures

- (i) Protest, censure, condemnation.
- (ii) Postponement, cancellation of official visits, meetings, negotiations for treaties and agreements.
- (iii) Reduction, limitation of scale of diplomatic representation:
  - (a) status of post.
  - (b) number of diplomatic personnel.
  - (c) number of consular offices.
- (iv) Severance of diplomatic relations.
- (v) Nonrecognition of new governments, new states.

2. Cultural and Communications Measures

- (i) Reduction, cancellation of cultural exchanges (scientific co-operation; educational links; sporting links; entertainment).
- (ii) Ban on tourism to/from target country.
- (iii) Withdrawal of visas for nationals of targets.
- (iv) Restriction, cancellation of telephone, cable, postal links with target.
- (v) Restriction, suspension, cancellation of overflight landing privileges.
- (vi) Restriction, suspension, cancellation of water transit/docking/port privileges.
- (vii) Restriction, suspension, cancellation of land transit privileges.

3. Economic measures

(a) *Financial*

- (i) Reduction, suspension, cancellation of aid: military, food, development, funds for technical assistance.
- (ii) Reduction, suspension, cancellation of credit facilities at concessionary/market rates.
- (iii) Freezing, confiscation of bank assets of target government.
- (iv) Confiscation of other assets belonging to the target.
- (v) Ban on interest payments to target.
- (vi) Ban on other transfer payments to target.
- (vii) Refusal to refinance, reschedule debt repayments (interest and principal).
- (viii) Control, ban on capital movements.

(b) *Commercial and Technical*

- (i) Quotas on imports from the target.
- (ii) Quotas on exports to the target.
- (iii) Restrictive licensing of imports/exports.
- (iv) Limited, total embargo on imports.
- (v) Limited, total embargo on exports.
- (vi) Discriminatory tariff policy (includes denial of most favoured-nation status).
- (vii) Restriction, cancellation, suspension of fishing rights.
- (viii) Suspension, cancellation of joint projects, industrial ventures.
- (ix) Cancellation of trade agreements.
- (x) Ban on export of technology to the target.
- (xi) Blacklisting of individuals/firms trading with the target.
- (xii) Reduction, suspension, cancellation of technical assistance, training programs.
- (xiii) Ban on insurance services.

4. Organizational penalties

(a) *Membership and Participation*

- (i) Rejection of admission.
- (ii) Rejection of credentials.
- (iii) Suspension.
- (iv) Expulsion.

(b) *Benefits*

- (i) Denial of loans, grants, technical assistance, etc.
- (ii) Removal of headquarters, regional office from target.

governments acting in concert — a process that has been described as "multiple unilateralism" or "minilateralism."

Common sense suggests that the larger the group of sanctioning states, the more effective the sanctions are likely to be, and that it will be particularly important to include in any program of economic denial "key" states on which the target is heavily dependent. But, there is also an "authority factor" to be considered, and sanctions might be expected to carry more weight when they are backed by an international body that determines that rules have been broken or standards ignored. In the aftermath of World War I, international sanctions were devised as an integral part of the new collective-security system to be provided by the League of Nations. It was hoped that the threat of universal ostracism set out in Article 16 of the League Covenant would deter any would-be aggressor from violating League rules about going to war.[1] League sanctions, as an automatic and thoroughgoing response to any such violation, were envisaged as penalties that states would prefer to avoid.

Within domestic societies, the role of deterrence and punishment is generally accepted, albeit with reservations. However, at the international level, there is no comparable framework or machinery of law and order. Voluntarism reigns supreme, and from the earliest days of the League of Nations, which had limited membership and did not include the United States, there was little support for the idea of automatic sanctions. Collective security was conspicuous by its absence. The only major case of sanctions, against Italy, was a complete failure and served to discredit both the League and the idea of international sanctions.[2] Italy's invasion of Ethiopia — a fellow member of the League — in October 1935 constituted a violation of the Covenant's provisions on resort to war, but the sanctions applied by League members were of limited scope and did not include a ban on oil exports, which might have been effective in halting Italy's military operations. The sanctions were also undermined by the revelation that Britain and France, the leading League powers, were secretly planning to offer Italy part of Ethiopia as a means of resolving the crisis.[3] In any event, the conquest of Ethiopia was successfully completed by May 1936; Italy was not expelled from the League, and sanctions were officially lifted in July.

Despite the failure of the League to prevent aggression and war, the idea of collective security, backed by sanctions, was revived and extended when the United Nations was established in 1945. This body appeared to have advantages both of experience and of membership over the League. Both superpowers were founding members and, in Chapter VII of the Charter, the Security Council was given executive authority to deal with threats to the peace as well as breaches of the peace and acts of aggression. Members of the U.N. undertook to seek peaceful resolution of their disputes (Article 33) and to obey Security Council decisions (Article 25). Nonviolent sanctions in any combination can be ordered (or recommended) by the Council; military measures can be recommended but not ordered because agreements under Article 43 to make forces available were never concluded. Mandatory sanctions obviously carry the maximum authority. But, once again, the idea of collective security proved to be unworkable, and international enforcement, a myth. Expectations that there would be consensus on wrongdoing or on what should be done about it ignore the reality of international relations where perceptions of delinquency can vary significantly and foreign- and domestic-policy considerations often rule out hostile action toward another state.

In the post–World War II era, the rapid onset of the cold war brought stalemate in the Security Council where the veto enjoyed by permanent members offered a convenient mechanism for Britain, France, China, the United States, and the Soviet Union to block resolutions with which they disagreed, particularly any that were seen as damaging to their own interests or those of their allies and clients.

If there is little likelihood that sanctions will be adopted, they will not be effective in deterring states from wrongdoing. In the history of the United Nations, consensus on mandatory economic sanctions has been achieved only with respect to Rhodesia.[4] Calls from the General Assembly for sanctions against the Franco regime in Spain; against Portugal while it held African colonial territories; and against South Africa and Israel have been largely ignored. One can argue, perhaps, that censure of state policy by the Security Council, even if it is not followed by a sanctions order or recommendations, confirms the status of measures adopted by members of the U.N. on a unilateral basis. For instance, Iran's failure to release the U.S. hostages in Tehran was deemed a threat to the peace by the Security Council, confirming wrongdoing and legitimizing U.S. sanctions (though not recourse to force); similarly, the Council encouraged members to adopt sanctions against South Africa in 1986. Such resolutions reveal the limits of consensus: it is obvious that stronger resolutions were — or would be — subject to veto.

Regional and limited member organizations can also decide — or recommend — that members should impose restrictions on their unilateral dealings with a fellow member. Organizational penalties are also likely in such cases. The suspension of Cuba from the OAS (see below) and of Egypt from the Arab League are cases in point. The affirmation of wrongdoing and sponsorship of penalties within an institutional framework invests the penalties with some authoritative international status that is lacking when sanctions are adopted on a unilateral basis without such backing. States have always been free to retaliate with countermeasures against acts that directly harm their interests, whether such acts are illegal or merely unfriendly, but injured states may also seek the support of others, claiming that the offender has violated international obligations. In the 1980s, there was a series of high-profile cases where sanctions were initiated by the United States who then sought to involve other Western countries, including Canada, Japan, and members of the European Community. The targets were Iran, the Soviet Union, Poland, and Libya, and the sanctions were adopted on a voluntary basis, without any institutional sponsorship. In some cases, as will be discussed later in this chapter, the grounds for retaliation as well as the appropriateness of particular measures became matters for dispute, which further weakened the status of the sanctions.

Selected Case Studies

Before considering major issues and problems raised by sanctions, it is useful to review several important cases of international sanctions, identifying in each case the occasion for sanctions, the sponsoring government(s) or organization, the measures adopted, the duration of the sanctions, and a summary of their overall effects, as far as these can be assessed. Limits of space preclude exhaustive treatment of all recent sanctions cases — which can be found in other works[5] — but it is obviously essential to give some account of the Rhodesian case, as the only instance of comprehensive U.N. sanctions. In addition, OAS sanctions against Cuba provide an example of regional action, and the recent cases of U.S.-led sanctions against Iran, the Soviet Union, and Poland illustrate the trend to unilateralism outside organizational frameworks. South Africa also requires attention as a continuing and unresolved problem.

Rhodesia

By 1988 Rhodesia was still the only case of comprehensive mandatory economic sanctions in the record of the United Nations. The illegal unilateral declaration of independence (UDI) by the white regime of Ian Smith in Rhodesia in November 1965 led to U.N. sanctions because Britain, the constitutionally responsible power, was in favour, and no other permanent member of the Security Council had an interest in using its veto. The UDI was unacceptable to Britain until greater progress had been achieved toward African majority rule; it was unacceptable to African countries until majority rule had been achieved.

Sanctions were imposed in the first instance by Britain, with support from Commonwealth countries, and included a total trade ban (except for humanitarian items); a ban on transfer payments to Rhodesia; its exclusion from the Sterling Area, the Commonwealth Preference Area, and the London capital market; a freeze of Rhodesian central-bank assets in Britain; and the denial of diplomatic recognition. A year later, in December 1966, the Security Council determined that the Rhodesian rebellion constituted a "threat to the peace" and ordered selective measures that included a ban on the export of petroleum and armaments to Rhodesia and an embargo on imports of Rhodesian tobacco, meat and meat products, asbestos, copper, chrome ore, and iron ore — all key commodities in Rhodesia's export trade.[6] Compliance with these sanctions was obligatory for all U.N. members. In 1968 they were extended to comprise a total economic boycott of Rhodesia.[7]

This program of sanctions did not signal an end to British negotiations for a settlement with the Smith regime. Talks and proposals continued over a period of 14 years, until late 1979, when the Lancaster House Conference agreed on terms that led to the emergence of Zimbabwe as an independent state in April 1980.[8] The conference, which brought together representatives of the Rhodesian government (by this time headed by a black prime minister), the two leading African nationalist groups ZANU and ZAPU united in the Patriotic Front, and the British government, was successful in drawing up a new constitution, securing a ceasefire, and providing for acceptable transitional arrangements. During the short pre-independence period, Rhodesia reverted to the status of a British colony.

Sanctions were lifted at the conclusion of the conference. They had played some part in undermining the capacity of the Rhodesian regime to survive but had not proved speedy or decisive.[9] The major factor in the regime's eventual capitulation was the growing scale of guerrilla warfare inside the country.

In economic terms, Rhodesia displayed a surprising ability to withstand the initial shock of sanctions and rapidly diversified agricultural production and expanded manufacturing industry. Blacks bore the brunt of unemployment. South Africa provided a lifeline for exports and imports, particularly imports of oil, and was a significant factor in the prolonged survival of the Smith regime. White solidarity in Rhodesia was also important: government and business co-operated closely in efforts to minimize the effects of sanctions, and a sophisticated international network developed for smuggling goods and laundering financial transactions. Monitoring systems set up by the Commonwealth Secretariat, and later by the U.N. Security Council, proved largely ineffective in closing holes in the sanctions "net."[10]

Cuba

Under U.S. leadership, the Organization of American States (OAS) suspended Cuba from membership early in 1962 in response to Fidel Castro's proclaimed Marxist-Leninist orientation, which was declared incompatible with the inter-American system.[11] The missile crisis in October of the same year brought OAS support for the U.S. naval quarantine, directed at Soviet and other ships carrying military equipment to Cuba, and in 1964 the OAS adopted further measures against Cuba when Castro was accused of subversive activities in Venezuela. A two-thirds majority of OAS members voted in terms of the 1947 Inter-American (Rio) Treaty of Reciprocal Assistance to embargo arms sales to, and trade with, Cuba, except for food and medicine. Diplomatic relations were also to be severed, although Mexico did not comply with this decision. Alongside these OAS measures went a much harsher set of U.S. sanctions that included the severance of sea and air links between the United States and Cuba, a freeze of Cuban assets, and a total trade embargo.[12]

The OAS measures were lifted in 1975, but U.S. measures remain in force. It is hard to judge the effects of the OAS measures in isolation from the U.S. program of denial that was obviously of much greater impact and forced the Cuban government to seek massive economic help from the Soviet Union. Politically, the sanctions were clearly unsuccessful in luring Castro away from communism; indeed, it seems likely that his position in Cuba was reinforced, rather than undermined, by external pressure.

Iran

The occasion for sanctions against Iran was the seizure by Iranian militants on November 4, 1979, of the American embassy in Tehran and 52 hostages, mostly U.S. diplomats. There was no doubt of the illegality of the Iranian government's conduct: it quickly became clear that it was not prepared to live up to its obligations under international law regarding the immunity and protection of diplomatic personnel and property. Time-honoured international customary law had established these rights, which are also codified in the Vienna conventions on Diplomatic Relations (1961) and Consular Relations (1963). Iran is a party to both conventions.

The United States, as the injured party, appealed to the United Nations Security Council for support and, on November 9, the Council unanimously called for the release of the hostages. In December, it threatened "effective measures" (i.e., sanctions) if Iran failed to comply. The United States also took its case to the International Court of Justice (ICJ), asking for provisional measures under Article 41 of the Court's Statute to address the situation urgently and for a judgement that Iran had violated its obligations to the United States and was required to make amends. The Iranian government declined to participate in the Court's proceedings, but the Court established its jurisdiction under the Vienna conventions and dismissed Iran's claims of prior U.S. wrongdoing as irrelevant to the issue under consideration. In its Order of December 15, 1979, the Court called for the immediate release of the hostages,[13] and it upheld the U.S. case in its judgement delivered on May 24, 1980.[14]

Regrettably, on January 13, 1980, the Soviet Union vetoed a U.S.-sponsored resolution for mandatory economic sanctions against Iran. Thus, although wrongdoing had been confirmed by both the Security Council and the ICJ, remedies were left to the United States and any other governments who might voluntarily offer support. The Carter administration imposed a series of sanctions between January and April 1980, beginning with a freeze of all Iranian assets (totalling $12 billion) in U.S. banks and their inventorization with a view to future confiscation; a ban on imports of Iranian oil, which was extended to a total embargo on trade with Iran, except for food and medicine; the withdrawal of visas for Iranians in the United States; and a ban on all financial transactions with Iran. Diplomatic relations were formally severed in April. In addition to these penalties, the Carter administration conducted intensive diplomatic negotiations with the Iranian authorities and, in April 1980, undertook a disastrously unsuccessful attempt to rescue the hostages. Their release was finally arranged with the help of Algeria's good offices on January 20, 1981, the day of Ronald Reagan's inauguration.[15]

The United States also looked to its allies for supportive sanctions, but they proved very reluctant to get involved. Finally, in April 1980, the members of the European Community and certain other countries, including Japan, imposed some limited trade restrictions. They did not sever diplomatic relations with Iran, and their measures were mainly of symbolic effect.[16]

All sanctions were lifted when the hostages were released, although a portion of the Iranian assets were placed in an escrow account and a United States–Iran claims tribunal was set up to adjudicate outstanding claims between the two countries.

The verdict on the efficacy of the U.S. sanctions was that they probably contributed to Iran's eventual willingness to release the hostages, particularly after the war with Iraq began in late 1979 and Iran needed funds to pay for armaments.[17] However, by the end of 1980, every drop of publicity had been squeezed from the hostages' detention and the Iranian government may also have been concerned that the incoming U.S. president, Ronald Reagan, would adopt stronger measures against it. Clearly the Carter administration had no alternative but to make some response to the egregious affront to its interests, which the hostage case represented, but the lack of support from other governments for the important principle of protection of diplomats in which all governments have a direct stake underlined the difficulty of developing a united front against wrong-doing, even in the most blatant of cases.

The Soviet Union: Intervention in Afghanistan

In December 1979, shortly after the seizure of the American hostages in Tehran, the Soviet Union sent its forces into Afghanistan. A pro-Moscow regime had been in power in Kabul since April 1978, but its continuation was threatened by internal unrest. Soviet troops installed a new leader, Babrak Karmal. This intervention, which extended the Soviet sphere of influence into a new region and was to last for a decade, aroused resentment in both Third World and Western governments. At the United Nations, the Soviet veto blocked Security Council action, but the General Assembly, meeting in emergency session in January 1980, adopted a motion of condemnation calling for the withdrawal of all Soviet forces. Voting was 104 to 18, with 18 abstentions. Censure of Soviet conduct was reiterated at all subsequent General Assembly meetings, but there was no recommendation for U.N. members to impose sanctions.

Soviet intervention in Afghanistan posed a further set of problems for the Carter administration, which was already trying to deal with the hostage crisis. It was seen as imperative to devise a response, initially on a unilateral basis. Early in January 1980, President Carter announced a series of measures designed to express disapproval of the Soviet violation of Afghanistan's sovereignty. The SALT II treaty was shelved, a limited grain embargo was imposed, restrictions on the export of high technology to the USSR were tightened, Soviet fishing privileges in U.S. waters were withdrawn, and a ban on participation in the Moscow Summer Olympics was proposed. The allies were then pressed to adopt similar measures, but only Britain and Canada offered strong support, ending preferential credit arrangements with the Soviet Union, curtailing official and cultural exchanges, and officially endorsing the Olympic boycott. In concert with Australia and the European Community, Canada also agreed to maintain grain exports to the USSR at "normal" levels. France and West Germany did not adopt sanctions and offered only limited support for the Olympic boycott. The grain embargo proved extremely unpopular with American farmers, and Republican presidential candidate Ronald Reagan promised to lift it if he were elected, a promise he fulfilled in April 1981.

With the exception of the grain embargo, the restrictions imposed by the United States and its allies were not lifted but tightened and extended as the crisis over Afghanistan merged with the crisis over Poland (discussed below). As far as efficacy is concerned, there was obviously no question of the sanctions themselves changing Soviet policy, but they may have served as a warning of harsher measures if the USSR went any farther. This warning was emphasized by President Carter's declaration, in his 1980 State of the Union address, that the Gulf area was of vital interest for the United States.

The grain embargo did not cause serious dislocation to the Soviet economy because the shortfall in imports from the United States was made up from other sources, particularly Argentina.[18] However, it did prove costly for the United States, and some scholars argue it was effective for that reason.[19] It is also important to remember that, if a response is needed to demonstrate purposiveness at home, economic sanctions are less dangerous than the use of military force. However, the disunity in allied ranks that was already visible over Iran, and was to worsen during the Polish crisis, was counterproductive. The perception of U.S. heavy-handedness was more pronounced against its allies than against the USSR.

Poland and the Soviet Union

Sanctions against Poland and intensified sanctions against the Soviet Union became an issue in December 1981 when the Polish military under General Jaruzelski took over the government, declared martial law, suspended the independent trade union, Solidarity, and detained its leaders. There were fears in the West that the Soviets would intervene militarily in Poland, which would certainly have posed a serious problem for NATO in terms of making a suitable response. The declaration of martial law in Poland did not violate international law, although human rights were obviously being suppressed. The Reagan administration responded promptly with a new set of sanctions against the Soviet Union, which it accused of complicity in the actions of the Jaruzelski regime. Negotiations for a new U.S.–Soviet long-term trade agreement were (temporarily) shelved; Aeroflot flights to the United States were suspended; and the ban on exports of high technology to the Soviet Union was tightened and extended to include equipment for the Siberian gas pipeline. The United States also imposed penalties on Poland: aviation and fishing privileges were withdrawn; food aid and export credits were cancelled; most-favoured–nation status was suspended; and Poland's application to join the International Monetary Fund was blocked. The allies were once again pressed to follow suit. However, they were even less convinced of the need for, or appropriateness of, sanctions in this case. The Soviet Union had not invaded Poland, and measures against Poland itself were seen as counterproductive. European concern was rather to preserve some East-West links and the remnants of détente. Britain, Canada, and Japan adopted very limited diplomatic and economic measures in February 1982, while France and West Germany showed little or no support for U.S. policy. The sharp division between the European and U.S. view of the situation grew worse in June, when the Reagan administration promulgated further regulations that banned the export to the Soviet Union by American and foreign firms of oil- and gas-related equipment, components, and technology, unless permission of the U.S. government was obtained. The refusal of European governments to accept this extraterritorial edict brought a serious rift in East-West relations; defiance by European firms led to their being blacklisted from receiving oil and gas equipment, technology, and services from U.S. sources. Finally, the row subsided in the fall of 1982 when the Reagan administration withdrew the offending regulations, but this did not erase the overall impression of allied disunity rather than concerted efforts to pressure the Soviet Union.

Sanctions against Poland were gradually lifted over the next few years as conditions eased in that country. At one point, Lech Walesa, the leader of Solidarity, appealed for their removal because they were causing hardship to the Polish people. Sanctions against the Soviet Union were also removed as better relations developed between the United States in Reagan's second term of office and the Soviet Union under its new leader, Mikhail Gorbachev.

In general, the measures directed at the Soviet Union were expressive rather than coercive. They were undertaken by the United States to signal disapproval and to reassure domestic constituencies and, by the reluctant Europeans, to support their principal ally. The measures taken by the United States with regard to the control of technology and particularly with regard to the pipeline — whose construction was delayed but not prevented — represented a continuation of its well-established anti-Soviet, anti-communist cold-war strategy policy. Denial of strategic goods and technology to the USSR had been official policy since the late 1940s, and the pattern of U.S. enthusiasm for, and Western European resistance to, extensions to the lists of embargoed items was a familiar one.[20]

South Africa

In considering the South African case, which is ongoing, there is obviously no problem in using the term "sanctions." The system of institutionalized racial discrimination known as apartheid, which denies any participation in the government of South Africa to its majority black population and imposes harsh penalties on all who seek reform, is rightly condemned by world public opinion as being completely unacceptable in terms of international human-rights obligations. In addition, the South African government has retained control of Namibia in defiance of U.N. and World Court rulings, and in recent years South African forces have carried out many raids into neighbouring countries, causing loss of life and damage to property.

Sanctions were recommended by the General Assembly as early as 1961; the Security Council finally declared the arms trade with South Africa a threat to the peace in 1977 and banned it.[21] South Africa was also expelled or forced to withdraw from a number of U.N. agencies including the World Health Organization (WHO) and the Food and Agricultural Organization (FAO). Members of the Organization of African Unity have banned diplomatic relations with South Africa, have denied it overflight rights, and have limited economic contacts. African members of the Commonwealth have also used that body to put pressure on South Africa. It was forced to withdraw from the Commonwealth in 1961; Britain's proposed arms sales to South Africa were strongly opposed in 1971; and sporting contacts have been banned since 1977. A new outbreak of unrest in South Africa and heavy repression by the authorities occurred in 1985. The result was an intensification of international pressure for sanctions, which was immediately reflected at the U.N. and in the Commonwealth. The United States and Britain continue to veto Security Council resolutions that would make sanctions mandatory, but they did not block Resolution 569, in July 1985, which encouraged U.N. members to adopt voluntary measures, and there were subsequently significant developments outside the U.N. In the Commonwealth, although Britain refused to accept the complete "package" proposed by fellow members, all other members agreed in 1987 to ban air links, the promotion of tourism, and new investment and bank loans to South Africa, and to impose embargoes on imports of arms as well as uranium, coal, iron and steel, and gold coins from South Africa and on exports of oil and nuclear goods and of computers for use by the South Africa security forces. Britain joined its European Community partners in imposing similar export embargoes, but EC import embargoes were limited to South African arms, iron and steel, and gold coins. In 1986 the United States Congress overrode a presidential veto to pass legislation that denied landing rights to South African airlines, banned the sale of oil and oil products to South Africa, and also prohibited the import of South African coal, iron and steel, uranium, textiles, food and agricultural products, and armaments. Japan also imposed some limited measures.

By 1987 a wide variety of sanctions against South Africa had been approved by many governments and organizations; but, they remained uncoordinated, and the level of implementation was often unsatisfactory. There were some unwelcome effects for South Africa, chiefly in terms of international isolation (pariah status) and as a result of disinvestment and other financial sanctions, but there was no indication at the time of writing that the sanctions were exerting any significant coercive effect on South African government policy. Without the full participation of Britain, France, West Germany, and Japan in a comprehensive program of economic sanctions, it is hard to see how this could realistically come about. It is worth noting, however, that black opposition groups in South Africa are generally in favour of stiffer sanctions, and the Commonwealth eminent-persons group argued that the absence of sanctions was an encouragement to the South African government not to undertake serious reform, thus increasing the possibilities of widespread racial war in days to come.[22] Further action at the United Nations can certainly not be ruled out.

Issues and Problems

Drawing on these cases for illustration, we can now discuss some issues and problems that are relevant to the analysis of sanctions and whose implications should be understood by policy makers.

The Intentions of Sponsoring Governments

The intentions of governments in imposing sanctions have been thoroughly and carefully studied in recent years. Analysts have become sensitive to the need to relate the "success" or "failure" of sanctions to the purpose(s) they were actually intended to serve and there is a clearer comprehension of the multiplicity of possible objectives and targets.[23]

If sanctions are defined as measures taken unilaterally or multilaterally in response to an unwelcome or unacceptable act by another government, it might be assumed that a change in conduct on the part of that government — or even a change of government — is the prime objective. Thus, Ian Smith's regime in Rhodesia should have abandoned its illegal rebellion; the Cuban people should have rejected Castro; Iran should have released the hostages; the South African government should enter into a serious dialogue with the majority of the population with a view to black enfranchisement. However, it is realistic to acknowledge not only that compliance may be too ambitious an objective but also that the intention of sanctioning governments may be less far-reaching. They may wish merely to administer a public rebuke that indicates displeasure but is not expected to bring about a major shift in policy. Sanctions may be largely symbolic in intent as well as in effect, demonstrating support for international standards and community values, signalling that the target's conduct has not passed unnoticed, and perhaps warning that a more severe reaction is to follow if its actions are repeated or extended. Sanctions against the Soviet Union over Afghanistan, and the measures adopted by the United States following the imposition of martial law and the banning of Solidarity in Poland, fell into this category. They were expressive and punitive, but not designed or expected to be coercive. Sanctions send messages to the people as well as the government of the target. OAS and U.S. sanctions against Cuba were intended to demonstrate to the Cuban people that the Castro government could not serve their interests,[24] while, in the case of South Africa, the message for blacks is one of support and encouragement in their struggle for fair treatment.

Sanctions may also be directed at the domestic audience in the state imposing them. They may be imposed to satisfy internal pressure groups and/or to reassure the public that its government is in control and can give leadership. Such reassurance may be particularly important in a pre-election period. Many Western governments find it necessary to respond to public opinion that demands action against South Africa; even if they do not have much confidence in the effectiveness of sanctions, they prefer not to leave the moral high ground to opposition parties or groups.

Sanctions may also be directed to third parties and to the wider international community, signalling displeasure with the ostensible target's policy and perhaps serving as a warning of the likely costs of misbehaviour. Alternatively, sanctions may be intended principally to support or satisfy allies, suggesting solidarity. The sanctions that allies of the United States reluctantly imposed on Iran, the USSR, and Poland are good examples. These different sets of objectives are not mutually exclusive, and governments may hope to achieve several of them simultaneously, but they impose different priorities and can even be contradictory. They will certainly affect the measures that are selected in each case.

Choice of Measures

The choice of a particular sanction or set of sanctions will reflect intention but it will also be closely linked to the estimated economic and political costs of imposition. Other things being equal, milder measures will be preferred; they are less expensive for the government adopting them, and if the target is not expected to change its policies as a result, there is no need to impose severe economic sanctions that will also hurt the economy of the sanctioning state(s). Although domestic interest groups may be in favour of sanctions, they will not wish to carry the brunt and other sectors of the economy, for example, farmers and manufacturers, will not welcome embargoes that damage their livelihood and prospects. A common set of measures can be specified by the Security Council, which has 15 members, 5 holding veto power, or by other organizations usually by majority vote, but in other circumstances governments are free to choose whatever measures they prefer. A smorgasbord of sanctions can be the result. The case studies outlined above illustrate the variety of factors that can influence governments to adopt some measures and reject others. British prime minister Margaret Thatcher has been adamant in refusing to place sanctions on South Africa, which would cause unemployment in Britain; her resolve is strengthened by her belief that sanctions will not "work" — a subject that is discussed below.

Efficacy

In judging the efficacy of sanctions it is important to remember that one cannot know with certainty what would have happened if they had not been applied. It is also important to distinguish between the economic effects of economic measures, insofar as they can be measured, and the extent to which they can be seen to have engendered political effects.

The conventional wisdom has been that economic sanctions may do economic damage but do not succeed in bringing political change. The failure of League sanctions against Italy; the long, drawn-out process of U.N. sanctions against Rhodesia; the apparent ineffectiveness of U.S.-led sanctions against Cuba, the Soviet Union, and Poland; all these cases seem to substantiate the claim that sanctions don't work particularly well.

For several reasons this judgement may be too facile. If the sanctions were designed primarily as signals, or were intended to satisfy a domestic pressure group or an ally seeking support, they may, in fact, have been quite efficacious. The first point, then, is that "success" must be related to intention. But there are cases where more was sought, and here one needs to probe deeper into the apparent "failures" of sanctions. On the one hand, it is possible to point to a poor choice of measures and to gaps and weaknesses in implementation. The latter are particularly well documented in the Rhodesian case. On the other hand, one must reckon with target resilience and adaptability and the difficulty of translating economic hardship into policy change. Both the target government's will to resist and its domestic support may solidify as a result of external pressures that can conveniently be blamed for all economic woes. And succumbing to pressure may be perceived as a greater sacrifice of values than resisting it and suffering hardship.

It is worth remembering that, under U.N. sanctions, which by 1968 covered all its foreign trade as well as many communication links, Rhodesia not only succeeded in exporting its mineral and agricultural products to all parts of the world, but also continued to receive adequate supplies of oil. It had been expected that the oil sanction would be particularly effective, but despite the official blockade of the Mozambique port of Beira by a British naval unit from 1966 to 1975, Rhodesia received oil through Mozambique (until it achieved independence from Portugal) and from South Africa thereafter. And this fact was known to the British government, which was actively reporting suspected cases of sanctions-breaking in other countries to the U.N. Sanctions Committee.[25]

South Africa was, of course, Rhodesia's lifeline. It ignored both the Security Council order for sanctions and its own obligations under the Charter and continued to provide a vital conduit for Rhodesian trade as well as paramilitary support. But the United States also violated its Charter obligations by importing Rhodesian chrome between 1971 and 1977. In the last analysis, it is generally agreed that guerrilla warfare did more than did sanctions to end the illegal rebellion in Rhodesia and pave the way for majority rule.

Other cases of sanctions show similar features: partial and delayed implementation of agreed measures and gaps in the sanctions front,[26] and target resourcefulness in developing substitutes, doing without, finding outside help, and smuggling.[27] The profit motive acts as a powerful stimulus to middlemen, and false certificates of origin and complex payments systems are hard to detect even if there is a will on the part of sanctioning governments or international secretariats to limit sanctions-busting.

The failure of the Reagan administration's efforts to oust General Noriega from power in Panama in early 1988 further illustrates the difficulty of translating economic damage into political change. The financial measures imposed by the United States included a freeze on Panamanian assets in U.S. banks and the diversion of payments owed to the Panamanian government into an escrow account on which Noriega could not draw. The U.S. dollar is the currency of Panama, and a serious cash-flow problem quickly developed that led to the temporary closure of all banks in Panama. General Noriega had difficulty in meeting the army payroll, and there was an abortive coup as well as some unrest among the civilian population. But his grip on Panama was not loosened but strengthened as a result of the crisis: anti-American sentiment grew stronger and the Reagan administration demeaned itself in unsuccessful negotiations for a deal with Noriega that would have involved his leaving the country in return for the dropping of drug-trafficking charges laid against him in the United States.[28]

Wider Effects of Sanctions

In considering the effects of international sanctions, particularly international economic sanctions, it is also important to recognize that economic pressure is not exercised in a vacuum, nor can it be turned on and off like a tap. We have already noted that the cost to various sectors of the domestic economy of the state(s) imposing sanctions may be severe, and may exceed any realistic expectations. Lost export earnings may be temporary, lost markets may be permanent; certain imports may be vital for national security; investors' confidence may be shattered by "freezing" financial assets. These are backlash effects. Spillover effects mean that third parties may be adversely affected, and the record of help for innocent "bystander" states is not encouraging. Zambia suffered hugely as a result of U.N. sanctions against Rhodesia and has never fully recovered; international assistance was nowhere near adequate.[29] Comprehensive sanctions against South Africa would also have serious effects for neighbouring front-line states and, while they may be willing to bear some of these burdens, there must be international concern for their fate, particularly if there is a low level of confidence that sanctions will actually bring political change in South Africa.

There are also ethical issues concerning the hardship that economic sanctions could entail for Third World targets and especially for the poorest and most vulnerable sections of their populations. And sanctions may produce new and unwelcome patterns of dependence. Zimbabwe is more dependent on South Africa as a result of sanctions against Rhodesia; Cuba became totally dependent on the Soviet Union for survival; Poland could have been driven back into the Soviet embrace; Panama may move closer to Cuba. Finally, there can be systemic effects that are hard to predict — or control. International financial relationships are so complex and far-reaching and, in terms of debtor/creditor nations, so precarious, that shocks to the system are best avoided. The debt crisis alone makes many countries inappropriate targets of economic sanctions.

Lessons of Experience

Our discussion, which is necessarily limited in scope, has revealed some of the complexities and dilemmas associated with international sanctions. Experience suggests that governments will be wise to consider their sanctioning policies carefully, particularly in respect of economic and political costs.

Where important international norms have been violated, there is certainly a case to be made for a collective sanctioning effort that, in both symbolic and practical terms, is likely to have more impact than are unilateral sanctions. And failure to support or reinforce important standards of behaviour, such as the protection of diplomats, will itself carry political costs. But there is also danger in striving too hard for group sanctions if this means alienation of allies and perhaps damage to institutional fabric.[30]

Second, it is important to consider whether economic sanctions will justify themselves in political terms. In economic warfare, which seeks to reduce the enemy's military capability, all loss for the enemy is gain for the other side, and both sides are engaged in hostile acts, but this case is not one where sanctions are intended to bring a policy change — whether this is the freeing of hostages in Iran, the end of martial law in Poland, the end of apartheid in South Africa, or the departure of General Noriega from Panama. Experience has shown the difficulty of predicting behaviour, and it may be realistic to see the role of international sanctions as contributory rather than decisive in producing political change. In any case, where economic and financial sanctions are under consideration, it will always be important to take into account not only ethical questions but also the possibility of backlash, spillover, and systemic implications.

In the future, with the possible exception of South Africa, U.N. sanctions seem unlikely, and the pattern of unilateral measures adopted by one or more states will probably continue. Motives will undoubtedly be mixed; there may be genuine outrage over aggression or inhumane policies; there can also be a perceived need to satisfy domestic or world opinion; to please an ally; even to demonstrate some capacity for response. Sanctions imposed for any or all of these reasons are only part of any government's foreign policy and must be reconciled with other goals. While expectations of their coercive efficacy should not be exaggerated, their utility as signals and as punitive measures ensure their continuing place in the repertory of state practice. This is a far cry from the concept of "international enforcement" set out in the U.N. Charter, but we have seen that this concept was always unrealistic. In fact, the existence of the veto may be an advantage in that it protects the Security Council from taking decisions that would not be implemented. For individual states who take retaliatory action themselves, and perhaps seek to associate others with it, an acknowledgement of the probable limits of what can be achieved would produce fewer mistakes and disappointments, while respect for community norms in their own foreign and domestic policy would also enhance their stature as instigators of sanctions.

NOTES

1. Article 16 of the Covenant reads in part: "Should any member of the League resort to war in disregard of its covenants under Articles 12, 13, or 15, it shall *ipso facto* be

deemed to have committed an act of war against all other Members of the League, which hereby undertake immediately to subject it to the severance of all trade or financial relations [and] the prohibition of all intercourse between their nationals and the nationals of the covenant-breaking State."

2. On the Italo-Ethiopian crisis, see Frank Hardie, *The Abyssinian Crisis* (London: Batsford, 1974); and A.J. Toynbee, *Survey of International Affairs, 1935*, vol. II (London: Oxford University Press, for the Royal Institute of International Affairs, 1936).

3. The Hoare–Laval Pact was drawn up privately in Paris in December 1935 by the British foreign secretary and the French prime minister. When details of the plan became known, public opinion in Britain was outraged and Hoare was forced to resign as foreign secretary.

4. The Security Council has been involved with sanctions in two other cases. In 1950 military measures against North Korea could be *recommended* because of the Soviet Union's temporary boycott of Council meetings — a mistaken tactic that no permanent member has ever repeated — and the Council banned the arms trade with South Africa in 1977.

5. See the select bibliography at the end of this chapter and particularly G. Hufbauer and J. Schott's *Economic Sanctions Reconsidered: History and Current Policy* (Washington, D.C.: Institute for International Economics, 1985).

6. Security Council Resolution 232 of December 16, 1966.

7. Security Council Resolution 253 of May 29, 1968.

8. See M. Doxey, "The Making of Zimbabwe: From Illegal to Legal Independence," *The Year Book of World Affairs* 36 (1982): 151–65.

9. See Harry Strack, *Sanctions: The Case of Rhodesia* (Syracuse: Syracuse University Press, 1978); and R. Renwick, *Economic Sanctions* (London: Croom Helm, 1982). See, too, William Minter and Elizabeth Schmidt, "When Sanctions Worked: The Case of Rhodesia Re-examined," *African Affairs* 87, no. 347 (1988): 207–37.

10. The Security Council Sanctions Committee began work in 1968 and submitted annual reports until its demise when sanctions were lifted in December 1979. Its main weapon was publicity, which was of very limited effect. See M. Doxey, *International Sanctions in Contemporary Perspective* (London: Macmillan, 1987), chap. 7.

11. This declaration was made at Punta del Este at the Eighth Meeting of Ministers of Foreign Affairs of the Organization of American States in January 1962.

12. See Anna P. Schreiber, "Economic Coercion as an Instrument of Foreign Policy: US Economic Measures against Cuba and the Dominican Republic," *World Politics* 25, no. 3 (1973): 387–412.

13. U.S. Diplomatic and Consular Staff in Tehran, ICJ *Reports*, 1979.

14. U.S. Diplomatic and Consular Staff in Tehran, ICJ *Reports*, 1980.

15. See Christopher Warren et al., *American Hostages in Iran: The Conduct of a Crisis* (New Haven: Yale University Press, 1985).

16. Canada maintained diplomatic relations until several American diplomats who were sheltered by the Canadian Embassy in Tehran had safely left the country.

17. See Robert Carswell, "Economic Sanctions and the Iran Experience," *Foreign Affairs* 60, no.2 (1981–82): 247–65.

18. See Robert Paarlberg, *Food Trade and Foreign Policy* (Ithaca: Cornell University Press, 1985); and John C. Roney, "Grain Embargo as Diplomatic Lever: A Case Study of the US–Soviet Embargo of 1980–81," in U.S. Congress, Joint Economic Committee, *The Soviet Economy in the 1980s: Problems and Prospects*, part II (Washington, D.C.: 1982).

19. See David Baldwin's *Economic Statecraft* (Princeton: Princeton University Press, 1985), 262–66; and R.N. Cooper, *Trade Policy as Foreign Policy* (Cambridge, Mass.: Harvard University Press, 1985).

20. See G. Adler-Karlsson, *Western Economic Warfare 1947–1967* (Stockholm: Almqvist and Wiksell, 1968); and A. S. Becker, ed., *Economic Relations with the USSR* (Lexington, Mass.: D.C. Heath, 1983), especially chap. 5 and appendix 5A.

21. Security Council Resolution 418, November 4, 1977.

22. *Mission to South Africa: The Findings of the Commonwealth Eminent Persons Group* (Harmondsworth: Penguin Books, 1986).

23. See, particularly, James Barber, "Economic Sanctions as a Policy Instrument," *International Affairs* 55, no. 3 (1979): 367–84; and James Lindsay, "Trade Sanctions as Policy Instruments," *International Studies Quarterly* 30 (Summer 1986): 153–73.

24. See U.S. Department of State, *American Foreign Policy: Current Documents 1964* (Washington, D.C.: 1967), 323–24.

25. See T.H. Bingham and S.M. Gray, *Report on the Supply of Petroleum and Petroleum Products to Rhodesia* (London: HMSO, Foreign and Commonwealth Office, 1978); and Martin Bailey, *Oilgate: The Sanctions Scandal* (London: Hodder and Stoughton, 1979).

26. See, particularly, P.J. Kuyper, *The Implementation of International Sanctions: The Netherlands and Rhodesia* (Aalphen aan de Rijn: Sijthoff and Noordhoff, 1978).

27. Strack, *Sanctions.*

28. The crisis in U.S.–Panamanian relations was fully reported in the press during March and early April 1988. On May 25 the Reagan administration announced the end of its campaign to oust Noriega and the end of negotiations with him. See the *New York Times*, May 26, 1988. The United States government did, however, resume its efforts to put an end to Noriega's rule in Panama which led, in early January of 1990, to Noriega's arrest.

29. See *The Front Line States: The Burden of the Liberation Struggle* (London: Commonwealth Secretariat, 1978).

30. See M. Doxey, "International Sanctions in Recent State Practice: Trends and Problems," in *Contemporary Problems of International Law: Essays in Honour of Georg Schwarzenberger*, ed. Bin Cheng and E.D. Brown (London: Stevens, 1988), 53–69.

SELECT BIBLIOGRAPHY

Baldwin, David. *Economic Statecraft*. Princeton: Princeton University Press, 1985.

Barber, James. "Economic Sanctions as a Policy Instrument." *International Affairs* 55 (July 1979): 367–84.

Daoudi, M.S., and M.S. Dajani. *Economic Sanctions: Ideals and Experience*. London: Routledge and Kegan Paul, 1983.

Doxey, Margaret. *Economic Sanctions in Contemporary Perspective*. London: Macmillan; New York: St. Martin's, 1987.

———. *Economic Sanctions and International Enforcement*. 2d ed. London: Macmillan, for the Royal Institute of International Affairs, 1980.

———. "International Sanctions: A Framework for Analysis with Special Reference to the U.N. and Southern Africa." *International Organization* 26 (Summer 1972): 527–50.

Galtung, Johan. "On the Effects of International Economic Sanctions with Examples from the Case of Rhodesia." *World Politics* 19 (April 1967): 378–416.

Hufbauer, Gary C., and J.J. Schott. *Economic Sanctions Reconsidered: History and Current Policy*. Washington, D.C.: Institute for International Economics, 1985.

Leyton-Brown, David, ed. *The Utility of International Economic Sanctions*. London: Croom Helm; New York: St. Martin's, 1987.

Lindsay, James. "Trade Sanctions as Policy Instruments." *International Studies Quarterly* 30 (Summer 1986): 153–73.

Losman, Donald. *International Economic Sanctions: The Cases of Cuba, Israel and Rhodesia*. Albuquerque: University of New Mexico Press, 1979.

Mayall, James. "The Sanctions Problems in International Economic Relations: Reflections to the Light of Recent Experience." *International Affairs* 60 (October 1984): 631–42.

Mitrany, David. *The Problem of International Sanctions*. London: Oxford University Press, 1925.

Nincic, Miroslav, and Peter Wallensteen, eds. *Dilemmas of Economic Coercion: Sanctions in World Politics*. New York: Praeger, 1983.

Renwick, Robin. *Economic Sanctions*. London: Croom Helm, 1981.

Strack, Harry. *Sanctions: The Case of Rhodesia*. Syracuse: Syracuse University Press, 1978.

STATE CAPITALISM

Maureen Appel Molot

In a 1978 article on state-owned enterprises, *The Economist* noted that "all governments, overtly or covertly, directly or at arms length, are in business."[1] That same publication, some seven years later, headlined another examination of state enterprises, "Privatization — everybody's doing it, differently."[2] How can we explain the difference in depiction of the role of the state in contemporary capitalism exemplified by these two articles?[3] Are states abandoning the business of business?

The 1980s have witnessed a heated debate in Canada, Britain, and elsewhere about the appropriate role of the state in the economy. For example, the Thatcher government in Britain has engaged in a massive sell-off of previously state-owned corporations such as British Telecom, British Gas, British Airways, and Rolls-Royce. In Europe, Japan, Africa, Latin America, and parts of Asia, the state has sold off a number of enterprises. In Canada, the Mulroney government proclaimed its intention to redefine and reduce the role of the government in the economy by, among other measures, selling a number of Crown corporations. By the end of its first term, the Tories had divested themselves of federal ownership of all or part of 14 enterprises and disbanded a number of inactive companies. A number of provincial governments have also sold government-owned corporations.

Before we can make sense of the current penchant for selling state assets, we need to understand why and how the state came to find itself in business. How can we explain state ownership of oil companies, resource-extraction companies, airlines, and banks? Have the conditions that originally prompted state ownership of firms actively engaged in competition with the private sector in the production and sale of goods and services changed? This chapter will argue that the growth of state-owned enterprises is a function of the changing global economy and that the conditions that occasioned the creation of state enterprises have not altered substantially. Rather, what we are witnessing is a re-evaluation of the modalities of state intervention, largely as a result of growing budgetary deficits and frustration with the tractability of state enterprises as instruments of public policy. State capitalism will not disappear, but the state is streamlining many of its investments, withdrawing from others, and seeking more flexible ways in which to intervene in the economy. The end is the same — the enhancement of national welfare in the context of a global economy in which capital and states compete with each other — but the means are changing as governments search for strategies to ensure competitiveness.

The chapter is divided into four sections: the first will discuss the emergence of state capitalism; the second, the changing character of state capitalism during the 1970s; the third, the move to privatization in the 1980s; and the fourth, the future of state capitalism in light of the international division of labour of the 1990s.

The Emergence of State Capitalism

By state capitalism we mean direct state intervention in the economy through the production of goods and services in profitable sectors for sale nationally and internationally in competition with private capital.[4] In other words, the state has become an economic actor in its own right, participating in the economy not only to establish the rules of the marketplace but also as a player, owning the means of production, hiring labour, selling goods, and investing at home and abroad.

The contemporary international political-economy literature gives us mixed intellectual signals with which to understand the phenomenon of state capitalism. The liberal-capitalist perspective on political economy places the individual or the firm, not the state, at the centre of economic activity. The market and the price mechanism are seen as the most efficient means for organizing domestic and international economic relations.[5] According to this view, state intervention should be kept to the minimum necessary to ensure the conditions under which the market will function, thereby promoting individual or corporate maximization of interests. The creation of state-owned enterprises can be justified only as a response to circumstances combining public need with the inability of private capital to meet it, such as the establishment of hydroelectric companies or the provision of transportation infrastructure in circumstances in which the private sector was not prepared to invest. These state enterprises service the private sector but are not expected to compete with it or, in the provision of infrastructural support for capital, engage in profit-making activities themselves.

Although there is considerable debate among Marxist theorists about the precise relationship of the state to capital,[6] there is general agreement that the purpose of state is to create and maintain the conditions that will facilitate the accumulation process. State intervention in the economy is understood as necessary, if not essential, for this purpose. Given the society-centred assumptions of Marxist theory, autonomous state action is considered virtually impossible by definition.[7] Where direct state intervention in production has been discussed by neo-Marxist protagonists, it has been explained as typical of a new stage of capitalist development marked by the concentration and centralization of capital.[8] In the context of the changing global economy, capitalist survival now necessitates direct state intervention in production. However, state-owned enterprises are purely instrumental and have no life of their own; that they might engage in competition with capital and pursue profits on their own is an idea incompatible with Marxist analysis.

Perhaps more useful in explaining state capitalism is the mercantilist perspective, which focusses not on the relationship between individuals or capital and the state — an intrasocietal relationship from which extrasocietal (i.e., international) activities follow, as in the two approaches just noted — but rather on the role of the state in ensuring national power and security within an international context. In the mercantilist view, governments "pursue economic policies that aim at the maximization of military and economic strength and self-sufficiency."[9] Neomercantilists thus envision the close and continuing involvement of the state in the economy, whether this involvement was the historical effort to accumulate gold and other precious commodities or the subsequent (late-19th-century) effort to promote industrialization and, thereby, national strength. In the contemporary global economy, competition between states prompts active government involvement to promote "economic growth and high living standards based on technical superiority in new industries."[10] The use of state-owned enterprises is one tool the state can employ in its pursuit of national advantage.

Also of relevance to an understanding of state capitalism is the recent international political-economy literature that argues that the state should be brought "back in" the debate on national-policy responses to global and domestic issues. Operating at a level of abstraction lower than that of the broad theoretical formulations of both liberalism and Marxism, this perspective suggests that state autonomy does exist, that states are able to formulate and pursue goals independent of particular societal interests. An understanding of why, when, and how states intervene in their economies and their capacity to spell out and implement policy can be attained only through systematic, historical, and comparative research on state activity in specific economic and societal situations.[11] In terms of state capitalism, this approach, like that of mercantilism, accepts state intervention as an inherent part of capitalist development and examines its changing rationales and modalities.

Although national experiences vary, state-owned enterprises have a long history in the political economies of Western Europe and Canada. The first ones were created before World War I, among the most notable being provincial hydro, telephone, and railway companies in Canada. During the interwar years there was some growth in the number of state-owned corporations: Canada established, among others, a national airline and a national broadcasting company; Italy created a number of state-owned enterprises, the most significant being the Istituto per la Ricostruzione Industriale (IRI) as a result of takeovers by the Mussolini government; and there were some limited nationalizations by the 1936 Popular Front government in France. But the first significant foray of the state into ownership or partial ownership of different sectors of the economy came in the post–World War II period, in response to ideological and pragmatic considerations that faced Western European governments. According to Stuart Holland, there were five main reasons for what he has called "the first generation nationalizations in Western Europe": the election of labour or social democratic governments (as in Britain) committed to public ownership of major sectors such as coal, steel, gas, and electricity; social or producer interests in reliable and reasonable-cost infrastructural services; the salvaging of uncompetitive industries whose collapse would have serious economic consequences in the postwar environment; punitive nationalizations of companies previously controlled by wartime collaborators (for example, Renault); and the concern that certain already-recognized high technology industries (nuclear-power engineering in Britain and France, for instance) were essential to national economic well-being.[12] Many, though not all, of these state enterprises were infrastructural (i.e., designed to service private capital) in sectors where demand was generated by other parts of the economy. By the early 1960s, in Holland's view, this "first postwar wave of nationalizations in Europe had come to an end and had given way to more flexible forms of public intervention. . . . Many of the nationalized concerns had failed to show profits at all or at least profits comparable with those . . . in the private sector."[13]

In Canada, the pattern was slightly different from that of Western Europe. As noted above, at the onset of World War II, a considerable number of important infrastructural enterprises, owned by either the federal or the provincial state, had been created to promote national integration and/or economic development. Some 28 new Crown corporations, 11 of which were directly involved in war production, including the manufacture of synthetic rubber, aircraft, and munitions, as well as research and development of sensitive technology and the mining and refining of uranium, were established during the war. At war's end, the federal government had a productive capacity in a number of sectors of increasing technological relevance, and retained under public ownership several strategic industries, among them Eldorado Mining (nuclear), Polymer Corporation (synthetic rubber), and Canadian Arsenals Limited (munitions), seen as important for postwar security, research, and defence. However, in the absence of political parties committed to public ownership, and with infrastructural industries then being nationalized in Western Europe already under state control, most of the wartime industries were either returned to their previous owners or sold to private capital.[14] The most significant state enterprises created in Canada in the postwar period were stimulative — financial corporations, such as Central Mortgage and Housing, the Exports Credit Insurance Corporation (later the Export Development Corporation), and the Farm Credit Corporation — rather than productive. As was the case in Western Europe, the character of state-owned enterprises in Canada, and the purposes behind their creation, would not alter until the 1960s.

By the late 1960s many West European governments had created what Holland termed "second-generation" state enterprises, which were "devoted to either the management or financing of industry."[15] In contrast to the earlier state ventures, many of which were rescue operations, the new ones were in the more dynamic sectors of the economy and had as their purpose the promotion of economic growth in a rapidly changing economic context of increasing interdependence.

Included among these state enterprises were new holding companies, designed to regroup and reorganize existing state firms, as well as a system of direct equity used by the state to promote joint ventures. In Italy, IRI diversified and expanded into high-technology sectors such as electronics. France attempted to improve the performance of its existing enterprises by regrouping its publicly owned aeronautical-construction firms, actively promoting the restructuring of such industries as steel, and using equity participation to create a new computer company. Sweden created a state holding company (Stats Foretag AB) to regroup a number of existing public enterprises and formed a machine-tools firm through the purchase of three private companies.[16] In Canada, the federal government created Petro-Canada, the Canada Development Corporation, and Telesat Canada, all of which were designed to promote Canadian ownership and control in industry generally or in sectors of growing economic and technological significance. Various provincial states also established public enterprises, primarily in the resource sectors, to ensure greater local control over activities of central importance to their economic vitality.[17]

How do we explain this change in state investment policy from a relatively passive form to that of more active participation in the economy? It would appear that, in both Europe and Canada, the answer lies in the changing character of the global economy, in particular, in the "new problems of economic management and government economic sovereignty posed by the opening of the EEC and the intensification of [the] multinational challenge."[18] By the 1960s, governments in virtually all advanced capitalist countries were faced with a relative loss of control over domestic economic development in an increasingly transnational world economy in which the internationalization of production was becoming the norm. With the speed of technological change and the recognized importance of new sectors such as electronics and computers, many states worried that, without direct intervention through equity participation to create "a national champion,"[19] their economies would lose out on this technology of the future and the spinoffs it would generate. Moreover, while growth in the developed market economies was consistent in this period, it was also uneven, resulting in regional disparities in investment and employment which were potentially politically costly to ruling elites. It was clear that the state would have to assume a more assertive role in order to stimulate economic growth and alleviate regional imbalances. State investment and state-owned enterprises that would reduce government dependence on private capital to achieve national goals were thus attractive to governments seeking new instruments of intervention.

The 1970s witnessed dramatic and continuing changes in the global economy, which prompted states in the advanced capitalist societies to create new state enterprises in sunrise sectors and holding companies for investment purposes, encourage existing enterprises to diversify and internationalize some of their activities, and change the basis of legitimation of state enterprises from expectations of support for private capital and domestic economic stimulus to those of profit. The main characteristics of the world economy by the mid-1970s — the end of the Bretton Woods system of fixed exchange rates, the growth of neoprotectionism, the sharp increases in energy costs, rapid technological advances that were altering manufacturing processes, recession, rising unemployment, and widespread fiscal crisis — are so well known (and discussed elsewhere in this volume) as to necessitate only enumeration here. An integral part of these changes was the growing internationalization of production as multinational corporations relocated some labour-intensive production in the Third World and formulated strategies of worldwide sourcing that permitted the subdivision of manufacturing through subcontracting and licensing agreements. Manufacturing no longer required that the product be made where it would be sold or that a production unit abroad be under the total control of its parent operation. As a result, a growing share of world trade was becoming intrafirm trade (i.e., transfers of goods between affiliated companies). In addition, in the 1970s, exports of consumer and capital goods from the newly industrializing economies of Asia entered world markets on a competitive basis for the first time. In response to this challenge, as well as to an increasingly competitive Japan and a world of rising oil prices, multinational firms in sectors such as steel, textiles, and petrochemicals were restructuring across national boundaries to ensure continuing competitiveness.

The Changing Character of State Capitalism

The breadth and rapidity of change posed serious problems for governments in terms of their ability to formulate and implement economic policies. States have jurisdiction nationally but the activities of major corporations had become global. Concerns about deindustrialization — the loss of manufacturing employment and the falling proportion of a country's share of world manufactured exports[20] — translated into pressures for protection of domestic industry and programs designed for reindustrialization to regain international competitiveness. In the words of the U.N. Development Organization, "this concern has given impetus to the gradual but steady increase in the degree of government involvement in the manufacturing sector."[21] Contributing to this increase was the slippage in adherence to the norms of trade liberalization as states adopted neoprotectionist measures to aid their domestic firms. In the 1970s, states would reorient their activities cognizant of the character of the global economy and new patterns of competition.

It is in this context that we find the emergence of a third generation of state enterprises[22] in many of the developed market economies — enterprises that moved the state into participation in internationally competitive industries alongside, and in competition with, private capital. Reacting in horror from an American perspective at the changing character of capitalism in Western Europe, R. Joseph Monsen and Kenneth D. Walters noted in 1983 that

> in some countries state-owned companies amount to nearly half of the industrial sector, including control of key industries. European governments now have a direct stake in over half of Europe's fifty largest companies. . . . Government companies in Western Europe make aluminum pans, airplane engines, tractors, computer software . . . office equipment, advanced electronic equipment, computers, and cars and trucks. . . . Although the private sector is for the moment still larger than the state-owned sector, the state-owned sector is beginning to dominate in more and more industries, and it expands to new products and new markets each year.[23]

What many governments did during the 1970s and after was to expand their state-owned sectors by creating new enterprises or strengthening the mandates of existing ones. Specifically, they encouraged the diversification, expansion, and internationalization of existing state-owned companies that heretofore had simply provided infrastructure for private capital or had not been previously seen as having the potential for new activities. A number came to see equity participation as an important instrument of public policy, alongside traditional grants, loans, and other fiscal incentives, and created joint ventures and state holding companies to facilitate government participation in the economy as investor and producer. Equally significant was the change in the basis of legitimation of state-owned enterprises as governments exhorted them to adopt business norms and make a profit.

Given the concerns about energy production in the 1970s, it is not surprising that state-owned energy companies expanded their activities to enhance security of supply and to invest in alternatives to oil, particularly natural gas and nuclear energy. In Britain, the Labour government created the British National Oil Company to exploit the then newly found North Sea reserves and replaced the Gas Council with the British Gas Corporation, which began to engage in research and exploration as well as production and retail-sales activities. One of France's two state-owned oil companies, Elf-Acquitaine, which had over the years become a fully integrated oil company, purchased U.S.-owned Texasgulf in 1981 and acquired other interests in areas such as chemicals, solar energy, and biotechnology. The Norwegian state oil company, Statoil, established to secure control over that nation's North Sea oil, evolved into a vertically integrated enterprise with full control over Norwegian oil supply, while Italy's Ente Nazionale Idrocarburi (ENI) rationalized its oil holdings and diversified into natural gas and nuclear energy. Petro-Canada quickly moved beyond its original exploration activities on Crown lands into natural-gas production, oil refining and retailing (the company is now Canada's second-largest oil and gas company), and joint venturing in offshore oil exploration.[24]

In the high-technology sector of aerospace, state investment gained a new prominence. The creation of a new state enterprise in Britain and the restructuring of existing state-owned firms in France had as their purpose not only concerns of national autonomy in defence production but also the search for world markets in an industry that has become increasingly export intensive and more oriented to the civilian airline industry. British Aerospace resulted from the amalgamation of three solvent aircraft manufacturers, purchased for strategic rather than salvage reasons. In France, aircraft manufacturers had long been under state control and, by 1970, had been reorganized into two large state-controlled firms, the Société nationale d'étude et de construction de moteurs d'avion (SNECMA) (89.6 percent state-owned), which produces aircraft engines, and Aerospatiale (98 percent state-owned), which produces a number of different goods, including aircraft, helicopters, tactical weapons, and ballistic and space systems. Both of these French state enterprises internationalized their activities, purchasing significant equity interests in commercial enterprises in Europe and Asia as well as North America.

Aerospatiale acquired an American helicopter company in 1974 that has operated competitively on both sides of the Atlantic. In addition to other instances of internationalization of operations (e.g., participation in a Brazilian joint venture to manufacture and sell helicopters in South America), Aerospatiale, like British Aerospace, continues to produce for domestic-defence needs. These two state-owned companies, in conjunction with the Spanish state's aerospace company and West Germany's minority state-owned firm, formed a consortium to develop and subsequently manufacture the now highly competitive Airbus.[25]

Beyond the movement into the sectors that had become prominent for security or high-technology reasons, governments promoted the commercialization of the activities of existing state enterprises. In basic resource industries, such as coal, the French state regrouped its holdings — on the one hand, to facilitate continuing coal supplies through domestic production and minority-equity positions in foreign coal-mining companies, and on the other, to permit diversification into petrochemicals and fertilizers, among other products. The Norwegian government secured majority control of Norsk Hydro and expanded its operations in Europe during the 1970s to acquire companies in the fertilizer, chemical, and plastics industries and, in the United States, established a subsidiary to manufacture and market its European-made aluminum tubes for the auto industry.[26] In Canada, provincially owned utilities (most notably, hydro and telephone companies) internationalized their activities by exporting production (electricity to the United States), diversifying product lines for sale abroad, and commercializing technology and technical expertise to penetrate foreign markets. No longer were the activities of these resource firms restricted solely to the provision of infrastructural services for the private sector.[27]

It was through the creation of subsidiaries and joint ventures by existing state enterprises that much of the diversification and internationalization occurred in this period. Expansion via subsidiaries was in accord with market logic (enterprise managers pursued normal corporate interests) and with political logic (governments could use existing corporations to expand their activities, thereby reducing, if not avoiding, the political costs of state intervention).

In France, many of the major state-owned enterprises — Renault, Elf-Acquitaine, Saint-Gobain, to name three — listed dozens of subsidiaries on their balance sheets; indeed, it was through their subsidiaries that these enterprises had expanded their operations abroad to become multinational. Cogema, a subsidiary of the French nuclear-energy company, invested in production in a number of foreign locations, including Canada in a joint venture with the Saskatchewan Mining Development Corporation, without any objection from the French government. Many state enterprises in Canada, both at the federal and provincial levels, particularly, though not solely, those in the energy and minerals sectors, created subsidiaries or participated in joint ventures to expand their range of operations. In West Germany, too, state-owned or -controlled firms expanded their activities dramatically in the 1970s by creating subsidiaries to diversify into new sectors. The German Monopolies Commission found in 1976 that the government was the most important shareholder in the country's top 100 companies.[28]

Salzgitter, the state-owned steel and engineering firm, expanded into the automotive parts business, Saarbergwerke AG had investments in coal (including a 25 percent interest in the Ashland Coal Company of the United States), coke, fuels, and machine-tools and rubber production, and Vereinigte Elektrizitaets und Bergwerks AG (VEBA), a company with a long history of full or partial state ownership, moved into petroleum, petrochemicals, aluminum, and glass manufacturing.

Italy's IRI provided an example for many states looking for a modality to facilitate equity participation in firms as an instrument of industrial policy. By the end of the 1970s, a number of countries, including France, Britain, Belgium, Austria, and Sweden, and the province of Quebec, had created government holding companies. These were not development banks or granting agencies to finance private capital but state institutions that were a constituent of industrial-restructuring policies and for which equity and the intent to participate in strategic management decisions were an integral part of their raison d'être.

The Labour government in Britain created the National Enterprise Board (NEB) in 1975 (it had established the Industrial Reorganization Corporation in 1966, which was disbanded by the Conservatives in 1970 and had been mandated to promote mergers and restructuring) to extend state participation in industry, particularly in high-technology sectors. The NEB assisted many small companies and managed the government minority holdings in commercial firms as well as newly nationalized companies such as Rolls-Royce and British Leyland. The Quebec government established the Société générale de financement (SGF) in 1962 to promote new commercial investments through full or partial ownership that would help to restructure the provincial economic base. During its first decade, SGF held shares in a variety of Quebec companies but did not serve actively as a tool of government policy. The SGF became a wholly state-owned holding company in 1972 and was subsequently directed by the government to concentrate its investments in five sectors deemed strategic for provincial economic development.[29]

Austria and Sweden also have state holding companies, though these were established to organize and direct existing state enterprises. Through Österreichische Industrieverwaltungs AG (OIAG), the Austrian state controls some of the major sectors of the economy (oil, chemicals, steel, and, more recently, microelectronics) and some of the largest firms in the country. Sweden's holding company, Stats Foretag AB, was mentioned above as a second-generation state enterprise established to allow the state to restructure its investments under one roof. By the end of the 1970s, it had diversified its activities into a number of sectors, its enterprises had created some 200 subsidiaries, and it had become Sweden's second-largest corporation in terms of assets, fourth-largest ranked by sales. Although the Austrian and Swedish state holding companies differ from those created solely to permit direct state equity investment in new industries, what all the holding companies have in common is their expansion of the role of the state as an investor and producer in the capitalist economy. Moreover, the holding company allows the state a flexibility with respect to its investments that the wholly owned state enterprise does not. This flexibility to invest — or divest, should priorities alter — becomes increasingly important, as we shall see, in the re-evaluation of state capitalism that begins in the wake of the changing national and global economic circumstance of the 1980s.

The final — and by no means least important — characteristic of state capitalism in the 1970s was the new emphasis placed by governments on profits. In an environment of fiscal restraint and concerns over public-sector expenditures, governments increasingly applied a business logic to the management of their public enterprises. Enterprise managers were expected to be attentive to "bottom line" considerations, to questions of efficiency, profitability, and competitiveness. Reports on public enterprises in a number of countries, France, Britain, and Canada, for example, suggested, in the phraseology of the British White Paper on nationalized industries, that "investment projects must normally show a satisfactory return in commercial terms" and "ensure that public investment earned a return which was comparable with that of private industry."[30] This emphasis on profitability was the logical follow-up to the already-commercialized character of state enterprises outlined above.

In a global economy in which state enterprises were confronting competition and responding to it by altering their style and horizons of operation, the adoption of private-sector norms to legitimate the activities of state capitalism seemed appropriate. The fact that many state enterprises never attained this profitability is another — and not insignificant — question. What the trend to commercialization revealed, however, is the character of state expectations of its competitive enterprises in the mixed economies of the 1970s.

The change in the size and the character of the state enterprise sector in the developed market economies can be illustrated by looking at the *Fortune 500* listings of the largest industrial corporations outside the United States over the 20-year period from 1963 to 1983. Leaving aside state petroleum companies from the Third World, in 1963 there were 14 state-owned enterprises, from seven European countries and South Africa, among the 200 largest non-American corporations on the *Fortune 500* list; of these, three were classified by Anastassopoulos et al. as multinationals, as having activities beyond their national boundaries. By 1973 the number of public enterprises on the *Fortune* list had risen to 18, again omitting the Third World state oil companies; of these, eight were multinationals. Ten years later, there were 28 state-owned companies among the largest 200 firms on the *Fortune 500* list; among them there were now 15 that were multinational.[31] There was only one Canadian firm — Petro-Canada — in the 28 on the 1983 *Fortune* list. When Canada's 500 largest industrial companies are ranked by sales, 32 wholly owned government enterprises (16 owned by the federal government and 16 by provincial governments) and another 22 with substantial government participation were included in the 1986 *Financial Post* table.[32] Not only have state-owned enterprises from the developed market economies become large in global terms, they also, not surprisingly, have contributed significantly to GNP, to gross fixed-capital formation, to value added, and to employment in the countries in which they are located.[33]

From the perspective of relative size, which is what the *Fortune 500* ranking measures, only nine state-owned firms from the Third World were included among the largest 200 on the list. Of these, eight were petroleum producers and one was a steel company. Anastassopoulos et al. categorize three of these large Third World state-owned companies as multinationals, suggest a fourth might well become a multinational corporation, and then note that another two state-owned enterprises, which were not large enough to make the top 200, fit their definition of multinational corporations and, in their view, that another six may diversify sufficiently to be so described.[34]

What is more significant than size in global terms is the significance of state-owned enterprises in the economies of developing countries. In most of the Third World countries for which data are available, state-owned enterprises dominate a variety of strategic sectors of the economy, frequently direct much of domestic credit, account for at least a quarter of the total fixed gross-capital formation and more than a quarter of the nonagricultural employment, play an active role in earning foreign exchange and in international trade, and often control a sizeable share of the value added in manufacturing.[35] Whatever the reasons for their creation — desire for national control over economic development, lack of indigenous entrepreneurs, dissatisfaction with the activities of multinational corporations, which, in many cases, led to nationalizations — state-owned enterprises of all "generations" are numerous in Third World countries.

We have argued here that the phenomenon of state capitalism can be understood only in context of the changing international division of labour and effort on the part of states to promote their own economies in the face of challenges from multinational corporations, the rise of neoprotectionism, and their weakened ability to control outcomes. In an effort to exert greater control over economic activity within their jurisdictions, governments have promoted the growth and diversification of their state-owned enterprises. As will be argued below, the commercialization of state enterprises was not without its difficulties. Questions about the viability of many of these enterprises in the light of the recession of the early 1980s, as well as the need for fiscal restraint, led governments in Western Europe and Canada, regardless of political philosophy, to re-examine the role of state-owned enterprises and to search for more flexible forms of state intervention.

State Capitalism in the 1980s

The reassessment of state capitalism that would occur in much of the world during the 1980s was presaged by the election of the Thatcher government in Britain in 1979. Privatization in Britain did not begin with a coherent set of objectives[36] but was an idea that had its roots in the Conservative Party's traditional support for private property and in the growing disillusionment with the performance of many state enterprises. The Conservatives historically had not been supporters of the nationalized industries and had denationalized the steel industry, for example. What distinguished the Thatcher government's divestment program from that of its predecessors was the strong neoconservative philosophy of the prime minister and her firm determination to recast the balance of public and private power in Britain. By the end of the government's second term, much of the infrastructural and industrial state sector created in Britain after World War II had been dismantled, and the state share of GDP had been reduced to approximately 6.5 percent from the 10 percent share held when the Conservatives were first elected.[37] Not only did the Conservative government di-est itself of those state-owned companies in competitive industries, it also began to sell public utilities where competition did not exist. Among the companies that have been sold in whole or in part are British Aerospace, Amersham International, British Airways, Britoil, British Telecom, and British Gas. Slated for sale are some of the country's water and electricity companies. The sales have raised many billions of pounds for the British Treasury — not an unimportant consideration in an era of fiscal restraint — and have clearly dramatically altered the balance in Britain between the state-owned and private sectors.

The British experience is not unique. Whether motivated by ideology, as is the case in Britain, Germany, Holland, Canada (federally, and in some provinces), and Japan, or pushed by fiscal restraints, as in Italy, Sweden, Spain, and much of the Third World, governments are reducing the size of their state sectors by outright sale of all or parts of their enterprises and by rationalizing and streamlining those they have decided to retain. In West Germany, divestment of state assets has occurred primarily through the reduction of government interests in a number of industrial, banking, and transport groups, for example, the sale of equity that lowered the state share in the industrial conglomerate Vereinigte Industrie-Unternehmungen AG (VIAG) and ended it in VEBA. In Holland, although a report on privatization was presented to the government in 1985, the Dutch state's first venture into privatization (other than contracting out of some services) is the sale of one-third of the state-owned chemical firm to the public.[38] Japan has sold part of its airline and part of Nippon Telegraph and Telephone. Austria has divested some of its holdings in the state oil-and-gas company. In France, the government under Jacques Chirac embarked on an ambitious program to privatize many of the sectors and firms nationalized by its Socialist predecessors, a program that has seen the sale of the multinational St. Gobain, the state banking group Paribas, and the divestment of 11 percent of the French government's holdings in the mixed-petroleum enterprise Elf-Acquitaine. In Canada, the federal government sold totally or in part 18 of its enterprises (some of which, such as CN Route and CN Hotels, were subsidiaries of companies that remained in state hands) between April 1984 and April 1988, dissolved eight companies, some of which were inactive, and arranged for the merger of Eldorado Nuclear with the Saskatchewan Mining Development Corporation, preparatory to the sale of what is now the world's largest uranium producer. A number of Canadian provinces, among them Quebec, Saskatchewan, Ontario, and British Columbia, have also privatized all or parts of enterprises no longer deemed essential to provincial economic well-being.[39]

Many Third World governments have similarly begun to reduce the size of the state sector by reducing their corporate holdings. The Mexican government, for example, has sold 75 percent of the state airline to the private sector and has closed, merged, or sold some 700 entities out of a total of 1155 state firms in the past six years.[40] In Africa, a number of governments have established divestiture committees or have instituted privatization programs, but actual sales have to date been far fewer than expected.[41] Brazil, Malaysia, Bangladesh, the Philippines, Thailand, and Turkey have also expressed interest in divestment.

Privatization is not without its difficulties, though some states have managed divestment more easily than have others. In Britain, most of the large sales of state enterprises have been public sales through the stock market rather than sales to an individual purchaser. To protect the state's continuing interest in companies deemed to operate in the national interest and to prevent any single investor from owning more than 15 percent of the company — Enterprise Oil, Amersham International, and British Steel, for example — the British government retained a "golden share" that, in effect, allows it a veto power. The government has also imposed limits on foreign shareholdings of previously state-owned firms and demanded undertakings with respect to job preservation and investment from potential purchasers of others.[42] These conditions, as well as the Thatcher government's decision to force Kuwait to reduce its stake in British Petroleum, suggest political limits to the withdrawal of the state from production. Even a neoconservative government retains statist interests that might demand direct intervention in corporate decision making.[43] In Canada, too, governments have not been prepared to permit unimpeded market forces to shape the future of privatized state enterprises and have imposed conditions on the sale of some corporations.[44]

Britain, as well as other political economies desirous of selling state assets, learned that the vagaries of the stock market and the ability of a national capital market to absorb large share offerings impose their own limitations on privatization strategies. Although the Thatcher government marketed its privatization policy in part as the creation of popular capitalism, the number of small shareholders who have retained their shares in the now-public companies is small.[45] Moreover, it is not clear that privatization has produced the desired goals of greater competition (giant public monopolies have become giant private ones) and reduced state involvement in the economy; in the British case, what has received considerably less attention is the vast array of regulatory agencies created to police the new private monopolies and the fact that at least one of these, British Gas, has been criticized by the state Monopoly and Mergers Commission for practising price discrimination.[46] Will Britons be concerned that a number of their local water suppliers have been purchased by French companies?[47]

Divestiture is considerably more difficult in the Third World than in the developed market economies. Many, if not most, of the enterprises targeted for sale in the less-developed countries are not profitable, and finding prospective buyers, to say nothing of buyers who will offer a price acceptable to the government, has been a challenge. Some potential investors lose interest as a result of state employment regulations and other policies. There is also greater commitment on the part of intellectual and political leaders to state ownership of basic industries in the Third World. As a result, in many developing countries, proposals for privatization have frequently been restricted to non-essential industries or to only a portion of the state's shares in a firm, with the hope that the performance of those enterprises remaining under state control can be improved.[48] As two analysts of privatization in Africa have noted, "the harsh physical environment, the relatively small supply of people with entrepreneurial and managerial skills, and antimarket and prostatist interests and ideologies all combine to make effective large-scale privatization unlikely."[49] Because divestiture frequently results in the sale of state assets to foreigners, it has raised the spectre of recolonization in Africa and has thus generated considerable opposition. Finally, weak local capital markets and the problems of obtaining bank financing complicate the divestment process.

Clearly, then, there has been some significant divestment of state-owned enterprises across many political economies. For many states, the reasons are fiscal — the state's inability to continue to support money-losing enterprises combined with large deficits that the sale of profitable enterprises would hope to reduce. For Britain and France, for example, the latter has certainly been the case; for many other countries the companies were sold well below their value or were simply disbanded. Ideology, the argument that the "state should be out of business," is a factor in privatization in Britain, as it is for some governments in Canada — the federal state and, among the provinces, particularly British Columbia. Problems of management, which included the ability (sometimes inability) of the state to persuade enterprise officials to do the state's bidding, and frustration with the incompatibility of commercialization with broader public-policy purposes, also led to some reconsideration of the state-owned enterprise as a tool of economic policy.

At the same time, as privatization has made headlines around the world, state capitalism has not disappeared. Sales of state-owned firms have sometimes generated large returns; nonetheless, the share of assets remaining under state control is impressive. Some divestitures, like those undertaken by Italy's holding company, IRI, have had as their purpose the strengthening of the financial position of the IRI group, not a diminution in the role of state-owned enterprises.[50] Moreover, at the same time as governments were selling companies, others owned by the same state were expanding their activities. For example, Petro-Canada purchased the refineries and retail outlets of Gulf Canada, and the state-owned oil companies of Venezuela and Brazil internationalized their operations by investing in exploration and production and marketing abroad.[51] France's state-controlled oil and chemicals group, Elf-Acquitaine, has become one of the five largest international oil firms operating in Britain as the result of its acquisitions of 25 percent of Enterprise Oil (Britain's largest independent North Sea operator), and the oil and gas assets of another British company,[52] and its metals group (Pechiney SA) has become the world's largest packaging company through its purchase of an American conglomerate.[53]

As a result of rationalizing their holdings, state-owned firms have emerged better able to face changing international competition, and many are seeking new investments. Joint-venturing is one way in which the state as capitalist can participate in new and potentially significant undertakings, yet reduce both the cost and the risk. Italimpianti, Italy's state-owned industrial group, has joined with the Venezuelan government to build an aluminum plant, and the Italian government is planning more such joint ventures in Latin America.[54] The West German state has agreed to a decision by Daimler-Benz, the car and engineering company, to take a 30 percent stake and eventual majority control in Messerschmitt-Bokow-Blohm GmbH, an aerospace firm in which governments currently have a controlling share; under the terms of the merger, the state will reduce its interest in the company, but will continue to hold a significant piece of what will become the second-largest aerospace firm in Europe.[55] Here we see another example of how divestment and continuing state participation in enhanced production opportunities can occur simultaneously. The behaviour of Quebec's Caisse de dépôt et placement over the last few years illustrates the same phenomenon of rationalization of holdings as part of a search for a flexible investment strategy that will generate returns for the state; over the last few years the Caisse has built a substantial foreign-equity portfolio and has increased its stake in large Canadian companies.[56] In sum, a significant state-enterprise sector remains in many developed market economies; it is employing new investment strategies, such as joint ventures, mixed enterprises, and transnational alliances, in an effort to be competitive and sufficiently adaptable to the ever-changing international division of labour.

The Future of State Capitalism

The sell-off of many state firms in the 1980s seems to suggest that the optimism of state capitalism — that state-owned enterprises could compete successfully alongside private capital in a number of important industries to enhance national economic advantage — was misplaced. If so, the liberal theorists who argued that the state had no place in production but rather had simply the responsibility to create an atmosphere conducive to private accumulation were right. The liberal argument might have some credibility were the characteristics of the global economy the ones depicted by those same liberal thinkers. But we know that the global economy is inordinately complex and that states are intervening more than ever in the pursuit of competitive advantage. Rather than a reduction in the role of the state, we are witnessing intensified neomercantilist competition as states vie for investment and markets and attempt to develop and promote industries on the leading edge of technology.[57]

With the increasing importance of knowledge-based production and continuing investment and divestment by multinational firms, this neomercantilist state behaviour is not likely to cease. This style of operation was exemplified by the French government in its privatization of the Compagnie Générale de Constructions Téléphoniques (CGCT) in 1987; the state entertained bids from three consortia, each involving a French firm and a foreign one that could offer technology or market access, and selected the one best suited to reducing the market power of American AT&T and creating a French-based firm able to compete for future European contracts.[58] Governments may be divesting many of their enterprises but those that remain state-owned are positioning themselves, through acquisitions and joint ventures, to be able to compete in the global economy of the next decade.

In sum, state capitalism as it was in the late 1960s and early 1970s is a phenomenon that is not likely to reappear. Divestment of state holdings in many political economies has proceeded so far as to be probably irreversible, since it is difficult to imagine governments in the future having the financial wherewithal, or indeed the ability, given the sale of some companies to diversified investors, to reacquire privatized enterprises.[59] At the same time, few governments "seem prepared to give up the option of maintaining a core of state-owned enterprises . . . [and] there is little evidence of a shift in sentiment so fundamental as to prevent the creation of a new crop of state-owned enterprises in the future."[60] To the extent that privatization programs were seen as a way to "get the government out of business," to strengthen the market at the expense of the state, or to rid the state of the problems of certain industries by selling the industries themselves, this perspective reveals a certain naïveté. Privatization will not free industry from state constraints — witness the restrictions on sales or the need to find new modalities to regulate newly privatized monopolies in Britain — nor will it free the state from concerns about the viability and competitiveness of industry. In the context of the new global economy, the state may have reduced its business holdings, but few states will have totally gone out of business.

NOTES

1. *The Economist*, December 30, 1978, 37.

2. *The Economist*, December 21, 1985, 71.

3. Many of the ideas in this chapter are developed more fully in Jeanne Kirk Laux and Maureen Appel Molot, *State Capitalism: Public Enterprise in Canada* (Ithaca: Cornell University Press, 1988).

4. Laux and Molot, *State Capitalism*, 11–12.

5. Robert Gilpin, *The Political Economy of International Relations* (Princeton: Princeton University Press, 1987), 27.

6. For a sense of this debate, see Fred Block, "Beyond Relative Autonomy: State Managers as Historical Subjects," in *The Socialist Register*, ed. Ralph Miliband and John Saville (London: Merlin, 1980), 227–42.

7. Theda Skocpol, "Bringing the State Back In: Strategies of Analysis in Current Research," in *Bringing the State Back In*, ed. Peter Evans, Dietrich Rueschemeyer, and Theda Skocpol (Cambridge, Mass.: Harvard University Press, 1985), 5.

8. Bob Jessop, *The Capitalist State* (Oxford: Martin Robinson, 1982).

9. R.J. Barry Jones, "International Political Economy: Perspectives and Prospects — Part II," *Review of International Studies* 8 (January 1982): 40.

10. Harry Johnson, ed., *The New Mercantilism* (Oxford: Oxford University Press, 1974), ix–x.

11. Skocpol, "Bringing the State Back In." See also Dietrich Rueschemeyer and Peter Evans, "The State and Economic Transformation," in *Bringing the State Back In*, wherein state-owned enterprises are briefly discussed (57–59).

12. Stuart Holland, "Europe's New Public Enterprises," in *Big Business and the State*, ed. Raymond Vernon (Cambridge, Mass.: Harvard University Press, 1974), 25–27.

13. Holland, "Europe's New Public Enterprises," 25.

14. Sanford Borins, "World War Two Crown Corporations: Their Wartime Role and Peacetime Privatization," *Canadian Public Administration* 25 (Fall 1982): 380–404.

15. Holland, "Europe's New Public Enterprises," 41.

16. Holland, "Europe's New Public Enterprises," 31–39; Charles-Albert Michalet, "France," in *Big Business and the State*, 105–25; and Stuart Holland, "Adoption and Adaptation of the IRI Formula: Britain, France, Canada, Australia, Sweden, West Germany," in *The State as Entrepreneur*, ed. Stuart Holland (London: Weidenfeld and Nicolson, 1972), 259–60.

17. Ottawa also engaged in some important rescue efforts during the late 1960s and early 1970s, creating the Cape Breton Development Corporation (Devco) to ensure the continuation of coal mining in Cape Breton and to promote industrial diversification in the region, and purchased de Havilland Aircraft of Canada and Canadair, both to save jobs and to continue the support of the aircraft industry, which was seen as having important industrial potential. In all these instances the rescue resulted from the restructuring decisions of multinational corporations.

18. Holland, "Europe's New Public Enterprises," 31.

19. The term is used by Raymond Vernon, "Government and Enterprise in Western Europe," by Charles-Albert Michalet, "France," and by Nicholas Jequier, "Computers," all in *Big Business and the State*.

20. Alec Cairncross, "What is De-industrialization?," in *De-industrialization*, ed. Frank Blackaby (London: Heinemann, 1979), 5–17; and Barry Bluestone, "Is Deindustrialization a Myth? Capital Mobility Versus Absorptive Capacity in the U.S. Economy," *The Annals* (September 1984): 39–51.

21. UNIDO, *Industry in a Changing World* (New York: United Nations, 1983), 10.

22. The term is used in Laux and Molot, *State Capitalism*, 24. The paragraphs on third-generation state enterprises are adapted from *Industry in a Changing World*, 24–35.

23. *Nationalized Companies: A Threat to American Business* (New York: McGraw-Hill, 1983), ix.

24. For information on state-owned oil companies, see Leslie Grayson, *National Oil Companies* (New York: John Wiley and Sons, 1981); Oystein Noreng, "State-owned Oil Com-

panies: Western Europe," in *State-Owned Enterprise in the Western Economies*, ed. Raymond Vernon and Yair Aharoni (London: St. Martin's, 1981), 133–44; Jean-Pierre Anastassopoulos et al., *Les Multinationales Publiques* (Geneva: L'Institut de Recherche et d'Information sur les Multinationales, 1985); and Larry Pratt, "Petro-Canada," in *Privatization, Public Policy and Public Corporations in Canada*, ed. Allan Tupper and G. Bruce Doern (Halifax: Institute for Research on Public Policy, 1988), 151–210.

25. On state-owned aerospace firms, see M.S. Hochmuth, "Aerospace," in *Big Business and the State*, 145–69; Anastassopoulos, *Les Multinationales Publiques*, passim; and Jeanne Kirk Laux, "The State and Reindustrialization: Public Enterprise Comparisons in the Aerospace Industry," a paper prepared for the Canadian Political Science Association Annual Meeting, Winnipeg, June 5–8, 1986. Aerospatiale and the German company each have a 37.9 percent share in the Airbus project, British Aerospace 20 percent, and Construcciones Aeronauticas SA (CASA), 4.2 percent. For information on Airbus, see Keith Hayward, *International Collaboration in Civil Aerospace* (London: Frances Pinter, 1986).

26. R. Joseph Monsen and Kenneth Walters, *Nationalized Companies* (New York: McGraw-Hill, 1983), 13.

27. On the export and international activities of Hydro Quebec, see Philippe Faucher and Johanne Bergeron, *Hydro-Québec: la société de l'heure de pointe* (Montreal: Les Presses de l'Université de Montréal, 1986).

28. Monsen and Walters, *Nationalized Companies*, 12.

29. On SGF, see Jorge Niosi, *Canadian Capitalism* (Toronto: James Lorimer, 1981), 108–10.

30. National Economic Development Office, *A Study of U.K. Nationalized Industries: Their Role in the Economy and Control in the Future* (London: HMSO, November 1976), 89. In France the call for a more efficient and profitable public sector came from the Nora Report (Groupe de travail du Comité interministeriel des entreprises publiques, *Rapport sur les entreprises publiques*, April 1967), and in Canada from a 1977 Privy Council Office report, *Crown Corporations*.

31. Anastassopoulos et al., *Les Multinationales Publiques*, 32–35. There were, in addition to the 15 European-based multinational state enterprises on the 1984 *Fortune 500* list, also three Third World state-owned oil companies that were identified as multinationals. Yair Aharoni discusses the reasons for the internationalization of state-owned enterprises in his *The Evolution and Management of State-Owned Enterprises* (Cambridge, Mass.: Ballinger, 1986), chap. 10: 340–76.

32. *FP 500* (Summer 1986). The editors of the issue noted (p. 66) that three other state enterprises qualified — Alberta Government Telephones, Eldorado Nuclear, and Potash Corporation of Saskatchewan — but failure to submit data on time prevented their inclusion. These figures do not include the privatizations that had begun by the time the rankings were published and that will be noted briefly below.

33. See Aharoni, *Evolution and Management of State-Owned Enterprises*, 17–23. Many of Aharoni's statistics are taken from Mary Shirley, *Managing State-Owned Enterprises* (Washington: World Bank Staff Working Papers Number 577, 1983).

34. Anastassopoulos et al., *Les Multinationales Publiques*, 34–35, 40–41.

35. Aharoni, *Evolution and Management of State-Owned Enterprises*, 17–26.

36. See David Heald and David Steel, "Privatising Public Enterprise: An Analysis of the Government's Case," in *Privatisation & Regulation — the UK Experience*, ed. John Kay et al. (Oxford: Oxford University Press, 1986), 58–77; and Yair Aharoni, "The United Kingdom: Transforming Attitudes," in *The Promise of Privatization*, ed. Raymond Vernon (New York: Council on Foreign Relations, 1988), 23–56.

37. *The Economist*, December 21, 1985, 71.

38. *Globe and Mail*, November 4, 1988, B17.

39. On the sale of state enterprises in Canada, see Laux and Molot, *State Capitalism*, 191–98; Maureen Appel Molot, "State Enterprise in Canada: Nationalization vs Privatization," in *Canadian Politics: An Introduction to Discipline*, ed. Alain Gagnon and James Bickerton (Toronto: Broadview, 1989); W.T. Stanbury, "Privatization in Canada: Ideology, Symbolism or Substance?" in *Privatization in Britain and North America: Theory, Evidence and Implementation*, ed. Paul MacAvoy et al. (Rochester: University of Rochester, Bradley Policy Research Center, William E. Simon Graduate School of Business Administration, 1988); and Allan Tupper and G. Bruce Doern, eds., *Public Corporations and Public Policy in Canada* (Montreal: Institute for Research on Public Policy, 1981). Among other European states, Austria has sold a significant part of its holdings in the oil company Österreichische Mineraloelverwaltung AG (OMV), as well as in Austrian Airlines; in Italy, IRI has been reorganized and some enterprises sold; and in Spain, the state holding company, Insituto Nacional de Industria (INI), was instructed to streamline its operations and get out of those sectors unable to meet international competition. Laux and Molot, *State Capitalism*, chap. 8, passim. New Zealand has also begun to privatize some of its state enterprises.

40. *Financial Post*, October 31, 1988, 15; and *Globe and Mail*, November 26, 1988, B6. This latter article also noted the sale of 90 percent of the state's share in the petrochemical firm Tereftalatos Mexicanos.

41. Thomas M. Callaghy and Ernest James Wilson III, "Africa: Policy, Reality or Ritual?" in *Promise of Privatization*, 179–230. For a general dsicussion on privatization in the Third World and its problems, see Eliot Berg and Mary M. Shirley, *Divestiture in Developing Countries*, World Bank Discussion Papers (Washington: The World Bank, September 1987).

42. British Aerospace and Rolls-Royce have both had the 15 percent foreign-shareholding ceiling broken, forcing foreign shareholders to sell excess shares, in some cases at a considerable loss. The latest foreign shareholders to appear on the share register are the first to be forced to sell, *Financial Post*, May 13, 1989, 25. The government imposed conditions on the sale of Short Brothers PLC of Belfast, *Financial Post*, May 23, 1989, 3.

43. Laux and Molot, *State Capitalism*, 187; and *The Times* (London), October 7, 1988, 25.

44. See Molot, "State Enterprise in Canada" for a discussion of the restrictions imposed on the sale of Air Canada and SaskPower bonds, and on the potential sale of Potash Corporation of Saskatchewan. The restrictions on the sale of one series of SaskPower bonds (to provincial residents only) were lifted in May 1989, *Financial Post*, May 24, 1989, 24.

45. For details on the dramatic decrease in the number of small shareholders with shares in privatized British companies, see Herschel Hardin, *The Privatization Putsch* (Halifax:

Institute for Research on Public Policy, 1989), 50–51. Hardin, as well as others, argues that many of the British firms were sold far too cheaply.

46. Allan Tupper and Bruce Doern, "Canadian Public Enterprise and Privatization," in *Public Corporations and Public Policy in Canada*. On the British Gas case, see *The Economist*, October 22, 1988, 67. For a discussion of the concern that privatization in Italy might reduce competition if public firms are purchased by powerful private-sector companies, see "The Italian Economy," *The Economist*, February 27, 1988, 31.

47. "Water Privatization: Big Business," *The Economist*, November 26, 1988, 62.

48. Raymond Vernon, "Introduction: The Promise and the Challenge," in *Promise of Privatization*, 11.

49. Callaghy and Wilson, "Africa: Policy, Reality or Ritual?" 179.

50. Vernon, "Introduction: The Promise and the Challenge," 16.

51. The Venezuelan state oil company, Petróleos de Venezuela, SA (PDVSA), has been cited as one of the companies interested in purchasing the refining and marketing assets of Texaco Canada, *Globe and Mail*, November 4, 1988, D8. For a discussion of privatization in Venezuela, see Janet Kelly de Escobar, "Venezuela: Letting in the Market," in *Promise of Privatization*, 57–90.

52. *Financial Times* (Toronto), December 26, 1988, 3.

53. *Financial Times*, November 28, 1988, 3

54. *The Economist*, October 1, 1988, 69.

55. *Financial Times*, November 14, 1988.

56. Caisse de dépôt et placement, *Annual Report 1988*, 14. The Caisse has holdings in British, French, Swiss, U.S., and Japanese multinationals. The Caisse now holds more than 10 percent of the shares of Moore Corp. Ltd., Provigo Inc., and Power Financial Corp., *Globe and Mail*, May 24, 1989, B9.

57. For a discussion of neomercantilism, see Gilpin, *The Political Economy of International Relations*, 395–96. For a discussion of how states attempt to promote comparative advantage, see some of the articles in Paul R. Krugman, ed., *Strategic Trade Policy and the New International Economics* (Cambridge, Mass.: MIT Press, 1987).

58. The consortium selected included Sweden's Ericsson as minority partner, *Le Figaro*, April 24, 1987, 13.

59. Tony Prosser, *Nationalised Industries and Public Control* (Oxford: Basil Blackwell, 1986), 97, 107.

60. Vernon, "Introduction: The Promise and the Challenge," 19.

SELECT BIBLIOGRAPHY

Aharoni, Yair. *The Evolution and Management of State-Owned Enterprises*. Cambridge, Mass.: Ballinger, 1986.

Anastassopoulos, Jean-Pierre, et al. *Les Multinationales Publiques*. Geneva: L'Institut de Recherche et d'Information sur les Multinationales, 1985.

Berg, Elliott, and Mary M. Shirley. *Divestiture in Developing Countries*. World Bank Discussion Papers. Washington: The World Bank, September 1987.

Feigenbaum, Harvey. *The Politics of Public Enterprise Oil and the French State*. Princeton: Princeton University Press, 1985.

Hardin, Herschel. *The Privatization Putsch*. Halifax: Institute for Research on Public Policy, 1989.

Holland, Stuart, ed. *The State as Entrepreneur*. London: Weidenfeld and Nicolson, 1972.

Laux, Jeanne Kirk, and Maureen Appel Molot. *State Capitalism: Public Enterprise in Canada*. Ithaca: Cornell University Press, 1988.

Prosser, Tony. *Nationalised Industries and Public Control*. Oxford: Basil Blackwell, 1986.

Shirley, Mary. *Managing State-Owned Enterprises*. Washington: World Bank Staff Working Papers Number 577, 1983.

Tupper, Allan, and G. Bruce Doern, eds. *Public Corporations and Public Policy in Canada*. Montreal: Institute for Research on Public Policy, 1981.

———. *Privatization, Public Policy and Public Corporations in Canada*. Halifax: Institute for Research on Public Policy, 1988.

Veljanovski, Cento. *Selling the State: Privatisation in Britain*. London: Weidenfeld and Nicolson, 1987.

Vernon, Raymond, ed. *Big Business and the State*. Cambridge, Mass.: Harvard University Press, 1974.

———, ed. *The Promise of Privatization: A Challenge for American Foreign Policy*. New York: Council on Foreign Relations, 1988.

Vernon, Raymond, and Yair Aharoni, eds. *State-Owned Enterprise in the Western Economies*. London: Croom Helm, 1981.

TRADE AND GLOBAL INTERDEPENDENCE

Jock A. Finlayson

Even a quick glance at the contents of political-science journals and the syllabi of international relations courses issued during the past decade will attest to the growing interest of political scientists in trade issues. This development has been stimulated by and is also related to the longer-term trend toward greater interdependence among national economies — a trend particularly evident in the case of the major industrial nations. Much contemporary literature on international relations is directly or indirectly concerned with the nature and consequences of global interdependence. Signs of increased interdependence in the world political economy are not difficult to find. The growing importance of trade in goods and services to most national economies, the extraordinary expansion of international capital flows and financial transactions, the acute sensitivity of national exchange rates to movements in interest rates in other countries, the progressive integration of global capital markets, and the rapid international diffusion of new technologies and technical knowledge — these developments all provide compelling evidence that, in the contemporary international system, economic interdependence is much more than a mere academic construct.

In simple terms, economic interdependence can be thought of as a situation whereby economic decisions or events taking place in one country influence those occurring in other countries. The degree of interdependence tends to rise, "the more one nation has to take into account what other states might do in charting their own international and domestic policy."[1] For economists, the concept of interdependence captures the idea that national economies have become more sensitive to one another. Virtually all states — even those that traditionally have been quite insulated from the world economy, such as the United States and China — have become more dependent on foreign trade and investment in the past quarter-century. However, the impact of increased interdependence and the emergence of more "open" national economies varies considerably among states. In particular, smaller states tend to be more affected — and constrained in their policy choices — by global economic interdependence than are larger states or those that deliberately choose to limit their transactions with the outside world.

Although liberal economists underline the broadly based economic benefits resulting from the specialization of industrial production and the expansion of trade flows that are hallmarks of interdependence, political scientists are more inclined to focus on the attenuation of national sovereignty and the increased vulnerability experienced by states in a more interdependent world economy.[2] The fetters on national sovereignty and heightened vulnerability associated with economic interdependence do not affect all countries equally. Typically, it is the smaller countries, whose domestic economies are more integrated with an international economy over which they exercise little real influence, that experience the most pronounced loss of national autonomy in economic decision making. But, in the past dozen years, even some of the largest and traditionally most insulated states have begun to see their scope for independent economic policy making narrow as they become more dependent on economic transactions with the rest of the world. The dramatic increase in U.S. dependence on both foreign capital and foreign goods in the 1980s provides an interesting case study of how dependence on the global economy has constrained the policy choices available to even the most powerful states.

This chapter explores one of the key arenas in which economic interdependence has evolved — the international trade system. In the next section, I discuss the structure, growth, and patterns of global trade. Following that, I examine the post-World War II international trade "regime" based on the General Agreement on Tariffs and Trade (GATT), and chart the gradual and uneven movement toward trade liberalization that has taken place under the GATT's auspices. I then consider the political and normative characteristics of the GATT regime, evaluate the foundations of postwar trade expansion and liberalization, and discuss the rise in the late 1970s and 1980s of what has been called the "new protectionism." The final section offers some brief concluding observations on interdependence and the future of the international trading system.

The Current Structure of World Trade

The spectacular growth of world trade since World War II is the most frequently cited manifestation of international economic interdependence. From 1948 to 1973, the volume of world trade (a measure that ignores the effect of prices) increased more than six times, rising on average by 7 percent annually. Since the mid-1970s, the international economy has become more unstable, in part because of the collapse of the Bretton Woods fixed-exchange-rate international monetary regime in the early 1970s and the twin oil crises of 1973–74 and 1979–80. As a result, both international and national economic-growth rates have declined. In this less-favourable environment, the pace of trade expansion has slowed somewhat, and protectionist pressures have intensified. As shown in Table 1, however, since 1960 real world merchandise exports have risen much faster than world production, normally by 1 to 2.5 percent each year. Even in the 1980–87 period — which witnessed the tail end of an oil crisis, a severe global recession, and the onset of more protectionist trade policies in many industrial countries — global exports grew faster than did world output. This trend continued in the

TABLE 1 Growth of World Merchandise Trade and Production (annual average percentage change in volume terms)

	1960–70	1970–80	1980–87	1987
Exports:				
Agriculture	4.0	3.5	1.5	4.5
Mining*	7.0	1.5	-1.5	1.0
Manufacturing	10.5	7.0	4.5	5.5
All merchandise exports	8.5	5.0	3.0	5.0
Production:				
Agriculture	2.5	2.0	2.0	-3.0
Mining*	5.5	3.0	-1.0	0.5
Manufacturing	7.5	4.5	3.0	4.5
All production	6.0	4.0	2.5	3.0

*Includes petroleum.

SOURCE: GATT, *International Trade 1987/1988*, vol. 1 (Geneva: GATT Secretariat, 1988), 3.

late 1980s: the volume of world exports was up by 5.5 percent in 1987, and an astounding 8.5 percent in 1988; these figures outstripped world output-growth in both years.

Since trade has expanded more quickly than have most national economies, the ratio of foreign trade to gross domestic product (GDP) has trended upward for virtually all countries since the 1950s. Table 2 (page 286) charts the evolution of merchandise exports and imports as a percentage of GDP for the seven leading industrial countries (the G7). Table 3 does the same, using a more comprehensive measure of trade that includes both merchandise trade and trade in services. Table 4 (page 287) provides data on the GDP share of exports of goods and services as of the mid-1980s for a number of other countries not listed in the previous tables. All of these tables show that while international trade has come to play a larger role in the economies of many states, significant differences continue to exist in the degree of trade dependence.

Taking the United States as an example, Table 2 reveals that merchandise exports as a share of U.S. GDP more than doubled between 1960 and 1980, before dropping sharply in the mid-1980s, mainly because of a substantially overvalued U.S. dollar prior to 1986. U.S. merchandise imports shot up even more dramatically, tripling as a proportion of GDP since 1960. Measured in real or volume terms (i.e., factoring out the impact of inflation), U.S. exports tripled between 1960 and 1986, while imports soared by more than 600 percent.[3] The broader measure of trade used in Table 3 provides a similar picture, except that in each year exports and imports amount to a somewhat bigger share of U.S. GDP. All of the other countries listed in tables 2 and 3 are currently more dependent on trade than is the United States — a situation that was also true in the 1960s and 1970s. In West Germany, for example, exports contributed more than 30 percent to GDP in 1987, while imports accounted for more than one-quarter of

TABLE 2 Merchandise* Exports and Imports as a Share of GDP for the Seven Largest Capitalist Economies (percent of GDP measured in domestic currency)

	1960		1970		1980		1987**	
	Exp	**Imp**	**Exp**	**Imp**	**Exp**	**Imp**	**Exp**	**Imp**
Canada	14.3	14.8	19.6	16.7	25.5	23.6	24.5	23.1
W. Germany	15.8	14.1	18.6	16.2	23.6	23.1	26.2	20.3
France	11.4	10.5	12.6	13.4	17.4	20.2	17.1	17.8
Italy	9.8	12.7	13.1	14.8	17.3	22.0	16.1	16.4
Japan	9.4	10.4	9.4	9.3	12.2	13.3	10.6	6.5
U.K.	14.3	17.8	15.7	17.7	20.6	21.6	19.6	23.0
U.S.	4.0	3.2	4.3	4.2	8.2	9.6	5.6	9.5

*Merchandise trade consists of trade in products; services are excluded. In the table, exports are measured FOB; imports, CIF.

**1986 rather than 1987 data used for Canada, France, Italy, and Japan.

SOURCE: International Monetary Fund, *International Financial Statistics Yearbook, 1988* (Washington: IMF, 1988).

GDP; similar figures also apply in the cases of Canada and the United Kingdom (Table 3).

Since 1980, international trade has expanded somewhat more slowly, and protectionism has gained strength in a number of industrial sectors resulting in a modest decline in the importance of trade as measured in terms of GDP for some countries. The central point, however, is that, for all of the countries listed in tables 2 and 3, foreign trade constituted a larger share of GDP in the 1980s than in the 1960s. The impact of this trend has been uneven. For example, according to GATT statistics, over the period 1960–86/87 the absolute increase in merchandise exports as a percentage of GDP was greatest in West Germany (10.4 percentage points), followed by Canada (10.2 points), Italy (6.3 points), France (5.7 points), the United Kingdom (5.3 points), the United States (1.6 points), and Japan (1.2 points). These findings underline the fact that, despite

TABLE 3 Total* Exports and Imports as a Share of GDP for the Seven Largest Capitalist Economies (percent of GDP measured in domestic currency)

	1960		1970		1980		1987**	
	Exp	**Imp**	**Exp**	**Imp**	**Exp**	**Imp**	**Exp**	**Imp**
Canada	17.3	18.5	22.5	20.0	28.2	26.4	27.1	25.9
W. Germany	20.1	17.4	22.6	20.5	28.5	28.7	31.6	26.2
France	13.9	11.3	15.8	15.2	21.5	22.7	21.3	20.3
Italy	12.1	13.9	15.8	16.5	19.8	23.9	18.5	18.1
Japan	11.4	11.0	11.3	10.2	14.9	15.8	13.2	13.1
U.K.	20.0	21.5	22.5	21.6	27.2	25.0	26.3	27.2
U.S.	4.9	4.4	5.6	5.5	10.2	10.7	7.5	10.7

*Trade in goods and services. Exports and imports measured on a national-accounts basis.

**1986 rather than 1987 data used for Canada, France, Italy, and Japan.

SOURCE: International Monetary Fund, *International Financial Statistics Yearbook, 1988* (Washington: IMF, 1988).

TABLE 4 Exports of Goods and Services as a Percentage of GDP* in Selected Countries

Country	% GDP (1987 or year indicated)
Bahrain (1986)	81
Malta	77
Mauritius	68
Belgium	65
Gabon (1985)	57
Malaysia (1986)	56
Jordan (1986)	46
South Korea	45
Fiji (1985)	44
Portugal (1985)	39
Norway	36
Saudi Arabia	36
Austria	35
Sweden	33
Costa Rica	32
Chile (1986)	31
New Zealand	28
Kenya (1986)	27
Finland	26
Peru (1985)	25
Malawi	23
Bolivia (1986)	23
Philippines	23
Spain	21
Nigeria (1985)	19
Colombia	19
Morocco (1986)	17
Australia	16
Argentina	15
Brazil (1986)	13
Pakistan	13
Burma	5

*Exports measured on a national-accounts basis.

SOURCE: International Monetary Fund, *International Financial Statistics Yearbook, 1988* (Washington: IMF, 1988).

the unprecedented attention paid to U.S. and Japanese trade performance by legions of scholars, journalists, and policy makers in the 1980s, these economic "superpowers" — they are the world's two largest economies — actually remain much less trade-dependent than do the vast majority of other industrial and developing nations.

Another statistic sometimes used to gauge the trade-orientation of national economies is the ratio of exports and imports to domestic goods production; because it excludes services, this ratio is a much less inclusive measure of national economic activity than is GDP. In 1950 the United States exported only 6.3 percent of its total domestic goods production. By 1970, this figure had risen to 9.2 percent, and, by the early 1980s, to almost 20 percent. Corresponding figures for U.S. imports as a proportion of domestic goods production jumped from 5.8 percent to 8.7 percent and then to 22 percent over this same period.[4] The reason that exports/imports as a share of domestic goods production suggests a more significant rise in the relative importance of trade than does the trade/GDP measure used in tables 2 and 3 has to do with the growing importance of services in the U.S. and other economies. Production of services now accounts for up to 60 percent of GDP in most developed industrial countries, while production of goods has fallen steadily as a proportion of GDP since the 1950s. Many services — for example, retail trade, community services, personal services, and public administration — do not enter international trade, and thus the health of many domestic service industries is not directly affected by international markets. In contrast, a growing proportion of domestic goods production is increasingly influenced by international competition. Goods continue to be far more extensively traded internationally than are services. More than 70 percent of the value of world trade is still made up of goods, with services comprising the other 30 percent. However, trade in services has expanded rapidly in the past decade — a trend that is posing new challenges to the GATT trade regime established in the late 1940s.

The commodity composition of world trade has changed significantly since World War II. Trade in manufactured products has grown much faster than that in raw materials, and thus the share of primary products in international commerce has fallen quite steadily. As shown in Table 1, since 1960, world manufactured exports have consistently increased faster than exports of agricultural and mineral raw materials (the latter also includes fuels). In the most recent documented period (1980–87), exports of manufactures went up on average 4.5 percent each year, while agricultural exports grew by only 1.5 percent and the volume of exports of mineral raw materials actually declined. Today, more than two-thirds of world merchandise trade is composed of processed, manufactured, and finished products, with the remainder accounted for by primary products (Table 5). The long-term trend toward a larger share for manufactured products in world merchandise trade is almost certain to continue. Only a sharp and sustained rise in the real price of petroleum could conceivably interrupt it in the decade of the 1990s.

While merchandise goods continue to dominate world trade flows, the proportion of services that can be traded across borders has risen in recent decades. Rapid development of communications and data-processing and information technologies has been at the heart of the expansion of tradable services. Tradable services include such items as transportation, telecommunications and computer services, data-processing, insurance, other financial services, cross-border consulting and professional services, and travel and tourism. According to the International Monetary Fund, trade in services now constitutes almost 30 percent of all world trade and is set to increase in the 1990s. In 1987, services trade

TABLE 5 Composition of World Merchandise Trade, 1987 (approximate percentage shares, by product)*

Product Category		Percentage Share
Food		10.1
Raw materials**		3.6
Ores and minerals		1.5
Fuels		11.4
Non-ferrous metals		1.9
Total Primary Products		**28.5**
Iron and steel		3.3
Chemicals		9.3
Other semi-manufactures		5.3
Engineering finished products, of which:		39.3
• specialized machinery	8.5	
• road motor vehicles	9.5	
• other machinery and transport equipment	11.9	
Textiles		3.2
Clothing		3.3
Other consumer goods		6.0
Total Manufactured Goods		**69.7**

Value of 1987 World Merchandise Exports: $2.49 trillion (U.S.)

*Figures do not add to 100 because commodities are not classified elsewhere (SITC section 9).

**Raw materials include raw wood, wood pulp, cotton and other textile fibres, horticultural products, hides and skins, and natural rubber.

SOURCE: GATT, *International Trade 1987/1988*, vol. 2 (Geneva: GATT Secretariat, 1988), table AB3.

amounted to $960 billion (U.S.), out of total world trade of $3.3 trillion. From 1979 to 1987, trade in services expanded much more quickly than trade in goods, rising by 240 percent as compared to 150 percent for goods.[5]

Although the composition of world trade has altered significantly, at the broadest level there has actually been considerable stability in the relative importance of the major groups of countries in international exchanges since the 1950s. The summary data provided in Table 6 show that in 1987, the three main

TABLE 6 World Merchandise Exports by Main Country Groupings, 1963–87 (percentage shares of value of world exports)

	1963	1973	1987
Developed countries*	67.1	70.8	69.9
Developing countries**	20.7	19.2	19.7
Eastern trading area***	12.1	9.9	10.4

*Developed countries: North America (except Mexico), Western Europe, Japan, Australia, New Zealand, and South Africa.

**Developing countries: all of Latin America and the Caribbean, Africa (excluding South Africa), the Middle East (including Israel), and Asia (excluding Australia, Japan, New Zealand, China, and other centrally planned economies in Asia).

***Eastern trading area: USSR, Eastern Europe, China, and other centrally planned economies in Asia.

SOURCE: GATT, *International Trade 1987/1988*, vol. 2 (Geneva: GATT Secretariat, 1988), table AB3.

country groupings — the developed capitalist economies (including Japan), the developing countries, and the Soviet bloc — accounted for roughly the same proportions of global merchandise exports as in 1963. It is striking that despite the myriad Third World states that have achieved independence in the past quarter-century and the dramatic increase of exports of manufactures from the newly industrializing economies (NIEs), the developed economies collectively have seen their share of total world exports *rise* slightly since the early 1960s. (LDCs' collective share of world exports of manufactures, however, has more than doubled during this period.)

TABLE 7 Destination of Exports from Major Country Groupings,* 1987 (percentage of exports sold to different groups of states)

	Exports to:		
	Developed Countries	**Developing Countries**	**Eastern Trading Area**
Exports from:			
Developed countries	78.6	17.6	3.8
Developing countries	68.6	24.5	6.9
Eastern trading area	27.5	19.3	53.2

*For definitions of country groupings, see Table 6.

SOURCE: GATT, *International Trade 1987/1988*, vol. 2 (Geneva: GATT Secretariat, 1988), table AB3.

An important characteristic of the international trade conducted by the industrial countries is that the bulk of it takes place *within* the developed-country group (the member states of the Organization for Economic Cooperation and Development — the OECD). For example, in 1987 trade among the developed countries accounted for 55 percent of the value of total world merchandise exports. And as indicated in Table 7, more than three-quarters of all exports by developed countries in 1987 went to other industrial economies. Only 18 percent of developed-country merchandise exports were shipped to the Third World, with less than 4 percent sold to Eastern-bloc customers. Unlike the developed countries, Third World states do not trade primarily with each other. Two-thirds of all developing-country exports are sold in industrial-country markets, with one-quarter exported to other developing countries and only 7 percent to the Soviet bloc. More than half (53 percent) of all exports from Eastern-bloc countries stayed within the bloc in 1987, with developed and Third World countries accounting for 27 percent and 19 percent, respectively.

A marked asymmetry thus exists between "North" and "South": the Northern economies exchange goods and services mostly with each other, whereas developing countries rely disproportionately on the North, both as an export market and as a source of imports. This trend explains why, in fashioning their trade policies, governments of developed countries tend to be preoccupied with other OECD member states, while the trade interests of LDCs experience a significant impact from economic performance and commercial policies of the industrialized nations. In short, even though developing countries have become more active participants in world trade — particularly in markets for manufactured products — in recent decades, the advanced industrial states have clearly maintained control over the world trade system.

TABLE 8 Shares of Top 20 Countries in World Merchandise Trade, 1987 (percentage share of world total, in value terms)

Country	Global Export Share	Country	Global Import Share
West Germany	11.8	United States	16.4
United States	10.2	West Germany	8.8
Japan	9.3	France	6.1
France	5.9	Japan	5.9
U.K.	5.3	U.K.	5.9
Italy	4.7	Italy	4.9
USSR	4.3	USSR	3.7
Canada	3.9	Canada	3.6
Netherlands	3.7	Netherlands	3.5
Belgium-Luxembourg	3.4	Belgium-Luxembourg	3.2
Total of Above 10	**62.5**		**62.0**
Taiwan	2.2	Switzerland	2.0
Hong Kong*	1.9	Spain	1.9
South Korea	1.9	Hong Kong*	1.9
Switzerland	1.8	China	1.7
Sweden	1.8	South Korea	1.6
China	1.6	Sweden	1.6
Spain	1.4	Taiwan	1.4
Singapore*	1.2	Austria	1.3
East Germany	1.1	Singapore*	1.3
Austria	1.1	Australia	1.1
Total of Above 20	**78.5**		**77.8**

*Includes substantial re-exports and imports for re-export.

SOURCE: GATT, *International Trade 1987/1988*, vol. 1 (Geneva: GATT Secretariat, 1988), 19.

Finally, turning from groups of countries to individual states, Table 8 lists the world's 20 top-ranked trading nations as of 1987. Once again the predominant role of the major capitalist countries is very apparent. Measured in terms of country share of total world merchandise imports and exports, the table shows that nine of the ten largest traders were developed capitalist states. The Soviet Union is the only member of the top ten that is not in the Western economic group (the OECD). The ten leading trading nations were still responsible for well over 60 percent of world merchandise trade (and for an even bigger share of services trade) in 1987. A small number of developing countries have entered the ranks of the world's top 20 traders in that they now account for more than one percent of world exports or imports. Rising exports of manufactured products from these NIEs have certainly magnified the adjustment pressures being experienced by the advanced industrial countries, but this trend has not yet seriously threatened the position of the North in world trade.

The GATT: Origins and Basic Principles

In the four decades since its creation in 1947, the General Agreement on Tariffs and Trade (GATT) has served as both the primary international institution for negotiations on trade-barrier issues as well as the main regulatory framework governing world trade. (The institution is usually referred to as the GATT, while the legal rules are outlined in the General Agreement and in a number of separate accords and protocols negotiated since the GATT was established.) Under its auspices, a host of complicated rules and intergovernmental arrangements have evolved to regulate the use of tariffs and other trade barriers by GATT members. There are currently 96 member states, including all of the Western industrial powers, a large number of developing countries, and a few Eastern-bloc states.

The GATT emerged from the prolonged process of global institution-building in the 1940s, which also saw the establishment of the United Nations, the International Monetary Fund (IMF), and the World Bank. The United States played by far the most influential role in designing this postwar regime and in shaping decisions on key issues. The original 23 GATT signatories were also engaged in wide-ranging negotiations aimed at creating the comprehensive International Trade Organization (ITO) that was to be the third leg (along with the IMF and the World Bank) of the postwar economic system. As outlined in the 1948 Havana Charter, the ITO was intended to have a very expansive regulatory scope, encompassing not only trade-barrier issues but also such matters as international-investment rules, the operation of commodity agreements, and restrictive business practices. In the event, the ITO and its Havana Charter never came into effect, in part because of strong opposition to certain of its provisions in the U.S. Congress. As a result, the much less comprehensive GATT accord — which regulates only trade barriers and is generally silent on other trade-related issues — was all that remained after several years of concerted negotiations during the last half of the 1940s.[6]

It is not possible to discuss here in any detail the manifold rules and various institutional arrangements that together help to define the contemporary GATT trade regime. Instead, only the main principles underlying the regime will be noted. Most of the substantive rules and specific trade accords negotiated under the GATT reflect these fundamental principles. A handful of key principles have been identified by scholars and international trade analysts:[7]

1. **Multilateralism and Nondiscrimination.** Central to the functioning of the GATT regime is the most-favoured-nation (MFN) or "nondiscrimination" principle. This principle requires that all GATT members apply tariff duties

and other trade barriers equally to imports from *all other GATT member states*. Often referred to as the "unconditional" MFN obligation, it is enshrined in a number of the GATT's substantive rules, including Article 1 of the General Agreement, which can be amended only with the unanimous consent of all GATT members. The American diplomats who were the primary architects of the postwar trade regime saw the MFN principle as an essential tool, not just to expand trade, but also to discourage the development of bilateral and regional trade blocs (such as the British Commonwealth) that discriminated against imports from other countries. However, they accepted a major derogation from the MFN principle when they agreed to include in the General Agreement a provision (Article 24) permitting the creation of regional free-trade areas, common markets, and customs unions. Since the 1950s such regional-trade schemes — beginning with the European Community — have proliferated. In the 1980s, for example, the EC has expanded to include 12 member-states, and the United States has negotiated bilateral free-trade pacts with Canada, its biggest trading partner, and with Israel. In large part because of this trend toward regional-trade arrangements, the share of global trade conducted on an MFN basis has fallen from more than 85 percent in the 1950s to, perhaps, 50 percent today.

2. **Trade Liberalization.** Although the GATT's rules do not compel member countries to eliminate tariffs and all other trade restrictions, the commitment to freer trade is a basic underpinning of the GATT regime. The General Agreement envisages that multilateral negotiations will be held periodically to lower trade barriers. In addition, several GATT rules and accords oblige countries to refrain from imposing certain types of trade barriers or else regulate the ways in which such barriers may be used. Examples include the General Agreement's restrictions on the use of quotas and quantitative restrictions on imports of manufactured goods, and various GATT rules governing the use of national technical standards, which can act as barriers to trade. In pursuit of the goal of trade liberalization, seven "rounds" of multilateral negotiations have been completed under the GATT; an eighth round, the "Uruguay Round," is currently underway and is not expected to end until the end of 1990 at the earliest. As discussed later, these multilateral negotiations have achieved much-reduced tariff levels, but they have proven less successful in reducing either the use of nontariff trade barriers (NTBs) or states' increasing reliance on market-sharing schemes and "managed trade" arrangements.
3. **Reciprocity.** Particularly among the developed countries, it has long been accepted that trade negotiations ought to be conducted on the basis of reciprocity and mutual advantage. At a general level, the principle of reciprocity suggests that countries that fail to comply with the provisions of an international agreement may be denied the opportunity to reap the benefits of that agreement. In the GATT context, reciprocity has meant

that trade concessions — for example, lower tariffs — usually are granted by countries only in exchange for similar concessions on the part of their main trading partners. In addition, GATT rules anticipate that a country harmed by another GATT member's trade actions will be free to take measures of "equivalent effect" to re-establish a "balance" of concessions between them. At heart, reciprocity is really a political rather than an economic imperative. In the context of international negotiations, national governments must often justify to skeptical domestic interest groups their own trade concessions by pointing to the benefits that have been won from major trading partners through the give-and-take of interstate bargaining.

In the early years following the creation of the GATT, the United States did not insist on strict reciprocity in its negotiations with the war-ravaged countries of Western Europe (or with Japan). In fact, during much of the 1950s, Washington allowed several European states suffering from shortages of hard currency to discriminate against imports from the United States in order to conserve their dollar holdings. (GATT rules permitted member-states experiencing balance-of-payments difficulties to restrict imports.) But by the 1960s, reciprocity was a firmly established principle, guiding trade negotiations among the industrialized countries. Around the same time, however, it came to be accepted that, owing to the underdeveloped state of their industries and the pressing need of their governments for revenue derived from tariff levies, Third World countries should not be required to make "reciprocal" concessions when negotiating with developed states in the GATT. Tariff preferences and other measures of "differential and more favourable treatment" for LDCs were explicitly endorsed by GATT members in 1971 and again in 1979, and most industrial countries instituted preferential (i.e., lower) tariffs on selected categories of imports from LDCs. In addition, developing countries convinced other GATT members to write more flexible rules concerning the use of nontariff trade barriers by LDCs. More recently, the United States and some other developed countries have insisted that, as LDCs mature economically, they are no longer "entitled" to benefit from any kind of preferential treatment and should be expected to participate fully in the reciprocal exchange of trade concessions in multilateral negotiations.[8]

4. **Transparency and Multilateral Surveillance.** An important GATT principle is that trade restrictions and countries' trade policies in general should be transparent and subject to ongoing scrutiny and evaluation in a multilateral forum. Numerous GATT rules are designed to allow states to monitor the policies and actions of their trading partners. Other rules require member-states to notify the GATT about decisions they have taken that could affect the trade interests of other countries. In addition, by imposing some limits on the ability of states to use quotas and other nontariff barriers to restrict trade, the General Agreement and the various intergovernmental codes and accords negotiated through the GATT express an explicit pref-

erence for tariffs — which are transparent and allow the price system to function — over NTBS, which are less visible forms of import protection and tend to thwart the operation of the price system. Students of international-trade policy have noted that improving the quality, quantity, and transparency of information about matters affecting international commerce is an essential element of multilateral trade liberalization, and is particularly valuable for smaller and weaker countries that lack the capacity to monitor global trading developments of their own.[9]

The Foundations of Postwar Trade Liberalization

Successive rounds of multilateral negotiations have brought about a marked decline in industrial countries' tariff and, to a much lesser extent, nontariff barriers. Of the first five GATT rounds, only the first, held when the General Agreement was negotiated in 1947, actually resulted in substantial tariff reductions, with the United States agreeing to cut its average weighted tariff by some 35 percent.[10] The following four rounds yielded meagre results, partly because the U.S. government was unable to win congressional authority to make large tariff cuts, and partly because of lukewarm enthusiasm for wide-ranging multilateral tariff liberalization on the part of some Western European countries (particularly those preoccupied with establishing the European Economic Community after 1957), Japan, and several other GATT member-states. Despite limited progress in the GATT, however, most of the internal exchange controls and currency restrictions instituted in Western Europe following the war were gradually phased out in the 1950s under the auspices of the Organization for European Economic Cooperation.

In the GATT itself, further broadly based multilateral tariff cuts were not implemented until the Kennedy Round (1963–67). During these negotiations, 16 industrial countries (including the six individual member-states of the European Community) agreed to slash their most-favoured-nation tariffs on nonagricultural imports by roughly 40 percent, with smaller reductions agreed to in respect of agricultural imports. With the conclusion of the Kennedy Round, average MFN tariffs on manufactured goods had been reduced through six rounds of negotiations by approximately 60 percent in the case of the United States, Western Europe, and Canada, and by 50 percent in the case of Japan.[11] The Kennedy Round also saw the beginnings of a major and ongoing campaign by developing countries — sparked by the creation of the U.N. Conference on Trade and Development (UNCTAD) in 1964 — to obtain more favourable treatment under the rules of the GATT regime.[12]

The Kennedy Round was hailed as the most impressive step toward freer multilateral trade in the 20th century. The next series of multilateral negotiations, the Tokyo Round (1973–79), also achieved considerable progress, with the industrial countries agreeing to further lower their tariffs on manufactured products by an average of 40 percent over the period 1980–87. Following the phase-in of these tariff cuts, post–Tokyo Round weighted-average tariff duties on manufactured imports for the major industrial countries fell to very low levels — 5 to 7 percent for the United States, Japan, and the European Community, slightly higher figures for Canada, Spain, and Australia. More important than these tariff cuts, however, the Tokyo Round also produced several new multilateral agreements (known as "codes") intended to update and liberalize existing GATT rules governing the use of key NTBs, notably in the areas of government procurement, subsidies/countervailing duties, dumping/antidumping duties, technical barriers to trade, customs-valuation methods, and import-licensing procedures. These codes represented the first major multilateral initiative to control and lessen the trade-distorting impact of NTBs.[13] But, in practice, GATT members have taken only limited steps to restrict the use of many NTBs. And even as the Tokyo Round negotiations came to a close, evidence was accumulating that the GATT regime was experiencing a serious erosion of its effectiveness and legal integrity because of the widespread proliferation of subsidies, quotas, and other nontariff measures.

Scholars and close observers of the international-trade system have identified several factors that have encouraged and smoothed the way toward increased trade and lower global trade barriers. Some of these are economic factors, while others have to do with political leadership and the distribution of power among states.

Prominent among the economic factors supporting trade liberalization and increased trade flows was the exceptionally favourable macroeconomic climate prevailing throughout much of the postwar era, especially in the 1950s and 1960s. The expansion of international trade from the late 1940s to the early 1970s, and the major tariff cuts negotiated in the 1960s, were unquestionably facilitated by the strong economic growth, buoyant labour markets, and general improvement in living standards enjoyed by the principal industrial economies during much of this period. A related contributing factor was the exchange-rate stability provided by the Bretton Woods international monetary regime, which prevented widespread currency fluctuations. In many countries, average real economic-growth rates over 1960–73 were almost twice as high as those recorded between 1974 and 1985. For the political analyst interested in international trade, robust economic growth is a suggestive variable for explaining liberalization because it helps to create conditions in which the process of industrial- and labour- market adjustment arising from increased trade, lower import barriers, and heightened economic interdependence can occur relatively painlessly. From this follows the unexceptional hypothesis that international trade liberalization is more apt to take place when economic growth rates are high. In looking at developments in the trade system since the early 1970s, it is thus perhaps not surprising that protectionist policies became more common, and the growth of world trade slowed, during a period when exchange rates became more unstable and the macroeconomic performance of most industrial countries deteriorated, as compared to figures for earlier postwar decades.

Yet it is essential to recognize that despite stronger protectionist pressures, weaker economic growth in the advanced industrial countries, and a less stable macro environment, international trade has continued to expand more quickly than global production during most of the past 15 years. Indeed, in both 1984 and 1988 the volume of world exports rose at record rates. This fact points to a central paradox of the modern trade regime — the simultaneous and continuing growth of trade, on the one hand, but national policies and measures that distort and impede the free international movement of goods, services, and capital, on the other. It also underlines the fact that the lowering of tariffs and other trade barriers has been only one of several factors behind the exponential rise in international exchanges of goods and services in the postwar era.

A second economic trend that has promoted increased trade and the reduction of trade barriers relates to the character of contemporary trade flows and the predominant role of multinational firms in structuring international production and exchange in many manufacturing industries. Traditional neoclassical trade theory predicted that commercial exchanges between countries would largely take the form of "interindustry" trade. Countries would specialize in and export products made by industries in which their particular national resource endowments allowed them to develop comparative advantages, and import goods produced by other industries located in foreign countries that had different relative resource or factor endowments. According to this view, with liberalized world trade, Country A would manufacture products from a particular industry (say, machinery) in which it had a comparative advantage, and export these products to Country B, which in turn would manufacture products from another industry (say, chemicals) and sell these to Country A. Those industries in which a country was not "competitive" — chemicals in the case of Country A above, and machinery in the case of Country B — would contract or even disappear as international trade expanded and became progressively freer.

This older theory of international trade rested on certain fundamental assumptions: that labour and capital are not mobile internationally, that all countries have equal access to technology (and, thus, have common production functions), that international markets are characterized by conditions of near-perfect competition, that comparative advantage is static, and that returns to scale in production are constant. These assumptions have been rendered untenable by the nature and evolution of postwar production structures and international trade flows. In the modern trade regime, capital is highly mobile, increasingly differentiated products and components are traded within specific industries and individual firms throughout all stages of the production process, a few multinational firms dominate world markets and production activity in many sectors, firms and governments both seek to gain technological advantages over their rivals, and foreign trade and investment are inextricably linked. Today, most trade in manufactured products among the developed countries actually occurs not between distinct industries, but rather *within* industries and individual multinational firms that have plants located in different countries ("intraindustry" and "intrafirm" trade). Many industrial countries are both exporters and importers of the same broad range of manufactured products. There has been a general convergence of industrial structures among advanced industrial states, with the result that not only is their distribution of output and employment between agriculture, industry, and services now quite similar, but the bulk of their mutual trade consists of exchanges within the same categories of manufactured products. Examples include transport equipment, chemicals, electronic products and components (including computer-related products), and all manner of specialized machinery. Up to two-thirds of intra-OECD trade in manufactures now takes the form of intraindustry exchanges.[14]

Closely related to the growth of intraindustry trade is the fact that a large portion of the exchanges that occur among the OECD economies actually consists of transfers of products, components, and services within individual multinational firms. These firms effectively structure global production and markets in many sectors and wield market power far greater than anything anticipated by the conventional trade models. Some studies suggest that intrafirm transfers now comprise up to half of the value of imports of a number of developed countries.[15] With their increasingly integrated global operations, multinational firms have brought about unprecedented internationalization of production as well as more concentrated market power across a wide range of industries. In the contemporary trade regime, multinational firms have a common interest in trade expansion and liberalization. They have been — and remain — the most potent international political constituency in favour of the free movement of goods, services, and capital.

Owing to the importance of intraindustry and intrafirm exchanges, trade liberalization among the industrial countries has been accompanied by less national specialization in the production and export of individual industries — and hence less pressure to phase out existing manufacturing sectors — than predicted by conventional trade theory. Instead, since the 1950s there has been a dramatic jump in trade in products belonging to the same industry. For the political analyst, one intriguing implication of intraindustry and intrafirm trade and specialization is that it produces fewer adjustment problems for national economies than does interindustry trade. A second important implication, recently noted by Susan Strange, is that governmental restrictions on trade — and negotiations concerning their use — appear to be of declining salience in determining the behaviour of multinational firms and the composition and flow of trade in manufactures among the advanced industrial economies. The forces underlying the convergence and increasing integration of production structures among the developed economies are today so powerful and pervasive that they often outweigh the impact of governments' commercial policies. In contrast, it is precisely in those economic sectors where interindustry specialization *has* posed clear threats to the survival of particular industries in developed countries — textiles, clothing, footwear, and above all, agriculture come to mind — that multilateral trade liberalization through the GATT has proven most difficult to achieve and governments' commercial policies have had their greatest effect.[16]

A final economic factor that has encouraged trade liberalization is the priority long given by trade negotiators to reducing tariffs rather than other types of trade barriers — an understandable priority in view of the high tariff rates maintained by so many industrial countries at the close of the war. While scaling back the degree of tariff protection afforded to domestic industry has often proven politically contentious for national governments, the fact remains that tariffs are relatively simple to deal with from the standpoint of international-trade bargaining. They are border measures that are readily quantifiable and that can be easily compared across countries and product categories. Most important, because tariffs are by definition imposed at the border by national governments to limit imports, international negotiations to lower tariffs have not normally raised politically sensitive questions of national sovereignty. In this respect, tariffs differ significantly from nontariff trade barriers, such as subsidies; "buy-national" government procurement policies; and national health, safety, and other technical standards. These and other NTBS may distort trade and impede foreign access to markets, but often they arise from national policy decisions that are primarily or partially domestic rather than international in character. Moreover, restricting the use of nontariff measures and harmonizing national standards and practices through international negotiations raise special difficulties because international regulation in these areas almost always clashes with the demonstrated preference of governments to preserve (and, indeed, enhance) their ability to make national choices in social and economic policy rather than have these choices dictated by the terms of international organizations and agreements.

International efforts to reduce and regulate the use of barriers other than tariffs have proceeded more tentatively, and with noticeably less success, than negotiations aimed at cutting tariff rates. And, as briefly discussed in the previous section of this chapter, GATT member-states have only just begun to address several important trade-related issues not previously subject to GATT regulation, such as investment, intellectual-property rights, and trade in services. It is difficult to avoid the conclusion that much of the liberalization achieved through the GATT since the late 1940s is attributable to the fact that, during the first six rounds of bargaining, negotiators concentrated on reducing the simplest and most straightforward type of trade barrier — tariffs. Whether GATT member-states will be prepared to commit themselves to abide by increasingly strict and more sovereignty-constraining international rules governing the use of a wide range of other trade-distorting policies remains to be seen.

Explaining Trade Liberalization: Political Factors

The post–World War II international economic system was put in place at a time when the relative political, military, and economic power of the United States was at its apex. As the undisputed leader of the noncommunist world, the United States not only exercised unrivalled influence but for many years displayed a willingness to underwrite the costs associated with constructing and sustaining postwar global arrangements in the security sphere as well as in the areas of trade and money. In the case of the GATT, for example, both the architecture of the General Agreement and the normative principles underlying the trade regime (especially nondiscrimination and liberalization) faithfully reflected prevailing American beliefs and policy preferences. According to the by now well-known theory of "hegemonic stability," the establishment of durable liberal international regimes depends critically on the existence of a dominant state willing and able both to enforce the disciplines of international agreements and to absorb the costs of maintaining these agreements. The theory predicts that the absence of a "hegemon" will both weaken and render international regimes less effective and lead to increased instability in the global political economy.[17]

There can be little doubt that the birth and early development of the multilateral trade regime owed much to American power and leadership. In the 1950s and 1960s, the United States essentially determined the scope and timing of tariff cuts in the GATT. In the early rounds of negotiations, the United States agreed to make disproportionate tariff reductions in order to encourage multilateral liberalization and facilitate the accession of new GATT members (notably Japan, in 1955). In the 1970s and 1980s, American dominance within the trade regime — and in the world economy generally — eroded. Today, for example, West Germany is the world's leading exporter; Japan is the most competitive and dynamic advanced industrial economy; the enlarged European Community constitutes the world's largest market; and the EC accounts for a significantly bigger share of total global imports than does the United States. Although it still has great influence, the United States can no longer either unilaterally set the GATT's agenda or determine the outcome of multilateral negotiations on trade issues. As predicted by the hegemonic model, the decline of the dominant state has coincided with a period of greater instability and an apparent weakening of the trade regime based on such criteria as respect for the GATT's legal rules, adherence to the principles of nondiscrimination and multilateral surveillance, and reliance on multilateral means of dispute settlement.[18]

The key issue that must be addressed here, however, is whether this attenuation of American hegemony has led to the unravelling of the trade regime. Despite mounting adjustment pressures and the declining effectiveness of some GATT rules, the fact remains that not only have the postwar arrangements governing international trade not collapsed, but exchanges of goods and services among states have continued to expand at an impressive rate. The GATT regime has not ceased to affect either the trade policies of member countries or the conditions under which a very large proportion of world trade takes place. Instead, as Keohane observes, a high degree of multilateral "co-operation," and an enduring belief by most countries in the overall benefits of trade liberalization and the need for international trade rules, have characterized the trade regime in an era of lessened American influence.[19] This situation suggests that, while the existence of a dominant power may be critical to the initial establishment of international economic regimes, a regime can persist following the erosion of hegemony if the most important states perceive a common interest in its maintenance and continuing effectiveness. In the context of the trade regime, the most powerful GATT members — the United States, the European Community, and Japan — have remained convinced of the need for a multilateral regulatory and negotiating body for world trade, even though they (and other GATT members) have periodically taken actions that are inconsistent with certain of the regime's principles and rules.

The New Protectionism

Scholars and trade-policy experts have devoted much effort in recent years to analyzing and cataloguing the various pressures confronting the GATT. These include, *inter alia*, the increased use of nontariff barriers and "managed trade" arrangements — many of which operate outside of the GATT and often violate its rules — by developed countries; the trend toward unilateral interpretations of trade rules by some major trading nations, notably the United States and the EC; the popularity of regional and bilateral trade arrangements; and the declining effectiveness of the GATT dispute-settlement system. Many believe that the cumulative impact of these and other developments has been to bring about a marked erosion of the capacity of the GATT's rules and principles to impart order, discipline, and some degree of coherence to the international trading system.[20] Other analysts stress the durability of the trade regime and the continuing commitment of most GATT members to liberalization and the existence of meaningful multilateral-trade rules.[21] It is instructive to note that the ultimate source of many of the infirmities allegedly besetting the GATT is the remarkable expansion of international trade that has taken place under its auspices since the 1950s — a development that has created difficult adjustment problems in many countries.

The most intractable long-term international trade-policy issue is how to deal with the exceptionally rapid growth of exports of manufactured goods from the newly industrialized countries (NICs), and the consequent intense adjustment pressures facing many advanced industrial economies. In 1963, developing countries accounted for only 4 percent of world exports of manufactures. A quarter-century later, this figure reached 15 percent, and it could conceivably rise to 20 percent by the end of the 1990s. Most of the increase is attributable to a handful of quickly industrializing East Asian developing countries — Hong Kong, Taiwan, South Korea, and Singapore. Today these "four dragons" are formidable international competitors across a wide range of markets for manufactured products. Several other LDCs — among them India, Brazil, Mexico, Malaysia, China, and Thailand — are fast becoming important competitors in world markets for certain categories of labour-intensive manufactures.

Governmental responses to contemporary adjustment and import pressures have taken on an increasingly protectionist character since the 1970s. Most responses have been motivated by the immediate problems facing particular domestic industries. Yet, at the global level, liberalization has continued to move forward in many industrial sectors in which trade consists largely of exchanges among the advanced industrial economies. There are, of course, some important exceptions to this, such as U.S. restrictions on auto and semiconductor imports from Japan and on all offshore steel imports, and European quotas on a wide range of imported manufactured goods from Japan. But while protectionist measures may have intensified in some areas of intra-OECD trade, they have become almost pervasive in industrial sectors where developing countries account for a rising share of global exports. Protection has been concentrated in a relatively small number of sectors: a few older capital-intensive industries characterized by surplus global capacity, such as steel and shipbuilding; and a larger number of more labour-intensive industries characterized by standardized production processes, mature markets, and extensive price competition, such as textiles, clothing, shoes, many consumer electronic products, and toys.[22]

In addition to the sectoral focus of much recent protectionism, the means by which import restrictions and controls are implemented and enforced have altered. Reliance on high tariffs alone to deter imports has become quite rare among the industrialized countries, even though above-average tariffs are levied by most developed countries on imports of many of the manufactured products in which the NICs have acquired a comparative advantage. Instead, developed countries have resorted to an array of nontariff barriers and "managed trade" arrangements, many of which entail an increased role for the state, both to limit import growth and to improve the competitive position of domestic firms and industries in international markets. The preferred instruments of contemporary import protection generally involve both explicit governmental intervention into international markets and the selective (i.e., discriminatory) targeting of particular products and producing countries. Among the most popular are internationally negotiated market-sharing arrangements such as "voluntary restraint" agreements (VRAs) and "orderly marketing" agreements (OMAs). These are negotiated between firms and/or governments from importing and exporting countries, with national governments always involved in enforcing the arrangements, even when they are not formally party to them. Although some developing-country suppliers have actually benefited from the higher prices and stability of market access sometimes provided by VRAs and OMAs, overall these arrangements serve to limit the opportunities available to LDC exporters to sell manufactured goods.[23]

Moreover, and more damaging to the legal integrity and political authority of the GATT regime, most market-sharing and managed-trade arrangements exist outside of the GATT system of rules, procedures, and multilateral surveillance. An exception is the international scheme for textiles and clothing, the Multi-Fibre Arrangement, which is part of the GATT. Under the MFA, individual exporting and importing countries periodically negotiate bilateral agreements that specify by how much imports of various categories of textile/apparel products may grow. Although exports of these products from developing countries have generally continued to increase under the MFA, LDCs have complained that the arrangement limits their growth prospects and singles them out for discriminatory commercial treatment. Because they are bilateral in character and discriminate among different categories of suppliers, all market-sharing and managed-trade arrangements —

including the MFA — conflict with the "nondiscrimination" principle that was long the cornerstone of the GATT regime.

Thus, the defining characteristics of what some economists have called the "new protectionism" are its focus on particular sectors and industries, on the one hand, and the escalating number of nontariff instruments — VRAS, OMAS, subsidies, and other nontariff barriers — by which it is implemented, on the other.[24] Estimates of the volume of global trade affected by the "new protectionism" vary, but there is wide agreement that the proportion has been rising since the mid-1970s. According to one analysis, in 1983 approximately 20 percent of total OECD nonagricultural imports from other OECD countries, and 34 percent of OECD nonagricultural imports from developing countries, were affected by market-sharing and managed trade arrangements or other types of nontariff trade barriers such as quotas, price controls, or import licences.[25] The Institute for International Economics calculated that, in 1985, up to 21 percent of U.S. imports were covered by some form of "special protection."[26] (It should be noted that the 1983 figures cited above do not include agriculture, which has long been subject to extensive governmental intervention in both domestic and international markets and, because of this, has always been treated separately during GATT negotiations.)[27] In sum, the "new protectionism" attests to the tendency of governments to resort to such devices as cartelization, VRAS, OMAS, and other nontariff barriers and national trade controls — often targeted at developing countries — as they respond to tougher import competition and adjustment problems in their domestic manufacturing sectors.

Conclusion: Interdependence and the Future of the Trade Regime

The current Uruguay Round of multilateral trade negotiations will determine whether the GATT is to remain central to the evolution of the postwar international-trade system. It will not, however, determine whether international trade and economic interdependence continue to increase. Growing international exchanges of goods and services and higher levels of interdependence are almost certain to persist because of the integration of both global capital markets and production structures and the rapid international diffusion of technological knowledge. While a "successful" outcome to the Uruguay Round negotiations would undoubtedly lend support to these long-term structural trends that are reshaping the global political economy, it is improbable that a less successful result would have a huge impact on trade flows. The institutional arrangements, rules, and intergovernmental understandings that together constitute the trade regime are best understood as part of what Susan Strange has called a "secondary" global power structure, one that is ultimately influenced by other, more important global power structures in the areas of production, finance, knowledge, and international security.[28] The roots of increased international exchanges and interdependence are mainly found in these primary international power structures rather than in the international trading regime itself.

Notwithstanding the fact that contemporary trade flows are affected by many factors other than trade barriers and governments' commercial policies, the GATT regime does appear to be at a crossroads. The most pressing challenge is to update and expand the GATT's regulatory structure to capture a larger share of global exchanges of goods and services. In particular, failure to expand the regulatory scope of the GATT regime to include key emergent trade issues and fast-growing economic sectors will render the regime less and less relevant to a widening proportion of total global trade. In addition to such perennial negotiating items as reducing tariffs and seeking to control agricultural protection, the Uruguay Round agenda includes several newer and more complex issues on which consensus — particularly between developing and advanced-industrial countries — will prove difficult to achieve. Four of these "new" trade issues deserve brief mention here.[29]

1. **Nontariff Barriers.** The NTB codes negotiated during the Tokyo Round began the process of refurbishing the General Agreement's rather skeletal rules on nontariff measures. While considerable progress has been achieved in some areas, in practice little has been done to reduce or effectively control those NTBs that have the greatest impact on international trade — notably, government subsidies, discriminatory government procurement, and the unilateral imposition by developed countries, acting outside of the GATT's rules, of restrictions against imports from LDCs that are deemed to cause market disruption (an issue on which the Tokyo Round negotiators failed to produce a code). Thus, a priority in the current Round is to extend and elaborate the existing GATT NTB codes and to negotiate revised "safeguard" rules designed to stem the proliferation of extralegal protectionist measures such as VRAs and OMAs.
2. **Trade in Services.** The United States, supported by several other developed countries, took the lead in pressing for the inclusion of trade in services in the Uruguay Round agenda. Since services account for a rising share of global trade and have remained outside of the GATT's regulatory structure, the development of an agreed multilateral framework for services is considered by many analysts to be essential to the GATT's long-term survival. However, GATT member states have vastly different economic interests and national priorities in this area. Many developing countries worry that new liberal rules governing trade in services will force their own service-producing industries to compete directly in LDC domestic markets with large multinational firms (e.g., banks, insurance companies, and communications firms) based in the United States, Europe, and Japan. Because of divergent national traditions and legal frameworks with respect to the regulation of service industries, opening up domestic markets to increased foreign competition and developing harmonized international rules for services, trade is certain to be a lengthy and politically contentious process. Already, for example, conflict has arisen within the OECD bloc on the extent to which concrete steps to improve market access for foreign

service-providers can be expected to result from the Uruguay Round. U.S. negotiators, apparently convinced that American firms enjoy a comparative advantage in many service sectors, have insisted that significant progress toward more open markets and liberalized rules must be made, while Japan and the European Community have exhibited more caution, and most developing countries have basically opposed the idea of negotiations on the whole question of trade in services. Since trade in services is new territory for the GATT, and basic information is lacking, Uruguay Round negotiators must grapple with a host of difficult statistical, measurement, and conceptual problems as they explore the prospects for new international agreements.

3. **Trade-Related Investment Measures (TRIMS).** The declaration launching the Uruguay Round called for multilateral negotiations on "trade-related investment measures." These include such measures as local-content requirements imposed on foreign manufacturers seeking to sell in a country's market and export-performance requirements imposed on foreign-owned firms. The absence of effective GATT rules on international investment has long been a peculiar lacuna in light of the fact that trade and investment are closely interwoven in an international economy dominated by multinational enterprises that enjoy wide latitude to produce, source, and sell their goods and services in a large number of separate national markets. Again, the developing countries are noticeably less enthusiastic than the major developed nations about the negotiation within the GATT of far-reaching international investment rules reflecting market-oriented principles.
4. **Intellectual-Property Rights.** The United States, the EC, and other developed countries have argued that stronger international measures are urgently needed to protect private intellectual-property rights. Intellectual-property rights are acquiring more importance as the global economy becomes more knowledge- and information-intensive. This broad field includes both traditional property rights such as patents, trademarks, and copyrights, as well as the issues of the pirating of new technologies (e.g., biotechnology and computer software) and of the sale of counterfeit goods by developing countries. Although some of these matters are covered by other international agreements and conventions, many developed countries favour using the GATT to tighten the protection afforded to intellectual-property rights attached to goods and services entering international trade. In addition to negotiations in the GATT context, direct bilateral pressure has been exerted by the Americans and West Europeans on the NIEs to improve their patent and copyright legislation and to impose tougher penalties on domestic firms that pirate foreign technologies and produce counterfeit goods.

In order to achieve progress on the issues canvassed above, GATT members will have to accept a much greater degree of harmonization and consistency in the design and application of national trade regulations than they have contemplated in the past. The quest for lower and more transparent nontariff trade barriers, and for agreed international rules in the areas of services trade, investment, and intellectual property, raises issues that are far more complex and politically sensitive than those that have surrounded traditional questions of tariff policy. The "new" trade issues that are such a vital part of the Uruguay Round negotiating agenda implicitly envisage a world in which national governments' policies, standards, and regulations with respect to both trade and commercial activity generally will tend to converge. While a trend toward policy convergence is already evident, the movement toward the integration of global production and finance has been much more dramatic. A growing gap thus exists in the trading regime between the "economic reality" of increasing interdependence and the policy response of governments and international institutions.

The inclusion of these new topics on the GATT agenda can be viewed as a belated effort by many GATT members to construct a more comprehensive trade regime, whose rules and principles will apply to a larger share of global exchanges of goods and services. Ironically, the Uruguay Round agenda testifies to the prescience of the original drafters of the ambitious 1948 Havana Charter for the International Trade Organization. The Charter was premised on the assumption that, to be effective, a global multilateral-trade institution had to address all of the most important commercial policy issues believed to affect international trade. In setting the agenda for the current Uruguay Round, the most powerful trading nations have apparently decided to breathe new life into the "old" goal of a comprehensive international-trade institution that guided the ITO negotiations more than four decades ago.

NOTES

1. Richard Rosecrance, Arthur Stein, and Alan Alexandroff, "Whither Interdependence?" *International Organization* 31 (Summer 1977): 426.

2. Robert O. Keohane and Joseph S. Nye, Jr., *Power and Interdependence: World Politics in Transition* (Boston: Little, Brown, 1977), 12–13; Robert Gilpin, *The Political Economy of International Relations* (Princeton: Princeton University Press, 1987), 17–18.

3. I.M. Destler, *American Trade Politics* (Washington: Institute for International Economics, 1986), 41.

4. Destler, *American Trade Politics*, 41.

5. International Monetary Fund, *World Economic Outlook* (March 1988); for a general discussion of services trade, see Jonathan David Aronson and Peter F. Cowhey, *Trade in Services: A Case for Open Markets* (Washington: American Enterprise Institute, 1984); and Brian Hindley and Alasdair Smith, "Comparative Advantage and Trade in Services," *World Economy* 7 (December 1984): 369–89.

6. On the negotiations leading to the creation of the GATT, see Richard Gardner, *Sterling-Dollar Diplomacy in Current Perspective* (New York: Columbia University Press, 1980); and William A. Brown, *The United States and the Restoration of World Trade* (Washington: The Brookings Institution, 1950); for a discussion of the failed ITO scheme, see William Diebold, *The End of the ITO*, Essays in International Finance (Princeton: Princeton University Press, 1952).

7. Kenneth Dam, *The GATT: Law and International Economic Organization* (Chicago: University of Chicago Press, 1970); Frank Stone, *Canada, the GATT and the International Trade System* (Montreal: Institute for Research on Public Policy, 1984); John Jackson, *World Trade and the Law of GATT* (Indianapolis: Bobbs-Merrill, 1969); Gerard Curzon and Victoria Price Curzon, "The Management of Trade Relations in the GATT," in *International Economic Relations of the Western World, 1959–1971: Politics and Trade*, ed. Andrew Shonfield (Oxford: Oxford University Press, 1976); Jock A. Finlayson and Mark W. Zacher, "The GATT and the Regulation of Trade Barriers: Regime Dynamics and Functions," in *International Regimes*, ed. Stephen D. Krasner (Ithaca: Cornell University Press, 1983).

8. For a lengthy discussion of the treatment of developing countries in the GATT legal system, consult Robert E. Hudec, *Developing Countries in the GATT Legal System* (London: Trade Policy Research Centre, 1987).

9. Jackson, *World Trade and the Law of GATT*, 124.

10. F. V. Meyer, *International Trade Policy* (London: Croom Helm, 1978), 137–38.

11. Stone, *Canada, the GATT and the International Trade System*, 64.

12. A detailed account of the Kennedy Round negotiations is provided by John Evans, *The Kennedy Round and American Trade Policy* (Cambridge, Mass.: Harvard University Press, 1971).

13. The Tokyo Round is examined by Gilbert Winham, *International Trade and the Tokyo Round Negotiations* (Princeton: Princeton University Press, 1986), and in GATT, *The Tokyo Round of Multilateral Trade Negotiations* (Geneva: GATT Secretariat, 1979).

14. The economics of intraindustry trade are analyzed in David Greenaway and Chris Milner, *The Economics of Intra-Industry Trade* (Oxford: Basil Blackwell, 1986), and Herbert Grubel and Peter Lloyd, *Intra-Industry Trade* (New York: John Wiley and Sons, 1975).

15. Gerald K. Helleiner, *Intrafirm Trade and the Developing Countries* (New York: St. Martin's, 1981).

16. Susan Strange, *States and Markets: An Introduction to International Political Economy* (London: Pinter, 1988), 184–85.

17. Charles Kindleberger, *The World in Depression* (Berkeley: University of California Press, 1973); Stephen D. Krasner, "State Power and the Structure of International Trade," *World Politics* 28 (April 1976): 317–47; Robert Keohane, *After Hegemony: Cooperation and Discord in the World Political Economy* (Princeton: Princeton University Press, 1984); Robert Gilpin, *U.S. Power and the Multinational Corporation* (New York: Basic Books, 1975); and Gilpin, *Political Economy of International Relations*.

18. Charles Lipson, "The Transformation of Trade: The Sources and Effects of Regime Change," in *International Regimes*, 235.

19. Keohane, *After Hegemony*, 188–90.

20. See, for example, John Jackson, "The Crumbling Institutions of the Liberal Trade System," *Journal of World Trade Law* 12 (March–April 1978): 93–106; and Hudec, *Developing Countries in the GATT Legal System.*

21. Finlayson and Zacher, "The GATT and the Regulation of Trade Barriers"; Keohane, *After Hegemony*; Lipson, "The Transformation of Trade"; and Strange, *States and Markets.*

22. For analyses of protectionist trends in the 1970s and 1980s, see Susan Strange, "Protectionism and World Politics," *International Organization* 39 (1985) 233–60; OECD, "Costs and Benefits of Protection," *OECD Observer* 134 (1985): 18–23; OECD, "Change and Continuity in OECD Trade in Manufactures with Developing Countries," *OECD Observer* 139 (1986): 3–9; and Sheila Page, "The Rise in Protection Since 1974," *Oxford Review of Economic Policy* 3 (Spring 1987): 1–3.

23. See David Yoffie, *Power and Protectionism* (New York: Columbia University Press, 1983), for a revealing account of how some LDCs have successfully adapted to VRAs and OMAs imposed by the United States.

24. Bela Balassa, "The New Protectionism and the International Economy," *Journal of World Trade Law* 12 (September–October 1978), was the first to introduce the term "new protectionism."

25. J. Nogues, A. Olechowski, and L. Winters, "Extent of Non-Tariff Barriers to Industrial Countries' Imports," *World Bank Economic Review* 1 (1986): 181–91.

26. Gary Clyde Hufbauer, Diane T. Berliner, and Kimberly Ann Elliott, *Trade Protection in the United States: 31 Case Studies* (Washington: Institute for International Economics, 1986).

27. Dale E. Hathaway, *Agriculture and the GATT: Rewriting the Rules* (Washington: Institute for International Economics, 1987).

28. Strange, *States and Markets.*

29. Gary Clyde Hufbauer and Jeffrey J. Scott, *Trading for Growth: The Next Round of Trade Negotiations* (Washington: Institute for International Economics, 1986); and Aronson and Cowhey, *Trade in Services.*

SELECT BIBLIOGRAPHY

Aronson, Jonathan David, and Peter F. Cowhey. *Trade in Services: A Case for Open Markets.* Washington: American Enterprise Institute, 1984.

Balassa, Bela. "The New Protectionism and the International Economy." *Journal of World Trade Law* 12 (September–October 1978): 409–36.

Brown, William A. *The United States and the Restoration of World Trade.* Washington: The Brookings Institution, 1950.

Curzon, Gerard, and Victoria Price Curzon. "The Management of Trade Relations in the GATT." In *International Economic Relations of the Western World, 1959–1971: Politics and Trade*, ed. Andrew Shonfield. Oxford: Oxford University Press, 1976.

Dam, Kenneth. *The GATT: Law and International Economic Organization.* Chicago: University of Chicago Press, 1970.

Destler, I.M. *American Trade Politics.* Washington: Institute for International Economics, 1986.

Diebold, William. *The End of the ITO.* Princeton University: Essays in International Finance, 1952.

Evans, John. *The Kennedy Round and American Trade Policy.* Cambridge, Mass.: Harvard University Press, 1971.

Finlayson, Jock A., and Mark W. Zacher. "GATT and the Regulation of Trade Barriers: Regime Dynamics and Functions." In *International Regimes,* ed. Stephen D. Krasner. Ithaca: Cornell University Press, 1983.

Gardner, Richard. *Sterling-Dollar Diplomacy in Current Perspective.* New York: Columbia University Press, 1980.

GATT. *International Trade, 1987/88.* Geneva: GATT Secretariat, 1988.

———. *The Tokyo Round of Multilateral Trade Negotiations.* Geneva: GATT Secretariat, 1979.

Gilpin, Robert. *The Political Economy of International Relations.* Princeton: Princeton University Press, 1987.

———. *U.S. Power and the Multinational Corporation.* New York: Basic Books, 1975.

Greenaway, David, and Chris Milner. *The Economics of Intra-Industry Trade.* Oxford: Basil Blackwell, 1986.

Grubel, Herbert, and Peter Lloyd. *Intra-Industry Trade.* New York: John Wiley and Sons, 1975.

Hathaway, Dale E. *Agriculture and the GATT: Rewriting the Rules.* Washington: Institute for International Economics, 1987.

Helleiner, Gerald K. *Intrafirm Trade and the Developing Countries.* New York: St. Martin's, 1981.

Hindley, Brian, and Smith, Alasdair. "Comparative Advantage and Trade in Services." *The World Economy* 7 (December 1984): 369–89.

Hudec, Robert E. *Developing Countries in the GATT Legal System.* London: Trade Policy Research Centre, 1987.

Hufbauer, Gary Clyde; Diane T. Berliner; and Kimberley Ann Elliott. *Trade Protection in the United States: 31 Case Studies.* Washington: Institute for International Economics, 1986.

Hufbauer, Gary Clyde, and Jeffrey J. Schott. *Trading for Growth: The Next Round of Trade Negotiations.* Washington: Institute for International Economics, 1985.

International Monetary Fund. *World Economic Outlook.* March 1988.

Jackson, John. "The Crumbling Institutions of the Liberal Trade System." *The Journal of World Trade Law* 12 (March–April 1978): 93–106.

———. *World Trade and the Law of GATT.* Indianapolis: Bobbs-Merrill, 1969.

Keohane, Robert O. *After Hegemony: Cooperation and Discord in the World Political Economy.* Princeton: Princeton University Press, 1984.

Keohane, Robert O., and Joseph S. Nye, Jr. *Power and Interdependence: World Politics in Transition.* Boston: Little, Brown, 1977.

Kindleberger, Charles. *The World in Depression.* Berkeley: University of California Press, 1973.

Krasner, Stephen D. "State Power and the Structure of International Trade." *World Politics* 28 (April 1976): 317–47.

Lipson, Charles. "The Transformation of Trade: The Sources and Effects of Regime Change." In *International Regimes*, ed. Stephen D. Krasner. Ithaca: Cornell University Press, 1983.

Meyer, F. V. *International Trade Policy*. London: Croom Helm, 1978.

Nogues, J.; A. Olechowski; and L. Winters. "Extent of Non-Tariff Barriers to Industrial Countries' Imports." *World Bank Economic Review* 1 (1986): 181–91.

OECD. "Change and Continuity in OECD Trade in Manufactures with Developing Countries." *OECD Observer* 139 (1986): 3–9.

———. "Costs and Benefits of Protection." *OECD Observer* 134 (1985):18–23.

Page, Sheila. "The Rise in Protection Since 1974." *Oxford Review of Economic Policy* 3 (Spring 1987): 1–3.

Rosecrance, Richard. *The Rise of the Trading State: Commerce and Conquest in the Modern World*. New York: Basic Books, 1986.

Rosecrance, Richard; Arthur Stein; and Alan Alexandroff. "Whither Interdependence?" *International Organization* 31 (Summer 1977): 425–72.

Stone, Frank. *Canada, the GATT and the International Trade System*. Montreal: Institute for Research on Public Policy, 1984.

Strange, Susan. *States and Markets: An Introduction to International Political Economy*. London: Pinter, 1988.

———. "Protectionism and World Politics." *International Organization* 39, no. 2 (Spring 1985): 233–60.

Winham, Gilbert. *International Trade and the Tokyo Round Negotiations*. Princeton: Princeton University Press, 1986.

Yoffie, David. *Power and Protectionism*. New York: Columbia University Press, 1983.

PART III

THE POLITICS OF DEPENDENCE

Parts I and II of this book have addressed the principal concerns of the Western industrialized world, with particular attention to physical and economic security. The politics of dependence, the subject of Part III, is quite different in that it arises out of, and deals specifically with, the politics of the less-developed world, and has some roots in traditional Marxist scholarship, which deals with the nature of imperialism and superordinate-subordinate relations. The principal approach to the politics of dependence is holistic and historical in nature and generally systemic in scope. Moreover, there is a normative predisposition toward finding solutions that allow for some greater measure of distributive justice.

The first chapter, by Malcolm Grieve, assesses the various causes and consequences of imperialism, paying particular attention to the notion of economic imperialism and to the various debates over the implications of imperialism. The remaining chapters in Part III address some of the key issue-areas in the ongoing conflict between existing and emerging structures. Timothy Shaw assesses the prospects for African development within the context of a new international division of labour. Elizabeth Riddell-Dixon tackles the question of technology within the same context, in an attempt to come to terms with the importance of technology and technology transfer in the demands from the less-developed countries for a more just and equitable world order. Andrew Fenton Cooper examines the changes that have taken place in the international political economy of food and agriculture, and David Haglund explores the changing significance of strategic minerals.

ECONOMIC IMPERIALISM

Malcolm J. Grieve

Why Study Economic Imperialism?

Imperialism has long been a major concern of scholars of international relations. For most of this time, a fairly straightforward definition of the subject of analysis was possible: an empire involved in direct military and political control over specific territories. The word itself derives from the Latin *imperium*, which the Romans used to refer to the incorporation of militarily defeated peoples under their direct political rule and command. The French and British languages share the word *empire*, referring to an era of supreme political and military rule, usually combined with the payment of some taxes or tribute to the central government. The French and British nations also shared the bulk of the land surface of the globe during the heyday of the European colonial empires, from about 1875 to 1925. *Imperialism* referred to their struggle to expand and protect the areas under colonial rule. Imperialism, then, in its distant origins and relatively recent great-power policy, is of central concern for classical (or realist) international relations scholars, who are concerned with the power relationships among states.

Since Marx's analysis of the dynamics of capitalism, the meanings attached to the concept of imperialism have broadened considerably. Some students of international relations would argue that the Marxist use of "imperialism" has resulted in a reduction of the analytical usefulness of the concept.[1] Wherever the blame for the devaluation of the concept lies, mention of imperialism today calls first to mind relations of economic exploitation rather than (or as a preface to) the earlier notion of coercive relationships among states of different capabilities. Some discussion of definition is necessary for understanding the meaning and the utility of economic imperialism. First, imperialism, although rooted in classical notions of armed domination, has come to be broadly associated with any relationship involving threat and submission. Economic imperialism simply takes this one step farther and implies that the threat-submission relationship can and does involve the production and exchange of goods and services.

This chapter provides an introduction to the debate over the definition and process of economic imperialism. By reference to some of the major authors in the field, it will be argued that many original aspects of imperialism remain in the international relations literature under different guises. Rather than direct reference to empires, we are more likely today to find discussions of "hegemonic" behaviour and duties (with *hegemony* defined as the proper authority of leading states to police those in their sphere of influence).[2] The contemporary literature refers to the rise and decline of U.S. leadership in its postwar role as a global hegemon. Earlier work in diplomatic history referred to a duty to extend and preserve the British Empire, or to pursue the French *mission civilatrice*. The change in preferred usage from "empire" to "hegemony" reflects the fact that imperialism has come to be understood as a negative concept, precisely because of its pejorative connotations of the extraction of economic value, which, in turn, stems from economic analysis of the causes and impact of British imperialism (both at home and abroad). There is something ignoble about a state policy focussed chiefly on securing economic benefits, either in the national interest or in the interests of a particular class, when contrasted with the real or rhetorical ambitions of securing order and spreading "civilized" values through military conquest and economic dominance.

Despite the credentials of imperialism as a concept in "power politics," it seems useful to state at the outset why a discussion of economic imperialism has a place in a Canadian volume on international relations. One might consider the following points in assessing the theoretical and practical value of the notion of economic imperialism. It is generally conceded by all but the most confirmed "realists" that economic relationships cannot be meaningfully separated from the political, military, or strategic concerns of states.[3] War remains an important focus of research in international relations. There is a substantial body of scholarship dealing with the relationship between capitalism, economic imperialism, and war. A major part of the theoretical-debate and empirical-research agenda in the past 20 years has focussed on alleged patterns and consequences of dependency theory, an offshoot from the literature on economic imperialism. International political economy of a less ideological type than the dependency school has shown that economic relations have a high and growing importance in defining prestige in the system of sovereign states.[4] Studies of complex interdependence also draw attention to the myriad connections between societies and extend our understanding of what constitutes international relations far beyond the realists' reconstruction of international politics (conceived as the interaction of discrete and unitary states). Once we look beyond the apex of power and alleged "national interests," we can begin to include a wider agenda for research, again including economic concerns.[5] Moving beyond definitions of international politics that centre on power and high-level security concerns leads us to consider the impact of nonstate actors on international relations. An interesting branch of international political-economy research considers the scope and extent of the influence that transnational corporations have on orthodox diplomatic and security concerns as well as their more obvious involvement with economic developments in both the Third World and developed economies.[6] If the literature of the left has any validity at all, imperialism presents a major problem for development prospects in the Third World. Development, of course, is part and parcel of the new focus upon middle-range, nonsecurity issues that now fall under the umbrella of international relations research. Finally, the official ideology of the Soviet Union, if not of the more pragmatic General Secretary Gorbachev, holds that *contradictions* or internal tensions in capitalism are the well-spring of aggressive Western foreign policy. Soviets charge that economic imperialism by the major capitalist states is the principal source of friction in the modern world. If we are to understand the perspective of Soviet theorists and perhaps the thinking of Soviet policy makers, it is necessary to understand the Marxist literature on economic imperialism.

In summary, economic imperialism is very much alive, both as a concern and as a theoretical framework for describing a set of international relations. This framework is being reinforced by a more general movement in the international relations literature to bring economic relationships and actors "back in" to the discipline. At this point, there is no need to pass judgement on whether the literature on economic imperialism has impeded or furthered the broadening of international relations theory and research. It can be safely asserted that no serious observer of international relations can function today without some understanding of international trade, international debt, and direct foreign investment. Most authors on economic imperialism contend that such relationships operate to the permanent and increasing disadvantage of those beyond the centres of capitalist power. The task of this chapter is to evaluate and review the debate over what constitutes economic imperialism, and who suffers and benefits from it. As a first step, let us consider some important points of definition concerning the involvement of the state in imperial activities.

Economic Imperialism and the State

As students of international politics, we need to know if policies supporting economic imperialism are forced upon decision makers by dominant groups within a given nation or are simply one means by which nations enter into a deeper political context for strategic position or security. Unless we take a position on this issue, it is difficult to know if the rising prominence of *transnational* corporations in world commerce signals an end to *national* economic imperialism. If we argue, as many neo-Marxists do, that imperialism is inherent in the world capitalist system, then it is not necessary that national policy makers involve themselves directly in the exploitation or domination of the weaker countries. Economic imperialism, according to this view, will result from the simple fact that some economies are able consistently to command a higher price for their goods and services, earning a kind of international monopoly rent. This position seems to be a rather broad one where the term "imperialist" becomes a disparaging remark to hurl at any group or individual whose behaviour we dislike. In order to retain something of the original meaning of the term, it is necessary to have state decision makers involved in the imperialist action at some point. The questions we should be asking are: At what point do public officials get involved in economic imperialism? Why do they act? How far does their influence run? These are not easy questions to answer, as earlier chapters in this volume, which examined the role of the state, have shown. Some preliminary points can be made concerning whether or not state officials typically act (1) in the national interest, (2) on their own behalf, (3) at the instigation of powerful economic classes, or (4) out of some combination of these three motives.

Let us further consider these three alternative perspectives on state involvement. First, establishing whether economic imperialism is in the national interest requires assessing not only the tangible flows of trade and investment, but the very intangible elements of prestige, national pride, and the like. To ask a Briton at the turn of the 19th century whether imperial policies were in the national interest would probably have provoked an incredulous or hostile answer. Most shared vicariously in the glory of the Empire "on which the sun never set." Marxists frequently ascribe the willingness of the English working class to support imperialist ventures and wars to a temporary false consciousness on the part of the masses. Hilferding, for example, argued that expansionism was given ideological justification by "deflection of the national idea and racial ideology" in the direction of imperialism.[7] Interestingly, a prominent non-Marxist historian of imperialism, D.K. Fieldhouse, took a similar view, arguing that modern imperialism was "the product of a national mass hysteria which led eventually to fascism and World War II." According to Fieldhouse, it was not business people and bankers who pushed the state toward support for economic imperialism but rather politicians who allowed their behaviour to be dictated by mass opinion.[8] Such motivation for imperialist policies runs pretty close to a popular notion of "national interest," at least in the short term.

The second possibility for state involvement suggests the triumph of "official" preferences over any private individual or group. When referring to the organizational source of these preferences, we generally look back to Max Weber's work on bureaucracy. Weber approved of the imperial enterprise, especially as conducted by his newly unified German state after 1871. He combined a focus on state roles and coercive characteristics with sociological accounts of imperialism, and argued that it was partly prestige considerations that led the European powers to engage in overseas expansion. The German ruling classes who occupied state roles had a vested interest in imperialism because the extension of national sovereignty increased their social prestige and buttressed what might otherwise have been waning social privilege and political prominence. Economic imperialism is explicable by reference to the preferences that officials had for extending or entrenching policies for which the bureaucratic apparatus was suited. Schumpeter's sociological reference to the persistent influence of the "warrior class" fits with this Weberian kind of explanation. While we cannot easily resolve whether the colonial office, army, or traders were most influential, we can say that noneconomic and nonsecurity motives must have underpinned the imperial scramble for possessions from 1870 on.

The third way to explain economic imperialism is to examine the purely economic returns of state intervention in foreign investment and international commerce. If we see economic imperialism simply as a matter of economic cost and benefit, it is reasonably easy to assess the rationality of imperial enterprise such as British rule in India. To assess the costs and benefits of imperial possessions, one must simply show that the monopoly on trading opportunities in controlled territories yields returns above the cost of preserving that monopoly. The heart of the current liberal critique of imperialism is that it simply did not repay the security costs borne by the imperial state, let alone the general costs of lost growth in world trade through the obstruction of national specialization and the laws of comparative advantage. Thus, liberal proponents of global free trade are quick to seek nonrational behaviour in their explanations of the European scramble for imperial possessions. It is interesting, however, to note that there was virtual consensus among classical economic thinkers before 1914 that the capitalist economy needed overseas markets and investment opportunities and that it might be necessary to obtain them by imperialist means.[9] We now accept that economic imperialism runs counter to liberalism and is inherently exclusive, since its essence is to establish a preferred trading position by formal control or informal threats. Economic imperialism is, broadly speaking, the opposite of free trade.

Most Marxists agree that economic imperialism does not serve the national interest of either the dominating state or the dominated peoples. They see benefits only to those with control over the investment of capital and the means of production. Classical liberal economists share this view on benefits, but for different reasons. They adhere to Ricardo and the alleged maximizing of growth that flows from free trade and the specialization of national economies in certain goods under comparative advantage. Notwithstanding the variations in the dependency school, which are discussed elsewhere in this volume, the Marxian critique of economic imperialism is that it is a policy adopted by imperial capitalist states at the behest or on behalf of the dominant class. One set of losers under this policy are the workers in the metropole (because capitalism can continue to grow without raising their living standards). Another set of losers are the workers in the periphery who are doubly exploited by foreign capital and indigenous compradors (collaborators). But, before we discuss the current forms and costs of economic imperialism, it will be of help to consider, a little more carefully, various theoretical positions.

Imperialism: The Debate Outlined

Marx and Marxists

Although Marxist analysis does not enjoy a monopoly in the literature on economic imperialism, a good deal of intellectual energy has been expended in analyzing Marx's discussion of capitalist dynamics in the European context and applying them to the contemporary North-South conflict. As one close adherent to Marxian thought has pointed out, "in no other field has Marxism succeeded in so influencing — even dominating — the thought of mankind."[10] Several excellent readers are available that provide an insight into the debate on imperialism among Marxists, and there is neither room nor need in this chapter for a full rehearsal of it.[11] It is the major points of contention that are important, and they can be summarized as follows.

First, did Marx care about the effects of economic imperialism in the Third World? There is only a scant and disparate collection of readings that address this question. Marx was passionate on the subject of the British subjugation of Ireland (the so-called Irish question), but he did not make explicit the similarities of the imperial relationship between England and Ireland and English domination of the Third World. Without question, the vast majority of Marxian analysis is concerned with European political economy. It is also possible to find in Marx's writing, and in his personal life, signs of what is now widely criticized as "Eurocentrism." One can find references, even in the crusading *Manifesto of the Communist Party*, to Third World examples of the "idiocy of rural life," which suggests that Marx was insensitive to the unique and distinctive cultures of Third World societies.

Second, what would Marx have said about the Third World if he had been able to find the time for the same level of detailed analysis he provided for Europe? While this question is a crucial one, the truth is that we just do not know what Marx's assessment of Third World development in the wake of European capitalism would have been. One author has suggested that Marx was quite worried that an indigenous development would take place in Asia that would confound the alleged universality of his theory of social dialectic.[12] Another compilation notes that occasional Third World references in his major works, together with his newspaper articles, suggest that Marx was speaking tongue-in-cheek when he sang the praises of the revolutionary role of the European capitalists as the major dynamic of world history. (Marx saw social change rooted in the relationship of various classes to the dominant means of producing goods and services and thus seemed to express admiration for the way in which the bourgeoisie overthrew the old feudal order.) Marx would, in this view, have conducted a more thorough condemnation of colonialism had time permitted.[13]

Third, can the dialectic of class struggle operate in poor countries during or after their subjugation to imperialism or is autonomous national development inhibited? This issue is central to the debate that goes on among neo-Marxists. Dependency scholars are especially prone to deny the potential for an indigenous process of class-formation and consequent development via class struggle. Others have gone through extraordinary intellectual contortions to prove that indigenous capitalist and proletarian social formations preceded and survived the impact of colonialism and economic imperialism.[14] If we look at what Marx himself had to say, there are not very many clues. He did make reference to a distinctive "Asiatic mode" of production that was neither primitive nor part of the dialectic. In broad terms, though, Marx's own polemic that the Third World has "no history" shows that he saw European capitalism as the dynamo of socioeconomic development for the whole world. Analyses targeted specifically at Third World social formations thus fall well outside the mainstream of Marxian thought.

Aside from these three questions, there remains the problem of the state and imperialism. Marxist analysis tends to assume that an explanation of imperialism is adequate if it is shown that imperialist policies serve the interests of important factions of the capitalist class. But, the most interesting aspects of the debate about imperialism centre on the balance of costs and benefits for the metropolitan economy. To infer imperialism in any profits made in the Third World is to depoliticize the concept and to inhibit research into the pressures confronting policy makers who decide how far and in what way to support their community of traders and investors overseas.

Lenin attempted to combine Marxian analysis of capitalism with some very practical concerns of fomenting and preserving the Bolshevik Revolution. These constraints may explain his borrowing heavily from Marx, from Hilferding, and from the British liberal economist Hobson in developing the "theory" of imperialism as a further stage after capitalism in the social dialectic. The importance attached to Lenin's pamphlet on imperialism rests in its enthusiastic adoption in the Third World, rather than in its theoretical merits. Lenin's thesis was that monopoly capital would naturally lead to rivalry and conflict between capitalist-dominated states. While not paying much attention to the specifics of development in the subject territories, Lenin generally saw the export of capital accelerating development in the Third World through provision of infrastructure, such as railways and ports.[15] His focus was on the metropoles, where he saw imperialism as having a reactionary impact; profits earned abroad made it possible to pay a segment of the working class at higher rates and thus to transform them into a conservative "labour aristocracy."

Bill Warren has elicited an often vigorous attack from fellow Marxists for his interpretation and application of Marx's Third World writing and for his consequent criticism of Lenin's theory of imperialism. Lenin, he argued, "ignored the major analytical achievements of Marxist economics in favour of a crude under-consumption buttressed by superficial observations by the bourgeois liberal propagandist Hobson."[16] (Underconsumption refers to the notion that capitalists had to seek markets abroad because, in their search for higher profits, they paid workers too little to keep the home economy growing.) Warren has also locked horns with dependency theorists over his controversial thesis that imperialism has operated to the benefit of the Third World in absolute terms and relative to the more-developed economies. The very process of imperial conquest was beneficial, according to Warren: "[Direct colonialism] acted as a powerful agent of progressive social change, advancing capitalist development far more rapidly than was conceivable in any other way, both by its destructive effects on pre-capitalist social systems and by its implantation of elements of capitalism."[17] As a Marxist, he is clearly not without reservations over the impact of imperialism on subject peoples; his thesis follows from the orthodoxy that the spread of capitalism furthers the process of class struggle and, hence, the achievement of socialism. He castigates those neo-Marxists who argue the pessimistic underdevelopment thesis for their reluctance to acknowledge the development in the Third World of a proletarian working class: "capitalism's gravedigger." One can criticize this position for being ethnocentric and deterministic. Still, it is hard to oppose Warren's distaste for the tendency of Third World leaders and dependency theorists to externalize the blame for the plight of their poor. It is also plausible that Third World leaders have found in dependency theory a marvellous ideology for deflecting responsibility from their part in economic failure. Such use of the ideology is especially condemning for a body of literature that claims to influence revolutionary praxis rather than simply to persuade scholars of an analytical position.

Paul Baran is credited as being the Marxist who brought the periphery more into the mainstream of analytical concerns for Marxists. While they varied with respect to timing, Marx, Lenin, and Warren all expected full capitalist development to occur in the Third World. Baran took a closer look at what was happening in the periphery of the capitalist system and suggested that these areas were experiencing a much different pattern of development from that experienced by the advanced economies. Like Lenin's, his analysis of capitalism centred on the problems associated with monopoly capitalism. Baran argued that monopoly capitalism led to a diversion of output from productive investment to wasteful uses in luxury consumer goods and military expenditures. He saw this waste as especially pronounced in the underdeveloped countries, where economic "surplus" that remained after profits had been repatriated was being absorbed by luxury spending of a small elite. Economic imperialism, then, was contributing to the stagnation of the Third World and not to its revolutionary development.[18]

Michael Barratt-Brown is not properly described as a Marxist, but his major works have been devoted to exploring the viability of the Marxist critique of imperialism. His main contribution has been to show that Keynesian analysis of the role of the state in providing the conditions for steady domestic economic growth is also a powerful means to explain foreign economic policy. (Keynes is credited with developing the theory that underpinned deficit spending by governments so as to avoid extreme troughs in the business cycle, such as the Great Depression of the 1930s.) Because of its focus on the role of state decision makers in economic affairs, Keynesian theory is a politically sensitive explanation of imperialism. Marxist theory, by contrast, argues basically that it is falling rates of profit at home that impel capitalists to pursue foreign markets and to dragoon the state into supporting and protecting them. Economic imperialism, according to Keynes, precedes capitalism and is at least as old as the mercantilist era of the 16th and 17th centuries, when Spain, for example, established its Mexican empire and British ships sought to pirate the proceeds. These risky ventures were pursued to accumulate wealth, which was seen as a measure and a source of national strength. Keynesian analysis of these older forms of imperialism and the more recent European empires combines economic motivation with state concerns in a way that no Marxists attempt. Keeping this Keynesian role of the state in mind, we can move on to examine theories of imperialism that find causes beyond the internal tensions and pressures of capitalism in the imperialist powers.

Liberals, Objectivists, and Peripheral Theorists

If any common theme can be found in the respected non-Marxist discussions of imperialism, it is a distrust of simple, monocausal explanations, such as Marxists offer, of the falling rate of profit and related capitalist concerns. The following section will cover some of these historical critiques of theories centred on economic causes. Unfortunately, the more detailed and accurate the analysis of imperialism, the more complex it becomes. Consider, for example, a useful distinction drawn among capitalists who tend to be treated as a homogeneous bloc by Marx and others. David Landes has observed that there was a real difference in the attitudes and the demands made by capitalists upon state officials, depending on the type of investments they had made: "businessmen at home . . . entertained far less illusions about the profitability of colonial ventures than the adventurers, chauvinists and statesmen who exhorted them to invest and become rich."[19] Landes is also noteworthy for his clear expression of the "objectivist" thesis that imperialism was inevitable because of the economic and military weakness of the periphery. According to this view, the European states played a role in economic imperialism only when the power vacuum in overseas territories left them no choice but to intervene in order to put a stop to "general plunder and piracy." Like the realists, with their theory of power politics, objectivists hold that the world system cannot long tolerate a vacuum in the distribution of power: weakness inevitably leads to domination by the strong. This line is taken by Ronald Robinson and John Gallagher, the influential and controversial analysts of Victorian imperialism whose thesis is basically one of peripheral pull rather than centre push. Contrary to the Marxist idea of an automatic bond between capital and state, Robinson and Gallagher find that the "official mind" was hesitant and distrustful of schemes leading to the expansion of empire. And opposing the notion of an internal dynamic for formal imperialism, they find that "the imperialist actions of the great powers were generally provoked by crises in third-world territories."[20] The Robinson–Gallagher argument is a step toward a political-security theory of imperialism. Even more interesting is their denial that the most intensive period of imperialism was driven by the interests of capital looking for foreign investors: "from the 1880s onwards economic expansion tended to follow territorial expansion: economic arguments were generally adduced as afterthoughts to justify territorial gains that had already taken place."[21]

D.K. Fieldhouse is prominent among those who argue that too much attention has been paid to the forces at the capitalist centre when accounting for imperial policies. While acknowledging that politicians in Europe were subject to pressure from public opinion to persist in the scramble for colonial possessions, Fieldhouse also noted "peripheral" causes of imperialism. A period of intensive and formal annexation of territory took place after 1870. In a persuasive critique of Hobson's allegations that this imperialism was forced upon the state by finance capital, Fieldhouse argues: "the obvious driving force of British expansion since 1870 appeared to lie in the explorers, missionaries, engineers, patriotic pressure groups, and empire minded politicians, all of whom had evident influence, and had demonstrable interests, other than those of investment, in territorial acquisitions."[22] Herein begins a movement to a "peripheral" explanation of imperialism. Fieldhouse certainly puts the locus of the explanation outside the inner sanctum of the dominant economic class, but he draws a rather broad causal picture and mixes state officials and public opinion in Britain with the influence of people actually working in the imperial territories. Still, it is useful to consider that the strongest pressure for formal imperialism came from those actually working in the field. (The same argument might be made today, concerning pressure to restructure or increase official development assistance.) Elsewhere, Fieldhouse argues more strongly for a peripheral dynamic to imperialism. He suggests two main forms: first, an informal arrangement with local peoples by traders and other "subimperial" people on the spot, and second, formal imperialism after the collapse of traditional methods of informal co-operation between native elites and Europeans.

While it is not his primary purpose, Schumpeter offers a sociological explanation for imperialism that implies some costs for the imperialist economy. He found a way to explain the economic irrationality of imperialism in the continued political influence of those whose predecessors had participated in classical imperialism of plunder and extortion of tribute. Families that had risen to social dominance in feudal times through armed prowess continued to influence policy in the more benign days of capitalist democracy. Schumpeter argued that strife and armed conflict among imperial powers did not derive from inherent expansionist pressures of capitalism. Rather, as a classical liberal economist, Schumpeter wished to demonstrate that growth could proceed under free trade and need not result in a clash over markets, materials, or labour. If nothing else, Schumpeter can claim for his theory the achievement of having predicted World War I. We can draw a comparison between Schumpeter's 19th-century irrational imperialists and the 20th-century military-industrial complex, which allegedly subordinates national security to the mundane interests of bureaucrats in maximizing their budgets in collusion with defence contractors.

For the liberal John Hobson, economic imperialism was a problem to be understood chiefly in terms of the effects that it had on the imperial economy itself. Hobson's theory of economic imperialism is relatively straightforward and elegant; unfortunately, it is also wrong in important respects. Critics have shown that Hobson was guilty of assuming causality in what was a mere correlation between expanding trade and the extension of formal empire. It is interesting to recall, then, that Lenin's analysis drew heavily on Hobson's "underconsumption" thesis.

Hobson argued that the failure of capitalists to pay a decent wage to their workers led to a crisis of underconsumption in the domestic economy. He understood the British Empire chiefly as a means to absorb the immense productivity (i.e., surplus) of British industry by securing foreign markets. More sophisticated in political analysis is Hobson's argument that the British state was influenced in its imperial policies by the need to find a home for the rapidly obsolescing (but still politically influential) landed aristocracy. Using James Mills's pithy phrase, Hobson described the British Empire as a "vast system of outdoor relief for the upper classes."[23] In Hobson's view, then, the British Empire was not exclusively economic in motivation; it yielded benefits restricted to a relatively small class of capitalists and an even smaller class of landed aristocrats. Imperialism was to be understood as an economic instrument of a politically influential class. The concepts of national interest, strategic goals, and cultural mission were seen by Hobson as a smokescreen for this basically economic imperialist motivation. He prescribed an increase in the wages paid to British workers as a means to escape the alternatives of empire and foreign investment.

Before moving on to consider in more detail the current manifestations of economic imperialism, it is useful to summarize from the foregoing debate just what we mean when we use the term. Here, we must return to the questions raised about the extent of participation by state officials in economic imperialism. Clearly, there is a consensus of sorts that some kind of influence must be wielded over the territories in the *imperium*. The key question that we cannot resolve fully is whether that influence is intentional or accidental, whether it is the product of deliberate state security policy or whether policy is rather tailored to promote the interests of powerful economic groups. The main questions raised during the debate, and some indications of the evidence required (or available) to address them, are the following.

Does economic imperialism provide benefits to the metropolitan economy as a whole, in part, or not at all? The kind of evidence applied to this question is typically large-scale, time-series data about flow rates of investment, expansion of trade, and growth in GNP. We can examine the evidence on the flow of goods, or better, the net value of trade from imperial possessions, and contrast it with the cost of installing the provisions for security. Such comparison would help us to evaluate the argument of the early classical liberal economists and the Marxists that imperialism was a necessary and beneficial aspect of growing capitalism. Note, however, that the mere existence of some evidence of net economic benefits does not necessarily mean that state involvement in imperialism was merely mercenary or undertaken at the behest of the capitalist class. Macrolevel data simply give us the confidence to explore the relationship further through examination of governmental records, memoranda, and so forth. According to Paul Kennedy's recent massive discussion of empire, we should not expect to find benefits in the long run. The costs of maintaining a global presence, in fact, lead to the ultimate waning of imperialist states as world powers; the United States may be the latest "overextended" state, with an economy currently suffering from the cumulative burden of its post–World War II empire.[24]

Does economic imperialism retard or advance the social, political, and economic development of subject economies? Again, the evidence to answer this question tends to be of a macro nature, even though the analysis of underdevelopment often calls for microlevel data, showing relative movements in standard of living of groups and classes at the periphery, such as urban-rural differences. Mere increases in gross national product or volume of trade may have to be discounted in developmental terms if the growth is at the expense of a narrowing economic base leading to lost self-sufficiency and dependence on imports for key commodities. Even if we could find a net gain in economic well-being, measured by sensitive indicators such as infant mortality and literacy rates, we might still want to qualify our assessment of the impact of imperialism as a development force. Economic imperialism may have political effects such as the weakening of sovereignty or the distorting of indigenous bureaucratic capacity, which are extremely difficult to measure.

Is economic imperialism an independent state policy or a result of socio-economic pressure? In other words, does trade follow the flag or lead it? This is the central question, from the point of view of our concern with the role of the state as a dynamic in economic imperialism. Imperialist policies tend to benefit at least part of a significant social group, but the data required to prove the influence of that group over state policy tend to be qualitative rather than quantitative. Marxists assert that, at best, the state can only be relatively autonomous from the demands and needs of the capitalist class. Keynesians argue that state intervention in the economy is increasingly motivated by broad public goals. And there is currently a lively revival of the debate concerning the centrality of state structures and socialization patterns in determining events ranging from implementation of public policy to social revolution.[25] It may be impossible to satisfactorily resolve the issue of state involvement in economic imperialism. Any comprehensive theory of imperialism is likely to oversimplify the reality that confronts the investors and policy makers of the day. Still, our review of the historical debate serves as a useful foundation for the discussion of contemporary economic imperialism. The days of direct colonial rule are past: economic dependence today is more likely to involve a complex relationship between international banks, transnational firms, intergovernmental agencies, governments, and influential national elites or classes.

Current Forms and Agents of Economic Imperialism

The poor are always with us, as the old adage goes, and for Marxists so, too, is exploitation. They tend to infer economic imperialism from the mere fact of inequality in living standards and in national economic performance. One of the most powerful images of exploitation is the extraction of mineral wealth from a poor country to feed the advanced industrial economy of a wealthy one. Exploitation is also demonstrated by the persistence of a low relative value for raw materials as compared with manufactured goods. Low prices paid for raw materials condemn the poor country to a perpetual role as a hewer of wood and drawer of water. In addition, the Third World may increasingly bear the environmental costs associated with production of mineral wealth through damaging processes such as strip mining, or with the manufacture of hazardous chemicals. This new "international division of labour" may come to be regarded as equally exploitative to the economic imperialism that incorporated Third World countries into the world capitalist system. This section looks at some important economic interactions between rich and poor states and asks whether they fit the mould of imperialist relations of threat and submission.

Direct Foreign Investment

The tendency to replace equity investment with direct foreign investment in mining, manufacturing, and marketing is one of the most striking changes to occur in the international political economy since World War II. Marx predicted that capitalism would spread throughout the globe, but he did not foresee the form in which that spread now seems most vibrant. Transnational capitalism is far removed from the nationally based venture capital that Marx considered; Lenin came only a little closer to predicting the future with his focus on monopoly capitalism. To the extent that markets in the communist countries are opened up to the giant transnational firms, we may even see a reversal in the revolutionary dialectic that Marx held would culminate in socialism. Our main purpose is to see whether there is a direct link between the "transnationalization" of capital and imperialist exploitation and domination.

Since the majority of the world's multinational corporations are based in the United States (though Japan is gaining some ground here), it is tempting to infer that American regional policies are primarily geared to protecting or promoting the interests of these firms. Those accepting this view usually cite the sorry episode in the early 1970s when Chilean president Salvador Allende was driven out of office and to his death in part because of an alliance between the Nixon–Kissinger White House and International Telephone and Telegraph (ITT), the giant multinational conglomerate. While there was doubtless collusion between corporate and state decision makers in this instance, it is hard to prove a systematic influence over U.S. policy by big business. Stephen Krasner has demonstrated, in fact, that State Department officials, at least, are relatively insulated from corporate pressures and tend to develop and stick to policies on the grounds of national interest, as they themselves would define it.[26] In any event, it seems hard to draw a direct line between the economic interests of U.S. corporations and U.S. foreign policy. If such a line existed, it might lead to more influence on the Japanese economy to accommodate concerns of American industry, rather than to pressure on the still-underdeveloped economies of Central America, where U.S. foreign policy is far more active.

Since there are not always immediate returns to direct foreign investment, it has been suggested that special dynamics are at work to impel the giant corporations to continue to invest where short-run profits are low. Even if we accept the notion that imperialism is led by the economic interests of the dominant class, it is often hard to explain why the major multinational firms pay so much attention to relatively insignificant markets, as, for example, the giant pharmaceutical firms do in East Africa. Students of the multinational corporations have found that a desire for long-range planning (backed by extensive resources) leads multinational corporations to take out insurance by establishing marketing footholds even in countries where aggregate purchasing power is weak. The charge that can be laid against these firms, as well as those earning large profits now, is that they inhibit the development of local commerce and subordinate national economic interests to the global marketing strategy set in corporate headquarters in European or North American capitals.[27] This strategy may include unfair competition with harmful effects, but it is hard to see how today's transnational capitalism can be compared to the direct state role in the annexation of colonial territories during European imperialism.

Transnational business has had a tremendous impact in the less-developed countries; but the extent and nature of state involvement in protecting or promoting these firms' activity varies so dramatically that it would be simplistic to attach the label "economic imperialism" to all direct foreign investment.

Trade

To allege economic imperialism in trade relations one has to adopt the perspectives of one of the neo-Marxist dependency scholars who find exploitation in differential wage rates between centre and periphery or in the whole process of exchange within the capitalist world economy. Raoul Prebisch, a Latin American economist and the first secretary general of the United Nations Conference on Trade and Development, argued that the development of the South had been unfairly restricted by trade and investment relations with the more-developed countries. His historical analysis alleged that economic imperialism was inherent in the nominally free exchange of goods between North and South. Apparently the economies of South America grew fastest during times of war or other crises that involved the European metropoles. This point was later elaborated by André Gunder Frank and by Latin American dependency theorists who are discussed in the next chapter.

Immanuel Wallerstein has argued that Marx's writings were pitched at the wrong level of analysis because trade had already spread capitalism throughout the world and created an integrated system by the 16th century. This system was one in which some areas extract profit through the mechanism of unequal exchange between raw materials and more highly processed goods. Thus, the class structures in various parts of the world resulted from their respective place in the world system. Holders of political power in the peripheral areas of the system would stay in office only so long as they facilitated the transfer of profit to the dominant metropoles by maintaining sufficient order for profitable trade and investment. This systemic division of labour contradicts orthodox Marxist theory, which sees the national capitalist revolution in 18th- and 19th-century Europe spilling over to shape the rest of the world through imperialism.[28]

While there are flaws in Wallerstein's analysis of the world system, it is useful to consider the possibility that obstacles are placed in the path of free trade by powerful states who wish to protect their relative advantage in the international political economy. Certainly, there are political implications to controlling the direction and content of trade, and the developed economies remain reluctant to drop tariff and nontariff barriers to the entry of goods from the Third World. However, there are enough exceptions to the rule of a fixed international division of labour (even given some possibilities for promotion from periphery to semiperiphery) that we cannot take trade relations alone as an indication of economic imperialism.

Private and Government Loans

According to critics of the contemporary international political economy, the major banks (and a good number of minor ones too) have been guilty of exploiting the desire of Third World countries to pursue rapid growth. The argument runs as follows. Faced with the huge increase in deposits by Arab states after the oil-price hike of 1973, European and American banks sought outlets for the capital by making loans to Third World states. The banks relaxed normal risk criteria in setting interest rates and found many Third World governments willing to guarantee loans for projects that turned out to have marginal or dubious commercial value. The willingness of countries to borrow was boosted by their expectations of finding export markets in the developed countries for the goods produced by factories financed with foreign loans. Instead, the world economy went into recession, and barriers against Third World exports were maintained or strengthened. From the late 1970s onward, Third World borrowers found that the burden of meeting their interest payments was stifling growth. At present, austerity measures are in place in many of the major borrowers (such as Mexico), which critics interpret as making the poor pay for the profligacy of Third World elites and for the unscrupulousness of international finance.[29]

Was this economic imperialism or bad luck? If we apply our criteria of state participation in imperialist relations of threat and submission, it is hard to sustain a view that the goal of the advanced capitalist states was to purposefully burden the Third World with debt. If anything, the policy makers in the North were guilty of allowing the financial markets to operate with insufficient regulation. Now that the debt problem is well and truly entrenched, however, it is possible to be more critical of "adjustment" policies imposed with the collaboration of the major capitalist states. They have imposed structural-adjustment conditions in return for extending further credit or for postponement of interest payments. Given the dramatic sociopolitical impact that they can have on subjected countries, control over conditions for debt relief offers as powerful an economic lever over the Third World as any used during the period of direct colonial rule. Low-income oil-importing countries are giving up autonomy in important domestic-policy areas because of the threat of losing access to further credit. Subsidies on basic foods, the wages of government employees, and exchange rates have been subjected to the "domination" of the IMF and other such creditor actions. Since it was Third World borrowing that kept the world's capitalist financial markets solvent after the oil-price hike, there is an added touch of injustice to the failure of the main players to find a way to relieve debts instead of merely rolling them over and forcing citizens in the Third World to tighten their belts.

Government-to-government loans have been grouped with other forms of bilateral aid as another aspect of economic imperialism. Cheryl Payer led the way among left-wing critics in her claim that official development assistance (ODA) actually tends to underdevelop the economy of the recipient countries in addition to lending political support to oppressive regimes.[30] Interestingly, some critics of aid from the right of the political spectrum argue that the same problems will result from aid. But the right wing alleges that it is the leaders of corrupt Third World governments who are exploiting both the poor in their own countries and the taxpayers in the rich who finance ODA.[31] It seems that the critics of aid are on shaky ground when they allege imperialism in the benefits that rebound to aid-givers through tying grants to purchases of goods and services in the donor state. After all, there are no sanctions for refusing aid, and only the poorest states now are forced to accept aid that they can't use. More serious and more sophisticated is the argument that the ODA system links bureaucratic elites in recipient and donor countries in a relationship that biases development policy toward unsuitable and inefficient investments. Such development policies result in continued patterns of dependency in trade and perhaps in further weakening the fibre of government decision making. Still, this is a long way from the extraction of tribute in the Roman *imperium*, and we are well-advised to treat the concept of imperialism in economic aid with caution.

Intergovernmental Organizations

It has become commonplace to find charges of undue political influence and economic injustice levelled at the major intergovernmental financial institutions. Space does not permit a full account, but most students of international relations are probably familiar with the argument that the International Monetary Fund (IMF) is not a truly intergovernmental organization because its policies are dominated by the voting power of the United States and other Western industrialized countries. It is further asserted that the conditions imposed by the IMF for balance-of-payments assistance are rigidly and unfairly applied to countries with questionable affiliation to the United States. Jamaica's socialist prime minister, Michael Manley, found IMF restrictions on public spending and price supports to be a recipe for social unrest and, ultimately, for the defeat of his government by pro-American Edward Seaga, who quickly won IMF support. A third point of criticism concerning the power of the IMF is that, without its approval for a government's program of readjustment, private banks will not offer the credit needed to maintain debt servicing and new investment. In its defence, the IMF claims that most of the social hardship caused by its conditions results from delays in calling for its teams of analysts and advisers. Still, it might be noted that, because of strict adherence to rules that were, after all, set by the major states in the system, the IMF has been taking money out of Africa over the past five years for repayment of earlier loans at a time when these countries are in great need and shunned by the private capital markets.

It seems to be stretching the term too far to label an intergovernmental organization as imperialist. Charges of economic imperialism can arise, however, when IMF actions are viewed as an instrument of U.S. policy. Just as the British state has been charged with imperialism in imposing a system of free trade on the world when this was to its advantage, the United States can be labelled as imperialist in imposing a debt regime that is unfavourable to borrowers. However, as was noted in the first part of this chapter, we tend to call this hegemonic activity rather than imperialism.

Conclusion

Is Economic Imperialism a Threat to Peace?

Historically, there is evidence to suggest that economic factors have played a major part in conflict among states. The literature contains a wide range of opinion, from those who see trade following the path paved by state security policies to those who argue that political and imperial ventures are forced on reluctant decision makers by bold traders and overseas investors. The contemporary scene contains much ambivalence. On the one hand, the primary sources of conflict in today's bipolar system centre on regional tensions and nuclear deterrence, neither of which has much to do with economic imperialism. On the other hand, there is reason to suppose that the continued expansion of transnational corporate activity is laying more American (and other OECD) capital open to the threat of nationalization. This threat may well pull the American state into a supporting or protecting role, as occurred when the Marines were sent by President Lyndon Johnson into the Dominican Republic.

A rather more subtle line of argument suggests that competition for markets, sources of raw materials, and the like has always been an important way in which states established prestige ranking and competed for increased capabilities. Economic imperialism becomes rather more than a subtext to the great game of military and strategic security. The campaign to win access to areas of present and potential value was not simply a means of building up the war-making capabilities of states but was an exercise in intrinsic symbolic and strategic importance. The "Scramble for Africa," for example, that took place among the European powers in the late 19th century can be seen as a state-initiated series of events rather than a consequence of commercial lobbying. Germany had lagged in both state-consolidation and economic modernization and thus found itself short of imperial possessions commensurate with its perceived status by the turn of the 20th century. Hence the argument that World War I was partly explained by perceptions of "status deprivation" on the part of German decision makers.

The question then becomes whether there are now similar feelings of deprivation that might lead to interstate rivalry expressed through economic imperialism. A reasonable prediction would be that states will continue to value economic performance as a means of ranking. Indeed, in an age where major-power conflict is deterred by the presence of nuclear weapons, economic competition may have taken an even more important place in state interaction. But the result need not be competition between the major powers for colonial possessions. Rather, economic competition is likely to take place in the negotiations of interdependence or, if we are unlucky, through protectionist interactions. The main economic cleavage will continue to be between North and South, but the most attention will be focussed on relations among advanced economies and the newly industrializing economies. Third World markets and raw materials will be secured not by imperialism but by co-operation of dependent elites and classes. Economic imperialism does not persist in any form that is likely to lead to interstate conflict.

Is Economic Imperialism a Threat to Development?

Most of the contemporary concerns of those critical of economic imperialism centre on development issues rather than on conflict. As a consequence, it is appropriate that we end this chapter with a summation of the applicability of economic imperialism to describe the relations between rich and poor countries and the various organizations that mediate the relationship. Clearly many areas of the Third World remain very much in the role of producers of raw materials with a low value added relative to the manufactured goods of the North. But it is also true that some areas of the periphery have succeeded in making the transition away from a political economy of dependence on raw materials. Would anyone argue that Hong Kong, South Korea, or Taiwan is the victim of imperialism? If so, there are many countries in the periphery that would willingly share their fate. These newly industrializing economies are highly integrated into the world economy and thus present problems for theories that see underdevelopment for Third World countries that participate in the world capitalist system.

In general I have argued that while the relations between rich and poor states involve varied and extensive costs for the Third World, we lack the evidence of direct state involvement in the "threats and submissions" that characterize economic imperialism. Some of the most prominent contemporary economic actors (such as transnational firms and intergovernmental financial institutions) are not "national" in the strict sense of the word, and their impact on development has to be assessed independently of competition between states for economic advantage.[32]

We cannot escape the great debate between those with faith in the developmental power of capitalism and those who deny it. Both orthodox Marxists and classical liberals believe that capitalism can and must spread throughout the world in order for every country to achieve its full material and social potential. Neo-Marxists and neoconservatives hold that relations between advanced and underdeveloped countries are unlikely to result in benefits for the "junior partners." Evidence for international economic exploitation can certainly be found today, but the forms in which it takes place are diverse and the effects often long-term. There is certainly room for caution in applying the concept of economic imperialism to these contemporary relations.

NOTES

1. See Karl Deutsch, *The Analysis of International Relations* (Englewood Cliffs, N.J.: Prentice-Hall, 1978), 263–76, for a discussion of imperialism as "highly unequal interdependence."

2. Robert O. Keohane, *After Hegemony: Cooperation and Discord in the World Political Economy* (Princeton: Princeton University Press, 1984). See also Michael K. Hawes, "Structural Change and Hegemonic Decline," in this volume.

3. For commentary on the steady incorporation of economic variables into the analysis of international relations, see Joan Edelman Spero, *The Politics of International Economic Relations*, 3d ed. (New York: St. Martin's, 1985); and David H. Blake and Robert S. Walters, *The Politics of Global Economic Relations*, 3d ed. (Englewood Cliffs, N.J.: Prentice-Hall, 1987).

4. See David Baldwin's critique of the pure realist position in his *Economic Statecraft* (Princeton: Princeton University Press, 1985).

5. The pioneering work is Robert O. Keohane and Joseph S. Nye, *Power and Interdependence: World Politics in Transition* (Boston: Little, Brown, 1977).

6. For a useful overview of work in this area, see Peter B. Evans, "Transnational Linkages and the Role of the States," in *Bringing the State Back In*, ed. Peter B. Evans, Dietrich Rueschmeyer, and Theda Skocpol (Cambridge: Cambridge University Press, 1985).

7. Cited in Wolfgang Mommsen, *Theories of Imperialism* (New York: Random House, 1980), 37.

8. D.K. Fieldhouse, *Theory of Capitalist Imperialism* (London: Longman, 1967).

9. Mommsen, *Theories of Imperialism*, 9.

10. Bill Warren, *Imperialism: Pioneer of Capitalism* (London: New Left Books and Verso, 1980), 3.

11. See Anthony Brewer, *Marxist Theories of Imperialism: A Critical Survey* (London and Boston: Routledge and Kegan Paul, 1980); Robert I. Rhodes, ed., *Imperialism and Underdevelopment: A Reader* (New York: Monthly Review Press, 1971); R. Owen and B. Sutcliffe, eds., *Studies in the Theory of Imperialism* (London: Longman, 1972).

12. Umberto Melotti, *Marx and the Third World* (Atlantic Highlands, N.J.: Humanities Press, 1977).

13. Shlomo Avineri, ed., *Karl Marx on Colonialism and Modernization: His Dispatches and other Writings on China, India, Mexico, the Middle East and North Africa* (Garden City, N.Y.: Doubleday, 1968).

14. See, for example, Nicola Swainson, *The Development of Corporate Capitalism in Kenya: 1918–1978* (London: Heinemann, 1979). The *Review of African Political Economy* has carried many contributions to the debate on Third World capitalism.

15. V.I. Lenin, *Imperialism: The Highest Stage of Capitalism: A Popular Outline* (Peking: Foreign Languages Press, 1975).

16. Warren, *Imperialism*, 4.

17. Warren, *Imperialism*, 9.

18. Paul Baran, *The Political Economy of Growth* (New York: Monthly Review Press, 1957).

19. Cited in Mommsen, *Theories of Imperialism*, 79.

20. Mommsen, *Theories of Imperialism*, 101.

21. Mommsen, *Theories of Imperialism*, 102.

22. D.K. Fieldhouse, "'Imperialism': An Historiographical Revision," in *Economic Imperialism: A Book of Readings*, ed. Kenneth Boulding (Ann Arbor: University of Michigan Press, 1972), 100.

23. J.A. Hobson, *Imperialism: A Study* (Ann Arbor: University of Michigan Press, 1965), 51.

24. Paul Kennedy, *The Rise and Fall of the Great Powers: Economic Change and Military Conflict from 1500 to 2000* (New York: Random House, 1987).

25. See Theda Skocpol, *States and Social Revolutions: A Comparative Analysis of France, Russia and China* (Cambridge: Cambridge University Press, 1979).

26. Stephen Krasner, *Defending the National Interest: Raw Materials, Investments and US Foreign Policy* (Princeton: Princeton University Press, 1978).

27. Richard Barnet and Ronald Muller, *Global Reach: The Power of the Multinational Corporations* (New York: Simon and Schuster, 1974).

28. See Brewer, *Marxist Theories of Imperialism*, 17–18.

29. Susan George, *A Fate Worse than Debt* (Harmondsworth: Penguin, 1988).

30. Teresa Hayter, *Aid as Imperialism* (Harmondsworth: Penguin, 1971).

31. See the collection of aid critiques by P.T. Bauer, *Equality, the Third World, and Economic Delusion* (Cambridge, Mass.: Harvard University Press, 1981), 66–155.

32. For a sophisticated discussion along these lines, see David G. Becker, Jeff Frieden, Sayre Schatz, and Richard Sklar, *Postimperialism: International Capitalism and Development in the Late Twentieth Century* (Boulder, Colo.: Lynne Rienner, 1987).

SELECT BIBLIOGRAPHY

Baran, Paul A. *The Political Economy of Growth*. New York: Monthly Review Press, 1957.

Barratt Brown, Michael. *The Economics of Imperialism*. Harmondsworth: Penguin, 1973.

Becker, David G.; Jeff Frieden; Sayre Schatz; and Richard Sklar. *Postimperialism: International Capitalism and Development in the Late Twentieth Century*. Boulder, Colo.: Lynne Rienner, 1987.

Boulding, Kenneth A., ed. *Economic Imperialism: A Book of Readings*. Ann Arbor: University of Michigan Press, 1972.

Brewer, Anthony. *Marxist Theories of Imperialism: A Critical Survey*. London: Routledge and Kegan Paul, 1980.

Cohen, Benjamin. *The Question of Imperialism: The Political Economy of Dominance and Dependence*. New York: Basic, 1973.

Fann, K.T., and D.C. Hodges, eds. *Readings in U.S. Imperialism*. Boston: P. Sargent, 1971.

Fieldhouse, D.K. *Theory of Capitalist Imperialism*. London: Longman, 1967.

Hayter, Teresa. *Aid as Imperialism*. Harmondsworth: Penguin, 1971.

Hobson, J.A. *Imperialism: A Study*. London: Allen and Unwin, 1938.

Jalée, Pierre. *The Pillage of the Third World*. New York: Monthly Review Press, 1968.

Kennedy, Paul. *The Rise and Fall of the Great Powers: Economic Change and Military Conflict from 1500 to 2000*. New York: Random House, 1987.

Lenin, V.I. *Imperialism: The Highest Stage of Capitalism: A Popular Outline*. Peking: Foreign Languages Press, 1975.

Lichtheim, George. *Imperialism*. New York: Praeger, 1971.

Luxemburg, Rosa. *The Accumulation of Capital*. New York: Modern Reader Paperbacks, 1968.

Magdoff, Harry. *The Age of Imperialism*. New York: Monthly Review Press, 1969.

Melotti, Umberto. *Marx and the Third World*. Atlantic Highlands, N.J.: Humanities Press, 1977.

Mommsen, Wolfgang. *Theories of Imperialism*. New York: Random House, 1980.

Niebuhr, Rheinhold. *The Structure of Nations and Empires: A Study of the Recurring Pattern*. New York: Charles Scribner's Sons, 1959.

Owen, Roger, and Bob Sutcliffe, eds. *Studies in the Theory of Imperialism*. London: Longman, 1972.

Rhodes, Robert I., ed. *Imperialism and Underdevelopment: A Reader*. New York: Monthly Review Press, 1971.

Robinson, Ronald, and John Gallagher. *Africa and the Victorians: The Official Mind of Imperialism*. New York: Anchor Books, 1968.

Schumpeter, Joseph. *Imperialism and Social Classes*. New York: A.M. Kelley, 1951.

Strachey, J. *The End of Empire*. London: Gollancz, 1959.

Warren, Bill. *Imperialism, Pioneer of Capitalism*. London: New Left Books, 1980.

Zeitlin, Irving M. *Capitalism and Imperialism: An Introduction to Neo-Marxian Concepts*. Chicago: Markham, 1972.

DEPENDENT DEVELOPMENT IN THE NEW INTERNATIONAL DIVISION OF LABOUR: PROSPECTS FOR AFRICA'S POLITICAL ECONOMY*

Timothy M. Shaw

The demise of the postwar Bretton Woods order in the early 1970s marked a period of economic instability as well as one of policy and paradigm disorder: both welfare economics and dependency began to lose their salience and influence. Though such turning points are now apparent with the hindsight of history, they were camouflaged through much of the 1970s by energy shocks, interest-rate rises, and foreign-exchange fluctuations. Ironically, just as the South was demanding a new international economic order (NIEO),[1] a new international division of labour was emerging: OPEC power and newly industrializing economy (NIE) growth marked not the rise but the demise of the Group of 77. Regrettably, much analysis and praxis within both South and North are still based on outdated assumptions. The conjuncture of the 1970s has not yet transformed paradigms, even if it has begun to change the global agenda. It has, however, brought development studies into the mainstream of the social sciences; issues of global debt, conflict, and environment are now inescapable in contemporary theory and policy.

The divergence and differentiation apparent in the South at the end of the 1980s[2] has had profound implications for theory and policy in the related areas of development studies and international relations. Despite a pronounced time lag, a few informed and enlightened analyses have appeared recently in both fields of study — from Nigel Harris's seminal *The End of the Third World* to Robert Gilpin's substantial *The Political Economy of International Relations.*[3] But, reflective of the tardiness of academic responses, the parameters of thinking in the two areas have been largely determined by reports and events of inter-

*This chapter draws on, but goes beyond, an earlier paper co-authored with Jerker Carlsson, "Issues in and Prospects for Cooperation between Africa and the International Community," presented at the OAU/ECA/African Development Bank (ADB) conference "Africa: The Challenge of Economic Recovery and Accelerated Development," at Abuja, Nigeria, in June 1987.

national organizations: the World Bank on structural adjustment and the Brandt and Palme reports.[4] If one particular approach has emerged from both academic and bureaucratic sources, it is political economy. However, within this approach there are distinctive, even antagonistic, strands — notably the nonmaterialist and materialist perspectives. Yet, it remains symptomatic of the age that political and economic forces are being juxtaposed once more, even if not integrated. The demise of Bretton Woods may eventually lead to a new paradigm and regime, but these appear to be quite distant and elusive at this point.

The concern of this chapter is that, in such an environment of uncertainty, the choices available to the least-developed countries (the so-called Fourth World), especially Africa, in the 1990s and beyond, are severely constrained not only by the immediate realities of structural adjustment but also by the continuing difficulties of the emerging global economy. The short-term agenda may be dominated by debt repayments and exchange rates, but the underlying issues are determined by internal and external inequalities in the South: the hierarchies of states and classes in the Third World that, in fact, already inform responses to the debt syndrome. No simple solution is conceivable today, if one ever was; rather, unequal opportunities are a function of uneven development.

In short, the twin transformations of internationalization and differentiation have come to define dependent development in the Third World at the end of the 20th century;[5] the result has been more dependence and less development for some states and classes than for others. The proletariat and unemployed and underemployed in Africa are particularly vulnerable and marginal in the new international division of labour. Conversely, the NIEs and the emerging bourgeoisies and peasantries of Asia and Latin America are among the more advantaged, particularly in a period of structural adjustment. However, informal sectors and illegal economies provide some compensation. If women's work and black markets are included rather than excluded, then the South is not as impoverished as it might appear to be from misleading and incomplete national accounts. Nevertheless, it is clear that most Africans have endured declining living standards over the last decade, while many in the NIEs of Asia and Latin America have enjoyed improved living standards, particularly those in the bureaucracy and industry of the NIEs.

Prospects for development, particularly in Africa, depend on a pair of dialectical responses appropriate to the current conjuncture. The first response has been indigenous policies in reaction to the difficulties and disappointments of inappropriate and unsustainable levels of structural adjustment — successive devaluations, intense deflation, privatization of welfare, desubsidization of services — from "austral" and "cruzado" plans in Latin America's NIEs[6] to rejection of Bank/Fund terms in Somalia and Zambia, plus comprehensive unicontinental or tricontinental policies from the Lagos Plan of Action and the Wass Report[7] to the Group of 77 and Brundtland reports. The second response has been broadly within the informal sector and has had myriad forms, from black markets in currencies and goods to drug smuggling: in general, a series of survival strategies by many different social groups in civil society that ignore and undermine the state. Thus, in some parts of the Third World, the state is simultaneously both beleaguered and bellicose: to protect itself in a period of structural adjustment (fewer resources for patronage and more challenges from antagonized groups), it may resort to militarism. Such an outcome is particularly likely when alienated communities resort to guerrilla tactics to resist or undermine the state: the ultimate weapon may be its only available response, given the erosion of alternative links as conditionality compels its shrinkage. Ironically, despite the apparent decline of the postcolonial state, most alternatives to Bank/Fund strategies fail to recognize, let alone capture, the potential of the informal sector: such is the ultimate feature or force of privatization.[8]

Although there is a continuing reluctance in official circles to treat issues of hierarchy and informality, in reality the diversification of states and sectors is already apparent in divergent debt negotiations and solutions. The disaggregation of the debt syndrome reveals the diversity of Third World countries and contexts, which have been exacerbated by the incidence of structural adjustment. The typology or matrix proposed by Roy Culpepper reflects de facto distinctions between big and small states, between debtors and creditors, and between private and public loans; Africa has the smallest, mainly official yet most serious, situation, whereas Latin America's is largest, private, but more resolvable.[9] By contrast, Asia's debt is less political and more manageable, at least at the global level.[10] Such distinctions symbolize and capture much of the new hierarchy in the South, which both diplomats and analysts have been reluctant to treat. Prospects for dependent development are inseparable from such categories. This chapter focusses on Africa but cannot exclude the rest of South and North, as interdependence and dependence both coexist and contradict.

Finally, the chapter treats the dialectics of Third World politics and policies, on the one hand, and international institutions and prescriptions, on the other. International organizations have evolved and proliferated: from basic needs to structural adjustment and from the Non-Aligned Movement (NAM) to South Commission. Ongoing debates about debt, devaluation, and development are concentrated in the Bank and the Fund but also preoccupy agencies in the United Nations. Yet, while cohesion in the South remains problematic, it would be naïve and misleading to disregard it. Given myriad links within the South treated below — including regionalism, continentalism, and tricontinentalism — it is premature to pronounce on its demise. Rather, the Third World's heterogeneity imposes limits on consensus and action; it does not exclude them. The global pluralism merely requires enhanced diplomacy and nuanced enquiry, two qualities in rather short supply as the 1990s unfold.

There are, then, three themes in this chapter. First, the old stand-off between modernization and dependence at the level of analysis, and between integration and disengagement at the level of *praxis*, has been updated within the new international division of labour to one between structural adjustment, on the one hand, and self-reliance, on the other. Second, within the established political economy *genre*, a renewed emphasis has been placed on the "political" and on the "radical" (i.e., the politics of economic contraction and redirection and the imperative of treating new forces and factors, from gender and informal sector, to environment and novel coalitions). And third, I extrapolate from past and present to speculate on possible policies and prospects in the 1990s for Fourth World states at the periphery of the new international division of labour: on how to turn marginalization to advantage in terms of authentic and sustainable development into the 21st century.[11]

Together, these themes serve to reinforce the trend back toward real political economy while also pointing to lacunae, given the new existential context. In particular, prospects for theories and policies of corporatism[12] and participation need to be addressed, given the transformation of both state and economy in much of the Fourth World over the last decade. Palpable shifts in property and power have taken place.[13] But, can a distinctive African capitalism characterized by informal exchange, co-operative institutions, and nongovernmental organizations (NGOs) fill the space vacated by the local state and international capital? Or is the decline of the African state, by contrast to the *dirigisme* of the NIE state, a further indication of the continent's marginality and vulnerability?[14]

In short, the benign and optimistic era of expansion in the postindependence period has long since gone and may never return, hence the centrality of the most recent (Uruguay) Round of the GATT, which may include services as well as manufactures. The decade of the 1990s (postneocolonialism?) is unlikely to be either as benign or as optimistic. Rather, it will pose a series of challenges for the periphery, which will be compelled to rethink its development assumptions and directions: more or less self-reliance? more or less privatization? more or less stability? The current discussions and uncertainties within the IMF/IBRD, GATT/OECD, and UNCTAD/South Commission mark the beginning of the new international division of labour.

Africa and the New International Division of Labour

The post–Bretton Woods order poses profound problems for both analysis and praxis everywhere, but especially in the Third and Fourth worlds. Despite the pretensions and intentions of the Fund and Bank, it is not yet clear whether they can re-create the level of economic order and growth, given the very different economic and strategic context in the 1960s. Annual economic summits have managed to contain crises but have not devised a post–Bretton Woods order. The African states, in particular, have now to plan in an environment of considerable uncertainty and volatility. The unsteady context became most apparent as droughts and conflicts increased the prospect of famine over the last decade. Both before and after the second Sahel drought, the continent had already begun to identify new constraints and possibilities: from Lagos Plan of Action (LPA) to Africa's Priority Programme for Economic Recovery (APPER).[15]

Yet, these and other official ideological declarations constitute only one part of an emerging redirection, as already indicated. For, just as the new international division of labour has resulted in changed expectations and relations among and within the advanced industrialized states — structural adjustment is a feature of contemporary economic history in the North as well as the South — so, it has caused dramatic shifts in the Third World. The official re-evaluation and unofficial redirection have not always been entirely compatible — de jure or de facto privatization and subnational or regional integration? — but together they mark a turning point in the African condition: from postcolonial to postneo-colonial periods.

Several of the features apparent in the new division of labour are interrelated: free and fluctuating exchange rates along with nationalization have encouraged portfolio rather than direct foreign investment; official development assistance (ODA) is unlikely to grow in real terms and will become more conditional; unstable and increasing costs of petroleum are encouraging the development of alternative sources of oil and gas; new technologies have led to an expanding global service sector and a decreasing salience for particular commodities; and the Pacific Rim rather than the North Atlantic will be the centre of innovation and accumulation. Hence, the problem of policy redirection: to treat short-term crisis or long-term conjuncture?

In most factors identified as central to the new division of labour, Africa tends to be the least-favoured continent: in terms of debt, industry, services, and technology, Africa trails Asia and Latin America. Parts of Africa, particularly Algeria, Côte d'Ivoire, Kenya, and Zimbabwe, are more engaged in the international system than others. However, the beneficiaries within even these states are few and the costs are high. Thus, the post–Bretton Woods order is more inequitable at all levels, with profound implications for African viability and stability.

It is already axiomatic that economic trilateralism (i.e., the United States, the EEC, and Japan) has been superseded by multipolarity, with the NIEs eroding the status and distance of the already industrialized. Yet, despite the promise of South-South exchange, much of the South still concentrates on the old North rather than on the new frontiers of capitalism concentrated around the Pacific Rim, the time warp of the nationalist generation. Nuclear bipolarity has not yet yielded to wholesale proliferation despite tendencies in that direction and in the militarization of much of the Third World. Interdependence has yet to transcend established North-South interregional lines of facilitating Africa's relations with the NIEs of Asia and Latin America.

Multilateralism is under threat everywhere as protectionism and trade disputes encourage bilateralism. Africa, with its 50 states, benefits most from multilateral contexts and loses most from bilateral contexts. Any attempt to restore multilateralism should be based on Africa's needs and Japan's recognition. For instance, NIE graduation into the OECD could be conditional upon investment in the continent.

Despite the unanticipated windfall — for most of Africa as well as the rest of the world — of a dramatic decline in energy prices in the mid-1980s, the recovery in the North has been uneven: persistent unemployment despite reduced inflation and increased indebtedness despite currency fluctuations. Ronald Reagan's rearmament binge has not financed a global recovery; rather, it has produced a massive U.S. debt in just a couple of years, leading to excessive imports from Japan and the Pacific Rim, initially of goods, but then of investment. The long-term response to U.S. vulnerability is not currency realignment but a fundamental shift in patterns of production: U.S. and other Western investment in Japan, Taiwan, and South Korea along with Pacific investment in the United States and the EEC. Despite the protectionist rhetoric, the long-term trend is toward increased inter-OECD investment rather than exchange. If the U.S. debt was controlled or Pacific Rim investment diverted in favour of Africa, then a new contract for the continent might be prepared; the draft agreed to in New York in mid-1986 is presently in danger of being honoured more in the breach, in part because it lacked an institutional expression.[16]

The marginal gains secured by the OECD in the wake of OPEC have not spilled over to advance the South. Instead, as noted below, South-South relations have become more problematic as their centrepieces — OPEC oil and NIE industrial exports in exchange for labour and commodity imports — have contracted. When such contraction is viewed in combination with declines in foreign assistance and investment, it appears that the 1980s have been anything but auspicious for the South. As the 1986 *OECD Economic Outlook* indicates, by contrast to more optimistic IBRD positions, even after a decade of marginal or negative growth,

> the main counterpart to the OECD's terms-of-trade gain has been a loss to the *developing countries* equivalent to as much as 3 percent of their combined GNP. Faced with this development, as well as reduced access to financing from private sources, many developing countries cut back their imports sharply over the past year — at a time when some of them had not fully digested earlier import reductions. The OECD projects that import compression will continue in many of these countries, albeit at a slower pace, over the year to come, even if their terms of trade do not change significantly, because pick-up of capital flows to most of these countries appears unlikely.[17]

The euphemism of "import compression" can be translated, of course, as increased infant mortality and malnutrition in the Third World and decreases in life expectancy and basic-needs satisfaction. The new rhetoric of "adjustment with a human face" or "growth for Basic Human Needs (BHN)" merely disguises palpable declines in Positive Quality of Work Life Index (PQLI) scores, which are likely to be exponential rather than transitional.[18]

Gerald Helleiner is quite right to be pessimistic, asserting that the IBRD's strictures may be insufficiently cautious: "sober as the World Bank's 1986 report is, it nevertheless significantly *understates* the degree of Africa's problems."[19] He warns, in particular, that

> the most immediate constraints upon improved sub-Saharan African economic performance are undoubtedly foreign exchange and the difficult international economic environment. There is plenty of room for policy improvement in many countries, but even the best performers in Africa are at present struggling with acute foreign exchange constraints. Unfortunately, the international prospects are not bright . . . no knowledgeable observers now predict any recovery in real agricultural or metals prices over the remainder of the 1980s.[20]

However, while Helleiner warns that the real crisis now is "institutional desertification," in which African regimes reveal uncertain capacity "to right themselves and their economies, to redress the enormous losses already suffered and to resume orderly progress,"[21] he fails to recognize the range of innovative informal adaptations at subnational levels: regional, peasant, female, and technological adaptations. The dialectic of African political economies persists despite (or because) of the vacillation of incumbent governments.

The remaining commodity sector can be characterized as a particular form of "casino capitalism" as the long-term trend is toward a secular decline in relation to manufactures (as well as to debt and services). Yet, a few countries, classes, and commodities may enjoy short-term windfalls; these include oil (Middle East war), coffee (frost in Brazil), or gold (currency instability). But such bonanzas do not compensate for overall long-term trends; they merely camouflage them. Compensating schemes such as the Integrated Programme for Commodities, enunciated at UNCTAD, or the Compensatory Financing Facility of the IMF, are moribund already, although the EEC's Stabilization of Export Earnings (STABEX) scheme has been helpful if insufficient. And because of extreme dependence on one commodity in a few cases, the foreign exchange and debt implications have been devastating:

> Commodity prices in real (purchasing power) terms are now at their lowest levels since the 1930s; overall they also failed to rise significantly with the sharp upturn in world economic activity during 1985–6. By mid-1986 the overall average was (in nominal terms) a quarter below that of 1980. . . . Between 1980 and 1985, the dollar value of merchandise exports from Zambia fell in every year. . . . Between 1970 and 1984 the ratio of debt-service repayments to total export receipts deteriorated 5- to 9-fold in Jamaica, Kenya, Mauritius, Nigeria, Uganda, and Zimbabwe.[22]

Although by global standards sub-Saharan Africa's debt is modest — just over $100 billion by the late-1980s — the development implications of escalating payments are considerable: over 70 percent of regional GNP and over 300 percent of exports.

> We are fully aware of the fact that shortcomings in development policies have contributed to the present debt crisis. However, it is evident that the major causes of our countries' debt servicing problems are external. . . . These include, *inter alia*, the deteriorating terms of trade . . . unprecedented rise in interest rates, sharp exchange rate fluctuations, deteriorating terms of borrowing and the reduction in the flow of concessional resources, the combined effects of which result in net capital outflow for most of our member states. In this regard, the 26 African LDCs have been the most seriously affected.[23]

Africa's debt may be modest *in toto*, but it has grown faster than that of other regions and is more official than private; hence, the centrality of the Paris rather than the London Club negotiations and the roles of the Bank and Fund. Africa's regular and repeated negotiations and reschedulings have not (yet?) meant recovery, and the United Nation's Wass Report on financing Africa's recovery suggests that these will extend into the 1990s.[24] They have already become a national and bureaucratic preoccupation, especially for states in decline. As Tom

Callaghy notes, "an important psychological side effect of these foreign economic relations is that scarce talent is constantly preoccupied by negotiations with external actors about adjustment issues, while attempting to implement previous agreements."[25]

Despite the centrality and symbolism of the debt, Callaghy, like Wass, cautions that no dramatic developments are likely on either side. Rather,

> modest expectations are in order on both sides. African states cannot expect any major beneficial structural or procedural reforms in the international political economy on the part of their Western creditors. Likewise, the latter cannot expect any significant restructuring of African regimes and economies or substantial improvement in their economic and debt performance. Western actors clearly determine most of the rules of the game, shaping the parameters of action, but African regimes do have some autonomy and room for maneuver.[26]

Although Africa's debt remains small by global standards, it has "grown faster than that of any other region," doubling in the first half of the 1980s. Its ability to manage this debt may be equally modest — initially many African states had little idea of how much they owed — and, as the state has shrunk, so too has its ability to repay. Belatedly, the Bank seems to be appreciative of the centrality of debt as well as of exchange rates; its most recent Africa report accordingly focusses on it and regionalism, another overlooked dimension that I treat below. Likewise, the U.N. Secretary General eventually received a report from his group of eminent persons on debt — *Financing Africa's Recovery*, the Wass Report — which will no doubt also animate the South Commission in its first few years. The U.N. report essentially tried to salvage the de facto compact arrived at during the mid-1986 special session: increased financial flows for states implementing structural adjustment reforms.[27]

African debt, like that of other regions, is not, of course, uncontroversial in origin. If Brazil can set a cap on its repayments, then so can Nigeria or Central African Republic. Not surprisingly, Zaire's debt and Mobutu Sese Seko's fortune are almost equal in size, and yet the private accounts cannot be taken to balance the official obligations. One possible means for the continent to reverse the capital flow, other than major incentives and ready convertibility, is to lay claim to Africans' overseas savings, which are not inconsiderable, a point that Wass reiterates.[28] In fact, of course, the most seriously affected, "debt distressed" African states have stopped paying interest, let alone repaying capital, as such payments exceed their GNPs, compared to a mere 50 percent for the other sub-Saharan states.

Capital flows to Africa, which were never massive despite the assertions of dependency theorists, have declined for a series of reasons.[29] First, "aid fatigue" in the North (as well as in the East and OPEC, two sets of rather mercurial donors) has led to reduced and conditional aid for purposes of emergencies, allies, and structural adjustment only. Second, declarations of indigenization and nationalization have made investors apprehensive — especially when alternative opportunities present themselves. Third, the new international division of labour has systematically reduced the demand for African minerals and markets. Finally, partly in response to Third World nationalism, multinational corporations (MNCs) began to unpackage their investment. New patterns of foreign direct investment include contractual arrangements for licensing, management, turnkey, subcontracting, leasing, or franchising contracts. Such packages attempt to minimize risks and foreign exchange costs, and often involve MNCs from the EEC or the NIEs. Such involvement opens up a range of possibilities that may now become more commonplace in a period of privatization. There is, however, one element or level of organization, production, and exchange, if not accumulation, that most analyses of the African crisis overlook: regionalism both within and around the continent. To be sure, it has suffered a somewhat chequered history; but to ignore its potential is to disregard the focus of considerable African diplomatic, strategic, and security activity.

Africa and the South: Regionalisms in the 1980s

One principal structural feature of the Second U.N. Development Decade was the changing organization of global production. By the early 1970s, international production had surpassed international trade as a vehicle for international economic exchange (i.e., the combined production of all multinational corporations abroad is now greater than the total value of goods and services that enter into trade between countries).

This internationalization process has interacted with two other phenomena. First, the internationalization of production has tended to run parallel with the process of economic differentiation in the South noted above. The minority of rapidly growing countries of the Third World are those that have been most clearly integrated into this emerging international network of production relations. Second, the petrodollar-fuelled expansion of international capital markets during the late 1970s and early 1980s contributed to an increased involvement by international finance capital with multinational-controlled/-owned productive enterprises, often in an alliance with the peripheral state. The new tripartite collaboration, among international finance capital, multinational corporations, and the state in the South, articulates international relations of production that are wholly consistent with escalating costs and risks characteristic of present-day raw-material explorations and industrial ventures.

The new-found wealth of the petroleum exporters and the rather sophisticated production structures of the NIEs have meant profound changes in the established structure of the South. Developing countries outside this group, by contrast, are still largely dependent on agriculture. Three decades of "development" have left them poorer than they were before.

The pattern of global industrialization, particularly in the last decade, has been responsible for a great divergence in economic performance within the South. The diversifying Latin American economies and the export-led Southeast Asian economies together constitute the NIEs. According to the OECD, there are ten in this group, none of them in Africa: Brazil, Greece, Hong Kong, Mexico, Portugal, Singapore, South Korea, Spain, Taiwan, and Yugoslavia. Most definitions of the common characteristics of these NIEs include: a rapid penetration of the world market for manufactures; a rising share of industrial employment; and, increases in real GDP per capita relative to the more advanced industrial countries.[30] By contrast, the majority of states in the South (the so-called Fourth World) lack all these criteria.

The related hierarchization of the South has thus created many countries with more or less permanent stagnation tendencies, as well as a few countries with structural characteristics that increasingly resemble the North and with favourable (although not very high) real growth rates. The performance of countries within the Fourth World has deteriorated in both relative and absolute terms when compared with that of the NIEs. Needless to say, most African countries share this experience of stagnation or decline.[31]

Judging by measures of economic production and trade performance, certain conclusions appear to be self-evident. First, there has been apparent economic differentiation in the South into, on the one hand, economies experiencing growth and structural change and, on the other hand, economies grown stagnant, or even declining, with traditional peripheral structural characteristics. Second, this economic differentiation is associated with the degree and type of integration of such countries into the capitalist world economy. An analysis of Africa's diplomatic, strategic, and economic relations with the international community predetermines the character of foreign policy and external relations, correlates of development orientation and direction.[32]

Political developments in the South do not always follow economic realities directly. However, there is usually a time lag at the political level, namely the formation of appropriate organizations and actions. The achievement of "Southern solidarity" is a case in point. Thus, despite the embryonic diverging economic situations experienced by the countries of the South, they managed to forge a stronger political unity than ever before during the early 1970s through various institutional venues (in particular, the Group of 77 and the Non-Aligned Movement).[33] The success of Southern leaders in presenting a united front manifested itself for the first time in the formulation of the demand for a new international economic order (NIEO) in 1974.

The theme of collective self-reliance, central to the NIEO process, and derivative of *dependencia* logic, contains the crucial element of economic co-operation. This has two aspects: first, the notion of co-operation for enhancing the developing countries' collective bargaining power vis-à-vis the outside world and, second, the notion of intensifying trade and other linkages within a South-South framework. However, the imperative of collective self-reliance also reveals the Achilles heel of the NIEO ideology. It is an ideology uneasily balanced on contradictory principles: greater interdependence between rich and poor worlds and independence from the former by the latter. In other words, the NIEO called for better links with the rich world, while, at the same time, attempting to "delink" itself from the North.

In response to the NIEO debate, a new element came to be included in the Northern strategy — internal reform and redistribution in the South. Redistribution of resources between the countries of the South (at the time, particularly, a transfer of wealth from the oil-exporting to the oil-importing developing countries); and domestic redistribution from within them. Thus, a link was made between international redistribution and internal reform. Without the latter, the former would not have any effect on the economic development of the poorest countries or peoples of the South. The symbolic and synthetic Brandt Report articulated this view in terms of concessions for international redistribution being made conditional upon internationally recognized measures of internal reform: such contractual "interdependence" is the basis of the mid-1980s understanding over debt relief for structural adjustment in the case of Africa.

The need for internal reform has already been admitted by Third World spokespersons. However, they have made their central point compatible with *dependencia* logic: namely, that the unequal pattern of income distribution inside the South has been generated by these countries' manner of insertion into the total world economy, and that this, in turn, presents bottlenecks for further economic development in the South. The "basic needs" approach was the logical outcome of this new orientation in Northern strategy. The conditionality associated with this approach was attacked by the Group of 77, who called it a diversion and intrusion — the conditionalities of modernization.

After 1975, the emerging facts of economic divergence among Southern countries made it difficult to translate general NIEO demands into specific policies and to maintain unity at any level other than rhetoric. As for the North, it readily seized upon the opportunities to contribute to an increasingly hierarchical South, with the accompanying differences in political goals. The North came to propagate the new perspective of "global management for an interdependent world": OECD and GATT rules on a global scale. This perspective was designed to forge and legitimate closer links between international business and global institutions, on the one hand, and repressive regimes of fast-growing developing countries, on the other: modernization for the late-20th century. Within this perspective, the twin problems of global inequality and poverty were redefined as problems arising not so much from international economic relations as from domestic social injustice and lack of internal reforms — hence, the new emphasis on "human rights" and "democratic development."

Characteristic of the dialectic between economic change and political debate has been the recent formation of two new Southern organizations, both related to nationalist counterdependence strategies. First, in an attempt to contain the impact of divergencies at the level of political economy, the NAM approved the creation of the "South Commission" at its 1986 summit in Harare: an important development in the encouragement and articulation of a distinctive Southern perspective on global issues, symbolizing intellectual and political autonomy.[34] And second, under Nigeria's sponsorship, a group of "like-minded" or "like-positioned" NIEs have formed a "Concert of Medium Powers": what we could call "newly *influential* economies." These sixteen intermediate states are concerned with reviving multilateralism and encouraging international development and peace by serving as a bridge between the North and the South: a diplomatic and strategic aspect of "graduation."[35]

During the last ten years, a considerable expansion has taken place in the relationship between the NIEs and the rest of the South. The initiative has usually come from the NIEs themselves, as the objective needs of their economic structures have required a rather determined strategy for developing alternative markets. It often reinforces historical regionalist roles in both economy and security.

The economic relations that have developed under the guise of "South-South" are markedly "neocolonial" in their character, where Africa, in particular performs its traditional role as a supplier of primary goods and as a market for industrial products.[36] It has been argued that this South-South "regional" exchange possesses certain qualitative aspects that differentiate it from traditional North-South patterns. For example, it has been argued that the terms of trade would be "fairer" to the South, as compared with traditional North-South exchange, and that technologies and goods would be more appropriate to the needs of Southern markets. Yet, little quantitative evidence is available in support of the first argument, and there are indications that the terms of trade are not substantially more beneficial to the weaker partner in this type of South-South exchange. It may very well be that we are dealing with more suitable forms of industrial technology (paradoxically enough, usually produced by Northern companies from their new locations in the South). However, this point is not currently self-evident.

More importantly, though, these large-scale relations cannot be said to contain any better prospects for structural change in the traditional peripheral structure of African economies than would traditional North-South exchange. Rather, I would argue, the main advantage to Africa from dealing with the NIEs is that such relations create new outlets for its products, possibilities for developing alternative trade arrangements, and access to alternative sources of technological know-how. As a consequence, Africa might also gain from a better bargaining position vis-à-vis the North, a subject for the South Commission.

The dynamic element in such Third World–Fourth World relations lies, to a considerable extent, in the extent to which the NIEs act as a catalyst to Fourth World economic growth. These dynamics can, through South-South relations, to which I now turn, be transferred to participating African countries, admittedly without significant structural development effects, at least not in the short to medium term.

Dependent Development in Africa: Beyond the 1980s

Although I am concerned with Africa's internal and external economic directions, these cannot be separated from changes within the continent's political economy, especially at regional, national, and subnational levels. Obviously, the imperative of reform and restructuring lies in the failure of previous development policies and contexts. But the incidence and impact of stagnation or contraction are uneven in Africa as elsewhere: some states and peoples have endured more than others. Therefore, support for adjustment — the identification and manipulation of majority "coalitions" — is problematic. Moreover, given the contraction in living standards already suffered by most Africans — decreases in income, services, basic human needs, and expectations — skepticism is a natural response to dramatic devaluations and privatizations. Finally, if the current direction is not vindicated in the early 1990s, alienation is likely to be widespread, with profound social, political, and strategic implications. What is to follow failures in structural adjustment — self-reliance or militarism? — is anyone's guess.

African economies remain, despite considerable postindependence efforts, largely agricultural in concentration and external in orientation, characteristics that, we will see, the Bank and Fund seek to foster rather than transcend. The rest of the world economy is increasingly preoccupied with its own persistence and expansion. The coincidence of externally oriented reforms with international protectionism is hardly auspicious unless Africa can produce new products that can find new market niches, along the lines of successful manufacturers and commodity exporters from the NIEs to Côte d'Ivoire. And it remains quite unlikely that all 50 states could adjust successfully simultaneously given commonalities among their products and positions (the "fallacy of composition" argument).[37] Moreover, the mutual impacts of reforms and protectionism on continental exchange are important, if neglected, elements in any African revival: will reoriented production reduce intra- and inter-African exchange even further?

The juxtaposition of international and continental trends does not, at first sight, appear to be promising: the future seems to hold global protectionism induced by low levels of growth and continental recession caused by underdevelopment, underfinancing, and drought. The orthodox projection from such an inauspicious conjecture would surely be limited prospects for African development, because of Northern preoccupations and disinterest. In short, we can expect OECD isolationism based on new technologies and new relationships.

However, three alternative scenarios can be identified for Africa based on apparent trends and interests, as indicated in my final section and extrapolated from extant perspectives. First, the World Bank's (and now the Wass group's) "optimistic" preference of "reform" based on new coalitions and resources may be realized, at least in some selected African states: Northern re-engagement. Second, the OAU/Economic Commission for Africa (ECA) official and "realistic" definition of self-reliance — continental, regional, and national self-reliance centred around a group of core African states — may be approached, given the northern retreat. And third, an unofficial and somewhat pessimistic conception of development may triumph: the decline, if not demise, of the state in Africa accompanied by a set of alternative structures — informal economies based on exchange, credit, women, and adaptive (especially agricultural) technologies in which rival systems flourish, often across national borders, exacerbating the shrinking of the postcolonial state. These three possibilities are related to alternative analytic approaches: modernization, *dependencia*, and radical, respectively.

Clearly, these three alternatives to any new international economic order or even Lomé IV are unlikely to be effected easily. (The Lomé convention of 1975 established special trading relations between the EEC and 46 African, Caribbean, and Pacific countries. At the outset, the Lomé agreement was hailed as a model for establishing the NIEO.) Rather, some mix of them is likely between and within states. As indicated in the earlier discussion, some countries, classes, and companies identify more readily with establishment (i.e., Bank or Commission) perspectives. Likewise, some interests encourage reform coalitions; others favour official self-reliance; and yet others advocate informal survival strategies. These may coexist for a while, as has occurred in Africa in the 1980s — the imperative of crisis and contraction — and official strategies may indeed attempt to incorporate the unofficial; but whether they can be rendered compatible over the medium term is another question. Yet, as Claude Ake has indicated, continuing global and continental contradictions make the sequence of structural adjustment followed by self-reliance ever more likely, especially if the resource "gap" widens further: "the strategy of collective self-reliance outlined in the LPA is becoming more attractive with each passing day. It is a potentially effective strategy for dealing with the current crisis and the new realities of the international environment."[38]

However, in the short term, the stand-off between LPA and *Agenda* as alternative and antagonistic worldviews[39] moderated over the first half of the 1980s. The Agenda of Action on the Establishment of a New International Economic Order began a campaign in the U.N. at the 6th Special Session in 1974, which led to the introduction of the NIEO and the integrated commodity program in Nairobi in 1976. Drought demanded attention and successor documents on both sides moved toward a middle ground: APPER and *Financing Adjustment with Growth*, respectively, plus now *Financing Africa's Recovery*. This new consensus, or at least truce between approaches and priorities, was most apparent in the run-up to the special session in mid-1986 for which the OAU/ECA submission identified sets of both indigenous and exogenous factors responsible for the contemporary malaise.[40] Yet although APPER recognizes short-term and indigenous problems it, like the LPA before it, still emphasized longer-term, exogenous causes as primary: "the current battle to save lives and to reduce the impact of hunger and famine should not be the only focus of international support and cooperation. Otherwise, the international community will be unwittingly contributing to making the emergency a permanent phenomenon."[41] Likewise, in explaining why LPA has been difficult to implement, APPER points to inherited external dependence, insufficient resources, elusive regionalism, and structural problems. It points in particular to a set of "extraneous factors": "the widespread, severe and persistent drought; the acceleration of the desertification process; persistent and destructive cyclones in the Indian Ocean; and the intensification of destabilisation attempts from South Africa on neighbouring African countries, especially the Front Line States."[42]

Yet, it also suggests that "if most of the measures recommended in the LPA had been implemented, the ravaging effects of the current world recession and drought on African economies would have certainly been minimised."[43] Thus, Africa's leaders criticize both themselves and the international system for the nonimplementation of the LPA, which is itself symptomatic of depressed and extroverted political economies.

If there is a new uncertainty and modesty in explanations and expectations of the global economy, there is considerable apprehension about the probable trends in Africa, a continent in considerable and seemingly exponential difficulty.[44] This apprehension is reflected in a new official openness toward policy failures and reforms as well as in a revisionist mood among scholars and statespersons (the forerunner of a possible postreform radicalism?).

African studies, and African-states and development studies, have begun to reflect this new postcrisis conjuncture. To be sure, established perspectives are restated still,[45] and no agreed paradigm has yet emerged to replace "modernization" or "decolonization": no intellectual as opposed to political "consensus" has been reached. Yet, there is a new format and excitement as novel issues — debt, environment, gender, informal sector, privatization, reform — are identified and debated, if not resolved. And a range of possible frameworks has been conceived and considered, from dependence and democracy to corporatism and capitalism.[46] This intellectual adjunct of reform is welcome, given the staleness and fruitlessness of established perspectives, whether of the modernization or the materialist persuasion.[47]

Africa is, then, at a crossroads. Temperamentally, as Ake indicates, its leaders are increasingly inclined to opt for greater self-reliance, recognizing that further extroverted integration is unlikely to be either possible or profitable. Pragmatically, however, the pressures to accept structural adjustment strictures are intense, leading to supposedly short-term compromises in the interest of external support, approval, and advice: the Wass compact. And the apparent options available to Africa may yet change if protectionism intensifies in the North because slow growth, especially of employment, and exponential debt lead to nationalist measures against Japan and the NIEs. Unless freer trade is advanced everywhere, Africa may have no choice but to become more self-reliant, nationally and continentally. Ironically, however, it has postponed such an advance toward self-reliance under pressure from external agencies that themselves lack the resources to deliver the massive amounts of concessional assistance needed to perpetuate extroversion — there is a \$1 billion to \$5 billion shortfall, depending on the year and on Bank/Fund replenishments.[48] Structural adjustment has, thus, raised hopes that it cannot begin to satisfy, especially if the majority of eligible states opt for "reform," the real fallacy of composition.

One indicator of the new consensus is the agreed but ambiguous concept of "reform" itself, which seems to have superseded more controversial terms such as "conditionality" or "structural adjustment." Somewhat akin to "basic human needs," reform passes the buck back from an unyielding world economy to impoverished peripheral polities. In particular, advocates of reform in the World Bank expect local ruling classes to assemble political "coalitions" to effect change — the usual mix of devaluation, desubsidization, privatization, and so on —

when the terms of such adjustments are usually quite unacceptable to the majority of the population.[49] Thus, a new "contract" is required between donors and recipients, based on mutual acceptability, in which resources as well as conditions for reform are agreed; the Wass Report represents the latest attempt to define and sustain such a compact.[50] Otherwise, reform will lead to repression or instability: the food-riots syndrome. The Bank cannot excuse its past policy mistakes any more than can African regimes, despite attempts to do so: "governments in Africa must be seen to have the prime responsibility for designing their adjustment and investment programmes and for coordinating aid and other financial flows."[51]

Although there is a new, albeit fragile, consensus on the imperative of such "reform," there is considerable divergence and disagreement about how to define its content — from purist laissez-faire to pragmatic interventionism (i.e., from minimal to substantial if not maximal state intervention). The range of issues stretches from exchange rates, subsidies, regulation, and ownership, to sectoral balancing. Despite the pressures to proliferate adjustment in Africa, skepticism remains about the appropriateness and efficacy of reform over the medium term, especially if defined to include basic human needs because of global resources and national reservations. Notwithstanding assertions of compatibility between Bank and ECA proposals reflected in the convergence of the former's third report and the latter's *Priority Programme*, the longer-term viability of reform is still in some doubt. As an Overseas Development Institute (ODI) briefing paper has suggested, "the Bank's overriding emphasis on the importance of the price mechanism raises the risk of neglecting infrastructure and other long-term constraints to growth."[52] And if the "liquidity gap"[53] is not bridged by novel and expanded forms of finance in addition to Bank/Fund and Wass proposals (e.g., from the Pacific Rim and the socialist states), then the promised benefits of postponed consumption may never materialize, leading to "back-sliding" from agreed packages:

> So far the shock of adjustment has been accompanied by relative political stability. This may suggest no more, however, than the capacity of most governments to ride out a squall. Once these changes are seen to be more or less permanent, governments are likely to face mounting political opposition to these reforms — a reflection that makes the lack of a long-term strategy for African development the more serious.[54]

And yet, as in the modernization era of "trickle-down," there still seems to be a widespread assumption among policy makers that basic human needs will be met through renewed growth, if not through redistribution. Nevertheless, despite accolades from the State Department about successful adjustment,[55] all the evidence in Africa points to the contrary: declining per-capita incomes lead to reduced taxation and national revenue, and so to poorer roads, hospitals, schools, and other services. Where the slack is being picked up, it is being done by informal institutions, notably by national and transnational NGOs. The for-profit multinational corporation may have largely abandoned the continent, but nonprofit transnationals have taken their place. The so-called success stories after such a short period of adjustment need to be treated cautiously: success for whom and for how long? And the concentration of resources on such "models" — Ghana and Zaire — means de-facto triage for the continent as a whole, so reinforcing inequalities.

Although there is widespread international recognition that the series of shocks over the last 15 years constitutes a turning point in the global political economy, there is a peculiar reluctance to recognize correlates such as the vitality of Africa's informal sector and the related vulnerability of the continent's economies. The old assumptions about neocolonial dependence — Africa was important enough to be rescued — were undermined by oil shocks and debt negotiations, and Africa's survival became closely linked to that of the informal sector. And yet, the political and personal "internalization" of these changes did not really occur, despite drought and decline; the LPA was grafted on to the established orthodoxies. Rather, it was not until the early 1980s, when structural adjustments were demanded, that official African perceptions changed, albeit reluctantly. And, even today, there is a lingering romanticism, despite all the evidence to the contrary, that the continent can still return to the halcyon days of the 1960s, although both global and African systems indicate otherwise.

If these issues constitute a new "radical" agenda for African studies,[56] a new "orthodox" agenda has been defined and proselytized by the World Bank: reform rather than anything more revolutionary. The Bank's package, along with that of the Fund, of devaluation, deregulation, privatization, revival of commodity exports, and debt-reschedulings has transformed the policy framework during the 1980s. Aspirations and arrangements that were unthinkable in the 1970s are now regarded as commonplace; growth is considered rather than development and adjustment rather than consolidation. This reform conundrum has led to an unseemly and unprecedented rush toward floats, auctions, privatizations, and renegotiations: the old days of state sectors, parastatals, controls, and BHN seem to be gone forever. The literature is now replete with comparative analyses of adjustment and anticipations of expansion — from Ghana and Zaire to Somalia and Zambia — despite emerging cautionary tales.[57]

However, some real skeptics remain, albeit in the minority,[58] and the radical perspective may yet return to prominence along the lines indicated by Ake if the new orthodoxy proves to be inappropriate and inadequate for the continent's crisis. In short, the Berg Report and LPA (and their respective successor documents) may indeed be compatible, at least in sequence. As difficulties arise with structural adjustment, mainly because of an ungiving world economy, so the necessity of self-reliance will become apparent once again; i.e., the supposed consensus bought time for reforms to work but, if these fail to be efficacious, then the LPA and APPER would exist as welcome fall-backs. The Wass Report and the mid-1988 U.N. review may constitute a last chance for the proposed contract to work.

The Bank is concerned about mobilizing domestic coalitions in Africa to support reform in the short term; however, why should the peoples of Africa welcome restraint programs when they were barely consulted, except perhaps in Nigeria's great "IMF debate"?[59] It should be even more perplexed about securing such support, or even permissiveness, in the longer term. For, as contraction comes to be seen as normal, so popular reactions and resistance will intensify: from religious extremism to food riots to populist associations. To be sure, some of the continent's difficulties predate restructuring. But the scapegoat will be external — IMF/IBRD — rather than internal — rapacious or inappropriate leaders. Debates about the efficacy and objectivity of IMF conditionalities will continue to rage[60] but, unless Africa has more than a few "success" stories, internal opposition will build against external deficiencies: a return to dependence as effect if not cause.

(In)stability of leadership and policy is, to be sure, a crucial ingredient, but the issue remains whether it is a dependent or independent variable. And its characterization is integrally related to mode of analysis, with substructuralists treating it as result and superstructuralists as cause. Clearly, the set of factors identified by Dharam Ghai are interrelated and reinforcing, as the sets of fast and slow growers both indicate.[61] But the balances between politics and economics and between internal and external factors remain controversial.

The role of the state, however conceived, is central in both instances of fast and slow growth, and between NIEs and LDCs. The new orthodoxy on the former suggests that the *dirigiste* state is crucial to rapid and sustained industrialization whereas, on the latter, the World Bank now calls for the shrinking of the state. Harris's rhetorical volume on the NIEs reflects the former, albeit with comparative elements — the Asian "gang of four" are quite dissimilar in recent history and political economy.[62] Likewise, Peter Evans's seminal study of Brazil's "triple alliance" suggests a central role for the state in semiperipheral industrialization.[63]

Nevertheless, if some of the Third World cannot be cavalierly dismissed from the new international division of labour, "Third Worldism" is increasingly hollow and vulnerable. In particular, the issue of "graduation" from Third to First worlds — forced on some NIEs by unilateral U.S. actions — is complicating current North-South relations, particularly in GATT's current "Uruguay Round." Ironically, it was such co-optation that Henry Kissinger sought in the early 1970s as a response to OPEC's invigoration of the South. However, in the late 1980s, the very success of the NIEs is undermining not only the South but also the North: protectionism is contrary to graduation; international and national capitalists are in competition.

Notwithstanding the generally unhelpful character of the global economy and ecology over the last one or two decades, the differential performances of African political economies has led ironically to a rediscovery of politics and policies as variables: ways in which different leaders, sectors, classes, and industries have responded. A succinct comparative analysis in this genre is provided by Ghai, who contrasts groups of fast and slow growers, recognizing distinctions among each according to reliance on minerals and agriculture and to basic needs performances. He concludes that political instability, export performance, terms of trade, resource inflows, foreign aid, natural-resources endowment, role of the state, and appropriate policy framework are all salient factors, with an emphasis on the first and last. Ghai argues that "robustness"[64] of economic performance is crucial, with Kenya, of all the fast growers, being the most "robust."

The major structural constraints on Africa are external and environmental as well as internal. Reginald Green points to the profound ecological challenge facing the continent as population growth without economic expansion serves to disrupt established land-people equations as well as optimistic Bank/Fund extrapolations. The famine periods of the 1970s and 1980s may, then, become normal rather than occasional as exponential desertification affects weather patterns in both long and short terms: "By the mid-1990s, if present trends continue, the 1983–5 'famine' years will be looked upon as 'good' harvest years compared with the poor harvests that followed."[65] Green cautions against any expectations of general, fast rehabilitation and redirection, given Africa's social history and the basic, ecological and economic, causes of contemporary declines: "the root problem is not any African disrespect for nature but the combination of rising populations, limited land of reasonable quality, and the failure to devise sustainable intensive cropping or pastoral systems. The traditional African . . . pastoral systems were ecologically sustainable but only with low population/land ratios."[66] Even the fast-growing political economies of the 1980s may become, then, the ecological catastrophes of the 1990s, coinciding with the termination of external debt renegotiations. I turn, in conclusion, to three distinctive medium-term scenarios, which reflect trends in international political economy as both analysis and praxis.

What Future for Dependent Development?

The continuing African crisis, compounded by tensions in the global economy, means that the 1990s are likely to be crucial in relation to the continent's development prospects.[67] Domestic reform is not enough; external support is critical. If Africa meets the terms of its conditionalities but international institutions and donors fail to meet theirs, then the implicit contract lapses, with profound implications for Africa's directions and prospects. Conversely, if cross-conditionalities are met on both sides, then at least some African political economies may yet revive and grow. A final possibility, not discussed in either diplomatic or academic circles, is that Africa will become, because of the uneven incidence of contradiction, stagnation, and expansion, a more unequal continent.[68] This trend toward inter- and intrastate inequalities has already been intensified over the last decade — from OPEC and coffee windfalls to drought, devaluation, and deflation — but the new concentration on "reform" has overshadowed notions of declining basic needs and rights, let alone exponential ecological decline. In this concluding section, I revive the themes of formal-informal, changing technologies, and international diplomacy–political economy dialectics in abstracting three possible scenarios for the remainder of this century.

The new orthodoxy of IMF/IBRD "reform" — debt-rescheduling and structural adjustment with de facto cross-conditionalities — has now been adopted by the majority of African and industrial states. It promises transformed policies and economies: the package of devaluation, deregulation, privatization, and commodity exportation. Its emphasis is on growth rather than development, and it is permissive of authoritarian regimes, providing they follow its dictates. The new "multilateral colonization" is quite unconcerned about noncompliant states (a new pattern of differentiation on the continent?) and has yet had insufficient time for testing: Ghana and Zaire are among the early purported "success" stories. The Fund/Bank assumption, even assertion, is that devaluation and deregulation will serve to revive and restructure African economies so that foreign-exchange income from commodity exports will finance debt-repayment and industrial rejuvenation. This new orthodoxy is, I believe, *optimistic*. There is little evidence that the global economy is expanding sufficiently quickly to absorb Africa's exports of raw materials (no neocolonialism in the new division of labour?). And it is so preoccupied with Northern trade wars and NIE graduations that Southern development is low on its agenda.[69] Unless new forms of assistance and investment are forthcoming — debt for equity? special drawing rights? aid from NIEs? democratic and environmental development? — the implicit "contract" will remain unfulfilled because of Northern perfidy, not Southern procrastination. The African agenda has been transformed because of Bank/Fund and related donor conditionalities, which the continent may attempt to meet while Northern partners fail to match.[70] But, if reform does not generate sustained revival, then social coalitions supportive of the new regime will evaporate or be alienated with profound implications in near and long terms, as indicated in the final, third scenario. In the latter, authoritarianism is disapproved of, whereas in this official projection, some militarization may be necessary to advance adjustment.[71]

Given alternative ECA/OAU proposals for greater self-reliance, somewhat sidelined in the first half of this decade by IBRD reports and reforms, Africa's exponential marginality in the global economy along with the minority of nonadjusting governments may yet renew their relevance and salience, as indicated by Ake. If adjustment packages are not sustained, because of regime exhaustion or social opposition, on the one hand, or external indifference or protectionism, on the other, then Africa may once again be thrown back onto its own devices. Because of prevailing Northern preoccupations, I consider the rediscovery of self-reliance to be *realistic* rather than idealistic, given the dictates of international diplomacy. The Bank has always asserted that its reforms were shorter-term and economistic and, therefore, compatible with longer-term and developmental ECA reformations. The transition from reform to restructuring may occur around the end of the decade if IBRD fails to mobilize sufficient international resources to meet its side of the tacit bargain. Moreover, nonadjusting states may have meanwhile enhanced their national self-reliance, while adjusting regional powers may be strengthened sufficiently to once again encourage regional self-reliance. And if the Bank fails to deliver, then continent-side collective self-reliance may be a necessity rather than desideratum. The only level or form of self-reliance that may not be either recognized or facilitated is that of subnational, informal enterprise, the centrepiece of our final, *pessimistic* scenario.

If neither Bank reform nor ECA self-reliance is realized, then a more pluralist or anarchistic scenario is possible — if not desirable. Neither African nor international bourgeois interests would gain if a variety of informal, populist, proletarian, even guerrilla, formations were released. Yet, if devaluation and adjustment fail, and self-reliance proves elusive, then social reactions could be multiple: the state could shrink farther, informal exchange and credit would expand, black markets might revive, and a variety of bandit or guerrilla warlords could establish de facto "microstates."[72] To be sure, such a pessimistic scenario is not only unlikely, it would be both fragmented and resisted: the external agencies that declined to support reform adequately might yet contain violent opposition, especially if East-West interests were stimulated and injected into essentially development situations of disinterest in militarization under this scenario. The trend toward domestic authoritarianism would be intensified, to protect vulnerable bourgeois privileges, and African "peace-keeping" operations might be stimulated, as a distinctive form of continental self-reliance. While such a scenario is problematic, it does at least represent a logical correlate of underdevelopment. And it might lead both African studies and development back to some of its earlier, presently overlooked, concerns with inequalities as well as with adjustments: class and ethnicity as well as reform and trickle-down.

Conclusion

Any estimation and evaluation of Africa's future position in the emerging international division of labour cannot escape from the inheritance of dependence and underdevelopment to cycles of ecology and economy. Thus, the dialectics of diplomacy-security with political economy and of formal-informal responses will undoubtedly continue, along with the primacy of links with the North, even if South-South relations, particularly those involving NIEs, do increase in salience somewhat. The importance of the latter, along with intra- and inter-African relations, will only increase as North-South connections decrease, either because of Northern protectionism or preoccupations or because of Southern preferences and resources. In retrospect, then, the current structural-adjustment preoccupations of the Bank and Fund may appear to be necessary corrections on the path toward self-reliance and development that ECA and other indigenous directions identified. To be sure, "distortions" in Africa have become widespread and extreme, but the external prescription consistently ignores changes in the global division of labour. As Northern preoccupations and preservation predominate, so Africa's self-sustainment will become an imperative. The lingering questions remain whether this imperative will be state-determined — variations of corporatism, if not of militarism[73] — or a function of privatizations of the heights of the economy and recognition of the resilience of the ubiquitous informal sector: questions that even the new political economy hardly addresses. As Toye notes, "the current dominance of the 'New Right' in the field of development policy" is a function not only of its ability to oversimplify but also of "important intellectual failures in the competing tradition of Marxist political economy."[74] The probable inability of the established "counter revolution in development policy" to facilitate Africa's escape from crisis means that the alternative neomaterialist approach may have a second chance: will it be able to seize it given the emergence of the new international division of labour? And will it impact upon social-science perspectives in general just as orthodox development studies and issues have begun to do?

A final footnote about a novel, responsive trend in Africa comparable to that in other parts of the Third World and related to both official and informal privatization: demands for democratic development. In the mid-1980s, a group of eminent Africans again posed the question, "Which way Africa?" Their declaration called for three interdependent fundamentals: "democracy, development and unity."[75] In situating Africa's economic crisis, they implicitly responded to World Bank conditions:

> The development of Africa cannot, under existing conditions, result from closer integration into the world economy. . . . Rigorous management of financial and monetary resources is indispensable for development and democracy in Africa and presupposes the participation of the people in the decision-making process. . . . Full repayment of our countries' debts would seriously mortgage our future and deprive Africa of the resources it needs to develop, while the adjustment policies involved might well destabilize the African production and social systems in the long run.[76]

NOTES

1. See Timothy M. Shaw, *Towards an International Political Economy for the 1980s: From Dependence to (Inter)Dependence* (Halifax: Centre for Foreign Policy Studies, 1980).

2. See Bahgat Korany, "Hierarchy within the South: In Search of Theory," *Third World Affairs 1986* (London: Third World Foundation, 1986), 85–100.

3. See Nigel Harris's seminal *The End of the Third World* (Harmondsworth: Pelican, 1987), and Robert Gilpin's *The Political Economy of International Relations* (Princeton: Princeton University Press, 1987).

4. See, for example, World Bank, *World Development Report 1987* (Washington: 1987); *Toward Sustained Development in Sub-Saharan Africa: A Joint Program of Action* (Washington: 1984); and *Financing Adjustment with Growth in Sub-Saharan Africa, 1986–90* (Washington: 1986); and Willy Brandt, *North-South: A Programme for Survival* (London: Pan, 1980); *Common Security: a Programme for Disarmament* (Palme Report) (London: Pan, 1982), and *Our Common Future: The World Commission on Environment and Development* (Brundtland Report) (Oxford: Oxford University Press, 1987). On the intellectual antecedents and contexts of these perspectives, see John Toye, *Dilemmas of Development: Reflections on the Counter-revolution in Development Theory and Policy* (Oxford: Basil Blackwell, 1987).

5. See Ankie M. M. Hoogvelt, *The Third World in Global Development* (London: Macmillan, 1982), especially 1–72.

6. See Aldo Ferrer, "Argentina's Foreign Debt Crisis," *Third World Affairs 1985* (London: Third World Foundation, 1985), 10–22; Carl B. Weinberg, "The Plans Austral and Cruzado: Self-directed Economic Adjustment vs IMF Conditionality," *Third World Affairs 1987* (London: Third World Foundation, 1987), 36–46; and John Crabtree, "Heterodox Stabilisation Policies in Argentina, Brazil and Peru," *Third World Affairs 1988* (London: Third World Foundation, 1988), 300–317.

7. See OAU, *Lagos Plan of Action for the Economic Development of Africa 1980-2000* (Geneva: International Institute for Labour Studies, 1981), and United Nations, *Financing Africa's Recovery: Report and Recommendations of the Advisory Group on Financial Flows for Africa* (New York: United Nations, 1988).

8. Cf. Timothy M. Shaw, "Alternative African Futures: Debates, Dynamics and Dialectics," Conference on the Future of Africa, Edinburgh, December 1987; and "Africa's Conjuncture: From Structural Adjustment to Self-reliance," *Third World Affairs 1988*, 318–37.

9. See Ray Culpepper, *The Debt Matrix* (Ottawa: North-South Institute, April 1988), and *Banking Regulation and Debt: A Policy of Flexible Response*, ODC Policy Focus Number 1 (Washington: 1988).

10. Cf. Cheryl Payer, "The Asian Debtors," *Third World Affairs 1988*, 283–99.

11. See Shaw, "Alternative African Futures."

12. See Julius E. Nyang'oro and Timothy M. Shaw, eds., *Corporatism in Africa: The Political Economy of Social Control* (Boulder, Colo.: Westview, 1988).

13. For an informed and comprehensive but nonmaterialist overview, see Donald Rothchild and Naomi Chazan, eds., *The Precarious Balance: State and Society in Africa* (Boulder, Colo.: Westview, 1988); cf. the more critical collection edited by Zaki Ergas, *The African State in Transition* (London: Macmillan, 1987).

14. For a dialectic, counterdependence perspective on Africa's pre-1980 economic history, see John Spender and Sheila Smith, *The Development of Capitalism in Africa* (London: Methuen, 1986).

15. See OAU, *Africa's Priority Programme for Economic Recovery 1986–1990* [APPER] (Addis Ababa: 1985).

16. See "UN Programme of Action for Africa's Economic Recovery and Development," *Africa Recovery*, February–April 1987: 12–14.

17. "Highlights from the *OECD Economic Outlook*, December 1986," *OECD Observer* 144 (January 1987): 36.

18. See "Children and Recession," *The State of the World's Children 1988* (Oxford: Oxford University Press for UNICEF, 1988), 23–31. See also Giovanni Cornia, Richard Jolly, and Frances Stewart, eds., *Adjustment with a Human Face*, 2 vols. (Oxford: Oxford University Press, 1987).

19. Gerald K. Helleiner, "Economic Crisis in Sub-Saharan Africa: The International Dimension," *International Journal* 41 (Autumn 1986): 749.

20. Helleiner, "Economic Crisis in Sub-Saharan Africa," 750.

21. Helleiner, "Economic Crisis in Sub-Saharan Africa," 749. See also Gerald K. Helleiner, ed., *Africa and the IMF* (Washington: International Monetary Fund, 1985).

22. "Commodities and the Commonwealth," *Commonwealth Currents* (December 1986): 9.

23. APPER, 5. See also John Loxley, *The IMF and the Poorest Countries* (Ottawa: North-South Institute, 1984).

24. *Financing Africa's Recovery*, 22.

25. Thomas M. Callaghy, "Between Scylla and Charybdis: The Foreign Economic Relations of Sub-Saharan African States," *Annals of the American Academy* 489 (January 1987): 158.

26. Callaghy, "Between Scylla and Charybdis," 162. See also Carol Lancaster and John Williamson, eds., *African Debt and Financing* (Washington: Institute for International Economics, 1986), and Trevor Parfitt and Stephen Riley, "The International Politics of African Debt," *Political Studies* 35, no. 1 (March 1987): 1–17.

27. *Financing Africa's Recovery*, especially 43. See also *Africa Recovery* 2 (March 1988): 1, 16–27.

28. *Financing Africa's Recovery*, 37.

29. See *Financing Africa's Recovery*, 11–13, 37.

30. See Harris, *End of the Third World*, and Jerker Carlsson and Timothy M. Shaw, eds., *Newly Industrialising Countries and the Political Economy of South-South Relations* (London: Macmillan, 1988).

31. See *Financing Africa's Recovery*; cf. Spender and Smith, *Development of Capitalism in Africa*.

32. See Timothy M. Shaw, "Peripheral Social Formations in the New International Division of Labour: African States in the Mid 1980s," *Journal of Modern African Studies* 24 (September 1986): 489–508.

33. See Timothy M. Shaw, "The Non-Aligned Movement and the New International Division of Labour," in *New Perspectives in North-South Dialogue: Essays in Honour of Olof Palme*, ed. Kofi Buenor Hadjor (London: Third World Book Review, 1988).

34. Shaw, "Non-Aligned Movement and the New International Division of Labour."

35. See A. Bolaji Akinyemi, "A Nigerian View of the World," *South Magazine* (London: March 1987), 26–28; *North-South News* (Ottawa: North-South Institute, Fall 1987); and "Nigeria: Concert of Medium Powers," *Africa Press Clips* 1, no. 2 (1987/88): 18.

36. See Carlsson and Shaw, eds., *Newly Industrialising Countries and the Political Economy of South-South Relations*.

37. See Tony Killick, *Adjustment with Growth in Africa? Unsettled Questions of Design and Finance* (London: ODI, February 1987).

38. Claude Ake, "How Politics Underdevelops Africa," OAU/ECA/ADB Conference on "Africa: The Challenge of Economic Recovery and Accelerated Development," Abuja, Nigeria, June 1987, 17.

39. See the original "Berg Report": *Accelerated Development in Sub-Saharan Africa: Agenda for Action* (Washington: World Bank, 1981). For discussion of it and alternative proposals and projections, see, *inter alia*, Adebayo Adedeji and Timothy M. Shaw, eds., *Economic Crisis in Africa: African Perspectives on Development Problems and Potentials* (Boulder, Colo.: Lynne Rienner, 1985); Robert J. Berg and Jennifer Seymour Whitaker, eds., *Strategies for African Development* (Berkeley: University of California Press, 1986); and John Ravenhill, ed., *Africa in Economic Crisis* (London: Macmillan, 1987).

40. "Africa's Submission to the Special Session of the UN on Africa's Economic and Social Crisis" (Addis Ababa: OAU/ECA, March 1986; E/ECA/ECM,1/1 Rev. 2), 7–9. On the intellectual roots of such dialectical positions, see Timothy M. Shaw, "Debates about Africa's Future: The Brandt, World Bank and Lagos Plan Blueprints," *Third World Quarterly* 5 (April 1983): 330–44.

41. APPER, 4.

42. APPER, 13.

43. APPER, 12.

44. See *The Abuja Statement from the International Conference on Africa: The Challenge of Economic Recovery and Accelerated Development*, June 1987 (Addis Ababa: ECA, 1987; ECA/87/75). See also Timothy M. Shaw, ed., *Alternative Futures for Africa* (Boulder, Colo.: Westview, 1982), and, with Olajide Aluko, ed., *Africa Projected: From Recession to Renaissance by the Year 2000?* (London: Macmillan, 1985).

45. Classic among the restatements of modernization orthodoxy is J. Gus Liebenow, *Africa Politics: Crises and Challenges* (Bloomington: Indiana University Press, 1986).

46. For an early attempt to incorporate new factors and articulate new frameworks, see Timothy M. Shaw, *Towards a Political Economy for Africa: The Dialectics of Dependence* (London: Macmillan, 1985).

47. See Shaw, "Alternative African Futures."

48. *Financing Africa's Recovery*, vi and 45, and *Financing Adjustment with Growth in Sub-Saharan Africa*, 4–5.

49. See "Stabilisation — For Growth or Decay?" *IDS Bulletin* 19 (January 1988): 1–80.

50. See "Compact for African Development: Report of the Committee on African Development Strategies," in *Strategies for African Development*, 557–85; and *Financing Africa's Recovery*, 43.

51. *Financing Adjustment with Growth in Sub-Saharan Africa*, 4–5.

52. ODI, *Sub-Saharan Africa: Economic Crisis and Reform* (London: February 1987), 4. See also Gerald K. Helleiner, *Growth-Oriented Adjustment Lending: A Critical Assessment of IMF/World Bank Approaches* (Geneva: South Commission, 1988).

53. J.D.A. Duddy, "Third World Liquidity Needs: A New Look," *Third World Affairs 1987*, 22.

54. ODI, "Sub-Saharan Africa," 4. See also Jeff Haynes, Trevor Parfitt, and Stephen Riley, "Debt in Sub-Saharan Africa: The Local Politics of Stabilisation," *African Affairs* 86 (July 1987): 343–66; and Reginald Herbold Green and Stephany Griffiths-Jones, "Sub-Saharan Africa's External Debt Crisis," *Third World Affairs 1986*, 17–32.

55. See Robert M. Press, "Economic Reform Brings Hopes — and Risks — to Africa," editorial, *Christian Science Monitor* 79 (April 21, 1987): 3. See also "Reform Statistics Study," *West Africa* 3629 (March 30, 1987): 625; and *Should the IMF Withdraw from Africa?* (Washington: ODC, 1987).

56. See Nzongola-Ntalaja et al., *Africa's Crisis* (London: Institute for African Alternatives, 1987), and James H. Mittelman, *Out from Underdevelopment: Prospects for the Third World* (London: Macmillan, 1988).

57. See, especially, John Loxley, *Ghana: Economic Crisis and the Long Road to Recovery* (Ottawa: North-South Institute, 1988); and Roger Young, *Zambia: Adjusting to Poverty* (Ottawa: North-South Institute, 1988).

58. See, for example, Norman P. Girvan, "Adjustment via Austerity: Is There an Alternative?" *IDA Dossier* 45 (January–February 1985): 45–54; and *Development and Peace* 7 (Spring 1986): 56–63.

59. See Timothy M. Shaw, "Nigeria Restrained: Foreign Policy Under Changing Political and Petroleum Regimes," *The Annals of the American Academy* 489 (January 1987): 40–50.

60. See Jahangir Amuzegar, "The IMF Under Fire," *Foreign Policy* 64 (Fall 1986): 98–119; and Henry S. Bienen and Mark Gersovitz, "Economic Stabilisation, Conditionality and Political Stability," *International Organisation* 39 (Autumn 1985): 729–54.

61. Dharam Ghai, "Successes and Failures in African Development, 1960–62," OECD Seminar on Alternative Development Strategies, Paris, January 1987.

62. See Harris, *End of the Third World*, passim.

63. See Peter Evans, *Dependent Development: The Alliance of Multinational, State and Local Capital in Brazil* (Princeton: Princeton University Press, 1979). See also Atul Kohli, "The State and Development," *States and Social Structures Newsletter* 6 (Winter 1988): 1–5.

64. Ghai, "Successes and Failures in African Development," 28. See also his "Economic Growth, Structural Change and Labour Absorption in Africa, 1960–85," UNRISD, Discussion Paper Number 1.

65. Reginald Herbold Green, "Food Policy, Food Production, and Hunger in Sub-Saharan Africa: Retrospect and Prospect," *International Journal* 41 (Autumn 1986): 769.

66. Green, "Food Policy," 798. See also Timothy M. Shaw, "Towards a Political Economy of the African Crisis: Diplomacy, Debates and Dialectics," in *Drought and Hunger in Africa*, ed. Michael H. Glantz (Cambridge: Cambridge University Press, 1987), 127–47.

67. See *Africa Recovery*, quarterly, from early 1987.

68. See also Shaw, "Alternative African Futures."

69. See *Resolving the Global Economic Crisis: After Wall Street* (Washington: Institute for International Economics, December 1987, Special Report Number 6).

70. Cf. *Financing Africa's Recovery*.

71. See Eboe Hutchful, "New Elements in Militarism," *International Journal* 41 (Autumn 1986): 802–30. See also Clive Thomas, *The Rise of the Authoritarian State in Peripheral Societies* (New York: Monthly Review, 1987).

72. See the caution of Olusewgun Obasanjo, "Debt and Drugs in the Third World," *New York Times*, April 15, 1987, and ODC, "The Drug Trade and Developing Countries," *Policy Focus* Number 4 (Washington: 1987).

73. See Nyang'oro and Shaw, eds., *Corporatism in Africa.*

74. Toye, *Dilemmas of Development*, 115.

75. See "Which Way Africa? For Democracy, for Development, for Unity. Declaration on Africa," *IDA Dossier* 54 (July 1986): 35–45.

76. "Which Way Africa?" 43. See also Peter Anyang'Nyongo, ed., *Popular Struggles for Democracy in Africa* (London: Zed, for UNU, 1987).

SELECT BIBLIOGRAPHY

Berg Report. *Accelerated Development in Sub-Saharan Africa: Agenda for Action.* Washington: World Bank, 1981.

Berg, Robert J., and Jennifer Seymour Whitaker, eds. *Strategies for African Development.* Berkeley: University of California Press, 1986.

Brandt, Willy. *North-South: A Programme for Survival.* London: Pan, 1980.

Carlsson, Jerker, and Timothy M. Shaw, eds. *Newly Industrialising Countries and the Political Economy of South-South Relations.* London: Macmillan, 1988.

Evans, Peter. *Dependent Development: The Alliance of Multinational, State and Local Capital in Brazil.* Princeton: Princeton University Press, 1979.

Gilpin, Robert. *The Political Economy of International Relations.* Princeton: Princeton University Press, 1987.

Harris, Nigel. *The End of the Third World.* Harmondsworth: Pelican, 1987.

Hoogvelt, Ankie M.M. *The Third World in Global Development.* London: Macmillan, 1982.

Korany, Bahgat. "Hierarchy Within the South: In Search of Theory." In *Third World Affairs 1986.* London: Third World Foundation, 1986.

Lancaster, Carol, and John Williamson, eds. *African Debt and Financing.* Washington: Institute for International Economics, 1986.

Loxley, John. *Ghana: Economic Crisis and the Long Road to Recovery.* Ottawa: North-South Institute, 1988.

Nyang'oro, Julius E., and Timothy M. Shaw, eds. *Corporatism in Africa: The Political Economy of Social Control.* Boulder, Colo.: Westview, 1988.

Our Common Future: The World Commission on Environment and Development [Brundtland Report]. Oxford: Oxford University Press, 1987.

Ravenhill, John, ed. *Africa in Economic Crisis.* London: Macmillan, 1987.

Rothchild, Donald, and Naomi Chazan, eds. *The Precarious Balance: State and Society in Africa.* Boulder, Colo.: Westview, 1988.

Shaw, Timothy M. "The Non-Aligned Movement and the New International Division of Labour." In *New Perspectives in North-South Dialogue: Essays in Honour of Olof Palme*, ed. Kofi Buenor Hadjor. London: Third World Book Review, 1988.

———. "Peripheral Social Formations in the New International Division of Labour: African States in the Mid 1980s." *Journal of Modern African Studies* 24 (September 1986): 373–94.

———. *Towards an International Political Economy for the 1980s: From Dependence to (Inter)Dependence*. Halifax: Centre for Foreign Policy Studies, 1980.

Spender, John, and Sheila Smith. *The Development of Capitalism in Africa*. London: Methuen, 1986.

Toye, John. *Dilemmas of Development: Reflections on the Counter-revolution in Development Theory and Policy*. Oxford: Basil Blackwell, 1987.

TECHNOLOGY AND THE NEW INTERNATIONAL ECONOMIC ORDER

Elizabeth Riddell-Dixon

Technology and technological innovation are cornerstones of the modern capitalist system. The cycle of innovation and obsolescence fuels the forces of change. Retaining control over the knowledge base and over techniques that foster innovation and change is critical in perpetuating the competitive advantage of industrialized states. Without it, cheaper labour would pose a serious challenge to the advanced industrialized countries of the West. Technology is likewise essential to less-developed countries (LDCs) for, without it, they are destined to perpetually lag behind the industrialized states, and will rely increasingly on labour-intensive forms of industrial production to compete in the global marketplace. Thus, without current technology, the prospects for their economic development are dismal.

This chapter sets out to examine the importance of technology and technology transfer to the demand from the LDCs for a more just and equitable new international economic order (NIEO). It begins with a brief overview of the demand for an NIEO. Then, it focusses on the importance of technology and technology transfers to LDCs, before addressing the serious ancillary problems impeding their successful harnessing of technology. Finally, the prospects for LDCs' securing the technology necessary for their economic development are assessed by examining the transfer-of-technology negotiations between developing and developed states at the U.N. Conference on Trade and Development (UNCTAD). Although not the only international body concerned with the transfer of technology, UNCTAD has held the most prolonged, direct negotiations on the process of transferring technology.[1] However, 25 years of meetings by its Transfer of Technology Committee, six negotiating sessions by its Intergovernmental Group of Experts on the International Code of Conduct for Technology Transfers, and its six conferences devoted solely to the issue of technology transfer have produced minimal results. Negotiations on crucial transfer-of-technology issues have frequently ended in stalemate. The inability to reach a compromise is not surprising, given the conflicting positions of developed and developing countries. For the LDCs, increased access to technology is vital to their development. For the industrialized states, the fundamental structural changes in the world economy that would be required in order to ensure technology for LDCs could threaten their economic ascendancy and the free-market ethos they have inherited. The conflict of cherished interests and values erodes the political will of either developed or developing states to compromise.

The New International Economic Order

The post–World War II era witnessed a dramatic increase in the number of newly independent states. Yet, this new-found sovereignty appeared hollow when it was launched in a global system that perpetuated their economic dependence on former colonial masters, countries that happened to have industrialized and developed economies. Patterns of trade and investment that had been established under earlier (colonial) periods continued to operate. The economic dependence of these new states, often referred to as "neocolonialism," undermined their political independence. Frustration increased as the gap between rich and poor countries, industrialized and emerging, widened. The LDCs blamed their chronic poverty and continued economic dependence on two principal factors: the exploitation engendered by historically conditioned relationships, which had made them extractive hinterlands in an evolving imperial world economy; and the structural discrimination of the present international trading system, which continued to promote the centrality, and hence the prosperity, of the Western industrialized countries at the expense of the economic development of the LDCs. As a consequence, the latter have become increasingly vocal in demanding not only larger quantities of aid on more generous terms but also, and more importantly, a new international economic order that would reduce the structural distortions in the world economy and thus permit a more equitable sharing of the world's resources.

Relations between the LDCs and the wealthy industrialized countries are commonly referred to as "North-South" relations and their interaction, the "North-South dialogue." The "North," so called because most of its members are located in the Northern Hemisphere, includes the industrialized countries of North America and Western Europe, as well as Japan, Australia, and New Zealand. These countries all have well-developed market economies, and all have relatively liberal-democratic political systems. The "South" comprises the LDCs, most of which are located in the Southern Hemisphere. Needless to say, there is enormous diversity within each grouping. The economic resources of New Zealand are dwarfed by those of the United States. The contrasts are even more startling when one compares the various states of the South. They include the newly industrializing economies (NIEs), such as South Korea and Singapore; the oil-rich states of the Organization of the Petroleum Exporting Countries (OPEC), such as Kuwait and Saudi Arabia; and such poverty-stricken, resource-poor countries as Mali, Haiti, and Somalia. The diversity in their political systems is enormous, encompassing democracies, totalitarian regimes, and monarchies. Some are aligned with the Western bloc, some are aligned with the Eastern bloc, and some are nonaligned. Given this diversity, the LDCs cannot be considered a monolithic bloc in any real sense. Nevertheless, they do share several important objectives: to end all traces of colonialism; to safeguard their sovereign jurisdiction by controlling their political, economic, and social affairs; and to accelerate their economic development.

The USSR and the Eastern European countries, which have industrialized, centrally planned economies, play a minor role in the North-South dialogue — both because they blame the South's problems on capitalist imperialism, past and present, and because their economic relations with the South are small relative to those of the North.

The origins of the North-South dialogue, as it became known in the 1970s, can be traced back to the early 1950s. The quest for an NIEO began in 1952 when the U.N. General Assembly passed a resolution for the "financing of economic development through the establishment of fair and equitable international prices for primary commodities and through the execution of national programmes of integrated economic development."[2] Three years later, in 1955, 29 LDCs met at the Bandung Conference in Indonesia, where they resolved to avoid military alliances within the sphere of either superpower and thereby to safeguard their political sovereignty. The Non-Aligned Movement (NAM) had taken root.

The U.N. General Assembly declared the 1960s the "Decade for Development," and its commitment was given added weight when, during the first year of the decade, 17 newly independent countries were admitted to its membership. Three years later, in 1963, the LDCs undertook their first collective action, presenting their demands to the General Assembly in the "Joint Declaration of Developing Countries."[3] The Declaration heralded a new era in North-South relations. The first U.N. Conference on Trade and Development (UNCTAD) followed in 1964, convened in response to pressure from the LDCs.

History was made at that 1964 meeting of UNCTAD, when 77 LDCs established a negotiating group, the Group of 77, to formulate and voice their shared demands. They believed that a common front would have greater bargaining strength than individual developing countries acting unilaterally. The Group of 77 achieved an early victory when, in spite of opposition from the Western industrialized countries, it was successful in having UNCTAD designated a permanent organ of the General Assembly.[4] UNCTAD was given authority to launch inquiries and discussions on issues it deemed salient to its mandate. Nevertheless, negotiations proceeded very slowly throughout the 1960s.

By 1970, it was clear that previous approaches to the economic development of Southern countries were not working. During the so-called Decade of Development, the gap between rich and poor countries had widened, not diminished. Furthermore, approximately half of the world's population was suffering from malnutrition; unemployment or underemployment; environmental pollution; and inadequate housing, sanitation, medical care, and education.[5]

To herald a new beginning, the 1970s were declared the "Second Decade for Development," but concrete actions were necessary to add substance to the rhetoric. The Group of 77 was becoming more militant, both because of frustration with the sluggish rate of progress during the 1960s and because of the success of OPEC in the early 1970s, which exemplified the power LDCs could wield if they acted in unison. OPEC's 1973 oil embargo demonstrated an effective use of an economic weapon against wealthy Western states by LDCs.

In the North-South dialogue, 1974 was an historic year. In response to the urging of the Group of 77, whose membership had grown to more than 95 states, the General Assembly held a special session in April 1974 to find ways of using the world's natural resources effectively so as to promote social justice throughout the globe. There, the Group of 77 presented a "Declaration and Program of Action on the Establishment of a New International Economic Order."[6] This was the first time that the demands for an NIEO had been put in a cohesive package and presented formally to the international community. The word "new" in the title implied a change from the existing system in which the LDCs exerted little influence in decision making and tended to be relegated to the role of providing Western industrialized countries with raw materials, cheap labour, and export markets.

The Declaration formed the basis for the subsequent "Charter of Economic Rights and Duties of States,"[7] which was adopted by the General Assembly on December 12 of the same year. The Group of 77 exercised its ever-increasing voting strength, albeit aided by the votes of the USSR and Eastern European countries, to pass the Charter in spite of opposition from such major Western powers as the Federal Republic of Germany, the United States, and the United Kingdom.

The Charter's principal demands can be summarized as follows:

a. the right of each state to choose its own political, economic, and social system in keeping with the will of its citizens;
b. the right of each state to complete and permanent sovereignty over its economic, political, and social affairs;
c. the right of each state to regulate the activities of multinational enterprises operating within its borders and to "nationalize, expropriate or transfer ownership of foreign property" (with payment of appropriate compensation) in order to safeguard the state's economic well-being;
d. changes to the international pricing system to maintain and increase the purchasing power of LDCs, especially those exporting raw materials;
e. the reduction of the tariff and nontariff barriers imposed by the North on Southern exports, especially manufactured goods;
f. a state's right to participate fully in international trade without discrimination based on its political, economic, or social system;
g. measures to alleviate the debt problems facing LDCs;
h. larger amounts of financial and technical aid to LDCs granted on more generous terms;
i. the right of LDCs to participate fully and effectively in international decision-making bodies, especially the International Monetary Fund, International Bank for Reconstruction and Development (World Bank), and

the General Agreement on Tariffs and Trade, and to make these bodies more sensitive to the needs and aspirations of LDCs; and

j. the promotion of technology transfers to provide LDCs with technology appropriate to their needs and resources at affordable prices and on a scale large enough to spawn indigenous research capabilities.

The list clearly identifies technology transfer as one of three cornerstones of the NIEO, along with trade and finance. The transfer of technology, however, also comprises part of several of the other demands, particularly the promotion of sovereignty, the treatment of multinational enterprises, debt relief, and foreign aid.

The Charter was a package of demands supported by the majority of the General Assembly and designed to establish a more just and equitable international economic order by giving the development of the LDCs priority over other considerations. Like all United Nations resolutions, it was not legally binding and, hence, its implementation depended on further North-South negotiation, which would translate the demands into practice. The task has not been easy; both North and South perceive the stakes to be high. The North has been reluctant to make concessions and has tended to consider the NIEO impractical, at best, or more seriously, a grave threat to the operations of free-market forces internationally. In addition, the industrialized West has been preoccupied with internal problems; specifically slow and uneven growth rates, a levelling-off of economic influence, and real conflict over the usefulness and efficacy of international economic institutions. To the LDCs, the NIEO is critical to their economic development and to closing the gap between rich and poor countries. Nowhere was this North-South polarization more evident than in the transfer-of-technology negotiations.

Technology and the NIEO

The importance of technology and technological innovation to the economic development of LDCs cannot be overstated. A.F. Ewing is not alone when he argues that "the almost total technological dependence of the vast majority of developing countries is the most important single reason for their poverty."[8] As is the case in so many areas critical to development, the LDCs depend on the North for technology. This is not surprising since

> about 95 percent of the world's research and development (R&D) capabilities are concentrated in the developed world, and 94 percent of the patents are held by individuals and organizations in developed market economies. Of the remaining 6 percent of patents 84 percent are held by foreigners, often for purposes of preventing the rise of local competition.[9]

The concept of technology transfers is far more complex than a one-time exchange of expertise or knowledge. Problems of costs, appropriateness, and self-sufficiency are intrinsically linked to the concept. Of these factors, LDCs cite cost, both direct and indirect, as the most serious impediment to obtaining technology.[10]

The word *transfer* suggests the conveyance of a property or right without cost. However, in actuality most technology is sold. Limited amounts of technology are given as foreign aid, but most transfers are strictly commercial transactions. The UNCTAD study *Major Issues Arising from the Transfer of Technology to Developing Countries* identifies three commercial methods of transferring technology.[11] In each case the method chosen affects the LDC's control over its economy. The LDC and its national enterprises maintain the greatest amount of autonomy when technology (e.g., foreign consultants, machinery and other capital goods) are purchased directly from various suppliers abroad. Under these circumstances, the purchaser can shop around for the package that best meets its requirements. Such control is lost when the transfer of technology comes with direct foreign investment by MNEs. MNEs provide entire technology packages comprising such vital resources as capital goods, industrial techniques, and managerial skills. The recipient becomes dependent on a single source of technology. Furthermore, such transfers are usually accompanied by restrictions on the use and distribution of the technology and the products that result from its use. Technology can also be acquired through a licensing or contractual arrangement with a foreign firm. In such cases, the contract determines the relative degree of control exercised by the supplier and purchaser. As the UNCTAD report points out, a combination of these three methods is usually involved in the transfer of technology.

More than 80 percent of all patents used in LDCs are foreign-owned.[12] Not only is the desire to make a profit the prime motivation for selling technology but prices are frequently kept high by oligopolistic competition. (Sellers of technology are few relative to the number of prospective buyers.) To meet these direct costs, LDCs and their domestic companies must use scarce foreign-currency reserves, exacerbating their already troubled balance-of-payments problems.[13]

While the direct costs of technology can be onerous, indirect costs often impose an even greater burden on LDCs. Indirect costs are the conditions frequently attached to technology transfers, and they take many forms. These "restrictive business practices" can include tying the transfer to the purchase of supplies, spare parts, and other equipment, frequently at prices higher than those charged by other suppliers. The time period during which the technology can be employed may be limited. The sale, especially the "re-exportation," of goods produced using the technology can be restricted. Prices or quantities of goods produced with the technology can be stipulated. The recipient of the technology may be prohibited from selling or otherwise disseminating the technology in the local economy or may need to seek permission of the original owner before so doing. All these factors limit the economic sovereignty of the developing country and the spread of technology within its borders.

Most technology is developed by the North to meet the needs of the North, and most technology transfers take place among and between Western industrialized states. Conversely, little technology is developed to meet the specific needs of LDCs. The technology of the North is capital-intensive and requires a relatively small but highly skilled labour force. Such requirements are broadly inappropriate for LDCs, where capital is scarce and labour is abundant but largely unskilled.

> Almost all world expenditures on science and technology take place inside the richer countries, and research and development are therefore quite naturally directed towards solving their problems by methods suited to their circumstances and resource endowments. The problems of the poorer countries, however, are not the same; for instance, they need research to design simple products, to develop production for smaller markets, to improve the quality of and to develop new uses for tropical products, and above all to develop production processes which utilise their abundant labour. Instead, emphasis is placed on sophisticated weaponry, space research, atomic research, sophisticated products, production for high-income markets, and specifically a constant search for processes which save labour by substituting capital or high-order skills.[14]

The application of Northern technology in LDCs can be exceedingly counterproductive. Such was the case when the Canadian International Development Agency (CIDA) undertook to design and build a modern bakery in Tanzania.[15] In 1969, the Tanzanian government asked Canada for assistance in building a modern, semi-automatic bakery in Dar es Salaam to replace the six existing traditional bakeries. Canada agreed, but insisted that Canadian technology be used, a technology that proved unsuitable for conditions in Tanzania on several scores. First, it was overly capital-intensive. Canadian loans were given on the condition that Canadian consulting services, design, and equipment were purchased. Second, the factory produced white bread, a luxury item that was not part of the traditional diet, from wheat that had to be imported. Unlike the small, traditional bakeries that ran on locally produced charcoal, the modern bakery ovens operated on fossil fuels, which also had to be imported. In addition to the problems of capital cost, social costs were incurred. Finally, the modern bakery provided fewer jobs than did the traditional bakeries — a serious disadvantage in a country with high unemployment. Furthermore, the Canadian technology employed was appropriate for the climatic conditions in Alberta, but not Dar es Salaam. "Its low ceiling, enclosed-wall architecture requires a complicated system of fans and vents to remove excess heat created by the ovens. In contrast, other bakeries in Dar es Salaam have simple, concrete foundations and high ceilings for air circulation — and they cost a fraction of the CIDA-sponsored building."[16] The technology used in the bakery project in Dar es Salaam was inappropriate because it consumed scarce capital resources, it exacerbated the balance-of-payments problem of Tanzania, it failed to utilize local resources (including labour) to the maximum, it was poorly suited to local climatic conditions, and it produced a luxury commodity instead of food for those in need.

But one should not conclude from this example that all capital-intensive, energy-consuming, and labour-saving technologies are wrong for LDCs. What is needed is a more comprehensive strategy to ensure that the technology used actually promotes the development of LDCs. As Klause-Heinrich Standke points out, "any technology that advances development can be considered appropriate technology."[17] But what is development? Clearly it implies a good deal more than economic growth. It also connotes the promotion of social equity within a society as well as between societies on a global scale. Hence, consideration must be given within LDCs to the poor as well as to the rich and to the rural population as well as to the urban. Technology should be geared not only to production but also to the distribution, marketing, and transportation of the goods produced.[18] Appropriate technology makes optimal use of local resources, while safeguarding the long-term health of the environment. Finally, it promotes interdependence among states rather than the dependence of the South on the North.

The direct and indirect cost of technology transfer for LDCs in the existing international economic system and the frequent inappropriateness of Northern technology to meet Southern requirements all point to the need for greater self-sufficiency on the part of the LDCs. More technology must be developed by the South to meet Southern needs. Given the close relationship between social needs and the economy, technology transfers must be regarded as ongoing processes rather than one-time sales or gifts. To import an inappropriate technology is to risk social calamity and further the state's economic vulnerability. To harness technology effectively requires sensitivity to community needs, and training and experience working with the technology. Buying a patent is no guarantee of acquiring expertise. Despite living in a developed economy, few of us would be capable of building a tractor engine, let alone of adapting it to meet new needs, even if we were given the blueprints. In most cases technology is useful only once it has been adapted to suit the particular needs, markets, and human and physical resources of the LDCs. Unless the complexities of the technology are understood, effective implementation will not be possible. Perhaps more importantly, it is only by working with technology that future invention and innovation can take place. Training and the acquisition of expertise in the present are, therefore, critical both to reducing the LDCs' dependence on foreign sources of technology in the future and to procuring their control over their own economic development.

As a long-term solution to the problem of technological dependence, the above strategy sounds straightforward, but it faces several impediments. First, there are the restrictive business practices, discussed earlier, that inhibit the dissemination of information and knowledge within LDCs. Second, the cultivation of indigenous expertise is undermined by the "brain drain" from LDCs to developed countries, often referred to as the "reverse transfer of technology." Many of the brightest and best-educated citizens of LDCs are sent to study at universities in the North. Of these students, a considerable number choose to remain in the North and hence fail to contribute to the economic development of their own countries.

The need for technology is obvious in LDCs. The impediments to their acquisition of technology and the expertise to use it effectively are serious and numerous. The gravity of the problem demands an examination of the North-South negotiations on technology-transfer issues at UNCTAD, an assessment of their progress, and a determination of the causes of their disappointing results.

UNCTAD

Nowhere have the LDCs' expectations of progress on the transfer-of-technology issue been higher than at UNCTAD. The issue has been debated since its very first conference in 1964. Throughout the 1960s, such debates focussed on technology to facilitate industrialization within LDCs, although, by the early 1970s, it was clear that a broader approach was required. The impetus for direct action to facilitate technology transfers from the North to the South came in 1974 when the Pugwash Conference on Science and World Affairs drafted a code designed to regulate technology transfers. The concept of a code was not new; the possibility of developing international rules to regulate technology transfers had been raised at UNCTAD I. But this was the first time that the rights and obligations of countries, especially the rights of the LDCs and the obligations of the developed states, had been clearly enumerated. The Group of 77, supported by the UNCTAD Secretariat, urged UNCTAD to carry on the work begun at Pugwash and to negotiate a legally binding code to govern technology transfers. Plenary meetings of UNCTAD were held only every three to four years, hence ongoing negotiations had to be delegated to subcommittees, groups, and special conferences held under the auspices of UNCTAD. At its next meeting, in May 1976, in Nairobi, Kenya, UNCTAD voted to establish an intergovernmental group of experts to draft an international code of conduct for technology transfers and called upon the U.N. General Assembly to call a conference to adopt the code and decide its legal status.[19] Over the next two years, the group of experts met six times before presenting their proposals to the Conference on the International Code of Conduct in the autumn of 1978.

The decision-making structure at the Conference on the International Code of Conduct paralleled that of UNCTAD itself. The 159 participating states are divided into four categories: Group A, the Asian and African states and Yugoslavia; Group B, the Western states; Group C, the Latin American countries; and Group D, the countries of Eastern Europe. In the negotiations, three groups were salient: the Group of 77 (comprising groups A and C), Group B, and Group D. As is true of the North-South struggle generally, the major controversy occurs between the Group of 77 and Group B. Group D shared many of the interests of the latter; in fact, the countries of Eastern Europe are no more generous than is the West in setting conditions for the transfer of their technologies. During the discussions, however, they tended to rely on the Group B countries to safeguard their shared interest, while publicly championing the LDCs' positions. In addition, the USSR has had some special axes to grind. It sought to end "political discrimination" by the West; in particular, it sought an end to NATO's restrictions on the export of strategic materials to the Eastern-bloc countries.

As is the case in most North-South negotiations, neither the Group of 77 nor Group B is monolithic. The initial push for a code came from the Latin American countries, many of whom were seeking international approval for their strict domestic legislation regulating technology transfers within their borders.[20] Their quest soon had the support of India and the Philippines. By contrast, many of the newly industrialized economies (especially South Korea) were never very enthusiastic about a legally binding code. With time, Thailand and Malaysia came to share South Korea's reservations, and by the later 1970s, even the newly industrialized economies in Latin America shared these reservations. As a result, the African states, Algeria in particular, were left as the main advocates of a code containing stringent obligations to promote the transfer of technology.

This diversity of position and inconsistency was not confined to the Group of 77; views varied considerably among the Group B countries. At one extreme, the U.S.-led "hardliners" (including the United Kingdom, the Netherlands, and Switzerland) preferred to have no code at all. However, realizing that this was impractical, they sought to make its provisions as weak as possible. At the other extreme, the "softliners" (Turkey, in particular, but also the Scandinavian countries) were sympathetic to the demands of the Group of 77 and hence were willing to make major concessions. Quite typically, Canada took a "moderate" position, along with Australia and New Zealand, supporting the code as long as its implementation was voluntary and its application was universal.

The notable differences in the Group B countries' overall responses and attitudes to the LDCs' demands were, in large part, rooted in the diversity of their interests. All of the Group B countries were both importers and exporters of technology, but the relative importance of these two activities was different for each state. For instance, there was a significant cleavage between the countries, such as the United States and Federal Republic of Germany, whose main concern was the protection of the overseas activities of their MNEs, and the states, such as Canada, whose principal concern was the limitation of foreign MNEs' control over their affiliates in other countries. Moreover, Canada, as a net importer of technology, was eager to ensure that the terminology used in the code read "technology-acquiring states" (rather than LDCs) and "technology-exporting countries" (rather than developed states). The LDCs were willing to accept this wording since "technology-acquiring states" applied to them just as well as did "LDCs."

UNCTAD was the negotiating forum preferred by the Group of 77 since the UNCTAD Secretariat also served as the Secretariat for the Group. The overlap eased the preparation of background material and position papers; in many ways it provided an indigenous technology transfer with the U.N. system. The Group B countries formally agreed to co-ordinate their policies for UNCTAD within the Organization for Economic Cooperation and Development, which served as a secretariat for their group.

Of the many contentious issues under negotiation, none proved more intractable than the treatment of multinational enterprises (MNEs). In light of their fundamental concerns for economic self-determination and sovereignty, the LDCs sought to enhance their bargaining strength in dealing with MNEs. The Group of 77 insisted, therefore, that the code include a list of restrictive business practices to regulate MNEs operating within their borders. The issue was so controversial that North and South never even agreed on the agenda for these negotiations, let alone on the substance of the provisions. At the broadest level, the Group of 77 wanted an open list of restrictions so that new controls could be added as deemed necessary, whereas Group B wanted a set list of restrictions so that the MNEs could operate in a stable environment. When it came to specifics, Group B opposed many of the Group of 77 proposals, among them any that undermined the protection accorded to owners of technology by patent legislation.

The problem of regulating the power of MNEs included the issue of technology transfers between a parent company and its affiliates. Should the code regulate such shifts of technology and thus superimpose a concern for the recipient's national interest onto the affairs of the MNE? Such transactions were of vital importance to the LDCs, since, on the one hand, MNEs were their major source of technology and, on the other, decisions within the boardrooms of the MNEs determined the production rights of affiliates. Thus, an MNE might allocate not only technological resources but also the right to use the corporation's marketing network to penetrate local, regional, or global markets. The use of this "product mandate" could have a profound impact on the economic potential of a branch plant or an affiliate.

Such decisions were critical to the LDCs. If technology transfers could be treated the same way as those occurring between totally unrelated enterprises, the less-developed country could play some role in defending its national interest and in determining its potential in the global economy.

For their part, Group B countries, sensitive to the needs of established economic and corporate relations, distinguished technology transfers between a parent company and its affiliates from those between totally unrelated enterprises. They sought to preserve the existing, special relationship between a parent company and its subsidiary. Their stand was rooted in their acceptance of the traditional structures of the established international economy and, more generally, the liberal theory of the firm. The insertion of LDC negotiations within that corporate structure would challenge the workings of the free-enterprise system.

Closely related to the issues of restrictive business practices and relations between parent companies and their affiliates was the highly fractious issue of extraterritoriality. The Group of 77's desire to have developed countries police the overseas activities of their MNEs to ensure that they conformed to the code's provisions was not surprising. After all, the LDCs perceived their bargaining position to be weak relative to that of the MNEs. If the developed countries were required to police the activities of MNEs headquartered in, or in legal terms "found in," their jurisdiction, they would have the leverage to make the MNE honour the code and, possibly more importantly, they would then be responsible for realizing a fundamental aspect of the NIEO — a responsibility they avoid as long as the MNEs are seen as independent actors in the free-enterprise system. If Group B countries accepted responsibility for global economic development, the host LDC and operating MNE could negotiate as relative equals, with the code establishing a legal context. Enforcement of the code would fall to governments acting in concert; the developing country registering a concern and the Group B country using its leverage to enforce it in the name of the international economic order. Such an arrangement would have the further advantage of minimizing the likelihood of conflict between host LDCs and MNEs operating within their borders, conflict that could otherwise have curtailed foreign investment. However, as is the case with international law, enforcement is a perennial problem.

Not surprisingly, obligations requiring home governments to ensure that the overseas activities of their companies conformed with the code's regulations were vehemently opposed by the Group B countries on the grounds that they had neither the right nor the desire to exercise such extraterritorial control. Instead, they favoured a voluntary set of guidelines directed primarily toward enterprises supplying the acquiring technology. Thus, it was limited to intercorporate relations. Otherwise, such governmental control over the private sector was not compatible with accepted norms in Western industrialized states, especially the United States and Mrs. Thatcher's Britain. Furthermore, acceptance of the concept of extraterritoriality at UNCTAD was seen to set an undesirable precedent, particularly to countries such as Canada that had always opposed attempts by the U.S. government to make Canadian subsidiaries of American MNEs or their officers subject to American law. The distinction between governmental intervention to control the MNE for somewhat altruistic ends was transformed in the minds of these middle-sized states into a concern that the government of a major Group B country housing an MNE might use its leverage to realize its own international priorities.

A second, and only slightly less controversial, set of issues related to the relative status of national legislation and international law in the regulation of technology transfers, and the rules and procedures for settling disputes. Both North and South recognized and supported the sovereign right of states to make and implement laws pertaining to technology transfers within their jurisdiction; but they differed on the extent of that right. The Group of 77 insisted that the sovereignty should be absolute and hence not limited by a need to conform to international norms. Group B, in contrast, contended that states had the right to legislate as long as its laws were in conformity with international law. Adherence to international norms was necessary, it argued, to safeguard the legitimate interests of suppliers of technology (particularly MNEs) and to create an environment of stable expectations that would facilitate and encourage transfers. Group B sought a commitment on the part of the LDCs to act in accordance with international law and advocated drafting a list of the measures to regulate technology transfers that could be included in national laws. When it came to the negotiation of a particular contract, Group B countries insisted on the right of the parties involved to mutually agree on which law would be applicable.

On the matter of dispute settlement, the delegates had to decide on the procedures and mechanisms for resolving disagreements arising out of contracts designed to transfer technology. For example, would a dispute over the meaning of a contract be negotiated or would it be referred to arbitration? Who would do the negotiating or judging? Whose laws would provide the framework within which the dispute would be resolved? Once again, the Group of 77 insisted the choice belonged to the country receiving the transfer, which meant that the dispute would, in most cases, be settled in the recipient country's courts, using its laws. Not surprisingly, Group B maintained that the mechanisms and procedures for settling disputes would have to be negotiated as part of the conditions of a contract to transfer technology. Its position reflected current practice, where most contracts involving transfers of technology specify that, in the event of a dispute arising between the parties to the contract, it will be referred to a specified body for adjudication and specific laws will apply. For example, contracts between Canada and the USSR usually designate the Swedish Board of Trade as the adjudicating body.

Given the controversial nature of the code, and its far-reaching implications not only for the economic development of LDCs but also for the scope of governmental responsibility in shaping the global economic order, it is hardly surprising that the North and South were polarized over both its legal character and the practical implications. The Group of 77 maintained that the code should be legally binding and that steps should be defined that would ensure its effective implementation. Group B argued that the code should comprise a set of voluntary guidelines that governments could urge their companies to follow when negotiating contracts involving technology transfers. Members of Group B were unwilling, however, either to pass legislation to make the code provisions operational within their jurisdictions or to force their companies to comply with the code's regulations. As the negotiations dragged on, there was an increasing realization, if not complete acceptance, among the LDCs that the code would not be mandatory.

The controversial nature of the issues discussed above resulted in a protracted and conflict-ridden conference. Its meetings began in 1978 and continued into the 1980s; but, according to members of the Canadian delegation, no concrete progress was made after 1980. Instead, negotiations degenerated into stalemate.

Prior to this, especially during the early years of the conference, some successes were achieved. For example, as the result of compromise by the Group of 77, agreement was reached on the issue of universality. The Group of 77 would have preferred to have the code apply only to transfers of technology between developed and developing countries. This interpretation would exclude the MNEs of newly industrializing LDCs from having to conform to the regulations of the code. Group B insisted that the code apply to all transfers of technology, regardless of the parties involved. They insisted on the terms "technology supplier" and "technology recipient," which were inclusive. The terminology clearly referred to the entities directly involved in the transactions, which in most cases were the MNEs themselves. Thus, it side-stepped governmental responsibility for the activities of MNEs. Furthermore, since many of the Group B states, like Canada, were recipients as well as sources of technology, they wanted to be able to take advantage of any benefits the code might offer. With time the Group of 77 accepted the concept of universality.

The high point in the conference came in 1980 when it appeared likely that the code would be accepted. But, hopes faded quickly when Brazil, and subsequently the African states, rejected it. Thereafter, the United States and the other "hardliners" became increasingly intransigent. On the issues relating to the treatment of MNEs, the obligations of states to enforce the code, the applicable law, and the settlement of disputes, the gulf between North and South was never bridged.

The UNCTAD experience was not atypical. The 1979 United Nations Conference on Science and Technology for Development was no more successful in adapting a code to regulate technology transfers than was UNCTAD. Moreover, the hardening of positions, especially on the part of the major Group B countries, in the later 1970s and early 1980s also undermined negotiations in other international fora.

At the Third United Nations Conference on the Law of the Sea, for example, the United States, United Kingdom, and Federal Republic of Germany all rejected the Law of the Sea Convention after nine years of intense negotiations, on the grounds that it discriminated against private enterprise and placed onerous obligations on developed countries. Among the provisions they rejected were those pertaining to technology transfer.

Throughout both the drafting of the proposed code and negotiations on its provisions, progress at UNCTAD was impeded by several factors. First, the mandate under negotiation was enormous, and largely unmanageable, encompassing restrictive business practices, the conduct of multinational corporations (each of which was the subject of an entire conference), and intellectual-property rights. The last was the focus of attention for the World Intellectual Property Organization.

Second, the interests of North and South clearly conflicted. The South wanted to secure its access to technology at an affordable price and to enhance its bargaining leverage with the MNEs. The North sought to safeguard technology owners, the MNEs in particular, from mandatory transfers and other undue restrictions on their freedom to act. The Group of 77 and Group B each perceived its interests to be vital and its grave reservations about the other group's positions to be justified; hence the conflict persisted.

Third, and most importantly, the political will to reach a compromise position was missing, especially during the late 1970s and early 1980s. The interests of the LDCs and Group B countries conflicted, and each saw its own interests as fundamental. A gain by one group was seen as a loss by the other. Furthermore, the United States, which would play a crucial role apropos the MNEs, took a very hard line during the four years of the Carter administration in an effort to win business votes in the next election. Needless to say, such a stance did not facilitate reaching compromises at UNCTAD. The Group of 77, for its part, was less and less able to exert pressure on Group B to compromise. The growing strength of the Southeast Asian and Latin American participants lessened their interest in the code and thus led to internal differences and dissension within the Group of 77, which undermined a strong united front. In fact by 1980, the African states alone were advocating a legally binding code.

Group D continued to give nominal support to the Group of 77's positions and to be critical of Group B's policies. Nonetheless, its endorsement of UNCTAD's efforts to promote technology transfers was clearly limited. It vehemently opposed any Group of 77 proposals to increase UNCTAD's administrative costs, facilities, and resources.

Finally, the decision-making process was not conducive to compromises. Each of the negotiating groups worked out its position before negotiating with the other groups. Hence, each arrived at the bargaining table with an inflexible stand that took little account of the other's interests. As Finlayson and Zacher point out,

> the LDCs tend to produce an extraordinarily ambitious package of proposals which is basically an aggregate of the disparate (and often conflicting) demands of the

> members. The developed countries often evolve a common position that is largely determined by the views of the least tractable of the Western bloc. It is hardly surprising therefore that . . . agreement is rare. As a brief from the government of the Netherlands once noted, decision-making in UNCTAD is characterized by a revised version of Gresham's law: "extreme positions drive out moderate ones."[21]

The combination of these four impediments (the extensive agenda, the conflict of interests, the lack of political will, and the nature of the decision-making process) deterred progress at UNCTAD's negotiations on technology transfer. It is extremely difficult to address each problem separately, since they are interrelated. The large mandate increased the number of contentious issues to be discussed. Divergent interests diminished the will to compromise, which in turn impeded the resolution of conflicts. Finally, the nature of the decision-making process intensified existing cleavages.

Conclusion

The issue of technology transfer remains an important aspect of the program to create an NIEO. It also illustrates the growing conflict and debate over the role of the state in regulating the returns of the international economy. Should Group B states assume responsibility for the redistribution of the rewards of the international economy? Or should each state maximize its own self-interest? The behaviour of the major Group B countries exemplifies adherence to the latter course, but so did the erosion within the Group of 77 with respect to support for a binding code. The recent shift of wealth and economic development to the newly industrializing economies, such as South Korea, Taiwan, and Singapore, poses a tough challenge to the traditional international economic order. Group B countries frequently respond with policies of retrenchment and the rigid promotion of their short-term economic interests. As rewards shift in the international system, Group B countries may increasingly have to make concessions to bolster their attractiveness to MNEs, thereby lessening their political power to reinforce the traditional world economy.

At the same time, the blossoming of the newly industrializing economies has implications for solidarity within the Group of 77 as the gulf between them and the least-developed countries widens. As was seen in the UNCTAD negotiations, the newly industrializing economies promote their own interests rather than those of the least-developed states, which begs the question: can the United Nations fill the void as the spokesperson for an international order in the realm of intellectual property that promotes the interests of the least-developed countries, or will the initiative remain with blocks of like-minded states using whatever leverage is available to them? The answer has profound implications for the transfer of technology and the NIEO. It has also provided insights into the role of the state in determining the returns from an increasingly global economy.

NOTES

1. Almost all of the U.N. specialized agencies working in the areas of science and technology have interests in technology transfer. For example, the World Health Organization is concerned about pharmaceuticals; the U.N. Educational, Scientific and Cultural Organization seeks to promote scientific research and the dissemination of knowledge; the Food and Agriculture Organization is concerned about developing expertise to facilitate greater agricultural productivity; the International Labour Organization is interested in training programs; the World Intellectual Property Organization deals with matters pertaining to patents; and the U.N. Industrial Development Organization examines the criteria for licensing arrangements. In 1979, the United Nations sponsored the Conference on Science and Technology for Development, whose mandate virtually duplicated the work of UNCTAD and which also failed to produce a code to regulate technology transfer. The transfer of technology has also been on the agenda of several other negotiations sponsored by United Nations, in particular those pertaining to restrictive business practices and the code of conduct for multinational enterprises.

2. United Nations, General Assembly, Resolution 623 (VII).

3. United Nations, General Assembly, Resolution 1897 (XVIII).

4. UNCTAD was established and its terms of reference outlined in General Assembly Resolution 1995 (XIX).

5. Jan Tinbergen et al. provide a useful discussion of these problems in *RIO: Reshaping the International Order: Report to the Club of Rome* (New York: The Club of Rome, 1976), 25–46.

6. United Nations, General Assembly, Resolutions 3201 (S-VI), and 3202 (S-VI).

7. United Nations, General Assembly, Resolution 3281 (XXIX).

8. A.F. Ewing, "UNCTAD and the Transfer of Technology," *Journal of World Trade Law* 10 (May/June 1976): 197. See also Hans Singer and Javed Ansari, *Rich and Poor Countries*, 3d ed. (London: George Allen and Unwin, 1982), esp. 37; and S.J. Patel, "The Technological Dependence of Developing Countries," *Journal of Modern African Studies* 12, no. 1 (1974): 1–18.

9. Ervin Laszlo et al., *The Objectives of the New International Economic Order* (New York: Pergamon, 1978), xvii–xviii.

10. Dennis Thompson, "The UNCTAD Code on Transfer of Technology," *Journal of World Trade Law* 16 (July/August 1982): 312.

11. UNCTAD, Secretariat, TD/B/AC.11/10/Rev. 2 (1975): 7.

12. Oseheimen Osunbor, "Law and Policy on the Registration of Technology Transfer Transactions in Nigeria," *Journal of World Trade Law* 21, no. 5 (1987): 27.

13. The OPEC countries are unique among LDCs in having large foreign currency reserves.

14. Singer and Ansari, *Rich and Poor Countries*, 50.

15. For further information about the case, see Roger Young, *Canadian Development Assistance to Tanzania: An Independent Study* (Ottawa: North-South Institute, 1983),

75–77; and Robert Carty and Virginia Smith, *Perpetuating Poverty: The Political Economy of Canadian Foreign Aid* (Toronto: Between the Lines, 1981), especially 71–74.

16. Carty and Smith, *Perpetuating Poverty*, 72.

17. Klaus-Heinrich Standke, "Appropriate Technology for the Third Development Decade," in *The Challenge of the New International Economic Order*, ed. Edwin P. Reubens (Boulder, Colo.: Westview, 1981), 142.

18. Standke, "Appropriate Technology," 142.

19. UNCTAD IV, Resolution 89, Nairobi, May 1976.

20. The Andean Common Market had already agreed in 1970 to a Uniform Code on Foreign Investment, which established terms for receiving technology on a regional basis.

21. J.A. Finlayson and M.W. Zacher, "International Trade Institutions and the North/South Dialogue," *International Journal* 36 (Autumn 1981): 732–65.

SELECT BIBLIOGRAPHY

Ahooja-Patel, Krishna; Anne Gord Drabek; and Marc Nerfin, eds. *World Economy in Transition*. New York: Pergamon, 1986.

Clark, N. "The Multi-National Corporation: The Transfer of Technology and Dependence." *Development and Change* 6, no. 1 (1975): 5–21.

Cole, Sam, and Ian Miles. *Worlds Apart: Technology and North-South Relations in the Global Economy*. Sussex: Wheatsheaf, 1984.

Eckaus, Richard S. *Appropriate Technologies for Developing Countries*. Washington: National Academy of Sciences, 1977.

Ewing, A.F. "UNCTAD and the Transfer of Technology." *Journal of World Trade Law* 10, no. 3 (1976): 197–213.

Ezegbobelu, Edmund Emeka. *Development Impact of Technology Transfers Theory and Practice: A Case of Nigeria, 1970-1982*. Frankfurt: Peter Lang, 1986.

Farrel, Trevor M.A. "Do Multinational Corporations Really Transfer Technology?" In *Integration of Science and Technology with Development / Caribbean and Latin American Problems in the Context of the United Nations Conference on Science and Technology for Development*, ed. D.B. Thomas and M. Wioncz. London: Pergamon, 1979.

Glaser, Edward M.; Harold H. Abelson, and Kathalee N. Garrison. *Putting Knowledge to Use: Facilitating the Diffusion of Knowledge and the Implementation of Planned Change*. London: Jossey-Bass, 1983, esp. chap. 13.

Heller, Peter B. *Technology Transfer and Human Values: Concepts, Applications, Cases*. New York: University Press of America, 1985.

Lall, Sanjaya. "Brandt on 'Transnational Corporations Investment and the Sharing of Technology.'" In *Third World Strategy: Economic and Political Cohesion in the South*, ed. Altaf Gauhar. New York: Praeger Special Studies, 1983.

Murphy, Craig. *The Emergence of the NIEO Ideology*. Boulder, Colo.: Westview, 1984.

Osunbor, Oseheimen. "Law and Policy on the Registration of Technology Transfer Transactions in Nigeria." *Journal of World Trade Law* 21, no. 5 (1987): 13–30.

Ravn, Hans F. *Technological Planning in Underdeveloped Countries.* Denmark: Eksamensprojekt, 1976.

Roffe, P. "UNCTAD Transfer of Technology Code." *Journal of World Trade Law* 18, no. 2 (1984): 176–82.

Reubens, Edwin P., ed. *The Challenge of the New International Economic Order.* Boulder, Colo.: Westview, 1981.

Stewart, F. *Technology and Underdevelopment*, 2d ed. London: Macmillan, 1978.

Thompson, Dennis. "The UNCTAD Code on Transfer of Technology." *Journal of World Trade Law* 16, no. 4 (1982): 311–37.

THE INTERNATIONAL POLITICAL ECONOMY OF FOOD AND AGRICULTURE

Andrew Fenton Cooper

The politics of food and agriculture have attracted considerable attention in recent years. The concern here derives, to a large extent, from problems with the supply and distribution of foodstuffs — problems that have been exacerbated by the food shock of 1972–74, the increasingly competitive and bellicose behaviour of the major agricultural trading nations, and the accelerated trend toward divergent economic approaches in the Third World. The main purpose of this chapter is to present an overview of some of the more significant of these complex problems, with special attention to their place in the wider literature on international political economy (IPE). An underlying theme of this chapter is the relative usefulness of a number of distinctive perspectives from this wider IPE literature in understanding food and agricultural issues. This chapter attempts to provide some theoretical underpinning for a better understanding of the international political economy of food and agriculture, and provide a broad range of views on future tendencies within the issue-area.

Regimes and the Erosion of Economic Liberalism

One approach to the international relations of food has been put forward by Raymond Hopkins and Donald Puchala in *The Global Political Economy of Food.*[1] Hopkins and Puchala suggest that food and agricultural issues in the post-1945 period can best be understood in terms of a distinctive system or regime, a regime in which different actors understand or are aware of the appropriateness and legitimacy of certain norms, rules, and decision-making procedures. On the basis of these norms, rules, and procedures, an element of international collaboration or pattern of regularized co-operative behaviour is built up in the issue-area.

Regime analysis has a number of attractions. As a framework, it facilitates taking a systemic view of a multifaceted issue-area such as food and agriculture. The regime is said to encompass all forms of transactions, including concessional ones, in the form of food aid and technology transfer, as well as those made in the commercial marketplace. At the same time, regime analysis allows for some discrepancies between attitudes and practices, on the one hand, and codified rules, on the other. Such analysis is extremely important for the food and agriculture regime in that the norms and rules (e.g., adherence to the principles of the free market, the free movement of technology, and the qualified acceptance of extra-market channels of food distribution) emphasized by Hopkins and Puchala are sometimes contradicted in practice. The best illustration of this sort of inconsistency came with the extension of an open-ended waiver to the United States in 1955, which put American trade-restricting practices outside the purview of the GATT.[2] Accordingly, although comprehensive, the regime discerned by Hopkins and Puchala in the food and agriculture issue-area may be said to have been a loose and informal one, frequently deviating from and containing exceptions to the strictures of its origin. Especially relevant here is the shift in the hierarchy among the norms within the regime. If the weight given to individual norms changes (to national self-reliance or sovereignty, for example, as opposed to the free transactions of produce), the regime itself may change.

The hierarchical nature of the regime, vis-à-vis the respective roles of the actors within an issue-area regime, also needs to be elaborated upon. As was the case in most areas in the postwar period, the United States was the dominant actor in the food system. By virtue of its willingness to take on the burden of the role of global food manager — and, specifically, to perform the role of stock-holder of last resort (or residual supplier) in grains in respect of both commercial and concessional transactions — the United States was instrumental in shaping the nature and extent of the regime itself. In many respects, the norms and rules of the food and agriculture regime reflected the liberal economic values championed (although not always practised) by the United States, values that included a commitment to comparative advantage, specialization, and the free and open exchange of goods and technology. Under such conditions, American politicians and bureaucrats argued that economic growth and efficiency could be maximized on a global level. Conversely, constraints of an illiberal nature were generally considered to be detrimental to those liberal economic values that formed the cornerstone of the postwar order.

Such a regime had a number of benefits for the major Western allies of the United States. Above all, the liberal flow of foodstuffs allowed Western Europe and Japan to secure cheap and secure supplies of foodstuffs, thus enabling those countries to concentrate on the reconstruction of their industrial plant and infrastructure after the disruptions of World War II. Japanese self-sufficiency measured in terms of the value of domestic production of food of agricultural origin as a percentage of total supplies, for instance, fell from 95 percent in 1955 to 73 percent in 1972.[3] Moreover, this pattern of exchange allowed these actors to benefit from the positive effects of technological transfer. To give just one illustration, the development of the modern European poultry industry was based on the import of American "breeder stock, formula feed, equipment (brooders, slaughterhouse machinery, automatic feeders, etc.), and technicians."[4]

Still, despite all of these benefits, suspicions about the principles of economic liberalism (and U.S. leadership) have plagued the advanced industrial countries.

The strength of these negative feelings was shown clearly by the establishment and extension in the European Community of the Common Agricultural Policy (CAP), and the retention by Japan (through the Basic Agricultural Law) of import quotas and other protective devices on a wide number of agricultural items, even after the 1961 liberalization of foreign-trade controls. In part, this resistance to the imposition of liberal economic principles reflects the clout of the protectionist-oriented farm lobbies in Western Europe and Japan. In both the EC and Japan, these groups were not only vociferous in their defence of specific sectoral interests but politically powerful; rural support has been critical for the ruling Liberal Democratic Party in Japan, the Gaullists in France, and the Christian Democratic–Free Democratic coalition governments in the Federal Republic of Germany.

This resistance has, however, also provided evidence of the continuing challenge that mercantilism poses to the post-1945 liberal order. For mercantilists, such as Charles de Gaulle, economic liberalism was simply a rationale for hegemony — a means by which U.S. power could be exerted (both directly, through governmental policy, and indirectly, through the activity of U.S.-based multinational corporations). As such, France's own national power had to be exerted diplomatically, strategically, as well as economically. From a narrower economic nationalist (or neomercantilist) perspective, the safeguarding of the values and interests of a society (including the rural way of life) was given much higher priority than economic efficiency. Concomitantly, greater weight was placed by neomercantilists than by economic liberals on the role of an activist or interventionist state. Rather than relying on market forces or other actors to produce prosperity, self-help had to be practised.

Although conflict-oriented (witness the so-called chicken war waged between the European Community and the United States from 1961 to 1964), the neomercantilist challenge did not constitute a fundamental one to the international food and agriculture order in the 1950s and 1960s. As long as the United States was willing to take on the burden of leadership, carrying out its responsibilities notwithstanding the short-term sacrifices it had to make to do so, the stability of that regime seemed secure. Reinforcing this point, there seemed to be clear signs that many of the illiberal practices of the EC's Common Agricultural Policy (the very symbol of mercantilism) were more likely to be rolled back than extended in the early 1970s if external circumstances had not intervened. Aside from the more vigorous pressure exerted by the United States for a more open trading system, pressure for the reform of the CAP was growing within the EC itself. The overall costs of the CAP, and the maldistribution of the rewards between large and small farmers, was and is a major irritant in European relations. The enlargement of the EC, and particularly the entry of Britain, added another significant push for more openness in agricultural trade within the Community.

What threatened to undermine the stability of the international food regime (as with the IPE more generally) were not the internal mercantilist practices of the EC or Japan. Rather, the threat to stability was a reflection of a series of external shocks. The critical period for the food regime came when it was confronted with the food crises of the early 1970s. The most dramatic of these shocks came in the form of natural phenomena — that is to say, the failure of crops caused by drought in Asia, the Soviet Union, North America, and Africa, and the change in ocean currents. These shocks were preceded, moreover, by signals that the regime leader was not only withdrawing from some of its commitments to the post-1945 regime (specifically, with respect to the international orderly marketing of grains) but it was attempting to impose new terms on the other countries based on its own definition of "equal treatment" (which ultimately involved the promotion of American exports). With this new emphasis on national self-interest, as opposed to international obligations, the Americans directed attention away from the anomalies and defects of the EC's CAP and Japanese-import restrictions, and onto their own declining will and capacity for maintaining and defending the international food and agriculture system.

Undoubtedly, the shift in the U.S. approach constrained the reform impetus in the EC and Japan. Mansholt, the Dutch commissioner of agriculture (and perhaps the most prominent advocate of CAP reform within the EC), made it quite clear that he considered the move by the United States in the late 1960s away from support for the International Wheat Agreement to be most unhelpful to the commission's efforts to restructure the CAP. Without some renewed commitment by the United States to maintain order in the world market, he warned, it could not be expected that the EC would be flexible on protectionism. The sense of uncertainly aroused by the change in the American approach to the IPE of food and agriculture was heightened by the confrontational language accompanying it. In the late 1960s and early 1970s, American politicians and officials repeatedly called upon their trading partners in the Western world to abandon or ease their impediments to access, and adhere more fully to the principles of open trade and investment. Nor were the actions of the United States any less blunt than its talk. One indirect sign of the American escalation with respect to the use of tactics designed to win concessions on agricultural trade came in the form of the "Nixon shock" in 1971. By effectively devaluing the American currency and introducing a surcharge of 10 percent on all dutiable imports, the Nixon administration hoped to gain some leverage in the upcoming trade negotiations.

These indirect measures were supplemented by more direct measures that were associated with the food crisis of 1972–74. The most traumatic of these initiatives was the sudden decision of the Nixon administration to place an embargo on the export of soybeans and soybean products in 1973. The embargo itself was extremely short-lived, lasting from June 27 to July 2, 1973, when it was replaced by export controls that continued through the rest of the summer. The decision to impose the embargo could be explained, retrospectively, as a "one-off" action designed to defend the interests of both domestic and foreign consumers during a time of reduced supplies (largely as a result of the vagaries of nature) and higher prices for protein. Despite these situational allowances, though, the economic and psychological impact of the embargo on the EC and Japan was profound. Whether interpreted as either (in the absence of prior consultation) a sign of poor crisis management or a blatant attempt to use American influence in the food sector ("to show something to the people who thought our economic strength was low"), the credibility of the United States as a reliable supplier of foodstuffs was seriously damaged.

The ultimate effect of these measures — compounded by the subsequent OPEC crisis — was to place the issues of autonomy and self-sufficiency with respect to foodstuffs on the top of the political agenda in Japan and the EC. Dependence on the United States for specific imports having become equated in the minds of European and Japanese opinion leaders with vulnerability and the loss of independent decision making, far less attention was paid to the idea of reform of illiberal trading practices and far more on building up and maintaining food security in keeping with a narrowly defined self-interest. If the United States was unwilling or unable to continue to provide adequate protection in the way of international food security, the industrial countries would look to address the security-of-supply issue. In other words, self-help was legitimized and encouraged at the expense of economic liberalism. As one leading American proponent of a market-oriented agricultural-trade approach has argued: "Americans must admit that our own temporary embargo . . . gave support to arguments for protectionism . . . [creating] a climate that continues to be deleterious to our efforts to assure reductions in barriers to trade in agricultural products."[5]

The EC and Japan had, broadly speaking, two options available to them as part of an overall strategy of assuring supplies of foodstuffs. The first of these options was simply to raise internal support prices for basic crops while relying less on agricultural imports. To a certain extent, this path was followed by Japan — especially with regard to the establishment of a two-million-ton emergency fund of rice and restrictions on the import of beef through such measures as the 1975 Beef Price Stabilization Scheme. Such an inward-looking approach had the inevitable consequence of generating new sources of conflict with the United States and other exporting countries over access to the Japanese market. As the president of the Brookings Institution suggested with respect to the American embargo and Japan's response: "It is not difficult to see how a pattern of thrust and parry could thus be established in U.S.-Japanese agricultural relations, which have hitherto been relatively free of tension."[6]

Japan did not extend this inward-looking approach to the point of autarchy. Rather, because of the physical limitations imposed on its own agricultural production, Japan meshed this first type of approach with a more outward-looking approach directed at the search for alternative sources of secure and cheap supplies of agricultural goods. This diversification strategy was, in turn, based on the more creative utilization of economic statecraft. Critical to this second approach was the establishment by Japan of a new set of bilateral relationships with various Third World countries that gave preferential treatment to the imports from those countries. One interesting example of this type of relationship was with Brazil, which received massive Japanese public- and private-sector support in the building up of its export capacity with respect to agricultural exports. The initial focus of this 'Brazilian fever' was on the soybean potential of that country; a potential abundantly realized as Brazil's production of soybeans grew from 20 000 bushels in the mid-1960s to more than 400 000 tons in 1976.[7] Over time, this Japanese interest in Brazilian agriculture has expanded to include other products, such as poultry and beef. Another significant example of intensified Japanese involvement in Third World agriculture, as part of a wide-ranging diversification strategy, may be found with reference to Southeast Asia, in countries such as Thailand. As in the case of Brazil, Japanese government and business concerns were instrumental in encouraging Thailand's exports of animal feedgrain (corn) and meat products. For instance, the Thai share of the Japanese market in boneless poultry increased quickly from 1.8 percent in 1975 to 8.5 percent in 1977, to 26 percent in 1980.[8]

The EC resorted to an outward-looking strategy to ensure food security in selective products where there was a "gap" in the CAP. The most notable example in this regard was, of course, the supply of protein feed materials. Parallel to the Japanese approach, the main thrust of the EC's effort to secure reliable and cheap sources of supply involved the development of feed production and export in South America, Asia, and Africa. Groundnut production in West Africa, manioc production in Thailand and Indonesia, and soybean production in Brazil were targeted by the EC in this fashion, as witnessed by the Community's distribution of technical aid for agricultural development; its promotion of joint ventures; and its establishment of institutional links such as the Lomé Agreement, the joint EC–ASEAN study group, and its support for the Amazonian Development Agency. This diversification approach not only spread the risk of alternative supplies of "strategic goods" for the EC members but created attractive new opportunities for West European investors.

In products covered by the CAP, the EC concentrated on increasing its own internal farm production through the continuation and expansion of high prices and open-ended intervention guarantees. In the context of the food crisis, the cost of this approach seemed to be well justified. Even the long-time critic of the CAP, *The Economist*, admitted in 1974 that "instead of the ogre it once appeared to be, the CAP is protecting the community from some of the unstabilizing effects of the price spiral."[9] The longer-term implications arising out of this food-security approach were realized only when the crisis receded in the late 1970s. This inward-looking, expansionist strategy pushed the EC's overall agricultural production well beyond the requirements of its own immediate food-security needs. By 1983, the degree of EC self-sufficiency in percentage terms was high in wheat (125), sugar (144), cheese (108), butter (123), beef and veal (104), pigmeat (101), and poultry (110).[10]

The move of the EC from a position of being a net-deficit to a net-surplus actor in a wide variety of agricultural products introduced new sources of tension into the IPE of food and agriculture. As massive "mountains" of agricultural produce accumulated in the post-crisis environment, the CAP was gradually "globalized" in the sense that the surpluses were incorporated into an emergent EC agricultural export strategy utilizing export subsidies or "restitutions." The EC justified this new approach on pragmatic grounds, arguing that it was better to subsidize consumers outside the Community (especially in the Third World) at a low cost than to subsidize the storage and preservation of stockpiles inside the EC at a high cost. To the traditional defenders of the CAP, nevertheless, an explicit export strategy also had the advantage of institutionalizing those surpluses.

The EC's efforts to "export the CAP's problems" posed a direct challenge to U.S. leadership in international agricultural transactions. In overall commercial transactions, the United States continued to lead, exporting $41.7 billion (U.S.) of produce in 1982, 70 percent more than in 1976.[11] The EC vaulted into second place, with agricultural exports valued at $27 billion in 1982, a 156 percent rise during the same six-year period. In terms of specific commodities, the EC had, by the early 1980s, become the world's largest exporter of some of the major agricultural exports, including poultry; the supplier of three-fifths of the international market in butter and dried milk; and the second-largest exporter of beef (after Australia); as well as a major exporter of grain and flour.

The impact of this challenge was felt in a variety of ways. At the level of values, there continued to be fundamental differences between the weight placed by the United States on a "free market" and the EC's emphasis on "sovereignty" and the "management" of international transactions. At the level of action, the increasingly aggressive export approach prompted a backlash from the United States. During the Carter administration and the early part (particularly prior to the November 1982 GATT Ministerial) of the Reagan administration, this response centred on a concerted attempt to win recourse through a revamped subsidy code of international trade under the GATT. Frustration over the slow pace involved in changing the formal rules governing export subsidies, however, encouraged Americans to "fight fire with fire." The clearest expression of this frustration was the decision by the United States, in January 1983, to openly subsidize the sale of one million tons of surplus wheat flour held in government warehouses to Egypt — a traditional European market. In doing this, the United States signalled to the other actors involved in food and agricultural trade that it was willing to resort to explicitly mercantilist practices to defend economic liberal values.

Toward an Agricultural Trade War?

Given the multiple tensions in the U.S.–EC and U.S.–Japan agricultural relationship, there has been a tendency to portray these relationships as openly hostile. The U.S.–Japan conflict over access to the domestic Japanese market broadened and deepened by the mid-1980s, to the point where the two countries appeared to be on a "collision course." [12] Even more dramatically, by the same time, a "ploughshares war" was said to have broken out between the EC and the United States. [13]

Viewing the agricultural relationship between the various Western allies as an essentially adversarial one offers a guide for an understanding of this issue-area. To be sure, the highly charged rhetoric of the main players (such as accusations by the French that the Americans were utilizing "gunboat" or

"Rambo" negotiating tactics) appears to justify this way of analyzing international food relations. Yet, despite this heated debate, the picture one gets of international food politics in the 1980s is not of an inexorable extension of mercantilism. Rather, it is of a more "segmented" nature,[14] in which there has been a considerable erosion of liberal economic practices in some areas and a substantial element of resilience in others. Although heated, the tension does not appear to have reached the point where a total collapse of the post-1945 order is imminent.

In attempting to account for the resilience of economic liberalism, two explanations seem plausible. One is that the decline of U.S. power and influence in the food and agriculture area has been overstated. If the United States is no longer the stabilizer of the food system, it may be argued that it continues to exert considerable leverage over the other key actors through the use of economic statecraft involving linkage and retaliatory tactics. This line of argument would appear to go some way toward explaining why Japan has backed down somewhat on the access question, and why the EC has hesitated both with respect to closing the internal holes in the CAP and with reference to the extension of its global export-subsidy program. It may also explain why both the EC and Japan have grudgingly agreed to have agriculture "on the table" in the Uruguay Round of the GATT.

Another possible explanation gives greater weight to the role of other actors as important stabilizers or rule-keepers in the international political economy of food and agriculture. There are at least three categories of these types of actors. First, there is the extensive network of international organizations involved in this issue-area. These organizations include recently created informal institutions such as the Western Economic Summit as well as the well-established formal organizations such as the Organization for Economic Cooperation and Development (OECD), the U.N. Food and Agriculture Organization (FAO), the international Wheat Council, and the GATT. All have been criticized in the past for being "talking shops" with little clout over the behaviour of individual states. More recently though, in the context of the ongoing attempt to "reform" world agriculture (i.e., eliminating distortions in trade) in the 1980s, these organizations have been given at least some credit both for persistence in providing a forum for discussions and more co-operative behaviour and for their efforts in providing technical data to buttress this activity. Many of the steps toward building consensus on the need and practicalities of reform have come out of the work of these institutions.

A second bulwark of economic liberalism has been the large number of multinational corporations (MNCs) extensively involved in global agriculture transactions. American agribusiness interests benefited substantially from the liberal economic order of the post-1945 period, in that the values of that regime facilitated the ability of those interests to gain access to foreign markets on a global basis. Understandably, therefore, the challenge to liberal values posed by neomercantilist tendencies has been perceived by many to be a serious problem in that economic nationalism tends to erode the position of the MNCs in the food system by distorting market forces, by creating uncertainty (as the adage states: "trade abhors tension but follows friendship"), and by necessitating the introduction of costly strategies designed by individual corporations to allow them to overcome protectionist barriers. Nor have the American-based MNCs been isolated in this resistance to neo-mercantilism. With the greater internationalization of agribusiness in the 1970s and 1980s the stake of non-American (especially West European and Japanese) as well as American-based corporations in open transactions has increased. Some of these concerns have taken advantage of diversified sources for raw materials. More innovatively, others have wanted to more fully integrate their operations abroad into the U.S. agribusiness model.

The third set of actors with an active interest in agricultural trade liberalization consists of those countries that were the long-standing supporters of the values and principles of the post-1945 food order. Of these countries, the most important have been Canada and Australia.[15] Traditionally, these two middle powers have placed considerable weight on "order" and "rules" in international agricultural transactions. In practice, this support for the post-1945 order has been reflected in the continuing diplomatic efforts made by both Canada and Australia to modify the practices of other actors that were at odds with the rules of that order. The strength of this commitment may be judged by the fact that, even subsequent to the shocks of the early 1970s, there remained a strong element in the Canadian and Australian approaches on agricultural issues that subordinated other goals to those centred on attempting to re-establish stability in world markets.

This commitment to orderly behaviour is not to imply that neither of these two countries has refrained from contemplating alternative (i.e., defection) strategies. On the contrary, during the late 1970s and early 1980s, there were indications in both of these countries of a possible shift toward a more state-centred agricultural approach, where Canada and Australia would aggressively compete with the United States and the EC for international agricultural markets. In Canada, the operationalization of a more mercantilist-oriented approach was associated with Canagrex, a (short-lived) state trading agency. In Australia, a shift to a more regional focus on agricultural trade was accompanied by the utilization of more creative trading practices, such as barter or countertrade. The two countries also parallel each other in the emphasis they have recently placed on the development of a "special relationship" with their prime trading partner. With respect to Canada the focus of attention has been the United States; in Australia's case, Japan.

Despite the availability of these options, perhaps the most interesting aspect of the Canadian and Australian approach in the 1980s with respect to the political economy of food and agriculture is the lingering faith both of these countries have in the old order. The most important sign of this faith is the leadership role embraced by both Australia and Canada in the creation of the so-called Cairns group as a coalition of reformist, "fair-trading" countries to act as a "third force" between the United States and the European Community. Consistent with Canadian and Australian efforts in the past, the main focus of this group (made up of 14 diverse countries) has been designed to constrain the "unacceptable" behaviour of other actors. As such, this group has criticized both the high internal support and external subsidy levels maintained by the European Community and moves made in the same direction by the United States. However, as in the 1950s and 1960s, this disapproval of the actions of others did not translate into direct retaliatory action. Rather, the coalition has tried to bring the two main players back in line through confidence-building measures and a renewed emphasis on dispute-settlement through the use of international institutions. While the long-term future of the Cairns group remains unclear, it has already achieved some success in terms of "agenda-setting" in the Uruguay Round.[16]

The Food Crisis in Global Perspective

The impact of change in the international food system has varied considerably among the countries outside of the First World. Some countries actually gained from the rapid shifts in agricultural and food supplies — from "surplus" in the 1950s and 1960s to "scarcity" in the early 1970s, to "glut" again in the 1980s. It is important to note here, though, that the most obvious winner in terms of international food transactions has not come from among Third World countries but from among the centrally planned economies of the Second World. The Soviet Union has been especially successful in capitalizing on its market power (that the Russians are buying is significant, given the size of purchases from the USSR) and its capabilities as an international economic negotiator. Utilizing the advantages of a single trading agency, considerable secrecy in terms of its own import needs and priorities, and its established credit-worthiness, the Soviet Union has been able to act in a decisive and co-ordinated fashion with respect to agricultural trade. The ability of the Soviets to position themselves to take advantage of market conditions was demonstrated most convincingly by the massive United States–USSR grain deal (the so-called Great Grain Robbery) of 1972. But, a number of other transactions could be mentioned in this context as well, not least the repeated efforts of the EC to ease their chronic dairy surpluses by selling supplies on attractive terms to the Soviets.

Even the grain embargo, which President Carter initiated to punish the USSR for invading Afghanistan, was remarkable for revealing how flexible the Soviets were in terms of their imports of agricultural produce. Rather than displaying "food power" by effectively denying the Soviets grain for human and animal consumption, the embargo opened up new possibilities by which the Soviets could play rival exporters off against each other. During the time of the embargo itself, the Soviets could exploit the fact that some of the major grain exporters (most notably, Argentina) were reluctant to co-operate with the United States in this case. Likewise, they could benefit from the frustration felt by the other exporting nations that did join in on the embargo (such as Canada and Australia), only to find themselves facing fiercer competition from the United States in other external markets.

In the aftermath of the embargo, the United States found itself in the embarrassing situation of having to buy itself back into the Soviet market through extremely generous export subsidies.[17] The main tool that the Americans employed was the Export-Enhancement Program (EEP). Based on the type of export subsidy used by the United States in the 1983 Egyptian-flour retaliatory action, this program has been drastically extended to cover not only its original targets (markets such as the Middle East and North Africa where the United States faced "predatory" EC competition) but specific markets (such as the Soviet Union and the People's Republic of China) where much of the competition came from non-EC sources. Although the United States did manage to firm up its position in the Soviet market by mid-1988, through the use of approximately $13 million under the EEP, the diplomatic cost of this effort was tremendous. Indeed, prompted by widespread feelings that it was becoming increasingly "hypocritical" on agricultural trade reform, the U.S. reversal of approach on export subsidies vis-à-vis the Soviet Union may be seen as having been the fundamental catalyst for the "fair traders" forming the Cairns group.

The impact of change on the Third World was much different. The overall feeling of the Third World toward the transformation in the political economy of food and agriculture has been a sense of grievance, arising out of a shared perception of unfavourable or inequitable treatment with regard to the post-1945 order. If considerable differences have arisen among the various Third World countries, they have remained relatively united in their demand for the replacement of the old order by a new order that would take into account the interests of the South. Thus, the reforms called for by the Third World (as, for instance, those made at the 1974 Rome Food Conference) have been as much in the political as in the economic realm, centred as they have been on the question of influence over the agenda in international organization. As one leading American international relations scholar has noted: "the programs put forth . . . by the Third World can be seen as an effort to lessen vulnerability and weakness by altering the rules of the game in various international issue areas."[18]

Looking more closely at the post-1945 food order, the sense of vulnerability and weakness of the LDCs stands out. This is not to suggest that the Third World did not receive some benefits from the establishment and maintenance of that order. Regime analysts are essentially correct when they highlight the fact that support for qualified acceptance of extra-market channels for food distribution facilitated the mobilization of aid efforts in emergencies. When a drought or floods hit in the 1950s and 1960s, a net of protection was provided through nationally held stockpiles of grain. In the wake of the Indian drought during the mid-1960s, for example, roughly one-fifth of the U.S. wheat crop was shipped to India. Many Third World countries also benefited from the commitment made by the United States and the other major actors within the order for technological transfer. During the 1950s and 1960s, a "Green Revolution" did take place in India and elsewhere in the Third World, as agricultural production was accelerated through the introduction of high-yield miracle seeds, oil-based fertilizers, farm machinery, and modern irrigation techniques.

To a certain extent, the post-1945 food order was almost too successful in the sense of building up expectations in the Third World. By stabilizing the political economy of food and agriculture in the 1950s and 1960s, the Third World was exposed to the shocks of the early 1970s. These shocks were quite traumatic. Given the oil crisis, the costs of utilizing Green Revolution technology in the Third World rose appreciably. More seriously still, the move from surplus to scarcity in terms of agricultural production (combined with the shift in U.S. agricultural policy toward a more free market–orientation) introduced a new element of uncertainty into international food and agricultural politics. With influential domestic, commercial, and strategic concerns all competing for scarce resources, the needs of the Third World were given reduced priority in the United States. The most tangible sign of the failure of the old order to deliver when it was needed most came with reference to the reduction in American food aid during the food crisis. The annual total volume of PL480 (food for peace) grain shipments dropped catastrophically from 10 008 604 tons in 1970, to 8 993 769 in 1972, 6 637 482 in 1973, and 2 916 470 in 1974.[19] What is more, the food aid provided in these years was increasingly politicized, a higher proportion being allocated to countries on strategic grounds rather than on grounds of economic need (with half of U.S. food aid in 1974 going to Vietnam and Cambodia).

Adjustment in the Third World was exceedingly difficult in comparison to the EC and Japan as the bulk of the countries in the Third World had limited capabilities to adapt to conditions in which grain prices quadrupled from 1972 to 1973. As *Agra Europe* bluntly put it: "The truth is . . . that food is always available to those with money to pay for it. . . . During the 1972–74 crisis no one in the EEC went short of bread or meat, they merely paid slightly more for their cereal-based foods."[20] With few reserves of foreign exchange, the issue in respect of the Third World was completely different. While Western Europeans and the Japanese had to make some limited economic sacrifices because of the food crisis, much of the population in the Third World has had to make far greater sacrifices.

A crucial question that has to be posed here is whether the food crisis can be viewed simply as an episode caused by the conjunction of a number of complex, unrelated circumstances or whether it must be seen as a result of long-term underdevelopment in the Third World. Using the dependency framework, the stress is on the latter view. This type of analysis pays less attention to short-term situational factors and more to the problems imposed by the structure of the international economic system itself. The fragility of the Third World in respect to the food crisis of the early 1970s was, according to this framework, conditioned not by system failure but by the very nature of the food system.

The dependency literature focusses on why and how agricultural production takes place in the Third World. The approach is holistic and historical, with a major theme being the impact of colonialism on Third World agriculture. The conclusions drawn by this literature are extremely pessimistic.[21] As a result of its colonial legacy, the Third World is said to be firmly locked into a distorted agricultural structure — characterized by an export profile dominated by a few cash crops (sugar, cocoa, coffee, bananas, tea, and so on); little diversification; little movement into new varieties of crops; and few linkages between agriculture and industry. The pattern of trade with the First World, therefore, is one of raw materials going out and processed goods coming in. To produce export crops most efficiently, plantations or large farms have continued to flourish. What technological advances are made in the Third World are restricted to cash crops at the expense of food crops such as roots and tubers for the domestic market.

The wider implications of what dependency theorists have called "the development of underdevelopment" or "growth without development" are manifold. The most obvious of these is that Third World countries have become increasingly dependent on imported produce at the expense of their own internal food security. This situation has been exacerbated by other factors such as taste transfer from the North to the South. According to Richard Barnet, "the major political impact of food aid has been to create a long-range dependency. The introduction of cheap surplus American wheat has changed dietary habits around the world."[22]

The value of dependency theory should not be discounted. Yet, this mode of analysis can be criticized for taking an overly deterministic position, in that it fails to capture the growing economic complexity within the Third World itself. Far from consisting of a monolithic entity, the Third World consists increasingly of a wide range of countries whose needs and interests in the issue-area of food and agriculture extend over a wide spectrum. While many Third World Countries continue to be locked into a less than favourable agricultural-export structure, other countries have done much to change their position within the international division of labour and to ensure their own food security.

Divergence in the Third World

The divergence between Third World countries in the issue-area of food and agriculture is most marked when a comparison is made between the bulk of the African countries and selected Asian and Latin American countries. For sub-Saharan Africa the agricultural problem in the 1970s and 1980s has not been "growth without development" but economic stagnation and deterioration. Over the 1960–80 period, aggregate food production has grown only slowly (approximately 1.8 percent), well below the growth rate for most of Latin America and Asia. More strikingly still, sub-Saharan Africa has been the only region where per-capita production has dropped over the past two decades. Concomitantly, food self-sufficiency has fallen in almost every country. Declining per-capita agricultural production combined with declining self-sufficiency add up to a situation of "serious concern";[23] the concern over whether Africa can survive is a real one.[24]

Part of the explanation for the poor performance by sub-Saharan countries in the 1970s and 1980s lies with the economic features emphasized by dependency theorists. As a World Bank report admitted, "the Sub-Saharan countries are 'locked' into a commodity-oriented structure of exports. This makes them highly vulnerable to the 'commodity problem' as characterized by heavy dependence on a limited range of exportable products, extreme price instability, and sluggish growth in export demand."[25] Indeed, sub-Saharan Africa has been extremely hard hit by the fall in prices of primary products as a result of oversupply, recession, and substitution.

The question remains, however, why the sub-Saharan African experience is so at odds with the experience in much of Latin America and Asia. To more fully understand the pattern of divergence within the Third World it is necessary to look more closely at internal variables as well. To begin with, the crucial impact of natural shocks on agricultural production in sub-Saharan Africa cannot be overlooked in any discussion of this issue. The vagaries of the weather in the sub-Sahel region stands out in this regard. Moreover, man-made factors have intensified these problems. While it is true that some of these factors can be attributed to the legacy of the past — not only economically, in terms of "monoculture" agriculture, dualistic research and development, and an infrastructure geared to external markets, but politically, in terms of weak state institutions and poorly defined borders. The effect of postindependence civil war and insurgency on agricultural production is highlighted by the case of Angola, in which the food self-sufficiency ratio dropped from 110 percent in 1964–66 to 64 percent in 1978–80.[26]

African leaders have to take some of the blame for the region's poor agricultural performance. The priorities of most of the postindependence governments have seemed in retrospect to have been misdirected.[27] This was particularly so with respect to the clear urban bias of many of these governments, a bias that not only showcased industrialization at the expense of agriculture but actually discouraged agricultural production through heavy taxation and a cheap food policy. As the World Bank report notes, "inappropriate domestic price and incentive policies lie at the heart of the agricultural problem."[28] Furthermore, these mistaken policies have had longer-term implications with respect to the environment, as underinvestment in agriculture has contributed directly to widespread soil degradation and erosion.

Is there the possibility that these mistaken policies can be reversed? The answer seems to be a cautious yes. Several African countries have recently moved in the direction of reorienting their priorities with respect to agricultural production. Indeed, there seems to be an emerging consensus that internal reform is necessary. The document *A Programme of Action for African Economic Recovery and Development*, submitted by African governments at the U.N. Special Session on Africa in 1986, was described by the World Bank as "a slow process of important policy change that is gaining momentum."[29] Contained in this reform package are proposals for a greater allocation of resources for agriculture, changes in the marketing system, more attractive prices for producers, additional storage and transport facilities, and more attention to problems relating to the soil.

Still, the success of this reform effort is in no way guaranteed. Domestically, opposition to this course of action is bound to be strong if more economic hardships are necessary — especially when these hardships may have to be made in conjunction with debt-restructuring. The status quo may seem, as in many cases it has in the past, an attractive alternative to demonstrations and riots in urban centres. Externally, there remains the danger that the reform effort may be blown off course by the continuation of intense competition among the major agricultural exporters. *South* magazine has summed up the situation by noting that "the farm policies of North and South interact in a ruinous way. Surpluses in the developed countries are dumped on world markets, depressing prices."[30] This dilemma could even get worse if there was an escalation in this competitive struggle. Certainly, few reform programs in sub-Saharan Africa could survive an all-out "ploughshares war." As a diplomatic representative from a West African country warned: "a price war between the major surplus countries would wreck our tediously developed self-sufficiency programme."[31]

Turning to those components of the Third World that have been more successful in pursuing their own needs and interests in the area of food and agriculture, two categories of countries must be examined. The first group is made up of a small core of Asian newly industrializing economies (NIEs), most notably South Korea and Taiwan. The second group consists of a much wider range of countries, including Latin American NIEs, such as Brazil and Mexico; emerging NIEs, such as Argentina and India; and potential NIEs, particularly Thailand and Indonesia. These countries are similar in that they have attempted to gain more manoeuvrability in the political economy of food and agriculture through an activist, state-backed approach. The fundamental difference between them, aside from the contrasts in their state-societal relationships, is in their respective goals. For the first group of countries, the attainment of food security has been predominant. For the second group, conversely, the central aim has been the diversification and upgrading of their agricultural production and trade.

As part of the more generalized push by South Korea and Taiwan toward export-led growth, a strong outward-looking food-processing industry has been developed in those two NIEs. Taiwan has specialized in pork products and fruit and vegetables (canned asparagus, bananas, and pineapples); South Korea has built up its processed meat and sugar-refining industries. Both of these NIEs have large corporations involved in food and agricultural trade based in them. South Korean food corporations on *South*'s list of the 600 largest multinationals are Samyang Food Co., Lotte Confectionery, Nhong Shim, Dong Bang Corp., and Haitai Confectionery. The largest Taiwanese corporations listed are President Enterprises Corps. and Wei Chaun Foods Corps.[32]

Despite this sort of economic activity, food security remains the essential element of South Korean and Taiwanese agricultural policy. Notwithstanding the pressure associated with industrial take-off, urbanization, and dietary change, the domestic agriculture of these NIEs has not been completely exposed to outside competition. In fact, heightened agricultural protection has accompanied strong economic growth. As one Australian study states, "the rates of growth in agricultural protection since the 1950s have probably been far more rapid in these East Asian economies than in any other region of the world."[33] While the South

Korean and Taiwanese markets have become lucrative for exporters, many of the barriers to those markets (especially for rice and meat) limit the extent to which they can be tapped.

What stands out in the South Korean and Taiwanese cases is how well they seem to fit the model of Japanese agricultural development (with all its neo-mercantilist manifestations) rather than the Third World model as understood by dependency theorists. The picture one gets is not of a weak state constrained by historical circumstances but rather of a state orchestrating a deliberative strategy to defend domestic agriculture. In both of the NIEs under review, farmers are an important source of conservative political support; such a defence (as in Japan) can be rationalized by reference to national security and the wider national interest.

The second, and in many ways the more interesting, of the two groups of countries has concentrated more fully on exploiting its food and agricultural potential. In this effort, it is important to note, this group does not seem to have been as "locked in" as early dependency theorists have suggested. Unlike sub-Saharan countries, these countries have had some success, at least, with diversification, producing new crops, and building up new linkages between agriculture and industry. According to the World Bank's *World Development Report 1988*, Brazil increased the value added in agriculture (in millions of current dollars) from 4401 in 1970 to 22 940 in 1986; Mexico, from 4330 to 11 467; Argentina, from 2438 to 8867; India, from 22 227 to 64 487; Thailand, from 1851 to 6962; and Indonesia, from 4340 to 19 531.[34]

The ability of Brazil and Thailand to adjust to the political economy of food and agriculture stands out. Brazil has moved in the 1970s and 1980s from a position befitting a stereotypical Third World commodity producer with an agriculture dominated by a few cash crops (coffee and sugar) to the point where it has a trading profile along the lines of the major agricultural exporters in the First World (exporting a wide range of produce including soybeans, maize, sesame, beef and poultry, a wide variety of fruit, and manioc). The speed and scale of this adjustment process may be judged not only by the soybean phenomenon but by the fact that Brazil has moved from the position of a net importer of poultry in 1975 to the role of a major exporter of poultry in the early 1980s, as well as becoming the world's largest exporter of orange-juice concentrate. The increased export of canned fruit and frozen concentrate, along with crushed soybean in the form of oil and meal, also shows that Brazil has managed to build up some light industries in the food-processing sector.

Although not yet the broadly based agricultural exporter that Brazil has become, Thailand presents a similar picture with respect to its approach to agricultural production and marketing. Since the 1960s, the Thai strategy has dramatically changed from concentration on rice production to the development of a more diversified agricultural economy that includes an additional range of products mainly for export.[35] These additional products have included maize, sugar, fruit and vegetables, poultry, and tapioca/manioc. Like Brazil, Thailand has also made an effort to increase the value-added component of its agricultural exports.

One significant indication of this effort is the sharp increase in the production of manioc chips and pellets in the 1970s and 1980s (filling approximately 95 percent of the world's demand for these products). Another comes in regard to the push by Thailand to become a major producer and exporter of frozen boneless broiler chickens. Still other signs of this pattern have emerged with the recent moves by Thailand to enter into the canned-fruit and -seafood industries.

Another aspect of interest with reference to the export strategies of Brazil and Thailand is their utilization of flexible and innovative marketing tools. First, these countries have made use of the increasingly popular practice of barter and countertrade to facilitate the trade of both traditional and nontraditional items. Brazil, for instance, has incorporated countertrade in a variety of deals within and outside of Latin America. Thailand, in a similar manner, has exchanged agricultural products through these sorts of practices with a variety of other countries. Second, Brazil and Thailand have encouraged the production and export of their agricultural goods through a wide array of governmental incentives ranging from infrastructural and input support to export subsidies. A common theme running through this group is the desire and the capacity of these countries to change and to elevate their position in the food and agriculture sector (and the international division of labour generally).

The diversification and upgrading of agriculture in selected Third World countries focusses attention ultimately on the new form of relationship forged between those countries and external nonstate and state actors (characterized in some of the second-wave dependency literature as associated dependent development).[36] Foreign capital and technological support have been instrumental in building and shaping many of the new agricultural industries in countries such as Brazil and Thailand in the 1970s and 1980s. Indeed, it seems unlikely that much of this development would have taken place at all without this outside support. In the case of the Thai manioc industry, the crucial role of the EC (with West German and Dutch investors) has been referred to. In the case of the Brazilian soybean industry, various Japanese interests (i.e., the Japanese government, quasi-governmental financial agencies such as the Japanese Export-Import Bank, and various elements of the private sector, including the general trading companies or sogoshoshas) were the prime movers. This type of support has since been replicated in a variety of other agricultural product-areas. In addition to their efforts in developing the Thai frozen-broiler chicken industry, Japanese interests have been instrumental in recent moves to establish the frozen-vegetable industry in that country.[37]

This type of corporate investment has as its bottom line reliable lower-cost production. In the case of the Thai poultry industry, to give just one illustration, the Japanese interests "decided to start a broiler operation in Thailand, together with a Thai partner, since maize, which is the major feed, is cheaper and wages are lower there than in Japan."[38] It goes without saying that noneconomic goals have been clearly subordinated to economic growth. As a consequence the social costs of such a strategy have been considerable, whether in the form of rural depopulation, increased social inequality, or environmental damage. In addition, the introduction of a new form of agricultural production has often meant the reduction or elimination of traditional staple foodstuffs. A case in point is the displacement of black beans in Brazil by soybeans.

From an economic perspective alone, however, these emergent links with international actors have had some considerable appeal for Third World countries. This is particularly true if these links are developed not on the more traditional basis of direct ownership but through more innovative and flexible means such as joint ventures and other forms of co-operative arrangement. Joining with external actors such as processors, shippers, and wholesalers, the LDCs may ensure the more efficient international promotion and distribution of their produce. In addition, a move toward association with powerful actors based in the First World may secure access to those markets in the face of competition from other exporters or the growth of protectionism. That is to say, by building up a set of transnational alliances, selective Third World countries may gain some added leverage in the global marketplace.[39]

Protectionism in the advanced industrial countries is an area of extreme importance to the Third World. Efforts by Third World countries to diversify and upgrade their agricultural exports tend to create additional sources of trade tension — the push by Third World countries generating at times a fierce backlash in the First World. As the World Bank has stated, "exports of processed products face escalating tariffs and other barriers in the industrial countries."[40] These "other" barriers, the so-called nontariff barriers (NTBS), take many forms. One important measure involves the imposition of various types of unilateral (and often arbitrary) controls on imports on the basis of health and safety standards, labelling, and product design. This form of NTB often involves product testing — and hence, delay and frustration. A second major type is the introduction of some form of quantitative restriction (QR) scheme or quota system, either through the imposition of unilateral restrictions or through a bilaterally negotiated "voluntary" restraint agreement (VRA).

To a considerable degree, it may be said that it is the ability or inability of Third World countries to resist and overcome protectionism in the North that determines their relative position in the food and agriculture regime. Looking at the various categories of Third World countries, there appears to be a considerable difference between the capacity of the sub-Saharan African countries, the East Asian NIEs, and the diversified agricultural exporters on this score. At the bottom end of the scale, the traditional commodity exporting countries of sub-Saharan Africa have the least room to manoeuvre. Constrained by the nature of their economic structures, these countries have little clout in the international political economy. When confronted by protectionism in the North, therefore, they can do little to deflect or escape such action. The consequences have often been devastating. The effect of the passage of measures in the 1985 U.S. Food Security Act (the so-called Farm Bill) reducing the import quota for sugar and other tropical products, for instance, was to "kill the ability of African countries to sell to the U.S. or compete in the international marketplace."[41]

The efforts of the sub-Saharan African countries to "manage" collectively their trading relations have been very disappointing. On a regional level, arrangements such as the Lomé Convention involving the EC and ACP (African, Caribbean, and Pacific) countries have not come up to the expectations of the Third World membership. When faced with a choice between the interests of EC agriculture and ACP exports, "agricultural interests override development policy aims."[42] The most obvious cases in point are sugar (with the EC pressuring the ACP countries to cut the yearly export quota); and beef (hard hit by the imposition of various export restrictions, most notably health regulations). On a global scale, attempts to regulate commodity prices and output through international commodity arrangements (such as the International Coffee Agreement) have likewise proved ineffective — with "strains in relations among producers" being "the critical problem."[43] Again the sub-Saharan African countries appear to be the main losers from this heightened competition, as, with the exception of tea, their share in world markets in agricultural produce has declined appreciably.[44]

In contrast to the weak bargaining position of the sub-Saharan countries, the East Asian NIEs have been able to gain some considerable leverage in the political economy of agriculture and food. South Korea and Taiwan have (in a manner similar to Japan) come under strong pressure from the United States and other major exporting nations to "open up" their domestic markets. However, these countries have been strikingly successful in resisting this pressure. In large part, this success has been the result of these NIEs' ability to use the agricultural liberalization issue as a bargaining chip in international negotiations — in the sense of exploiting their commercial purchasing power as an instrument to gain advantages for their own exports. One vital element of this approach has been the playing-off of the various competing exporters — through the manipulation of import barriers such as quotas and licences.

The diversified agricultural exporters may be seen to occupy a position in between the two other categories of Third World countries. By developing a more sophisticated coalition-building strategy vis-à-vis state and corporate actors, these countries can increase their influence in the area of food and agriculture. One aspect of this approach may be the greater exploitation by these countries of their own purchasing power (particularly technology) along the lines of South Korea and Taiwan. Another aspect may be the use of direct foreign investment as a means of getting more clout in First World markets (Mantrust, Indonesia's largest food processor, has for example recently purchased the brand Chicken of the Sea in order to increase its market share in the United States). In addition to this sort of activity, however, will come various attempts to forge a variety of coalitions on a state-to-state basis. Regional groups (such as ASEAN) are one important long-standing aspect of this sort of activity. Cross-cutting, issue-oriented coalitions constitute a newer variation on this theme. The Cairns group may be a pioneer in this regard. Although not without its internal tensions (for instance, on the principle of differential and more favourable treatment for Third World countries), this group is significant not only because of the leadership role played by Australia and Canada but because it encompasses many of the most competitive of the Third World agricultural exporters.

Through the utilization of these various sorts of instruments, the diversified Third World agricultural exporters should be able to better cushion the impact of First World protectionism. Thailand, for example, has been able to win tariff concessions on the import of boneless chicken into Japan — largely through the collective pressure exerted by ASEAN. When dealing with First World countries on an individual basis, this group of Third World countries retains a far stronger bargaining position than do the sub-Saharan countries. Again, Thailand is an especially interesting case. As noted above, during the scarcity crisis of the early 1970s Thailand was encouraged to produce feed in the form of cassava pellets/chips for the EC market. However, when the crisis receded, the Community attempted to settle on a voluntary restraint agreement with Thailand. The result of the extended negotiations on this issue cannot be seen as a victory for the Thais. The "gentleman's agreement" implemented in 1981 severely cut back cassava exports. However, the introduction of "orderly" marketing did not involve the worst-case scenario either; that is to say, the agreement was not unilaterally imposed on Thailand by the EC. As such, the Thais were able to drag the talks on until they were able to win concessions with respect to the assurance that there would be no trade diversion on the part of the EC and that the EC would compensate Thailand for agreeing to the cuts in cassava exports by an aid package to facilitate further agricultural diversification in Thailand.

Conclusion

The predominant theme of this chapter has been change in the international political economy of food and agriculture in the 1970s and 1980s. The question of how profound these changes have been differs according to the mode of analysis utilized. From a liberal economic perspective, what is important is the resilience of the post-1945 order. Although the potential for the complete collapse of the fundamental values and rules of that order has been acknowledged, great emphasis has been placed on the stabilizing elements within that order. Such elements are significant not only for the old champions of the old order but also for those Third World countries that have geared their economic strategy to an export-oriented approach.

In terms of the prescription for the future, the liberal economic agenda continues to lay great weight on the reaffirmation of the centrality of market forces. This is not to say that the need for some reforms — designed to correct some of the flaws of the international order and to protect the more vulnerable actors within that order from shocks — has not been recognized. Equity, however, remains generally subordinated to efficiency and growth as a means for Third World countries to change their position in the IPE of food and agriculture.[45]

In contrast, a neomercantilist perspective attributes the success of countries in the food and agriculture area to "self-help." What has been emphasized is the ability of actors with a food surplus in either the First World (the EC) or the Third World (most notably, Brazil) to change their position in the division of labour through deliberate statist strategies. The same is true for those actors with a food deficit whose first priority is food security. In both cases, actors are viewed as having a wide range of choices at their disposal.

Unlike the liberal economic perspective, with its attention to collaborative activity as a restraining force, the neomercantilism prescription is not a benign one. The increased autonomy and greater allowance for the use of economic statecraft by individual actors suggests that there are going to be both winners and losers in the international political economy of food and agriculture. From this perspective, the future holds that a pattern of increased fragmentation and competitiveness among actors will occur with respect to both industrialized countries and Third World countries. The major source of conflict in this latter context will be between the diversifying export-oriented countries and the food security-oriented countries in the Third World. One indication of the extent of the bitterness contained within this emergent pattern may be seen in the mounting attacks by Asian agricultural exporters on South Korea's "parasitic, mercantilist view of trade."[46] Another source of tension stems from the different needs and interests of the "fair trading" Cairns group countries, on the one hand, and the GATT Food Importers' Group, on the other.

The dependency perspective, in turn, has focussed more and more on the position of those countries of sub-Saharan Africa. Increasingly reliant on a small number of commodities (and facing continuing deterioration in their terms of trade), these countries remain highly marginalized and vulnerable in the political economy of food and agriculture.[47] In the absence of a concerted agricultural rehabilitation and recovery effort in the region (or alternatively, an effective international management approach with reference to buffer stocks of essential foodstuffs), it would seem likely that the situation in sub-Saharan Africa has the potential of getting much worse before it has any possibility at all of getting better. The crucial factor here would appear to be the impact of man-made and natural shocks (or, as in 1972–74, a combination of both).

This chapter has, in examining the political economy of food and agriculture in the 1970s and 1980s, taken a rather eclectic approach. In focussing on the liberal-economic, neomercantilist, and dependency perspectives, it has attempted to highlight how all of these modes of analysis are useful in capturing the essence of particular aspects of this complex and wide-ranging issue-area. At the same time, given the extent of change at the international level and the diversity of national approaches designed to cope with those changes, it is not surprising that all of these perspectives have gaps and inconsistencies as well. A future research agenda in this, as in other areas of the international political economy, should then not only focus on "extracting and integrating central themes" from each of these perspectives. It should attempt to "synthesize" these approaches by "injecting an original focus on the national level along with sub- and transnational forces."[48] By utilizing a combination of these approaches, it would seem possible to gain a more complete and consistent understanding of the food and agriculture issue-area.

NOTES

1. Raymond F. Hopkins and Donald J. Puchala, eds., special issue of *International Organization* 32, no.1 (1978). See also Donald J. Puchala and Raymond F. Hopkins, "International Regimes: Lessons from Inductive Analysis," *International Organization* 36 (Spring 1982): 245–75.

2. See, for example, T.K. Warley, "Western Trade in Agricultural Products," in *International Economic Relations of the Western World*, vol. 1, ed. Andrew Shonfield (London: Oxford University Press, for the Royal Institute of International Affairs, 1976), 345–48; Gilbert R. Winham, *International Trade and The Tokyo Round Negotiation* (Princeton: Princeton University Press, 1986), 152–53.

3. Fred H. Sanderson, *Japan's Food Prospects and Policies* (Washington, D.C.: The Brookings Institution, 1978), 11.

4. Ross B. Talbot, *The Chicken War: An International Trade Conflict between the United States and the European Economic Community, 1961–64* (Ames: Iowa State University Press, 1978), 65.

5. D. Gale Johnson, "Food Reserves and International Trade Policy," in *International Trade and Agriculture: Theory and Policy*, ed. Jimmye S. Hillman and Andrew Schmitz (Boulder, Colo.: Westview, 1979), 247. See also Reiko Niimi, "The Problem of Food Security," in *Japan's Economic Security: Resources as a Factor in Foreign Policy*, ed. Nobutoshi Akao (Aldershot: Gower, for the Royal Institute of International Affairs, 1983), 169–96.

6. "Foreword," in Sanderson, *Japan's Food Prospects and Policies.*

7. Leon Hollerman, *Japan's Economic Strategy in Brazil: Challenge for the United States* (Toronto: Lexington, 1988), 226.

8. N. Poapongsakoran, "The Commercial Broiler and Swine Industries in Thailand," in *Food Policy Analysis in Thailand*, ed. T. Panayotou (Bangkok: Agricultural Development Council, 1985), 280.

9. "Agriculture: Wait and See," *The Economist*, December 28, 1974, 55.

10. D. Gale Johnson, Kenzo Hemmi, Pierre Lardinois, *Agricultural Policy and Trade: Adjusting Domestic Programs in an International Framework*, A Report to the Trilateral Commission (New York: New York University Press, 1985), 109. See also European Commission, *The Agricultural Situation in the Community: 1982 Report* (Brussels: 1983).

11. Figures taken from Paul Lewis, "Europe's Farm Policies Clash with American Export Goals," *New York Times*, February 22, 1983, 1, 5.

12. "Collision Course: Can the U.S. Avert a Trade War with Japan?" *Business Week*, April 8, 1985, 50–55. See also Steve Lohr, "Japan, by Shielding Farmers, Rankles Its Trading Partners," *New York Times*, February 23, 1983, 1, 3.

13. N. Butler, "The Ploughshares War Between Europe and America," *Foreign Affairs* 62 (Fall 1983): 122.

14. David R. Mares, *Restructuring the International Market: Theoretical Considerations and a Mexican Case Study* (New York: Columbia University Press, 1987), 13. See also

Andrew Fenton Cooper, "The Protein Link: Complexity in the U.S.-EC Agricultural Trading Relationship," *Journal of European Integration* 11, no. 1 (1987): 31–45.

15. Andrew Fenton Cooper, "Agricultural Relations Between Western Nations: Canadian Approaches," in *Canadian Agriculture in a Global Perspective: Opportunities and Obligations*, ed. I.S. Knell and J. English (Waterloo: University of Waterloo, 1986), 69–85.

16. P. Gallagher, "Setting the Agenda for Trade Negotiations: Australia and the Cairns Group," *Australian Outlook: The Australian Journal of International Affairs* 44 (April 1988): 3–8. The other members of the Cairns group are Argentina, Brazil, Chile, Colombia, Fiji, Hungary, Indonesia, Malaysia, New Zealand, the Philippines, Thailand, and Uruguay.

17. Robert L. Paarlberg, *Fixing Farm Trade: Policy Options for the United States* (Cambridge, Mass.: Ballinger, for the Council on Foreign Relations, 1988), 5. See also Robert L. Paarlberg, "The 1980–81 US Grain Embargo: Consequences for the Participants," in *The Utility of International Economic Sanctions*, ed. David Leyton-Brown (London: Croom Helm, 1987), 185–203.

18. Stephen D. Krasner, "Third World Vulnerabilities and Global Negotiations," *Review of International Studies* 9 (October 1983): 242.

19. Michael B. Wallerstein, *Food for War — Food for Peace: United States Food Aid in a Global Context* (Cambridge, Mass.: The MIT Press, 1980), 62.

20. Agra Europe, Special Report No. 19, *The Common Agricultural Policy's Role in International Trade* (London: 1983), 64.

21. See, for example, Samir Amin, *Accumulation on a World Scale* (New York: Monthly Review Press, 1973); André Gunder Frank, *Capitalism and Underdevelopment in Latin America* (New York: Monthly Review Press, 1972).

22. Richard J. Barnet, *The Lean Years: Politics in the Age of Scarcity* (New York: Simon and Schuster, 1980), 158.

23. Shamsher Singh, *Sub-Saharan Agriculture: Synthesis and Prospects*, World Bank Staff Working Papers, Number 608 (Washington, D.C.: The World Bank), 3.

24. Jennifer Whitaker, *How Can Africa Survive?* (New York: Harper and Row, 1988). This title echoes the words of Edem Kodjo, the secretary general of the Organization of African Unity, who stated, at the first African economic summit, in Lagos, in April 1980: "The future seems to be without future. And we are blithely told that if things go on in the same way, only five to nine of the fifty or so African countries will be able to survive for any length of time. This is indeed an apocalyptic prospect but it reflects better than any speech what lies in store for us. . . . The very survival of Africa is at stake." Quoted in Albert Bressand, "The Time for Painful Rethinking," in *Power, Passions, and Purpose: Prospects for North-South Negotiations*, ed. Jagdish N. Bhagwati and John Gerard Ruggie (Cambridge Mass.: The MIT Press, 1984), 60.

25. Singh, *Sub-Saharan Agriculture*, 5.

26. Singh, *Sub-Saharan Agriculture*, 30.

27. See, for example, "Editorial: People Are to Blame," quoted in Naomi Chazan and Timothy M. Shaw, eds., *Coping with Africa's Food Crisis* (Boulder, Colo.: Lynne Rienner, 1988), 1. Robert Bates explores this theme in considerable detail in *Markets and States in Tropical Africa* (Berkeley: University of California Press, 1981).

28. Singh, *Sub-Saharan Agriculture*, 10.

29. "Policy Reform in Sub-Saharan Africa," *World Development Report 1988* (New York: Oxford University Press, 1988), 28.

30. Melvyn Westlake and Kevin Watkins, "Farm Trade Wars," *South*, November 1987, 9.

31. Quoted in Heimo Claasen, "Battle for the Stomachs of the World: Grain of Truth on Both Sides," in *German Tribune*, August 17, 1983.

32. "600 South," *South*, August 1987, 14–24.

33. Kym Anderson and Yujiro Hayami, *The Political Economy of Agricultural Protection: The Experience of East Asia* (Sydney: Allen and Unwin, 1986), 4.

34. The World Bank, *World Development Report 1988*, 234–35.

35. Dow Mongkolsmai, "Thailand," in *Food Trade & Food Security in ASEAN and Australia*, ed. Anne Booth, Cristina C. David et al. (Kuala Lumpur and Canberra: ASEAN–Australia Joint Research Project, 1986), 145.

36. See, for example, Peter Evans, *Dependent Development: The Alliance of Multinational, State, and Local Capital in Brazil* (Princeton: Princeton University Press, 1979).

37. Tomio Shida, "Japanese Bypass 'Dragons'; Target Low-cost Asia Nations," *The Japan Economic Journal*, September 24, 1988, 4.

38. Kunio Yoshihara, "General Trading Companies in Thailand," in *Current Development in Thai-Japanese Economic Relations, Trade and Investment*, ed. Medhi Krongkaew (Bangkok: Thammasat University Press, 1980), 260.

39. See, for example, United Nations Centre on Transnational Corporations, *Transnational Corporations in Food and Beverage Processing* (New York: United Nations, 1981), 56–57.

40. Singh, *Sub-Saharan Agriculture*, 11.

41. "Restricting African Exports is Bad Trade Policy," letter by Randall B. Purcell, Director, Curry Foundation, *New York Times*, June 20, 1986, 30.

42. Agra Europe, *Common Agricultural Policy's Role in International Trade*, 36. John Ravenhill concludes: "What is very evident . . . is that there is no potential for a significant growth in ACP exports of CAP products in the future," *Collective Clientelism: The Lomé Conventions and North-South Relations* (New York: Columbia University Press, 1985), 162–63.

43. Jock Finlayson and Mark Zacher, "The Third World and the Management of International Commodity Trade: Accord and Discord," in *An International Political Economy*, International Political Economy Yearbook, vol. 1, ed. W. Ladd Hollist and F. LaMond Tullis (Boulder, Colo.: Westview, 1985), 215.

44. Singh, *Sub-Saharan Agriculture,* 20.

45. See, for example, Johnson, Hemmi, and Lardinois, *Agricultural Policy and Trade.*

46. See, for example, Phillip Bowring, "Reaping the Whirlwind," *Far East Economic Review* 11 (September 1986): 139.

47. See, for example, Bob Sutcliffe, "Africa and the World Economic Crisis," in *World Recession & the Food Crisis in Africa*, ed. Peter Lawrence (Boulder, Colo.: Westview, 1986), 18–28.

48. Jerker Carlsson and Timothy M. Shaw, eds., *Newly Industrializing Countries and the Political Economy of South-South Relations* (London: Macmillan, 1988), 6.

SELECT BIBLIOGRAPHY

Anderson, Kym, and Yujiro Hayami. *The Political Economy of Agricultural Protection: The Experience of East Asia*. Sydney: Allen and Unwin, 1986.

Barnet, Richard J. *The Lean Years: Politics in the Age of Scarcity*. New York: Simon and Schuster, 1980.

Chazan, Naomi, and Timothy M. Shaw, eds. *Coping with Africa's Food Crisis*. Boulder, Colo.: Lynne Rienner, 1988.

Cooper, Andrew Fenton. "Agricultural Relations Between Western Nations: Canadian Approaches." In *Canadian Agriculture in a Global Perspective: Opportunities and Obligations*, ed. I.S. Knell and J. English. Waterloo: University of Waterloo Press, 1986.

———. "The Protein Link: Complexity in the US–EC Agricultural Trading Relationship." *Journal of European Integration* 11, no. 1 (1987): 31–45.

Gallagher, P. "Setting the Agenda for Trade Negotiations: Australia and the Cairns Group." *Australian Outlook: The Australian Journal of International Affairs* 44 (April 1988): 3–8.

Hillman, Jimmye S., and Andrew Schmitz, eds. *International Trade and Agriculture Theory and Policy*. Boulder, Colo.: Westview, 1979.

Hollerman, Leon. *Japan's Economic Strategy in Brazil: Challenge for the United States*. Toronto: Lexington, 1988.

Hopkins, Raymond F., and Donald J. Puchala, eds. Special Issue of *International Organization* 32 (Summer 1978).

Johnson, D. Gale; Kenzo Hemmi; and Pierre Lardinois. *Agricultural Policy and Trade: Adjusting Domestic Programs in an International Framework*. A Report to the Trilateral Commission. New York: New York University Press, 1985.

Lawrence, Peter, ed. *World Recession & the Food Crisis in Africa*. Boulder, Colo.: Westview, 1986.

Mares, David R. *Restructuring the International Market: Theoretical Considerations and a Mexican Case Study*. New York: Columbia University Press, 1987.

Paarlberg, Robert L. *Fixing Farm Trade: Policy Options for the United States*. Cambridge, Mass.: Ballinger, for the Council on Foreign Relations, 1988.

Sanderson, Fred H. *Japan's Food Prospects and Policies*. Washington, D.C.: The Brookings Institution, 1978.

Singh, Shamsher. *Sub-Saharan Agriculture: Synthesis and Prospects*. World Bank Staff Working Papers, Number 608. Washington, D.C.: The World Bank, 1983.

Talbot, Ross, B. *The Chicken War: An International Trade Conflict between the United States and the European Economic Community, 1961–64*. Ames: Iowa State University Press, 1978.

Wallerstein, Michael B. *Food for War — Food for Peace: United States Food Aid in a Global Context*. Cambridge, Mass.: MIT Press, 1980.

Warley, T.K. "Western Trade in Agricultural Products." In *International Economic Relations of the Western World*, vol. 1, ed. Andrew Shonfield. London: Oxford University Press, for the Royal Institute of International Affairs, 1976.

Whitaker, Jennifer. *How Can Africa Survive?* New York: Harper and Row, 1988.

THE NEW GEOPOLITICS OF MINERALS: THE CHANGING SIGNIFICANCE OF STRATEGIC MINERALS*

David G. Haglund

Twice in this century, resource questions have emerged as major issues in international politics. The first time was during the period between the two world wars; the second dated from the 1973 OPEC oil-price increase and lasted into the early 1980s. Although the specific commodities and actors involved in the politicization of resources may have varied between the two eras, in one fundamental respect the eras were similar: each featured a concern on the part of industrialized states about access to what have come to be called "strategic minerals." Alone among raw materials, strategic minerals have been deemed indispensable building blocks for industrial, military, and political power. More so than with any other class of commodities, the question of *access* has characterized policy planning and policy making in respect of strategic minerals. Such has been and remains the case, not because minerals are the materials most essential to sustain human existence, for food and water are clearly more important in this regard, but rather because of the inequitable manner in which mineral wealth has been distributed among countries.

Differential distribution militates against self-sufficiency in minerals for all countries in a way that differential distribution of technology and other factors of production does not militate against agricultural self-sufficiency for most. Seeds, know-how, fertilizer, manpower, and to an extent even water, are transferable; so, in a physical (if not economic) sense, agricultural autarchy is a policy that all but the very ill-situated can contemplate. Indeed, countries have commonly moved beyond contemplation to the actual implementation, with varying degrees of costliness, of policies of agricultural self-sufficiency. If, in agriculture, autarchy is possible, but at a price, the same cannot be said for minerals, even taking into account the wonder-working properties of modern

*A longer version of this chapter appears as Chapter 1 in David G. Haglund, ed., *The New Geopolitics of Minerals: Canada and International Resource Trade* (Vancouver: University of British Columbia Press, 1989).

technology, for *no* country has a sufficiently ample resource base to allow it to produce all the minerals it needs. The words of C.K. Leith, a leading minerals analyst of the interwar period, remain in this regard as relevant today as they were a half-century ago: "It is a costly and, in the long run, a futile effort to create by enactment something which was not created by nature."[1] Not only will every state lack some important mineral needed by its industries but many have lacked, and will continue to lack, a wide range of such industrial inputs. Lacking domestic sources of needed minerals, states have sought and will continue to seek foreign sources of supply.

Thus, for minerals, as for no other commodity, the most salient international political concerns centre on the question of access. It is sometimes assumed, usually by those analysts who find persuasive the idea that a "resource war" has raged between the superpowers, that resource conflict is a recent phenomenon of international politics. To those who think this is so, Hanns Maull's observation that minerals have been implicated in international political rivalry for thousands of years comes as a needed and timely reminder.[2] In what follows, I will argue, mindful that it might be chronologically fallacious to do so, that the 20th century, much more than any other, has witnessed the most significant developments in the international politics of strategic minerals. In developing my argument, I will resort to a comparative-historical, or "diachronic," mode of inquiry. This method allows for a comparative analysis of the relevant aspects of the access question as it has arisen in two discrete eras, and seems especially well-suited, if not obligatory, for an investigation that presumes to ask whether there is, in fact, a "new geopolitics" of minerals. Before attempting to answer this question, it would be well to resolve two related conceptual/definitional matters, namely the relevance to political analysis of the concept "geopolitics" and the meaning of "strategic minerals."

Geopolitics: A Conceptual Analysis

Among contemporary political scientists, particularly those who specialize in international relations, geopolitics is only beginning to recover from the fall from conceptual grace that occurred in the aftermath of World War II.[3] Before the fall, geopolitics had been as much, if not more, in fashion among students of international politics as was integration, interdependence, regimes, or any of the other theoretical problems that attracted scholarly attention in subsequent years. The causes of the fall are varied. The imperative of changing intellectual fashion is one, but not the most important, reason for the abandonment of explicitly "geopolitical" analysis. Nor is the capture of geopolitics (to the extent it still exists in Anglo-American academia) by political geographers anything other than a symptom, not a cause, of its abandonment by political scientists. There are several explanations of the demise, among which three stand out as being especially worthy of attention.

The first is that the method of approach we call geopolitics had become tainted by association with the pre–World War II German "science" of *Geopolitik* — a pseudoscience that, in *some* ways, was similar to the geopolitics of leading British and American theorists such as Halford Mackinder, Alfred Mahan, James Fairgrieve, and Nicholas Spykman, but was fundamentally characterized by its normative stress on the necessity of German expansionism.[4] Indeed, the taint-by-association syndrome is still with us, and has dissuaded at least one scholar from situating his work on the assessment of world power plainly within the corpus of geopolitical writing. That scholar, Ray S. Cline, has noted that his decision to label his own approach "politectonics" was, in large measure, a function of there being no suitable concept now in use that better conveyed the shifting realities of the international power system, the subject of Cline's inquiry. *Geopolitics* could have suited his purposes, but unfortunately, it "fell into disrepute some time ago."[5]

If some have shunned the concept primarily as a matter of etiquette, still more have refrained from employing it out of the conviction that it is simply too imprecise to serve as an effective tool for political analysis. To be sure, political scientists have long learned to live with the fact that, ultimately, theirs is a discipline whose concepts can never be submitted to the test of truth in any objective, certifiable form. We all are reminded, more often than is perhaps necessary, of the definitional problem that confronts us, but we do try to come to grips with this problem by adopting reasonably succinct operational definitions that are, at minimum, internally consistent within the arbitrary limits we establish for them. From this perspective, the primary drawback of the term geopolitics is that it is conceptually so broad that it can and does mean all things to all people. That it is prone to manipulation by those who are most comfortable with deterministic theories and models is only an added deficiency, for the basic flaw is its ambitiousness. Once we have been told, as a frequently cited definition of the concept puts it, that geopolitics is "the study of political phenomena (1) in their spatial relationship and (2) in their relationship with, dependence upon, and influence on, earth as well as on all those cultural factors which constitute the subject matter of human geography (anthropogeography) broadly defined," what else is left to say?[6] The past two decades have not been propitious ones, certainly not in the realm of international relations scholarship, for the cultivation of geopolitical or any other kind of "grand" theories. Is it surprising, then, that geopolitics should have been caught up in what Kal Holsti has labelled "the retreat from theoretical utopia"?[7]

A third case made against geopolitics as a useful concept for analysis is that it is obsolete. According to this view, whatever merit geopolitical grand theory may have had in former years, in the nuclear age the theory has diminished utility. Not only have spatial considerations (for example, being a maritime power as opposed to being a land-based power) been said to have undergone a reduction of importance in the post–World War II decades, but so even have other geographical phenomena, such as the importance of raw materials as either a cause of war or as a means of carrying on a war.[8] The diminished-utility thesis has an obvious affinity with John Herz's well-known argument that the onset of the nuclear age constituted a "Great Divide" between an international politics rooted in the concept of territoriality and one in which that concept has been stripped by technology of most of its meaning.[9] Although exponents of the diminished-utility perspective would not be prepared to argue that political implications of geography are irrelevant, the thrust of their critique leads them to concentrate upon other, nongeographical, factors as the primary variables in international politics.

The case against geopolitics, however stated, seems to have been persuasively made as far as most political scientists are concerned, but it should not be supposed that the concept is without its defenders. As noted above, Ray Cline approves of the concept of geopolitics, but does not like to call it that. Someone who likes both concept and label is Colin Gray, who urges a revival of explicitly geopolitical analysis, because, in a world faced with the threat of an expansionary Soviet Union, "the concepts contained in the classic literature of geopolitics were never so relevant to international political reality as they are today."[10] According to Gray, one could do much worse than to construe the then Soviet threat in terms of a struggle between a Mahanian insular empire (composed of the United States and its allies) and a Mackinderesque "Heartland" empire (composed of the Soviet bloc). The stakes of the struggle, or so it seemed a decade ago, were none other than control of the Eurasian-African "Rimlands," the importance of which Nicholas Spykman stressed some 40 years earlier.[11] They, it was maintained, remained the key to global mastery.

Although I have chosen to title this chapter "The New Geopolitics of Minerals," I do not subscribe to the view that a revival of geopolitics on the grand scale is either imminent or desirable. In some measure, geopolitics as a concept of political analysis *is* flawed, and does deserve the relative neglect into which it has fallen. That being said, however, it is apparent that whatever one's views on the concept, the *word* itself is far from disappearing from common usage, where it most typically appears in a context intended to connote some vague relationship between political phenomena and geography. One can scarcely open a newspaper or tune in to a news broadcast without being apprised of the geopolitical implications of whatever happens to form the subject at hand.

The price of gold, we are often informed, seems to be constantly responding to "geopolitical" events. Oil remains topical, and whatever the current marketing prospects for crude, there seems to be no shortfall in the demand for analysis of "the geopolitics of oil." Other minerals have not been without their perceived geopolitical implications. Soviet and southern African domination of production and reserves of chromium, platinum, manganese, cobalt, and other metals was held not too long ago to be "developing into an ominous geopolitical threat to the industrialized countries of the West."[12] Nor have minerals been the only occasion for a resort to geopolitical musings.

For all the problems associated with it as an analytical tool, I would argue that it still is possible to put geopolitics as a *concept* to scholarly service, provided we avoid falling into the former bad habit of asking it to do too much. If we are unable, in any event, to banish the word, we might as well be able to agree that, in the context of our limited inquiry into strategic minerals, it possesses some helpful conceptual properties — properties that would allow us to speak meaningfully of the "geopolitics of minerals." If we accept, as Harold and Margaret Sprout suggest, that geopolitical hypotheses seek to account for international distributions of power and influence by reference to geographical factors, we can perhaps reduce the concept of geopolitics to those factors that clearly have not been affected significantly by the post-1945 changes in the international political environment that are held to have made the bulk of geopolitics obsolete. Again following the Sprouts, let us accept that geopolitical hypothesizing in the past has fallen into three general categories, namely, hypotheses that sought to account for power and influence differences primarily as: (1) a function of *geographical configuration* (e.g., Mahan and Mackinder); (2) a function of *climate* (e.g., Ellsworth Huntington); (3) a function of security of *access* to needed raw materials.[13]

It seems that, to the extent a case against geopolitics has been made and serious defects have been associated with geopolitical hypotheses, that case has been most successfully made against those hypotheses that focus on *configuration* (because of technological changes, especially in respect of nuclear-weapons delivery systems) or *climate* (because of inherent deterministic tendencies associated with this kind of hypothesis). It *used* to be thought, fairly early in the post–World War II era, that raw materials, too, had lost much of their former significance, but, as I shall argue below, by the early 1970s it once again became apparent that raw materials, minerals in particular, continued to be highly significant variable factors affecting the distribution of international power and influence.

It is my contention that it does make sense to speak of a "geopolitics" of minerals, if by that we mean that we are really concerned not with the size and shape of continents or the influence of climate upon history, but rather with the international political significance of the continuing differential distribution of mineral wealth. Because this distribution pattern is a function of geography, the political problem of access becomes by definition a matter of "geopolitical" importance; it cannot be otherwise. But, if it seems clear that there is an operational geopolitics of minerals, it needs to be determined whether there is a *new* such geopolitics and, if so, how it differs from the old. Prior to making such a determination, however, it remains for us to attend to the second conceptual/definitional matter cited above.

Strategic Minerals: What Are They?

In the preceding section, "minerals" and "strategic minerals" were used interchangeably. In reality, not all minerals are strategic; however, for the kind of minerals that are commonly involved in international trade — that is, for those that are, ipso facto, constituents of the access problem — the distinction between "ordinary" and "strategic" minerals quickly blurs. Without too much exaggeration, one could paraphrase Shakespeare's Hamlet and state that there is nothing either strategic or nonstrategic but thinking makes it so. Like most concepts, that of strategic minerals possesses inherent expansionary tendencies.

Much has been written, especially in the past decade, about "strategic minerals." Though the concept itself dates back to the 1930s, strategic minerals have recently become an increasingly familiar part of the vocabulary of scholars interested in the study of international-resource questions. The discipline of political science has witnessed a swelling of the ranks of those who analyze the international politics of strategic minerals, and the cognate discipline of economics is similarly paying more attention to the study of these commodities, albeit with a different focus. Nor is it just in the social sciences that one encounters this interest, for concomitant with the increase in governments' concern with commodities issues over the past decade has been a growing reliance of policy makers upon the minerals expertise of such "hard" scientists as geologists and mining engineers.

Few would disagree that strategic minerals have been attracting attention of late; where the disagreement arises is over what they are. Like other political concepts, strategic minerals is shaded by nuance and characterized by ambiguity, suggestive of what British philosopher W.B. Gallie calls "essentially contested concepts" — concepts that are at minimum appraisive and complex. A hallmark of such concepts is that "the proper use of [them] inevitably involves endless disputes about their proper uses on the part of the users."[14] Though evidently not one of the more exotic or momentous examples, the concept of strategic minerals has engendered debate as to its proper use, and not only for members of the scholarly community; on occasion, it has also taken on policy relevance.

The first explicit use of "strategic minerals" as a connotative expression occurred in the United States during the interwar years. The label may have originated in the United States, but the concept owed its existence primarily to the recognition on the part of the major European combatants during World War I that modern wars of attrition depended more upon a state's capacity for industrialization and its ability to ensure a continuing flow of vital industrial inputs than upon such qualitative factors as leadership and combat morale.[15] Among the vital industrial inputs, none was held to be as essential for war-fighting capability as were minerals. And among the minerals, iron ore and coal were accorded pride of place.[16] There were, however, already signs by the end of that war that petroleum was likely to become the most important energy commodity in international trade, and perhaps the most important of what would soon come to be known as "strategic" minerals. By the middle of the 1920s, French statesman Aristide Briand could remark, with only slight exaggeration, that "international politics today are oil politics."[17] During the remainder of the interwar period, oil gained in perceived geopolitical significance, as was reflected not only in the oil diplomacy of the great powers but also in the appearance of a body of literature that sought to establish a causal link between scarcity of oil (and other minerals) and the increased incidence of international conflict.[18]

It is perhaps ironical that the label "strategic minerals" should have been developed in the United States, for during neither World War I nor the interwar years was that country terribly dependent upon imports for most of the minerals held to contribute to military power.[19] Nevertheless, U.S. mobilization efforts in 1917 and 1918 had been affected to an extent by shortages of specific materials, which were enumerated during the immediate postwar period when the War Department drafted a list of the 28 materials (not all of which were minerals) that had presented wartime supply difficulties. During the 1920s, this list, called, after its author, the "Harbord List," was expanded by the commodity committees operating within the War Department's planning branch. In the course of the committees' work, the label "strategic minerals" was introduced, and was followed, in the 1930s, by a further analytical category, "critical materials."[20]

In the ensuing decades the definition of strategic materials (of which strategic minerals is a subset) underwent some refinement. By 1939, the concepts of strategic and critical materials had been developed by the U.S. Army and Navy Munitions Board: *strategic* connoted those items deemed essential for defence, the supply of which came in whole or in large part from foreign sources, and for which strict conservation and other control measures would be necessary in wartime; *critical* referred to items also held to be essential for defence, but whose wartime supply was, though problematical, not as much so as that of the strategic materials. However, the two concepts were collapsed into the new expression "strategic and critical materials" when, in an attempt to remove some of the ambiguities associated with the 1939 definitions, the Munitions Board decided in 1944 that henceforth "strategic and critical materials [were] those materials required for essential uses in a war emergency, the procurement of which in adequate quantities, quality, and time is sufficiently uncertain for any reason to require prior provision for the supply thereof."[21]

Notwithstanding the Munition Board's desire to clarify the terminology, its omnibus definition of "strategic and critical" has really not been of much analytical use. The "strategic and critical" wording continues to enjoy U.S. governmental endorsement, but there has been growing dissatisfaction with it, both within the United States and abroad. In section 12 of the U.S. Strategic and Critical Materials Stockpiling Act of 1979, strategic and critical materials are those "that (A) would be needed to supply the military, industrial, and essential civilian needs of the United States during a national emergency, and (B) are not found or produced in the United States in sufficient quantities to meet such need."[22] Critics of this definition object to it on two grounds, one cosmetic, the other substantive. The cosmetic objection, voiced by the National Strategy Information Center, is that two words are being employed, "like Tweedledee and Tweedledum," where one word would be adequate.[23]

Those who raise the substantive objection do so primarily because they feel that not only is the current official U.S. definition too broad to have any analytical precision but it focusses on the wrong set of issues. In short, the definition fails to provide guidance either for the purposes of scholarly inquiry or, more importantly, for the making of materials policy.[24] Some have called for the outright abolition of the term "strategic minerals," while others have urged that its use be severely restricted.

Prominent among those who wish to see usage of the term drastically restricted is the group of minerals experts at the British Geological Survey (BGS) in London, who, in 1982, gave evidence to the Committee of the House of Lords that was studying the strategic-minerals position of the European Community.[25] One of the BGS minerals analysts, Alan Archer, has written that it would be preferable if the term "strategic minerals" were to fall into disuse, because its inherent ambiguity has led to the concept's becoming so broad as to be practically useless. "In short, the term's traditional military or defence meaning has been so abused and its wider meaning is so obscure that, as an adjective applied to minerals, 'strategic' has little or no value."[26]

One who would agree with most of the Archer criticism is Hans Landsberg, an economist with Resources for the Future in Washington. Landsberg does not necessarily advocate the outright abolition of the term, but he would prefer that it be used sparingly. Instead of the scores of items often intended, Landsberg would confine the category to a mere handful of commodities, including chromium, manganese, cobalt, and the platinum-group metals, as well (presumably) as oil.[27] Not only is "strategic minerals" analytically flawed, but it is a potentially costly concept, as the proliferation of such minerals tends to reinforce a political perception that minerals access is threatened on a broad front. In turn, the implication seems to be that industrialized countries should adopt materials policies that are more comprehensive (and expensive) than most can reasonably afford, whereas the problem of guaranteeing access to vitally needed materials, preferably at stable prices, can be solved more economically if the number of minerals is minimized. This tack is justified if the restrictionists' argument that "vulnerability" is a defining characteristic of strategic minerals is accepted.[28]

Before this argument is discussed, the case made by those who would conceive of strategic minerals in the broad sense should be examined. For the broad-interpretationists, the category "strategic minerals" embraces all those minerals held in the U.S. Strategic Stockpile, as well as some of the "essential" and imported items that are not stockpiled, such as iron ore, phosphate, and molybdenum.[29] For broad-interpretationists there are really only two major defining characteristics: such minerals as are deemed strategic must be, in some sense, essential to national defence, and they must, to some important degree, be imported.

Given these two defining characteristics, it is not difficult to account for the enlargement of the strategic-mineral category in recent decades. Not only is "essential" vague and therefore easily expandable, but "national defence" has become more elastic over time, *pari passu* with the broadening of the idea of national security that has occurred in the post–World War II years. National security has always been an ambiguous symbol, but it is arguable that, in the interwar period, it was more narrowly focussed on the question of a state's *physical* security, while today it includes both physical and *economic* security. It has even been suggested that the latter has been gaining in importance, as a result of the "domestication" of the international political system, which is increasingly concerned with the distributive processes that had been the preserve of the state.[30]

That security depends on a healthy economy as much as, if not more than, it does on anything else has gained widespread international acceptance. According to those holding this point of view, among them former West German chancellor Helmut Schmidt,

> the world economic crisis of today is at least as great a strategic danger to the cohesion of the West as anything we have talked about so far. It is strategic danger because it does spread social and political unrest in our countries, and it entails the danger of national economic protectionism against each other within the West.[31]

The economic dimension of security takes on added significance when it is placed in the context of the West's acknowledged dependence upon imports for such minerals as oil, which are self-evidently essential.[32] President Reagan expressed his concern that disruptions in supply of important raw materials, especially minerals, "could have serious consequences for United States and allied security by disrupting capabilities to produce military and essential civilian goods either in a declared national emergency or wartime mobilization."[33]

U.S. Bureau of Mines official John D. Morgan has pointed out that the link between economic and physical security can justify a very broad interpretation of strategic minerals. "Viewed in this context adequate supplies of virtually every known material are a strategic necessity."[34] What to the broad-interpretationists seems a logical extension appears an *extension ad absurdum* to others. Making practically every material strategic, say the restrictionists, obscures the very significance that the label "strategic" was originally intended to convey.

What was, or should be, connoted by the expression "strategic minerals" are, to the restrictionists, the properties known as "vulnerability" and "criticality." Their principal objection is that the broad-interpretationists equate import dependence with the vulnerability of consuming states to supply disruptions, and thereby miss the original point of the concept of strategic minerals. The conditions that bear on whether or not countries are vulnerable to supply disruptions include: (a) the degree of concentration of production of the mineral in question; (b) the identity of the supplying countries; (c) whether there are alternative supply prospects (including domestic alternatives); (d) the opportunities for substitution; (e) the opportunities for recycling and conservation; and (f) the presence of stockpiles in the consuming countries.[35]

The example of the American experience with nickel serves as a good illustration of why import dependence should not be equated with vulnerability. Canada has always been by far the principal source of U.S. nickel, and remains so.[36] Because of contiguity and a general similarity of outlook on most major foreign-policy issues, Americans have tended to look upon Canadian supply "as equivalent to a domestic source."[37] As one prominent minerals analyst of an earlier generation put it, "the possibility that Canada would sever diplomatic relations with the United States and cut off our nickel supply seems no more likely than the possibility of a revolt in northern Minnesota and the consequent cessation of the iron ore supply from that region."[38]

The minerals specialists at the BGS, when they attempt to define strategic minerals, also introduce the idea of "criticality." Criticality, as employed here, is not to be confused with its usage in the above-mentioned official U.S. definition of "strategic and critical" materials (where it is the "Tweedledum" of an adjectival pair). Rather, it corresponds to the more frequently employed term, "essential," though perhaps it is a bit more elegant when used as a noun than would be "essentiality." In other words, criticality, to the restrictionists, need carry no ascription as to the source of the mineral (i.e., whether domestic or foreign), but instead is a function of the importance of the mineral to the military and industrial well-being of a country.

While the restrictionists may, indeed, have logic on their side in arguing that vulnerability, not import-dependence, and criticality should serve as the analytical foci, it is less clear that their strictures against a broad usage of "strategic minerals" merit adherence. Even if we could police the use of concepts, would we be warranted in insisting that "strategic minerals" be accorded a greatly delimited currency? For all its flaws, it may be more difficult to dispense with the concept of strategic minerals than to retain it. The restrictionist case illustrates some of the difficulties associated with the attempt to avoid employing the offending concept, for it possesses some problems of its own, the most important of which I shall call the fallacy of ethnocentrism.

Since vulnerability to supply disruption is not associated with all minerals, as it clearly is not, the restrictionists would have us reduce the vulnerability issue to its proper dimensions by getting rid of most of the strategic minerals and calling strategic only those that everyone would agree are worth worrying about. The objection to this proposition is contained in the proposition itself, for consensus is never possible to achieve on the list of worrisome minerals of the present, let alone on those that might cause or have caused concern in another era. Adopting the logic of restrictionism would oblige us incessantly to qualify strategic minerals by indicating to whom and at what period they were or are strategic, a process that would be clumsy at best, ridiculous at worst. Indeed, the logical consequence of restrictionism must be abolitionism, for of what utility to discourse would be a concept so encumbered by qualifications that it could possess no meaning if left on its own?

The broad-interpretationists, who also insist that, to be strategic, a mineral must, to a significant degree, be imported, similarly commit the ethnocentric fallacy. The problem with requiring that import dependence be a necessary (though not a sufficient) condition in determining whether a mineral is strategic to any given country is that it becomes logically absurd to speak of states being *exporters* of strategic minerals, unless, of course, they are also importers of the same item (which they often are not). Import dependence may be an interesting phenomenon in and of itself, but it is no sine qua non for determining whether a mineral is or is not strategic.

What has happened over several decades to the concept of strategic minerals is what usually happens to essentially contested concepts, especially political ones.

They grow, both because their very contestedness (or ambiguity) encourages expansion, and because the conditions extant when they first came into use have changed. T.D. Weldon has written of the effect that changing conditions have on concepts, and though Weldon was a political philosopher and not an expert on minerals, his words are worth pondering. Facts change, writes Weldon, and this requires that adjustments be made in the way we express facts. The adjustments can be of two kinds: we can invent a new technical word or concept to reflect the change, or we can expand a familiar word or concept. "Usually the second method is preferred, partly because it avoids more confusion than it creates, indeed it seldom confuses anybody but political philosophers, and partly because the extended use has often come to be adopted uncritically in the natural course of events."[39]

We have seen that both the broad and the restrictionist interpretations of "strategic minerals" are flawed; each conveys a certain amount of analytical confusion, which in turn has potential policy implications. The problem with "strategic minerals" cannot, however, be overcome by restricting its use, not least importantly because it is in the nature of things for expanded concepts that have entered into demotic usage to resist abandonment. It may be that they are used in ways we would prefer they not be used, but that they *will* be used is not at issue. One book dedicated to showing policy makers how to avoid shortages in strategic minerals starts out by confronting the definitional problem — and surrendering to it. Pursuing the logic of the restrictionists, Bohdan Szuprowicz arrives willy-nilly at the conclusion of the broad-interpretationists when he writes that "the definition of what is truly a strategic and critical material will vary not only from country to country but also among industries and even enterprises within each country."[40] Szuprowicz is not advocating the proliferation of strategic minerals, but if all consumers are free to decide what does or does not deserve the label, it is hard to see how proliferation, or confusion, could be avoided.

Since the purpose of words is to clarify, not obscure, meaning, perhaps a truce between the contending definitional camps can be arranged. A case can be made, paradoxically, both for a broad usage of the term strategic minerals *and* for the argument that ultimately what is important about such minerals is the extent to which consumers (or supplies) are vulnerable. This case would rest on the assumption that those minerals deserving to be described as strategic should fulfil two admittedly subjective conditions. They must be deemed essential to the national security (either in the narrow military sense or in the wider understanding that equates national security with economic well-being); and they must be traded internationally to a significant degree. This second condition recognizes that, in a world where all states are self-sufficient in minerals, no minerals are strategic, but at the same time avoids the ethnocentrism of defining strategic minerals solely from the perspective of the importing countries.

The attractiveness of such a proposal would perhaps be greater for those countries, like Canada, for whom strategic minerals are more important export than import commodities. At the very least, one could then speak and write logically of Canadian *exports* of strategic minerals, and have it understood that what was being referred to were those minerals in international commerce that were essential to at least *one* (and usually to more than one) of Canada's trading partners.

A principal drawback, however, would be that in out-broadening the broad-interpretationists, such a construct would lead to most base metals being listed as strategic. To a degree, this problem is already in existence, as a glance at the common minerals (e.g., lead and zinc) contained in the U.S. National Defense Stockpile indicates. More to the point, there really is no a priori reason for excluding common minerals from the "strategic" category; minerals such as iron ore were widely considered to be highly strategic not so very long ago and, if Brian Skinner and others are to be believed, might again be so considered.[41]

To summarize, the strategic-mineral category *is* flawed and, for the most part, the restrictionist critique is legitimate. Knowing only that a mineral is strategic really does not tell us whether any particular country might have grounds for considering itself vulnerable to supply disruptions. If it were possible to "uninvent" words, perhaps minerals analysts would all be better off if the concept could be abolished. But it is not, and as the passage from Gallie quoted above would indicate, one can expect that not only will strategic minerals continue to be a topic of discussion, but that the discussion will involve endless disputes about the term's "proper" meaning.

From the above discussion, it might be concluded that the minerals-access problem has assumed greater importance over time as a factor in international politics; in short, that today the geopolitics of minerals is of vaster significance than ever before, if for no other reason than the proliferation of strategic minerals in our era. I would caution against such a conclusion. What can be stated unequivocally is that minerals retain their political meaning, that they are a part of geopolitics that has not been rendered obsolete in the decades since the end of World War II. But to go beyond that statement requires an analysis that contrasts the various dimensions of the contemporary access problem with those of the only other in which minerals problems were anything like as relevant, namely, the interwar period. Let us, therefore, seek to determine what changes have occurred over time in respect of several issues that are directly related to, and at times derivative of, the differential distribution of minerals. For the purposes of analysis, I have selected the following issues: minerals as a cause of international conflict; minerals as a factor contributing to military potential; and the issue of scarcity. These categories are not meant to be exhaustive, but it is intended that they be illustrative of the most important changes that have transpired in the geopolitics of minerals over the past half-century.

Minerals as a Cause of International Conflict

Because war or the threat of war remains the most serious problem confronting the international political system, any analysis of the geopolitical significance of minerals must begin with their relationship to the larger problem of international conflict. Although the relationship can be traced back through centuries, given the obvious part that minerals have had in the evolution of military technology, it is really only in the 20th century that minerals have appeared as a reason *for*, and not merely a means *of*, fighting. World War I constituted a watershed insofar as minerals were concerned; prior to 1914, states appeared relatively indifferent to (or unconscious of) the access problem, either because of greater minerals self-sufficiency (as in the case of the United States and the British Empire) or because of confidence that what was lacking could always be provided through the channels of untrammelled free trade. To be sure, wars in the 19th century had wrought substantial redistributions of minerals, as a consequence of the rearrangement of boundaries, but even the highly redistributive (in the minerals sense) Franco-Prussian War did not arise because of a desire on the part of either belligerent to acquire mineral wealth. Although, in retrospect, it appeared that the war had in fact been an "exchange of blood for iron," archival research has revealed that minerals did not figure in the decision of either side to go to war.[42]

It was really only the experience that all belligerents encountered with materials supply during World War I that underscored the strategic relevance of minerals in modern wars of attrition. As C.K. Leith observed, "the war brought a rude awakening to the fact that no nation could be sure of a steady supply from abroad. . . . As for the Central Powers, the acute shortage of essential minerals which they experienced was a very considerable factor in their ultimate defeat."[43] More rudely awakened than any of the other participants was Germany, for whom the interwar years witnessed what a contemporary political scientist termed a "real claustrophobia in . . . national psychology."[44] This predisposition became especially pronounced after the advent to power of Hitler in 1933, for, under the Nazis, Germany incessantly argued for a more "equitable" distribution of the earth's mineral and other raw-materials supply, which meant, *at minimum*, that Germany's lost African colonies be restored to it. The German case for a new international economic order rested, as does the more recent argument for the new international economic order (NIEO), on a concept of "equality" that was nothing if not ambiguous. Apart from this similarity, however, the arguments made for changing the international economic status quo in the interwar years were of a radically different nature from more contemporary arguments for equality, in that Germany, the leader of the minerals "have-nots," was nonetheless one of the wealthier countries on earth.

It was not, of course, a more equitable division of wealth that Hitler sought, but of territory, for territorial redistribution seemed to offer a way out of Germany's minerals dilemma.[45] As German leaders interpreted their country's position, autarchy (or self-sufficiency) in mineral and other raw-materials supply offered the only chance of living as an equal with the other powers; but to the others, autarchy could only mean territorial expansionism, or imperialism. Germany had never been particularly well-situated with regard to minerals, even when it had an overseas empire, but losing the war in 1918 had meant the loss of Lorraine iron ore as well; and from being nearly self-sufficient in this one mineral in 1914 Germany became largely dependent in the interwar years on imported iron ore, mostly Swedish. Nor was iron ore an exception; in fact, Germany possessed self-sufficiency in only two of the 35 raw materials that were, at the time, held to be necessary for modern warfare — coal and potash.[46] Besides iron ore, it lacked (in many cases completely) the following minerals, most of which were essential for the normal operation of an industrial economy, and *all* of which were essential for a society contemplating war: petroleum, copper, nickel, sulphur, tungsten, titanium, tin, manganese, chromium, lead, mica, graphite, industrial diamonds, quartz crystal, and bauxite.

But if Germany showed that losing a Great War could have serious minerals consequences, Japan and Italy demonstrated that being on the winning side did not necessarily imply any easy solutions to the problem of mineral maldistribution. If anything, Japan's minerals situation was worse than Germany's, since, of the raw materials essential to modern industry, Japan possessed only sulphur and artificial nitrates in abundance. Italy was in a better minerals position, but only marginally; it was dependent on imports for all the essential minerals except bauxite, mercury, and sulphur.[47] Together, the above three states constituted what came to be called the "have-not" countries. Contrasted with their plight was the comfortable minerals situation of the "haves": the United States, Great Britain and its dominions and colonies, and the Soviet Union. Between them, the United States and Great Britain alone controlled some two-thirds of global mineral reserves, and the United States was far and away the world's leading producer of minerals.[48]

In ascribing significance to various factors implicated in the outset of World War II — and in this connection it might be wiser to date the beginning of the war in the Pacific from the Japanese invasion of Manchuria rather than from Pearl Harbor — one must be extremely careful to avoid succumbing to reductionist theories of causation. It is surely impossible to isolate any single "cause" of the war, but high on the list of predisposing conditions has to be the mineral-access problem. That there was a widespread conviction during the interwar period that differential minerals distribution posed a threat to peace is a matter of record. Hjalmar Schacht, director of the Reichsbank, was only stating the conventional wisdom when he wrote that "a nation which is cut off from the essential necessities of life must be a source of unrest in the world."[49] By 1937, the time Schacht was writing, Italy and Japan had launched wars of territorial conquest that were explicitly justified by reference to each state's need for more "living-space." In the case of Italy, conquests in Africa did not do much to redress minerals shortages (and did even less to relieve so-called population pressure at home), but Japan was able to secure some needed minerals, getting coal, low-grade iron ore, and magnesium from Manchuria and North China.[50]

To recapitulate, it is not possible, nor is it my purpose, to argue an immediate causal link between the minerals question of the interwar years and the origins of World War II. But it does seem that T.S. Lovering's assessment, made some 47 years ago, has stood well the test of time. According to Lovering, "the immediate causes of the second world war were clearly psychological and political; but the immediate causes grew out of social conditions, and the social conditions in turn were profoundly affected by the distribution and control of raw materials."[51] More recently, Alfred Eckes, Jr., has observed that, apart from the political and social causes of the war, "there was also an important structural problem — the uneven global distribution of raw materials among industrial states — that contributed directly to the collapse of world peace."[52]

However conceived, the conclusion appears inescapable that the minerals-access problem was an important factor in the breakdown of world order during the late 1930s. Put into contemporary terminology, we might say that access issues were highly contributory to "East-West," or interbloc, tension. Would it be possible to make the same kind of statement in respect of the other era with which our analysis is concerned, the period from 1973 to the early 1980s? That is, were minerals-access questions of as much perceived importance in Moscow and Washington at the start of this decade as they were in Berlin, Rome, and Tokyo, on the one hand, and London and Washington, on the other, during the 1930s?

To answer this question requires that we differentiate between conflict on the scale of a world war — that is, the kind of war between superpowers that might start out as an exchange of tactical nuclear weapons but that would quickly escalate into an all-out strategic exchange — and conflict that is more clearly containable. It may be that the latter type of superpower conflict will ultimately prove to be a conceptual impossibility, but it is at least arguable that we have already had, in the form of several proxy wars of the past decade or so, evidence that armed-superpower rivalry need not lead to a war to the finish. The point is important, for if what is meant by "war" is the nuclear equivalent of World War II, then minerals access will not likely — barring an epidemic of insanity in Washington and Moscow — constitute an important cause of war ever again. Thus, in the context of East-West tension, one clear distinction between the "new" and the "old" geopolitics of minerals would be that, as a reason for fighting a major war, as a war aim, minerals-access problems are not likely to result in a serious threat to world peace.

Having said that, there still exists the likelihood that minerals-access will remain at least an incidental source of tension between West and East. Because it is primarily the Western industrialized states for whom the question of access is deemed a vital interest, given the greater relative self-sufficiency in minerals of the Soviet Union, the question of resort to arms to preserve access to raw materials is one that has occasioned not a little interest in the West (especially in the United States) in the post-1973 years.[53] Initially, most of the speculation about preserving access with force focussed on the question of Persian Gulf oil.[54] When the access fears first surfaced in the mid-1970s, the Soviet Union was not considered to be the primary cause of any future supply distribution; hence, use of force, to the extent it was contemplated at all, was considered in the context of strictly regional issues, and not in the broader framework of East-West relations.

But with the decline of détente and the growing perception in parts of the West that the Soviet Union was running out of oil — a perception fed by a series of 1977 CIA reports that have subsequently been radically modified — policy planning in Washington began to assume as a first principle that Soviet expansion into the Gulf area might soon occur as a direct consequence of the Soviet need for foreign oil. It quickly became apparent that the Soviets might continue enjoying self-sufficiency in oil for some time to come, so those who still preferred to regard Soviet meddling as the leading threat to Western access began to concentrate on another presumed motive: Soviet desire to cripple, or "cannibalize," Western economies by interfering with their supply of Persian Gulf oil.[55]

Although there never was any solid evidence upon which to rest the contention that the Soviets were, in fact, out to menace Western oil supply, analysts in the West did not refrain from extending their assumptions about oil to other strategic minerals. What Soviet power might portend for oil supply, it apparently also could portend for other mineral imports. There seemed to be two main concerns. The first was that the Soviets, by building up their navy, might eventually be strong enough to interdict Western sea lanes.[56] The other was that the Soviets would step up their political and military involvement in southern Africa, with the view to making Western access to the region's mineral wealth more problematical. In this regard, it is important to note the high degree of concentration of certain strategic minerals. Twenty-five percent or more (and usually it is more) of total global production of the following minerals takes place in the southern African region (which comprises Angola, Botswana, Congo, Lesotho, Mozambique, Namibia, South Africa, Swaziland, Tanzania, Zaire, Zambia, and Zimbabwe): diamonds, vanadium, platinum-group metals, chromite, cobalt, and manganese.[57]

Despite the fears of such observers as Frank Barnett, head of the New York–based National Strategy Information Center, that "the age of détente is shading into the era of the resource war,"[58] it bears repeating that an important — perhaps the most important — implication of the new geopolitics of minerals is that as a potential source of armed conflict between rival world-power blocs, minerals simply do not possess the significance that they had in the interwar years. On this most relevant issue, I believe that Ruth W. and Uzi B. Arad are correct in writing that

> the undeniably growing importance of raw materials and the politics of using or securing them will probably be conducive to a less stable world . . . [in which] . . . there will be more international disputes involving access to resources. But all are likely to fall short of causing major upheavals that may lead to war.[59]

Minerals as a Factor Contributing to Military Potential

Military potential, like strategic minerals, is a 20th-century concept. In fact, the two concepts stemmed from the same period, the interwar years. The evolution of both is, in large measure, testimony to the impact of the great "lesson" of

World War I: that modern wars of attrition would be won by those states that had the most secure resource bases, and lost by those that did not.

In its early years, the concept of military potential was known by another name, "war potential." But irrespective of which label was employed, the basic idea connoted was of a reserve of "national resources available for producing and maintaining armed forces. Whenever a nation creates or expands military forces in peace and war, it mobilizes military potential."[60] Given the amplitude of such a definition, it is no surprise that military potential should be a difficult concept to measure, for not only are "objective" constituents of national power, such as population, GNP, or energy production, factored into the overall equation, but so too are such subjective qualities as sociopolitical structure, and patterns of culture. With due regard to the inherent flaws of any attempts to formulate numerical indices of the power potential of various states,[61] I would, nevertheless, maintain that one can, with a reasonable degree of validity, address the manner in which the concept of military potential has evolved across historical eras, with particular attention to the changing role of minerals as ingredients of military potential.

Probably the most significant difference between the "new" geopolitics of minerals and the "old," in the context of military potential, is the extent to which earlier hypotheses were founded on assumptions that were heavily deterministic. Recent analyses of military potential have placed much emphasis on the capabilities of modern industrial societies to utilize substitution and technology to free themselves from the "dictates" of geography. In the interwar years, however, no such stress on voluntarism was present. Instead, states were held to be truly captives of their resource bases, which were conceived of in static terms. A country either had mineral deposits, or it did not; and, if it did not, there was not much likelihood of it ever becoming a great power. This view was based on the fact, which the Great War had convincingly demonstrated, that military potential was a direct function of the capacity for industrialization, "and since large-scale industrialization presupposes a ready availability of vast quantities of the basic industrial raw materials, nature, through her unequal distribution of these, has rigidly set a limit to the number of states capable of achieving the status of Great Powers."[62]

The post–World War II decades have witnessed a markedly different understanding of the role of minerals in overall military potential. Ironically, it was the example of Germany during the war that brought about a reinterpretation of earlier, deterministic, assumptions that stressed a strong and direct link between minerals and power. It will be recalled from the preceding section that fear of losing access to needed minerals had been a major concern of German foreign policy in the 1930s; both within Germany and elsewhere, it was widely assumed that, without access to essential minerals, Germany could not hope to become a great power.[63] Germany did, of course, acquire substantial mineral holdings through its early wartime conquests in Europe, but the net effect of these conquests was only to reduce, not to eliminate, its overall import dependence. Thus, it was with a sense of incredulity that postwar students of military potential pondered the German wartime experience; for contrary to what World War I had "predicted," the experience of Germany in World War II seemed to indicate that access to minerals was not, after all, vital for the purposes of waging a major war. Technology and substitution, both of which assumed a greater degree of administrative skill than had been the case in the Germany of 1914–18, were held to have been instrumental in Germany's fighting as long as it had, given its relatively meagre minerals endowment. Significantly, if Germany could have accomplished so much with so little, then the dependence-minimizing options seemed to be promising, indeed, for more well-endowed countries such as the United States, which emerged from the war in 1945 facing potential supply shortages in nonfuel minerals for the first time, or so it seemed, in its history.[64]

In a celebrated article that appeared in the inaugural volume of *World Politics*, Edward S. Mason drew an analogy between what the Germans had accomplished and what he thought the United States and other industrialized powers could achieve. Noting that, although Germany's consumption of essential minerals had remained constant from 1938 to 1944, German military production had actually increased by 300 to 400 percent, Mason concluded that "it is quite clear . . . that Germany managed to fight a first-class war on very small quantities of 'essential' raw materials. . . . The moral, for our purpose, seems to be that the potentialities of raw material substitution and replacement in a modern economy are enormous."[65] Other analysts drew on the German experience to reach conclusions similar to Mason's. The new geopolitics of minerals, it appeared, promised to be substantially different from the old, because industrial and, therefore, military potential were in the process of being freed from the shackles of geographic determinism.

Mancur Olson, Jr., was one of the new breed of analysts who minimized the contribution of minerals to military potential. Earlier, deterministic, statements of that relationship were examples, said Olson, of the "physiocratic fallacy," in that they proceeded from the erroneous assumption that all wealth flowed from the production of primary goods. Olson's thesis was not that minerals were irrelevant to defence; it was rather that "the experience of the two world wars and a glance at the opportunities for substitution reveal that shortages of primary products need not always be fatal to a nation at war."[66] Far less qualified was the view articulated a decade later by Charles L. Schultze. Writing a few short months before the oil-supply crisis of autumn 1973, Schultze advanced the proposition that "the national security of the United States depends in no important way on securing access to raw materials, markets, or sea lanes abroad, and securing or protecting such access cannot reasonably be used as the rationale for a foreign policy."[67]

Schultze's argument has merit if, and only if, national security is conceived of in the narrow sense of physical security. Clearly, the most dangerous challenge the United States faces in a military sense inheres in the destructive capability of the Soviet nuclear arsenal. The same holds, *mutatis mutandis*, for the Soviet Union. In the worst case of a major nuclear war between the superpowers, mineral reserves cannot constitute anything but a trivial asset, if an asset at all. As World

War I *seemed* to indicate, wars of attrition required substantial military potential in the form of capacity for industrialization. Whether World War II — at least, the German experience in that war — disconfirmed the lesson of World War I remains an open question (frankly, I am skeptical of the Mason thesis), but what cannot be questioned is that World War III, were it to involve nuclear weapons, would not be much of a war of attrition. And, in that sense, minerals would matter hardly at all.

But if military potential is, as I suspect it is, enmeshed in the same kind of conceptual broadening process that has seen national security come to mean security in an economic as well as a physical sense, then surely the military potential of stronger economies — no matter how measured, no matter what it signifies — has to be greater than that of weaker economies, all other things being equal.[68] According to the broader view of national security, a NATO alliance not beset with supply problems for oil and other strategic minerals must be a stronger NATO than one beset with such difficulties. The point is that, while the new geopolitics of minerals is, indeed, less deterministic than the old insofar as the relationship of minerals to military potential is concerned, it remains the case that minerals-access issues possess meaning in the *military* context. The experience of Western industrialized states in the post-1973 years has led analysts of minerals questions to draw back from the more sanguine assumptions of the 1945-to-1973 period. It has not proved possible, despite the very impressive gains forged by technology, for modern economies to reduce very much their need for imports of certain essential minerals.

Individual minerals may and do become irrelevant for military purposes as a result of technological developments. An outstanding example of this is the case of natural nitrates, which were rendered dispensable as a result of breakthroughs achieved by German chemists who, stimulated by the British disruption of Germany's Chilean nitrate supply during World War I, succeeded in economically synthesizing nitrates, a success that ultimately doomed the Chilean nitrate industry. But, to be sustainable over the long term, substitution made possible by technology must be economic (or at least not terribly uneconomic), and in this regard the German interwar experience with synthetic-fuel production is instructive; for although technology did enable Germany to satisfy nearly half its domestic oil consumption from coal by the late 1930s, it was at a heavy price (about four times the per-barrel cost of imported oil) — a price that had to redound to the ultimate detriment of overall German industrial performance and, hence, military potential.

Nor is economics the only drawback to more widespread resort to what one geologist has scornfully termed the "technical fix."[69] Even assuming economic-substitution possibilities, technology remains a two-edged sword. It may and does eliminate dependence on some minerals, but usually at the cost of creating dependence on others. As Nazli Choucri and Robert North have argued, "the more advanced the level of technology . . . the greater the variety and quantity of resources needed by that society."[70] An illustration of this tendency was provided by the U.S. experience during the interwar period, when a search for mineral substitutes for items that were on the strategic list uncovered 34 new materials (among which were beryllium, lithium, and magnesium), many of which were produced outside the United States.[71]

A further instance of the limited capabilities of technology to find substitutes is the continuing problem that advanced industrial societies, Canada included, have encountered in trying to reduce their dependence upon imports of certain essential minerals. One of the striking similarities between the new geopolitics and the old consists in the inability of states to do away with their need for particular strategic minerals. Two of the most important such minerals were strategic to most industrialized states during the interwar period and remain so today: manganese and chromium, both essential for steel-making purposes, neither with an economic substitute (indeed, for manganese there is no substitute at all).[72] The list of such hard-to-replace items could be expanded, with oil being an obvious inclusion.

The Issue of Scarcity

Technology may have limits, but it should be stressed that the underlying problem of strategic minerals — that is, the very reason they *are* strategic — is not that they are on the verge of depletion, but rather that they are differentially distributed throughout the world. If the pattern of global minerals distribution were somehow made more uniform than it is, the question of access would, in theory, be less an international political issue and more a purely domestic one, as each country sought to satisfy consumption from its own reserves. Actual physical, or geological, scarcity has not to date been a serious problem, and in this respect there is again similarity between the new geopolitics of minerals and the old. Paradoxical as it might seem, and despite the gargantuan minerals consumption of the industrialized and industrializing world over the decades since the end of World War II, "reserves of nearly all mineral commodities are larger today than in the early postwar period."[73] However, if the actuality of physical depletion looms no larger today than it did a half-century ago, the *perception* that it is a growing danger has been more pronounced in the post-1973 era than it was in the interwar years. In the earlier period there was, to be sure, intermittent concern (particularly in the immediate aftermath of World War I) over the physical supply of certain minerals, above all oil. Perhaps more so than anywhere else, there was in the United States of the early 1920s a perception that oil reserves could not last much beyond another decade. Some students of minerals questions even predicted that "our children will in all probability see the end of the petroleum industry."[74] Ultimately, the fear of imminent exhaustion of oil reserves proved to be self-correcting, for among other things it motivated the American government to practise "resource diplomacy," thereby helping American companies to establish their presence in oil provinces outside the Western Hemisphere. So intensive and successful was the search for new oil fields (both in the United States and elsewhere) that, by the end of the 1920s, the "menace" of physical depletion of oil had been put to rest, at least for several decades.

By the early 1930s, no informed student of minerals would have deemed the world mineral problem to be one of scarcity. Far from scarcity, it was glut that seemed to be plaguing mineral production. As a result of improvements in the technology of mineral extraction, the real price of minerals tumbled throughout the 1920s, and the market for them was characterized by oversupply, notwithstanding that demand for minerals was constantly on the rise during the decade. But, the onset of the depression caused demand to fall, making a bad situation worse for mineral (and other commodity) producers.[75] In 1937, the Raw Materials Committee of the League of Nations reported that, to the degree the world had a minerals problem at all, it was chiefly a function of the inability of consumers to pay for them, not of the world to produce them. Analysts in Great Britain and elsewhere did not fail to note the incongruity between the global oversupply of minerals and the clamant demands of Germany for a more "equitable" distribution of territory. "Among the many irrational features of international affairs today," wrote H.D. Henderson, "there is none more ironical than the voicing of the demand for more 'living-space' by the leader of a great European industrial nation at this particular juncture of the world's history. For never was living-space a less real problem for the people of Western Europe."[76]

The response made by Germany (and to a lesser extent the other "have-nots") to the charge that minerals were in such abundance during the 1930s that, in effect, their acquisition had never before been *easier*, was to point up the deficiencies of trade as a means of remedying the access problem. In an ideal world, stated Hjalmar Schacht, trade could resolve the access question, just as it had in the era before the Great War, when Germany and other minerals-deficient countries could and did procure supply in free international markets. But the global trade regime prevailing in the 1930s was a far cry from that of the prewar period, a situation that, to Schacht, suggested that "it is either silly or cynical . . . for foreign commentators to declare that Germany can buy raw materials in the world market at will." Such purchase of materials was impossible, as Germany's leading economist saw it, because Germany lacked foreign exchange, and it lacked foreign exchange because it was becoming increasingly harder for its manufactures to penetrate foreign markets in the protectionist environment.[77]

Economists in Britain and other "have" countries were being more than a little naïve in expecting international trade to do for minerals consumers in the protectionist 1930s what it had been able to do in the earlier, more liberal area that Asa Briggs characterized as "the *belle époque* of interdependence."[78] However, German (and Italian and Japanese) demand for minerals in the 1930s was in large measure a function not of the dictates of a normal peacetime economy but rather of an economy rapidly preparing for war. How else explain the anomaly of "have-not" economies, all of them well-launched on ambitious rearmament programs, consuming many more minerals in the late 1930s than they did in the prosperity era of a decade before?[79] The debate over trade as a means of settling access problems in any case totally overlooked what should have been obvious to everyone: that trade itself, as Albert O. Hirschman has brilliantly argued, cannot lead to the depoliticization of minerals questions precisely because trade was, is, and probably always will be an eminently political process. It is so because, whether intended or not, it inevitably affects the power position of states. The effect is twofold: because trade can enhance a state's military potential by supplying essential minerals, it was said by Hirschman to possess a property known as the "supply effect"; and because it could serve as a direct source of power, through the fostering of asymmetrical dependencies, it possessed an "influence effect."[80]

I will have some further comments about trade as a means of ensuring access, but for the moment let us return to the question of scarcity as it has been formulated in the post-1973 years. The argument that minerals are becoming less abundant globally takes two distinct forms: the first, and more common, variant is that depletion, whether in the physical or economic sense, is the principal threat to future supply; the second, which has gained in plausibility in the past few years, is that scarcity will be a function neither of physical nor of economic depletion, but rather will have political causes.[81]

It will be recalled that in the post-1973 years, much more so than in the interwar period, there has been a quickened sense of anxiety about the possibility of the depletion of global mineral reserves. There is, of course, nothing new about the notion that nonrenewable resources must, in a finite world, sooner or later become exhausted. Depletion — whether in the physical sense of things actually running out, or in the economic sense of their becoming too expensive for the world to use — has been a theoretically interesting proposition ever since the time of Malthus and Ricardo. The germane question, and the one for which no one has been able to supply a definitive answer, concerns the amount of time it will take before either economic (Ricardian) or physical (Malthusian) scarcity sets in. In the early years of the 1970s, it began to appear that Ricardian scarcity was closer to reality than the most optimistic (or "Cornucopian") viewpoint had held it to be. Minerals shortages were, in fact, starting to crop up by late 1973, as accelerating demand among OECD consumers temporarily outran supply. OPEC was in the process of shocking world oil consumers with its unprecedented use of "resource power." And the Club of Rome had begun to publicize its dramatic findings that nonrenewable resources were rapidly disappearing.

This is not the place to detail the methodological problems associated with the Club of Rome findings as published in the controversial work *Limits to Growth*.[82] However, one central fallacy of that report does merit stating: the assumption that *reserves* were what was most important about global mineral supply. The concept of reserves is a dynamic one; reserves may indeed decline, as the Club of Rome report noted, but they also can and do increase. Whether dynamic or not, they are not the most relevant conceptual category around which to base a series of assumptions about the probability of scarcity. Reserves simply mean the quantity of minerals in deposits that can be profitably exploited under current economic and technological conditions.[83] Far more important conceptually than reserves are the earth's total *resources*, for the former are but a subset of the latter. Put differently, resources become reserves through a combination of discovery and improvements in either technology or price (or both). Copper provides an example of the distinction between reserves and resources. A century ago, the average grade mined was about 3 percent; by 1960, it was 0.72 percent. In current terminology, only the 3 percent ores would have been classified as reserves in 1882, while all ores of lower copper content would have been resources.[84] Thus, one can account for the otherwise paradoxical tendency of copper reserves to expand at the same time the consumption of copper has been increasing, a situation characteristic of the post–World War II decades; for although "known" global reserves of copper were 100 million tons in 1945 and consumption was 93 million tons between 1945 and 1970 alone, by the end of the 1970s world reserves stood at more than 300 million tons.

Total global mineral resources are truly, as geologist James Boyd described them, "large enough to stagger the imagination."[85] And it would take a feverish imagination, indeed, to conjure up a probable Malthusian future. But is a Ricardian future as improbable, and if it is not, how far away is it? All that can be said in respect of this twinned question is that *doctores scinduntur*, the scholars are divided. Minerals economists tend to be more optimistic than geologists about the prospect of staving off a Ricardian future.[86] In any case, hardly any knowledgeable student of minerals, whether economist or geologist, envisions the onset of Ricardian scarcity until the next century, at the earliest. And whether or not economic scarcity does become manifest even then, all would agree, depends upon whether "the race between the cost-decreasing effects of new technology and the cost-increasing effects of depletion is won by the latter."[87]

Far more problematical is the prospect facing consumers that access will become more difficult as a result of politically induced scarcity. Political scarcity can be a function either of the withdrawal of capital investment on the part of multinational mining companies frightened by increased "resource power" in many parts of the Third World, or of supply disruptions occasioned either as an incidental consequence of political turmoil in a producing country (as happened with cobalt in Zaire in the late 1970s) or as an intended consequence of Soviet attempts to render Western economic security more tenuous. Concerning this second aspect of political scarcity (the potential disruption of supply, whether intended or not), suffice it to note that there was growing concern in the West a few years ago that such disruptions might be the most likely causes of shortages in the 1980s. We now know this concern to have been misplaced.

Here I would like to address briefly the possibility that political scarcity may be brought about as a result of increasingly assertive LDC governments attempting to extract more economic rent from multinational minerals producers operating within their boundaries. Here is a further way in which the new geopolitics of minerals differs sharply from the old, for in the interwar period many of the minerals-producing regions were outright colonies of European consuming states, and those that did have de jure sovereignty were (with the exception of Mexico and Bolivia in the late 1930s) unwilling or unable to challenge the terms that governed the operations of foreign extractive enterprises.

With rapid decolonization in the post–World War II decades, and with the declining ability of the United States to preserve its "hegemonic position" in world politics, economic power seemed to be shifting to a greater or lesser degree toward the developing states; especially was this so by the mid-1960s. Their exercise of "resource power" was given an apparently powerful fillip when OPEC launched its successful price action in 1973, and for a time it appeared that cartels in other minerals would make supply increasingly costly and risky.[88] One effect of LDC assertiveness was "an enormous shift in the location of new mineral activity," which was increasingly, by the mid-1970s, taking place in countries considered more hospitable to private foreign capital — countries such as the United States, Canada, Australia, and South Africa.[89] During the 1966–72 period, American mining and smelting investment in developing countries had amounted to some 40 percent of such investment in developed countries (mostly Canada and Australia); but, by the end of 1977, the developing countries' share had declined to only 32 percent of that of the developed countries. Nor was there anything exceptional about the behaviour of American-based multinationals, for mining firms domiciled in other consuming countries likewise undertook a relative shift in the locus of their operations.[90]

By the mid-1970s, the emerging view of scarcity was that it was more likely to be caused by political than economic developments in future — primarily political developments attending the climb up the "learning curve" of more assertive LDC governments eager to exert greater control over their mineral wealth. Whatever the particular modalities chosen by the LDC governments in attempting to assert their "resource power" (embargoes, cartels, and unilateral price-administration schemes were some of the possibilities mentioned), minerals experts in the West were becoming increasingly convinced that "we should . . . look more to the political context than to economic theories to assess the present and potential difficulties in international transactions in raw materials."[91] But the recession of the early 1980s would lead to a drastic and rapid reassessment of the postulated link between political forces and minerals scarcity. Indeed, in some minerals (e.g., copper) it became common to encounter arguments that held political manipulation (in the event, for reasons related to balance-of-payment and employment-maintenance imperatives) to be the principal source of glut![92]

Conclusion

Despite the several and important ways in which minerals-access questions of the post-1973 years differ from those of the interwar period, there is a strong undercurrent of continuity crossing the two historical eras. What has *not* changed is that access to minerals continues to be ultimately a function of political processes, and, as a result, the access question remains today what it was in the 1930s — a matter of "geopolitical" concern. It has proven impossible for the international political/economic order that emerged out of World War II to bring about a depoliticization of minerals, despite some optimistic assertions made in the early 1960s about the potentialities of increasing interdependence between nations to do just that. Indeed, to the extent that interdependence can be considered to be coterminous with, or rather reducible to, vulnerability interdependence, a thesis provocatively advanced by David Baldwin,[93] it must come to connote not a *solution* to the access problem, but rather a confirmation of its most worrisome feature, from the perspective of the industrialized countries — namely, the vulnerability of consumers. To be sure, the vulnerability worries of industrialized consumers vary in step with the vagaries of the business cycle, and, by the end of the 1980s, the tightening of mineral markets was promising once again to raise the issue of mineral supply higher on the political agenda of developed Western countries.

NOTES

1. C.K. Leith, *World Minerals and World Politics: A Factual Study of Minerals in Their Political and International Relations* (New York: Whittlesey House, McGraw-Hill, 1931), 104.

2. Hanns W. Maull, *Raw Materials, Energy and Western Security* (London: Macmillan/ International Institute for Strategic Studies, 1984), 7.

3. At least in Anglo-American precincts of the discipline, for, as John Child and others have noted, elsewhere the "geopolitical" tradition retains its allure. See John Child, "Geopolitical Thinking in Latin America," *Latin American Research Review* 14 (1979): 89–111; John Child, *Geopolitics and Conflict in South America: Quarrels among Neighbors* (New York: Praeger, 1985); Judith Ewell, "The Development of Venezuelan Geopolitical Analysis since World War II," *Journal of Interamerican Studies and World Affairs* 24 (August 1982): 295–320; Stephen M. Gorman, "Geopolitics and Peruvian Foreign Policy," *Inter-American Economic Affairs* 36 (Autumn 1982): 65–88; John D. Young, "L'explication interthéorique en relations internationales: Quelques jalons pour une synthèse du réalisme structurel americain et de la géopolitique française contemporaine," *Études Internationales* 18 (June 1987): 305–28; and Patrick O'Sullivan, *Geopolitics* (New York: St. Martin's, 1986).

4. Two interesting studies of *Geopolitik* and its relationship to geopolitics, both written during World War II, are Andrew Gyorgy, *Geopolitics: The New German Science*, University of California Publications in International Relations, vol. 3 (Berkeley: University of California Press, 1944); and Johannes Mattern, *Geopolitik: Doctrine of National Self-Sufficiency and Empire*, Johns Hopkins University Studies in Historical and Political Science, series 60, no. 2 (Baltimore: Johns Hopkins Press, 1942). A prewar, and more sympathetic, treatment of the work done by Karl Haushofer's Geopolitical Institute at Munich is provided in Richard Hartshorne, "Recent Developments in Political Geography, II," *American Political Science Review* 29 (December 1935): 960–64.

5. Ray S. Cline, *World Power Assessment, 1977: A Calculus of Strategic Drive* (Boulder, Colo.: Westview, 1977), 3.

6. Ladis K.D. Kristof, "The Origins and Evolution of Geopolitics," *Journal of Conflict Resolution* 4 (March 1960): 34.

7. K.J. Holsti, "Retreat from Utopia: International Relations Theory, 1945–70," *Canadian Journal of Political Science* 4 (June 1971): 165–77.

8. Harold J. Barnett, "The Changing Relation of Natural Resources to National Security," *Economic Geography* 34 (July 1958): 188–201.

9. John H. Herz, "Rise and Demise of the Territorial State," *World Politics* 9 (July 1957): 473–93.

10. Colin S. Gray, *The Geopolitics of the Nuclear Era: Heartland, Rimlands, and the Technological Revolution* (New York: Crane, Russak, 1977), 12. Also see, by the same author, *Maritime Strategy, Geopolitics, and the Defense of the West* (New York: National Strategy Information Center, 1986); and "Keeping the Soviets Landlocked: Geostrategy for a Maritime America," *National Interest*, no. 4 (Summer 1986): 24–36.

11. Nicholas John Spykman, *America's Strategy in World Politics: The United States and the Balance of Power* (New York: Harcourt, Brace, 1942). The other classics of geopolitical literature are Alfred Thayer Mahan, *The Influence of Seapower upon History, 1660–1783* (Boston: Little, Brown, 1897); and Halford Mackinder, *Democratic Ideals and Reality: A Study in the Politics of Reconstruction* (New York: Henry Holt, 1942).

12. Bohdan O. Szuprowicz, *How to Avoid Strategic Materials Shortages: Dealing with Cartels, Embargoes, and Supply Disruptions* (New York: John Wiley and Sons, 1981), ix.

13. Harold and Margaret Sprout, "Geography and International Politics in an Era of Revolutionary Change," *Journal of Conflict Resolution* 4 (March 1960): 152.

14. W.B. Gallie, "Essentially Contested Concepts," in *The Importance of Language*, ed. Max Black (Englewood Cliffs, N.J.: Prentice-Hall, 1962), 123. Also see William E. Connolly, *The Terms of Political Discourse*, 2d ed. (Princeton: Princeton University Press, 1983), chap. 1: "Essentially Contested Concepts in Politics."

15. Klaus Knorr, *The War Potential of Nations* (Princeton: Princeton University Press, 1956), 35–37.

16. In the early postwar period, iron and coal were generally considered to be of "basal" importance to industrial capacity, and hence to military potential. In the words of one writer, distribution patterns of iron and coal deposits had "repeatedly changed the balance of power throughout the world." Edwin C. Eckel, *Coal, Iron, and War: A Study in Industrialism Past and Future* (New York: Henry Holt, 1920), 96.

17. Quoted in P.H. Frankel, *Essentials of Petroleum: A Key to Oil Economics*, rev. ed. (London: Frank Cass, 1969), 3.

18. A contemporary popular treatment of the topic is Ludwell Denny, *We Fight for Oil* (New York: Knopf, 1928). Contemporary scholarly treatments include: Leith, *World Minerals and World Politics* and "Mineral Resources and Peace," *Foreign Affairs* 16 (April 1938): 515–24; and Norman Angell, *Raw Materials, Population Pressure and War*, World Affairs Books, no. 14 (Boston: World Peace Foundation, 1936). For a recent scholarly discussion, see Stephen D. Krasner, *Defending the National Interest: Raw Materials Investments and U.S. Foreign Policy* (Princeton: Princeton University Press, 1978), 106–19.

19. For an analysis of America's relatively favourable position in respect of mineral and other raw-material supply, see Brooks Emeny, *The Strategy of Raw Materials: A Study of America in Peace and War* (New York: Macmillan, 1934).

20. Franklin P. Huddle, "The Evolving National Policy for Materials," *Science* 191 (20 February 1976): 654; Alfred E. Eckes, Jr., *The United States and the Global Struggle for Minerals* (Austin: University of Texas Press, 1979), 43.

21. Quoted in Percy W. Bidwell, *Raw Materials: A Study of American Policy* (New York: Harper and Bros./Council on Foreign Relations, 1958), 32–33.

22. U.S. Federal Emergency Management Agency, *Stockpile Report to the Congress: October 1981–March 1982* (Washington: September 1982), 27.

23. National Strategy Information Center, *Strategic Minerals: A Resource Crisis* (Washington: Council on Economics and National Security, 1981), 34.

24. The definitional problem is discussed in some detail in U.S. General Accounting Office, *Report to the Secretary of the Interior: Actions Needed to Promote a Stable Supply of Strategic and Critical Minerals and Materials* (Washington: June 1982).

25. United Kingdom, House of Lords, Select Committee on the European Communities, *Strategic Minerals*, sess. 1981–82, 20th report (London: Her Majesty's Stationery Office, 1982).

26. Alan Archer, "Definition of Strategic Minerals and the Means Currently Available to the United Kingdom Government to Identify Strategic Sources and Requirements," in *Availability of Strategic Minerals* (London: Institution of Mining and Metallurgy, 1980), 2–3.

27. Hans H. Landsberg, *Minerals in the Eighties: Issues and Policies* (Oak Ridge, Tenn.: Oak Ridge National Laboratory, Program Planning and Analysis, 1982), 20–21.

28. Phillip Crowson, *Non-Fuel Minerals and Foreign Policy* (London: Royal Institute of International Affairs, 1977), 3.

29. V. Anthony Cammarota, Jr., "America's Dependence on Strategic Minerals," in *American Strategic Minerals*, ed. Gerard J. Mangone (New York: Crane, Russak, 1984), 30.

30. Arnold Wolfers, " 'National Security' as an Ambiguous Symbol," *Political Science Quarterly* 67 (December 1952): 481–502; Wolfram F. Hanreider, "Dissolving International Politics: Reflections on the Nation-State," *American Political Science Review* 72 (December 1978): 1276–87.

31. Interview with Jonathan Power, *Manchester Guardian Weekly* 7 (March 7, 1982), 8. Others adopting an inclusive interpretation of national security include Maull, *Raw Materials, Energy, and Western Security*, chap. 1: "Minerals, Markets and Security"; Lester R. Brown, *Redefining National Security*, Worldwatch Paper no. 14 (Washington: Worldwatch Institute, 1977), 6; and Richard N. Cooper, "Natural Resources and National Security," *Resources Policy* 1 (June 1975): 192–93. For a recent theoretical treatment of national security, see Barry Buzan, *People, States, and Fear: The National Security Problem in International Relations* (Brighton, Sussex: Wheatsheaf, 1983).

32. Few would dispute Robert Lieber's claim that "oil is a resource . . . nearly as essential as food or water." Robert J. Lieber, "Cohesion and Disruption in the Western Alliance," in *Global Insecurity: A Strategy for Energy and Economic Renewal*, ed. Daniel Yergin and Martin Hillenbrand (Harmondsworth: Penguin, 1982), 347.

33. U.S. Executive Office, *National Materials and Minerals Program Plan and Report to Congress* (Washington: April 1982), 12.

34. John D. Morgan, "Future Demands of the United States for Strategic Minerals," in *American Strategic Minerals*, 60.

35. Amos A. Jordan and Robert A. Kilmarx, *Strategic Mineral Dependence: The Stockpile Dilemma*, The Washington Papers, vol. 7, no. 70 (Washington: Center for Strategic and International Studies, Georgetown University, 1979), 18–19; Hans H. Landsberg and John E. Tilton, with Ruth B. Haas, "Nonfuel Minerals," in *Current Issues in Natural Resource Policy*, ed. Paul R. Portney (Washington: Resources for the Future, 1982), 91–95.

36. John I. Cameron, "Nickel," in *Natural Resources in U.S.–Canadian Relations*, vol. 2, *Patterns and Trends in Resource Supplies and Policies*, ed. Carl E. Beigie and Alfred O. Hero, Jr. (Boulder, Colo.: Westview, 1980), 87; U.S. Bureau of Mines, *Mineral Commodity Summaries, 1989* (Washington: Department of the Interior, 1989).

37. John M. Dunn, "American Dependence on Materials Imports: The World-Wide Resource Base," *Journal of Conflict Resolution* 4 (March 1960): 118.

38. T.S. Lovering, *Minerals in World Affairs* (Englewood Cliffs, N.J.: Prentice-Hall, 1943), 237.

39. T.D. Weldon, *The Vocabulary of Politics* (Harmondsworth: Penguin, 1953), 26–27.

40. Szuprowicz, *How to Avoid Strategic Materials Shortages*, 1.

41. Brian J. Skinner, "A Second Iron Age Ahead?" *American Scientist* 64 (May–June 1976): 258–69. The "strategic nature of iron ore has been highlighted in the debate in Sweden on whether that country's iron ore exports to Germany prolonged World War II." The thesis that they did is argued in Rolf Karlbom, "Sweden's Iron Ore Exports to Germany, 1933–1944," *Scandinavian Economic History Review* 13, no. 1 (1965): 65–93. Rebuttals include Alan S. Milward, "Could Sweden Have Stopped the Second World War?" and Jorg-Johannes Jager, "Sweden's Iron Ore Exports to Germany, 1933–1944," both in *Scandinavian Economic History Review* 15, no. 1 (1967): 127–47.

42. Michael Howard, *The Franco-Prussian War: The German Invasion of France, 1870–1871* (New York: Macmillan, 1961), 40–41. German statesmen actually would have preferred to receive Belfort instead of the Lorraine iron-ore fields as a prize of war, but in the face of strenuous French opposition to the transfer of the former, they settled for part of Lorraine. But so poorly formed was their knowledge of the Lorraine fields that the Germans left more than half of the Lorraine deposits in French hands. In any event, not until the discovery of the basic Bessemer, or Thomas–Gilchrist, process in 1879 would the high-phosphorous Lorraine ores become practical for steel-making. Eckel, *Coal, Iron, and War*, 56–58.

43. Leith, "Mineral Resources and Peace," 515–16.

44. Robert Strausz-Hupé, *Geopolitics: The Struggle for Space and Power* (New York: G.P. Putnam and Sons, 1942), 99–100.

45. R.R. Kuczynski, *"Living-Space" and Population Problems*, Oxford Pamphlets on World Affairs, no. 8 (Oxford: Clarendon Press, 1939), 5.

46. Moritz J. Bonn, *The Crumbling of Empire: The Disintegration of World Economy* (London: George Allen and Unwin, 1938), 209; David L. Gordon and Royden Dangerfield, *The Hidden Weapon: The Story of Economic Warfare* (New York: Harper and Bros., 1947), 8; C.K. Leith, J.W. Furness, and Cleona Lewis, *World Minerals and World Peace* (Washington: The Brookings Institution, 1943), 47.

47. Leith, "Mineral Resources and Peace," 519–21; Robert C. North, "Toward a Framework for the Analysis of Scarcity and Conflict," *International Studies Quarterly* 21 (December 1977): 569–91.

48. Emeny, *Strategy of Raw Materials*, 23–24; J. Hurstfield, "The Control of British Raw Material Supplies, 1919–1939," *Economic History Review* 14 (1944): 26–27.

49. Hjalmar Schacht, "Germany's Colonial Demands," *Foreign Affairs* 15 (January 1937): 228.

50. Leith, Furness, and Lewis, *World Minerals and World Peace*, 48.

51. Lovering, *Minerals in World Affairs*, 84.

52. Eckes, *United States and the Global Struggle for Minerals*, 58.

53. James A. Miller, Daniel I. Fine, and R. Daniel McMichael, *The Resource War in 3-D: Dependency, Diplomacy, Defense* (Pittsburgh: World Affairs Council of Pittsburgh, 1980); U.S. House, Committee on Foreign Affairs, Subcommittee on Africa, *The Possibility of a Resource War in Southern Africa*, 97th Cong., 1st sess. (Washington: U.S. Government Printing Office, July 1981). For a critical analysis of this perspective, see Jock A. Finlayson and David G. Haglund, "Whatever Happened to the Resource War?" *Survival* 29 (September/October 1987): 403–15.

54. See, in particular, two articles by Robert W. Tucker: "The Purposes of American Power," *Foreign Affairs* 59 (Winter 1980/81): 241–74; and "Oil: The Issue of American Intervention," *Commentary* 59 (January 1975): 21–31. Also relevant is Geoffrey Kemp, "Military Force and Middle East Oil," in *Energy and Security: A Report of Harvard's Energy and Security Research Project*, ed. David A. Deese and Joseph S. Nye (Cambridge: Ballinger, 1981), 365–85; and David G. Haglund, "The Question of Persian Gulf Oil and U.S. 'Vital' Interests," *Middle East Focus* 7 (September 1984): 7–11ff.

55. This thesis was advanced in Robert Moss, "Reaching for Oil: The Soviets' Bold Mideast Strategy," *Saturday Review* (4 April 1980): 14–22; and Edward Friedland, Paul Seabury, and Aaron Wildavsky, *The Great Détente Disaster: Oil and the Decline of American Foreign Policy* (New York: Basic, 1975), 50.

56. Robert L. Pfaltzgraff, Jr., "Resource Issues and the Atlantic Community," in *Atlantic Community in Crisis: A Redefinition of the Transatlantic Relationship*, ed. Walter F. Hahn and Robert L. Pfaltzgraff, Jr. (New York: Pergamon, 1979), 299. American concern for the security of sea lanes is conveyed in U.S. Department of the Navy, Chief of Naval Operations, *U.S. Lifelines: Imports of Essential Materials — 1967, 1971, 1975 — and the Impact of Waterborne Commerce on the Nation* (Washington: U.S. Government Printing Office, 1978).

57. Ruth W. Arad and Uzi B. Arad, "Scarce Natural Resources and Potential Conflict," in Ruth W. Arad et al., *Sharing Global Resources* (New York: McGraw-Hill, 1979), 71–72.

58. Preface to Gray, *Geopolitics of the Nuclear Era*, vii.

59. Arad and Arad, "Scarce Natural Resources," 104.

60. Klaus Knorr, *Military Power and Potential* (Lexington, Mass.: D.C. Heath, 1970), 15. Also see the same author's earlier work, *War Potential of Nations*, 40–60, for a conceptual analysis of military potential.

61. Ray S. Cline has devised a formula for measuring the perceived power of states, even though he concedes that some of his variables are impossible to quantify. The formula states that $Pp = (C+E+M) \times (S+W)$, where Pp = Perceived Power; C = Critical Mass (or Population plus Territory); E = Economic Capability; M = Military Capability; S = Strategic Purpose; and W = Will to Pursue National Strategy. Cline, *World Power Assessment*, 34. For an interesting review of various scholars' efforts to operationalize power, see James Lee Ray, *Global Politics*, 3d ed. (Boston: Houghton Mifflin, 1987), chap. 6: "Comparing States and Foreign Policies."

62. Emeny, *Strategy of Raw Materials*, 1. Also see George Otis Smith, ed., *The Strategy of Minerals: A Study of the Mineral Factor in the World Position of America in War and in Peace* (New York: D. Appleton, 1919), 26; Russell N. Fifield and G. Etzel Pearcy, *Geopolitics in Principle and Practice* (Boston: Ginn, 1944), 37–38; and Leith, *World Minerals and World Politics*, 142.

63. C.W. Wright, "Germany's Capacity to Produce and Consume Metals," *Mineral Trade Notes*, Special Supplement no. 4 (Washington: U.S. Bureau of Mines, November 1936), 34.

64. Eckes, *United States and the Global Struggle for Minerals*, 121–24; Dunn, "American Dependence on Materials Imports," 106–7; Michael B. Stoff, *Oil, War, and American Security: The Search for a National Policy on Foreign Oil, 1941-1947* (New Haven: Yale University Press, 1980), 209.

65. Edward S. Mason, "American Security and Access to Raw Materials," *World Politics* 1 (January 1949): 151–53.

66. Mancur Olson, Jr., "American Materials Policy and the 'Physiocratic Fallacy,'" *Orbis* 6 (Winter 1963): 680.

67. Charles L. Schultze, "The Economic Content of National Security Policy," *Foreign Affairs* 51 (April 1973): 523.

68. This, of course, is the argument currently being made, *inter alia*, by Paul Kennedy and David Calleo, about the security consequences of relative economic decline. See Paul Kennedy, *The Rise and Fall of the Great Powers* (New York: Random House, 1987); and David P. Calleo, *Beyond American Hegemony: The Future of the Western Alliance* (New York: Basic, 1987).

69. Preston E. Cloud, Jr., "Realities of Mineral Distribution," *Texas Quarterly* 11 (Summer 1968): 108.

70. Nazli Choucri and Robert C. North, "Dynamics of International Conflict: Some Policy Implications of Population, Resources, and Technology," in *Theory and Policy in International Relations*, ed. Raymond Tanter and Richard H. Ullman (Princeton: Princeton University Press, 1972), 87–88. Also see Andrew Scott, *The Dynamics of Interdependence* (Chapel Hill: University of North Carolina Press, 1982).

71. Eckes, *United States and the Global Struggle for Minerals*, 54–55.

72. Harry N. Holmes, *Strategic Materials and National Strength* (New York: Macmillan, 1942), 36–38; G.A. Roush, *Strategic Mineral Supplies* (New York: Macmillan, 1939), 31–69, 97–129; Leonard L. Fischman, *World Mineral Trends and U.S. Supply Problems* (Washington: Resources for the Future, 1980), 15–16; Michael W. Klass, James C. Burrows, and Steven D. Beggs, *International Minerals Cartels and Embargoes: Policy Implications*

for the United States (New York: Praeger, 1980), 135–36; U.S. Congress, Office of Technology Assessment, *Strategic Materials: Technologies to Reduce U.S. Import Vulnerability* (Washington: U.S. Government Printing Office, 1985), 27.

73. John E. Tilton, *The Future of Nonfuel Minerals* (Washington: The Brookings Institution, 1977), 9.

74. Eckel, *Coal, Iron, and War*, 118.

75. J.W.F. Rowe, *Primary Commodities in International Trade* (Cambridge: Cambridge University Press, 1965), 79–83.

76. H.D. Henderson, *Colonies and Raw Materials*, Oxford Pamphlets in World Affairs, no. 7 (Oxford: Clarendon Press, 1939), 30.

77. Schacht, "Germany's Colonial Demands," 229.

78. Quoted in Kenneth N. Waltz, *Theory of International Politics* (Reading, Mass.: Addison-Wesley, 1979), 140.

79. Herbert Feis, "Raw Materials and Foreign Policy," *Foreign Affairs* 16 (July 1938): 579.

80. Albert O. Hirschman, *National Power and the Structure of Foreign Trade* (Berkeley: University of California Press, 1945), 14–15. For other discussions of German utilization of trade as a political weapon in the 1930s, see Cleona Lewis, *Nazi Europe and World Trade* (Washington: The Brookings Institution, 1941); and Herbert Feis, *The Changing Pattern of International Economic Affairs* (New York: Harper and Bros., 1940: rept. ed., Port Washington, N.Y.: Kennikat Press, 1971).

81. John E. Tilton and Hans H. Landsberg, "Nonfuel Minerals — The Fear of Shortages and the Search for Policies," in *U.S. Interests and Global Natural Resources: Energy, Minerals, Food*, ed. Emery N. Castle and Kent A. Price (Washington: Resources for the Future, 1983), 48–80.

82. Donella H. Meadows et al., *The Limits to Growth* (New York: Universe Books, 1972). For critical analyses of this report, see Eric Ashby, "A Second Look at Doom," *Encounter* 46 (March 1976): 16–24; and Harold J. Barnett, "Energy, Resources, and Growth," in U.S. Congress, Joint Economic Committee, *Resource Scarcity, Economic Growth, and the Environment*, Hearing before the Subcommittee on Priorities and Economy in Government, 93rd Cong., 1st sess. (Washington: U.S. Government Printing Office, 1974), 171–90.

83. G.J.S. and M.H. Govett, "The Concept and Measurement of Mineral Reserves and Resources," *Resources Policy* 1 (September 1974): 47.

84. James F. McDivitt, *Minerals and Men: An Exploration of the World of Minerals and Its Effect on the World We Live In* (Baltimore: Johns Hopkins Press, Resources for the Future, 1965), 68–71.

85. James Boyd, "Minerals and How We Use Them," in *The Mineral Position of the United States, 1975-2000*, ed. Eugene N. Cameron (Madison: University of Wisconsin Press, 1973), 7.

86. T.S. Lovering, "Non-Fuel Mineral Resources in the Next Century," *Texas Quarterly* 11 (Summer 1968): 128–29.

87. Tilton, *Future of Nonfuel Minerals*, 92.

88. For analyses of the viability of "resource power," see Carmine Nappi, *Commodity Market Controls: A Historical Review* (Lexington, Mass.: D.C. Heath, 1979); and Robert L. Rothstein, *Global Bargaining: UNCTAD and the Quest for a New International Economic Order* (Princeton: Princeton University Press, 1979).

89. British–North American Committee, *Mineral Development in the Eighties: Prospects and Problems* (London, Montreal, and Washington: 1976), 14–15.

90. Raymond F. Mikesell, *New Patterns of World Mineral Development* (London, Montreal, and Washington: British–North American Committee, 1979), 24; Edward R. Fried, "International Trade in Raw Materials: Myths and Realities," *Science* 191 (February 20, 1976): 646.

91. Harald B. Malmgren, *The Raw Material and Commodity Controversy*, International Economic Studies Institute Contemporary Issues, no. 1 (Washington: IESI, 1975), 6.

92. See Aleksander Markowski and Marian Radetzki, "State Ownership and the Price Sensitivity of Supply: The Case of the Copper Mining Industry," *Resources Policy* 13 (March 1987): 19.

93. David A. Baldwin, "Interdependence and Power: A Conceptual Analysis," *International Organization* 34 (Autumn 1980): 471–506.

SELECT BIBLIOGRAPHY

Crowson, Phillip. *Non-Fuel Minerals and Foreign Policy*. London: Royal Institute of International Affairs, 1977.

Eckes, Alfred E., Jr. *The United States and the Global Struggle for Minerals*. Austin: University of Texas Press, 1979.

Feis, Herbert. *The Changing Pattern of International Economic Affairs*. New York: Harper and Bros., 1940. Rept. ed. Port Washington, N.Y.: Kennikat Press, 1971.

Gray, Colin S. *The Geopolitics of the Nuclear Era: Heartland, Rimlands, and the Technological Revolution*. New York: Crane, Russak, 1977.

———. "Keeping the Soviets Landlocked: Geostrategy for a Maritime America." *National Interest*, no. 4 (Summer 1986): 24–36.

———. *Maritime Strategy, Geopolitics, and the Defense of the West*. New York: National Strategy Information Center, 1986.

Gyorgy, Andrew. *Geopolitics: The New German Science*. University of California Publications in International Relations, vol. 3. Berkeley: University of California Press, 1944.

Hanreider, Wolfram F. "Dissolving International Politics: Reflections on the Nation-State." *American Political Science Review* 72 (December 1978): 1276–87.

Hirschman, Albert O. *National Power and the Structure of Foreign Trade*. Berkeley: University of California Press, 1945.

Krasner, Stephen D. *Defending the National Interest: Raw Materials Investments and U.S. Foreign Policy*. Princeton: Princeton University Press, 1978.

Kristof, Ladis K.D. "The Origins and Evolution of Geopolitics." *Journal of Conflict Resolution* 4 (March 1960): 15–51

Maull, Hanns W. *Raw Materials, Energy and Western Security*. London: Macmillan/International Institute for Strategic Studies, 1984.

O'Sullivan, Patrick. *Geopolitics*. New York: St. Martin's, 1986.

Pfaltzgraff, Robert L., Jr. "Resource Issues and the Atlantic Community." In *Atlantic Community in Crisis: A Redefinition of the Transatlantic Relationship*, ed. Walter F. Hahn and Robert F. Pfaltzgraff. New York: Pergamon, 1979.

PART IV

PERSPECTIVES ON WORLD POLITICS

The three previous sections of this book have dealt with power, interdependence, and dependence, each conforming broadly to a particular view of world politics — to realism, transnationalism, and globalism, respectively — and each taking a particular view with respect to the role of the state, the structure of the international system, and the need for change. World politics is, as the introduction notes, a dynamic and perplexing business. Moreover, it is not enough to possess the analytic tools to deal with the world as we know it; we must be able to account for change over time.

The six chapters in Part IV attempt to address the changing character of international relations scholarship and to come to terms with a dynamic world. Larry Pratt examines the logic of traditional realism, using the Peloponnesian War as a paradigm for war itself. He holds that the episodes, individuals, and phenomena of Thucydides's time have some universal meaning. Michel Fortmann and William George examine strategic studies as a separate analytic enterprise, arguing that events in the 1980s have not diminished the usefulness of this approach. R.B.J. Walker notes that the understanding of social and political life is a notoriously contentious enterprise. He pays particular attention to the different philosophical contexts of current international relations research and then examines some of the broader ontological, ethical, and ideological dilemmas faced by the discipline. Constantine Melakopides argues that cynical realism, in particular, and IR theory, in general, ignore the moral point of view. He asks why IR theorists are generally oblivious to the obvious links between moral concerns and international behaviour. Kim Richard Nossal examines an approach to the study of world politics that has, in the last three decades, experienced a dramatic rise in popularity, and then, as quickly, fallen out of fashion as a way to conceptualize, and understand, international relations. Finally, James Keeley explores the preoccupation of neorealist scholars with the notion of international regimes.

WAR AND EMPIRE: THUCYDIDES AND INTERNATIONAL POLITICS

Larry Pratt

> The sufferings which revolution entailed upon the cities were many and terrible, such as have occurred and always will occur, as long as the nature of mankind remains the same, though in severer or milder form, and varying in their symptoms, according to the variety of the particular cases. In peace and prosperity states and individuals have better sentiments, because they do not find themselves suddenly confronted with imperious necessities; but war takes away the easy supply of daily wants, and so proves a rough master that brings most men's characters to a level with their fortunes.
>
> (Thucydides, III. 82)[1]

What may be called the classical theory of international politics was first elaborated by Thucydides, an Athenian historian, in the midst of a great and terrible war for supremacy fought by Sparta and other Greek city-states against Athens and its empire from 431 to 404 B.C. He was the first writer in the Western tradition to develop a method for a precise empirical study of contemporary international affairs, the first to narrow the focus of historical inquiry to war and politics, and also the first to bring a "scientific" outlook to the study of power politics and the analysis of the deeper causes of war.

The Peloponnesian War, as it is called today, found its origins in earlier military struggles between the expanding Persian Empire and the Greek cities and in the subsequent growth of the Athenian Empire. So rapid and threatening was the expansion of Athens, so tyrannical its rule over its subject-cities, that it finally forced its traditional military rival, Sparta, to fight for its independence and to put an end to Athenian hegemony. The 27-year war that followed, wrote Thucydides, "was the greatest movement yet known in history, not only of the Hellenes, but of a large part of the barbarian world — I had almost said of mankind" (I.1). It ended in 404 with the complete defeat of Athens and its empire, an event that signalled the beginnings of Sparta's ascendancy under Lysander.

What made this the "greatest war" was not the magnitude of its operations or the heroism of the combatants but the immense suffering, disorder, and destruction that it introduced into the Greek system. Never had so many cities been taken and laid desolate; never had so many people been banished or slain in war and internal revolutions; never had Greece endured so many unexpected disasters, among them "that most calamitous and awfully fatal visitation, the plague" (I.23). The war was a tragedy, yet it was man-made. It was not inexplicable. By studying with great care its "real" causes and its impact upon the Greek world, we might uncover universal truths about, say, the nature of war and the relationship between justice and power. Thucydides had set out to write a history of the war between Athens and the Peloponnesians, "beginning at the moment that it broke out" (I.1), in the belief that it would be more worthy of relation than any war that had preceded it, and he wrote it for posterity, as his greatest translator, the 17th-century English philosopher Thomas Hobbes, put it, "to instruct and enable men, by the knowledge of actions past, to bear themselves prudently in the present and providentially towards the future."[2] If man's nature — or human nature — is unchanging over time, then, through the dispassionate reconstruction of the past or of contemporary history, we may learn, not how to predict or control the future or banish war, but to understand the complexity of decisions and events and the fragility of our own political and moral order in the face of that "rough master," war, and all its attendant disorders. Those who made the effort to study his account, Thucydides believed, would also come to understand their own time as well as his. Unlike the renderings of the poet Homer and Thucydides's somewhat older rival, Herodotus, his own history would be as exact and unsentimental as he could make it:

> The absence of romance in my history will, I fear, detract somewhat from its interest; but if it be judged useful by those inquirers who desire an exact knowledge of the past as an aid to the interpretation of the future, which in the course of human things must resemble it if it does not reflect it, I shall be content. In fine, I have written my work, not as an essay which is to win the applause of the moment, but as a possession for all time. (I.22)

This chapter attempts to show how Thucydides's *The Peloponnesian War* can be used to study the basic and enduring elements of international politics — such as imperialism, the causes of war, the nature of alliances, ideological revolutions, great-power interventions, the fate of small states, and the impact of domestic politics on the international actions of states. These are the central elements in Thucydides's anatomy of power and justice in the Greek system of warring city-states, and they are woven together in a brilliant sweeping theory of the rise of the Hellenic cities through the development of navigation, commerce, and seapower, followed by the outward expansion of the dominant cities, first as hegemons, or leaders of coalitions, and then as ruthless imperial powers, leading finally to the great and inevitable war for supremacy between the Athenians and Spartans. It is a deeply pessimistic theory in which cities and statesmen are repeatedly driven by fear and expediency to place power ahead of any considerations of what is fair and just; not justice but fear is the force that moves the system.[3]

None of this is directly asserted by Thucydides in his history of the war; he seldom speaks or comments on events, and is as famous for his silences and understatement as for his powerful antithetical style. "Such was the end of Plataea, in the ninety-third year after she became the ally of Athens" (III.68), he concludes, after describing Sparta's calculated massacre of 200 Plataean soldiers to please her own Theban allies. The text is meant to comment on the moral conduct of both Athens and Sparta, leading us to reflect on the fate of small cities caught up, like kindling between burning logs, in a war of great powers. Few out of many returned home, he says of the destruction of the Athenian expedition to Sicily. We do not need the author to tell us the meaning of these events. His narrative and the carefully crafted speeches of the statesmen and military leaders draw the reader into a deeper understanding of the war and the motives of the belligerents. The fact that Thucydides's own opinions and judgements are seldom stated and that he forces us, in effect, to live through the war and to experience its most disturbing episodes, observing for ourselves how war levels everyone's moral standards, only makes the effect more vivid and unforgettable. As Hobbes cautioned the readers of his translation, Thucydides rarely attempts to speak directly to his audience or to make his own views known, and yet he "doth secretly instruct the reader, and more effectually than can possibly be done by precept." He was, Hobbes wrote, "the most politick historiographer that ever writ."[4] Hobbes himself learned from Thucydides's account of the Peloponnesian War of the failings of democracy, and that fear is a cause of wars between states while the absence of fear is a cause of civil wars. Hobbes's statement that there can be no justice where, as in international relations, there is no common sovereign is simply an echo of what, according to Thucydides, the Athenians told the Spartans on the eve of the war — namely, that it has always been the law that the weak should be ruled by the strong, justice being the exclusive prerogative of the latter.

Power

Thucydides analyzes international politics as the struggle for power among the dominant city-states and empires of his time: the objects of the struggle are to defend one's own security and autonomy, to dominate others, and to gain supremacy over all states. The system of powers sketched in his history of the war seems remarkably similar to our modern system of states: an unstable system of many small states ruled by a handful of great powers and regulated by the institutions of diplomacy, alliances, and war;[5] it is a multiplicity of powers without common government — an international anarchy. In peace, as in war, international politics is a competition for advantage in which decisions and alignments are based on the bonds of interest or on grounds of necessity, not on shared moral values. What determines success and greatness in the international system is power — power and its effective use by statesmen. But what is power?

Power is the capacity of a city, first, to be able to defend itself and to prevent others from dictating to it, and, second, to rule over others. Policy is determined by self-interest, and it is natural — a law of nature — that those who have power should use it to rule those who lack power. A speaker in Thucydides's history of the war refers to freedom as the right to rule others. Freedom to oppress others is valued as much by the Greeks as is freedom from oppression. This law of the stronger, which Thucydides analyzes in several sections of his work dealing with the Athenian Empire, is deeply rooted in human nature; but, so too is the natural tendency for smaller states to resist imperialism by forming coalitions and aligning themselves with other powers.[6] The drive for power is thus not confined to hegemonic actors — those who have or want supremacy; the weaker states are equally compelled by fear to acquire power, since without it there can be neither security nor independence.

At the end of the second Persian invasion of Greece, which had seen the Athenians abandon their city and take to their ships and defeat the Persian navy at Salamis, Athens signalled its unwillingness to accept Spartan leadership by rebuilding its walls and agreeing to head an anti-Persian league. Themistocles encouraged the Athenians to complete their wall, in spite of Spartan opposition, partly out of fear of another invasion and partly as a demonstration of Athens's new status. He told the Spartans that Athens was able to distinguish both its own and the general interest; that when the Athenians had abandoned their city, they had done so without consulting the Spartans.

They now saw fit to have a wall for their city "for without equal military strength it was impossible to contribute equal or fair counsel to the common interest" (I.90–91). Her naval power, her success in war, and her raising of the wall gave Athens a claim to share the leadership of the Greeks. Themistocles was also responsible for the development of Athenian naval power between the wars with Persia: he "first ventured to tell them to stick to the sea and forthwith began to lay the foundations of empire" (I.93).

Is justice a constraint on the despotic use of power? Between the strong and the weak, according to the Athenians in their brutal encounter with the small neutral island of Melos, there are no relations based on justice; power decides all. The Athenians arrived with overpowering might to force the Melians to become tribute-paying subjects of the Athenian Empire, and they were unwilling to discuss any claims based on justice. The highly stylized "dialogue" that follows (the only one in the work) is a commentary by Thucydides on the tyranny of the Athenian Empire and the meaning of the law of the stronger in war:

> *Melians.* "So you would not consent to our being neutral, friends instead of enemies, but allies of neither side?"
>
> *Athenians.* "No; for your hostility cannot so much hurt us as your friendship will be an argument to our subjects of our weakness, and your enmity of our power."
>
> *Melians.* "Is that your subjects' idea of equity, to put those who have nothing to do with you in the same category with peoples that are most of them your own colonists, and some conquered rebels?"
>
> *Athenians.* "As far as right goes they think that one has as much of it as the other, and that if any maintain their independence it is because they are strong, and that if we do not molest them it is because we are afraid; so besides extending our empire we should gain in security by your subjection, the fact that you are islanders and

> weaker than others rendering it all the more important that you would not succeed in baffling the masters of the sea." (V. 94–97)

In other words, the Melians are to be reduced or destroyed in the wider interests of the Athenian Empire, an empire that wages war with tribute and ships raised from its island-subjects. Not to enslave or lay waste Melos would set an unfortunate precedent; *pour encourager les autres* the Athenians are prepared to act as tyrants. Anticipating the arguments, if not the language, of Hobbes, they assert the right of dominant powers to rule:

> [You] know as well as we do that right, as the world goes, is in question only between equals in power, while the strong do what they can and the weak suffer what they must. . . . Of the gods we believe, and of men we know, that by a necessary law of their nature they rule wherever they can. And it is not as if we were the first to make this law, or to act upon it when made: we found it existing before us, and shall leave it to exist forever after us; all we do is to make use of it, knowing that you and everybody else, having the same power as we have, would do the same as we do. (V. 89, 105)

The Melians resist, hoping for the intervention of the gods, or of Sparta, or of luck; but, as the Athenians rightly warn them, safety cannot be purchased with hopes. Melos is conquered, its male population put to death, its women and children sold for slaves, and the island colonized by Athenians. The fate of small neutral states in a war between great powers — Belgium in 1914, Norway and Denmark in 1940 — is decided by considerations of power and military strategy and not by those of justice or law.

It is concrete power — military force — that, in the last analysis, settles the great international conflicts. Thucydides is the first analyst to insist that the power of any state is based, first and foremost, on its relative military strength and its reputation in war. Political and military action are the *erga*, "works," by which we judge human greatness. They also give us the only reliable criteria with which to compare the power of cities,[7] or, for that matter, states. Sparta, the greatest military power in Greece, and Athens, its dominant naval power, lead rival hegemonies in the bipolarized Hellenic system in the decades before the war: it is Sparta's army and Athens's navy, plus their reputations in the wars against Persia, that allow them to claim the title of hegemons. In the opening paragraphs of Book I of his history, Thucydides reviews earlier and prehistoric Greece in order to make the point that no earlier wars were of great moment, but also to emphasize the role of seapower in the development of the leading cities. Naval supremacy is the basis of imperialism in Thucydides's view, and the Athenian Empire is only the latest stage in a process that stretches back to the legendary Minos of Crete. Minos cleared the seas of pirates and made it possible for the coastal populations to acquire wealth, and for self-interest to begin to divide the new settlements into rulers and ruled: "For the love of gain would reconcile the weaker to the domination of the stronger, and the possession of capital enabled the more powerful to reduce the smaller towns to subjection" (I.8).

The navies of the Hellenes became "an element of the greatest power" to those who cultivated them, supplying revenue and dominion to the tyrants of Greece until they were put down by Sparta.

Seapower provides security; security is necessary for the accumulation of economic resources. But a great navy also can be used to support a policy of expansionism, to coerce, and to inspire fear. This is how Athens uses her naval power in dealing with her allies and with truculent neutrals. It has always been thus, Thucydides implies: the overlordship of Agamemnon, who led the Greek expedition against Troy, was recognized by his Greek allies because of his "superiority of strength" rather than because of any oaths of loyalty that bound Helen's suitors to follow him. He had a navy "far stronger than his contemporaries, so that, in my opinion, fear was quite as strong an element as love in the formation of the confederate expedition" (I.9). (Fear and love: Thucydides here anticipates Machiavelli, who argues that, since men love at their own pleasure and fear at the prince's pleasure, a wise prince will found himself on that which is his — that is, on fear.)[8] Thucydides is also asserting that Homer's heroes[9] were men moved by ordinary human passions and needs — by fear, self-interest, the desire for profit; the nature of man is unchanging. It was the power of Agamemnon's fleet and the fear it inspired, not Greek friendship and unity, that created the alliance that destroyed Troy.

Throughout the classical period in Greece, Athenian naval supremacy rested upon one sort of warship, the trireme, a long slender ship manned by 170 rowers; the ship's chief armament was the ram mounted as an extension of the keel. Athens maintained fleets of 200 to 400 triremes and thousands of rowers (many of them mercenaries), highly trained and constantly at sea. Control of her island empire and of her trading routes depended on the expertise of the navy and its ability to put down revolts through the rapid mobility of a fleet maintained in a high state of readiness. Naval excellence is the chief source of power in Periclean Athens.

What gives a city its greatness, then, is its power, and its power (and wealth) are based on its arms and its military might and reputation. It is not its architecture, its culture, or its commerce that constitutes its true "works"; these are but appearances of greatness, and no "exact observer" — i.e., Thucydides — will compare cities on the basis of appearances.

> For I suppose if Lacadeaemon [Sparta] were to become desolate, and only the temples and the foundations of the public buildings were left, that as time went on there would be a strong disposition with posterity to refuse to accept her fame as a true exponent of her power. And yet they occupy two-fifths of the Peloponnese and lead the whole, not to speak of their numerous allies without. Still, as the city is neither built in a compact form nor adorned with magnificent temples and public edifices, but composed of villages after the old fashion of Hellas, there would be an impression of inadequacy. However, if Athens were to suffer the same misfortune, I suppose that any inference from the appearance presented to the eye would make her power to have been twice as great as it is. (I.10)

Greatness is achieved through success in war and rule over others. Pericles, leader of the war party at Athens, argues that individual happiness ought to be subordinated to "national greatness," and that if Athens has the greatest name in the world,

> it is because she has expended more life and effort in war than any other city, and has won for herself a power greater than hitherto known, the memory of which will descend to the last posterity; even if now, in obedience to the general law of decay, we should ever be forced to yield, still it will be remembered that we held rule over more Hellenes than any other Hellenic state [and] that we sustained the greatest wars against their united or separate powers. (II.64)

Pericles implies that the power of a state declines inevitably; yet, his argument is that Athenian capital and naval power can defeat Sparta.

Internal Politics

Power is also dependent on the domestic makeup of a regime. In the worst case, cities at war can become enfeebled by stasis, factionalism, and civil strife that destroy their capacity to act. Thucydides provides a brilliant diagnosis of stasis on the island of Corcyra after civil war breaks out between the oligarchic and democratic parties (III. 82–85), but his work also shows that Sparta and Athens display domestic instabilities and divisions that impair the effective use of their power. Sparta, the dominant state in the Peloponnesian League, is inhibited to the point of paralysis by the rigidity of her constitution and social structure, a state of affairs that permits Athens's rising power to go unchallenged until a major war is all but inevitable. Praised by Thucydides for her stable constitution and moderate conduct of foreign affairs but criticized by her own exasperated allies for being slow to fight Athens, Sparta rejects the leadership of the Hellenic system because of her great fear of a revolt by her growing slave population — the helots. Although she is a feared military power, Sparta is a reluctant warrior-state because she rightly fears the revolutionary consequences of war; she also fears the contagion of democratic ideas; and she is distracted by problems in the Peloponnese region. Distrustful of Athenian-sponsored democracy and its spread through the Aegean system, Sparta practises a cautious quasi isolationism in foreign affairs, observing the growth of Athens's power but confining herself to the maintenance of her indomitable hoplite army and resisting all temptation to challenge Athens at sea.

Sparta's fear of revolution acts as a brake on her use of power. Even after accepting the necessity to resist Athens, she avoids the overextension of power that brings down most empires. But Sparta's lethargy has also allowed the Athenians to transform their alliance into a highly centralized maritime empire that threatens the autonomy of every other state; her failure to use her power is itself a cause of the war. Her allies, led by Corinth, bitterly complain that Sparta, a great power with the duty to preserve the general welfare in return for the honours accorded her, was not living up to the responsibilities of hegemony: "the true author of the subjugation of a people is not so much the immediate agent as the power which permits it having the means to prevent it" (I.69). However, as Thucydides notes, when the Spartans finally did agree to declare war, they did so "not so much because they were persuaded by the arguments of the allies, as because they feared the growth of the power of the Athenians, seeing most of Hellas already subject to them" (I.88). Survival, not the duties of supremacy, forced Sparta to make war on Athens.

If Sparta was a city at rest and on the defensive, Athens was a state constantly in motion, a rising power encroaching on the freedom of other states. The Corinthians, trying to arouse Sparta, provided an entertaining caricature of Athens in Book I of Thucydides's history. The Athenians were addicted to innovation, adventurous beyond their power, acquisitive, constantly improving:

> Thus they toil on in trouble and danger all the days of their lives, with little opportunity for enjoying, being ever engaged in getting: their only idea of a holiday is to do what the occasion demands, and to them laborious occupation is less of a misfortune than the peace of a quiet life. To describe their character in a word, one might truly say that they were born into the world to take no rest themselves, and to give none to others. (I.70)

The domestic politics of Athens encouraged this restlessness; it also undermined the policy of the state and, according to Thucydides, cost Athens her empire. From the beginnings of the Athenian Empire in the 450s under Pericles, there was a close link between democracy at home and overseas expansion. Pericles, in opposition to his political rival, Cimon, intended to convert the Athenian alliance — the Delian League — into an empire or protectorate, and to force Athens's dependencies to underwrite her navy and to finance the construction of a massive program of public works in Athens. As the navy expanded, the thetes, or rowers of the warships, were incorporated into the Athenian democracy. Aristotle identified the "naval throng" as the true founders of the democracy in Athens. Pericles introduced state-pay for jury duty and other services, so that increasing numbers of citizens would have a material interest in democracy, and forced the allies of Athens to pay for it. He had great temples and magnificent public buildings, hugely popular with the masses, erected by the unemployed of Athens and again paid for by allied contributions. Pericles intended to make the citizens of Athens an elite subsidized by the subject-peoples: each new costly measure to deepen democracy at Athens led the Athenians to apply what Thucydides called "the screw of necessity" (I.99) to its Greek allies. When Pericles came under political fire in the Athenian Assembly for gilding the city with allied monies, as if it were a vain woman decorating herself with costly jewels paid for by prostitution, he replied that the allies owed the tribute for the "protection" afforded them by the Athenian fleet: the surplus would be applied to public works, which would provide employment for the Athenians and everlasting glory for the city.[10] He backed this up with very strong imperial actions to crush any signs of revolt by the allies. It was fear of the revenge that these states would take against Athens for her brutal use of her power that made the Athenians unwilling to dismantle the empire.

Democracy and empire were, then, inseparable in Periclean Athens. The Athenians, as will be shown, had key strategic as well as economic interests at stake in the empire, but considerations of domestic politics also promoted imperialism. Undoubtedly, the development of Athenian democracy was one of the key factors in the city's rise in international status, but Thucydides's own account of the war raises troubling questions about the capacity of the *demos* to make prudent decisions and to put up with the suffering and unpredictability that accompany prolonged conflict. Thucydides, himself an aristocrat, is deeply skeptical of Athens's democracy, particularly in its conduct in the war after the death of Pericles, and his portrayal of the empire as a cruel tyranny may be coloured by his view of the *demos*. He shows that the Athenians, discouraged by the plague and invasions by the Spartans, quickly turned against Pericles and that, following his death, Athens was badly led by demagogues and politicians who occupied themselves with private cabals for the leadership of the commons, by which they not only paralysed operations in the field, but also introduced civil discord at home. This produced a great many mistakes, including the fateful decision to invade Sicily in 415 while the war with Sparta was still underway.

Thucydides blames Athens's subsequent defeat in Sicily, the real turning point in the war, on the lack of support at home for the overseas expedition rather than on the original decision to intervene: "Nor did they finally succumb till they fell victims of their own intestine disorders" (II.65). A fickle *demos*, enthusiastic for the invasion of Sicily and intolerant of any criticism of the scheme, forces the removal of Athens's most able leader, Alcibiades, on trumped-up charges of sacrilege; then replaces him with Nicias, a superstitious but honourable man who had opposed the expedition from the outset. Nicias proves to be a timid military commander, and the Athenian expedition — the pride of Greece — is trapped in Sicily. Its destruction is inevitable. Nicias is unable to tell the people of Athens the truth because of what he knows about them. Faced with defeat, he chooses to die in Sicily rather than to withdraw his forces and face dishonour at the hands of the Athenians:

> he was sure the Athenians would never return without a vote of theirs. Those who would vote upon their conduct, instead of judging the facts as eye-witnesses like themselves and not from what they might hear from hostile critics, would simply be guided by the calumnies of the first clever speaker. . . . For himself, therefore, who knew the Athenian temper, sooner than perish under a dishonourable charge and by an unjust sentence at the hands of the Athenians, he would rather take his chance and die, if die he must, a soldier's death at the hand of the enemy. (VII.48)

Athenian democracy cannot long outlive the great disaster in Sicily: the final book shows the city riven by stasis in the form of oligarchic coups, political intrigues, and changes of government. Whether domestic divisions caused the military defeats or the defeats caused stasis in Athens is difficult to say.

Thucydides, a conservative man, believes in the value of stable institutions and moderate leaders; he loathes party factionalism and political extremism; and he is profoundly pessimistic on the subject of human nature. The nature of war is such that it may create revolutionary disorder or stasis in societies (including those that try to stay out of the conflict) and so proves a rough master that brings most men's characters to a level with their fortunes. In the revolution in Corcyra (a paradigm for *stasis* generally), the lust for power arising from greed and ambition brought on violence and extremism of many kinds, and the moderate class of citizens perished in the struggle. War, a violent teacher, releases the ungovernable passions of men:

> In the confusion into which life was now thrown in the cities, human nature, always rebelling against the law and now its master, gladly showed itself ungoverned in passion, above respect for justice, and the enemy of all superiority; for revenge would not have been set above religion, and gain above justice, had it not been for the fatal power of envy. (III.82–84)

Real Causes

Thucydides, a social scientist as well as an historian, is preoccupied with the problem of causation in the relations of states and empires. A recent study argues that "his greatest single contribution was consciously to develop and formulate an account of political causation in terms of deep cause and superficial, announced pretext."[11] Rejecting all religious and superstitious explanations of, say, the growth of empires or the causes of a great war, he looks for the deeper political, economic, and sociological interests of cities and their leaders, attempting to link motives to state actions, and the decisions of states to the changing pattern of power politics. His preference for *contemporary* history as the only true one arises from his conviction that so many events of the distant past have, through the passage of time, been robbed of historical value by the poets and chroniclers "enthroning them in the region of legend" (I.21). War being a social and political phenomenon, its causes must be sought in the relationships of states and the decisions of men — not in legends or oracles.

Thucydides's history of the war, in explicit contrast to that of his older contemporary, Herodotus, chronicler of the Persian-Greek wars, unfolds without the interventions of the gods. Herodotus thought that the Trojan War occurred because "the Divine was laying his plans that, as the Trojans perished in utter destruction, they might make this thing manifest to the world: that for great wrongdoings, great also are the punishments from the gods"; and he attributed the Persian invasion of Greece in 480 to a series of visions that finally persuaded the Persian ruler, Xerxes, that he must make mankind his slaves.[12] The power that rules the world of man — be it the jealous gods, fate, or the daimons — reveals itself through signs and oracles, and in these are to be found the causes of the great wars and the origins of great empires. But the gods and oracles are nowhere implicated in Thucydides's account of the immediate and deeper causes of the Peloponnesian War; while he cannot deny that some men (e.g., Nicias) are influenced by piety and oracles, nowhere does he attribute to nonhuman forces the slightest responsibility for the terrible war and related disasters that befell Greece after 431. He looks for human causes and explanations. Only men and states have power in his formulation.

His main concern is to separate the underlying "real cause" of the war from the events that served as a pretext for the conflict and from the stated grievances of the two sides prior to the declaration of hostilities — grievances that would hardly justify the terrible war that will follow. His second concern is to formulate a definition of the real cause in terms of *power* and shifting relationships of power between states, and for this he will be criticized by later historians for neglecting economic and social factors. However, for the student of international politics, his highly compressed statement endures "as the prototypic statement of how we usually express the causes of war"[13] as an instance of power politics: "The real cause I consider to be the one which was formally most kept out of sight. The growth of the power of Athens, and the alarm which this inspired in Lacadaemon, made war inevitable" (I.23).

It was, in other words, a war over power and imperialism — Athenian imperialism. The real cause of the war was the gradual and inexorable process whereby the Athenian-led alliance, the Delian League, formed after the great victories over Persia in 480 and 479, was converted into the Athenian Empire by the 450s, and then began to encroach upon the autonomy and security of Sparta and its allies. The shifting balance of power in Athens's favour not only threatened Sparta's position as a hegemon, but also placed her in a situation where she would sooner or later have to accept the terms of Pericles or go to war. Sparta's leaders feared a further decline in their power relative to that of Athens, a further worsening in their security position and that of their allies, and this fear of the future was their prime motive in going to war. Though traditionally "slow to go to war except under the pressure of necessity," the Spartans finally decided "that they could endure it no longer, but that the time had come for them to throw themselves heart and soul upon the hostile power, and break it, if they could, by commencing the present war" (I.118). It was, to express it another way, a war of fear, and not only for Sparta.

What made the war "inevitable" ("necessary," in Pericles's words) — and also so intractable once it began — was that it was a war between rival hegemonies for control of the whole Greek system of city-states. Sparta's final ultimatum, that Athens leave the Hellenes independent, called into question the very existence of the Athenian Empire, albeit half a century too late. Sparta's ultimatum ought to have been delivered much earlier, when Athens began to turn her alliance into an empire (i.e., when the treasury of the Delian League was moved to Athens from Delos in 454–453). Few alliances outlive a victory over the common enemy: that among Sparta, Athens, and other Greek cities had dissolved in recriminations over Sparta's failure to prevent the Persians from twice ravaging Athenian lands and properties. Withdrawing from the wider coalition of Greek cities into Peloponnesian isolation, and displaced as the unchallenged leader of the system after Persia's defeat in 480–479, Sparta had accepted a divided hegemony with Athens and then watched as the latter built up her walls and naval power and appropriated the economic resources of her allies. What had begun 50 years earlier as a voluntary anti-Persian coalition under Athenian leadership was, by the time the war commenced in 431, a very unpopular system of imperial power and rule (a "tyranny", according to Pericles himself) that gave Athens strategic control of the entire Aegean and its trading routes, great financial reserves, unparalleled naval power, and a famous democratic system for export. Athens ruled by force, she was ruthless in putting down revolts, and her appetite for new conquests seemed to grow with the eating. Sparta was correct to be afraid, but very late to challenge the threat; only the domestic tensions discussed earlier can explain her acquiescence in the face of successive challenges from the younger and bolder empire in the 50 years after the rout of the Persians. Her isolationism and the Persian retreat gave Athens far too much room to expand.

Fear and Empire

If the growth of Athenian power was the source of Sparta's fear, what was the "real cause" of Athens's expanding power? What lay behind the rising Athenian Empire? The influence of the democracy on the empire has been discussed and will not be rehearsed here. The Athenians themselves, who make no apologies for having acquired an empire or trying to keep it, add three other important reasons why they are "compelled" to be imperialists and to fight Sparta rather than make concessions. The reasons are given in a speech delivered in Sparta by some anonymous Athenian envoys on the eve of the war: it is the first Athenian speech recorded in the Thucydides's history, and it is remarkable for what it tells us about the perceptions and intransigent mood of the Athenians at the opening of the war. Although they are in Sparta on other business, the envoys have been prompted to ask leave to address the assembly in order to reply to some warlike speeches of Corinth and to other members of the Spartan alliance. The Athenians' aim is not to defend themselves on specific charges, but to deter Sparta from hasty decisions. They wish to call attention to the great power of Athens, and to refresh the memory of the old and enlighten the ignorance of the young from a notion that their words might have the effect of inducing them to prefer tranquillity to war — in order, deterrence. However, the speech is also a remarkable justification (rare in private, let alone public discourse) of the rule and the empire of a great power. Far from offering concessions to Sparta and her allies, the Athenian envoys will assert that they were forced or compelled to build up their empire, and that power rather than justice must regulate relations between cities. Only calculations of interest can explain the Spartans taking up the cry of justice, the Athenians state, for the rule has always been that the weaker must give way to the stronger, and justice is merely "a consideration which no one ever yet brought forward to hinder his ambition when he had a chance of gaining anything by might" (I.76).

The Athenian position is that they acquired their empire without violent means in the aftermath of the Persian wars, "because you [Sparta] were unwilling to prosecute to its conclusion the war against the barbarian, and because the allies attached themselves to us and spontaneously asked us to assume the command" (I.75). The empire was at first a voluntary one, and it came to Athens because of her daring and courage and military success in defeating Xerxes, but also because no one else was there. Thereafter, they were driven by necessity:

> And the nature of the case first compelled us to advance our empire to its present height, fear being our principal motive, though honour and interest afterwards came in. And at last, when almost all hated us, when some had already revolted and been subdued, when you had ceased to be the friends that you once were, and had become objects of suspicion and dislike, it appeared no longer safe to give up our empire, especially as all who left us would fall to you. (I.75)

Fear — first, of Persia, then of the hatred and desire for revenge of her own allies and of Sparta — was the dominant motive in Athenian imperialism, according to the Athenians themselves, just as fear of Athenian imperialism was Sparta's main motive in going to war. After fear comes honour (or prestige) and interest (or profit). But security is the prime value of the state, for without it the others cannot be realized. Fear, prestige, profit: this is a useful grouping of state motives, which closely resembles the motives for war suggested by Hobbes, Thucydides's translator — i.e., safety, reputation, gain — and the classification of wars of Martin Wight, a modern realist who was influenced by both Hobbes and Thucydides — i.e., wars of fear, wars of doctrine, and wars of gain.[14] Within this tradition, much of our thinking about the causes of war is really an elaboration of Thucydides's ideas about the nature of fear and security dilemmas in an anarchic and dynamic system of states dominated by two competing superpowers.

The cause of the war was that which had been born in fear and now rules by fear — the Athenian Empire. Athenian fears of Persia were no doubt real and legitimate: the city had been sacked, its population forced to take to the sea. This largely explains why Athens agreed to assume control of the Delian League, but only greed can explain why she transformed the League into her own empire. Her fear now is of the consequences of losing the empire (i.e., that Athens may receive the same brutal treatment that she gives her allies). No one disputes her empire's true nature: indeed, it is attacked or defended as a selfish despotism by eight different speakers in Thucydides.[15] In the words of Pericles, its arch-proponent, the empire is "a tyranny; to take it perhaps was wrong, but to let it go is unsafe" (II.63). The naval empire and its financial tribute are decisive for Athens in war, so much so that the Athenians believe they are forced to put down any revolt with the utmost severity and to put up with the hatred of the allies. Thucydides wrote of the empire's formative years:

> Of all the causes of defection, that connected with arrears of tribute and vessels, and with failure of service, was the chief; for the Athenians were very severe and exacting, and made themselves offensive by applying the screw of necessity to men who were not used to and not disposed for any continuous labour. (I.99)

The Athenians are by no means the only rulers who severely punish defectors, but they certainly stand to lose the most by failing to crush revolts. Pericles's strategy for an Athenian victory in the war is for the people to abandon land and property outside Athens,

> to come into the city and guard it, and get ready their fleet, in which their real strength lay. They were also to keep a tight rein on their allies — the strength of Athens being derived from the money brought in by their payments, and success in war depending principally upon conduct and capital.

Athens, which sets the assessments of allied contributions of money and ships, received 600 talents of silver annually from the allies; and she has enormous reserves (6000 talents) raised from the booty of empire (II.13). Pericles, who expresses the fear and "compulsion" as much as the arrogance of the empire, warns the Athenians against being provoked into battles on land with the numerically superior armies of the Spartan alliance: "a reverse involves the loss of our allies, the source of our strength, who will not remain quiet a day after we become unable to proceed with forces against them" (I.143). This is a remarkable admission of the vulnerability of Athens to uprisings in her empire, and it lends an ominous meaning to the admonition to keep "a tight rein" on the allies. The logic of fear and necessity, invoked to justify the most extreme acts of war, is what will lead the Athenian warships to Melos.

Conclusion

The collapse of the Greek city-states into the conflict now known as the Peloponnesian War came about because of the unabated aggrandizement of the Athenian naval empire and because Sparta, largely for internal reasons, acquiesced in the Athenian takeover of the leadership of the all-Greek alliance against Persia. The expansion of great powers is a product of two causes: domestic pressures and the weakness of surrounding powers. The growth of Athenian power externally was partly driven by the radicalization of the democracy and the efforts of leading politicians to link the *demos* to the glory and tribute of empire, and partly by the retreat of Sparta into uneasy isolation. Sparta's disinclination to challenge Athens was a major reason why the bipolar system or divided hegemony of fifth-century Greece failed, and the source of the failure was her unique internal situation. The efforts of Spartan diplomacy were primarily deployed to meet the needs of internal security, not to complement the use of her acknowledged military power to frustrate and contain the rising empire of Athens. Sparta's passivity amounted to a policy of appeasing Athenian imperialism. However, Athens is portrayed by many speakers in Thucydides as insatiable, for she is seeking an end to her insecurity through a universal empire. Sparta will therefore get war, but on unfavourable terms, by temporizing.

Thucydides shows with great clarity the security dilemmas that confront all states, including great powers, in an international anarchy; an anarchy that is the fundamental characteristic of international politics without a government. The Greek system of city-states, a multiplicity of independent sovereigns with no common government, was capable of achieving temporary unity in the face of external threats, but there was as yet no Rome capable of turning the quarrelsome Greek cities into obedient provinces. (This finally occurred in the second century.) The ties of nationality and race were observed by Thucydides, but they were not strong enough to counter the pull of fear and necessity in the creation of alliances; co-operation was almost entirely based on calculations of power and self-interest. War was a permanent condition in this system (from 497 to 338, Athens was at war for three years in every four) such that it came to be viewed by all Greek thinkers as inevitable and a product of human nature. A speaker says in Plato's *Laws* that what men call peace is merely an appearance; in reality, all cities are by nature in a permanent state of undeclared war against all other cities.[16]

If war is inevitable, so is the struggle to dominate and rule others. Only by overcoming the resistance of all other powers and founding a universal state can a great power escape from the security dilemma that is common to all. Thus, Athens's aim is to enslave every other state in order to free herself of insecurity. "We assert that we are rulers in Hellas in order not to be subjects," the Athenians tell the Sicilian city of Camarina, "and liberators in Sicily that we may not be harmed by the Sicilians; that we are compelled to interfere in many things, because we have many things to guard against" (VI.87). Sparta also is a liberator, "liberator of Hellas," and she will emerge from the war as the successor to the Athenian Empire.

The reader of Thucydides's history of the Peloponnesian War will find in its pages no statements setting out the basic precepts or laws of international relations; yet, it is to this one great book that we owe many of our fundamental and enduring ideas about the struggle for power and justice among states. The primacy of war and peace; the causes of war as the focus of inquiry; power defined as military and political power; the nature of the international anarchy; the expansion of powers; the tensions between justice and the interests of states. These questions, which were first posed by Thucydides on the basis of his observation of a single great war, are at the heart of the classical tradition of international politics. Because he believed that human nature is unchanging, he thought that the reader who took the time to study his "greatest movement" would discover the real causes and nature, not just of a specific war, but of all war. The fact that we still read Thucydides in order to understand our own world system suggests that he did indeed write "a possession for all time." He is, in my view, our pre-eminent theorist on war and peace.

NOTES

1. Thucydides, *The Peloponnesian War*, trans. Richard Crawley (New York: The Modern Library, 1981). Parenthetical text references are to this edition.

2. Richard Schlatter, ed., *Hobbes' Thucydides* (New Brunswick, N.J.: Rutgers University Press, 1975), 6.

3. Clifford Orwin, "Justifying Empire: The Speech of the Athenians at Sparta and the Problem of Justice in Thucydides," *Journal of Politics* 48 (February 1986): 80.

4. Schlatter, *Hobbes' Thucydides*, 18.

5. Sir Frank Adcock and D.J. Mosley, *Diplomacy in Ancient Greece* (London: Thames and Hudson, 1975).

6. Russell Meiggs, *The Athenian Empire* (Oxford: Clarendon Press, 1972), 388–91; and W. Robert Connor, *Thucydides* (Princeton: Princeton University Press, 1984), 147–57.

7. Simon Hornblower, *Thucydides* (London: Duckworth, 1987), chap. 1.

8. Niccolò Machiavelli, *The Prince*, trans. George Bull (Harmondsworth: Penguin, 1961), chap. XVII.

9. Homer,*The Iliad*, trans. William Cullen Bryant (Boston: James R. Osgood & Co., 1872), Book One.

10. Plutarch, *The Age of Alexander: Nine Greek Lives*, trans. Ian Scott-Kilvert (Harmondsworth: Penguin, 1973), 178–79; also Meiggs, *Athenian Empire*, chaps. 8 and 9.

11. Hornblower, *Thucydides*, 30.

12. Herodotus, *The History*, trans. David Green (Chicago: University of Chicago Press, 1987), 2.120 and 7.18–19.

13. Martin Wight, *Power Politics*, 2d ed. (London: 1986), 132.

14. T. Hobbes, *Leviathan* (London: 1986), 1.13.61; Wight, *Power Politics*, 138.

15. There is, however, important evidence in Thucydides's own narrative that the empire enjoyed considerable support from the *demos* in key allied cities. See G.E.M. de Ste. Croix, "The Character of the Athenian Empire," *Historia* 3 (1954–55).

16. Plato, *Laws*, trans. R.G. Bury (London: Heinemann, 1926).

SELECT BIBLIOGRAPHY

Connor, W. Robert. *Thucydides*. Princeton: Princeton University Press, 1984.
Hobbes, T. *Leviathan*. London: 1986.
Homer. *The Iliad*. Trans. William Cullen Bryant. Boston: James R. Osgood & Co., 1872.
Hornblower, Simon. *Thucydides*. London: Duckworth, 1987.
Machiavelli, Niccolò. *The Prince*. Trans. George Bull. Harmondsworth: Penguin, 1961.
Meiggs, Russell. *The Athenian Empire*. Oxford: Clarendon Press, 1972.
Plato. *Laws*. Trans. R.G. Bury. London: Heinemann, 1926.
Plutarch. *The Age of Alexander: Nine Greek Lives*. Trans. Ian Scott-Kilvert. Harmondsworth: Penguin, 1973.
Thucydides. *The Peloponnesian War*. Trans. Richard Crawley. New York: The Modern Library, 1982.
Wight, Martin. *Power Politics*. 2d ed. London: 1986.

BRIDGE OVER TROUBLED WATERS: LINKING STRATEGIC STUDIES AND INTERNATIONAL RELATIONS

Michel Fortmann and William L. George*

The story of strategic studies as both an academic discipline and a policy science might well be described as a success.[1] The growth of the discipline has been steady throughout the postwar era, with the creation of independent research institutes as well as specialized chairs of strategic studies in major universities bearing testimony to the field's popularity. In the United States, in particular, the increase in the number of foreign-policy and security-studies "think tanks" has been impressive, with more than a thousand private, nonprofit research centres currently in existence, roughly half of them university-based.[2] Furthermore, strategic analysts have been able to participate in and attain influence upon the policy-making process. Both the arrival of the so-called defence intellectuals at the Pentagon and the creation, in Canada, of the Directorate of Strategic Analysis in the Department of National Defence testify to the institutionalization of the field.[3]

Events during the 1980s have not diminished the relevance of strategic studies. Quite the contrary, there has been a reaffirmation of strategic studies as an important policy science, as this anecdote of Lawrence Freedman's indicates:

> When I first decided in the early 1970s to specialize in the field of nuclear weapons and arms control I almost felt cheated when, in May 1972, America and Russia signed the first SALT Treaty. As détente and arms control seemed perfectly logical and even inevitable, I suspected I had chosen my speciality just as it was losing practical relevance. I wondered if I ought to change to, say, urban planning instead. In 1980 I related this story at a conference at LSE [the London School of Economics] and afterwards a fellow came up to me and admitted that he was in urban planning and wanted to get into arms control![4]

*William L. George is with the Directorate of Strategic Analysis at the Department of National Defence. The views and opinions expressed in this chapter are those of the authors and do not represent the opinions of the DND or the Government of Canada.

Whether as a policy science or an academic discipline, strategic studies (especially in the United States) has unquestionably had a tremendous impact on how people think today about issues of international security.

Despite this evident success, strategic studies has never really been universally acknowledged as a genuine social science by academics; indeed, the field has been severely criticized by some scholars. Their attack has triggered an ideologically charged debate, one effect of which has been the appearance of a deep split, throughout the modern nuclear era, between strategic analysts and peace researchers.[5] Notwithstanding the polemical nature of this debate, some important questions have been raised, among which the following stand out: Where should we look to uncover the roots of contemporary strategic studies? How is the discipline related to the field of international relations? With which strand of international relations is strategic studies most compatible? In addition, many methodological and ethical considerations still remain insufficiently explored.

Consequently, the primary purpose of this chapter is both to synthesize and to focus further the main criticisms made against strategic studies. Its other objective is to investigate the theoretical foundation of the field, drawing attention to some avenues that promise to solidify its epistemological, conceptual, and theoretical bases. In the end, the student of strategic studies should have a better understanding of both the objectives and the limitations of the field. Throughout, we seek to emphasize the importance of the link between international relations and strategic studies.

This chapter is divided into two sections. The first examines some of the most celebrated accusations made against strategic studies. We argue that these charges are of limited relevance, as they are directed against one particular strand of the discipline: classical strategy. Moreover, we believe that, because of the polemical nature of the attack, serious theoretical and conceptual deficiencies of the field are left unaddressed.

The second section attempts to link strategic studies to a core theoretical paradigm, at the same time suggesting new research avenues. In this section, our objective is to demonstrate the complementary nature of new scholarship in both strategic studies and international relations. To this end, we conclude that the future success of strategic studies as a social science lies in its ability to broaden its analytical focus and implement a more ambitious and innovative research program.

The Strategic-Studies Strawman

Many sharp criticisms have been levelled against strategic studies. While these charges come from various sources, the most common ones are those elaborated by the proponents of peace studies, who tend to be deeply negative.[6] Two different sorts of accusations are typically made. These relate to theoretical and methodological matters, and to moral and ethical integrity. We examine these in turn.

At the level of theory and method, strategic-studies practitioners have been depicted as warmongers who "take for granted the existence of military force and confine themselves to considering how to exploit it."[7] To them, the international system is Hobbesian in that it is characterized by anarchy, chaos, and state egoism; for them, order is established by the rule of the fittest, and the only way states can assure their survival is through the maximization of power.[8] Thus, it is legitimate for states to use military force and to attempt to impose their hegemony. However, with all states constantly planning for the worst, the spiral effect of "worst-case planning" heightens the probability of undesired armed aggression, as each actor perceives war to be unavoidable.[9]

This emphasis on states and the balance of power leads to the best-known of the charges levelled against strategic studies, that of ethnocentrism.[10] While it is noted that the practice of strategy is widespread, its study is mostly a Western phenomenon. More specifically, it is argued that Western strategic analysis, because of its constant obsession with the Soviet Union, can be of little explanatory power for issues that do not hinge on the East-West balance. In particular, it is often observed that American strategic analysis suffers from acute analytical narrowness.[11] It is said to embody a particular national style that values pragmatism and technological solutions and generates ahistorical and, more importantly, apolitical scholarship.[12]

Furthermore, it has been often suggested that strategic theory is too abstract and complex. As a result, it is and must remain of little relevance to the politician, for the theorists are simply not in tune with the realities of the policy-making environment. Their indifference toward public opinion also draws severe criticism, as Colin Gray notes: "strategists, so the argument might proceed, presume that the arcane logic of strategic theory is beyond the grasp of the common man, and if anything, a little understanding would probably be a dangerous thing."[13] In the end, the problem of strategic analysis, in the United States above all, lies in its inability to play a useful role in the public debate. By either rubber-stamping the prevailing ideas of the government, or by utilizing a set of baffling concepts and jargon that transcend common sense, (American) strategic studies has failed in its political enterprise. It has not become the catalyst of better policy.[14]

In this regard, the American experience, as described above, has generated several important moral accusations. First, the language and logic of strategic analysts is depicted as frightening, especially for the layman. The cool manipulation of attack scenarios typical of strategic analysis, which imply the deaths of millions of people, can be a troublesome thought, indeed. As Michael Howard states, "Force sounds so strong, so calm, so authoritative, violence sounds so romantic, so revolutionary, so self-expressive, both in fact mean killing and maiming people in various vile ways."[15] Hence, strategists too often can lose sight of the implications of their work. Furthermore, in the nuclear era, strategists seem to have become so accustomed to the idea of nuclear war that they sometimes appear devoid of human sensitivity. Thus, it is charged, their fascination with the manipulation of violence has created a beast without ethics.[16]

Second, critics have argued that strategists indulge in a moral double standard, on the one hand approving the actions of certain states, while, on the other, condemning other states for similar behaviour. Thus, because of their worldview (mostly anticommunist), and of their perceptions of good and bad in the international system, strategists are said to support brutal actions by their preferred states — actions believed to be necessary to counter negative "evil" forces.

In truth, the importance of the strategic-studies normative agenda should not be underestimated. A particular latent characteristic of this agenda is a narrow definition of security. As such, the strategist's definition of security revolves around the interests of the state he serves, and thus operates to the detriment of a broader approach that emphasizes global peace and harmony.

Despite the polemical nature of the above-cited charges, they are quite serious. Their principal deficiency, however, lies in their narrow depiction of strategic studies. The critics assume that strategic studies is an homogeneous discipline; this perception of the field is inaccurate and misleading. Contemporary strategic studies should rather be characterized by the merger of several academic disciplines. History, political science, sociology, psychology, law, economics, operational research, and systems analysis have all contributed to the development of strategic studies. Therefore, the story of modern strategic analysis is more one of competing strands than of a single dominant approach.

For instance, the recent work of Barry Posen and Jack Snyder illustrates fairly well a particular strand of strategic studies, one that is preoccupied with the sociological dimension of security policy making.[17] At the opposite end of the spectrum, the work of Herman Kahn and Ashton Carter exemplifies a more military/technical approach to the subject matter.[18] Thus, what needs to be understood at the outset is that contemporary strategic studies is hardly united in its sins, as has been suggested, especially in the peace-research critique. Consequently, it would be wrong to suggest that classical strategy and contemporary strategic studies are synonymous. While one could argue that some of the mistakes of classical strategy are being replicated by contemporary strategic analysis, the mainstream of the latter discipline is characterized by an effort to go well beyond classical military thought. More specifically, contemporary strategic studies appears to be driven by the desire to comprehend conflict, and the link between armed coercion and the conduct of international politics, more thoroughly.

In essence, strategic studies may best be depicted as a divided discipline in search of a unifying framework. We will return to this vital issue later. The discipline, however, is also haunted by its past. It is precisely toward this past that the bulk of the attacks against the field are directed. Unfortunately, peace researchers did not seem fully to realize the thrust of their criticisms. They put modern strategists — hawks, doves, and owls — in the same category as Napoleon, Clausewitz, and a host of "dead German generals," thus confusing the issue hopelessly. They do not pursue their analyses far enough, nor do they try to explain why a certain breed of modern strategists behaves the way they do. In fact, much of the criticism appears premised on an incomplete assessment of the origins and development of classical strategic thought.

The Poisoned Legacy

Traditionally, strategic analysis has been the private domain of military professionals. With few exceptions, they were the first historians and philosophers of war, and their work can be traced back to antiquity.[19] In more recent history, Machiavelli may be cited as one of the founding fathers of classical strategic analysis. He had observed the decisive role that military power played in politics, and had concluded that the survival and the greatness of the state depended on this power. "New military institutions and new processes in warfare," he observed, were "the most urgent and the most fundamental requirements" of his time: "a man newly risen to power cannot acquire a greater reputation than by discovering [these] new rules and methods."[20] Henceforth, the strategist's purpose was to observe war so as to discover the principles that could make the military apparatus of his master more efficient.[21] With its emphasis on creating "scientific guides to war," early strategic studies came to be defined as a primitive policy science, rather than as an analytical and explanatory undertaking. Thus, military strategy and strategic studies became synonymous.

Most noteworthy definitions of the field have emphasized this aspect. B.H. Liddell Hart's, for example, has become an institutional standard, positing, as it does, that strategy is "the art of distributing and applying military means to fulfil the ends of policy."[22] Indeed, what this definition implies is that policy, although commanding strategy, lies outside its boundaries. Thus, this approach naturally generated an uncritical and apolitical type of analysis insofar as the *ends* of statecraft were concerned.

For subscribers to this view, strategic studies is limited to a very narrow line of inquiry. While many strategists have made their own particular mark, they have all essentially been analysts of combat rather than sociologists of war.[23] Not surprisingly, the field of strategic studies has often been perceived as an advanced form of military tactics.

Nor has the introduction of nuclear weapons in the arsenals of major military powers altered this bias in many strategic analyses. While strategy has been defined in a broader sense, it is often still associated mostly with the "means" part of the "means-to-end" equation, as illustrated by Robert Osgood's observation that "military strategy must now be understood as nothing less than the overall plan for utilizing the capacity for armed coercion — in conjunction with the economic, diplomatic, and psychological instruments of power — to support foreign policy most effectively by overt, covert, and tacit means."[24] Reiterated is, thus, the belief that the role of strategic studies lies at the juncture between military considerations and political interests. Under this view, the strategic analyst is more an interpreter than a social scientist.

This narrow approach toward strategic studies has recently been reaffirmed by such authors as Osgood, Edward Luttwak, and Colin Gray, and by the upsurge of interest in geopolitics.[25] Were the evolution of strategic studies from Machiavelli to Gray to be seen in a linear manner, then the field could truly be depicted as a static craftsmanship rather than as an evolving branch of science. With its emphasis on "how" rather than "why," strategic studies could stand in relationship to political science much as accounting does to economics.

Strategy under the classical tradition is a science of action (a "how to do it" science) or, more specifically, a praxis.[26] The classical strategist perceives war as a straightforward clash between two or more unitary actors. Moreover, it is assumed that both the people and armies of each actor are subservient to the war effort of each nation, much in the same way that pieces of a chess game are to respective players.[27]

Despite the fact that most classical strategists posit a subordination of military means to political ends, little thought has been given to how political and military authorities co-ordinate their actions. In an attempt to bypass this issue, some classical strategists have sought refuge in an ideal type of societal leadership, one that combines military and political authorities.[28] For others, who wished to reaffirm the validity of the state-centric (or unitary-actor) approach, analytical comfort was derived from the concept of grand strategy.[29] This concept presupposes that states or groups of states can and should co-ordinate and direct the totality of their resources to the promotion and affirmation of political objectives pursued in a war effort. Grand strategy constitutes an extension of military strategy in the realm of domestic and foreign policy, and indeed becomes a totalitarian concept in its appeal for a plan that might "integrate the political, economic and military strategy and prepare the state for a total war whether hot or cold."[30] This approach, apart from its dubious political connotations, possesses all the flaws of the classical tradition, especially that of ignoring the social and political environment that sustains the viability of such a strategy.

Neoclassical strategists such as Edward Luttwak and Colin Gray have suggested that grand strategy should be interpreted as both a more ambitious and a less diffident version of what is known as national security policy.[31] Grand strategy, in their eyes, is more ambitious than national security policy because it implies offensive moves and victories. However, national security policy is disdained because it is perceived to carry a defensive connotation. What this type of scholarship lacks is any sociological explanation of the war phenomenon. As with classical theories, neoclassical military thought either minimizes or negates the importance of domestic political or economic considerations as explanatory elements in the origins, conduct, and results of wars.

In summary, then, classical military thought has not really investigated the relationship between war and politics. More specifically, attempts to comprehend the origins and causes of wars have not dominated the classical strategist's agenda.[32] In the classical tradition, war is treated as a physical phenomenon, something that is largely apolitical. To be sure, not all classicists so regarded war: in this context, the principal source of Clausewitz's long-lasting popularity resides in his tentative, yet important, reflection on the political nature of war.

Perhaps the volatile nature of the political and technological dimensions of war contributed to their prevailing neglect in the classical tradition. Be that as it may, one can state with some confidence that classical strategic thought retains limited currency in the rapidly changing nuclear era.[33] As some scholars have indicated, there is an important dichotomy between classical strategy and contemporary strategic studies, one that is rarely recognized, but nevertheless takes the form of a major structural difference between the two approaches. From grand strategy all the way down to tactics, the classical tradition represents an integrated approach with a consistent logic, the purpose of which has been and remains to devise rules of military victory. By contrast, contemporary strategic studies is not as homogeneous, encompassing, as it does, many schools of thought and analytical foci, among which are nuclear strategy, conventional strategy, revolutionary warfare, and arms control.

This diversified character of contemporary strategic studies appears to be a source of additional insight into the field; at the same time, it may constitute an important limitation, for the absence of an overall analytical focus has prevented contemporary strategic studies from having a sound and consistent theoretical base.[34] In this regard, the principal challenge for contemporary strategic analysts is to pick up where the classical strategists left off, and to find a theoretical framework that will permit them to understand more thoroughly both the classical legacy and the historical database. If they are truly to be social scientists, they must not only transcend the peace-studies critique, but more importantly, they must cut the umbilical cord with classical strategy. The dead Germans should be allowed to rest in peace.

In Search of a Theory of Strategic Studies

It is our contention that the basic sin of strategic studies as an institutionalized field of inquiry has been to stick too closely to its historical (traditional) legacy and, hence, to reduce the study of war to the art and science of armed conflict. Their preoccupation with the clash of arms has blinded experts to the fact that wars and their outcome must be seen as products of larger social, political, and economic structures and processes. Of course, the battles of Midway, Trafalgar, and Verdun are important events that deserve to be studied, for some quite valid reasons. We wonder, however, whether the study of war at the operational level should not be the task of the soldier whose job it is to win battles, rather than that of the political scientist whose responsibility it is to search for the more fundamental determinants of conflict. Is it more important for political scientists to learn from the technical mistakes of the Japanese commanders during the Pacific war or to seek to explain why Japan initiated the conflict in the first place?

This, perhaps rhetorical, question underscores the point that strategy, the art of the general, depends to a large extent on the analysis of the international political and economical system, and that, in the absence of that analysis, war is condemned to remain a grammar without a logic, a speech without meaning. Consequently, if the strategic analyst wishes to be a social scientist, he or she must never stray too far from the fold of international relations.

If our observation is valid, it follows that the first item on the strategic-studies research agenda should be an inquiry into an appropriate conceptual and theoretical framework from among the various paradigms international relations can and does offer. Unfortunately, until very recently, this item had been neglected by strategic analysts, with the result being a regrettable absence of theoretical debate in the major journals of the field. There has been, and still is, a very active theoretical debate about wars, conflicts, and international crises outside the boundaries of strategic studies, in the fields of international relations theory and foreign policy. It is in that direction that the quest for answers to theoretical queries should be initiated, and in the following pages we attempt to critically analyze that literature. We seek above all answers to two questions: What type of theory do we need? What purpose will it serve?

To begin with, we need a theoretical framework that takes account of the phenomenon of war as a recurring type of interstate relation and tries to explain it on sociopolitical grounds. It should be a framework in which strategy, interpreted as "the art or science of shaping means so as to promote ends in any field of conflict," retains relevance.[35] We need a general theory broad enough to embrace the different levels of analysis essential to the understanding of war, one that warns us of the dangers of reductionist approaches that favour one level at the expense of others. Our theory should be unabashedly a heuristic device, which should at the same time be adaptive enough to evolve by integrating new explanatory elements.[36] As A.J.R. Groom notes, theory is a necessary prerequisite to disciplined analysis of *political* issues: "The fact of the matter is that we cannot think without a theory: facts do not speak for themselves, we impose meaning on them."[37] Finally, we should be attentive to the competing ideological assumptions that underlie the different paradigms we examine. Theories often present themselves as sanitized intellectual instruments, but it is well to remember that they are all skewed according to the specific worldview (*Weltanschauung*) of their adherents. This fact of life should neither be denied nor celebrated, but simply taken as a given.

Competing Paradigms of Conflict: The Continuing Relevance of Realism

For a number of years, three competing paradigms — the realist, the liberal (or pluralist), and the structuralist (or Marxian) — have informed the theoretical debate in international relations.[38] To each of them can be attached a specific subfield specializing in the study of conflict. For example, strategic studies is typically associated with realism, peace research with structuralism, and conflict research with the liberal model. As all three of the paradigms offer views on conflict, they satisfy our first criterion and, therefore, become of interest to us. At this stage of our inquiry, we seek neither to judge the validity of the three approaches nor to dissect them in detail. Rather, our aim is to determine which of the three theoretical niches is the most fitting one for strategic studies.

We wish to consider whether strategic analysts should divorce themselves from the realist model, and instead become peace researchers. Alternatively, if realism should remain their conceptual home, to what extent can the other paradigms contribute to their understanding of war?

Let us begin this analysis with the liberal model. There are at least four reasons why it would be difficult to reformulate strategic studies so as to make it consistent with this approach. First, although the paradigm does take conflicts into account, it conceives wars and power relations between states primarily as a small set of maladaptive and dysfunctional behaviours that are nested in a broad universe comprising all kinds of interactions between all kinds of units. The liberal model might offer a good start for a sociology that would explore the sources of conflict between individuals and groups (both inside and across state boundaries), but it also would tend to neglect *interstate* relations as a basis for explanation. To take one example, in the Cyprus conflict the liberal model would instruct us to learn about political culture and social traits or characteristics of the Greek-Turkish communities rather than to study the policies of the governments involved. Without denying that such an approach would, indeed, offer some useful insights for the understanding of certain conflicts, it is also clear that strategic studies as it now exists would become marginalized within such a framework. Additionally, political science itself would be only one of the many disciplines involved in this strand of conflict research, and not necessarily the most important one.

The liberal model comprehends power-driven relations as being only an extreme case on a continuum between totally peaceful (legitimized) exchanges and war. Legitimized relations it takes to be normal, adaptive, and rational, and, therefore, more important to study than their opposite. This orientation is based on the assumptions that men are not naturally aggressive or driven by an instinct to dominate, and that aggression or war is simply a learned reaction to certain environmental conditions. In other words, military strategy, the conduct of war, or the use of military threat is only rarely, if ever, a rational enterprise.

In a nutshell, then, the liberal paradigm sees human behaviour and interactions as basically nonantagonistic, provided that their nature is correctly understood by the actors involved. In this perspective, strategy (conceived as the method by which individuals or groups may coerce other actors through threats, even if for the common good) is perceived as a dysfunctional undertaking condemned to disappear in a world where nonstate-centric, legitimized interaction becomes the rule. In this context, the only surviving precept of classical strategy would be "know your enemy" — to which would be added, "understanding, not power, is the key to peace."

We should also note that the liberal model represents a tough problem in terms of the level of analysis. It does not, obviously, hold the state to be the central actor on the international stage. To the contrary, transnational actors and forces that are not amenable to governmental control are more and more seen as the driving mechanisms of international relations. Were one to accept this depiction, then one's legitimate focus of analysis should become the individual, and the set of interactions of which he or she partakes.

On the one hand, the liberal model could be labelled reductionist because it focusses on the societal level and tends to downplay the state, its structure, and the international system as explanatory factors. On the other hand, the model might be accused of holism because it applies the principle of rationality (i.e., cost-benefit analysis) to all kinds of human interactions at all levels. Conflict, for example, between individuals, states, ethnic groups, and industries, is seen as being the same phenomenon, obeying the same laws, despite the differences and idiosyncracies specific to each level. In this important sense, then, the liberal paradigm fails to satisfy our third criterion, namely, that it be resistant to reductionism.

Finally, it bears stressing that the liberal model is far from being the most powerful or theoretically rich approach to the field of international relations. Above all, it continues to suffer from the lack of a "powerful synthesis of its basic precepts and policy implications which would compare with the work of Carr, Morgenthau and Waltz among the realists."[39] The liberal model still relies heavily on its most persuasive specialized studies to maintain its reputation.

Whatever may be the demerits of the liberal model, we can find still more compelling reasons for strategic-studies researchers to refrain from attaching themselves to the structuralist paradigm. Indeed, the emphasis that the latter places upon the underlying "structure" of international relations to explain interstate violence is closely related to the works of such founders of political sociology as Durkheim and Marx. Structure, in their usage, means any set of theoretical concepts that determine or constrain the otherwise mysterious contingencies of concrete political events. As noted by Richard Little,

> when people [or states] interact, they create systems. These systems are defined by enduring characteristics. Individuals may come and go, but the structures of the system persist. The task of the social scientist is to identify these structures and determine how they affect social actions. They must also be concerned with the development and transformation of these structures.[40]

Now, an emphasis on structural realities can be considered as quite legitimate, as long as it does not reach the point of mania, stripping the individual, the group, or the state of any freedom as a decision-making unit. This is, regrettably, precisely the route modern structuralist-Marxism and its offshoot, radical peace research, have taken, in their rejection as "naïve humanism" of the study of politics at the subsystemic level.[41] According to this perspective, political actions, decisions, and events must be seen in essence to be the outcome of some constraining structure and not as phenomena understandable per se, or even as additional explanatory factors. Strategic studies, defined as the analysis of states' conflictual behaviour, would accordingly be considered irrelevant insofar as it did not focus exclusively on the structure of the international system. Hence, a purely structuralist approach to strategic studies might resemble one of those medieval paintings in which the battles of men on the ground have their (more important) counterparts in the contests of angelic hosts in the sky.[42] This approach could well be labelled "epiphenomenalism," because

> if we are to understand political reality we have to come to grips not only with its determinate aspects but most particularly with its creative, adaptive, problem-solving aspects, for it is this last characteristic which is the essentially human property, and which is the unique mechanism and explanatory challenge of the social sciences.[43]

Need we add that, after all, problem solving is what strategy is all about?

It is clear, then, that pure structuralism cannot be the proper theoretical home for strategic studies, and not just because of the defects of reductionism and neopositivistic arrogance. A further deficiency of peace research, apart from its being strongly influenced by the structuralist-Marxist tradition, is its involvement in political activism. As such, in the 1960s and 1970s,

> instead of conducting research in order to discover the causes of war and violence . . . [radical peace researchers] were . . . suggesting that they already knew the answers to those questions. Thus, research was not only no longer desirable in their eyes, but apparently no longer necessary. The answers were more or less in and the issue was one of acting on those answers.[44]

With structural violence and imperialism being defined as the systemic roots of war, the purpose of many peace researchers became "to conceive of science as an activity that brings about a new world."[45] How would that "new world" be brought about? Not through peaceful change and nonviolent means, but through revolution. Thus, this brand of peace research became a species of inverted strategy, one, moreover, that demonstrated all the worst tendencies and excesses of classical strategic thought.

To be sure, peace research, as well as conflict research, should not be judged exclusively according to the shortcomings and biases of the theoretical paradigms with which they are customarily associated. The works of David Singer, Bruce Russett, and Bruce Bueno de Mesquita can hardly be put in the same category as those of Johan Galtung.[46] It should also be admitted that "outsiders" such as Singer, Russett, and Bueno de Mesquita — who certainly deserve more attention because of the outstanding scientific and ethical qualities of their writings — are themselves still in search of a theoretical port of call, and therefore are in a situation similar to that of some of their colleagues in strategic studies. This raises the question of whether it is possible to dispense with abstract and value-laden theorizing and concentrate instead on methodology and empirical research. The answer is obvious, but nonetheless deserves to be stated: there is no such thing as apolitical, "pure" social science. Strategic studies, peace research, and conflict research, like all social sciences, cannot divorce themselves from human values and politics.

In this regard, operational research and systems analysis could be taken as perfect illustrations of ancillary, apolitical applied methodologies that attempt to reduce the phenomenon of war to a management problem; thus, they cannot be used as models in our quest.[47] For strategic analysts, as for peace researchers, there is no escape from the twin facts that one's ethical and political values help determine the research issues one addresses, and that a theoretical framework, paradigm, or simply a worldview is essential to keep these values visible and explicit, reducing the likelihood of contaminating the results.

To summarize our argument thus far, it is clear that, notwithstanding many interesting features, neither of the alternative paradigms in international relations theory provides a satisfactory perspective for the reformulation of strategic studies. By simple elimination, one would be entitled to warn insecure strategists against reneging prematurely on their traditional creed of realism (or one of its more recent offshoots, "structural realism").

Nonetheless, the strident and persistent critique directed at realism from all quarters requires that a closer look at this last paradigm be taken, and that the following questions be examined: What are its assumptions? Are they still valid? Has the paradigm been open to debate? Did these debates make a difference? Has realism evolved as a consequence? Finally, is the paradigm, in its present form, flexible enough to take into account the most fruitful critiques addressed to it by its challengers?

As far as the assumptions of realism are concerned, it is difficult to surpass the summarization crafted by Colin Gray:

> First [on the international scene] the principal actors are, and will continue to be, states. Transnational actors are most unlikely to effect more than marginal modification to the states system. Second, states seek to secure a cost-effective measure of control over their external environment. They seek influence over other states both as a goal and as an end in itself. Third, the absence of supra state authority means that every state is the final arbiter of the worth of its cause, while the relative strength of states and state groupings interacting in non-lethal or lethal conflict, [is] the final arbiter of the success of the engaged causes. Fourth, moral principles and notions of justice are far from irrelevant in interstate relations, but such considerations are always liable to be sacrified to the ethic of expediency. In the name of state security, anything and everything is permitted but there generally are convincing reasons why states hesitate before resorting to the grimmer end of "anything or everything." Fifth, interstate politics are far from being in a constant state of war all against all . . . but crisis and war are ever present possibilities. Sixth, if a state is presented with the opportunity to secure influence abroad at reasonable costs, that opportunity will probably be taken. And finally, there are no happy endings — indeed, there are few endings at all. A world balkanized into separate security communities must always live in the shadow of the risk of war.[48]

As such, it can be said that contemporary realists share a cautious view of the world whereby armed conflict, even though made improbable by nuclear threat, always remains possible because of the absence of a supranational authority, as well as of an accepted body of rules regarding the settlement of disputes. Even if this worldview is neither peaceful nor reassuring, it certainly cannot be faulted on its lack of "realism," in the common use of the term. After all, there were 22 wars underway in 1987, more wars than in any previous year in recorded history,[49] and this statistic strongly suggests that power politics rather than legitimized relations continues to be the rule in international relations. Moreover, it shows that strategy, far from being a dying art, remains an important part of statecraft, deserving of serious attention.

Judged on its assumptions, then, realism undoubtedly presents a set of plausible explanatory, fundamental, and integrated propositions that satisfy the conditions of theory-building. In addition, it endows international relations with a unique specificity that distinguishes the field from domestic politics and international economics, law, or sociology. The milieu of realism is characterized by anarchy — which does not mean chaos — and the rule of the game for the participating actors (the states) is self-help. Nevertheless, realism is not about economics but politics, i.e., "a social process characterized by activity involving rivalry and cooperation in the exercise of power and culminating in the making of decisions for a group."[50]

In essence, realism in its current form still offers a solid theoretical framework upon which to build. Moreover, and contrary to structuralist-Marxism, it has evolved. It has distanced itself from the blunt, state-centric assumption of power-maximization that was typical of classical realism. Specifically, the theoretical focus of contemporary realism has shifted from the state to the system; in other words, the international political structure is now seen as a "constraining and disposing force on the interacting units within it," and that "to the extent that dynamics of a system limit the freedom of its units, their behaviour and the outcome of their behaviours become predictable."[51] Realism, however, in expanding its framework, has not lost sight of the state as a relatively free decision-making unit. What it has done is to identify those variables that set limits on the range of human choice.

Contemporary realism, contrary to what is often argued, does not ignore transnational factors, nor does it reduce the state to an opaque billiard ball. In fact, it is "highly cognizant of the role of domestic politics and of the actor's choices within the constraints and incentives provided by the system."[52] What it does, though, is to give precedence to the system as the privileged source of explanation, and to the state as the principal actor on the international scene. To that extent, domestic politics and transnational forces may be perceived as secondary explanatory factors that can be introduced when state behaviour does not conform to the predictions of the model.

Finally, the contemporary realist paradigm, again contrary to what has been said, does not pretend that power politics is the only type of interaction between states. In fact, the paradigm can be and is quite compatible with international co-operation. Yet the conditions under which co-operation can emerge among egoists without a central authority are still open for debate, and realists may be criticized for paying too much attention to "power-maximization" as the basic driving force of state policy. However, it is important to note that realism has been remarkably open to constructive criticism, and the continuing debate that was triggered by Waltz's major contribution a decade ago is solid proof of this.

In summary, the interparadigm debate reveals that realism has, at this moment, "no credible competitor." As John Young has written, regarding contemporary realism: "only one intellectual tradition espousing a coherent set of paradigmatic assumptions can be said to have met [the] elementary criteria for viable theorizing consonant with the standard operating procedures of scientific inquiry."[53] However, this does not mean that today's realist thinking should be taken as gospel in all its aspects. The interparadigm debate demonstrates that challenges and criticisms are necessary to keep realism from ossifying into a dogma; it asks questions and raises problems that, in turn, force the researcher to define an agenda for the future. Indeed, as long as theoretical debating does not turn into scholastic navel-gazing, it should be esteemed as a vital element for the development of the paradigm. As such, modern strategists should not hesitate to acknowledge that they are, "without apologies," realists, and that the theoretical state of the field largely supports them in that acknowledgement.[54]

The Way Ahead: Some Avenues for Research

Strategy, within the contemporary realist framework, may be understood as a particular type of policy whose dynamics can be analyzed at the three interrelated levels of domestic politics, the state, and the international system. One of these levels, the state, acts as the basic decision-making unit, the two others as sets of constraining forces. One can then explain strategy as the product of this interaction and relate it to the broader dynamics of the international system, which, in turn, opens up more abstract, but nonetheless important, avenues regarding the principles governing that system: How, when, and why does conflict occur? Can it be controlled or managed and, if so, how? Is stability achievable and, if so, under what conditions? Those and many other questions then become the core of the strategist's (qua scientist's) research agenda, and it must be strongly emphasized that this agenda is totally different from that of the military strategists. In other words, military "sciences" are still relevant for the civilian, university-based strategist, but as an object of study instead of as a research guide.

We must next ask: are the principal parameters of the contemporary realist framework the best guides to define what Lakatos called a scientific program, that is, "a set of rules telling us what paths of research to avoid and what path to follow"?[55] The immediate answer might seem to be, no. Indeed, the value of a research program inheres in the *challenges* it offers to the core assumptions of the paradigm. By the same token, it should be noted that those assumptions — the reigning orthodoxy, as it were — itself can pose very strong challenges. Stanley Hoffmann remarked of Hans Morgenthau that

> the very breadth of his brushstrokes, the ambiguities hidden by his peremptory pronouncements . . . and even more the sleights of hand entailed by his pretense that the best analytic scheme necessarily yields the only sound normative advice — all of this incited readers to react and, by reacting, criticizing, correcting, refuting, to build upon Morgenthau's foundations. Those who rejected his blueprint were led to try other designs. He was both a goad and a foil. (Indeed, the more one agreed with his approach, the more one was irritated by its flaws, and eager to differentiate one's own product.) A less arrogantly dogmatic scholar, a writer more modest would never have had such an impact on scholarship. . . . Humane skeptics invite nods and sighs, not sound and fury; and sound and fury are good for creative scholarship.[56]

In other words, there seems to be a creative dialectical relationship between orthodoxy and heresy, with the usefulness of the former residing largely in its catalytic role. Consequently, realism and strategic studies may, after all, fulfil Lakatos's criteria for a progressive research program, because modesty, balance of judgement, and "humane skepticism" do not appear to be the foremost qualities of practitioners in the field of strategic studies.[57]

It is puzzling to note that neither strategic- nor security-studies researchers have found the knack of building a systematic research program, despite a constant clamour for "new approaches" to international security.[58] The latest efforts in this direction have been disappointing, because they either remain unsystematic or they confine strategic studies to its traditional "agenda." A representative of the latter problem is Barry Buzan's newest book, which argues that strategic studies should concentrate on the variable of military technology and its effect on political relations within the international system. "Any other approach," adds Buzan, "would risk making international relations subordinate to strategy, and so biasing the whole study of the international system towards relations of conflict and away from relations of harmony and indifference."[59] From our point of view, this attitude is gravely misleading because it seems to imply that strategic analysts do not belong in the field of international relations. They are, or should be, first and foremost, international relations specialists, because the development of their specialized field (i.e., strategy) depends critically on theories explaining how the international system works and evolves, and it is inconceivable that they should not be involved with the conceptual debates that will determine the future of strategy as a scholarly pursuit. In addition, to suggest that strategic studies might "invade" or otherwise "pollute" international relations seems to us to denigrate international relations, which is a strong and enduring discipline. Consequently, we argue that a strategic-studies research program should contain, at one and the same time, a traditional agenda focussing on such issues as strategy and defence policies *and* an innovative or progressive agenda that would concentrate on relevant international relations theoretical questions, which could be of crucial importance for the development of the field. Mindful of the strong emphasis in the strategic-studies traditional agenda on Western defence and security issues, we would suggest the development of an alternative "traditional" agenda, whose purpose would be to explore defence-related phenomena specific to other parts of the world.

The traditional research agenda itself would include five research areas (see the appendix to this chapter). First, at the level of strategies and military doctrines, there is a clear need for a general theory of strategy that would enable the analyst to compare and evaluate strategies as theoretical contructs. A similar claim could be made regarding the operational evaluation of strategies and the analysis of their impact on policy. How, for example, do we as social scientists rate such doctrines as "deep strike," or such concepts as area defence? What is the political meaning of these models? The absence of clear answers to these questions obviously indicates the need for a research effort in this direction. Only in the area of the origins of military doctrines, where researchers such as Barry Posen, Jack Snyder, and Donald Snow have attempted to design models explaining the development of strategic doctrines, has some ground been broken.[60] Research on the history of the nuclear age should correct some widely held misconceptions about the evolution of nuclear forces and strategy. Prenuclear history also deserves greater attention, especially World War II, which has been neglected by strategic-studies specialists. Moreover, if some attention has recently been accorded current conventional strategy, much of this has been dissipated on descriptions, "bean counting," or military-technical commentary at the expense of sound analysis and explanation. As for unconventional strategy, the subject was neglected for a full decade, and did not begin to attract renewed interest until the 1980s.[61]

In the area of defence-policy analysis, strategic studies is on much safer ground, if only because theories and models that are used in this sector are solidly rooted in the literature on foreign policy.[62] More specifically, decision-making theory, psychological concepts such as perception, bureaucratic-politics models, and organizational analysis all offer a wide range of heuristic instruments that enable one to better comprehend the formation of defence and security policies.[63] Nevertheless, some lacunae remain. We need to know more about legislative bodies, pressure groups, and public opinion on defence policies. Defence economics and its impact on defence-policy making constitutes a largely unexplored field for most strategic-studies researchers.[64] And, few efforts have been made to promote a general theory of defence-policy development.

Regarding arms control, the four proposed research subfields indicated in the appendix to this chapter are self-evident. A large amount of valuable work has already been done in these areas, and in some other related subfields (which have not been mentioned for the sake of brevity). It is important to emphasize, however, that the status of arms control, both as policy and as theory, is still ambiguous. Indeed, in 1985, after almost 30 years of frustrating experience, many strategic-studies specialists could still not say if arms control was a dying policy, one slowly going out of fashion, or an enduring reality of the nuclear era, deserving of more attention than it was getting as a modest subset of East-West diplomacy. This ambiguity can perhaps be explained by the fact that arms control has often been narrowly defined as an independent technical enterprise, detached from the larger framework of political relations between states.[65] Arms control should instead have been perceived as one specific form of interstate dialogue, devoid of meaning if not related to the system of co-operative/competitive relations between two or more states. In other words, a theory of arms control needs to rest on a theory of international security co-operation.

As far as military technology is concerned, who could dispute Barry Buzan when he says that "technology defines much of the contemporary strategic agenda, and generates much of the language in which strategy is discussed"?[66] To a large extent, what has been said about the study of strategy can be said about military technology: we lack theories, relevant concepts and hypotheses, and sound scientific empirical research. One student of the issue has perceptively observed that the study of military technology is viewed with some suspicion in academic circles,

> because things military are distasteful and technology . . . appears esoteric . . . or trivial. . . . [Military-technology studies] are viewed as lacking scholarly rigor and intellectual substance in part for good reason: some of the early writers in [the] field

> were buffs and enthusiasts, more intent on communicating their own predilections than on surveying their topics critically and analytically.[67]

The net result is that basic research in the field of military technology has been neglected, even though strategists take delight in the extensive use of the technical jargon of the trade. However, some efforts have been made to reinvigorate the field with academic rigour: R&D studies have given way to a wider range of case histories regarding weapons development.[68] Furthermore, technological assessments seem to have attracted renewed attention, especially in Europe.[69] Lastly, Barry Buzan's new book should be considered as an indication of a rejuvenation of military-technology research.[70]

Finally, international-security studies designate the large area where strategic studies and international relations overlap. More specifically, research conducted under this heading focusses on the study of wars and interstate competitive/co-operative relations within the framework of the international-security system. Moreover, it is important to note that this fifth item on our traditional agenda is perhaps the one that has been most heavily influenced by the realist paradigm in its classical form. But, a large gap has opened at this level between the study of war and the study of international-security relations; each subfield has developed its own theories and concepts, although both areas should have been closely associated because the conditions for peace and security can be inferred from the sources of conflict. In this regard, we posit that this area would probably benefit the most from the theoretical debate that stems from the next item on our proposed research agenda.

Our suggested "progressive" theoretical agenda is composed mainly of innovative and tentative proposals. In essence, what we advocate is that strategic studies join the international relations debate and concentrate its attention on specific and relevant concepts that challenge its core assumptions and its general worldview. Of course, one does not expect strategists to willingly undermine their credos, but it might be hoped that the dialectics of doubt and orthodoxy will permit the realist paradigm to transcend its categories while maintaining its ascendency, as it has done in the past. In this context, five concepts attract our attention, because of their importance in the current international relations debate and their relevance for strategic studies.

Security is probably the core concept of strategic studies. States are concerned with self-preservation, not with seeking to maximize power for power's sake. On the contrary, recognizing a trade-off between self-aggrandizement and self-preservation, they realize that a relentless search for universal domination may jeopardize their security. In other words, security is the ultimate goal of strategy, not victory or power or hegemony. Paradoxically, although the term itself is widely used by strategists, "when we search for a conceptual literature on security relatively little comes to hand, and there is certainly nothing equivalent to a coherent school of thought like the realists on power."[71] Considering the importance of the concept, research on security should certainly be a priority for strategic-studies analysts. One such analyst, Barry Buzan, has already made, in *People, States and Fear*, an essential contribution to our understanding of the concept, and in doing so has freed security from the strait-jacket of national security and related it to both the subnational level (individual security) and to the international-systemic one (international security). This milestone book opens new doors and, at the same time, raises unanswered questions that cry out for further research. As Buzan notes: "if security is placed in its proper, larger perspective, then strategic studies is free to make its important, specialized contributions to the study of the national security problem, without the suspicion that it is the front for vested interests in the domestic game of national security policy-making."[72]

Another concept, power, has attracted some recent attention precisely because the prevailing literature on the subject, although massive, has been perceived as unsatisfactory on several counts. David Baldwin has detected three common biases that distort the analysis of power, defined as the principal means by which a state seeks to attain security.[73] The first is the tendency to "exaggerate the fungibility of power resources," that is, to overstate the ability of a state to harness *all types* of resources to fulfil its security needs in *all kinds* of contingencies. The second is the practice of regarding military power resources as the "ultimate" power base — a base whose efficacy is often overestimated. The third, Baldwin terms the overemphasis "on conflict and negative sanctions at the expense of emphasis on cooperation and positive sanctions." Baldwin instructs strategists, wisely in our view, to go back to the drawing board and undertake a thorough review of the concept of power. New and interesting angles have already been formulated. For example, it has been demonstrated that power and interdependence are closely associated concepts that imply, in practice, that power relations cannot be analyzed separately from the larger web of interstate relations.[74] In other words, a dominant state in military terms may, at other levels (e.g., trade), depend heavily on the very states it seems to dominate. Indeed, all parties to this type of interchange control some assets valued by the others, and consequently are induced to co-operate, at least to a certain extent. In fact, most if not all interesting international relations involve this contrasting mixture of power/dependence and conflict/co-operation. A conceptual analysis of power should be regarded as one of the most worthwhile research prospects for strategic studies, as it returns the concept of co-operation to the realm of strategy.

This leads naturally to our third and fourth conceptual challenges: the twin notions of regime and security co-operation, which have triggered a fascinating debate over the past decade.[75] In essence, this debate opposes realists, who hold firm to their traditional notions of state-egoism and balance of power, to a new breed of sophisticated liberals (or pluralists), who argue not only that states may learn to co-operate but also that their co-operation will tend toward institutionalization in the form of regimes (i.e., a set of principles, rules, and norms that govern states' interactions).[76] As the debate stands today, several fruitful arguments have been presented, but its most interesting feature is that it resembles a real dialogue, one that challenges strategic studies to explore new and uncharted territory, namely, strategies for co-operation as opposed to strategies of conflict.

Lastly, it has often been argued that realism does not properly account for changes in the structure of international relations. If one stresses, for instance, the system-maintenance function of "hegemonic stability," then how can one explain the cyclical rise and fall of hegemons? How does one explain the decline of Rome, Britain, or France, without resorting to clichés such as decadence? And, how does one account for the wars that, often if not always, accompany the fall of one hegemon and the rise of another? Is peaceful change impossible, and if so why? These questions have barely been touched upon in the strategic-studies literature. Yet, they are of utmost importance, because they point to the systemic roots of war. In this perspective, Robert Gilpin's *War and Change in World Politics* and Paul Kennedy's *Rise and Fall of Great Powers* are good examples of the type of research needed.[77]

Finally, the proposed strategic-studies research agenda would be incomplete if it did not also stress the need for more area research. More specifically, one should beware of generalizations inspired by ethnocentric security frameworks when attempting to understand politicomilitary situations in other parts of the world. Indeed, security issues in Latin America or Africa cannot be understood in the same manner as similar issues in Europe or North America because they do not reflect the same realities.[78] In other words, strategic studies are in dire need of area specialists in order to interpret the realities of Third World conflicts and defence policies in their own terms. Stephanie Newman rightly notes that, "while much has been written in recent years about the flow of arms to these states, there has been little systematic research on their defense doctrines."[79] As the number of wars and domestic conflicts continues to increase in these regions, the importance of tackling such issues grows.

Conclusion

Even though strategic studies may be alive and well in 1989, the field's practitioners should not "rest on their laurels." No doubt, many criticisms levelled against strategists in the last two decades have been misplaced. Nevertheless, important deficiencies continue to plague contemporary strategic studies. Basically, it is a fragmented discipline and lacks a solid and dynamic theoretical foundation. To solve this problem, we have suggested that the only viable alternative for strategic studies is to return to the fold of international relations. More specifically, in order to regain some homogeneity, strategic studies should clearly identify its home paradigm or worldview. Realism was and remains the best choice for such a "home paradigm," for we believe that the dynamism and the progressive character of the debate inspired by realism in the past ten years puts it unquestionably at the cutting edge of international relations theory.

APPENDIX

PROPOSED STRATEGIC-STUDIES RESEARCH AGENDA

A. Traditional Research Agenda

1. *Strategies and Military Doctrines (conventional, unconventional, nuclear)*
   a. General theories of strategy
   b. The roots of strategy: development of strategic doctrines
   c. Operational evaluation of strategies and doctrines
   d. Political analysis of strategies and doctrines: study of their impact on policy
2. *Defence and Security Policies*
   a. General theories of defence/security formation
   b. Decision making, psychological, leadership studies
   c. Analysis of bureaucratic politics
   d. Study of organizational structures and processes
   e. Analysis of specific political forces and behaviours (legislative bodies, pressure groups, media, public opinion)
   f. Defence economics: defence resource allocation, defence industrial-base studies, military-industrial complex, etc.
3. *Arms Control*
   a. General theories of arms control
   b. Arms-control policy making (see defence and security policies)
   c. Analysis of arms-control negotiating dynamics
   d. Analysis of the interactions between arms control and its international environment
4. *Military Technology*
   a. Development of military technology: R&D studies
   b. Military technology and strategy
   c. Military technology and politics
   d. Military technology and interstate competition: arms race; arms-trade and -transfer studies (including nuclear proliferation)
5. *International-Security Studies*
   a. General theories of war and conflict; their causes, their course, and their impact in systemic terms (polemology, conflict research, geopolitics)
   b. Studies of interstate competition in normative or analytical terms (i.e., power-balancing, international-crises studies, threat assessments, etc.)
   c. Alliances and interstate co-operation in the area of security

B. "Progressive" Theoretical Agenda (by key concepts)

1. Concept of security
2. Concept of power and interdependence
3. Concept of regime
4. Concept of co-operation
5. Concept of change in international relations

C. Mid-level Research Agenda; Specifically for Non-Western Security Issues

1. Comparative defence and security policies
2. Comparative strategies
3. Comparative conflict analysis (i.e., studies of Third World conflicts)
4. Military power and politics in less-developed countries (i.e., military regimes and their impact on politics and society)
5. North-South relations in the area of security and defence
6. South-South relations in the area of security and defence
7. Regional security studies (i.e., South East Asia, Central America, etc.)

NOTES

1. It certainly has been depicted in this manner in such publications as Lawrence Freedman, "Outsiders' Influence on Defence Policy — Part I: The Development of the Think Tank," *Journal of the Royal United Services Institute for Defence Studies* 127 (March 1982): 13–18; Gregg Herken, *Counsels of War* (New York: Knopf, 1985); and Fred Kaplan, *The Wizards of Armageddon* (New York: Touchstone, 1983).

2. James A. Smith, "Private Players in the Game of Nations," *The Washington Quarterly* 11 (Summer 1988): 19.

3. For example, see Colin S. Gray, *Strategic Studies and Public Policy: The American Experience* (Lexington: The University Press of Kentucky, 1982); and John Gellner, "Strategic Analysis in Canada," *International Journal* 33 (Summer 1978): 493–505.

4. Freedman, "Outsiders' Influence," 14.

5. See Philip Green, "Strategy, Politics, and Social Scientists," in *Strategic Thinking and Its Moral Implications*, ed. Morton Kaplan (Chicago: Center for Policy Study, University of Chicago, 1973), 39–68; and Hedley Bull, "Strategic Studies and Its Critics," *World Politics* 20 (July 1968): 593–605. The idea of a polemical split between strategic studies and peace research is more thoroughly developed in Michel Fortmann, "Les études stratégiques, défense d'une discipline," *Études Internationales* 17 (décembre 1986): 767–84.

6. Fortmann, "Les études stratégiques," 767–70.

7. Bull, "Strategic Studies and Its Critics," 599.

8. A.J.R. Groom, "Paradigms in Conflict: The Strategist, the Conflict Researcher and the Peace Researcher," *Review of International Studies* 14 (April 1988): 105.

9. Michael Howard, "The Strategic Approach to International Relations," *British Journal of International Studies* 2 (April 1976): 73.

10. Ken Booth, *Strategy and Ethnocentrism* (New York: Holmes and Meier, 1979).

11. Ken Booth, "The Evolution of Strategic Thinking," in *Contemporary Strategy I: Theories and Concepts*, ed. John Baylis, Ken Booth, John Garnett and Phil Williams (London: Croom Helm, 1987), 55–63.

12. See Lawrence Freedman, "The Study of War: Indignation, Influence, and Strategic Studies," *International Affairs* 40 (Spring 1984): 207–19.

13. Colin S. Gray, *Strategic Studies: A Critical Assessment* (London: Aldwych, 1982), 117.

14. See Colin S. Gray, "What RAND Hath Wrought," *Foreign Policy*, no. 4 (Fall 1971): 111–29; and Bernard Brodie, "Why Were We So (Strategically) Wrong?" *Foreign Policy*, no. 5 (Winter 1971/72): 151–61.

15. Michael Howard, "Too Serious a Matter: Politicians and the Pentagon," *Times Literary Supplement*, September 6, 1974, 946.

16. See Morris Janowitz, "Towards a Redefinition of Military Strategy in International Relations," *World Politics* 28 (July 1974): 478.

17. See Barry Posen, *The Sources of Military Doctrines: France, Britain, and Germany Between the World Wars* (Ithaca, N.Y.: Cornell University Press, 1984); and Jack Snyder, *The Ideology of the Offensive: Decision-Making and the Disaster of 1914* (Ithaca, N.Y.: Cornell University Press, 1984).

18. For example, see Herman Kahn, *On Thermonuclear War* (New York: Macmillan, 1969); and Ashton B. Carter, John D. Steinbruner, and Charles A. Zarket, eds., *Managing Nuclear Operations* (Washington: The Brookings Institution, 1987).

19. See, for example, Thucydides, *The History of the Peloponnesian War*, ed., in translation, Sir Richard Livingstone (New York: Galaxy, 1960); and Xenophon, *The Persian Expedition*, trans. Rex Warner (New York: Penguin, 1949).

20. Quoted in Felix Gilbert, "Machiavelli: The Renaissance of the Art of War," in *Makers of Modern Strategy: From Machiavelli to the Nuclear Age*, ed. Peter Paret (Princeton: Princeton University Press, 1986), 11.

21. Stephen M. Walt, "The Search for a Science of Strategy: A Review Essay on Makers of Modern Strategy," *International Security* 12 (Summer 1987): 140–65 (see, specifically, 141–44).

22. B.H. Liddell Hart, *Strategy: The Indirect Approach*, 6th ed. (London: Faber and Faber, 1967), 335.

23. John E. Tashjean, "The Classics of Military Thought: Appreciations and Agenda," *Defense Analysis* 3 (September 1987): 246.

24. Robert E. Osgood, *NATO: The Entangling Alliance* (Chicago: University of Chicago Press, 1962), 5.

25. See, for example, Edward N. Luttwak, *Strategy: The Logic of War and Peace* (Cambridge, Mass.: Harvard University Press, 1987); Colin S. Gray, "Across the Nuclear Divide — Strategic Studies, Past and Present," *International Security* 2 (Summer 1977): 24–46; and Colin S. Gray, *The Geopolitics of the Nuclear Era: Heartland, Rimlands, and the Technological Revolution* (New York: Crane, Russak, 1977).

26. Irnerio Seminatore, "Evolution de la pensée stratégique 1945–1985," *Stratégique* 35, no. 1 (1985): 144; and Louis Le Hégarat, "La Stratégie, théorie d'une pratique?" *Défense nationale*, 40e année (mars 1984): 51–67.

27. Michael Howard, *The Causes of War* (Cambridge, Mass.: Harvard University Press, 1984), 88.

28. See Clausewitz's thoughts on this subject as discussed in Michael I. Handel, "Clausewitz in the Age of Technology," *Journal of Strategic Studies* 9 (June–September 1986): 73–74.

29. The term "grand strategy" was first thoroughly defined by B.H. Liddell Hart in *Strategy* (New York: Praeger, 1954), 336.

30. Julian Lider, *Military Theory* (New York: St. Martin's, 1983), 6.

31. See Edward N. Luttwak, *The Grand Strategy of the Soviet Union* (New York: St. Martin's, 1983); and Colin S. Gray, *The Geopolitics of Super Power* (Lexington: University Press of Kentucky, 1988).

32. As noted by Hervé Couteau-Bégarie in "L'histoire militaire entre la pensée stratégique et la nouvelle histoire," *Stratégique* 35, no. 4 (1985): 67.

33. Michael Howard, "The Classical Strategists," in *Problems of Modern Strategy*, ed. Alastair Buchan (New York: Praeger, 1970), 75–76.

34. Laurence Martin, "The Future of Strategic Studies," *Journal of Strategic Studies* 3 (December 1980): 95–96.

35. The quote is from Bull, "Strategic Studies and Its Critics," 593.

36. See Gabriel Almond and S.J. Genco, "Clouds, Clocks, and the Study of Politics," *World Politics* 29, no. 4 (1977): 504.

37. Groom, "Paradigms in Conflict," 97.

38. See Michael Banks, "The Inter-Paradigm Debate," in *International Relations: A Handbook of Current Theory*, ed. Margot Light and A.J.R. Groom (London: Pinter, 1985), 7–25. "Structuralism" in this context should not be confused with "structural realism."

39. Banks, "Inter-Paradigm Debate," 17.

40. Richard Little, "Structuralism and Neo-Realism," in *International Relations*, 75–76.

41. See P. Bourdieu, J.C. Chamboredon, and J.C. Passeron, *Le métier de sociologue* (Paris: Mouton/Bordas, 1973), 32.

42. K.R. Minogue, "Political Epiphenomenalism: The Quest for Political Reality," *Political Studies* 20, no. 4 (Fall 1972): 467.

43. Almond and Genco, "Clouds, Clocks, and the Study of Politics," 497.

44. J. David Singer, "An Assessment of Peace Research," *International Security* 1, no. 1 (Summer 1976): 123–24.

45. Groom, "Paradigms in Conflict," 111; Johan Galtung, *Essays in Peace Research* (Copenhagen: Ejlers, 1975), 256.

46. See Bruce Bueno de Mesquita, *The War Trap* (New Haven: Yale University Press, 1981); Bruce Russett, *The Prisoners of Insecurity* (San Francisco: Freeman, 1983); J. David Singer, *Wages of War: 1815–1965* (New York: Wiley and Son, 1972); and Johan Galtung, "A Structural Theory of Aggression," *Journal of Peace Research* 1 (1964): 95–119.

47. For examples of this school of thought, see E.S. Quade, "Analysis for Military Decisions," *RAND Papers*, no. R-387-PR, November 1964; and Alain C. Enthoven and Wayne K. Smith, *How Much Is Enough? Shaping the Defense Program 1961–1969* (New York: Harper and Row, 1971).

48. Gray, *Strategic Studies and Public Policy*, 190–91.

49. Ruth Leger Sivard, *World Military and Social Expenditures 1987–1988*, 12th ed. (New York: World Priorities, 1987), 6.

50. John D. Young, *International Political Theory, Political Science and the Interparadigm Debate: The Natural Selection of Realism*, Occasional Paper no. 19 (Kingston: Queen's Centre for International Relations, 1987), 4.

51. John Gerard Ruggie, "Continuity and Transformation in the World Polity: Toward a Neorealist Synthesis," in *Neorealism and Its Critics*, ed. Robert O. Keohane (New York: Columbia University Press, 1986), 133; also see Kenneth N. Waltz, "Reductionist and Systematic Theories," in *Neorealism*, 60. There has been an unfortunate degree of confusion

concerning the meaning of "neorealism," in large part because of the misleading title of the volume that Keohane edited, which focusses on the controversy attending the theoretical propositions of Kenneth Waltz. Whatever else he may be (and we suggest "structural realist" is as good a label as any), Waltz does not appear to us to be a "neorealist."

52. Robert O. Keohane, "Theory of World Politics: Structural Realism and Beyond," in *Neorealism*, 183.

53. Young, *International Political Theory*, 6.

54. Gray, *Strategic Studies and Public Policy*, 188.

55. Imre Lakatos, "Falsification and the Methodology of Scientific Research Programmes," in *Criticism and the Growth of Knowledge*, ed. I. Lakatos and A. Mustgrave (Cambridge: Cambridge University Press, 1970), 116–22; as cited in Keohane, "Theory of World Politics," 161.

56. Stanley Hoffmann, "An American Social Science: International Relations," *Daedalus* 106 (Summer 1977): 45.

57. No offence is intended. On the contrary, according to our argument we need more divas, not fewer.

58. Joseph S. Nye, Jr., and Sean M. Lynn-Jones, "International Security Studies: A Report of a Conference on the State of the Field," *International Security* 12 (Spring 1988): 20–21.

59. Barry Buzan, *An Introduction to Strategic Studies: Military Technology and International Relations* (New York: St. Martin's, 1987).

60. Posen, *Sources of Military Doctrines*, 34–80; Snyder, *Ideology of the Offensive*, 15–40; and Donald Snow, *Nuclear Strategy in a Dynamic World* (Birmingham: The University Press of Alabama, 1981), 12–22.

61. See Michael T. Klare and P. Kornbluh, eds., *Low Intensity Warfare: Counterinsurgency, Proinsurgency, and Antiterrorism in the Eighties* (New York: Pantheon, 1988).

62. Consult the following major texts on the subject: Graham Allison, *Essence of Decision: Explaining the Cuban Missile Crisis* (Boston: Little, Brown, 1971); Morton Halperin, *Bureaucratic Politics and Foreign Policy* (Washington: The Brookings Institution, 1974); John D. Steinbruner, *The Cybernetic Theory of Decision* (Princeton: Princeton University Press, 1974); and R. Hilsman, *The Politics of Policy Making in Defense and Foreign Affairs: Conceptual Models and Bureaucratic Politics* (Englewood Cliffs, N.J.: Prentice-Hall, 1987).

63. Several of these approaches are presented in a systematic and comparative form in J. Reichart and S. Sturm, *American Defense Policy*, 5th ed. (Baltimore: Johns Hopkins University Press, 1983), 493–718; also see D. Murray and P. Viotti, *The Defense Policies of Nations: A Comparative Study* (Baltimore: Johns Hopkins University Press, 1982).

64. A few scattered exceptions may be mentioned: see Jacques Gansler, *The Defense Industry* (Cambridge, Mass.: MIT Press, 1980); W.J. Weida and F. Gertcher, *The Political Economy of National Defense* (Boulder, Colo.: Westview, 1987); and A. Mintz, *The Politics of Resource Allocation in the US Department of Defense* (Boulder, Colo.: Westview, 1988).

65. This "technical" approach to arms control has been criticized by Robin Ranger, *Arms and Politics 1958–1978* (New York: Basic Books, 1980). It is important to note, however, that we do not agree with Ranger's interpretation of the problem.

66. Buzan, *Introduction to Strategic Studies*, 17.

67. Alex Roland, "Technology and War: A Bibliographic Essay," in *Military Enterprise and Technological Change*, ed. M.R. Smith (Cambridge, Mass.: MIT Press, 1985), 348.

68. Important texts on this subject are Edmund Beard, *Developing the ICBM* (New York: Columbia University Press, 1976); Ted Greenwood, *Making the MIRV: A Study in Defense Decision-Making* (Cambridge, Mass.: MIT Press, 1976); Harvey Sapolsky, *The Polaris System Development* (Cambridge, Mass.: Harvard University Press, 1972); and Lauren Holland and Robert Hoover, *The MX Decision* (Boulder, Colo.: Westview, 1985).

69. For example, see Marlies ter Borg and M.J.W. Tulp, *Defense Technology Assessment: Improving Defense Decision-Making* (Amsterdam: Nederlandse Organisatie voor Technologisch Aspectenonderzoek, September 1987).

70. Buzan, *Introduction to Strategic Studies.*

71. Barry Buzan, *People, States and Fear* (Chapel Hill: University of North Carolina Press, 1982), 3.

72. Buzan, *People, States and Fear*, 257.

73. David A. Baldwin, "Power Analysis and World Politics: New Trends Versus Old Tendencies," *World Politics* 31, no. 1 (1978): 192.

74. See Robert O. Keohane and Joseph S. Nye, Jr., *Power and Interdependence: World Politics in Transition* (Boston: Little, Brown, 1977); and Robert O. Keohane and Joseph S. Nye, Jr., "Power and Interdependence Revisited," *International Organization* 41 (Fall 1987): 724–53.

75. See Robert Jervis, "Cooperation Under the Security Dilemma," *World Politics* 30, no. 2 (1978): 167–214; Ernest Haas, "Why Collaborate? Issue Linkage and International Regimes," *World Politics* 32, no. 3 (1980): 357–405; Robert Jervis, "Security Regimes," *International Organization* 36, no. 2 (1982): 357–79; Charles Lipson, "International Cooperation in Economic and Security Affairs," *World Politics* 35, no. 1 (1984): 1–24; Joseph S. Nye, Jr., "Nuclear Learning and U.S.-Soviet Security Regimes," *International Organization* 41, no. 3 (1987): 371–402; Robert Jervis, "From Balance to Concert: A Study of International Security Cooperation," *World Politics* 36, no. 1 (1985): 58–79; Kenneth Oye, "Explaining Cooperation Under Anarchy: Hypotheses and Strategies," *World Politics* 35, no. 1 (1985): 1–25; and Robert Jervis, "Realism, Game Theory and Cooperation," *World Politics* 40, no. 3 (1988): 317–49.

76. Jervis, "Security Regimes," 357.

77. See Robert Gilpin, *War and Change in World Politics* (New York: Cambridge University Press, 1981), and Paul Kennedy, *The Rise and Fall of the Great Powers* (New York: Random House, 1987).

78. See A. Bozeman, "Political Intelligence in Non-Western Societies: Suggestions for Comparative Research," in *Comparing Foreign Intelligence*, ed. R. Godson (New York: Pergamon-Brassey's, 1988), 115–55.

79. Stephanie Newman, ed., *Defense Planning in Less Industrialized States* (Lexington: Lexington, 1984), 2.

SELECT BIBLIOGRAPHY

Bull, Hedley. "Strategic Studies and Its Critics." *World Politics* 20, no. 4 (July 1968): 593–605.

Buzan, Barry. *An Introduction to Strategic Studies: Military Technology & International Relations*. New York: St. Martin's, 1987.

———. "Peace, Power, and Security: Contending Concepts in the Study of International Relations." *Journal of Peace Research* 21, no. 2 (1984): 111–25.

———. *People, States, and Fear: The National Security Problem in International Relations*. Chapel Hill: University of North Carolina Press, 1983.

Fortmann, Michel. "Les études stratégiques, défense d'une discipline." *Études Internationales* 17 (décembre 1986): 767–84.

Freedman, Lawrence. "Has Strategy Reached a Dead-End?" *Futures* 11 (April 1979): 122–31.

———. "Indignation, Influence and Strategic Studies." *International Affairs* 40 (Spring 1984): 207–19.

———. "Outsiders' Influence on Defence Policy — Part I: The Development of the Think Tank." *Journal of the Royal United Services Institute for Defence Studies* 127 (March 1982): 13–18

Garnett, John. "Strategic Studies and Its Assumptions." In *Contemporary Strategy I*, ed. John Baylis, Ken Booth, John Garnett and Phil Williams. London: Croom Helm, 1987.

Gray, Colin S. "Across the Nuclear Divide — Strategic Studies, Past and Present." *International Security* 2 (Summer 1977): 24–46.

———. *Strategic Studies: A Critical Assessment*. London: Aldwych, 1982.

———. *Strategic Studies and Public Policy: The American Experience*. Lexington: University Press of Kentucky, 1982.

Groom, A.J.R. "Paradigms in Conflict: The Strategists, the Conflict Researcher and the Peace Researcher." *Review of International Studies* 14 (April 1988): 97–115.

———. "Strategy." In *International Relations: A Handbook of Current Theory*, ed. Margot Light and A.J.R. Groom. London: Pinter, 1985.

Howard, Michael. "The Strategic Approach to International Relations." *British Journal of International Studies* 2 (April 1976): 67–75.

Keohane, Robert O. "Realism, Neorealism and the Study of World Politics." In *Neorealism and Its Critics*, ed. Robert O. Keohane. New York: Columbia University Press, 1986.

Legault, Albert. "Vingt-cinq ans d'études stratégiques: essai critique et survol de la documentation." In *Analyse des relations internationales: approches, concepts et données*, ed. B. Korany. Montréal: Gaetan Morin, 1987.

Martin, Laurence. "The Future of Strategic Studies." *Journal of Strategic Studies* 3 (December 1980): 91–99.

HISTORY AND STRUCTURE IN THE THEORY OF INTERNATIONAL RELATIONS

R.B.J. Walker

The explanation of social and political life is a notoriously contentious enterprise, and the Anglo-American discipline of international relations is no exception. As with so many other disciplines that have been shaped by the broader ambitions of postwar social science, controversy has occurred largely on the terrain of epistemology. All too often, the more far-reaching epistemological problems posed by those who seek to understand what is involved in making knowledge claims about social and political processes have been pushed aside in favour of more restricted concerns about method and research technique. Narrowing the range of potential dispute in this manner has undoubtedly enhanced an appearance of professional solidarity. But it has also obscured many of the more troublesome, and in my view much more important, fractures visible to anyone now canvassing contemporary debates about the general nature and possibility of social and political enquiry.

In this chapter, I want to draw attention to some of these fractures, and to indicate their significance for currently influential discussions of appropriate research strategies in the analysis of world politics.[1] To begin with, I distinguish between different philosophical contexts in which appropriate research strategies may be judged. Here, I reflect on a recent assessment of these strategies offered by Robert Keohane, who judges them primarily in the context of epistemological and methodological criteria. I then explore some of the broader ontological, ethical, and ideological dilemmas that are at stake in the literature that Keohane discusses. I am especially concerned with the tension between the atemporal structuralism that informs currently fashionable socioscientific approaches (in particular the theory of international regimes and structural realism), and approaches that stress the priority of historical interpretation.

While my primary intention is simply to insist on the significance of themes that are played down in Keohane's analysis rather than to pursue them in any detail, I also argue in favour of three broad conclusions. First, I affirm the priority of history, and thus of approaches that stress interpretation, practice, and the critique of reification. Second, I insist that differences between approaches to world politics must be addressed at the level of basic ontological assumptions:

the possibility of empirical research strategies is a significant but decidedly secondary matter. Third, I suggest that the contemporary analysis of world politics poses fundamental questions of political theory — questions that remain interesting and provocative despite socioscientific attempts to reduce them to problems of utilitarian calculation and empirical testing.

Beyond Hegemony, Before Epistemology

In a recent text, first delivered as a presidential address to the International Studies Association in 1988, Robert Keohane offered what was, in some respects, a generous assessment of the different perspectives currently used to examine developing patterns of interstate co-operation.[2] Distinguishing between his own widely influential "rationalistic" orientation and positions that he identified as the "reflective" approach, Keohane was relatively sympathetic to the contributions of those who have criticized the rationalists for their reliance on ahistorical utilitarian presuppositions adapted from liberal microeconomics and public-choice theory. Moreover, his claims for the explanatory power of the rationalist or utilitarian position were relatively modest. The text as a whole was written as an invitation to a more constructive dialogue between what have been characterized as potentially complementary schools of thought.

Nevertheless, the central argument of the text was bold and blunt: the reflective school has "failed to develop a coherent research program of their own" — coherent, that is, in the sense that it bears comparison with the paradigmatic research program exemplified by the structuralist models of Kenneth Waltz or the utilitarian categories that constitute the theory of international regimes. An encouraging opening toward a positive assessment of the plurality of theoretical perspectives was thereby quickly closed off by privileging a highly specific — not to say philosophically contested — account of what a proper research program should look like.

It is not difficult to find evidence of the continuing influence of similar claims that scholarly controversies should be resolved on the privileged terrain of empirical method. These claims have been especially tenacious in international relations, although even here they have begun to seem curiously old-fashioned. One of the significant achievements of the debates about socioscientific explanation in the 1960s and 1970s has been a much greater awareness of the controversial character of what social science is or should be. Invocations of the logic of explanation in the physical sciences have become relatively rare, not least because our understanding of what is involved in even the most precise sciences is sharply contested. The general lesson that seems to have been drawn is not that empirical social science is impossible or undesirable, but that its achievements and possibilities ought to be placed in a more modest perspective.

This lesson is reflected in Keohane's emphasis on the context-specific character of generalization, as well as in the emphasis on model-building in the work of the utilitarian rationalists more generally. The hope, of course, is that the models offered for empirical testing can transcend their origins as analogical or metaphorical speculation. Whether the utilitarian images that have been deployed recently to explain interstate co-operation are successful in this respect will undoubtedly remain contentious. And some students of world politics will continue to be more fascinated by the social, political, ideological, and philosophical conditions under which a liberal-utilitarian account of human action can aspire to hegemony in a discipline that continues to raise far more interesting questions than it provides plausible answers.

Meanwhile, those concerned with what it means to study social and political life have turned away from the largely discredited positivistic accounts of scientific explanation to a much broader arena of philosophical debate, one in which the explorations of literary theorists are treated at least as seriously as pre-Kuhnian dogmas about cumulative scientific knowledge. Some have been impressed by the vitality of interpretive or hermeneutic procedures, especially where the old Cartesian assumption that language can be separated from the world in which it participates is resisted. Some have become immersed in controversies generated by the revival of political economy — controversies in which it has been relatively difficult to erase fundamental philosophical and ideological differences through the claims of universal method. Others have been drawn into forms of critical theory associated with, say, the Frankfurt School or poststructuralism and thus into long-standing controversies about modernity and late/counter/post-modernity. Whatever one makes of such trends, they undoubtedly reflect a different intellectual atmosphere than prevailed when the discipline of international relations became institutionalized as a major branch of social science some three decades or so ago.[3] Keohane was and is clearly aware of these developments. But, in affirming a more socioscientific account of what a proper research agenda should look like, he minimized much of their significance and complexity.

This minimization is apparent initially from the very broad range of perspectives that Keohane grouped together as exemplars of the reflective approach. They include the broad sociological influences on the work of John Ruggie, Hayward Alker's explorations of dialectical logics, Friedrich Kratochwil's concern with analytic philosophies of action, and the postmodernist sensitivities that have guided Richard Ashley's critical commentaries on the modernist impulses affirmed by the utilitarians. If we add all those who have resisted the charms of socioscientific theories of international relations by drawing on neo-Marxist forms of political economy, theories of ideology and discourse, or critical and interpretive forms of political thought, the ranks of the reflective school could be made to swell considerably. And, if we then think about the potential range of ontological, ethical, and ideological commitments that are likely to be held by such a diverse group of scholars, Keohane's hope for some kind of convergence with the insights of utilitarian rationalism seems rather exaggerated.

In this sense, much of Keohane's discussion is reminiscent of the quite misleading exchange in the 1960s between "scientific" and "traditionalist" approaches to international relations. Keohane's judgement reflects epistemological preoccupations, and is reinforced through an undiminished confidence in the promises of modern social science. However, as with the earlier exchange, many of the crucial differences between the utilitarian rationalists and the historically inclined reflectivists extend to prior and even more contentious problems, many of which have long been assumed to call the claims of modern social science into question.

In the earlier exchange, debate was largely preoccupied with contrasting accounts of what scientific explanation involves and how the more historical and even philosophical concerns of the traditionalists might be updated through the judicious application of appropriate method.[4] Yet, in initiating the debate, Hedley Bull offered a critique of the pretensions of scientific method that rested less on claims about knowledge as such than on arguments about the very nature of world politics. Scientific method was inappropriate, he argued, because of what world politics is. He was especially concerned with the dangers of the "domestic analogy," that is, the transfer of philosophical and theoretical premises derived from the analysis of political community within states to the analysis of relations between states. After all, from the classical Greek accounts of life in the *polis* to more recent accounts of the persistence of the state as the dominant expression of political power, interstate relations have been treated as quite fundamentally different from political life within states, in both their essential character and potential.

Unfortunately Bull's underlying concerns about whether interstate relations or world politics are, in principle, any different from politics within states were quickly translated into more limited epistemological questions about how analysis should be conducted. While initiated on the ground of an ontological dualism — statist community and the society of states, or in the unfortunately more common rendition, community and anarchy — debate quickly turned to the claims of an epistemological monism. Consequently, where Bull articulated a traditional claim that relations between states are distinctive enough to justify a separate discipline and different research strategies (not to mention an account of the relation between knowledge and power, or truth and violence, that would seem scandalous in the context of theories of political life within states), socioscientific approaches have affirmed a fundamental continuity. Hence, the possibility, so eagerly grasped by those searching for empirically testable models, of transferring assumptions, metaphors, research strategies, and accounts of rational action from one context to the other.

Nevertheless, Bull's concerns cannot be made to disappear quite so easily. It may now be common to speak of "interdependence," to analyze international regimes, or to enquire about the potentials of international organization, but few would argue that we have moved from a world of statist communities to a global community. The early-modern European account of political life as the establishment of relatively autonomous political communities coexisting in territorial space has yet to be superseded by a coherent account of a common planetary identity or a cosmopolitan human community. The epistemological claim to a universally applicable scientific method thus coexists quite uneasily with the contrary claim, articulated variously in ontological, ethical, and ideological forms, that human life is essentially fragmented. Similar problems have beset students of comparative politics or anthropology, where they have generated considerable controversy. In international relations, they have captured the attention of a few critical theorists and defenders of the more traditional approaches represented by Bull, but for the most part they have gone unnoticed, obscured by the achievements of what can now plausibly pass for the socioscientific orthodoxy.

Keohane's more recent discussion poses similar difficulties. Many of the differences between the positions he examines arise far more from disagreements about what it is scholars think they are studying than from disagreements about how to study it. The latter depend in large part upon the former. To attempt to turn all theoretical disputes into differences over method and epistemology is to presume that we have acceptable answers to questions about what kind of world it is that we are trying to know. This is a rather large presumption, as Keohane partly — but only partly — recognizes. Moreover, even if Keohane's distinction proves useful at some level, it is not altogether clear why the methodological prescriptions of the utilitarian rationalists should be treated as the successful orthodoxy on whose terms the contributions of the reflective school should be judged. It might be argued, for example, that there are very strong continuities between the work of the reflective theorists — Kratochwil and Ashley especially, though quite distinctively — and the work of Bull and others who begin their work by attempting to come to terms with the historically constituted distinction between politics within and between statist communities.[5] Keohane's polarity might then be reversed by suggesting that utilitarian rationalism merely adds some interesting analytic models and a distinctive vocabulary to traditions of considerable standing and achievement. Claims about what constitutes orthodoxy in this respect can vary considerably, depending on the cultural and temporal horizons of the claimant.

In any case, the appropriate context in which to situate Keohane's discussion is less the controversy about social science than the even earlier "great debate" between realists and idealists. While it is against the obvious limitations of that debate that the promises of social science were articulated in the first place, the categories through which that debate was constituted have remained very influential. In fact, far from being merely one of a series of debates that have characterized the history of the discipline, the distinction between political realism and political idealism has provided the broad, but severely restricted, context within which other disputes about appropriate method or the priority of state-centred accounts of world politics could occur at all.[6] Framed within this distinction, "metaphysics," "ethics," and "ideology" have become the names for roles in an old and obviously decrepit Manichean theatre. Tamed in this way, it is hardly surprising that they have been marginalized in favour of the louder and seemingly more up-to-date claims of social science. Nevertheless, as Keohane moves closer and closer to the primary themes that distinguish utilitarian rationalists from historically inclined reflectivists, the echoes of this older debate become much clearer.

To draw attention to the connection between current controversies and this older debate is certainly not to suggest that the categories of either realist or idealist can now offer much useful guidance. As roles in a Manichean theatre, these terms have served primarily to close off serious discussion in a manner that has helped to insulate the discipline of international debate ever since. Rather, the categories of realist and idealist, as they were deployed in these debates — and as they have since come to provide convenient labels and systems of classification — should be understood as the primary sites at which the basic assumptions governing the study of world politics have been left to congeal in forms that require little further exploration. As such, they provide a place to begin, and a place at which awkward questions may be deferred. Within their stylized horizons, it is possible to honour all those who, for some reason, are revered as contributors to the distilled wisdom of tradition. Thucydides, Machiavelli, Hobbes, Rousseau, and the rest may then commune with more modern masters such as E.H. Carr, Hans J. Morgenthau, and their even more modern disciples.

Much of the literature that Keohane seeks to judge as contributions to empirical social science can also be understood as attempts to re-engage with the philosophical and theoretical dilemmas that were packed away when the categories of realist and idealist were constructed as the appropriate arena in which dispute could be permitted to occur in an orderly and unthreatening manner. Unpacking these categories, it is possible to reformulate questions about, say, the relationship between claims to legitimate political community within states and the legitimacy of violence in relations between political communities; or the relative claims of people as human beings and people as citizens; or the tension between power and knowledge, as this has been mediated by the claims of state-sovereignty.

Such questions have come to be treated largely as the preserve of those toiling in the vineyards of social and political theory. They certainly raise all the awkward philosophical themes designated as ontology, ethics, ideology, or even the relation between theory and practice. These are themes that most scholars in the discipline of international relations have been loath to confront, except on terms permitted by the discipline's great debates. These are also themes that are at play in the differing perspectives canvassed by Keohane. To enquire into patterns of interdependence or dependence, or the emergence of international regimes and institutions, is to work both within and against inherited accounts of the possibility of political community. These accounts, I believe, are inherently problematic in ways that are systematically obscured by ahistorical utilitarianism and the categories of realist and idealist alike.

The assumption informing the alternative reading of contemporary perspectives on world politics to be sketched here, therefore, is that the central task confronting students of world politics at this juncture is not the refinement of utilitarian calculation or socioscientific method, but a renewed engagement with questions to which the categories of realist and idealist constitute only a great refusal. These categories fix historically contingent answers to questions about the nature and location of political community, questions that are necessarily reopened by any attempt to understand what such terms as international regime, or international institution, or interdependence and dependence, and especially *world* politics, can possibly mean.

Keohane rightly emphasizes the significance of historical interpretation for all those who have challenged the structuralist tendencies of the utilitarian rationalists, and it is this theme that I want to dwell on here. For, one way of reframing an account of current debates about approaches to world politics is to emphasize how contrasting perspectives have tended to privilege either history and time, on the one hand, or structure and space, on the other. The tendency to privilege either history or structure rests upon historically constituted philosophical options. To emphasize one or the other is to generate distinctive theoretical puzzles. These options and puzzles explain part — but only part — of what is at stake in the opposition between realism and idealism. They also underlie many of the distinctive claims made on behalf of the criticisms voiced against socioscientific forms of structural realism and regime theory. Moreover, the categories through which the privileging of either history or structure is sustained are themselves the product of distinctive historical conditions. They now tend to freeze or reify complex philosophical questions into a permanent problem: either an eternal debate between realists and idealists or a progressive struggle to establish a properly empirical social science against the recalcitrant metaphysicians, ideologists, historicists, hermeneuticists, or critical theorists. Neither of these legacies seems likely to advance our understanding of the transformative character of contemporary world politics very far.

In exploring the tension between history and structure in the analysis of world politics in an introductory and schematic manner, I want to suggest that it provides a much clearer indication of what is at stake in many current debates in this context than is possible by fixing the discussion on the terrain of epistemology or method. Beginning with history, I move on to structure before returning to problems raised by Keohane's delineation of the options before us.

History, Structure, and Reification

Once upon a time, according to a well-known story, the world was not as it is now. Precisely what it was like is not clear. Accounts vary, depending on when and where once-upon-a-time is supposed to have occurred. Records and memories are notoriously deceptive, and require careful coding and interpretation. The skills of the storyteller are judged more by the expectations of the audience than by the authenticity of the stamps in some time-traveller's passport. Even so, this particular story remains evocative. It tells of feudal modes of production, hierarchical arrangements of power and authority, and medieval forms of life and consciousness. This story can be told in many different versions and under many different titles. The version that concerns me here might be called "life before international relations."

The telling of this story is often short and snappy, a preface to an equally concise dénouement: feudalism gives way to capitalism, more modern forms of life and consciousness emerge, and political community gradually coheres around the sovereign claims of state. This story, in turn, has a sequel, full of plots etched deeply in the contemporary imagination. This sequel has come in two quite distinctive, but mutually interdependent variations.

One, especially favoured by those who refer to their stories as histories of social and political thought, impresses us with accounts of the progressive emancipation of statist political communities and the emergence of modern conceptions of freedom, justice, and rationality. Another, favoured by an apparently more hard-bitten breed who refer to their scripts as theories of international relations, depress us with tragic tales of violence, intrigue, and the triumph of might over right. In both versions, however, the story about how the world was not as it is now recedes into the background, and we are gripped instead by seemingly more topical tales of the world that has become what it is.

References to accounts of medieval life or of the complex transformations of early-modern Europe as mere stories may seem excessively flippant, given the massive and erudite literature that has undoubtedly advanced our understanding of these phases of human experience. Nevertheless, this literature is not invoked very often in the contemporary analysis of world politics. Significant exceptions to this general rule are not difficult to find, but, for the most part, influential strategies of analysis have been framed against a highly generalized story about when, where, and how interstate politics emerged as an appropriate object for scholarly reflection. In this sense, the well-known stories continue to exercise a powerful hold over categories of analysis and methodological strategies. At least four groups of puzzles are implicated in these stories — puzzles that regularly enter into ongoing discussions about what the analysis of world politics ought to involve.

One set of puzzles arises from the rather sharp disjunction between the comfortable rhythms in which the best-known stories about the early-modern period have been reiterated and the untidy, even recalcitrant, evidence that enters into the deeply contested accounts offered by contemporary historians. While old distinctions between ancients and moderns remain deeply entrenched in popular accounts of where we have come from, the role of these distinctions as a legitimation of modernity against the presumed darkness that came before is readily transparent. While the grand narratives of Marx and Weber continue to offer crucial insights into the conjunctures of forces responsible for the emergence of capitalism, modernity, and the state, simple linear trajectories and unicausal theories have been sharply qualified by the details of multiple transitions. While we may remain impressed by the rapidity and scale of the socioeconomic innovations of the 16th and 17th centuries or the spectacular intellectual achievements of the Renaissance, it is increasingly clear that the transformations of the early-modern period grew out of processes that had already been underway for a considerable period. Continuities have come to seem at least as important as ruptures. Complex interactions between mutually causal forces now seem more impressive than the residual prejudices of a self-celebrating modernity.[7]

In short, the simple story of life before international relations — a story of an absence against which the presence of contemporary international relations can be defined — has become quite implausible. Yet, while often prepared to admit the inadequacy of the conventional stories, theorists of international relations are easily drawn into an affirmation of them as a convenient myth of origins. By identifying when interstate relations began and providing a sharp contrast with what came before, these stories offer a powerful account of what interstate politics must be, given what it has always been since the presumed beginning.

Without such a myth of origins, of course, a number of rather basic questions from the philosophy of history begin to assert themselves. To what extent does our interpretation of contemporary interstate politics depend on particular readings of macrohistory? To what extent might these readings be challenged by, say, anthropologists, or by macrohistorians who are more reluctant to place early-modern European experiences at the centre of their analysis? To what extent are these readings caught up in unacknowledged assumptions about progress, or evolution, or eternal return? To what extent is our understanding of the possibilities of contemporary transformations constrained by our assumptions about the historical processes that have made us what we are now? Threatened by the implications of such questions as these, a retreat to a clear point of origin, from which contemporary trajectories may be delineated and continuities generalized, can seem very comforting. Nevertheless, it has rarely escaped the notice of the more astute political commentators that the capacity to construct a myth of origins signifies enormous political advantage.

Similar questions are at play in a second set of puzzles that regularly beset analysts of world politics, puzzles that arise from competing accounts of the most appropriate point at which to identify the origin of the modern states-system. Once we move away from the most caricatured accounts of life before and after the rise of the state, the variety of presumed points of origin can be quite striking. Two options have been especially popular. One is to focus on the emergence of the state as a distinctive and relatively autonomous form of political community in late 15th-century Europe. Another is to stress the period in which claims of state-sovereignty became formalized and codified in international law. Here the Peace of Westphalia of 1648 serves as a crucial demarcation between an era still dominated by competing claims to religious universalism and hierarchical authority and an era of secular competition and co-operation among autonomous political communities. But, there are also analysts who would direct our attention to an earlier period. They may want to push accounts of relatively autonomous state authority back farther into the feudal era, or more usually, point to analogies between early-modern Europe and the states-systems of antiquity. And others prefer to focus on later dates on the grounds that, say, only in the 18th century does the states-system generate recognizably modern procedures and "rules of the game," or that only later still do we discover a system of relations between properly national states. Taking things to rather absurd extremes, it is even possible to derive the impression from some textbooks that interstate politics is an invention of the 20th century.

This rather elastic identification of points of origin again raises very serious questions about what an analysis of world politics ought to involve. To engage with the literature on the emergence and development of the states-system is to be impressed by the transformative quality of both the state and the character of relations between states. States can then appear to us as historically constituted and always subject to change. Distinctions between, say, the absolutist state, the nation-state, the welfare state, and the national-security state become very interesting. The Canadian state is likely to be a significantly different phenomenon ten years after the operationalization of the Canada–U.S. Free Trade Agreement than it is now. And yet this historicity of states is at odds with a contrary sense that, whatever their historical transformations, states and states-systems exhibit certain regularities across time. Scholars do claim to be able to make plausible analogies between, say, the struggles of Athens and Sparta and our own epoch. Canadian spokesmen on defence policy will continue to justify their proposed procurements in the name of Canadian sovereignty — a sovereignty that fixes a claim to permanence and continuity in the identity of Canada as an ongoing political community.

In this way, the perspectives of history begin to give way to those of structure. Sometimes this takes the form of definitions of some sort of permanent essence, of accounts of the interstate system as in principle always anarchical, for example, or of the state as always a maximizer of power, status, or its own welfare. Sometimes it takes the form of the comparative analysis of various structural configurations, of the differences between multipolar and bipolar systems, for example, or of systems with and systems without a dominant actor. In either case, the historicity of states and states-systems recedes into the background, and world politics begins to turn into a permanent game, one that can appear to have conformed more or less to the same rules since time immemorial.

This apparent continuity, this sense of permanence or at least repetition, is particularly attractive to scholars who seek to develop an explanatory science of the politics of states-systems. Problems from the philosophy of history are difficult to negotiate. The historicity of states-systems leads to the contentious constructions of historical sociology or political economy. Discontinuity and historical transformation have long been viewed as serious threats to the accumulation of objective knowledge. One cannot step into the same river twice, say some. We have only managed to interpret the world while the point is to change it, say others. Against temporal flux, contingency, idiosyncrasy, and revolutionary praxis, the identification of structural form offers an alluring possibility of a universalizing objectivity.

This leads directly to a third set of puzzles, those that arise from claims that there is, indeed, a firm body of knowledge about the character of interstate politics enshrined in the "great tradition" of international theory. This account of a tradition may take a number of quite distinctive forms. Three primary versions have been particularly influential: the permanent debate between realism and idealism; the repetitious monologue spoken by those who have somehow been conscripted into the army of realists; and — the most interesting version — the account of a tradition of international relations theory as a negation of a presumed tradition of political theory.[8] In all three cases, crudely anachronistic interpretive procedures have served to obscure another version of the contradiction between history and structure. Thucydides, Machiavelli, Hobbes, Rousseau, and the rest appear to us as quite unproblematic figures, often in disguises that make them quite unrecognizable to anyone who examines the textual evidence we have of them. That each of these figures is open to sharply differing interpretations has mattered little. The history of political thought turns into an ahistorical repetition in which the struggles of these thinkers to make sense of the historical transformations in which they were caught are erased in favour of assertions about how they all articulate essential truths about the same unchanging and usually tragic reality: the eternal game of relations between states.

Following from this, a fourth set of puzzles arises from the historically constituted character not only of the state and the states-system but also of the categories in which we seek to understand how the states and the states-system participate in the dynamics of contemporary world politics. This puzzle is perhaps the most disconcerting of all. It is always tempting to minimize the significance of the historical experiences through which crucial concepts and ways of speaking have been formed. The longing for timeless categories has exercised a profound influence on many of those we associate with rationalism in the more philosophical sense of this term. Yet, it is possible to trace the history of the term "state," "sovereignty," "individual," "culture," "security," or many of the other terms we now take for granted, and in doing so we discover how they emerged in response to specific historical conjunctions and contradictions. Accounts of history as a sharp break between life before international relations and life since international relations easily distract attention from the historically specific meanings embodied in concepts and categories that can so easily appear to transcend their historical contingency. The categories and concepts we have learnt to use with such facility, almost without thinking, easily appear natural and inevitable. Their contested history is soon forgotten.

Structures, Meanings, and Practices

The story having been written, and sedimented into received accounts of origins, traditions, and analytical concepts, attention may be turned to the architecture of structures. Grand structures having emerged, it is possible to enquire into their modes of operation, their mechanisms and determinations, their forms and their functions, their regularities and repetitions. Indeed, some of the most familiar and enduring analysis of world politics often has been facilitated by a certain forgetting of history.

In its more extreme forms, structuralist analysis tends toward universalism. It is associated historically with attempts to identify the universal principles of reason, or myth, or language, the deep structures that inform the spatial variety and temporal variability visible on the surface of things. In practice, however, structuralist analysis is itself subject to considerable variation, partly with respect to the number of structural patterns that may be identified, and partly with respect to the way that, under critical inspection, structural patterns always seem to mutate into processes of historical transformation.

It is in this context, for example, that it is possible to identify Thomas Hobbes as a paradigmatic thinker. Because individuals are autonomous and equal under conditions of scarcity, Hobbes suggests, they necessarily find themselves in a position of perpetual insecurity. Each individual's struggle to enhance his or her own security increases everyone else's sense of insecurity. Hence, the imagery of both the "state of nature" and the "security dilemma." In contrast (and contrary to the usual direct translation of the fictive state of nature into an account of the security dilemma between states), Hobbes argues that precisely because states are both unequal and much less vulnerable than individuals, they are in a significantly different structural relationship to each other than are individuals. Among (protobourgeois) individuals, Hobbes argues, structural relations of insecurity demand a superior sovereign power for an ordered polity to be constituted. Hence, the powerful resolution of the relation between sovereign individuals and sovereign states through a contract that is both freely entered into and necessitated by structural conditions. Among states, by contrast, structural conditions of inequality suggest other ordering principles in what is nevertheless a "state of war," although Hobbes himself does not much concern himself with what these principles might be.

It could be argued, of course, that, in contemporary world politics, both the proliferation of nuclear weapons and the legal principle of sovereign equality have begun to make Hobbes's account of relations between individuals a more instructive guide to the dynamics of interstate relations than Hobbes himself suggests. For the most part, however, despite continuing references to Hobbes as a theorist of international anarchy, most accounts of world politics presume that the equality condition is absent. Conflict there may be, insecurity certainly, but structuralist accounts of world politics are just as likely to show how insecurity arises from patterns of hegemony, hierarchy, and penetration as from autonomy and equality.

The primary candidate for the most important structural form in world politics has been the balance of power, especially among those who identify the subject of world politics specifically as relations between states. Here we find the familiar themes of the consequences of different distributions or polarities of power, and of the presence or absence of great or hegemonic powers. These lead directly to a concern with, say, the nature of alliances or the transformations induced by the deployment of weapons of mass destruction and the regularized rituals of nuclear deterrence. When patterns of hegemony begin to seem especially significant, attention may turn to the difficulty of distinguishing the dynamics of states-systems from those of empires.

Other contenders for the primary structuring principles of world politics arise from those who situate the dynamics of interstate relations within a broader account of an international or global political economy. Here, the range of perspectives is particularly striking. Much of the literature on international regimes is often classified under this rubric. But the liberal categories of economic analysis deployed by this literature set it apart from more explicitly mercantilist or Marxist traditions that also inform contemporary political economy, especially outside the narrow ideological confines of the United States. Some, for example, Robert Gilpin, seek to combine liberal-economic categories with a more mercantilist or "realist" account of the state, especially in the context of contemporary disruptions and transformations in international trade and finance. Some, for example, Immanuel Wallerstein, echo Adam Smith in their stress on the determinations of a global division of labour and a world market, minimizing the autonomous role of the state while stressing the relations between centre and periphery in a world system. Others, for example, Robert Cox and Stephen Gill, begin — in my view, more helpfully — with a concern for the global structuring of relations of production, and thus emphasize the transformation of state practices in response to the contemporary global reorganization of production currently in progress.[9]

To canvass the range of structuralist accounts of world politics in this way is to become aware of the diversity of philosophical, theoretical, and ideological assumptions that can be embraced under the heading of structuralism. In this sense, Keohane's category of rationalists is just as much in need of differentiation as is his fusion of reflective approaches. But equally striking is the difficulty of distinguishing between structuralist and historical analysis.

Keohane recommends a greater openness to the reflective approach, partly because it would complement the ahistoricism of the rationalists. But, once we move away from the explicitly utilitarian models of regime theory, it is clear that accounts of the character of historical change are already built into many accounts of the structural forms of world politics. These accounts may not be entirely convincing, falling back, for example, on notions of change as alterations in the distribution of power in a system that remains essentially the same, or on accounts of history as either a sequence of repetitive cycles or a linear road from darkness to light. Nevertheless, it is probably fair to say that few students of world politics would argue that structuralist analysis can be divorced from a concern with history and change. There is a "plain common sense" view that both perspectives are obviously necessary. Some might argue, for example, that purely structural analyses of balances or power are intrinsically interesting, and that formal modelling or ahistorical ascriptions of utilitarian behaviour to states are entirely justified, as long as a complementary historical perspective is also encouraged. Even so, both the superficial tolerance of "plain common sense" and the division of academic labour can easily obscure some of the characteristic difficulties experienced by structuralist analysis in understanding the historical political practices through which structural forms have been constructed.

Again it is helpful to reflect upon the supposedly paradigmatic quality of Hobbes's thinking for the analysis of world politics. Hobbes builds upon a fairly radical reworking of philosophical categories within the broad context of the scientific cosmologies associated with the early-modern period. He is impressed, for example, with the unchanging character of reason, the spatial regularities of Euclidean geometry, and the possibility of grounding the language of social explanation in a firm foundation of precise definitions. Unlike Machiavelli before or

Rousseau after, he pays very little attention to history, at least not in the passages for which he has become a realist icon. Instead we find a classic expression of life before and life after the social contract, a shrinking of historical time and human practice to an ahistorical moment of utilitarian calculation informed by reason and fear.

Again, it is possible to identify a range of difficult puzzles that have beset those who have followed Hobbes in their privileging of structural form. Even if we try to avoid questions about whether structures can be said to exist, it is still necessary to engage with complex philosophical interrogations that converge on the question of what a structure is. Many of these arise from the contemporary emphasis on relationality rather than substance. Understood as part of a broader challenge to Newtonian metaphysics, contemporary structural analysis conflicts with popular accounts of the world as an accumulation of things. Some people may kick tables to affirm the material solidity of the "real world," but the demonstration is unlikely to be convincing to anyone familiar with categories of contemporary physics.

With a stress on relationality come questions about how one understands the distinction between the parts of a structure and the "emergent properties" that arise because, as it is often said, "the whole is greater than the sum of its parts." Hence, the dilemma, especially familiar in sociological theory, of whether social explanation should begin with an account of "society" or with the behaviour of "individuals." Hence also, some of the central dilemmas of the theory of international relations: the delineation of distinctions between individual, state, and states-system in the so-called levels-of-analysis typology, for example, or controversies about whether the states-system should be considered to have an autonomous logic of its own or to be part of a broader system of global political economy. The concept of causality also becomes problematic in this context, especially given that most popular accounts of causality are still informed by images of billiard balls colliding in a Newtonian universe. And with causality come questions about determinism, particularly about whether structural forms should be understood as constraining or enabling.

In pursuing questions like these, however, questions about the relationship between structure and history are never far away. Thus, contemporary structuralism does not exhibit the same attachment to timeless universals as do the earlier forms of axiomatic rationalism. On the contrary, as it has been used by anthropologists and theorists of language, structuralism has become more preoccupied with understanding the rules of transformation than with identifying patterns of continuity. More crucially, as a broad philosophical and theoretical movement, one associated with the work of Claude Lévi-Strauss and Louis Althusser, for example, structuralism mutated rather rapidly into what has become known as poststructuralism. And one of the central insights of poststructuralism, explored especially by theorists of language from Fernand de Saussure to Jacques Derrida, has been that structural patterns are constituted through historical processes of differentiation. The emphasis on relationality is pursued in a temporal direction, with the well-known result that poststructuralist analysis has come to be indicted for all the sins previously associated with those who insisted on the historicity of human existence. The indictment, of course, is invariably issued in the name of objectivity and universal standards, although it is the historically constituted nature of the capacity to issue the indictment in the first place that poststructuralism has sought to challenge.

As if this is not enough, questions about whether structures do, in fact, exist, will not go away. They are especially important for attempts to construct a theory of international regimes. The very term "regime," like similar uses of the term "governance," attempts to capture phenomena that seem to have a status that is somewhere between a concrete institution and a more or less invisible field of forces generated by structural determinations. The term "international organization" is also quite problematic in this respect, caught, as it is, between accounts of such specific institutional arrangements as the United Nations, and inchoate attempts to forge an analysis of processes that are neither interstate relations as conventionally understood nor readily understandable as precursors of some kind of world state.[10]

Such interrogations lead into some of the most difficult conceptual terrain in contemporary social and political theory. They ought to give pause to anyone attempting to keep discussion of contrasting perspectives on world politics to questions about epistemology and method. Even those who adhere most rigorously to an empiricist conception of research discover that they have to struggle with interrogations of this kind. Kenneth Waltz's accounts of systemic explanation and the levels of analysis typology or Robert Gilpin's attempt to reconcile modernist social science with an essentially historicist account of a classical tradition of theories of international relations clearly involve taking positions on these questions. Their positions may or may not be satisfactory, but their work has to be judged, at least partially, in terms of how far their more empirical work is both shaped and constrained by their prior ontological commitments.[11]

A second set of puzzles follows directly from such considerations, for, in practice, answers to these more philosophical problems are often articulated in the form of metaphors, analogies, and models derived from other areas of human experience. Here, it is as well to remember that metaphors, analogies, and models are a crucial aspect of theory formation, even in the more rigorous sciences. They assist in conceptual clarification and the development of systems of classification. It may well be that much of what we understand to be scientific analysis has been articulated against the dangers of misanalogy or the slippages in meaning that are intrinsic to metaphorical reasoning; that is, against the very possibilities that are often celebrated in the realms of literature and art. But again, the conventional distinction between the sciences and humanities obscures more than it reveals. In the analysis of social and political life, especially, textual strategies and literary devices are a characteristic part of even the most formalized modelling.

Two subthemes are especially important here. One concerns the tendency to draw analogies between relatively simple structures in order to explain ones that are more complex. The role of images taken from Newtonian mechanics or Darwinian biology is relatively familiar and has generated long-standing debate about the reductionist character of so much functionalist explanation in sociology.[12] In the analysis of world politics, the concept of a balance of power itself clearly has an analogical quality, and leads to questions about whether, say, the notion of equilibrium it implies is sufficiently nuanced to comprehend the dynamics of great-power diplomacy or the dialectics of nuclear deterrence. Similarly, many of the ideas articulated under the rubric of social-choice theory or utilitarian accounts of substantive rationality have a distinctly reductionist quality. In part this quality derives from a methodological individualism, whereby it is assumed that social processes can be explained in terms of the behaviour of individuals, as if individuals somehow exist prior to society. In part it derives from literary inventiveness, as when something called the "Prisoner's Dilemma" is presumed to bear some relation to what goes on under conditions of incarceration.

A second subtheme concerns the circulation of the metaphors and analogies used to analyze world politics within a broader cultural and political economy. Social and political explanation constantly draws on and collides with the imagery, prejudices, and ways of speaking of the society being explained. To move, for example, from a structuralist account of a balance of power to one of nuclear deterrence is to work within a cultural context in which the meaning of "equilibrium" or "security" or a "nuclear umbrella" is mediated by complex cultural codes of which strategic analysts are themselves only partly aware. Moving from structural analysis to metaphors and analogies, we can quickly become entangled in a complex politics of language or discourse.[13]

This leads directly to a third group of puzzles, those that focus on the relationship between structures and human consciousness or practice. Some of the most intense debates about structural analysis in modern social and political theory have occurred on this terrain, not least because structuralism has seemed to imply the erasure of human subjectivity. In the context of world politics, versions of this problem have occurred in debates about whether a balance of power should be understood as an automatic mechanism to which statesmen simply respond appropriately or inappropriately, or whether it should be regarded as a practice or policy that statesmen have developed on the basis of long historical experience.

Something similar is involved in the different accounts of international cooperation and regime-formation. In an extreme utilitarian approach, for example, human action is explained in terms of the rules of efficient conduct, rules that have a certain structural necessity. It is in this context that "normative" behaviour is interpreted as following the prudential rules of utility maximization. This is clearly not the only available account of human action, or of what normative behaviour involves. Even Max Weber, whose account of instrumental rationality is often invoked by utilitarian analysts, tended to see modernity not as a simple embrace of instrumental rationality, but as an intensifying clash between the meaningless rules of efficient action and a struggle to give meaning to life in a disenchanted world. And those who begin their account of human action in an analysis of, say, labour or language, are unlikely to be persuaded by the limited claims of utilitarian efficiency. To begin with the constitutive character of labour or language is to challenge the fundamental premises on which a utilitarian account of social and political life is grounded. There is nothing very novel about this. It merely serves as a reminder that the distance between Keohane's categories covers some rather deeply rooted and enormously complex differences among those who seek to understand social and political life.

To make matters worse, it is always possible to raise a still further group of puzzles about how our prevailing understanding of such terms as structure and history is itself informed by historically constituted accounts of the concepts of space and time. Here metaphysics enters with a vengeance. Questions about ethics and ideology cannot be far behind. For some, of course, this would be enough to bring on a bad case of positivist vertigo. But in a discipline in which the reflections of, say, Machiavelli, Kant, or St. Augustine have not been entirely obliterated by the myth of a tradition, it should come as no surprise.

From International Relations to World Politics

While introducing his analysis of the relative merits of the rationalistic and reflective approaches, Keohane affirms his commitment to a socioscientific analysis of world politics by explicitly marginalizing the themes I have tried to sketch here. In his view, he says, it

> will not be fruitful . . . indefinitely to conduct a debate at the purely theoretical level, much less to argue about epistemological and ontological issues in the abstract. Such an argument would only take us away from the study of our subject matter, world politics, toward what would probably become an intellectually derivative and programmatically diversionary philosophical discussion.[14]

The problem, however, is that Keohane's discussion is full of ontological and epistemological claims that are left abstract; his account of an empirical research program is dependent upon ontological (as well as ethical and ideological) commitments; and in marginalizing problems that have long been central to (non-empiricist) philosophies of social science, he diverts attention from the serious philosophical and political problems that are at stake in even postulating a subject matter called world politics. This is not, I should re-emphasize, to underestimate the importance of serious empirical research, merely to suggest that there is rather more involved in postulating such concepts as interdependence, regimes, or international institutions than the formulation of an empirical research program. As even conventional neo-Kantian philosophies of science have insisted time and time again, the appropriate conceptualization of the problem already prefigures the solution. It is not a matter of arguing about ontological and epistemological issues in the abstract. Philosophical commitments are already embedded in such concepts as state or states-system, such typologies as the level of analysis distinction and utilitarian accounts of rational action. The ideology-laden distinction between social science and sociopolitical theory, between empirical and normative forms of enquiry, simply cannot be sustained, no matter how much it may have legitimated disciplinary divisions and claims to professional expertise.

To advance such concepts as interdependence or international regime is already to admit the significance of historical transformation. But, to begin with history is to encounter problems that are usually encountered under the heading of the philosophy of history. Given the difficulty of some of these problems, it is perhaps not entirely surprising that they are so often marginalized and resolved in favour of ahistorical accounts of continuity and structural form. This has even happened to the interpretation of such a central figure as Machiavelli, who is invoked, perhaps more than anyone else, as the prototypical theorist of international relations. Despite the prime place he occupies in the myth of a tradition, his concern with the relationship between time (*fortuna*) and the possibility of *virtu* in a political community is rarely taken seriously in this context. Machiavelli's questions, in fact, are hardly discussed at all. Hobbes has been much easier to assimilate, for, with Hobbes, temporal questions are subordinated to historically specific accounts of structural form. For all his reputation as the devil incarnate, Machiavelli has been reified and tamed. Yet, Machiavelli's questions about the relationship between time or history (an era of accelerating transformations) and the possibility of new forms of political community seem much closer to what is involved in speaking about interdependence, or regimes, or world politics than are Hobbesian-style structuralist models.[15]

Similarly, many of the older realists were deeply preoccupied with questions about the philosophy of history. Many explicitly invoked an Augustinian contrast between time and eternity to explain the tragic conditions of life on earth. Others responded to the relativistic implications of a loss of faith in the grand vision of historical progress. To read older realists such as Carr, Morgenthau, Herz, and Niebuhr is to be struck by the intensity of their philosophical and even theological concerns with time and history. As such, their writings stand in the sharpest possible contrast with those of contemporary structural or neorealists. Unfortunately, however, their concern with history was rarely serious enough. It usually amounted to little more than the negation of Christian views of eternity or Enlightenment views of progress — a negation understood to be especially appropriate for a realm, interstate relations, that was itself understood as the negation of that political community in which perfectibility on earth was at least approachable, the state.

A sensitivity to history and time is always in danger of being undermined through reification. This *is* the essential complaint brought against the utilitarian approach by those who are identified with reflection. Historical practices are analyzed as ahistorical structures. Conscious human practices are erased in favour of structural determinations. But problems of temporality rarely disappear entirely. Attempts have even been made to analyze temporal process in terms of structural pattern. The flux of time has been portrayed as teleological or dialectical necessity. The history of human consciousness has been portrayed in relation to the generative structure of grammar. The logic of scientific explanation has been extended from the sciences of inert matter to encompass patterns of probability in historical practices. But such strategies have always encountered powerful opposition. The historicity of human experience remains deeply problematic.

These are not simply abstract considerations, to be deferred as somehow merely theoretical or philosophical. They are at play in the concrete practices of intellectual life. Claims about a point of origin, a tradition, or an essentially timeless form known as the state have had an enormous impact on what world politics is assumed to be, and thus on what it means to participate in or offer a legitimate account of world politics. Questions about the relationship between reified structures and conscious human practices are at the heart of — though they are resolved in distinctive ways by — the dominant ideological forces of modern political life.

Just as these remarks do not imply that empirical research is unimportant, neither do they mean that structuralist analysis has nothing to offer. Still less, that the questions pursued by the utilitarian rationalists are trivial. On the contrary.

Questions about processes of interstate co-operation and discord, the emergence of new patterns of interdependence and dependence, the appropriate conceptualization of regimes or institutions, the globalization of production, distribution, and exchange, or the changing character of state-formation in response to economic and technological transformations, functional problems, and political struggles are obviously crucial. Contemporary world politics is, as Keohane rightly emphasizes, "a matter of wealth and poverty, life and death." Indeed, these questions should be understood in relation to the possibility of thinking about political life at all in the late 20th century. They put in doubt the political categories that assume, with both Machiavelli and Hobbes, a fundamental distinction between political life within states and political life between states — the distinction that is constitutive of the discipline of international relations as we now know it. The questions are undoubtedly crucial, but the inherited categories of international relations theory do not necessarily offer the sharpest articulation of what they involve.

Structuralist analysis is also important, but so, too, are the persistent problems that structuralist analysis brings with it. A Kenneth Waltz has to wrestle with the relative merits of systemic and reductionist forms of explanation, choosing — contentiously — to resolve competing metaphysical claims through a reifying typology of the individual, the state, and the states-system as the essential components of the "real world." Others try to reconcile conflicting accounts of the primary structure as either the states-system, on the one hand, or a more inclusive global political economy, on the other. In both cases, it is possible to see powerful tensions between the claims of structure and those of history.

These tensions have characterized much of contemporary intellectual life. They have been a familiar theme even within North American social science. Attempts to employ functional explanation or cybernetic and systems analysis, for example, have quickly attracted the charge of conservatism on the grounds that mechanistic and biological models systematically downplay the significance of human consciousness and political struggle. In a broader context, existential or phenomenological humanism was once challenged by the structuralisms of Claude Lévi-Strauss or Louis Althusser, which were then challenged, in turn, both by reassertions of humanism and, more iconoclastically, by the nonhumanist historicism of the poststructuralists and postmodernists. In the background, of course, lie all those complex, yet stylized, codings in which Hegel's universal history challenges Kant's universal reason, or Aristotelian teleology follows Plato's geometrically inspired account of unchanging forms. In contemporary social and political theory, the tension between structure and history remains especially acute in ongoing debates about the relative significance of structure and action (and, thus, of explanation and interpretation) and about the status of modernity. It is no accident, therefore, that claims about the promise of a socioscientific approach to world politics should be challenged by positions that draw from the interpretive and critical techniques of hermeneutics and deconstruction.

It seems reasonable to expect that the need for accounts of world politics that are somehow both structuralist and historically informed will continue to be urged. Keohane's hope for an eventual synthesis of utilitarian and reflective approaches can be read in this way. So can several other major theoretical perspectives that are, for some reason, excluded from Keohane's discussion: the society-of-states perspective associated with Hedley Bull, for example, or forms of political economy that seek to extend Marx's account of capital as an historically structured and always transformative process. It is certainly likely that greater attention will in future be given to understanding the historical interplay between the structuring of the states-system and the structuring of global relations of production, distribution, and exchange. But, again, the limitations of traditions that privilege either politics or economics draw attention less to the problem of a particular academic discipline than to tendencies that inform the most influential currents of social and political theory in general.

Yet, if it is reasonable to urge the necessity of both structuralist and historical sensitivities, then it is also necessary to insist that empirical social science holds no monopoly on what this might bring. It might bring about a greater concern for the reifying practices that have been so powerful in accounts of a tradition of international relations theory, or in the more extreme presumption that a state is a state is a state. It might force open serious philosophical questions that have been closed off by the categories of realist and idealist, or by the pretense that neo- or structural realism is just an updated account of eternal realist principles. It might focus greater attention on the principle of state sovereignty as the crucial practice through which questions about human community are fixed within a spatial metaphysics that is sharply at odds with the historically constituted claims of the state. It might even focus attention on the deeply rooted categories through which we pretend to know just what space and time are.

All of which is to identify the analysis of world politics with a much broader account of social and political enquiry than is usual in the specific discipline of international relations. For, if questions about interdependence, dependence, regimes, and institutions are taken seriously — that is, as possibly putting into question the early modern European accounts of what political community can be, given the passing of life before international relations — then it is not clear that such explorations are any less significant than, in need of subsumption into, or just a prelude to a utilitarian and empirical social science. Rather, it is to suggest that vague and obscure hypotheses about the existence of something called world politics involve a claim to historical and structural transformation that throws historically derived concepts and disciplinary divisions into rather serious doubt. Consequently, the difficulty of analyzing political life at this historical juncture remains more impressive than the achievements of theories of international relations. It is this difficulty, and not the extravagant presumptions of modernist social science, that demands our immediate attention.

NOTES

1. In this chapter, I refer to international relations as an academic discipline; to world politics as an array of political practices that extend beyond the territoriality and competence of single political communities and affect large proportions of humanity; and to interstate relations or the politics of states-systems as the narrower array of practices constituted through interactions between states. All these terms are highly problematic, in ways that serve to underline the significance of questions about the character and location of political community in the late 20th century. International relations, for example, reifies a specific historical convergence between state and nation; references to states-systems tend to encourage a conflation of accounts of the state as a territorial space and as governmental apparatus; while world politics is used to refer to global political processes that largely escape prevailing analytical categories. The horizons of our language in this respect reflect the limits of traditions of political analysis that depend on a distinction between community within states and noncommunity (relations, anarchy, war) between them. For a brief elaboration of this argument — which forms the subtext of this chapter — see R.B.J. Walker, *State Sovereignty, Global Civilization and the Rearticulation of Political Space*, World Order Studies Program Occasional Paper No. 8 (Princeton: Center of International Studies, Princeton University, 1988). For more speculative discussions, see R.B.J. Walker, *One World, Many Worlds: Struggles for a Just World Peace* (Boulder, Colo.: Lynne Rienner; London: Zed Books, 1988) and Richard A. Falk, *The Promise of World Order* (Philadelphia: Temple University Press, 1987). In the specifically Canadian context, see Warren Magnusson and R.B.J. Walker, "Discentering the State: Political Theory and Canadian Political Economy," *Studies in Political Economy* 26 (Summer 1988): 37-71. For an important but neglected discussion of the historical context, see Andrew Linklater, *Men and Citizens in the Theory of International Relations* (London: Macmillan, 1982). For helpful discussions in the context of contemporary social and political theory, see John Dunn, *Western Political Theory in the Face of the Future* (Cambridge: Cambridge University Press, 1979), and *Rethinking Modern Political Theory* (Cambridge: Cambridge University Press, 1985).

2. Robert O. Keohane, "International Institutions: Two Approaches," *International Studies Quarterly* 32 (1988). See also Keohane, ed., *Neorealism and Its Critics* (New York: Columbia University Press, 1986).

3. Typical discussions include Richard J. Bernstein, *Restructuring of Social and Political Theory* (Philadelphia: University of Pennsylvania Press, 1976); Brian Fay, *Critical Social Science* (Cambridge: Polity Press, 1987); John G. Gunnell, *Between Philosophy and Politics: The Alienation of Political Theory* (Amherst: University of Massachusetts Press, 1986); and William E. Connolly, *Political Theory and Modernity* (Oxford: Basil Blackwell, 1988).

4. The main papers from this debate were collected in Klaus Knorr and James N. Rosenau, eds., *Contending Approaches to International Politics* (Princeton: Princeton University Press, 1969).

5. Hedley Bull, *The Anarchical Society* (London: Macmillan, 1977). Cf. Friedrich N. Kratochwil, *Rules, Norms and Decisions* (Cambridge: Cambridge University Press, 1989); Richard K. Ashley, "Living on Border Lines: Man, Post Structuralism and War" in *International/Intertextual Relations: The Boundaries of Knowledge and Practice in World Politics*, ed. James Der Derian and Michael Shapiro (Lexington: Lexington Books, 1989); and Richard K. Ashley, "The Geopolitics of Geopolitical Space," *Alternatives* 12 (October 1987): 403–34.

6. The most instructive formulations of the realist-idealist distinction remain E.H. Carr, *The Twenty Years' Crisis, 1919–1939* (London: Macmillan, 1939; 2d ed., 1956); and Hans J. Morgenthau, *Scientific Man Vs Power Politics* (Chicago: University of Chicago Press, 1946). They are especially instructive when read not as founding texts of the theory of international relations, but as belated formulations of dilemmas associated with early 20th-century German historicism as these dilemmas were mediated through the work of Karl Mannheim and Max Weber. See Stephen P. Turner and Regis A. Factor, *Max Weber and the Dispute over Reason and Value* (London: Routledge and Kegan Paul, 1984).

7. See the relatively accessible discussions in R.J. Holton, *The Transition from Feudalism to Capitalism* (London: Macmillan, 1985), and Michael Mann, *The Sources of Social Power*, vol. 1 (Cambridge: Cambridge University Press, 1986).

8. It is the most interesting, I have argued elsewhere, because it clarifies the connection between the contemporary usages of categories like realist and idealist and the early modern spatio-temporal resolution of questions about the possibility of political community offered by the principle of state sovereignty, a resolution that is also constitutive of international relations as a field of enquiry. See R.B.J. Walker, "*The Prince* and 'The Pauper': Tradition, Modernity and Practice in the Theory of International Relations," in *International/ Intertextual Relations*.

9. Robert Gilpin, *The Political Economy of International Relations* (Princeton: Princeton University Press, 1987); Immanuel Wallerstein, "The Rise and Future Demise of the World Capitalist System: Concepts for Comparative Analysis," *Comparative Studies in Society and History* 16 (1974): 387–415; Robert W. Cox, *Production, Power and World Order: Social Forces in the Making of History* (New York: Columbia University Press, 1987); Stephen Gill and David Law, *The Global Political Economy: Perspectives, Problems and Policies* (Baltimore: Johns Hopkins University Press, 1988); and Stephen Gill, *American Hegemony and the Trilateral Commission* (Cambridge: Cambridge University Press, 1989).

10. See the important analysis in Friedrich Kratochwil and John Gerard Ruggie, "International Organization: A State of the Art on an Art of the State," *International Organization* 40 (Autumn 1986): 753–76.

11. For a more extended discussion see my "Realism, Change and International Political Theory," *International Studies Quarterly* 31 (March 1987): 65–86; and "The Territorial State and the Theme of Gulliver," *International Journal* 39 (Summer 1984): 529–52.

12. In international relations, the adequacy of these images becomes especially important in the literature on systems analysis. For a helpful discussion see Richard Little, "Three Approaches to the International System: Some Ontological and Epistemological Considerations," *British Journal of International Studies* 3 (1977): 269–85.

13. On this theme see Der Derian and Shapiro, eds., *International/Intertextual Relations*; and Shapiro, *The Politics of Representation* (Madison: University of Wisconsin Press, 1988).

14. Keohane, "International Institutions: Two Approaches."

15. For an argument to this effect see "*The Prince* and 'The Pauper.'"

SELECT BIBLIOGRAPHY

Cox, Robert W. *Production, Power and World Order: Social Forces in the Making of History*. New York: Columbia University Press, 1987.

Der Derian, James, and Michael J. Shapiro, eds. *International/Intertextual Relations: The Boundaries of Knowledge and Practice in World Politics*. Lexington, Mass.: Lexington Books, 1989.

Descombes, Vincent. *Modern French Philosophy*. Trans. L. Scott-Fox and J.M. Harding. Cambridge: Cambridge University Press, 1980.

Giddens, A. *Central Problems in Social Theory: Action, Structure and Contradiction in Social Analysis*. London: Macmillan, 1979.

Gill, Stephen, and David Law. *The Global Political Economy: Perspectives, Problems and Policies*. Baltimore: Johns Hopkins University Press, 1988.

Hawthorn, Geoffrey. *Enlightenment and Despair: A History of Social Theory*. 2d ed. Cambridge: Cambridge University Press, 1987.

Keohane, Robert O. *Neorealism and Its Critics*. New York: Columbia University Press, 1986.

Kolb, David. *The Critique of Pure Modernity: Hegel, Heidegger and After*. Chicago: University of Chicago Press, 1986.

Linklater, Andrew. *Men and Citizens in the Theory of International Relations*. London: Macmillan, 1982.

Linklater, Andrew. "Realism, Marxism and Critical International Theory." *Review of International Studies* 12 (1986): 302–12.

Mann, Michael. *The Sources of Social Power*. 3 vols. Cambridge: Cambridge University Press, 1986– .

Schmidt, Alfred. *History and Structure: An Essay on Hegelian-Marxist and Structuralist Theories of History*. Trans. Jeffrey Herf. Cambridge, Mass.: MIT Press, 1981.

Seung, T.K. *Structuralism and Hermeneutics*. New York: Columbia University Press, 1982.

Smith, Steve, ed. *International Relations: British and American Perspectives.* Oxford: Basil Blackwell, 1985.

Walker, R.B.J. *One World, Many Worlds: Struggles for a Just World Peace.* Boulder, Colo.: Lynne Rienner; London: Zed Books, 1988.

———. "Realism, Change and International Political Theory." *International Studies Quarterly* 31, no. 1 (1987): 65–86.

Wendt, A.F. "The Agent-Structure Problem." *International Organization* 41 (Summer 1987): 336–70.

ETHICS AND INTERNATIONAL RELATIONS: A CRITIQUE OF CYNICAL REALISM

Constantine Melakopides

On Ethics, Morality, and Statecraft

Ethics is a discipline concerned with the examination, justification, and evaluation of motives, actions, and their consequences. Its subject matter, therefore, consists of judgements, decisions, and behaviour to which we apply such predicates as right and wrong, good and evil, and fair and unjust, or such concepts as misery, oppression, alienation, dignity, well-being, and self-realization. In spite of popular misconceptions, ethics is a discipline of enormous *practical* import: it helps us to clarify the nature of convoluted and agonizing problems; to provide solutions when available and, even when unavailable, to tell us why; to offer grounds or reasons for the justification of actions or omissions; to show the fallacies of untenable claims about moral issues; and to determine and reveal the values by which we choose to live.

A terminological clarification is necessary at the outset, because the terms "ethical" and "moral" are used in a variety of ways, reflecting the substantive preferences for a particular theory or view (e.g., Kantian, Christian, or utilitarian). To avoid begging the substantive question of which particular theory is the correct one, and to reflect common philosophical practice, the terms "ethical" and "moral" will be used interchangeably in this chapter. The context should make clear whether "ethical" means "moral" in the sense of "morally good" (or "morally acceptable"), or whether it means "about ethics" or "related to ethics," even if what it refers to is "immoral." For instance, there is no contradiction in saying (as I shall do below) that "Cynical Realism" is an immoral ethical view, since it denies the moral point of view. As for the meaning of "the moral point of view," here again no substantive ethical theory will be assumed; rather, the term typically refers to the commonly shared point of view that accepts the centrality or significance of ethical concepts and of the role of morality in social life, the concern for human well-being, the denial that egoism assumes this point of view, and the stress on the sympathetic impulse. It follows, of course, that cynics and egoists may disagree with much in the following discussion (and also that some readers may discover that cynicism and egoism in international relations, as in morality generally, are very narrow, and lonely, points of view).[1]

It is my argument that the analysis of international relations (IR) must, by definition, give pride of place to the moral point of view. For, as with all behaviour, that of international actors — i.e., states, statesmen, groups, movements, international organizations, transnational corporations, and ordinary citizens — cannot escape ethical judgements in terms of the appropriate predicates and concepts. If anything, an even stronger case could be made for the application of the moral point of view to international relations, since IR's agenda affects the life and well-being of myriad people and includes the apocalyptic possibility of nuclear omnicide.

Given that acts and omissions on the world scene might involve any or all of war, subversion, intervention, oppression, racism, exploitation, overpopulation, starvation, malnutrition, nuclearism, alienation, or environmental degradation, it is clear that no theory of international relations could be complete without a full examination of such phenomena and of their causes. Nor could it be complete without providing concrete proposals on the range of actions needed for the urgent handling of the present-day global malaise. As J. David Singer recently put it,

> specialists in world affairs have a special responsibility to not only teach and conduct high-quality research, but to address the major problems confronting the global village. . . . The human condition is, on balance, morally unacceptable. Too many of our fellows continue to die prematurely from war, terrorism, assassination, poverty, starvation, disease, and even more of them suffer untold misery, pain, and degradation en route to the grave.[2]

Academic discourse on world politics, however, has all but ostracized such work, as demonstrated by the near silence on ethical issues in IR books, articles, and university courses. Typical rationalizations of this silence seem to consist of one of the following claims: either that "morality is alien" to international politics; or that it is only incidental or peripheral to it; or that ethics in IR is at best *sui generis*, since it "derives" from the premises of *realpolitik* and *raison d'état*, and has somehow acquired an autonomy on the basis of these premises.

Such claims, and the associated points of view, are fallacious, as this chapter will try to show. It is quite remarkable, however, that, whereas most theorists of world politics are either reticent about or hostile toward the investigation of international morality, concrete actions of moral content are ever-present in the real world of international behaviour. Indeed, to appreciate that theorizing about international ethics is lagging behind the *realities* of international relations, consider such empirical manifestations of the links between morality and world politics as the following:

1. Judgements using ethical predicates are employed continuously about international behaviour by statesmen, governments, journalists, analysts, and ordinary citizens. They often describe the human condition as "morally unacceptable," in J. David Singer's manner; and they praise or condemn concrete cases, crises, actions, or omissions.

2. Praise and condemnation of actions or omissions in the international arena are central in the decisions, actions, and proposals of international organizations, agencies, and committees, such as those of the United Nations. Celebrated recent cases include the Brandt Commission reports, *North-South: A Programme for Survival* (1980) and *Common Crisis* (1983), and the Bruntland Commission report, *Our Common Future* (1987).
3. International legal principles and practices are clearly premised on ethical foundations demonstrating the possibilities of universalizing consensus (already widely present on the declaratory level) regarding aspects of justice, equality, human dignity, harmony, and co-operation. In particular, examples of such principles include the rules *pacta sunt servanda* (i.e. treaties are binding), the principles of self-defence and of nonintervention, and the laws of war. Well-known examples of legal agreements of moral content include international legislation on human rights, such as the U.N. Charter (Article l), the Universal Declaration of Human Rights (1948), the Declaration on Colonialism (1960), and the Declaration on the Elimination of Racial Discrimination.
4. Finally, and equally important, there is a host of tangible actions of a positive or constructive international ethical content that falls under the following indicative categories: the demonstrations of massive care and material aid to victims of natural catastrophes (such as famines and earthquakes); the sustained economic, technical, and educational aid to Third and Fourth World states and their peoples; the moral support and material assistance given to victims of human-rights violations, through publicizing their plight and expressing readiness to help them via immigration measures, economic sanctions against the offending states, and benign (i.e., nonmilitary) forms of intervention; the self-imposed restraints by states on the use of force and the public outcry against such use or its continuation (as dramatically demonstrated by the American people during the Vietnam War); the bilateral and multilateral agreements on ecological issues and concerns of a regional or a planetary scope (such as the recent Vienna Convention for the Protection of the Ozone Layer and the Montreal Protocol, and the emerging pressures on Brazil regarding the Amazon rain forest); the recognition and legislation by international and intergovernmental institutions of the need to curtail uninhibited greed by multinational corporations; the celebration by world public opinion (through rallies, massive demonstrations, or even electronically transmitted music concerts) of solidarity with the victims of South African racism; and expressions by U.N. representatives and their General Assembly votes of ethical stances on various issues, such as the condemnation of the Soviet invasion of Afghanistan and South Africa's apartheid regime.

If such examples provide tangible manifestations of the links between moral concerns (judgements, decisions, and actions) and international behaviour, why is it that theorists of international politics are generally oblivious to such links and have, with few exceptions, failed to account for them? And why have they concentrated primarily on observing violence and war, while evading, for the most part, the examination of the other plights of humanity and the recommendation of the means urgently needed to confront them?

This chapter seeks to answer these questions, as well as to examine the emerging normative alternatives (that is, theories that attempt to ground international politics on solid ethical foundations, demonstrating thereby that international activities need not be condemned permanently to the status of violence and conflict but can enhance dignity, co-operation, and need-satisfaction). In the next section, I shall suggest some of the philosophical and methodological reasons that have misled international relations scholars into supposing that ethics can be severed from their analyses. Following that, I examine critically the current orthodoxy of "Political Realism" on the ground that its work remains at best incomplete (as long as it evades the explicit consideration of the ever-present moral dimension), and at worst fallacious (because some of its versions do contain unacknowledged ethical stances, which render it self-contradictory, while others exhibit erroneous views about political morality). I then survey briefly some recent normative theories that go beyond Realism and point the way to an ethically grounded international relations theory and practice. Finally, I summarize the argument and offer modest suggestions on fruitful directions for further analysis.

Why Has There Been No International Relations Ethical Theory?

Any attempt to organize and analyze the raw material of international relations is found, on reflection, to be based on tacit or explicit methodological and epistemological assumptions that underscore it, support it, give it coherence and direction. Should these assumptions be problematic or untenable, the entire structure will, on probing, shake and possibly collapse. The majority of influential theorists of international relations appear to have subscribed to a view of political study and social science characterized by the following central convictions: (a) that the purpose of their work is to describe, explain, and possibly predict; (b) that moral prescriptions have no place in such "scientific" endeavours; and (c) that what needs to be sought after are *facts*, not "values" — for the two are, and must remain, distinct.

These views together constitute a positivistic, deterministic, and "value-free" approach to IR analysis, one, moreover, whose ancestry is located in the traditional aspiration of social science to emulate the methods and techniques of the natural sciences. And although its drawbacks are by now well known, such a commitment is so deeply entrenched and self-perpetuating that no amount of methodological-philosophical challenge has succeeded in shaking this "faith."[3] To enter fully into this debate would take us far afield; therefore, let me here record only a few crucial points.

First, if the aspiration to scientific rigour entails that social "facts" exist for all to see, then positivist social science (including IR) should have proven its case long ago. Manifestly, this has not been so. To reply that the facts are there but some do not see them because of "ideological" blinkers or methodological distortions is, simply, to concede the point that such postulated facts are, in reality, composites or syntheses that contain evaluative ingredients. But, this would be to acknowledge that pure facts do not exist. Indeed they do not, and they are therefore subject to interpretations, some of which, admittedly, are better than others.

Second, "descriptions" cannot be pure (or uncontaminated by values) either. Therefore, *a fortiori*, explanations in social science (including IR) cannot attain the status of *causal* demonstrations in any strict sense of causation. It thus follows, further, that no *certain* "predictions" can be expected: predictions are merely projections into the future, which assume the truth of "lawlike generalizations." This view becomes untenable, since nothing like "laws" have ever been shown to exist in international relations, although some occasionally think they have discovered them. It thus transpires that the "scientific" project in IR (like that in social science in general) is a *sui generis* enterprise that must consciously acknowledge its evaluative content — that is, its value choices, preferences, and commitments. While this by no means entails that values stand outside the *rational* domain of discourse, it does imply that values must be made explicit and then defended as such.

Third, the positivist or neopositivist assumptions of many IR theorists often appeal to a philosophical stereotype known as the "Is/Ought Dichotomy" or "Hume's Guillotine." It amounts to the belief that "values cannot be derived from facts." The belief, in other words, is that no amount of facts can imply an evaluative conclusion; from this, such further conclusions are drawn as that values are nonempirical, that they are merely emotive or subjective, and that no evaluative position is demonstrably better than another. If, however, we know that facts are not pure (i.e., without concomitant values) in the first place, there is no reason that values cannot indeed be derived from facts (in some broad sense akin to logical support). For instance, with minimal assumptions that are themselves empirical or factual, the description of a set of human needs that must be satisfied for an elementarily human life can solidly support the value of need-satisfaction to obtain and maintain such a life.

Fourth, and finally, if the positivism of these theorists is thus shown to be seriously defective in its epistemological-methodological foundations, their hostility to normative discourse is often sublimated by appeals to "meta-ethical" claims about the nature and the application of ethics. Thus, such theorists may, and often do, hold that widespread ethical disagreements only prove the futility, the subjectivity, or the irrationality of the relevant moral proposals; that morality has been developed for the personal or private sphere and is therefore inapplicable to the public, including the international, domain; and that even if moral truths were available, their implementation in practice would clearly be limited, if not nonexistent. Hence, the link between ethics and international relations is, at best, tenuous.

That such views have constituted a formidable challenge to normative theorizing in IR must readily be admitted. And yet, consider, first, that our earlier brief empirical account has demonstrated that the link between morality and international relations is abundantly real. Second, in contradiction to the claims of futility, subjectivity, and so on that are based on stressing disagreements, our empirical account demonstrates the wide moral consensus that exists on a variety of ethical issues and concerns, as shown by the judgements, decisions, and concrete actions of individuals, groups, governments, institutions, and international organizations. Therefore, actual ethical international behaviour demonstrates that there is ample room for cultivating transevaluative agreements, and that the antinormativists' fixation on ethical disputes (on which much of their challenge turns) is quite suspect. Third, such ethical consensus is based on shared moral premises, which can be the foundation for the creation of additional ones. Therefore, the difficulties in reaching a broader implementation of moral truths should not be confused with the nonexistence of such truths, just as the actual violation of moral principles is not to be confused with the absence of such principles. Fourth, what is needed in international ethics is to organize our material and thinking, by suggesting the reasons for ethical disputes, the grounds for moral agreement and behaviour, as well as the ways in which ethics and international relations can forge even stronger empirical links. Finally, it is noteworthy and ironic that, despite their disclaimers, antinormativists cannot escape the ethical predicament. Those who are silent on the matter leave untouched the "morally unacceptable" human condition, thereby implying their lack of concern for, or interest in, this condition. Their position, nonetheless, is, or entails thereby, a statement about ethics. Those who have taken a less negative stance toward values have either confined their ethical claims to a limited range of ethically relevant material or have committed various fallacies, as we shall see. In most cases, therefore, one can perceive their implicit satisfaction with the status quo.

While deeply disconcerting (given the "morally unacceptable" condition of the world), this may not be very surprising. The antinormative schools of thought are behaviouralism and especially some varieties of political realism, which may or may not otherwise have any affinity with behaviouralism. With a handful of exceptions, these schools are happy to leave the structure of things international as it is.[4] Their inherent conservatism, then, has restricted their capacity to engage in the ethically founded changes that are urgently needed. My discussion will not address directly the types of claims about ethics made by all "realists," even if (and perhaps because) realism is in some sense indisputably hegemonic in the realm of international relations. Rather, I will concentrate on a particular variant of realism, which I call "Cynical Realism," and which the late Robert Osgood has labelled "big-R" Realism.[5]

Cynical Realism and Morality

The four theses or assumptions about morality held by "big-R" Realists are: Cynicism, Amoralism, Skepticism, and Prudentialism. Note that, because this is a long, variegated, and complex tradition that regards as its founding fathers Thucydides, Machiavelli, and Hobbes, it is inevitable that not all of its practitioners would exhibit all four theses or assumptions, while some contemporary Realists may even be totally silent on their ethical or meta-ethical stance. The four positions form a continuum; the beginning of it stands squarely outside morality, parts of it subvert morality, and its end touches morality's periphery. Our account, thus, will associate specific scholars with a particular thesis or assumption and treat them as representatives of the continuum that is, in any event, intimately linked with the epistemological, methodological, and meta-ethical positions of antinormativism that were criticized above.

To be sure, Cynicism is a view that may be interpreted in one of two ways: either as a refusal to accept the existence (or the relevance) of the moral point of view, or as an endorsement of the inevitability or justifiability of immorality in international behaviour. Thus, under the former interpretation, it flows into Amoralism; under the latter, it may be seen as an "ethically relevant" stance that simply upholds the negation of the moral point of view. A celebrated instance of Cynicism is contained in Niccolò Machiavelli's *The Prince*, a work that Realism has adopted as part of its canon. Typical of its view of morality is the following:

> So a prince should not worry if he incurs reproach for his cruelty so long as he keeps his subjects united and loyal. By making an example or two he will prove more compassionate than those who, being too compassionate, allow disorders which lead to murder and rapine. These nearly always harm the whole community, whereas executions ordered by a prince only affect individuals.

Although Machiavelli's thought is the object of perennial hermeneutic debates, there is little doubt that his preoccupation was with "the security of the state," to which end he was prepared, as are contemporary Realists, to allow the use of even unconscionable means. As for his view of human nature, which lays behind his cynicism, the following is telling:

> One can make this generalization about men: they are ungrateful, fickle, liars and deceivers, they shun danger and are greedy for profit; while you treat them well, they are yours. They would shed their blood for you, risk their property, their lives, their children, so long . . . as danger is remote; but when you are in danger they turn against you. . . . The bond of love is one which men, wretched creatures that they are, break when it is to their advantage to do so; but fear is strengthened by a dread of punishment which is always effective.[6]

That similar views on a static and nonperfectible human nature are entertained by Realism is well known and gives rise to their celebrated "pessimism" about human nature. Morgenthau, for instance, shared this view, as shown at least by his conviction that "human nature, in which the laws of politics have their roots, has not changed since the classical philosophies of China, India, and Greece endeavoured to discover these laws," and by his approval of George Washington's view that "few men are capable of making a continual sacrifice of all views of private interest, or advantage, to the common good. It is vain to exclaim against the depravity of human nature on this account."[7] In addition, such present-day crypto-Machiavellians as Henry Kissinger have clearly adopted Cynicism. Two students of his theory and practice have described his view of how statesmen must work for values of "stability" and "balance of power":

> They must be able to manipulate events and people. They must play the power game in total secrecy, unconstrained by parliaments, which lack the temperament for diplomacy. They must connive with "the largest possible number of allies." They must not be afraid to use force when necessary, to maintain order. They must avoid ironclad rules of conduct; an occasional show of "credible irrationality" may be instructive. They must not shy away from duplicity, cynicism, and unscrupulousness, all of which are acceptable tools for statecraft. They must never burn their bridges behind them. And if possible they must always be charming, clever, and visible.[8]

In sum, Cynical Realism holds that, in view of the alleged nature of human beings, the imperatives of national security, the conflict among nation-states, and the consequent "anarchy" of international intercourse, the life of world politics sits comfortably with the kind of behaviour that is typically regarded as the height of immorality.

Amoralism, for its part, is adopted by Realists whenever they argue or imply that ethical claims at most arise and function in the realm of private or interpersonal morality. By definition, then, they are made irrelevant or inappropriate to behaviour in the international arena; for, in the Realists' view, this arena is the one where states ("primarily") act and interact.

Such a definition of morality, however, is arbitrary. Since morality is concerned with goodness or badness, right or wrong, fairness or injustice, the presumption exists in favour of the simple extension of the moral point of view to *any* relations that can give rise to these predicates. After all, morality is concerned with the well-being of human beings and with the conditions relevant to this well-being. As we noted, a case can easily be made that international morality may be more important and even primary today: for its denial does involve actions that pertain to massive misery, oppression, or annihilation; it may be caused by exploitation, poverty, or the imposition of foreign wills on human beings; and it may involve nuclear war. In other words, it is arguable that, in the complex and interdependent present world, in some respects international morality may be a *prerequisite* for private morality. In any event, it is certainly the case that the rules and principles of "private morality" (such as the duty to abstain from causing pain or the obligation to keep promises) do apply to international morality *by analogy*. Therefore, the burden of proof of the alleged nonextensibility of ordinary morality to the international sphere rests with Realism.

Here Realism's retort may take the form of reiterating the state-centric thesis and the argument from *raison d'état*. It may claim that the international system is primarily populated by states; that states have their own interests that are distinct from those of individuals; and that statesmen cannot apply the rules of ordinary morality to their own behaviour, since this may be counterproductive, naïve, or catastrophic. This reply of Realism is succinctly expressed by Hans Morgenthau's *Politics among Nations*. His "Six Principles of Political Realism" contain such statements as these:

> Realism maintains that universal moral principles cannot be applied to the actions of states in their abstract universal formulation, but they must be filtered through the concrete circumstances of time and place. . . . Both individual and state must

> judge political action by universal moral principles, such as that of liberty. Yet while the individual has a moral right to sacrifice himself in defense of such a moral principle, the state has no right to let its moral disapprobation of the infringement of liberty get in the way of successful political action, itself inspired by the moral principle of national survival.[9]

Morgenthau's view of morality, so influential in Realist circles, suffers from both ambiguity and amateurism. It is remarkable that Morgenthau contradicts himself by using "universal moral principles" as both applicable per se and as qualified by "the concrete circumstances." He also cannot decide whether any abstract "universal moral principle" is more or less applicable than national survival, although "national survival" is, of course, itself such a "universal moral principle." If so, how are we to decide between, say, liberty and national survival? What is clear is only that "successful political action" emerges as Morgenthau's most important criterion of all. But, if this is indeed his considered opinion, what is the meaning of "universal moral principles" that he already endorsed? And what is the relation of "successful political action" to morality? Perhaps one answer is provided:

> There can be no political morality without prudence; that is, without consideration of the political consequences of seemingly moral action. Realism, then, considers prudence — the weighing of the consequences of alternative political actions — to be the supreme virtue in politics. Ethics in the abstract judges action by its conformity with the moral law; political ethics judges action by its political consequences.[10]

Morgenthau's conceptual difficulties are now compounded: first, his definition of prudence as akin to consequentialism is idiosyncratic and highly damaging, as we shall see later in this section; second, to call the consideration of political consequences "the supreme virtue in politics" is a mere assertion without argument, and is seriously debatable; third, his claim that "ethics in the abstract" appeals to "the moral law" is unjustified, because it is only one view of ethics, namely the Kantian one, that insists on such supreme principle and because consequentialism is a major tradition at the heart of ethics; and fourth, the suggestion that "political ethics" uses only "political consequences" as its criterion is a false assertion that ignores motives and means, while also begging the very question that Morgenthau undertook to handle.

Morgenthau's classic programmatic account of the ethics of Realism contains serious fallacies that thoroughly undermine its credibility. These fallacies, however, are part and parcel of Morgenthau's considered beliefs about ethics. And, about his beliefs, we can say with assurance only that they try to *subsume* morality under political expediency, in Machiavelli's manner. The state seems to him to point to interests, first among which is "national survival," and, following which, statesmen will have to decide on an ad hoc basis what they regard as the politically expedient thing to do. The point is made explicitly by Morgenthau when he performs another artificial distinction of the moral and the political domains by declaring that "the moralist asks: 'Is this policy in accord with moral principles?' And the political realist asks: 'How does this policy affect the power of the nation?'

(Or of the federal government, of Congress, of the party, of agriculture, as the case may be.)" But, such a thesis about ethics, beyond its artificiality, suffers from the absence of any principles or rules whereby action can be guided. It is, thus, presumably left to statesmen to decide for all of us. Realism's moral centralism is, therefore, another feature of its inherent elitism and conservatism. In any event, as an "ethical" stance, Morgenthau's version of Amoralism is fundamentally unprincipled, or opportunistic, and therefore pernicious. It provides implicit licence to statesmen's amoral or immoral behaviour, since it can condone it on grounds similar or identical to those discussed under Cynicism.

The third position found among Realists is that of Moral Skepticism. It may be associated with Amoralism in that it may also deny entirely the relevance of ordinary moral principles and values to international relations. But, in some of its more sophisticated formulations, such as that of Hedley Bull, it may allow for the *partial* relevance of ethical judgements to our domain, by stressing the difficulties or limits of moral application.

Bull focussed primarily on a discussion of justice and order in IR. Unprepared to prescribe the centrality of justice to the discipline, Chapter 4 of *The Anarchical Society* emphasized that justice is "really" relevant only to interstate relations, for it is by virtue of the international system's being a *states*-system that negotiations, bargaining, and the like confer rights and duties on nations and states: "Because states are the main agents or actors in world politics, ideas of interstate justice provide the main content of everyday discussion of justice in world affairs."[11] What Bull calls "individual or human justice," that is, "the moral rules conferring rights and duties upon individual human beings," exists in some sense, but is, for him, essentially a permanent headache of states, hence the states' representatives discuss it only "in a muted voice": for the full implementation of justice would imply limits to the authority of states or the undermining of the state's claim to loyalty. In this manner, Bull proceeds to undermine completely the reality of "cosmopolitan or world justice," understanding by this term "ideas which seek to spell out what is right or good for the world as a whole, for an imagined *civitas maxima* or cosmopolitan society to which all individuals belong and to which their interests should be subordinate." Bull sarcastically suggests that such ideas are entertained primarily by Utopians or those ignorant of the present realities of the world: "There is, indeed, no lack of self-appointed spokesmen of the common good of 'the spaceship earth' or 'this endangered planet.' But the views of these private individuals, whatever merit they may have, are not the outcome of any political process of the assertion and reconciliation of interests."

Bull's claims, then, reflect the Realist fetishism of present global political arrangements as uniquely capable of legitimizing moral arguments: in his view, to "define the interests of humankind is to lay claim to a kind of authority that can only be conferred by a political process."[12] This view, however, once again confuses the implementation of a valid idea with the very validity of the idea. It is what I shall call "the sociological fallacy" of Realism that runs through much of its ethically relevant writings and is responsible for an additional problem.

By its fixation on the implementation problem, Realism not only downplays the moral successes of the human community already attained, but also constitutes an impediment to the dissemination of moral truths by erecting formalistic barriers in the manner exemplified by Hedley Bull's discussion.

Moreover, the sociological fallacy leads Bull to another transparent fallacy at the close of his discussion of justice and order. After openly admitting that order must have priority over justice, he adds that "it should not be taken to be a commanding value," and hence "the merits of a particular case" should decide. Bull, however, as did Morgenthau before him, provides no set of criteria that could guide our decisions and our actions. He does show an odd reliance on consensus after the fact, that is, the adoption of political agreement as pointing to the legitimizing justice as opposed to the other way round:

> Today, for example, it may be argued that there is a consensus in international society that the sovereignty of colonial powers over their subject territories is not legitimate, and that violence waged against such powers for the aim of national liberation is just. But this consensus did not exist in the early decades of the anti-colonial struggle, and if indeed it exists today, it is a consequence of that struggle.[13]

In truth, however, it is not consensus that creates truth: consensus can only reflect or recognize it. If it is just to fight for national liberation now, it must have been just even earlier, given the *reasons* that this should be so. Therefore, it should be irrelevant whether consensus exists or not among states or Realist scholars. This contextualization of morality would have made it "unjust" to fight *unless* consensus existed — which is absurd. (Nazism would *not* be "true" even if Hitler had won the war.)

Thus, Bull's fetishism of order raises its erroneous head, and so, once again, the whole set of Realism's assumptions — state-centricity, national interest, power, and order — determines artificially the limits of moral applicability. Morgenthau's "political morality" is thus reiterated, although we are still in the dark as to who would make moral decisions, and under what rules, save for "states." This is the more remarkable because Bull admits that this state of affairs entails that "the institutions and mechanisms which sustain international order . . . necessarily violate ordinary notions of justice."[14] But, to be consistent with the methodological, meta-ethical, and political commitments of Realism, Bull is bound to such a morally unacceptable conclusion.

The final assumption of Realism to be examined briefly is that of Morgenthau's Prudentialism. Recall that Morgenthau was quoted earlier endorsing "prudence" — in the sense of "the weighing of the consequences of alternative political actions" — as "the supreme virtue in politics." I called this definition of prudence "idiosyncratic," because it seems synonymous with utilitarian or pragmatic consequentialism, whereas, traditionally, "prudence" is identified with self-regarding considerations, self-love, or enlightened self-love. The difficulty, then, with prudentialism as posited by Morgenthau can be expressed thus: his "prudence" means either (1) the state must act in self-love, come what may, in which case the consequences can indeed be bleak or even catastrophic; or (2) the state, when acting, must seriously consider the consequences of its actions, in which case some actions will be unwarranted. Morgenthau seems unaware of the paradox. And it is, of course, a paradox because meaning 1 would contradict other principles of Realism, such as order, the state's security, or the satisfaction of the "national interest." As for 2, it would force the state to abstain from a whole host of actions that would have satisfied the Realist canon — especially power-maximization. Therefore, meaning 1 leads to action that can be counterproductive, while meaning 2 leads to counterproductive inaction. Surely, this could not have been what Morgenthau had in mind.

Moreover, if Morgenthau's "prudentialism," in conjunction with his amoralism, entails that *all* states should behave in a selfish or self-regarding manner, it follows that Morgenthau's ethics can be a recipe for imbalance, disorder, or chaos, all of which blatantly contradict the Realist agenda. If, however, Morgenthau meant to suggest that only *our* state should so behave, then this analogue to moral egoism is not a morality, contrary to what Morgenthau supposed by speaking of "no political morality without prudence." Indeed, "the prudential point of view is not the moral one. The moral point of view is *disinterested*, not 'interested.'"[15]

In any event, the *scope* of Morgenthau's ethical concerns is so narrow that the incompleteness of Realism follows as a matter of course. In *Politics among Nations*, Morgenthau's framework is delimited by his main question: "What kind of international ethics, international mores in the form of world public opinion, and international law is there to delimit, regulate, and civilize *the struggle for power among nations* . . . ?"[16] This framework restricted the terms of subsequent Realist discourse. Absent from this framework are such questions as relate to human rights, distributive justice, Third World poverty, overpopulation, malnutrition, starvation, illiteracy, racism, alienation, and global ecological degradation. Answers to these questions are not provided by mainstream Realist thought, for its core terms of reference all but preclude the cultivation of the normative agenda. Its moral reticence (derived from amoralism or cynicism, skepticism or "prudentialism") ended up in resistance to the moral point of view. It transpires, therefore, that Realism has been only an ethos, not an ethics.

But the ethical poverty of Realism has profound consequences for the validity of the doctrine: at best, it proves to be *incomplete* (and hence unacceptable as such), because it refuses to handle its chosen subject matter from the moral point of view. At worst, it is a fallacious or erroneous doctrine, because its "ethical poverty" entails its failure to fully describe, explain, and predict the nature and course of international relations. Therefore, the critique of Realism from the ethical standpoint supplements the critique of Realism's core premises and assumptions, in addition to the foundational assumptions of the epistemological and methodological kind discussed in the previous section. Thus, consider that (a) its conception of *human nature* as evil, fallen, and nonperfectible is based on a mere dogmatic *definition* that is oblivious or blind to factual counterevidence; (b) the assertion that the international system is *state-centric* is misleading since it downplays the remarkable changes in the number and nature of international forces and actors prominent in recent decades, ranging from multilateral international organizations to functional institutions, to transnational groups and movements, to multinational corporations; (c) the focus of *security*, therefore, has also changed: its former grounding in exclusively military preoccupations is now replaced by a manifold rooting that also involves commercial, financial, integrational, functional, cultural, and ecological concerns; (d) *power*, therefore, has already witnessed profound change in its character and range; (e) the *rationality* assumption of realism — drawing both on "the rational actor" model and the hidden assumption of the state as a unitary entity — must, therefore, also be abandoned or severely revised; and (f) the realist notion of *national interest* must also be transcended, if only because its content cannot any longer be inimical to collective solutions to the urgent global problems and needs.[17]

Robert O. Keohane has captured succinctly the predicament of international relations once the assumptions of Realism have been critically assessed. After noting many of Realism's weaknesses (except for its ethical poverty), and its pessimistic implications, including a chaotic international political economy and global nuclear war, Keohane wrote, "complacency in the face of this prospect is morally unacceptable. No serious thinker could, therefore, be satisfied with Realism as the correct theory of world politics, even if the scientific status of the theory were stronger than it is."[18] Having concluded that "Realism, furthermore, is better at telling us why we are in such trouble than how to get out of it," Keohane proposed that the need "to find a way out of the trap means that international relations must be a policy science as well as a theoretical activity,"[19] and hence, "what we need to do now is to understand peaceful change by combining multidimensional scholarly analysis with more visionary ways of seeing the future."[20]

Beyond Realism: Toward a Statist/Cosmopolitan Synthesis?

The Statist/Cosmopolitan synthesis is, indeed, the preoccupation of *normative* analysis. It stands in full or partial conflict with Realism, since it either begins from the need to establish practical ethical answers to international problems or revises Realism by appealing for ethical help to alternative systems of thought.

Scholars who have resisted severing their ties with realism (and perhaps even with Realism) include Stanley Hoffmann and Joseph Nye, Jr. In *Duties Beyond Borders* and *Nuclear Ethics*, respectively, they create syntheses of conceptual-moral frameworks with a view to offering ethical proposals regarding urgent IR problems.[21] Their work, which respects and at times draws on that of Michael Walzer,[22] attempts a thorough revision of Realism, being also a reminder that pure (or "utopian") normative flights that evade political conditions and constraints will be counterproductive.

But some "more visionary" authors are also trying to meet the twofold need for politically relevant proposals grounded on refined ethical categories, assumptions, and solutions. Here belong such scholars as Richard Falk and his associates in the World Order Models Project (WOMP), as well as Charles Beitz, Henry Shue, Peter Singer, and Richard Ashley.[23] Their work appeals explicitly or indirectly to a set of "cosmopolitan" theses and assumptions. "Cosmopolitan" is used in deference to Kant and his vision of a world ethics founded on peace and applying to the community of nations.

A tripartite division of major schools of thought thus emerges concerning the questions of international morality, questions that may be formulated as follows:

1. Is there a set of recognizable moral rules, principles, rights, and obligations?
2. If so, what are the subjects and the scope of this set?
3. What are the grounds used by scholars regarding items 1 and 2?
4. How can the content of the normative set be implemented in the real world of IR?

As we already know, the answers of Realism range from the adamant refusal to accept the existence of such a normative set to the insistence on self-regarding (state-promoting) rules only, to the partial and idiosyncratic admission that some rules may exist but are, at most, related to "the struggle for power" among states. On the other side, Cosmopolitanism presents an ambitious alternative that stands in unambiguous contrast with Realism, but is burdened by the accusation of "utopianism." And in the middle, Statism — or "the morality of states" (Beitz) or the "state moralist" approach (Nye) — borrows concepts and values from both Realism and Cosmopolitanism and leans on the side of the former when it answers item 4 above.

The central features of all three schools are presented in Table 1 (page 520). Given the complexity of the material, some simplification is inevitable. Cosmopolitanism has not been distinguished in any subschools, to underline its unity. Realism, however, deserves to be presented in two versions. Cynical and Amoral Realism, as well as Skeptical Realism and Morgenthau's "Prudentialism," are presented together because, although their philosophical and meta-ethical assumptions are distinguishable (as we have seen), they approach similarly most normative questions and adopt similar goals, justifications, and favoured means.

In the remainder of this section, then, I shall try to clarify some of the points of Table 1 and amplify some grounds given by Statism and Cosmopolitanism to support their normative answers. The discussion will be schematic and at times impressionistic, since our purpose is primarily to introduce the normative projects of the two schools and to stimulate further research. To this end (and because of space constraints), our discussion will be occasionally illustrated by only two concrete moral cases — duties to noncompatriots and interventionism — while the crucial issue of nuclearism will not be covered. A number of authoritative works have treated the nuclear issue, which is, in any event, unrepresentative of the broader debate that is now beginning among Realists, Statists, and Cosmopolitans and is also burdened by serious strategic, technological, technical, socioeconomic, and geopolitical factors that still await systematic assessment.[24]

TABLE 1 Three Approaches to Values in International Relations

Ethical and Political Values	Realism		Statism	Cosmopolitanism
	Cynical or Amoral	Skeptical or "Prudential"		
Classic Sources	Machiavelli, Hobbes, Treitschke	Thucydides	Grotius, Vattel, Pufendorf, Locke, John Stuart Mill	Aristotle, Grotius, Rousseau, Kant, Mill, Marx
Main Political Ends	State power; security; order in international system; national interest		Sovereignty and autonomy of states; peaceful international order	Human community; human needs; and human rights
Main Political Means	State power; great-power management	State power; balance of power; diplomacy of "Prudence"	Action by states and statesmen, and by international institutions	Global changes via international law and national and personal practices
Justification of Ends/Means Political	Human nature as evil, the state as supreme value; systemic anarchy; order first	Human nature as corrupt; national interest; systemic anarchy; order first	Human nature as perfectible; cautious meliorism; institutional reformism; order and then justice	Justice first, for need satisfaction, human rights, "self-realization" (but also order to prevent nuclear annihilation)
Value Foundations	Egoism; self-love; pessimism; *raison d'état*	Relativism; pessimism; national egoism; "Prudentialism"	Liberalism; states rights (ultimately derived from human rights); common states interests; contextualism	Human needs; basic rights; common humanity; peace; liberalism; socialism; ecological humanism
International Moral Rules	Nonexistent	Hardly any	Many, derived by analogy from domestic morality, possible to expand in the future	Many moral principles and conventions; international law; expansion of universal morality on the basis of human needs, human rights, ecological sanity, etc.
Subjects of International Morality	Nonexistent	States	States rights (but also recognition of rights of disadvantaged persons)	Persons
Moral Scope	As narrow as possible (self-regarding or state-regarding)	Very narrow (state-regarding, with few general norms admitted)	Broader than Skeptical Realism, much narrower than Cosmopolitanism	Very broad
Duties to Foreigners	None	None or virtually none	Limited (but possible to expand) because of national boundaries	Many, given that duties are to persons, and boundaries should not count
Interventionism	Yes, for self-regarding reasons	Ambiguous	No, with specific exceptions	Yes, for other-regarding reasons (i.e., to satisfy human needs and rights)
Representative Modern Scholars	Morgenthau, Kissinger	Morgenthau, Bull, Hoffmann*, Nye*	Hoffmann, Walzer, Rawls*, Nye	Falk, WOMP scholars, Nye, Ashley, Keohane*, Beitz, Shue, Peter Singer

*Scholars not commonly included in that category

To begin with, just as Realists appeal to Thucydides, Machiavelli, and Hobbes in arguments from authority, Statists can refer to such predecessors as natural-law scholars, international jurists, and classical liberal philosophers, from Grotius, Pufendorf, and Vattel, to John Locke and John Stuart Mill. Whereas Realism draws on the tradition of inherent human conflict and "anarchy" (both as Hobbesian state of nature and as an absence of an overarching international authority), the liberal Statists are optimistic about the possibilities of a peaceful and orderly international society, based primarily on the sovereignty and autonomy of states as well as the satisfaction of the needs and rights of individuals.

Thus, according to Stanley Hoffmann's self-portrait, he is "one of those old-fashioned and increasingly dinosaur-like types, a liberal"; hence, his belief in the "perfectibility of man and society, and particularly in the possibility of devising institutions, based on consent, that will make society more humane and more just, and the citizens' lot better," as well as his related conviction that injustices "must be fought."[25] Hoffmann's programmatic theses also involve the following: that questions "about morality — including the morality of foreign policy decisions — are questions about the rights and duties, as well as about the happiness and burdens, of individuals"; that his position is therefore "reformist or meliorist, not revolutionary"; which means that "he is addicted to the search for a better, less destructive, more tolerant alternative to an unbearable or nefarious status quo." Finally, his personal experiences (under the Nazi occupation of Europe) can explain "a lifelong, perverse preoccupation with world wars."

Hoffmann's worldview, therefore, reflects the Statists' liberal premises and is clearly distinct from Realism — in terms of human nature, main political ends and means, value foundations, the existence of international morality, and the subjects and scope of this morality. But his stylish and eloquent discourse is rather unsystematic, often convoluted, and overly qualified. While Hoffmann once confesses entertaining a "philosophically untidy and politically elastic notion" (on contextualism in duties toward noncompatriots), one may generalize and apply this notion to many of his arguments. And while he can also be credited with some meticulous ethical investigations that skilfully draw on the rich liberal tradition, Hoffmann's umbilical cord still connects him with the body of Realism — given his constant preoccupation with order and his fear that he may lapse into "utopianism" unless he handles "the world as it is."[26]

The problem, then, is not one of consistency (espousing liberalism while flirting with "the unbearable or nefarious status quo"); it is that Hoffmann is rather elusive about the strategies and tactics required to put his normative suggestions into practice. But, in the absence of a clear agenda for action (or at least clear pointers to action), Realism may still win the day — cynically, amorally, or skeptically. Thus, the states-system survives intact Hoffmann's contribution; and his duties beyond borders amount to minimalist proposals for limited, cautious change, essentially through government elites and other status quo instrumentalities.

Joseph Nye's *Nuclear Ethics* might well be placed in the Statist school, despite his declaration that he opts for a "realist-cosmopolitan synthesis." The declaration may be confusing: first, on a variety of normative issues — from value foundations to the subjects and scope of international morality, to duties toward foreigners, to interventionism — Nye's entire work pays tribute to Statist-liberal values, i.e., the tradition rooted in 19th-century economic and philosophical liberalism, which, on matters pertaining to our concerns, may now include the works of Michael Walzer and Hoffmann's *Duties Beyond Borders*. Second, Nye's value foundations centrally include "a sense of humanity" and duties flowing from the *definition* of "humanity," while they acknowledge the clear possibility of evolving "a stronger sense of community beyond the nation-state for the future."[27] All these Cosmopolitan notions are anathema to Realism. But they are theoretically compatible with the Statist framework of Hoffmann and others, as well as with Nye's other major contribution, *viz.* his work with Robert O. Keohane that produced *Power and Interdependence*.[28] Finally, Nye's "synthesis" of Realism and Cosmopolitanism looks like a shotgun marriage; given their radical antitheses on every normative item (see Table 1), the synthesis in question may only mean this: that Nye favours Cosmopolitan normative aspirations but retains a Realist skepticism about political applications. But this combination is very much what Hoffmann's school — i.e., liberal Statism — reflects.

Be that as it may, two points are already emerging: first, the normative differences between Statism and Cosmopolitanism, on the one hand, and all forms of Realism, on the other, are differences *in kind*; and while Statism and Cosmopolitanism differ on some evaluative emphases, most such differences seem reconcilable, being only *of degree*. Second, Statism is cautious or conservative in terms of normative implementation: whereas for most Realists this issue does not arise (since there is no set of moral rules or duties to implement), Cosmopolitanism can criticize Statists primarily for lack of commitment and boldness concerning the political application of normative proposals. Thus, while scholars such as Hoffmann and Nye dread the spectre of "utopianism," Cosmopolitan Richard Falk may place Statism outside the "system-transforming strategies" for world order, as either "system-reforming" or "system-maintaining."[29] Before, however, we consider the issue of implementation, let us identify the normative similarities and differences of Statism and Cosmopolitanism.

As Table 1 suggests, Statists and Cosmopolitans do agree on the following values: (1) that Realism's political goals of power, military security, and "national interest" prove to be narrow and must be transcended; (2) that moral values, and especially justice, are and ought to be at work in international relations; (3) that international moral rules and principles are natural extensions of the appropriate norms of domestic society; and (4) that duties toward noncompatriots exist and can be defended as such.

Statism and Cosmopolitanism, however, disagree on the emphases they put on the following: (1) state boundaries seem to Cosmopolitans to have questionable moral significance, while Statists place strict conditions on their transcendence; (2) whereas Statists see states, Cosmopolitans see persons, as the principal subjects of international morality; (3) in terms of moral scope, Cosmopolitans defend an expanding international morality, while Statists are cautious lest the sovereignty of states be violated in a morally or politically illegitimate manner; (4) while Statists are most sensitive about "order," Cosmopolitans emphasize the normative priority of "justice"; and (5) concerning intervention, while Statists begin with a principled refusal to accept it *unless* some conditions are met, Cosmopolitans opt for its principled endorsement *if* some conditions are met.

On reflection, then, one senses that the normative sets of the two approaches are, indeed, reconcilable and that their differences (given the solidity of their compatibility) derive more from concern over practical *implementation* than from an evaluative *foundation*. Ample evidence for this is provided by Nye's own synthesis. For Nye (like Hoffmann) reiterates his respect for "the realities of the way the world is organized into states at this stage in history."[30] However, his values are certainly grounded in approaches that Cosmopolitans share: that is why he called his approach "cosmopolitan-realist." In addition, Nye derives "positive" and "negative" duties toward others from such typical Cosmopolitan conceptions as the meaning of "humanity" and "sense of humanity." Thus, Nye could appeal to such authorities as Hume, Rousseau, Kant, and John Stuart Mill, as all Cosmopolitans can. Furthermore, Nye skilfully builds on the very notion of moral reasoning, which includes the criterion of impartiality.[31] Therefore, duties toward noncompatriots, for instance, can be established by endorsing moral impartiality — as one must: for one can uphold the idea of "moral partiality" only on pain of self-contradiction. Finally, Nye's "three-dimensional ethics" wisely endorses moral reasoning on the basis of motives, means, and consequences.[32] He is thus effective in combining the religious influences on the moral life with J.S. Mill's consequentialism and the Kantian stress on purity of motives. But this point, as all previous normative steps, most Cosmopolitans can all too happily endorse.[33]

Now, if Nye's eclectic value foundations can readily be shared by Cosmopolitans, so could most Cosmopolitan values be shared by liberal Statists (such as Hoffmann and Nye). Thus, as Richard Falk summarized them, the values agreed upon by the World Order Models Project of the Institute for World Order are entirely compatible with the Statist project: "minimization of collective violence; maximization of collective well-being; maximization of social and political justice; and maximization of ecological quality."[34] The "globalist ideology" advocated by this Cosmopolitan movement intends to harmonize various elements of the relevant influences. According to Falk, this ideology "draws on" *liberalism* ("to check abuses of state power in the relations between governments and people"); *socialism* ("to depict a humane set of economic relationships based on societal well-being"); *ecological humanism* ("to reorient the relations between human activity and nature"); and *global modelling* ("to put complex interactions of societal processes at various levels of organization into a dynamic, disciplines framework").[35] More concretely, the values that Falk has been defending consistently are peace; economic well-being ("satisfaction of basic human needs, together with a movement toward equality between and within societies"); social and political justice ("realization of non-economic human rights for individuals and groups"); ecological balance ("achievement of environmental quality, conservation of resources, preservation of endangered species"); and "humane governance."[36]

In view of Nye's "cosmopolitan-realist" declaration and Hoffmann's liberal-ideological self-portrait, the two approaches manifestly exhibit a normative kinship that can draw on a common traditional heritage. Consider, for instance, the satisfaction of human needs and the duties associated with them. Both Statists and Cosmopolitans can employ the moral naturalism of Aristotle and draw on his insight that these needs are, in fact, the impetus behind the formation of the human family, the clan, the village, and the *polis*.[37] Both schools may anchor on this empirical truth new biological-social-ecological needs of human universality. From such empirical foundations, the normative deductions can be unproblematic: for N stands for minimal biological-social-ecological needs (e.g., for safe food, clean water, unpolluted air, etc.) that must be satisfied for human life to be sustained; and if we grant human life as a self-evident or indubitable value, then it follows that N must be satisfied. Therefore, the duty to satisfy minimal human needs follows as a matter of *logic*. Thus, Statists and Cosmopolitans can be in total agreement on one more value foundation. (Of course, so could Realists, if they decided to accept the relevance and centrality of the moral point of view.)

The possibility of normative convergence between Statists and Cosmopolitans may be further demonstrated by recalling a host of traditional ethical arguments to which Cosmopolitans appeal and which Statists can endorse without violating any of their valued premises. Such arguments may include: (1) enlightened utilitarian considerations of maximizing human well-being and minimizing pain and distress; (2) the nonutilitarian consequentialism of the kind Peter Singer employed in his admirable papers on famine relief and the duties of the citizens of affluent nations;[38] (3) the neo-Marxist theory of human interests initiated by Jurgen Habermas and applied to IR theory by Richard Ashley;[39] (4) the international applications of John Rawls's theory of justice that, in its neocontractarian foundations, can be used as a vehicle for "the equal moral claims of all persons" and for criticizing the inequity and unfairness resulting from the present distributive criteria of the international economic institutions and arrangements (IMF, World Bank, etc.).[40] Finally, Henry Shue's non-Aristotelian but equally compelling argument about basic rights and their implications for U.S. foreign policy can be accepted in principle by Statists, given the persuasiveness of Shue's remarkable assault on the moral relevance of national boundaries.[41]

It therefore transpires that Statists and Cosmopolitans draw on the same broad ethical traditions that inform enlightened and viable political arrangements; that they agree on the necessity and validity of applying the moral point of view to IR; that once they agree on any relevant grounds — from consequentialist to "logical," to those based on human needs or basic rights — that it is *true* that, say, "famine, malnutrition and illiteracy are evil," they then can proceed to negotiate consensus about the means to combat such evils; and that, in the final analysis, debate will continue (as it must) on the best or most appropriate methods or means to meet the moral challenges of the human community.

It follows that, essentially, only questions of implementation separate the two normative approaches to international relations: should we proceed primarily in terms of states or international organizations? Is international law, and its spreading instruments and institutions, one of our best moral bets? Are moral duties as broad as Cosmopolitans insist, or more limited, as Statists often argue? And if the views of the former are accepted, how can we begin to satisfy those duties? Should "humanitarian intervention" be favoured and expanded or would this become a form of unconscionable meddling in other peoples' affairs for self-regarding, even cynical, reasons?

In general, the Statist replies are predicated on pragmatic solutions that accept the Statist given and try to build upon it. International organizations, however, are also seen as instruments or vehicles for moral change, as are groups and strata within societies, such as the intellectuals, the media, and the educational system.[42] Nye, in fact, goes a lot farther, toward "a Kantian type of future": he acknowledges that

> the development of transnational institutions and contacts may gradually transform domestic attitudes toward sovereignty and the use of violence to defend the state. The development of transnational interests, organizations, and communication may encourage growth of multiple loyalties that soften the claims of the sovereign state and of groups that help to bridge the cultural parochialisms of different peoples.[43]

Here, of course, Nye has spoken as a Cosmopolitan. But Cosmopolitans are not themselves divorced from the deep appreciation of the realities of the present states-system. In fact, while Falk has employed the language of "planetary citizenship" and of "the wholeness of the human race," he can be as hard-nosed about political practice as his Statist colleagues. He has, indeed, elaborated on the political and quasi-political means and mechanisms of implementing the cosmopolitan vision throughout his voluminous writings. What emerges clearly from the work of WOMP is a multidimensional picture of normative implementation that involves studies to "engage the attention of public opinion and government leaders"; theoretical work to inspire a manifold movement for globalist reform by mobilizing "a variety of groups working in widely disparate arenas for peace and justice, often in opposition to official state policy"; building "a more ambitious transnational consensus on the direction and shape of an acceptable world order solution"; and the assumption of "a political stance that is more populist than is characteristic of system maintainers or system-reformers," and is based on the "globalist ideology" mentioned above. In short, the political agenda of the World Order Models Project "seeks to promote an ethical and ecological flourishing in a political setting that joins solidarity of sentiments to diffusion of structure, power, wealth, and authority." Thus, regarding such work, Falk emphasizes two parallel commitments: "a commitment to *normative change* (i.e., change associated with positive values) and a commitment to *political relevance* (i.e., proposals sensitive to issues of feasibility)." Regarding the latter, Falk reveals the pragmatism of the Cosmopolitan project by including such premises as "an overriding concern with minimum order, especially in superpower relations" and "an image of feasibility (e.g. ten to one hundred years) not restricted to the exceedingly short horizons of governmental leaders (one to five years)."[44]

Conclusion

I have argued that Realism is primarily responsible for the ethical underdevelopment of international relations theory. Given that ethics cannot be severed even from the "description, explanation and prediction" of the subject matter of IR (since ethics conditions the choice of our concepts, methods, problems, and answers), it follows that what I have called the "ethical poverty" of Realism renders it a defective theory. When one considers that many of Realism's theses and assumptions are erroneous from the logical, epistemological, and empirical points of view, the tenability of Realism becomes highly problematic. And, given that the state of the world is morally unacceptable, and that theory must react and guide practice, Realism's evasion of the normative dimension renders it, at best, incomplete and, at worst, untenable as such.

In reaction to the ethical poverty of Realism and in order to handle the world's manifold malaise, a number of scholars have recently turned to the investigation of normative issues in international relations. While both Statists and Cosmopolitans transcend Realism by recognizing the centrality of ethics in IR, Statists are cautious about thorough global change, whereas Cosmopolitans advance bold proposals for the profound transformation of the world. But, because Statism and Cosmopolitanism share, as shown, solid normative foundations, their differences seem reconcilable. That is why I intimated above that there are good prospects for an ultimate Statist-Cosmopolitan synthesis.

In any event, the emerging normative debate among Realism, Cosmopolitanism, and Statism clearly entails the rehabilitation of ethical analysis at the heart of IR. Thus, new intra- and interdisciplinary work should yield fresh insights on the precise nature of the normative reconcilability of Statism and Cosmopolitanism, the character of their shared ethical foundations, the aspects of Realism that have to be revised and retained, and the viability of an additional synthesis regarding the political implementation of their normative proposals. It is crucial that we refine our views on the politics of transition to a post-Realist phase in international theory and practice. But normativists must also demonstrate the empirical sophistication and solidity of their moral suggestions; that is, they must produce compelling connections of their alternative descriptions and explanations with their proposed global institutional structures. It is also necessary to refine and harmonize the various strands of Statist and Cosmopolitan prescriptions, so that new grand theories can further challenge the theoretical (and actual) predominance of Realism.

The challenge from Realism cannot of course be underestimated, especially if couched in stark cynical or skeptical terms, amounting to "why be moral in international relations?" The retort here may take various forms, including throwing the ball immediately into the challenger's court by asking whether Realism sees the world as morally acceptable. In addition, one may stress that international morality (like all morality) entails its own justification (since to feed is better than to starve and to educate is better than to kill); that progression toward an ethically richer world manifestly implies satisfaction for each contributing individual; and that international morality includes tangible positive consequences for its contributors.

To be sure, on the question of political will, Statists have tended to stress "common interests," while Cosmopolitans emphasize our "common humanity." Given, however, the nature and urgency of many current plights — from nuclearism to Third World misery, to global ecological disasters — it may be already hard to distinguish "common humanity" from "common interests." When the ethics of the global village is finally written, no such distinction could probably be made on the majority of issues.

NOTES

1. For a brief and clear introduction to the ethical discourse, see William Frankena, *Ethics* (Englewood Cliffs, N.J.: Prentice-Hall, 1963). For recent developments in ethical theory, see *New Directions in Ethics: The Challenge of Applied Ethics*, ed. Joseph P. DeMarco and Richard M. Fox (New York and London: Routledge and Kegan Paul, 1986).

2. J. David Singer, "The Responsibilities of Competence in the Global Village," *International Studies Quarterly* 29 (September 1985): 245, 259.

3. Michael Banks, "The Evolution of International Relations Theory," in *Conflict in World Society: A New Perspective on International Relations*, ed. Michael Banks (Brighton: Wheatsheaf, 1984), 16, attributes this to "prominent mainstream scholars."

4. Exceptions would include E.H. Carr, John Herz, and J. David Singer.

5. Robert E. Osgood, *Ideals and Self-Interest in America's Foreign Relations: The Great Transformation of the Twentieth Century* (Chicago: University of Chicago Press, 1953).

6. This quotation and the one above are from Niccolò Machiavelli, *The Prince*, trans. George Bull (Harmondsworth: Penguin, 1975), 95, 96–97.

7. Hans J. Morgenthau, *Politics among Nations: The Struggle for Power and Peace* (New York: Knopf, 1967), 4, 8.

8. M. Kalb and B. Kalb, *Kissinger* (Boston: Little, Brown, 1974), 47.

9. Morgenthau, *Politics among Nations*, 10.

10. Morgenthau, *Politics among Nations*, 10.

11. Hedley Bull, *The Anarchical Society: A Study of Order in World Politics* (London: Macmillan, 1977), 82. All quotations in this paragraph are from pp. 82–85.

12. Bull, *Anarchical Society*, 86.

13. Bull, *Anarchical Society*, 98.

14. Bull, *Anarchical Society*, 91.

15. Frankena, *Ethics*, 18.

16. Morgenthau, *Politics among Nations*, 223 (emphasis added).

17. In addition to Michael Banks, another recent, accessible, and decisive critique of the major (nonethical) assumptions of Realism is Robert O. Keohane, "Realism, Neorealism and the Study of World Politics" and "Theory of World Politics: Structural Realism and Beyond," in *Neorealism and Its Critics*, ed. Robert O. Keohane (New York: Columbia University Press, 1986).

18. Keohane, *Neorealism*, 198.

19. Keohane, *Neorealism*, 198.

20. Keohane, *Neorealism*, 200.

21. Stanley Hoffmann, *Duties Beyond Borders: On the Limits and Possibilities of Ethical International Politics* (Syracuse: Syracuse University Press, 1981); Joseph S. Nye, Jr., *Nuclear Ethics* (New York: Free Press, 1986).

22. See Michael Walzer, *Just and Unjust Wars: A Moral Argument with Historical Illustrations* (New York: Basic Books, 1977), and "The Moral Standing of States: A Reply to Four Critics," *Philosophy and Public Affairs* 9 (Spring 1980): 209–29.

23. See, for example, Richard Falk, "Toward a New World Order: Modest Methods and Drastic Visions" in *On the Creation of a Just World Order*, ed. S.H. Mendlovitz (New York: Free Press 1975); "The World Order Model Project and Its Critics: A Reply," *International Organization* 32 (Spring 1978): 531–45; *The End of World Order* (New York: Holmes and Meier, 1983); and Richard Falk and Samuel S. Kim, "World Order Studies and the World System," in *Contending Approaches to World System Analysis*, ed. William R. Thompson (Beverly Hills: Sage, 1983), which provides references to other works by WOMP scholars, such as J. Galtung, S.S. Kim, A. Mazrui, S.H. Mendlovitz, and R.B.J. Walker. See also Charles S. Beitz, *Political Theory and International Relations* (Princeton: Princeton University Press, 1979), "Bounded Morality: Justice and the State in World Politics," *International Organization* 33 (Summer 1979): 405–24; Beitz, "Recent International Thought," *International Journal* 43 (Spring 1988): 183–204; Henry Shue, *Basic Rights: Subsistence, Affluence and U.S. Foreign Policy* (Princeton: Princeton University Press, 1980); and "Exporting Hazards," in *Boundaries: National Autonomy and Its Limits*, ed. Peter G. Brown and Henry Shue (Totowa, N.J.: Rowman and Littlefield, 1981); Peter Singer, "Famine, Affluence, and Morality," *Practical Ethics* (Cambridge: Cambridge University Press, 1979); Richard Ashley, "Political Realism and Human Interests," *International Studies Quarterly* 25 (June 1981): 204–36; and Robert W. Cox, "The Poverty of Neorealism," in *Neorealism*.

24. See Jonathan Schell, *The Fate of the Earth* (New York: Knopf, 1981); Anthony Kenny, *The Logic of Deterrence* (Chicago: University of Chicago Press, 1985); Russell Hardin et al., eds., *Nuclear Deterrence: Ethics and Strategy* (Chicago: University of Chicago Press, 1984); Gregory S. Kavka, *Moral Paradoxes of Nuclear Deterrence* (Cambridge: Cambridge University Press, 1987); and Nye, *Nuclear Ethics*.

25. All quotations in this paragraph are from Hoffmann, *Duties Beyond Borders*, 8–10.

26. Hoffmann, *Duties Beyond Borders*, *passim*. Cf. Hoffmann's "The Problem of Intervention," in *Intervention in World Politics*, ed. Hedley Bull (Oxford: Clarendon Press, 1984), 27.

27. Nye, *Nuclear Ethics*, 34, 39, and 41.

28. Robert O. Keohane and Joseph S. Nye, Jr., *Power and Interdependence: World Politics in Transition* (Boston: Little, Brown, 1977).

29. Richard Falk, *End of World Order*, 46ff.

30. Nye, *Nuclear Ethics*, for instance, 34.

31. Nye, *Nuclear Ethics*, 36.

32. Nye, *Nuclear Ethics*, 20ff.

33. For instance, Falk, *End of World Order*, chaps. 3, 11, and 13.

34. Falk, *End of World Order*, 53.

35. Falk, *End of World Order*, 54.

36. Falk, *End of World Order*, 306.

37. Aristotle, *Politics* (Harmondsworth: Penguin, 1964), Book I, esp. chaps. 1 and 2.

38. Peter Singer, "Famine, Affluence, and Morality," and "Reconsidering the Famine Relief Argument," in *Boundaries*.

39. Ashley, "Political Realism and Human Interests."

40. See Charles Beitz, *Political Theory and International Relations*, and Robert Amdur, "Rawls' Theory of Justice: Domestic and International Perspectives," *World Politics* 29 (April 1977): 438–61.

41. Shue, *Basic Rights*.

42. Hoffmann, *Duties Beyond Borders*, 225–28. Robert Keohane, *After Hegemony: Cooperation and Discord in the World Political Economy* (Princeton: Princeton University Press, 1984), 247–57, endorses cosmopolitan values but fastens on cautious revisionism of international economic regimes.

43. Nye, *Nuclear Ethics*, 130–31.

44. Falk, *End of World Order*, 54–55, passim.

SELECT BIBLIOGRAPHY

Ashley, Richard K. "Political Realism and Human Interests." *International Studies Quarterly* 25 (June 1981): 204–36 .

———. "The Poverty of Neorealism." *International Organization* 38 (Spring 1984). Reprinted in *Neorealism and Its Critics*, ed. Robert O. Keohane. New York: Columbia University Press, 1986.

Beitz, Charles R. *Political Theory and International Relations*. Princeton: Princeton University Press, 1979.

———. "Bounded Morality: Justice and the State in World Politics." *International Organization* 33 (Summer 1979): 405–24.

———. "Recent International Thought." *International Journal* 43 (Spring 1988): 183–204.

Bull, Hedley. *The Anarchical Society: A Study of Order in World Politics.* London: Macmillan, 1977.

Eayrs, James. *Diplomacy and Its Discontents.* Toronto: University of Toronto Press, 1971.

Falk, Richard. *The End of World Order.* New York: Holmes and Meier, 1983.

Falk, Richard, and Samuel Kim. "World Order Studies and the World System." In *Contending Approaches to World System Analysis*, ed. William R. Thompson. Beverly Hills: Sage, 1983.

Hoffmann, Stanley. *Duties Beyond Borders: On the Limits and Possibilities of Ethical International Politics.* Syracuse: Syracuse University Press, 1981.

———. "The Problem of Intervention." In *Intervention in World Politics*, ed. Hedley Bull. Oxford: Clarendon Press, 1984.

Keohane, Robert O. "Realism, Neorealism and the Study of World Politics." In *Neorealism and Its Critics.*

———. "Theory of World Politics: Structural Realism and Beyond." In *Neorealism and Its Critics.*

Morgenthau, Hans J. *Politics among Nations: The Struggle for Power and Peace.* New York: Knopf, 1967.

Nye, Joseph S., Jr. *Nuclear Ethics.* New York: Free Press, 1986.

Shue, Henry. *Basic Rights: Subsistence, Affluence and U.S. Foreign Policy.* Princeton: Princeton University Press, 1980.

Singer, Peter. "Famine, Affluence, and Morality." *Philosophy and Public Affairs* 1 (Spring 1972): 229–43.

Walzer, Michael. *Just and Unjust Wars: A Moral Argument with Historical Illustrations.* New York: Basic Books, 1977.

OPENING UP THE BLACK BOX: THE DECISION-MAKING APPROACH TO INTERNATIONAL POLITICS

Kim Richard Nossal

The purpose of this chapter is to examine an approach to the study of world politics that has, in the last three decades, experienced a dramatic rise in popularity, and then, as quickly, dropped out of fashion as a way to conceptualize about, and understand, international relations. In order to assess the usefulness of this approach, we need to survey its rise in the 1950s, its growth in the 1960s, and then its decline in the late 1970s and 1980s.

The "Old" Art: Billiard Balls and Black Boxes

Until the early 1950s, the dominant analysis of the foreign-policy decisions of states was marked by two interrelated analytical and methodological assumptions: that states were unitary actors and that states acted according to the precepts of a means-end rationality.

First, states tended to be conceived of as singular units, or unitary actors. They were seen essentially as billiard balls: impermeable and opaque, knocking against one another on the felt-covered slate of international politics.[1] To these units, qua units, could be attributed phenomena we usually associate with, and reserve for, individual human beings: goals, intentions, decisions, and actions. It is a conception that pervaded scholarly discussions of international politics a generation ago and, indeed, continues to inform how many politicians, members of the media, and the wider public perceive — and analyze — the actions of states. Thus, for example, we commonly speak of France seeking to harmonize the European Community's policies on textile imports; of the Soviet Union urging Vietnam to settle its differences with China; or of the United States invading Grenada. Some claim that this propensity to attribute goals, intentions, and actions to the abstraction of the state is merely a convenient shorthand. To say that the United States invaded Grenada is certainly a more economical way of saying that the leader of the governing apparatus of the geographical and political entity known as the United States sought to end what he saw as unwanted and illegitimate extrahemispheric influence in the affairs of the geographical and political entity known as Grenada, and so exercised the authority vested in him by the basic law of the United States to issue an order to several units of the armed forces of the United States to launch an armed attack against Grenada and seize control from those who wielded political power locally, an order that was successfully carried out. The brevity of the shorter formulation, it is commonly argued, does not hide any meaning, since, regarding common parlance, everyone understands precisely what the shorthand is intended to convey. But, to dismiss such conceptions as mere shorthand is to miss the critical analytical assumption that is made: "the United States" is conceived of as a unitary entity, something that can have goals, take decisions, and engage in action. The specification of exactly who is formulating those goals, making the decisions, or taking the action is therefore unnecessary because, at bottom, it is immaterial: the president, the soldiers who obey his commands, and the United States, are, for all practical intents and purposes, one and the same.

A second strand had to do with the methodological assumption that tended to be made about the essential rationality of these unitary entities. Most analyses of international politics must proceed without access to the documentation and data on the decision process, which invariably is kept secret by the state. Because the actual details of the process by which decisions were arrived at remains hidden, the analyst must depend heavily on assumptions about the process of decision if he or she is to reconstruct decision meaningfully. One way to undertake such a reconstruction was to impose the assumptions of rationality on states. The logic of this argument suggests that we can better analyze state behaviour if we assume that states are rational actors; in other words, if we assume that they have clear goals and employ the means best suited to achieving those goals. For example, Hans J. Morgenthau, the doyen of postwar students of international politics, is frequently cited as the key proponent of the "rational actor" assumption.[2] To be sure, Morgenthau appears to argue that it is necessary for the analyst of foreign policy to assume a particular kind of rationality on the part of decision makers:

> We put ourselves in the position of a statesman who must meet a certain problem of foreign policy under certain circumstances, and we ask ourselves what the rational alternatives are from which a statesman may choose . . . and which of these rational alternatives this particular statesman, acting under these circumstances, is likely to choose.[3]

Taken out of context, the quotation is indeed suggestive. But it is misleading, for Morgenthau was one of those students of international politics who decried the ahistorical analytical tendencies of both practitioners and publics. Instead, he sought to develop a theoretical perspective on the relations of states, the primary tenet of which was that leaders of states act in terms of interest defined as power. Such a tenet, Morgenthau went on to argue, "allows us to retrace and anticipate, as it were, the steps a statesman — past, present, or future —

has taken or will take on the political scene" by examining those steps on the assumption that they represent a rational search for "power."[4] In other words, Morgenthau was seeking to explain and predict the relations of states without having to know the exact details of the inner workings of the decision-making process in each state.

If the quotation taken out of the broader context of Morgenthau's argument does his theoretical perspective a disservice, it remains nonetheless a not unreasonable characterization of how much of what happens in foreign policy tended to be analyzed by students of international relations before the 1950s, and indeed tends to be analyzed by foreign offices, the media, and the informed public today. Since the manner in which a state arrives at the decisions that shape its actual behaviour in international politics is unknown, the foreign-policy decision-making process of states was commonly conceived of as a "black box," the inner workings of which remained largely hidden from view and could only be guessed at until the diplomatic historians could get their hands on the diplomatic records for the period.

"Art" or "Science"? The "New Frontier"

These two assumptions, taken together, had an oddly equalizing effect on the study and analysis of international affairs, for they served to make everyone a potential foreign-policy expert. By employing these two assumptions, it was (and remains) well within the capacity of any intelligent and reasonably well-informed person to engage in "armchair analysis" about the actions and behaviour of the great (or not so great) powers. James N. Rosenau may have bemoaned the fact that "most people, officials and ordinary citizens alike, consider themselves to be as qualified or as unqualified as the next person in international affairs,"[5] but such was the inexorable consequence of thinking about international politics in terms of billiard balls and black boxes.

One of the principal reasons why virtually everyone can dabble in the analysis of international politics lies in the nature of the discipline itself, particularly as it emerged within the university over the last century. The discipline of international politics had by the outset of World War II not developed in a manner similar to those of many other areas of scholarly inquiry in the 20th century where an emphasis tended to be placed on setting the scholar of that discipline apart from those of other disciplines, and indeed from society at large. It is axiomatic that theory, methodology, and vocabulary are the principal means by which "experts" in a particular field of human knowledge set themselves apart from the rest of society. In some disciplines, such exclusion is frequently designed to protect not only the political community as a whole but also the parochial economic interests of the expert practitioners themselves against the predations of competitors in the marketplace. Thus, for example, few citizens can claim "instant expertise" in medicine, law, or architecture, primarily because such expertise — and the common and legal recognition thereof — is beyond the reach of all but those who have invested a considerable number of years acquiring the elements of a theoretical body of knowledge, mastered both the methodology and vocabulary necessary for the practice of these areas of human knowledge, and then served a period of apprenticeship before being admitted to a state-sanctioned closed fraternity that provides formal and legitimate certification of "expertise." Such a process of exclusion, it might be noted, involves a trade-off: communities agree to allow these experts to eliminate competition, thereby keeping prices for their services high, but in return are saved (for the most part) from quackery, and from the damage to the common weal that would ensue. But, the exclusion also extends to eliminating credible claims to expertise by outsiders: a political scientist who would pronounce on such matters as antibody formation in macrophages, the application of *stare decisis* in a particular wrongful-dismissal suit, or the anticipated load and stress factors in the design of multistorey apartment buildings, would simply lack credibility and justifiably be dismissed as a quack, and perhaps even a danger to public safety.

By contrast, there seems to be no such reaction in the area of international affairs. Any well-informed doctor, lawyer, or architect, simply by employing assumptions of rationality applied to unitary actors in international politics, could express his or her views on the latest developments in international affairs without comparable fear of derision or dismissal by the "expert" foreign-policy analyst. For, before the 1950s, there was little effort to build the kind of expertise that would have allowed the political scientist to exercise a similar kind of exclusionary monopoly over the analysis of foreign affairs; students of the relations between states had been historically either unwilling or unable (or, more probably, both) to set themselves apart and claim an exclusionary expertise by cloaking their discipline in the shrouds of a distinctive set of theories, methods, and vocabulary that could put comprehension and analysis beyond the ken of the ordinary informed citizen.

At the end of World War II, the dominant approach to the study and understanding of international politics in the academy was, in fact, little different from the approach being taken by officials and publics. To be sure, diplomatic historians sought to uncover the motivations for particular policies and courses of actions by looking at the process by which sets of decisions were arrived at by different leaders in international affairs. However, their approach tended to be intuitive, eclectic, and ultimately idiosyncratic, as there was no explicit and agreed-upon framework for examining the behaviour of states, and no set of clear theoretical laws to guide analysis. Rather, analysis depended on examining, in a seemingly ahistorical and unsystematic fashion, a variety of possible explanatory factors that could reasonably account for a particular decision of a particular state at a particular time.

In political science, the approach was not very different. Charles McClelland termed it, somewhat disparagingly, the "wisdom outlook," because it depended on studying the accumulated wisdom and understanding of the relations among states inherited from those in the past who have tried to understand the essence of international politics. In this view, "students are advised, at the beginning, to concentrate their studies in diplomatic history, on the great books of commentary and political philosophy, and on the biographies of famous practitioners of the diplomatic arts." In doing this, the student has the opportunity to develop "an 'understanding' that is not quite intuitive; it is more a synthesis constructed privately from both particular facts and general meanings. Each student must build up such understanding by his own individual intellectual effort over a long period of time."[6]

Likewise, James Rosenau characterized foreign-policy analysis in political science as little more than a series of case studies of current events, or the foreign-policy decisions of single countries, analyzed unsystematically, unscientifically, and impressionistically. Such analysis was marked by an unwillingness on the part of political scientists in international politics to theorize, to see broader patterns, to assume that there was an underlying order in the foreign policies of states and search for and elucidate that order. Indeed, as Rosenau has noted, many academic analysts of international politics seemed to proceed on the assumption that their field was impossible to theorize about because of its complexity and fundamental unpredictability. Sometimes, this assumption was made quite explicit:

> When it comes to studying foreign policy in its various manifestations . . . the social scientist . . . [is] asked to explain and predict attitudes whose complexity makes a mockery of the few "scientific" tools we have. . . . To attempt generalizations and constructions of models that will give us a rigorous scientific understanding and prediction of foreign policy is a hopeless task.[7]

As a result of such attitudes, Rosenau continued, foreign-policy analysis rarely led to "a body of rigorously tested knowledge or even a coherent set of testable propositions." Instead, foreign-policy analysts in political science provided "only illustrations from past experience and informed impressions of present practice." In other words, they offered little more than the kind of knowledge that "can be acquired by reading a good newspaper." Even more damning was the charge that scholars of international politics in the university were just like (horror of horrors!) ordinary citizens: "like the journalist and the intelligent citizen, he bases his foreign policy assessments and recommendations on untested impressions rather than on a rigorously substantiated body of knowledge."[8] In short, foreign-policy analysis was ahistorical; because it proceeded intuitively, it was unsystematic; because it tended to focus on a single country, it was atheoretical. It remained an "art" rather than a "science."

Putting an end to this unsystematic, intuitive, and atheoretical analysis was the primary goal of the so-called behaviouralist revolution that swept the United States in the 1950s and 1960s. Working on the belief that the methods and assumptions of the natural sciences could and should be employed in the social sciences, many American social scientists sought to replace the impressionistic analysis employed by "traditional" students of international politics with a more rigorous, "scientific" method. Cumulative knowledge-building was to replace the scattered grapeshot of single-country case studies undertaken without any specific attempt to "build theory." Foreign policy would be examined to derive generalizations about state behaviour rather than to account for the particular policies of a particular country at a particular time. Scholars committed to the scientific method — those Rosenau would call "pioneers" and "frontiersmen"[9] — would boldly push out the boundaries of the new discipline, generating the testable and falsifiable "if-then" propositions so desperately needed to create a general theory of international politics.

To this end, the systematic collection and organization of data would replace the traditional method of an intuitive examination of relevant research materials. The careful creation of common databases would permit other social scientists to reproduce experiments, allowing for the independent confirmation or disconfirmation of theoretical postulates. The new research methods and technologies of the postwar world could also be brought to bear to aid in this task. In particular, the spread through academe of the computer would render such previously labour-intensive tasks as the collection of objectively identifiable event data more easily accomplished; the statements of leaders could be subjected to content analysis; the voting behaviour of the growing number of states at the United Nations could be manipulated and analyzed in a matter of seconds. With the application of statistical techniques — from crude factor analysis to more sophisticated regression analyses — relationships between variables could be rigorously and scientifically established.

In short, with new thinking, new methods, new techniques, and new goals, the ungainly and untidy discipline of the politics among nations could be transformed. Indeed, for some, the growth of a positive social science of international politics was seen as having positive normative implications, such as providing a means of eliminating war.[10]

"Art" as "Science": The "Framework for Analysis"

Behaviouralism would lead postwar scientists in numerous, and often divergent directions, but those interested in foreign-policy studies and international politics would be led to trying to make the analysis of the behaviour of states more systematic. But where to begin? The obvious place was with how the decisions of states were made, for there existed no explicated systematic method for examining and analyzing the process by which state behaviour was decided. Thus, it is not surprising that many of the efforts at making the study of foreign policy more "rigorous" and more "scientific" in the 1950s and 1960s were aimed at elucidating a framework for the analysis of foreign-policy decisions that could provide a "standard" for all students to follow.

This quest gave rise to a proliferation of art — or more precisely, artwork — in the literature on foreign-policy analysis, as a succession of scholars sought to represent schematically their ideas about how one might systematically analyze and theorize about the behaviour of states. Typically, this artwork — and, more importantly, the assumptions that lay behind it — would be a variation of a basic input-output model. One schematic box would represent the "input" var-

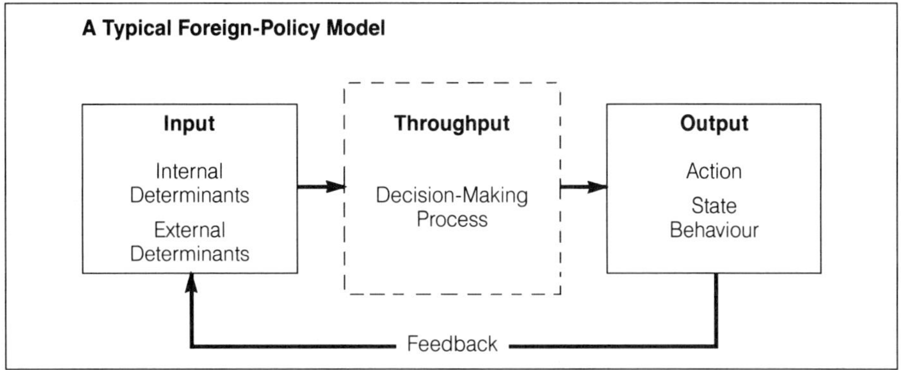

iables. This would be connected by an arrow to another box — the "decision," or "throughput," box. Another arrow would lead to an "output" box, representing the state's action. Usually, an arrow would be placed leading from the "output" box back to the "input" box, representing the "feedback loop" — the inexorable consequences of a state's actions in the international realm that would in turn have an impact on the input variables.

Filling each of these boxes was the first task of the would-be systematic analyst of foreign-policy decision making. Much of the initial work fixed on the input box, which had to be filled with the appropriate variables for examination if these independent variables were to eventually explain the content of the output box (or the dependent variable). The "output" box, by contrast, tended to be left blank, for that which was to be explained tended to be inclusively, but unspecifically, labelled simply "decision" or "action." The "throughput" box, representing the actual process of decision, was seen as important but hard to actually see in practice — hence the common reference to a "black box."

The work by Richard C. Snyder, H.W. Bruck, and Burton Sapin, first published in 1954, and republished in 1962,[11] is generally understood to be "pioneering"[12] work in this area. Their model proceeds on the explicit assumption that a detailed examination of a state's decision-making process is one of "only two ways of scientifically studying international politics" (the other being "the description and measurement of interaction"). They argued, against the orthodox assumptions that states were unitary actors behaving according to precepts of rationality, that state behaviour was more properly the outcome of a decision process dominated by human beings in "situations" that required decision and action. Thus, they sought self-consciously to "rid ourselves of the troublesome abstraction 'state'" by focussing on those who are authoritatively placed to take decisions and actions on behalf of the state — i.e., the process by which the state's leaders came to their decisions.

Their model sought to identify the dominant factors that determine outputs, or state actions, defined as the outcomes of decisions taken by the state's authoritative decision makers. Since decisions are taken in the context of "situations," Snyder, Bruck, and Sapin divided the "settings"[13] in which decisions are made into "internal" and "external" components. The external environment sought to examine the influence of such factors as the "nonhuman environment," "other cultures," "other societies," "societies organized and functioning as states," and "government action." The internal setting included nonhuman environmental factors, such as geographic location, societal factors, and the "human environment," specifically the culture and the population. Importantly, both the internal setting and the decision-making process itself affected, and were affected by, "social structure and behaviour," which included such variables as "major common value orientations," "major institutional patterns," "major characteristics of social organizations," "role differentiation and specialization," "groups," and "relevant social processes," such as opinion-formation, adult socialization, and the "political" process.[14] To understand foreign-policy decisions, in other words, one had to examine the impact of international politics, domestic politics, and the governmental process on the decision maker, and understand the individual's own psychology and perception of his or her environment.

All of these variables, it was assumed, would "determine," or "explain," foreign-policy outcomes in some way. However, the scheme proposed by Snyder and his associates had no predictive capacity. Indeed, whatever the scientific pretensions of its authors, it was little more than a heuristic "framework for analysis" — a means to help researchers organize their research efforts, rather than to predict that, in a certain situation, a particular variable would explain a particular outcome or foreign-policy decision. Thus, implicit in the model was the possibility that an exploration of all of the variables would reveal that, for example, State A's decision to use force against State B five years ago could be primarily attributable to "internal" factors, while State C's decision to use force against State D today could be accounted for primarily by reference to "external" variables. Whether State E would use force against State F five years from now was simply beyond the capacity of the model to predict. However, even though the Snyder framework did not pose such explanatory linkages, it did, as Hermann and Peacock have suggested, indicate that an answer to the central question posed by the framework — why do foreign-policy decision makers take the decisions they do? — would "require the introduction of the entire panoply of theory and research on human behaviour from the psychology of perception to organizational behaviour, from the analysis of communications networks to the examination of societal norms and values."[15]

Most of the subsequent attempts to elucidate a theoretical "framework" for the analysis of foreign policy amounted to little more than an elaboration of this initial effort. It is important to note that artwork featuring interconnected black boxes continued to be an essential component of this intellectual enterprise, or so it would appear from the propensity of modellers to seek to represent their models in diagrammatic fashion. While, mercifully, foreign-policy analysis was spared the pictographs so common in discussions of decision making in business-administration texts, artistic variations on the black box continued to make their appearance in schematic models of the foreign-policy decision-making process. They have included cubes,[16] funnels,[17] optical lenses,[18] decision trees,[19] and concentric circles.[20]

Basic to all this subsequent modelling was a refinement of the "input" box: "explanatory" variables linked by arrows to foreign-policy outcomes tended to proliferate, becoming, in the process, more complex. For example, Karl W. Deutsch's so-called cascading model of communication flows in foreign-policy decision making, in its "disassembled" 8 variants, includes 144 "black boxes" and 193 arrows that come in 2 colours and 4 distinct forms (circular, broken, bold, and normal).[21] However, these arrows, while they may serve to lend a patina of the scientific to the enterprise, are, in reality, little more than a quaint academic legerdemain. For, as Marion Levy has pointed out, social scientists, including foreign-policy analysts, have long been prone to embrace what he called the "fallacy of indeterminate representation" in using arrows in their models. While arrows may conjure up the rigours of vector analysis, the truth is that, in most social-science modelling, all these arrows really mean is that the author thinks that there is some kind of relationship — usually unspecified — between the variables so connected.[22] Like the model elaborated by Snyder and his associates, therefore, much of the subsequent "theoretical" modelling in foreign-policy decision making was bereft of "theory": these models lacked explanatory (i.e., predictive) capacity; they could not be operationalized without resorting to intuitive, judgemental, and essentially traditional methods; and, most importantly, they could not, by their very nature, generate that most sought-after of behavioural grails — the "if-then" hypothesis.

Developing a *predictive* capacity was the key goal of James Rosenau, who, it might be noted, generally eschewed arrow-heavy diagrams in his modelling. Rosenau's own contribution to frontiersmanship came in a 1966 article, which took aspects of the heuristic model advanced by Snyder, Bruck, and Sapin and developed them further.[23] First, Rosenau took the welter of independent variables suggested by Snyder and his associates and made them more manageable by reducing both their number and their complexity. Rosenau speculated that the behaviour of states could be accounted for by one of the following "determinants": "individual,"[24] role, governmental, societal, or systemic. In other words, a foreign-policy output could be attributed to the individual traits of a particular decision maker; to the role that the decision maker found himself or herself occupying; to the governmental process of decision; to the nature of the society on whose behalf the decision maker was operating; or to the nature of the international system in which the state operated.

Rosenau went well beyond Snyder and many other modellers. His search for theory led him to formulate a "pretheory" of foreign policy. As he put it, before one can build a house, one has to transform the raw materials (trees and clay) into comparable units of construction (bricks and boards), and have some idea as to how one will fit them together into a coherent whole. So, too, with "building" a "house of theory." His goal was to lay the groundwork for theory proper by making bricks and boards. As a means of developing some greater explanatory capacity for his model, he began by speculating on the relative *potencies* of these variables. For example, does the individual variable "explain" foreign-policy behaviour better than any or all other variables? Can we better understand the behaviour of states in international politics by reference to societal demands or pressures on a decision maker rather than by reference to other possible determinants? How important, in other words, are these variables relative to one another? The answer to such questions, of course, is that "it depends" on what one is seeking to explain. Thus, Rosenau took his "pretheoretical" analysis three steps farther. First, he "pretheorized" that the relative potency of these variables would vary, depending on the attributes of the state whose actions were to be explained. The attributes Rosenau selected were size, nature of the economy, and nature of the polity: employing simple dichotomies (large/small; developed/underdeveloped; open/closed), he emerged with eight types of societies, ranging from large/developed/open, such as the United States, to small/underdeveloped/closed societies, such as Ghana. In each of these cases, he speculated on how the five determinants could be ranked in importance. Thus, he theorized that, in the case of the United States, the roles of the individual decision makers would be the strongest determinant of foreign-policy behaviour, while their individual characteristics would be least likely to explain decisions. In the case of Ghana, by contrast, one could expect that the individual variable would be most potent, while the societal variable would be least important.

However, Rosenau recognized that such hypothetical rankings would be too abstract without a further specification of the dependent variable — or, to be more specific, until the actual policy outcome was elaborated more clearly. Moreover, one could not talk about particular policy areas without also taking into account the desire and the capacity of states to exercise influence and power vis-à-vis other states and in the process affect their decision making. For states, because of their varying power, had a varying capacity to resist the importunities of others in the international system. Rosenau's second step was to layer onto the dichotomous attributes noted above a further one — penetrated/non-penetrated — raising the number of society types to 16. Third, he specified four "issue areas" — with examples having an impact on foreign policy and international politics: the "territorial area" (conflict over Berlin, Cyprus, statehood for Quebec); the "status area" (recognition of the People's Republic of China, civil rights in South Africa); "human resources area" (the "population explosion"); and the "non-human resources area" (East-West trade, economic development of India). For his final elaboration of his "pretheory," Rosenau collapsed these four issue areas into three — "status," "non-human resources," and "other," and layered them onto the 16 society types, creating in the process 48 categories for hypothesizing about the relative potencies of his five variables, represented in an accompanying chart by their first letter or letters. The result is 48 lists of lower-case letters, the exact ordering of which, it should be noted, seems to be the result of Rosenau's intuition, and is not completely explained in the text.[25]

Rosenau's model provides a series of intuitive guesses, and an implicit call for applying them to reality. For example, in a small, developed, open, penetrated polity such as Canada, will decisions in the non-human-resources area be influenced primarily by systemic factors, and least of all by individual variables? It — and the 47 other hunches — remained untested. But did this model contribute to "theory"? To be sure, unlike Snyder's model a decade earlier, parts of Rosenau's "pretheory" generated a considerable degree of research and shaped the way in which other students in the field approached the analysis of decision making.[26] One not insignificant measure of the influence of his "pretheory" is the widespread use of his five determinants, or "sources," in textbooks on both foreign policy and international politics,[27] and the degree to which his categorization of determinants have become a standard in numerous explanations of foreign policy. As Hermann and Peacock have noted, however, Rosenau's attempts to further refine the model by specifying dichotomous types and different issue-areas have been frequently ignored, in part because these parts of the "pretheory" were not well specified.[28]

In the genre of the general "framework for analysis" of foreign policy, the last significant offering was that developed by Brecher, Steinberg, and Stein in 1969.[29] Their work developed aspects of that of both Snyder and Rosenau. For example, Brecher and his associates sought to make clearer the fact that decision makers operated in both an "operational" and a "psychological" environment. Brecher et al. thus brought the focus back to the individual decision maker and the patterns of human-information processing, a focus that had been stressed by Snyder in the mid-1950s, but had been lost in Rosenau's formulations in the mid-1960s. Another major contribution of the Brecher approach was the more careful elucidation of what kinds of external systemic factors would act on decision makers. Eschewing both Snyder's general approach, which had simply focussed on "other countries," and Rosenau's highly unspecific "systemic" variable, which had simply lumped *all* external variables together into one undifferentiated mass, Brecher and his associates sought to disaggregate the external variable into pieces that corresponded more intuitively with the actual conditions of states. Thus, in the Brecher model, there was the broad global system in which a state found itself; but states and their leaders also have more local foci. Brecher suggested that a state's regional subsystem would have an effect on outcomes. Likewise, most states have major bilateral ties, and so the model also included a "dominant bilateral" subsystem.

Beyond "Art": Opening Up the Black Box

By the end of the 1960s, the artwork approach to the study of foreign-policy decision making had seemingly run its course. As I will argue below, the modelling in this area has had considerable utility, but grand theory–building, as we have seen, was not one of its significant consequences. To be sure, the modelling movement spawned a great deal of research into related areas, such as crisis decision making and simulation; it also invigorated a number of large data-collecting projects, such as the Comparative Research on the Events of Nations (CREON) project.[30] But another of the lines of inquiry opened by the decision-making approach to foreign policy was occasioned by a signal failure of the approach as it was conceived in the 1950s and 1960s. That was the failure of such modellers as Snyder, Rosenau, or Brecher to uncover one of the boxes in the model: the "black box" of decision — the "process" or "throughput" box — still remained shrouded and largely uninvestigated.

It would be left to the successor generation of the original "pioneers" to explore more closely the actual decision-making process and, by doing so, open up the black box that had been largely ignored by those who had sought to create a framework for foreign-policy analysis. This group of students, it should be noted, would lack the pseudoscientific pretensions of the earlier students in the field. While they were not unconcerned with theorizing writ large, their methodology and their aims would straddle the boundaries between the traditional and behavioural approaches. The work of this group would take two principal directions: exploring the processes by which governments, as organizations, make decisions; and exploring further, as Snyder and his associates, and Brecher, Steinberg, and Stein had suggested, the psychological processes of individual decision makers, particularly the ways in which they perceived (and misperceived) their "realities." The purpose of this section is to examine briefly these two strands by examining some suggestive major works that emerged from this period as exemplars of each approach.

The process by which governments, as complex organizations, took the decisions that defined state action and behaviour in international politics was the concern of a number of scholars. Among them was Roger Hilsman, an academic who served as a senior official in the U.S. State Department in the early 1960s. In his work, *To Move a Nation*, Hilsman argued that the actual process of decision — in other words, how the different agencies of the state processed a decision from initiation to implementation — would have an impact on the outcome of the decision itself. In his view, "policy-making is politics," and one has to look to the bureaucracy as a *political* agency rather than merely as an *administrative* agency neutrally implementing decisions of political leaders. In this observation, Hilsman, and others who would adopt this perspective, was reflecting the results of the shifts in how the administrative apparatus of the state was seen in the postwar period. Beginning in the 1950s, American students of public administration would increasingly reject the famous 19th-century formulation of President Woodrow Wilson, who, in an earlier incarnation as a political scientist, had claimed in 1887 that "administration lies outside the proper sphere of politics."[31] In the context of domestic American politics, scholars were increasingly prone to focus on the *political* role of bureaucrats; it was the application of this perspective to the formulation of American foreign policy that underlay the approach taken by Hilsman and others.

If Hilsman had pointed the way in his discussion of foreign-policy decision making in Washington, Graham T. Allison systematized and made more explicit the assumptions. Allison's concern was to demonstrate the essential fallacies of the rational-actor assumptions discussed at the outset of this chapter and to demonstrate how and why state behaviour resulted from a process that was not always rational. His work[32] thus sought not only to critique the approach of traditional students of international politics, such as Hans Morgenthau, and therefore to provide us with a new perspective on the behaviour of states, but also to bring to the study of foreign-policy decision making some of the work and perspectives of students of the domestic decision-making process. His "governmental politics," or, as it has commonly come to be known, "bureaucratic politics" model of decision making was premised on a number of assumptions. First, the decision-making process itself was, at bottom, a struggle for power between value-maximizing governmental actors — bureaucrats, elected and appointed officials — "in positions." These officials had different conceptions of interest, depending not only on which department of government they were from but also on a variety of other, often idiosyncratic, factors. Issues were dealt with, not by all bureaucrats and decision makers, but by a limited number interacting with each other on a series of "action channels," a process of winning, losing, and compromising that produced the "final outcome." Allison termed it a *resultant* to distinguish it from a *result*, which carried with it a connotation of rationality. Though not without its critics,[33] the bureaucratic-politics perspective provided a useful heuristic means to explore foreign-policy decision. It became widely used, and widely quoted. While difficult to apply to specific decisions, because it depended on access to information about the interactions of officials, which was not readily available, it did serve to alert students of foreign policy to the tensions, incompatibilities, and conflicts of interest among officials, and the intensely political "pulling and hauling," to use Allison's phrase, that occurred as policy was being made.

One of the assumptions made by Allison and other bureaucratic-politics enthusiasts was that decision makers would have divergent conceptions about interest. In part, this divergence was the result of their different locations within the state, and the frequently divergent policy preferences to which such locations gave rise. However, it was also partly the result of differences in perception — in other words, differences in how individual decision makers saw reality. Allison's model notes the importance of perception and misperception, but does not explore it fully. A second strand in foreign-policy decision-making analysis, therefore, sought to expand on the observation originally made by Snyder and his associates in 1954 that foreign-policy decision makers operated within environments, and that how they saw their environment was critical to understanding their responses, which would be manifest in a state's decisions — an assumption restated with greater clarity by Brecher, Steinberg, and Stein in 1969. A great deal of research had flowed in the 1960s from the work of Snyder and the Sprouts in the 1950s, drawing, in particular, on studies in psychology that were being "imported" and applied in political science. This literature attempted to come to terms with how foreign-policy decision makers saw their world, and to determine how perception affected policy outcomes. The most cogent synthesis of much of this work came with the publication, in 1976, of Robert Jervis's work on perception and misperception in foreign-policy making.[34] Drawing on earlier observations, Jervis sought to demonstrate the processes by which decision makers fashioned their views of the world; more importantly, Jervis demonstrated how foreign-policy decision makers, like all human beings, are prone to misperceive their environment and act on those misperceptions. Jervis sought to generate specific hypotheses on perception and misperception as a guide for understanding the cognitive process of decision.

Two works that sought to combine elements of both these approaches should be mentioned here. Irving Janis's exploration of the intersection of misperception and the decision-making process led him to examine how the supposedly rational actors in foreign-policy decision making can "make mistakes." He suggested that the dynamics of the small group that typically characterizes decision making had an impact on outcomes, and hypothesized that members of these groups misperceive critical aspects of their environment because of the existence of a strong psychological drive for consensus within the group that dampens a search for possible alternatives. Using cases in American foreign policy, Janis explores four "fiascos" and two cases where consensus was not present, and suggests both some broad generalizations about the operation of a phenomenon he characterized as "groupthink." Like Allison, Janis was concerned about applying his perspective, proposing a well-argued normative conclusion about preventing groupthink.[35]

John Steinbrunner, like Allison and Janis, was committed to an exploration of the inadequacies of the rational analytical assumptions about foreign-policy behaviour so common in many analyses of international politics and foreign policy. Steinbrunner begins by asserting that the process of decision is infinitely more complex than the logic of the rational decision-making model would allow. In particular, he suggests that much of human "decision making" does not follow the rational process usually assumed. Humans must process vast amounts of information under conditions of great uncertainty, and must make value trade-offs of complex proportions. This complexity is magnified when humans must make decisions in the context of organizations. Such complexity, he suggests, involves a process well beyond the comprehension capacity of the rational model. The rational model assumes both the capacity for assessing the full range of alternatives, and a relatively predictable environment. Rather, Steinbrunner suggests a more appropriate and productive approach, what he calls the "cybernetic" paradigm, which is, in fact, a graft of a cybernetic model of decision making with a discussion of the cognitive processes by which the human mind processes information and "decides" on action. Central to his argument is that humans, whether in positions of political authority or not, do not make decisions involving a tremendous amount of information and intense uncertainty by adopting a rational model. Instead, they are subject to the distortions that can come with the selective processing of information, attachment to preconceived value trade-offs, and a very limited number of reasonable alternatives. To demonstrate the applicability of this alternative way of assessing foreign-policy decision making, Steinbrunner examines the issue of nuclear-weapons sharing in NATO using cybernetic, rather than rational-actor, assumptions.[36]

Beyond the Black Box: Going Grand Again

The decision-making approach to the study of international politics proved to be a 30-year process of unpeeling an onion — taking the "billiard ball" of the

1940s, and trying to strip away successive layers of the policy process in the hope of revealing the core. This approach has involved a continual disaggregation: from specifying the broad "external" and "internal" factors, to specifying the actual process of decision, to trying to delve into the very psyches of the decision makers themselves. By the early 1970s, the focus of inquiry in foreign-policy analysis had thus developed to the micropolitical.

The problem was that such micropolitical analysis lost sight, or proceeded in ignorance, of the macropolitical, or the broader political contexts within which perceptions were formed, bureaucracies operated, governments existed, and decisions were made. In particular, the decision-making approach tended to lack both a theory of the state and a theory of international politics. Adherents of the decision-making approach tended to take the relationship of the modern state apparatus to both the domestic polity and the international context in which the state operated for granted, or as a given. Likewise, the decision-making approach frequently operated on the assumption that international politics could be best understood as the sum of the decision-making processes of the individuals making decisions on behalf of their states: foreign-policy decision making *was* international politics.

By the end of the 1970s, such ideas had been rejected by those on what had become the new "new frontiers" of the discipline. These students argued that a deeper understanding of international politics was not to be found in delving more microscopically into the processes by which individual policy makers made their decisions, but rather in exploring the broader international and domestic contexts within which foreign-policy decisions are made. The international-politics literature in the late 1970s and throughout the 1980s was thus dominated by studies that concentrated on the macropolitical level. Broad theoretical perspectives emerged on the state (mirroring the movement in other areas of political science to "bring the state back in");[37] on the nature of the international system;[38] on the impact of anarchy on state behaviour;[39] and on the constraints and imperatives of operating within a capitalist world economy.[40] By the end of the 1980s, "new" approaches (frequently new applications of old ideas — regime theory and game theory are but two examples) dominated the output of the major university presses and journals in international politics. In this welter of "newness," the scientific foreign-policy modellers, who had once been so "new" themselves, became sidelined, no longer in the vanguard. Despite Rosenau's continued propensity to make bold claims for the approach — he declared in 1973, for example, that comparative foreign policy had all the attributes of a "normal science"[41] — the approach no longer dominated the field.[42]

Conclusion

This chapter has sought to trace what Hermann and Peacock have termed the "boom and bust quality"[43] of the decision-making approach to the study of international politics. It has argued that the foreign-policy decision-making approach enjoyed a short-lived heyday during the 1960s, but was eventually supplanted by alternative ways of looking at international politics. The fall of the decision-making approach can be attributed to the milieu in which it emerged, and to its own intellectual unsustainability.

First, the fall of the approach should be placed within the larger intellectual milieu within which it rose. The approach has to be seen as symptomatic of a larger phenomenon — the faddish nature of the study of international politics after the end of World War II. As Kal Holsti has noted, one of the distinguishing features of the discipline after 1945 is the degree to which its students have resisted theoretical and methodological orthodoxy, with the result that "international theory is in a state of disarray."[44] One of the reasons for this resistance is the pervasive and persistent search of students of international politics for "newness." This search, it can be argued, has been driven in the first place by the nature of the international system after 1945 and, in the second place, by the nature of the American university system.

The supposedly "new" phenomena of the postwar world seemed to demand the abandonment of "traditional" approaches to international politics as being without relevance in a world dominated by nuclear weapons and delivery systems capable of previously inconceivable destruction, transnational actors putatively supplanting the state, rising pollution of the global "commons," endemic shortages of food and other resources, persistent underdevelopment in much of the world, the globalization of capitalist production, the crisis of capitalism, the rise of globalized information and communication, or the decline of great-power hegemony. Such "new" phenomena surely demanded "new" approaches.

The technologically driven catalysts for "newness" were given an additional fillip by the explosive growth of postsecondary education in all industrialized countries after 1945, producing a concomitant growth in the number of academics engaged in research and writing on international politics. However, as Holsti noted,[45] they were working within the structures of a university system that would greatly affect the individual scholar's search for gain, safety, and reputation (to borrow the universals claimed by Thucydides and Hobbes). Membership and success in the postwar university system depended on meeting both the norms of the emerging discipline, reflected in the criteria used by reviewers of scholarly journals and university presses, and the expectations of university managers who viewed publications as a condition of tenure, promotion, and remuneration. Permeating this structure was and is the notion of knowledge "production," which puts a premium on discovery and, therefore, on "newness." This focus would manifest itself most clearly in international politics in the continual "invention" of "new" approaches to the study of international relations, with an emphasis on "theory."[46] Scholars with "new" ideas, who produced "seminal" or "pioneering" works, could claim a place in the pantheon; those who worked with these ideas could claim that they were on the "cutting edge of the discipline" (as it is so often and so pretentiously called). From this vantage point, both position and reputation were more easily assured.

This relentless search for newness, however, carries with it one inexorable and, in the long run, humbling, consequence: what is at one time new becomes old, and therefore of declining value in a system that puts a premium on newness. Such has been the inevitable fate of virtually all of the works that were in their day on the "cutting edge." The decision-making approach became "older" faster, because it could not sustain itself intellectually against the erosive effects of the succeeding waves of new "theoretical" approaches that came rolling in after it. To be sure, the Canute-like inundation was made easier because of the original claims — and the intellectual hubris — of many of its proponents, who might usefully have reminded themselves of the warning in Proverbs 16:18 before setting pen to paper. The fall of the decision-making approach was indeed all the harder, given the puffery and immodesty of the theoretical pretensions of many of its enthusiasts and their dismissal of the "traditional" approaches to international politics as "old" and therefore passé and irrelevant. The lofty promise of the "frontiersmen," who were boldly going where no one had gone before to carve theory out of the wilderness, simply could not be sustained over the longer term. The decision-making approach did not yield a "partial theory," much less a "general theory," of international politics. Thus, even those who seek refuge in the quaint notion that one can create so-called middle-level islands of theory that will one day be connected with each other in one great continent of "General Theory" were to be disappointed with the results of the approach.

If the decision-making approach is assessed as a theory of international politics, it will most assuredly fail the test. But, if assessed in more modest terms, shorn of its pretensions, the literature on decision making does have considerable utility for the student. Its primary contribution, it can be argued, is not as a means of generating "knowledge" defined in terms of a set of falsifiable if-then hypotheses based on a set of objectively observable data, but rather in providing a heuristic device for the analysis of the key microphenomena of world politics — the decisions of states. It is particularly useful for those who seek to understand the behaviour of a particular state at a particular time. For the frameworks for analysis created by Snyder, Bruck and Sapin; Rosenau; and Brecher, Steinberg, and Stein alert the student of foreign policy to a range of phenomena that must be examined to gain an understanding of the process by which a state's leaders make their decisions. The contributions of Allison, Janis, Jervis, and Steinbrunner alert us to the dynamics of human perception and interaction that may affect outcomes. To note that the student has to be armed with other assumptions about the broader political, social, and economic environments, both domestic and international, in which these dynamics occur is to take nothing away from the contribution they make to our understanding of the foreign-policy process.

The stress here, in sum, is on developing an "understanding" of international phenomena. Reading the works explored in this chapter will provide no "general" theory of either international politics or foreign policy; they will not provide the shortcut that will reveal why the leaders of states behave as they do. But, when read in combination with a range of other works on international politics, they will, to turn McClelland's disparaging words quoted above back on him, help one develop "an 'understanding' that is not quite intuitive; it is more a synthesis constructed privately from both particular facts and general meanings. Each student must build up such understanding by his own individual intellectual effort over a long period of time."

NOTES

1. A number of authors, including Arnold Wolfers and J.W. Burton, use this analogy: see Burton, *Systems, States, Diplomacy and Rules* (Cambridge: Cambridge University Press, 1968).

2. For example, Graham T. Allison, *Essence of Decision: Explaining the Cuban Missile Crisis* (Boston: Little, Brown, 1971), 26.

3. Hans J. Morgenthau, *Politics among Nations: The Struggle for Power and Peace*, 5th ed. (New York: Knopf, 1973), 5.

4. Morgenthau, *Politics among Nations*, 5.

5. James N. Rosenau, *The Scientific Study of Foreign Policy* (New York: Free Press, 1971), 29.

6. Charles McClelland, "International Relations: Wisdom or Science?" in *International Politics and Foreign Policy: A Reader in Research and Theory*, ed. James N. Rosenau, rev. ed. (New York: Free Press, 1969), 4.

7. Kenneth W. Thompson and Roy C. Macridis, "The Comparative Study of Foreign Policy," in *Foreign Policy in World Politics*, ed. Roy C. Macridis, 2d ed. (Englewood Cliffs: Prentice-Hall, 1962), 26–27, quoted in Rosenau, *Scientific Study of Foreign Policy*, 34. Fourteen years and three editions later, Thompson and Macridis would maintain that view: see their fifth edition (1976), 23.

8. Thompson and Macridis, "Comparative Study of Foreign Policy," 30.

9. See Rosenau's comments in the preface to *International Politics and Foreign Policy*, xvii, and elsewhere in his introductory remarks to the selections in the collection. Perhaps not surprisingly, the scholar as "pioneer" pushing outwards on the "frontier" of international politics was the metaphor of choice for many American students of foreign policy, such as Rosenau, who embraced the behavioural "scientific" approach in the 1950s. But, to the degree that the "frontier" in American culture tends to conjure images of taming both wilderness and "uncivilized" peoples, the metaphor also says a great deal about how the "frontiersmen" viewed the classical works on international relations of Chinese, Greek, Indian, and European cultures, some predating the "pioneers" by two and a half millennia.

10. See, for example, the comments of Kenneth E. Boulding, "The Learning and Reality-Testing Process in the International System," in *Image and Reality in World Politics*, ed. John C. Farrell and Asa P. Smith (New York: Columbia University Press, 1967), 13.

11. Richard C. Snyder, H.W. Bruck, and B. Sapin, *Decision-Making as an Approach to the Study of International Politics* (Princeton: Foreign Policy Analysis Project, Princeton University, 1954); Snyder, Bruck, and Sapin, eds., *Foreign Policy Decision-Making: An Approach to the Study of International Politics* (New York: Free Press, 1962).

12. Joseph Frankel, *Contemporary International Theory and the Behaviour of States* (Oxford: Oxford University Press, 1973), 64; Rosenau, who had been Snyder's graduate student in the early 1950s, had made a comparable claim in his introductory comments to the selection by Snyder, Bruck, and Sapin reprinted in the reader he edited, *International Politics and Foreign Policy.*

13. Cf. the "environmental" approach adopted by Harold and Margaret Sprout, which argues that foreign-policy decisions are taken and executed in different environments, or, to use the term they prefer, "milieus." See their *Man-Milieu Relationship Hypotheses in the Context of International Politics* (Princeton: Princeton University Center of International Studies, 1956); *Ecological Perspective on Human Affairs* (Princeton: Princeton University Press, 1965).

14. See Snyder, Bruck, and Sapin, *Foreign Policy Decision-Making.*

15. Charles F. Hermann and Gregory Peacock, "The Evolution and Future of Theoretical Research in the Comparative Study of Foreign Policy," in *New Directions in the Study of Foreign Policy*, ed. Charles F. Hermann; Charles W. Kegley, Jr.; and James N. Rosenau (Boston: Allen and Unwin, 1987), 23.

16. Charles F. Hermann, "International Crisis as a Situational Variable," in *International Politics and Foreign Policy*, 415.

17. Charles W. Kegley, Jr., and Eugene R. Wittkopf, *American Foreign Policy: Pattern and Process* (New York: St. Martin's, 1979), 10.

18. James M. Keagle, "Introduction and Framework," in *Bureaucratic Politics and National Security: Theory and Practice*, ed. David C. Kozak and James M. Keagle (Boulder, Colo.: Lynne Rienner, 1988), 18.

19. Margaret G. Hermann, Charles F. Hermann, and Joe D. Hagan, "How Decision Units Shape Behaviour," in *New Directions*, 334.

20. Roger Hilsman, *To Move a Nation* (Garden City, N.Y.: Doubleday, 1967), 541–44.

21. Karl W. Deutsch, *The Analysis of International Relations*, 3d ed. (Englewood Cliffs, N.J.: Prentice-Hall, 1988), 128–31. The "model assembled" (p. 132) is, not surprisingly, a tangle of arrows.

22. Marion J. Levy, Jr., "'Does It Matter If He's Naked?' Bawled the Child," in *Contending Approaches to International Politics*, ed. Klauss Knorr and James R. Rosenau (Princeton: Princeton University Press, 1969), 101–3.

23. James N. Rosenau, "Pre-theories and Theories of Foreign Policy," in *Approaches to Comparative and International Politics*, ed. R. Barry Farrell (Evanston: Northwestern University Press, 1966), 27–92.

24. It should be noted that, in the original formulation, Rosenau termed this the "idiosyncratic" variable. Because the term seemed "misleading," it was abandoned in favour of the term "individual." See *Scientific Study of Foreign Policy*, 108, n. 42.

25. Part of the reason for the ordering was revealed in what Vasquez terms the most famous footnote in the field. Footnote 45 claimed, almost as an afterthought, that there would be a relationship between the ordering of the variables and the size, or power, of a state. For a discussion, see John A. Vasquez, *The Power of Power Politics: A Critique* (New Brunswick, N.J.: Rutgers University Press, 1983), 59.

26. It has been frequently remarked that the Snyder framework was so complicated that it was applied only once — by Glenn D. Paige, *The Korean Decision* (New York: Free Press, 1968); Rosenau's "pretheory" generated greater interest because of the relatively greater ease of operationalization. See Hermann and Peacock, "Evolution and Future of Theoretical Research," 22–24.

27. For example, Kegley and Wittkopf combine Rosenau's "source" categories with Campbell's "funnel of causality." See *American Foreign Policy*, 10.

28. Hermann and Peacock, "Evolution and Future of Theoretical Research," 24.

29. Michael Brecher, Blema Steinberg, and Janice Stein, "A Framework for Analysis on Foreign Policy Behavior," *Journal of Conflict Resolution* 13, no. 1 (1969): 75–101.

30. For a discussion of these directions in the study of international politics, see Vasquez, *Power of Power Politics*, 47–77.

31. Cited in David C. Kozak, "The Bureaucratic Politics Approach: The Evolution of the Paradigm," in *Bureaucratic Politics and National Security*, 4.

32. The fullest exposition is to be found in Allison, *Essence of Decision*.

33. The most cogent is Robert J. Art, "Bureaucratic Politics and American Foreign Policy: A Critique," *Policy Sciences* 4 (December 1973): 467–90.

34. Robert Jervis, *Perception and Misperception in International Politics* (Princeton: Princeton University Press, 1976).

35. Irving L. Janis, *Victims of Groupthink: A Psychological Study of Foreign Policy Decisions and Fiascoes* (Boston: Houghton Mifflin, 1972).

36. John D. Steinbrunner, *The Cybernetic Theory of Decision: New Dimensions of Political Analysis* (Princeton: Princeton University Press, 1974).

37. For example, Stephen D. Krasner, *Defending the National Interest: Raw Materials Investments and U.S. Foreign Policy* (Princeton: Princeton University Press, 1978).

38. For example, the emergence of the so-called neorealist perspective: see Robert Gilpin, *War and Change in World Politics* (Cambridge: Cambridge University Press, 1981); Kenneth N. Waltz, *Theory of International Politics* (Reading, Mass.: Addison-Wesley, 1979); Robert O. Keohane, ed., *Neorealism and Its Critics* (New York: Columbia University Press, 1986).

39. Robert O. Keohane, *After Hegemony: Cooperation and Discord in the World Political Economy* (Princeton: Princeton University Press, 1984); Robert Axelrod, *The Evolution of Cooperation* (New York: Basic, 1984); Kenneth A. Oye, ed., *Cooperation under Anarchy* (Princeton: Princeton University Press, 1986).

40. For a good review of the huge literature that has developed on international political economy, see Robert Gilpin, *The Political Economy of International Relations* (Princeton: Princeton University Press, 1987).

41. James N. Rosenau, "Restlessness, Change, and Foreign Policy Analysis," in *In Search of Global Patterns*, ed. James N. Rosenau (New York: Free Press, 1976), 369–76.

42. The "pioneers" who had blazed such "new" trails in the theoretical wilderness in the 1950s and 1960s were fully cognizant of the degree to which the international politics

literature had become dominated by other approaches by the late 1980s. It can be best seen by the degree of self-criticism — sometimes amounting to self-flagellation — in many of the contributors to Hermann, Kegley, and Rosenau's *New Directions in the Study of Foreign Policy.*

43. Hermann and Peacock, "Evolution and Future of Theoretical Research," 15.

44. K.J. Holsti, *The Dividing Discipline: Hegemony and Diversity in International Theory* (Boston: Allen and Unwin, 1985), 1.

45. Holsti, *Dividing Discipline*, 130.

46. A survey of the titles in the bibliographies in Vasquez's *Power of Power Politics* and Hermann, Kegley, and Rosenau's *New Directions in the Study of Foreign Policy* reveals work in international politics on the following types of theory: adaptation, attribute, balance-of-power, bargaining, causal-attribution, cognitive, communication, conflict, cybernetic, decision-making, deterrence, events-research, exchange, field, game, information-processing, integration, international, mood, organization, realist, role, simulation, strategic, structural-realist, and systems. To this must be added works relating to theories of aggression, alliance-formation, anarchic co-operation, arms races, blackmail, dependence, foreign aid, imperialism, international crisis-behaviour, international interaction, the military-industrial complex, multinational politics, political coalitions, political instability, public international law, and the state.

SELECT BIBLIOGRAPHY

Allison, Graham T. *Essence of Decision: Explaining the Cuban Missile Crisis.* Boston: Little, Brown, 1971.

Art, Robert J. "Bureaucratic Politics and American Foreign Policy: A Critique." *Policy Sciences* 4 (December 1973): 467–90.

Brecher, Michael; Blema Steinberg; and Janice Stein. "A Framework for Analysis of Foreign Policy Behavior." *Journal of Conflict Resolution* 13, no. 1 (1969): 75–101.

Hermann, Charles F.; Charles W. Kegley, Jr.; and James N. Rosenau, eds. *New Directions in the Study of Foreign Policy.* Boston: Allen and Unwin, 1987.

Janis, Irving L. *Victims of Groupthink: A Psychological Study of Foreign Policy Decisions and Fiascoes.* Boston: Houghton Mifflin, 1972.

Jervis, Robert. *Perception and Misperception in International Politics.* Princeton: Princeton University Press, 1976.

Paige, Glenn D. *The Korean Decision.* New York: Free Press, 1968.

Rosenau, James N. "Pre-theories and Theories of Foreign Policy." In *Approaches to Comparative and International Politics*, ed. R. Barry Farrell. Evanston: Northwestern University Press, 1966. Reprinted in Rosenau, *Scientific Study of Foreign Policy.*

———. *The Scientific Study of Foreign Policy.* New York: Free Press, 1971.

———, ed. *International Politics and Foreign Policy: A Reader in Research and Theory.* Rev. ed. New York: Free Press, 1969.

Snyder, Richard C.; H.W. Bruck; and B. Sapin, eds. *Foreign Policy Decision-Making: An Approach to the Study of International Politics.* New York: Free Press, 1962.

Steinbrunner, John D. *The Cybernetic Theory of Decision: New Dimensions of Political Analysis*. Princeton: Princeton University Press, 1974.

Thompson, Kenneth W., and Roy C. Macridis. "The Comparative Study of Foreign Policy." In *Foreign Policy in World Politics*, ed. Roy C. Macridis. 2d ed. Englewood Cliffs, N.J.: Prentice-Hall, 1962.

THE LATEST WAVE: A CRITICAL REVIEW OF REGIME LITERATURE*

James F. Keeley

In the late 1960s, the preoccupation of mainstream international relations theorists in North America with realist-defined issues of military security began to break down. Trade, investment, and monetary developments led to a rediscovery of economics as a factor in international political life. A literature on interdependence and transnational relations began to develop. Other issues, such as the management of the environment, also arose as themes in international relations. In 1975, the journal *International Organization* presented a special issue, "International Responses to Technology," which might be seen as representing an early approach to the issue of international regimes.[1] In 1977, Robert O. Keohane and Joseph S. Nye, Jr., produced *Power and Interdependence*, which tried to come to grips with interdependence and world politics, in part through the analytical device of "regimes."[2] In 1982, another special issue of *International Organization* focussed explicitly on the regimes concept.[3] Since that time, regimes have constituted a significant, though debated, focus in the North American international relations literature, with *International Organization* as the major forum for their discussion and exploration.

The regime literature does not present a coherent whole, although it does display certain strong tendencies. The general concept of a regime points broadly to regularized, conscious, co-ordinated, long- (or at least medium-) term patterns of behaviour, ostensibly co-operative in nature, by which states (and other actors?) seek to manage their coexistence. It defines and approaches a general problem-area of international relations as occurring within and constituting ill-defined and possibly quite unstable communities. This orientation puts it somewhat at odds with that of realism, in which a zero-sum competition over national security among unified, rational state actors is the root formulation. Although one might argue that it is nowhere required by the concept, regimes tend to be approached to some degree as fairly benevolent, if not also voluntary, management devices created and maintained by dominant states. The literature thus tends to focus,

*The author wishes to thank Sheila K. Singh for her comments on an earlier draft; he is responsible, however, for all statements made here.

above all, on the great powers, and, in some cases, has an ideological and apologetic content as well as an empirical and/or a theoretical one. It also shows a tendency to be drawn into the old dispute between liberals and realists.

In the following pages, we shall survey very briefly a few main points in the regime literature, noting some concepts, themes, analytical devices, problems, and applications.

Some Fundamentals

International actors exist in a web of relations that allows both individual and co-ordinated, as well as co-operative and competitive, behaviour. These actors, seeking to manage their affairs and their environments, exist in at least a weak social situation. In this setting, the existence of others implies possibilities for both resistance and co-operation, and for shared as well as competing or independent interests and judgements on the part of others: the "war of all against all" does not capture its complexity. Regimes are management devices in this weak society. As such, they are affected, in part, by "objective" factors at work in the international system regardless of the knowledge or perceptions of actors; but they also can and do reflect how these actors define and understand their situations. Thus, we find in the dominating definition of international regimes, Krasner's, a strong emphasis on essentially psychological and normative factors, on how actors understand and organize their world:

> Regimes can be defined as sets of implicit or explicit principles, norms, rules, and decision-making procedures around which actors' expectations converge in a given area of international relations. Principles are beliefs of fact, causation, and rectitude. Norms are standards of behaviour defined in terms of rights and obligations. Rules are specific prescriptions or proscriptions for action. Decision-making procedures are prevailing practices for making and implementing collective choice.[4]

Regimes thus touch on the creation, transformation, and action within *social* constructions of reality as much as they do upon an objectively defined reality. If this conceptualization is accepted, then the realist concentration on "objective facts," such as distributions of power, is inadequate as the sole basis for an understanding of international relations. How actors understand their world is not fully predictable on the basis of power alone; thus, how they attempt to organize their world cannot be fully predictable on this basis, either. Rather, an analysis limited strictly to power implicitly operates within assumptions about the possible existence and the character of such understandings. A difficulty arises, however, in that the primary non-Marxian alternative to realism is some variant of liberal pluralism; thus, the old debate identified in earlier chapters of this volume tends to be revived in a new guise in the regime literature.

Some problems occur in Krasner's definition. There seem to be difficulties in identifying its components (principles, norms, etc.) in specific cases. Aggarwal thus relegates principles and norms to a "metaregime" existing somewhere above a specific regime of rules and decision-making procedures, and presumably informing a variety of such specific regimes.[5] This approach shifts rather than solves the problem, and the identification problem leads to others. Given sufficient looseness in defining principles and norms, just about any groups of behaviours could be dumped into a box labelled "regimes" and treated as if they somehow formed a coherent whole: the criteria for identifying and distinguishing among regimes are not well developed. This is a matter of some importance to Krasner's definition, since he proposes that changes of principles and norms be regarded as changes *of* regimes, while changes of rules and decision-making procedures be regarded as changes *in* regimes. A diminished ability to identify and distinguish among these components would also affect attempts to examine regime change, since what is changing may, therefore, be difficult to specify.

A problem also arises concerning relations among regimes (assuming we do not treat them as essentially isolated). Aggarwal's approach does lead to one ordering possibility: that some, more specific, regimes may be connected to, "nested" in, or otherwise dependent on, other broader regimes in a hierarchical relationship. So, he suggests, trade and monetary regimes are ultimately located within a structure of the international distribution of power. In similar terms, we might argue that specific formalized regimes may exist within a structure of broader and more fundamental concepts of international law. In a parallel vein would be some arguments about "issue-structural" versus "overall structural" explanations of changes in specific issue-areas, the theoretical problems of increasing incongruities between power distributions in different issue-areas in an issue-structural analysis, and the possibility that some forms of power and some issue-areas are ultimately dominant, are "trumps," however difficult or costly to play.[6] The nesting argument, then, has potential, although we should not ignore the possibilities for more complex and flexible and less hierarchical relationships as well.

Assuming we can identify the principles, norms, rules, and decision-making procedures of interest — that we can, in effect, specify a regime in at least useful, although not necessarily definitive terms — what are its other key characteristics? Listed here are six important considerations regarding the appearance and sustainability of regimes.[7]

1. **Formation:** whether contractual, imposed, or spontaneous.[8] There is a tendency to assume a contractual model, aided no doubt by the convenience of focussing on international organizations and on formal multilateral arrangements as key mechanisms for and definitive statements of international regimes. The idea of an imposed order points out the possibility of malevolent or coercive regimes, while the contractual approach favours a view of regimes as voluntary and benevolent, and encourages liberal analyses. The idea of a spontaneous order suggests the fundamental, although largely ignored, relevance of international customary law as a basic example of a regime (as well as a basic regime in "nesting" approach).
2. **Strength:** the degree of compliance with regime rules. This consideration is connected to a focus on processes of regime creation and erosion. In

the regime literature, it centres largely on the theme of hegemonic stability, and is connected to analyses drawn from the collective-goods literature. Another approach, that of Haas, links regime strength with cognitive rather than power considerations.[9]

3. **Form:** here again, there may be a tendency to identify regimes with formal international organizations, or at least formal multilateral statements of principles. As already noted, however, a consideration of the procedures, institutions, and character of international customary law, which are highly decentralized, might modify this tendency.
4. **Scope:** the range of issues covered by a regime. This consideration touches on the very definition of the issue-area within which the regime is operating. Haas starts at this point in treating regimes as disputable packages of specific issues, brought together in more or less strong and stable, and thus more or less changeable, regimes.[10]
5. **Modes of resource allocation:** the means used to distribute resources or, we might suggest, rights. These could be markets and private right systems, or some form of joint-management system. Some argue that a tendency exists in the literature, deriving perhaps from collective-goods analyses and ideas of "global commons," to focus on, if not favour, joint-management schemes.[11]
6. **Actors:** this term permits a variety of actor types to be involved in international regimes — states, private actors, individuals, international organizations, and so on. By and large, states are regarded as the dominant actors in international regimes.

In terms of basic theoretical orientations to the concept of international regimes, Krasner has identified three positions.[12] The key question here seems to be, "Do regimes matter, or are they mere epiphenomena?" The positions are:

1. **Structuralism**: argues that regimes are epiphenomena, manifestations of the distribution of power, rather than having a significant independent existence or effect. In such a formulation, regimes are variables dependent on power. This position is readily identifiable as realist.
2. **Grotianism**: the opposing position, one that argues the significant existence and effects of regimes: that regimes are independent variables in their own right, permeating international life. The very concept of regimes, as Krasner notes, tends to favour this position, since it argues their importance for study as causal factors, whereas the structuralist position would see them primarily as outcomes, and perhaps only as incidental outcomes at that.
3. **Modified structuralism**: the classic, uneasy middle ground. This position incorporates elements of realism, including a focus on states and a concern for state power, while arguing that regimes do have effects on international behaviour that make them worth studying. Thus, regimes are seen as being

> significant intervening variables between power and outcomes. Aside from organizing behaviour, regimes may affect actor definitions of interest or the distribution of advantages and disadvantages, two possibilities of interest from a Grotian perspective as well.

Krasner himself identifies the Grotian position with liberalism; thus, the old realist-liberal debate is revived rather than being transcended by this formulation.[13] This association with the old debate is a fundamental limitation on the ability of regime theory to point to new directions in the analysis of international relations, assuming that it can resolve its other difficulties.

Approaches and Themes

Although the regime literature is not strongly organized around any one theory, a number of thematic points do seem to recur in various combinations. As an illustration of some of these, we will look at two major and connected streams of thinking in the literature: the use of rational-actor analyses and the "theory of hegemonic stability." These are strongly associated with the modified-structuralist position, itself the main theoretical path of development in the regime literature. They deal with or arise from two basic questions: how do regimes form? and why do they form? This chapter focusses mainly on the latter question. The specific focus of individual scholars will, of course, vary, and each stage in this argument is subject to its own disputes. There are also approaches that operate outside of these lines of analysis, at least to some degree.

Why do states resort to international regimes to organize their coexistence? Rational-actor analyses derived from economics provide one way of searching for the answer. Presumably, if actors engage in relatively co-operative behaviour, they do so because the pay-offs are greater for such behaviour than for unilateral efforts. A classic statement of this possibility — and of its difficulties — is found in the Prisoner's Dilemma game. In such a game, both parties can be better off by co-operating, rather than by competing with each other: it is a non-zero-sum game in which each may benefit. However, either party may be better off if it lets the other engage in co-operative behaviour and then exploits this situation by refusing to co-operate in turn. Since both parties realize this, there is a strong tendency for defection to occur and, thus, for both parties to suffer (or at least do less well than they could) because of their inability to solve the problem of co-operation. If, however, this game is repeated many times, there is a greater chance that co-operative patterns of behaviour may become established, as there is both an opportunity for learning that co-operation pays off and that trust may be possible, and a potential penalty for defecting in the loss of future benefits from co-operation.[14]

A different, yet related, line of reasoning is found in theories of collective goods.[15] These goods are indivisible (their enjoyment by one does not reduce the amount available for enjoyment by others) and freely available (if they are available to any in a group, they are available to all). In many cases, actors may be unable to provide these goods for themselves by unilateral action, and thus may require co-ordination to obtain them. In other cases, one or a few large actors may be able to provide the good to others, although not necessarily in such quantities as might be desired. In either case, a major problem may be the "free rider" — an actor who receives the goods but refuses to contribute resources for its supply. If there are enough free riders, the level of resources available for its supply may be insufficient to meet the demand, or even to allow the provision of the good in any quantity at all. Again, we face a problem of co-ordination to achieve mutual benefits.

What benefits might regimes offer? Specific, concrete gains might be obtained by regulating otherwise potentially costly or destructive behaviour in certain issue-areas. In the absence of such co-ordination, oceans may be overfished or polluted, trade may be hindered by protectionism or special bilateral arrangements, and so on. However, since regimes are solutions to problems of co-ordination for mutual benefit, in this capacity they may, themselves, be treated as collective goods. Among the more general and abstract benefits offered by regimes as solutions to co-ordination problems, Keohane notes the following:[16]

1. Regimes increase the predictability of behaviour, insofar as they set out rules or guidelines to which actors are expected to adhere. As uncertainty is reduced and the expectation of regular, beneficial co-operation develops, costly hedging against defection by others (which can include being prepared to defect oneself) can be reduced or avoided.
2. Regimes provide generalized sets of rules, including those regarding rights and liabilities, which might then be applied in a variety of relevant relationships among sets of actors, rather than leaving them to work out fresh rules for each such relationship. Aside from the simplicity and predictability thus achieved, this system reduces the difficulty of working out new bilateral relations by allowing the parties to draw on existing structures of rules. Conversely, these rules may render illegitimate, and thus more costly, certain other kinds of agreements and relationships. Thus, regimes may provide standardized, agreed-upon formulas and procedures to help actors govern their relations. Once such a framework exists, it is easier to use it again than to create a new framework. So, for example, the International Atomic Energy Agency's safeguards system could acceptably replace a network of bilateral arrangements, providing a set of standardized obligations and rights acceptable to suppliers and recipients, and thus be seen as less of an intrusion on sovereignty than were bilateral safeguards. Once the principle and the practice of international safeguards had been accepted, the IAEA system could be drawn upon and modified in creating the system of non-proliferation treaty safeguards.
3. Under some circumstances, regimes may reduce differentials among actors in the information available to them. By reducing asymmetries in information, they may make agreement more likely by reducing fears of being

taken advantage of. They may also create greater "transparency" in agreements among other parties, so that actors have a better idea of what others are doing in their agreements. Here, again, the IAEA's safeguards systems could serve as an example.

The "theory of hegemonic stability" follows particularly from the collective-goods approach. It argues that regimes may be characteristically, if not necessarily, dependent on action by a single, highly capable actor that is able to underwrite the costs of organizing a regime, which then becomes available for other actors.[17] Provision of a collective good by one capable actor is one response to the problem of co-ordination, although free riding by others may make the supply of the good less than optimal. It is not that co-ordination by a group of actors is impossible, but rather that it is more difficult to achieve than action by one or a few powerful actors. Such an actor may simply impose its system, or it may make some effort to persuade others of the desirability of its activities, or it may try to take the interests of others into account in an effort to reduce enforcement costs. Thus, while regime theory points out the benefits of co-operation, the construction of a regime to obtain these may require, or at least be favoured by, substantially unilateral action by the powerful.

If we accept this account of the creation of a regime, what happens should the hegemon decline? Strict adherence to the theory argues that a regime will decline as the hegemon loses the power to reward co-operation and punish defection. This line of reasoning favours a structuralist position. A more Grotian or modified-structuralist argument is that actors may learn to co-operate and, therefore, may come to value a regime (thus, that regimes may affect, perhaps transform, the interests and the interest calculations of participants). The possibility then exists that a regime, even if established by a hegemon, may survive that actor's decline as other capable actors come to its support.[18]

A final element, somewhat undeveloped, that could be connected to this stream of thinking concerns the role of domestic politics. In this, the regime literature might build on examinations of the interaction between foreign (especially economic) policy and domestic political institutions and structures.[19] When the focus is on a hegemon, this element would tend to centre on the internal politics of that actor, for example, the response of its population to the relative increase in the burden of maintaining the regime as its relative capability declines.

Rational-actor analyses and the theory of hegemonic stability have become major foci of thinking in the regime literature: the former offers a set of powerful and attractive analytical devices, while the latter offers an apparently powerful hypothesis. Taken together, they draw on elements associated with structural realism, yet they may also be adapted to liberal analyses and conclusions, seemingly bridging the gap between these schools.[20] Certain difficulties and problems arise, however, in these two foci and from their interconnection.

First, both the "free rider" emphasis in collective-goods analyses and the concentration on the hegemon tend to assume the legitimacy of the regime and the general desirability of the goods it provides. Neither requires, but both tend to invite, treatments of regimes as benevolent, desirable, legitimate, and voluntary. Thus, although in one form it seems realist in character, the theory of hegemonic stability seems to have been developed along mainly liberal lines. Robert Gilpin's work demonstrates that this liberal tendency need not arise: he treats hegemons as creating regimes for their own benefit, rather than implicitly or "objectively" acting for the good of the entire community.[21] Oran Young, as already noted, allows for regimes to be created through imposition and spontaneous development as well as through contractual means. Although Krasner identifies Young with the Grotian position, Young's recognition of imposed regimes in particular would seem to challenge his easy placement in this camp.[22] There are, in any event, alternatives to this fundamental tendency in these streams.

Second, both collective-goods analyses and the theory of hegemonic stability tend to approach nonhegemonic actors primarily as presenting problems to be solved by a dominant state acting on behalf of all right-thinking persons. They are actors that must be organized by the hegemon, because of their own lack of capabilities (if not also the attractiveness of free riding), for the sake of the community as a whole. A strong and widely used theory of regimes from a non-hegemonic perspective does not seem to exist as yet.

Third, it is worth noting that the theory of hegemonic stability seems to be used particularly in studies of economic issues (the major focus of the regime literature itself) but less, and more questioningly, in security-area studies. Perhaps power is less concentrated in the security area than in economics, although the theory should still apply within blocs.[23] It is at least interesting, and a challenge for older realist theories of international relations, that the favoured economic regime (formed on liberal principles) should seem to be identified with the principle of hegemony,[24] while classic realism prefers the balance of power in security affairs. Perhaps liberals are the true supporters of hegemony? However, one might argue that the differences in the handling of the security and the economic realms merely reflect differences, from the perspective of a dominant state, between relations within and relations among hegemonic systems. More generally, it is intriguing that the utility of regime theory is questioned most in the area most amenable to a basic realist approach, while it is very widely used in an area in which liberal economic analyses (with attendant implicit or explicit political assumptions) are most strongly entrenched. It is a curious attempt, perhaps, to provide particularly structural-realist underpinnings for a liberal economic analysis.

Fourth, there is a close connection between the theory of hegemonic stability and the perception of a decline in U.S. power. Thus, for critics such as Susan Strange, the theory of regimes more generally reflects a specifically American set of preoccupations.[25] One might more generally suspect that the theory, particularly as it points to the erosion of regimes with the decline of the hegemon, might readily degenerate into a form of special pleading for rising states to support the order of things created and favoured by that hegemon. Beyond this is the empirical question of whether or not American hegemony really is declining.[26]

Fifth, it is not, in fact, clear just how well the theory of hegemonic stability works. Keohane, prominent in its development, has been careful to note its ambiguities and inadequacies.[27] Others have seen fit to modify it, or to challenge it more substantially.[28] The simplicity of the theory, its connections with both the well-developed analytical devices of rational-actor models (thus, with apparently rigorous theory) and currently popular structural realism, yet also its relationship to both liberal regimes and analyses and to American concerns, has its attractions despite these limitations. As well, the absence of a well-developed alternative capable of outweighing these factors may account for its persistence in the face of difficulties. If no other approach can replace it, but a sense of its inadequacies spreads, it might persist as a negative starting point, a source of anomalies, for theoretical and empirical work.

A final feature of rational-actor models is that they focus on certain technical difficulties in convergence processes among actors, rather than on the substance of the expectations and understandings among which this convergence is supposed to occur. The benefits of such a well-developed set of analytical devices, in laying bare the implications of interdependent decision making, among other things, are clear and attractive, as are their associations with one variety of realism. However, they may tend to encourage assumptions of shared orientations and judgements on substantive issues on the part of actors, or the alternative of the imposition of one solution on others, which might then be justified through various arguments. In either case, the substantive content of a dispute may be ignored or treated as unproblematic, with the focus then falling on the processes and problems of organizing action. This focus is not objectionable in itself, but it does overlook the implication in the Krasner definition that *how* people understand their world may affect their activities, and thus their attempts to organize action, within that world.

While the combination of rational-actor analysis and hegemonic-stability theory is the best developed in the literature, it is by no means the only possibility, as the work of Gilpin and Young, among others, demonstrates. One intriguing alternative is found in the early framework proposed by John Ruggie.[29] This framework was centred on the two concepts of a negotiated collective situation and a negotiated collective response. The former focussed particularly on the nature of the interdependent relationship among actors, while the latter was concerned with the objectives and the forms of response adopted by those actors in dealing with this situation. These components, being rather better developed than the "principles, norms, etc." of the now-dominant definition, perhaps could have avoided some of the difficulties that definition faces. While it kept open the possibility for game-theoretic and related analyses, this framework also placed emphasis on understandings of the situation. Unfortunately, the framework does not seem to have been strongly developed into a theory, and was displaced by the later lines of analysis.

Related to this early framework, however, is the work of Ernst Haas on cognitive factors in international regimes.[30] Haas focusses on how actors understand individually, and construct jointly, their situations and especially how they construct the issue-areas governed by regimes. Depending on the degree of consensus on these understandings, on the means by which issues are connected within the regime, and the bargaining styles of the participating actors, regimes may be more or less vulnerable to changes in power and knowledge. For example, issue-areas and regimes held together by "tactical linkage," short-term efforts to extract quid pro quos, may be particularly vulnerable because they lack any other source of coherence than immediate advantage. Haggard and Simmons note the predictive difficulties of a cognitive approach, in part because of the problem of predicting knowledge and in part because of the need to incorporate power considerations.[31]

Mention should also be made of the work of Friedrich Kratochwil on the concept of norms and on the power and functioning of social conventions.[32] Kratochwil draws particular inspiration from the Scottish philosopher David Hume. While some implications of his work can be directed to the question of regime change, it is, as he points out, also relevant to the question of why and how regimes work in the first place. His approach, as well as those of Ruggie, Haas, and perhaps Young, is less dominated by rational-actor techniques of analysis and emphasizes the social character of regimes. In this, these approaches open up regime theory to considerations drawn from the realm of sociology, for example, the work of Durkheim and more recently Foucault, and even to analyses that could draw on the work of Ludwig Wittgenstein on the use of language.[33] These approaches generally place more stress on how actors interpret and understand their world, and are less tied to the fundamental model of rational, individualized actors acting on the bases of power and calculations of self-interest. They are, thus, free to depart substantially from both realist and liberal assumptions about actors and about international relations. Such freedom also means, however, that the methods, theoretical statements, and conclusions that these sorts of approaches will produce will clash somewhat with the more standard methods, approaches, and conclusions of the discipline.

Some Applications

The concept of a regime is quite loose. The term could be used by a variety of scholars, within a variety of approaches, and with a varying level and character of theoretical content. "Regime" would well be, or become, a mere buzzword as a result, the latest fashionable term in a discipline somewhat prone to fashion. One can, therefore, expect a wide range of applications of regime notions, or at least a widespread use of the term, in a variety of empirical areas of study. The listing given here is intended, however, to cover applications of a more or less theoretically conscious nature. The breadth of actual applications suggests the pervasiveness of the phenomenon touched on by regimes (or, at least, the truth of the biblical injunction "seek and ye shall find"). It suggests the potential importance of regime theory in bringing co-operative behaviour and the concept of an international society into the heart of international relations theory, thereby mounting a serious challenge to contemporary realist theory.

Early realms of interest were the broad areas of environmental regulation and technological co-operation. These were the foci for the "International Responses to Technology" issue of *International Organization*, a portion of *Power and Interdependence*, and the work of M'Gonigle and Zacher.[34] In the narrower area of nuclear nonproliferation, Rochlin provides an illustration of an application of an early Haas–Ruggie approach, while Schiff's is a later application; Smith tests hegemonic stability theory in the nonproliferation context more recently.[35] Other areas have included food, human rights, and international law.[36]

In the troubling area of security, Jervis, in particular, has been a leading writer, although Haas, Lipson, and Nye, among others, have also been at work.[37] The relative nature of power (and, thus, the tendency to zero-sum rather than non-zero-sum games), and the high stakes and costs of errors and thus the particular allure of hedging against defection in the military-security area, among other factors, appear to pose substantial problems for regime development. This area, then, seems to present a limiting case for regime theory.

It is, above all, in the broad area of international economic relations — generally, in trade and in monetary relations — that regime analyses have proved to be most popular, and where the theory of hegemonic stability has been most often applied or tested. Kindleberger, Aggarwal, Zacher, Keohane, Krasner, and others have been active in this area.[38] It is particularly here, as well, that the curious combination of liberalism and realism in the regime literature is strongest.

Outside of the major stream identified here, associated with a combination of rational-actor analyses and hegemonic-stability theories, there are a variety of writers. Gilpin, Young, Haas, Kratochwil, Ruggie, and Rochlin have already been noted in this regard, but they are by no means the only ones.[39]

International Regimes: New Wave or New Fad?

The literature on international regimes has grown quickly over the last decade, but does this concept represent a new, potentially a very substantial, departure in the discipline of international relations, or is it merely one of a series of fads, as some have charged? Some significant reviews of the literature point to a variety of problems facing it: it is too tied to American concerns and perceptions, it is vague at key points, it is state-centric, it tends to be biassed toward liberal and status-quo orders, and so on.[40] At the same time, at least some see hope for it, although their prescriptions to cure its ills may vary. Young, for one, holds out some aspiration for the concept "reintegrating the subfields of international politics, economics, law, and organization."[41]

This survey of the regime literature has itself been rather negative in tone, finding that literature to be flawed in some fundamental ways, but it would not simply dismiss regimes out of hand. The concept could be simply the latest fad, or could succumb to its many problems, yet, if that were to be its fate, it would be a tragedy for the discipline. The regime concept allows a fruitful extension of a line of thinking that has opened up, particularly since the recognition of interdependence in the theoretical literature, that actors (states and others) are caught in a set of strategic interdependent relations of both zero-sum and non–zero-sum character, that these actors both act within and create systems of regularized behaviours and expectations, and that their understandings of the world constitute significant factors in international relations.

This set of considerations points both to some central problems currently facing regime theory and to a direction for a response. On the one hand, regime theory could challenge structural realism, which seems to offer little grasp on social or community phenomena because of its fixation on power and on a theory that is hamstrung by an unreasonable parsimony. The international world, it seems, may not be, or at least may not necessarily be, a Hobbesian state of nature; indeed, the whole "state of nature/state of war" formulation may be not only highly conditional but also seriously misleading. Simplistic realism — and structural realism is simplistic — simply will not do. Thus, and conversely, too ready and uncritical an adoption of realist devices and reasoning, in an attempt to protect the concept of regimes from realist attacks, could be harmful. On the other hand, the defects of a liberal analysis, as well as of an analysis assuming that American concerns, attitudes, and perceptions are synonymous with those of everyone else (or, at least, of all right-thinking actors), are also clear, however attractive such analyses may become when writers turn from theory to prescription. One fundamental problem of regime theory, then, is that it has been placed in a continuum between a simplistic realism and an apologetic and hopeful liberalism. In such a contest, over the long term one would expect the liberals to be "mugged by reality." It would not, after all, be the first time for them.

The existence of other streams of thinking besides rational-actor analyses and liberal-oriented hegemonic-stability theory points to both an opportunity and a danger in the future of that literature. An escape from tendencies to treat regimes as Good Things (and from U.S. preoccupations about regimes), even if some aspects of a rational-actor analysis were retained, could open up regime thinking to serious questions arising primarily on the political-theoretical Left, in the realm of international political economy. It could broaden and deepen our understanding of regimes as reflecting communities or a rough international society. If regime theories are perceived, however, as apologetics for liberal orders and for the United States, one can expect that this possibility will be lost as the regime baby is rejected along with the liberal/U.S. bathwater, as liberal analyses fail, and as American concern over the global position of the United States waxes and wanes.

If this is what happens — that is, if the current lines of development of regime theory persist — then the concept will turn out to be a fad. If, however, the question, the problem, of international society can be posed in regime theory in a way that escapes the limitations of structural realism while not sliding into the liberal camp (or adopting alternatives such as therapeutic do-goodism or utopian Marxism), then the possibility for a genuinely new development in international relations theory presents itself. Such innovation would require some backtracking from the currently dominant line of theoretical development in the regime literature that has captured the regime concept in a debate primarily between a realism that rejects it and a liberalism attempting to use realist theories, devices, and approaches to support liberal analyses. We are not required to turn away from power and from disputes as central factors in political life. Neither are we required to forgo the use of rational-actor analyses as ways of gaining insights into the implications of interdependence. Regime theory gives us a chance to build on the insights of realism while escaping the restrictions of its structuralist formulation. It gives us a chance to move beyond the old liberal-realist debate, to draw on philosophical, sociological, and other sources of insights that could liberate us from this debate, and thus possibly to grapple more successfully with a world that fits neither a narrow realist nor a liberal perspective. It gives us a chance to bring real political philosophy — real inquiries into the character of political life, rather than the special pleadings and schemes of ideologues and apolitical utopians or their equally sterile rejection in the name of the eternal verities of power — back into the study of international relations.

NOTES

1. John G. Ruggie, ed., "International Responses to Technology," a special issue of *International Organization* 29 (Summer 1975).

2. Robert O. Keohane and Joseph S. Nye, Jr. *Power and Interdependence: World Politics in Transition* (Boston: Little, Brown, 1977).

3. This was later reissued as Stephen D. Krasner, ed., *International Regimes* (Ithaca: Cornell University Press, 1983).

4. Krasner, *International Regimes*, 2.

5. Oran R. Young, "International Regimes: Toward a New Theory of Institutions," *World Politics* 39 (October 1986): 106–7; Vinod K. Aggarwal, *Liberal Protectionism: The International Politics of Organized Textile Trade* (Berkeley: University of California Press, 1985), 4, 16–20.

6. Aggarwal, *Liberal Protectionism*; Keohane and Nye, *Power and Interdependence*, 11–22, 42–54.

7. Save as otherwise noted, these are drawn from the listing in Stephen Haggard and Beth Simmons, "Theories of International Regimes," *International Organization* 41 (Summer 1987): 496–98.

8. Oran R. Young, "International Regimes: Problems of Concept Formation," *World Politics* 32 (April 1980): 349–51.

9. For example, Ernst B. Haas,"Why Collaborate? Issue-Linkage and International Regimes," *World Politics* 32 (April 1980): 357–405.

10. This is a major element in Haas's "cognitive" approach to regimes. See his "Why Collaborate?"

11. For example, John A.C. Conybeare, "International Organization and the Theory of Property Rights," *International Organization* 34 (Summer 1980): 307–34.

12. Krasner, ed., *International Regimes*, viii, 5–10, 355–68.

13. There are other possibilities: some regime theorists who employ the "theory of hegemonic stability" also draw to some degree on Gramsci's concept of hegemony, a Marxian notion. See, for example, Robert O. Keohane, *After Hegemony: Cooperation and Discord in the World Political Economy* (Princeton: Princeton University Press, 1984).

14. See Robert Axelrod, *The Evolution of Cooperation* (New York: Basic Books, 1984), for an examination of the development of co-operation over time in a Prisoner's Dilemma situation. For a critique of Axelrod, see Joanne Gowa, "Anarchy, Egoism, and Third Images: The Evolution of Cooperation and International Relations," *International Organization* 40 (Winter 1986): 167–93. For some approaches to regimes using Prisoner's Dilemma and other game-theory analyses, see, for example, Arthur A. Stein, "Coordination and Collaboration: Regimes in an Anarchic World," in *International Regimes*; and Kenneth A. Oye, "Explaining Cooperation under Anarchy: Hypotheses and Strategies," *World Politics* 38 (October 1985), later published as Kenneth A. Oye, ed., *Cooperation under Anarchy* (Princeton: Princeton University Press, 1985).

15. See, for example, Mancur Olson, *The Logic of Collective Action: Public Goods and the Theory of Groups* (Cambridge, Mass.: Harvard University Press, 1965).

16. Keohane, *After Hegemony*, 85–109.

17. See Keohane, *After Hegemony*, 31–46, for a discussion of hegemony and the theory of hegemonic stability.

18. Keohane, in *After Hegemony*, holds out this possibility.

19. See, for example, Peter J. Katzenstein, "International Relations and Domestic Structures: Foreign Economic Policies of Advanced Industrial States," *International Organization* 30 (Winter 1976): 1–46; and Peter J. Katzenstein, ed., *Between Power and Plenty: Foreign Economic Policies of Advanced Industrial States* (Madison: University of Wisconsin Press, 1978). Haggard and Simmons, "Theories of International Regimes," 513–17, call for increased attention to domestic political factors to correct an excessive reliance on systemic, especially structural, theories.

20. Keohane, in *After Hegemony* (e.g., p. 9), is quite clear about this.

21. Robert Gilpin, *War and Change in World Politics* (Cambridge: Cambridge University Press, 1981). Haggard and Simmons, "Theories of International Regimes," 502, characterize Gilpin's approach as a "malign" view of regimes. It might be more accurate simply to note that it is nonliberal.

22. See note 8 above.

23. For a study of the East European case, see Valerie Bunce, "The Empire Strikes Back: The Transformation of the Eastern Bloc from a Soviet Asset to a Soviet Liability," *International Organization* 39 (Winter 1985): 1–46.

24. See, for example, Stephen D. Krasner, "State Power and the Structure of International Trade," *World Politics* 28 (April 1976): 317–47.

25. Susan Strange, "*Cave! Hic Dragones*: A Critique of Regime Analysis," in *International Regimes*.

26. For example, Bruce Russett, "The Mysterious Case of Vanishing Hegemony; Or, Is Mark Twain Really Dead?" *International Organization* 39 (Spring 1985): 207–32; and Susan Strange, "The Persistent Myth of Lost Hegemony," *International Organization* 41 (Autumn 1987): 233–60.

27. Robert O. Keohane, "The Theory of Hegemonic Stability and Changes in International Economic Regimes, 1967–1977," in *Change in the International System*, ed. O.R. Holsti, R.M. Siverson and A.L. George (Boulder, Colo.: Westview, 1980). See also *After Hegemony*, 35–39.

28. See, for example, Timothy J. McKeown, "Hegemonic Stability Theory and 19th Century Tariff Levels in Europe," *International Organization* 37 (Winter 1983): 73–92; Peter F. Cowhey and Edward Long, "Testing Theories of Regime Change: Hegemonic Decline or Surplus Capacity?" *International Organization* 37 (Spring 1983): 157–88; Arthur A. Stein, "The Hegemon's Dilemma: Great Britain, the United States, and the International Economic Order," *International Organization* 38 (Spring 1984): 355–86; Duncan Snidal, "The Limits of Hegemonic Stability Theory," *International Organization* 39 (Autumn 1985): 579–614; and Roger K. Smith, "Explaining the Non-Proliferation Regime: Anomalies for Contemporary International Relations Theory," *International Organization* 41 (Spring 1987): 253–81.

29. John G. Ruggie, "International Responses to Technology: Concepts and Trends," *International Organization* 29 (Summer 1975): 557–84.

30. See note 9 above.

31. Haggard and Simmons, "Theories of International Regimes," 509–13.

32. For example, "On the Notion of 'Interest' in International Relations," *International Organization* 36 (Winter 1982): 1–32; "The Force of Prescriptions," *International Organization* 38 (Autumn 1984): 685–708.

33. See also Friedrich Kratochwil and John G. Ruggie, "International Organization: A State of the Art on the Art of the State," *International Organization* 40 (Autumn 1986): 753–76. On Wittgenstein, see, for example, Hanna F. Pitkin, *Wittgenstein and Justice* (Berkeley: University of California Press, 1972).

34. See notes 1 and 2 above; R. Michael M'Gonigle and Mark W. Zacher, *Pollution, Politics, and International Law: Tankers at Sea* (Berkeley: University of California Press, 1979). See also "Restructuring Ocean Regimes," special issue of *International Organization* 31 (Spring 1977): 151–384.

35. Gene I. Rochlin, *Plutonium, Power, and Politics: International Arrangements for the Disposition of Spent Nuclear Fuel* (Berkeley: University of California Press, 1979); Benjamin J. Schiff, *International Nuclear Technology Transfer: Dilemmas of Dissemination and Control* (Totowa, N.J.: Rowman and Allanheld, 1984); Smith, "Explaining the Non-Proliferation Regime."

36. Raymond F. Hopkins and Donald J. Puchala, eds., "The Global Political Economy of Food," special issue of *International Organization* 32 (Summer 1978); Jack Donnelly, "International Human Rights: A Regime Analysis," *International Organization* 40 (Summer 1986): 599–642; Robert H. Jackson, "Quasi-States, Dual Regimes, and Neoclassical

Theory: International Jurisprudence and the Third World," *International Organization* 41 (Autumn 1987): 519–50.

37. Robert Jervis, "Cooperation under the Security Dilemma," *World Politics* 30 (January 1978): 167–214; "Security Regimes," in *International Regimes*; "From Balance to Concert: A Study of International Security Cooperation," in *Cooperation under Anarchy*; Ernst B. Haas, "Regime Decay, Conflict Management and International Organizations, 1945–1981," *International Organization* 37 (Spring 1983): 189–256; Charles Lipson, "International Cooperation in Economic and Security Affairs," *World Politics* 37 (October 1984): 1–23; Joseph S. Nye, Jr., "Nuclear Learning and U.S.–Soviet Security Regimes," *International Organization* 41 (Summer 1987): 371–402. See also Stein, "Coordination and Collaboration," 299–304.

38. See Krasner and Oye, and previous notes, for various authors and studies. Charles P. Kindleberger, *The World in Depression, 1929–1939* (Berkeley: University of California Press, 1975), while not explicitly linked to regime theory, has been influential; see also Kindleberger, "Dominance and Leadership in the International Economy," *International Studies Quarterly* 25 (June 1981): 242–54; Aggarwal, *Liberal Protectionism*; Jock A. Finlayson and Mark W. Zacher, "The GATT and the Regulation of Trade Barriers; Regime Dynamics and Functions," in *International Regimes*; Zacher, "Trade Gaps, Analytical Gaps: Regime Analysis and International Commodity Trade Regulation," *International Organization* 41 (Spring 1987): 173–202; Keohane and Nye, *Power and Interdependence*; Keohane, *After Hegemony*; and Stephen D. Krasner, *Structural Conflict: The Third World Against Global Liberalism* (Berkeley: University of California Press, 1985).

39. For example, Roger A. Coate, *Global Issue Regimes* (New York: Praeger, 1982). See also Richard L. O'Meara, "Regimes and Their Implications for International Relations Theory," *Millennium* 13 (Winter 1984): 1–13.

40. For example, Strange, "*Cave! Hic Dragones*"; Haggard and Simmons, "Theories of International Regimes"; Young, "Toward a New Theory of Institutions"; James N. Rosenau, "Before Cooperation: Hegemons, Regimes, and Habit-Driven Actors in World Politics," *International Organization* 40 (Autumn 1986): 849–94.

41. Young, "Toward a New Theory of Institutions," 105.

SELECT BIBLIOGRAPHY

Aggarwal, Vinod K. *Liberal Protectionism: The International Politics of Organized Textile Trade*. Berkeley: University of California Press, 1985.

Axelrod, Robert. *The Evolution of Cooperation*. New York: Basic Books, 1984.

Conybeare, John A.C. "International Organization and the Theory of Property Rights." *International Organization* 34 (Summer 1980): 307–34.

Gilpin, Robert. *War and Change in World Politics*. Cambridge: Cambridge University Press, 1981.

Gowa, Joanne. "Anarchy, Egoism, and Third Images: The Evolution of Cooperation and International Relations." *International Organization* 40 (Winter 1986): 167–86.

Haas, Ernst B. "Why Collaborate? Issue-Linkage and International Regimes." *World Politics* 32 (April 1980): 357–405.

Haggard, Stephen, and Simmons, Beth A. "Theories of International Regimes." *International Organization* 41 (Summer 1987): 491–517.

Keohane, Robert O. *After Hegemony: Cooperation and Discord in the World Political Economy*. Princeton: Princeton University Press, 1984.

Keohane, Robert O., and Joseph S. Nye, Jr. *Power and Interdependence: World Politics in Transition*. Boston: Little, Brown, 1977.

Krasner, Stephen D., ed. *International Regimes*. Ithaca: Cornell University Press, 1983.

Kratochwil, Friedrich. "The Force of Prescriptions." *International Organization* 38 (Autumn 1984): 685–708.

Kratochwil, Friedrich, and Ruggie, John G. "International Organization: A State of the Art on the Art of the State." *International Organization* 40 (Autumn 1986): 753–76.

Olson, Mancur. *The Logic of Collective Action: Public Goods and the Theory of Groups*. Cambridge, Mass.: Harvard University Press, 1965.

Oye, Kenneth A., ed. *Cooperation under Anarchy*. Princeton: Princeton University Press, 1985.

Ruggie, John G., ed. "International Responses to Technology." Special Issue of *International Organization* 29 (Summer 1975).

Snidal, Duncan. "The Limits of Hegemonic Stability Theory." *International Organization* 39 (Autumn 1985): 579–614.

Young, Oran R. "International Regimes: Problems of Concept Formation." *World Politics* 32 (April 1980): 331–56.

———. "International Regimes: Toward a New Theory of Institutions." *World Politics* 39 (October 1986): 104–22.